KU-845-263

GOVERNING URBAN AMERICA

McGRAW-HILL SERIES IN POLITICAL SCIENCE

Joseph P. Harris, CONSULTING EDITOR

ADRIAN · Governing Urban America
ADRIAN · State and Local Governments
BONE · American Politics and the Party System
CHASE · The United Nations in Action
EBENSTEIN · Political Thought in Perspective
FERGUSON AND McHENRY · The American Federal Government
FERGUSON AND McHENRY · The American System of Government
FERGUSON AND McHENRY · Elements of American Government
FIELD · Governments in Modern Society
FRANK · Cases on the Constitution
GOSNELL, LANCASTER, AND RANKIN · Fundamentals of American National
    Government
GOSNELL, LANCASTER, AND RANKIN · Fundamentals of American Government
GROSS · The Legislative Struggle
HAAS AND WHITING · Dynamics of International Relations
HARTMANN · Basic Documents of International Relations
HARTMANN · Readings in International Relations
HOLLOWAY · State and Local Government in the United States
LEONARD · Elements of American Foreign Policy
LEONARD · International Organization
McCLOSKY AND TURNER · The Soviet Dictatorship
MANGONE · A Short History of International Organization
MILLETT · Government and Public Administration
MILLETT · Management in the Public Service
NEUMANN · European and Comparative Government
PIERSON AND GIL · Governments of Latin America
PRITCHETT · The American Constitution
REED · Municipal Management
RIEMER · Problems of American Government
ROCHE AND STEDMAN · The Dynamics of Democratic Government
RODEE, ANDERSON, AND CHRISTOL · Introduction to Political Science
STRAUSZ-HUPÉ AND POSSONY · International Relations
SVARLIEN · An Introduction to the Law of Nations
TURNER · Politics in the United States: Readings in Political Parties and Pressure
    Groups
TURNER AND VIEG · The Government and Politics of California
VANDENBOSCH AND HOGAN · The United Nations: Background, Organization,
    Functions, Activities
WALDO · Ideas and Issues in Public Administration: A Book of Readings
WILSON · The American Political Mind
WILSON · Police Administration

6 00 020004 6   TELEPEN

Students and External Readers	Staff & Research Students
DATE DUE FOR RETURN	**DATE OF ISSUE**
25. 06. 86.	17 FEB. 1983
25. 06. 86.	14.MAR 83 2 631
24. 06. 87.	

Any book which you borrow remains your responsibility
until the loan slip is cancelled

GOVERNING
URBAN AMERICA

Charles R. Adrian

Professor of Political Science
and Director, Institute for
Community Development and Services
Michigan State University

SECOND EDITION

McGRAW-HILL BOOK COMPANY, INC.

New York   Toronto   London   1961

243160
Am Sr.
1st ed JS 331 A4

GOVERNING URBAN AMERICA. Copyright © 1955, 1961 by the McGraw-Hill Book Company, Inc. Printed in the United States of America. All rights reserved. This book, or parts thereof, may not be reproduced in any form without permission of the publishers. *Library of Congress Catalog Card Number* 61–9465

00423

The government of cities is a part of the political process. Since this is the case, I believe that a course in American city government should be taught as a part of the offerings of political science in the liberal arts tradition. I have tried to write this textbook with that purpose in mind. It will, therefore, not serve as a handbook for the local government official, and it will not teach applied administration to a student who is a would-be city manager. Perhaps it may inspire a few students to take further courses toward a career in municipal administration, but that is not its major purpose. Principally, this textbook will, I hope, teach the college student, whether a political science major or otherwise, some of the things he, as a citizen, needs to know about his city and its governmental operations.

I have made three basic assumptions in writing this book. One is that a general text on city government should deal not only with structure and policy making, but also with functions and administrative operations. This volume is designed to be used as the text for either a one- or a two-semester course, but the current trend toward a single-semester course has been considered in the allocation of space. A second assumption is that city government is meaningful only if studied as part of the whole urban culture. I have therefore made considerable use of the materials of urban sociology, social psychology, and other related disciplines. A third assumption is that the process of urban government is primarily a *political* process. I have emphasized this point throughout the text. Functions are discussed from the point of view of what the lay citizen needs to know, and emphasis has been placed upon current issues of policy. The administrative organization of functions is not ignored, but detailed treatment of technical engineering and administrative problems has been omitted in the belief that these are properly material for professional courses in public administration as distinguished from academic courses in political science. I believe that municipal government is a matter not alone of administration of a professional quality, but also of interests protecting their stake in a local political process—a process that does not differ fundamentally from that on the state or national level.

This second edition is made possible by the encouraging reception that was given the book in its original form, and by the great amount of new research materials that have appeared in the last six years. The fact that the municipal government field has become one of the most active areas in the advancement of political science theory has made this revision a special pleasure.

A number of changes have been made with this revision. In particular, I have attempted to carry much further the analytical approach I rather cautiously advanced in the first edition. As a result, the chapters from 16 on have been recast with greater emphasis given to the role of competing interests in the municipal policy-making process. The chapter on administration has been completely changed and a separate chapter on financial administration is offered. In addition, urbanization, the politics of suburbia, and the decentralization of urban areas have been stressed.

I should like to acknowledge the helpful advice and criticism of those who reviewed the first edition for me, as well as of those who gave me their reactions based upon the use of the book in the classroom. Their numbers are too great to make individual credits possible, but this fact does not minimize the importance of their contribution to the revision.

It is conventional, and quite proper, to add that all errors of fact and all disputable conclusions are my responsibility alone.

Charles R. Adrian

CONTENTS

Preface v

1. The Trend Toward an Urban Nation 1
2. Suburbia 43
3. Ideas about Local Self-government in America 70
4. Municipal Elections 90
5. Intergroup Activity and Political Power 119
6. Urban Political Organization 147
7. The Law of Municipalities 166
8. Forms of Government 197
9. Executive Officers 232
10. The City Council 255
11. Government in Metropolitan Areas 274
12. Intergovernmental Relations 293
13. Administration 305
14. The Municipal Bureaucracy 332
15. Revenues and Expenditures 349
16. Financial Administration 378
17. Public Safety 388
18. Public Utilities and Transportation 417
19. Urban Housing 444
20. Land-use Policies 457
21. Public Health and Welfare 468
22. Governing Urban American Tomorrow 486

Index 501

vii

Chapter 1

THE TREND TOWARD AN URBAN NATION

The college student of today is, according to the best available estimates, by all odds a favorite to spend his lifetime in an urban community. This textbook is designed to help him, as a lay citizen, gain a better understanding of the operation of city government. Particular stress is laid throughout the text upon the issues in city politics that are political in nature, that is, issues that are controversial and possess alternative patterns of solution. As such, these issues may require the ordinary citizen to make a choice and take a stand, either at the polls or as a member of an interest group.

There are many possible approaches to the study of political institutions. In this book, the emphasis is placed upon a study of the *political process* with the objective of supplying to the reader a method that will provide him with *a tool for the analysis of political events* that affect him and his society. No attempt is made to supply details concerning the thousands of urban communities in the United States. Such information is available in the nearest library and the footnotes list ample citations. Neither is there an effort made to outline a set of ethical norms for the reader's guidance, since analysis requires an objective, or amoral, examination of relevant data if understanding of politics is the goal. A word of warning, however: Although the author has tried to avoid introducing his own preferences into the materials of the book, values—the beliefs one holds dear—are an essential ingredient in the decision-making process of politics. When one votes, or joins a group that seeks to influence governmental policy, or otherwise takes political action, he uses his sense of values of what is right or wrong, good or bad, in deciding what to do. At such times, personal values are of critical importance. However, to introduce one's personal preferences into an analysis of the political process is to blur the image: this the author has tried to avoid doing. But no reader should assume that "one choice is as good as another," or that "no matter what I do, things will turn out the same anyway." The analysis given in this book does not imply or justify such conclusions.

1

The Theoretical Model. Government is only one of the institutions of social control. It is not necessarily more powerful than some of the others—the family, the church, the school (which in America is commonly a part of government), the voluntary social agency, the business or professional association, the trade union, the business firm, the social club, or others. The role that government plays varies with the culture. In some primitive societies, it is almost nonexistent. In nineteenth-century America, people generally believed that most decisions determining the pattern of society should be made outside of government. Today, they wish to involve government in an ever greater number of decisions, though still in fewer than may be found in some other countries, such as in Denmark, a democracy, or in the Soviet Union, an authoritarian state.

The question of which aspects of social organization are to be controlled by government alone or by government acting in conjunction with other institutions is decided in America by the groups that are influential enough to be able to affect political decisions. The level of services provided by government, the means of financing them, and the method of organization for their administration are all also decided by this same means. The process is essentially one in which people of like values and interests band together into groups, with these groups seeking to influence members of all branches of government at every place where significant policy decisions are made. The decision makers are called upon to balance the various competing interests and to effect compromises among them. In the ideal model, every individual in society would have his every interest represented in the political process in proportion to its relative weight. In practice, such a nice balance would be achieved only by accident. Instead, some interests are better able to act effectively than are others, and hence public policy comes closer to their wishes than to those of competing but less effective interests. Yet, almost no group of today converts its desires into public policy without some modification by competing interests. Even the most powerful interest must make some concessions to others.

In responding to the many groups that seek its favor, a government tends to react not to a single public, but to a number of them. Each public constitutes an interest affected by government or a clientele group for one of its many services. Not only are there conflicts and usually ultimate compromise over which services are to be provided and over the level or quality of each service, but also various clientele groups compete against other groups for allocation of such funds as can be secured by government from citizens who have competing uses for the money that might be taken in taxes or service charges.

Interest groups are tied together internally and relate to members of other groups and to government officials in a variety of ways, all of which are affected by an elaborate system of political values and attitudes which tend to channel the behavior of both leaders and rank-and-file members. Group leaders—like public office seekers—are usually specialists in political communication, which involves the manipulation of value symbols, attitudes, and ideas. Groups, through their leaders, conduct unending campaigns to establish favorable political environments for their own goals. In the policy-making process, the cultural values of society are applied to various aspects of human behavior so as to control them in a manner that is considered desirable by the politically effective groups. In the case where politically effective groups are in competition rather than agreement with one another, the values are applied in a manner that is considered acceptable by the competing groups, usually through compromise.

This model for analysis is developed throughout the chapters that follow. Although it may not be easy to understand when it is stated in the abstract version presented here, the parts of the model will not be difficult to understand as they are developed separately, with illustrations and further detail.

The material in this book, then, seeks to fit contemporary municipal governments into their place in an age of mass communication and mass education. To the extent the author has succeeded, the reader is provided, not with a mass of detail or a series of hortatory essays, but with a tool for the analysis of politics.

THE CITY AND THE URBANITE

The City Today. American city government has matured rapidly in the last fifty years. Unlike most state and county governments, cities have undergone extensive modernization of their structure, so that they are prepared to furnish the services demanded by modern society. Most city political machines and bosses have disappeared. The remaining ones are adopting policies more appropriate for the environment they now find themselves in. Blatant corruption and spoilsmanship have given way before the need for governmental services performed by technical specialists.

The realities of government in the contemporary American city are not well understood by the typical citizen. The folkways and folk tales of Americana saddle city government and city politicians with a stereotype that has little basis in fact. The stereotype does, however, have a *historical* basis.

The Public Attitude toward City Governments. Nearly everyone has at one time heard of the famous comment by the great British political scientist Lord Bryce, who called "the government of cities the one conspicuous failure of the United States." That statement was made more than sixty years ago. Yet many Americans think of it as being appropriate today. Partly for this reason, citizens, including college students, have developed a cynicism regarding municipal governments, especially the governments of the larger municipalities that make up the core cities of metropolitan areas. It is worthwhile, therefore, to inquire into the following causes, which formerly resulted in corrupt and incompetent city government.

1. *Rapid Growth of Cities.* In the first place, difficulties in achieving confidence in city government are partly a product of the rapidity with which the American city grew after the Civil War. This nation was predominantly an agricultural one until (roughly) the last half of the nineteenth century, and its democratic traditions were oriented toward the frontier and the farm, not toward the city. The same traditions do not necessarily fit each of them equally well. Furthermore, effective *democratic* government is built largely upon a sound foundation of customs, attitudes, and traditions that require time to build and to work into the normal behavior patterns of a society. A nation of farmers cannot overnight discover methods for the effective government of industrial cities. Furthermore, when blossoming cities of the nineteenth century had added to their populations shiploads of immigrants, ignorant of the customs, laws, beliefs, and even language of an adopted country, the problems of government became a thousandfold more complex.

2. *City as Creature of State.* A second factor is to be found in the position of the city as a creature of the state. With minor exceptions (to be discussed in Chapter 7), the relationship of a city to the state in which it is located is the relationship between a child and its parent. A city can perform only those functions authorized for it by state law. These functions generally apply in: (1) matters in which the city acts simply as the agent of the state, and (2) matters of local concern. An example of the former is the protection of the public health; of the latter, the provision for transit service. American courts historically have given a very narrow interpretation to the powers of cities. This has been based on the theory that, if in doubt, power belongs to the sovereign state and not to one of its corporate subdivisions. The result has been that the state legislature—usually dominated by small-town merchants and lawyers who are inexperienced in city social patterns—has often not given the city the power needed to deal with local problems. This situation may lead to dissatisfaction, cynicism, and a tendency on the part of the public to look elsewhere for the solution of the problems of the city. The typical citizen, casually interested in politics and law, is not concerned with *why* the city cannot perform a function felt to be needed

—he wants it done, and if the city cannot do it, he will look for another unit of government that can and will.

Especially restrictive of the power of the city to perform services wanted by its citizens has been the state-imposed limitation upon the power of the city to tax. American cities have been, and still are, overwhelmingly dependent upon a levy that was designed to fit the needs of a frontier society—the general property tax. Because legislatures have not been anxious to allow cities to use other types of taxes, municipalities often have found that their limit of services renderable comes at whatever point the property tax seems to reach a saturation point. Again the impatient and annoyed citizen is likely to turn to the state or national government for a service for which the city has no money.

Picayunish control over local matters has been carried to such an extent by many state legislatures that cities have sometimes been given almost no chance to decide any really important matter for themselves. This type of action by the lawmakers turns the legislature into nothing less than an *administrative* overseer of city government. While the practice appears to be on the decline today, it continues in many states to give the citizen the impression that the really important decisions are made, not in the city hall, but in the state capital and that, therefore, city government is not of sufficient consequence to rate his attention. Such supervision by the state government has also had its adverse affect upon the municipal officeholder, whose creativity becomes dulled and discouraged by being constantly told that he is exceeding or is in danger of exceeding his authority. When his powers are interpreted narrowly by the courts and he must go to the legislature whenever he wishes to make a departure from customary policy, the city official begins to orient his job toward the annotated statutes and the opinions of the attorney general, instead of toward the economic and sociological needs of the city. The ordinary citizen, impatient with legalism, is likely to view the plight of the harassed official without sympathy. The explanations he hears will sound to him like excuses for inaction.

3. *Experience in Depression.* A third item discouraging citizen faith in city government stems from the experience of the Great Depression that began in the fall of 1929. Municipalities, supported by a tax base often deceivingly inflated by the artificial real estate boom of the twenties, found themselves financially unable to meet the suddenly enormous costs of the public relief load, the costs of the municipal payroll, or the costs of the interest upon bonded indebtedness.[1] In many parts of the United States, states had to shore up the finances of their cities, and then the

---

[1] On the impotence of municipal government during this period, see David A. Shannon (ed.), *The Great Depression* (Prentice-Hall, Inc., Englewood Cliffs, N.J., 1960), chap. 3.

national government had to do the same for the states. The reformer, the New Dealer, and the ordinary citizen, seeking to overcome the paralyzing depression, turned from the city to the state, and especially to the national government, for aid and support. The phenomenon of a municipality nearly or actually bankrupt in a time of great public need is well remembered by millions of persons alive today. The memory does not enhance the prestige of our cities.

4. *Corruption.* A fourth consideration has been the persistency with which American cities have been plagued with varying degrees of corruption. It has become a veritable tradition in our larger municipalities and has affected a great many of our cities of any size, at one time or another in history. Corruption may enter city government, in the first place, as a result of the commonplace lack of public interest in the operations of the city which permits lax administration. Dishonesty and irregularities breed a greater lack of interest and a cynicism which merely allows for more of the same. Another cause stems from circumstances which demand that city officials enforce formally enacted laws that do not accord with the prevailing public mores. Examples of this may be found in the case of liquor prohibition during the twenties, and of gambling today.[2] Such anomalies place city officials in positions of great temptation, yet the same citizens who drink illegal liquor or insist upon gambling will be among those who will censure public officials who do not enforce the law. Individual Americans are quite capable of expecting tougher moral fiber in their public officials than they themselves possess.

Corruption is far less widespread and certainly less overt today than it was formerly. Yet in 1948 Philadelphia was rocked by a series of scandals during which embezzlers were uncovered in the city's purchasing department, amusement-tax division, and other agencies. In 1959, a number of Chicago policemen were found to have been operating as part of a burglary gang. At about the same time, in New York, a variety of charges were made alleging maladministration or corruption in connection with a slum-clearance program, the inspection of meat retailers, and the purchasing of salt for snow removal. A borough president was charged with having accepted a large gift from a real estate operator who was doing business with the city.

5. *Apathy.* Finally, however, we must face the fact that whenever our cities have not been governed in a fashion that satisfies the high expectations of the citizen, the cause may be found in general public apathy. The ordinary citizen is a busy person with many demands upon his time. As a consequence, he must budget his interests—and municipal

---

[2] The effect of organized crime upon our cities will be examined in chap. 17; the influence of the old-time boss as a "broker of privilege" will be considered in chap. 6.

government has rated a low priority. This has been true in part because the city dweller has viewed his local government as one that performs primarily routine service functions. Who, he wants to know, can become interested in such prosaic problems as the supplying of water, the maintenance of streets, the disposal of sewage? Are these not routine matters to be handled by civil servants? Why should he concern himself? Unfortunately for the welfare of city government, many advocates of the reform movement of a few decades ago advanced the misconception that municipal government is nothing more than the application of the principles of "good business management" from which the politician ought properly to be excluded.[3] Undoubtedly, city governments exist primarily to render services to patron-citizens. These services, however, are often far from routine, and the existence of alternative approaches to public policy offers the basis for lively citizen participation in genuine political issues. Much of this book will be taken up with the consideration of nonroutine political issues in urban functions.

Until recent decades, citizen interest was often at low ebb because "respectable people" thought they could not be connected (at least not openly) with city administrations that all too often were under the control of a boss or a machine or were cooperating with professional criminals. It was uncommon for a representative of the "best people" of the community to become involved in municipal politics prior to the advent of the reform movement in the 1880s, which helped to make that sort of thing respectable. Even today, many persons still believe that city politics is corrupt, and hence to be shunned by good citizens. Such viewpoints severely retard efforts to achieve adequate, able, and modern city government.

The high mobility so characteristic of contemporary American cities, combined with the extreme heterogeneity of their populations, has militated against most people having a sense of "belongingness" in the community. This in turn has resulted in a low degree of civic pride and morale, which produces lack of interest in the local political process. Irvin S. Cobb once said, "There is this to be said for New York City: it is the one densely inhabited locality—with the possible exception of Hell— that has absolutely not a trace of local pride." Mr. Cobb to the contrary notwithstanding, the same problem exists in most large cities.

Another aspect of low citizen interest may be found in factors related to the phenomenon that the psychologists call identification. The individual, in his fantasies—in his daydreaming—tends to associate himself with the heroic, the "important" things in life. The dramatic, glamorous activities of the national government attract the layman, appeal to his imagination, and help him to form opinions about controversial matters on

[3] This movement, its philosophy, and its results will be reviewed in chap. 3.

this level of government, but the commonplace problems of health and of police and fire protection will have much less appeal. When the President of the United States discusses national problems over radio and television and asks for the assistance and support of the citizen, the individual is flattered. If, however, the mayor of the city appears on the television screen to talk to the citizenry about the daily problems of the municipality, the response of the citizen is not likely to be the same. Unless the mayor is an unusual individual, the citizen is likely to switch to another channel. His busy mind, with a thousand attractions calling for attention, can be directed only toward those things that are "important" or "interesting."

It can be seen, therefore, that many factors have combined to produce the cultural image of municipal government that exists today. Of all of them, however, the most important is the failure of the lay citizen to take a full measure of interest in the government that is the most intimate, the most observable, and the closest to him of all the coercive agents of society. The ordinary citizen must understand that whenever governments fail him in performing a demanded service, whenever there is a lack of imagination, of ability, or of zeal on the part of city officials, and whenever there is a lack of honesty in city government, it is because the citizenry has not insisted that it be otherwise.

METROPOLITAN PANORAMA

Cities come in all sizes and shapes. Some are large, some are small. No two are exactly alike. We can speak of statistical averages and "typical" cities, but we can only approximate what we would find if we were to give an intensive examination to any one city. An impressionistic glance may, however, furnish a few generalizations which can be examined in greater detail farther on in this text.

What, then, are the characteristics of the metropolis? It is a smoky, grimy sea of television aerials, noisome slums, bright neon signs, impatient traffic, mammoth factories with fantastic productive capacity, manicured suburbs desperately seeking to imitate a fond memory of a county-seat town in grandfather's day, with its frenetic citizens earnestly striving to be as exactly like the next-door neighbor as possible, dreading a slip that might engender the anathematic charge of being "different." It is a Champaigne fair of conflicting cultures where thousands of human beings live in close proximity to other thousands whom they dislike in one degree or another because—though they would not so state it—their values and cultural habits do not coincide. For the human being dislikes what he fears, he fears much that he does not understand, and there is much in the modern city that he does not understand. It is a land of coolness in a

Figure 1-1. City Hall, Birmingham, Ala. Victorian and "General Grant gothic" city halls are giving way to modern buildings in contemporary design. The change is symbolic of the change that has taken place in city government. SOURCE: Courtesy of C. E. Armstrong, Birmingham, Ala.

nation of supposedly friendly people, where émigrés from rural places find an absence of the primary social relationships to which they are accustomed, and where people, in the midst of the greatest possible variety of activities, often lead basically dull lives, although they seek to hide that fact from their own consciousness.

The City Hall. The people of the city have little interest in their local government and treat it with a lack of respect which, in their opinion, is its due. Somewhere downtown in an area sadly lacking in parking space —as is the entire city, for that matter—stands a hideous monstrosity decorated with Victorian gingerbread and contemporary pigeon droppings. This is the city hall. The interior of it is a prime example of poor utilization of space, and the taxpayers meet an abnormally large light bill, since the windows would not furnish adequate natural light if the building were located in the center of the Sahara (but see Figure 1-1).

The city officialdom is headed by the mayor, who is quite likely to be a man of broad smiles, firm handshakes, and modest talents. There are probably several other elective administrative officials—most of them glorified bookkeepers or file clerks, but the public insists upon electing them.

The members of the city council are perhaps somewhat more difficult to classify. Depending upon the city, a few or even perhaps most of them may be men chosen from the business and industrial world, who often are more concerned with the interests of the groups that selected them to run for office than with trying to determine a concept of the public interest. The council is apt to include in its membership one or more representatives of organized labor, who similarly are primarily concerned with labor interests. Usually it includes several lawyers, often those who are politically ambitious and who would use membership in the council as a steppingstone to higher political careers. It is not uncommon for lawyers to run for the council in the hope that the prestige and public notice gained in councilmanic membership will advance them in their profession. There may be a number of political hacks on the council: men who know nothing but the art of politics and to whom defeat would spell threatened starvation.

Although the citizen may pay little attention to local politics, he is quite likely to consider himself a very competent "Monday morning quarterback." While he is quick to offer criticisms of state and national officials, he is even more convinced of his competence in evaluating problems of municipal government. Furthermore, since municipal officials are close at hand, it is much easier for the citizen to make his complaints known.

Services of the City. Transportation is a real problem in the city. Not only is there a serious shortage of parking facilities, but there is probably no form of public transportation that can serve even generally as a substitute for the auto. The bus and streetcar system is operating at a deficit, be it privately or publicly owned, chiefly as the result of one simple fact: in 1918 there was one automobile for every eighteen people, today there is one for every four. Of course, the inadequacy is blamed on just about anything but this. If a private company owns the system, the pundits are screaming for purchase by the city. If the city is already in possession, the fault is found to lie with this misguided application of un-American socialism and the whole system should be returned post-haste to private hands. (Not that any entrepreneur in his right mind would undertake to buy it.) If no other scapegoat can be found, the fault must lie with "politics."

Expressways, belt lines, and cutoffs are beginning to appear several decades after their need first became apparent. The sunken highways do hurry you downtown, but they do not help you park the auto once you arrive there.

The Urban Personality. The streets of the city are not likely to have the fascinating names of those in a European metropolis. Our cities must have efficiency, not uniqueness. Many an American town is laid out with consecutively numbered streets running in one direction. The streets running at right angles to these may well be numbered "avenues." In 1952, the city of Toledo changed Wausonoquette Boulevard to 290th Street, and in one American city unimaginative residents petitioned the council to give a new name to a street called Spike's Alley. The main artery of Philadelphia is called simply Broad Street; Columbus has High Street; Davenport, Second Street. Although Boston has the Hoosac Docks, most of its place names sound as dull as the love life of a Puritan. Even mighty New York shows its tourists such names as Madison Avenue, Wall Street, Fifth Avenue and, at best, Broadway. At least in Manhattan. Of course Brooklyn does somewhat better with the Gowanus Canal and Flatbush Avenue.

All is not lost, however: there is Cane Run Road in Louisville; Sepulveda Boulevard and Topanga Canyon Avenue in Los Angeles; Cottage Grove Avenue in Chicago; and John R. Street in Detroit. St. Louis has Gravois; Minneapolis, Nicollet; Atlanta, Ponce de Leon; and Omaha, Saddle Creek Road. Even the nation's capital has Fighting Alley and Donnybrook Lane. Probably no city in America can come close to legendary New Orleans with its properly romantic street names: Canal, Carondolet, Bourbon, Beauregard, and the immortal Rampart Street. Nor are all American cities named for the local frontier banker, or called -burgs, -cities, -villes, or -ports. To name only a few, there is Fuquay Springs, Conshohocken, What Cheer, Aliquippa, San Luis Obispo, Wauwatosa, Irondequoit, Nacogdoches, Walla Walla, and Waxahachie. The chances are, however, that the First National Bank stands at the corner of Third Street and Sixth Avenue in Williamsburg.

Unlike the cities of Europe, each of which possesses a distinctive individuality, American cities for the most part have a dull monotony about them. To be sure, there are exceptions. There is only one Boston, New Orleans, New York, Atlantic City, San Francisco, or Washington. But the typical city has little to distinguish it as a personality. It has failed to develop its own individuality, to exploit latent traditions, to use its every opportunity to make the community a place where life is richer because of its own particular attributes. In the past, most pillars of the community and local politicians have been too busy in a frenetic world to concern themselves with such an expendable as local color.

Chaotic Development. Inadequate planning and land-use controls are a part of the picture, for somehow the concept of individual initiative and individual use of one's own property has been misinterpreted to mean a right to damage property values of others indiscriminately and to destroy the physical beauty and utility of an area. On the fringe of the city in particular will you find chaotic land use. Although the suburbanite has taken a deep interest in land-use controls—they represent a major governmental technique for molding the community to suit his image of a desirable life style—much damage has usually taken place before a planning commission is established and controls made effective.

The City Is a Playground. From the hinterland for miles around, people flock to the city when they seek recreation and relief from the chores of every day. The informal amusement patterns of rural America have given way to commercialization. The metropolis offers the theater, the symphony or an occasional opera, professional sports, the public dance hall, skating, billiards, and bowling. The saloon and its more elaborate relative, the night club, interest many. Some wish to visit museums, art galleries, zoos, parks, beaches, or playgrounds.

Any kind of recreation demanded by its hordes of people will be furnished by someone within the city. In a day when people feel more than ever the need for escape from the humdrum, gambling serves as a way out for increasing numbers. Except for operations at the gaudy track laid out in the suburbs, this business is illegal, to be sure, but it is controlled by a syndicate of gangsters who welcome its illegality. This same syndicate is likely to be involved in furnishing other illegal services: prostitution and narcotics. Illegal occupations produce enormous problems for the police—and city officials receive no sympathy from a public that simultaneously demands law enforcement and illegal services.

The City Is a Magnet. In comparison with the rural life that once dominated America, contemporary city life produces more crime, especially of the organized and professional type, more neurotics, more insanity, more lung cancer (possibly because of the greater amount of hydrocarbon irritants in its polluted air), greater extremes of wealth and poverty, more social and economic interdependence and hence more insecurity, more juvenile delinquency, more wrecked marriages, more suicides, and more deaths per thousand people.

Why, then, do increasing numbers of people come every year to the metropolis? And why do those who are already there only *talk* about giving up the struggle and taking "a little place in the country"? Because there is in the city a greater freedom for individually chosen behavior patterns; greater tolerance of diversity (but only in the more crowded parts of the city); more and better schools at all educational levels; a greater variety of entertainment mediums; far more institutions of fine art —libraries, museums, theaters, art cinemas, symphony orchestras, and the ballet; and a much greater opportunity for advancement in accord with the American pattern of values.

The city contains greater extremes of wealth and poverty than does the country, but for most people it means a higher standard of living. It suggests more material things and more of an opportunity for "the good life." The older pattern has been reversed: ours is now a society based largely upon urban values, with the rural dweller more and more imitating the ways of the urbanite. The contemporary American dream is housed among the millions in our cities.[4]

PORTRAIT OF A SMALL CITY

The metropolis, as it has just been described, is only part of the picture. In addition to those large cities of over, say, 100,000 people, there are a number of middle-sized cities in the United States ranging within the general limits of 40,000 to 100,000 people. Smaller than these and less complicated politically, but still a most important part of America, are hundreds of small cities.

The County Seat Today. Storville (we shall call it) is a Middle Western city of about 5,000 inhabitants. While it is hardly possible to pick out *the* typical small city in America, or even one for a particular section of the country, Storville certainly reflects many of the characteristics of a city of its size, and its governmental pattern is not atypical.

Storville is a county seat and trading town in a dairy region. It contains a goodly number of elderly retired farmers, but many of its young people have left to live in larger cities. There are several small manufacturing plants in town, all of them unionized, but the unions are not active in local politics, as they would be in a large city. Most of the people of the community have conservative political, social, and economic views, and they are Republicans in state and national elections. Churches are important local institutions—there are eight of them to serve the city and its rural trading area.

The local school board is building new schools, partly because Storville is growing in size, but largely because of the consolidation of school districts and the closing of surrounding "country schools." People in the city feel they are paying too great a share of the cost of educating the rural students.

The Manager, the Council, and Local Politics. Storville has operated as a council-manager city since the middle 1920s. The present manager, the city's sixth, is a civil engineer. He is about fifty years old, has spent most of his life in private employment, and is now serving in his second city as manager.

The council, which is elected at large, consists of five men, all of whom are under forty-five, except for the mayor. One is a grocer, another operates a men's store, a third is a hatchery owner, and the fourth is a plant superintendent in a middle-sized city forty-five minutes away by automo-

[4] For unfavorable criticisms of the contemporary city and of urban life, see E. T. Peterson, *Cities Are Abnormal* (University of Oklahoma Press, Norman, Okla., 1946), and Lewis Mumford, *The Culture of Cities* (Harcourt, Brace & World, Inc., New York, 1938).

bile. The mayor, who presides over the council and has no veto power, is a motel operator, is fifty-eight years old, and has had eighteen years of experience in city government—much more than any of the council-men. He shares policy leadership with the manager.

Elections are on a nonpartisan ballot and campaigns on an informal, personal basis. There is some pressure-group activity before the council and at elections, but most relationships between candidates or office-holders and the public are direct. State and county politicians do not take part in city campaigns. There is no single outstanding political leader in the city, although on some matters of local public policy people defer to the judgment of the president of the local bank. The principal interest groups in Storville politics are the chamber of commerce, acting for the downtown merchants, the League of Women Voters, and the American Legion. The last time an incumbent councilman decided to retire, the Legion solicited support in the community for one of its leaders and he was elected to fill the vacated seat.

Councilmen try to determine the public's viewpoints on important is-sues through personal contacts. They have no direct way of measuring their success in discovering cross-section opinions, but they believe that they "do all right"—at least an incumbent is seldom defeated for re-election.

Issues and Problems. The people of Storville are quite satisfied with their police department. It consists of a chief, seven policemen, two patrol cars, and a two-way radio system, and it enjoys a close relationship with the county sheriff's office. The fire department suits them, too. It has a paid chief with one full-time fireman. Other members are volunteers, each of whom has a radio in his home for receiving fire calls.

Water supply—from deep wells—is adequate, although another well will be needed in a few years. The manager will recommend that it be built at the east end of town—in the direction of population movement. The cost of water in Storville is nearly twice that of the largest cities in the state, since there is no large volume of sale which would reduce unit costs.

The city is faced with greater problems, however. County taxes are poorly equalized, and the city dweller pays a disproportionate share of them. City property taxes are high and produce many complaints. Stor-ville, from the time sewers were first installed, has dumped its raw sewage into the local river. This practice is creating a hazard to fish and to human health, so the city, under pressure from the state, must now raise $350,000 for a sewage-treatment plant.

The capital-improvements program of the city has not kept pace with the increase in the number of people—or automobiles. The greatest num-ber of complaints heard by councilmen and the manager deal with the condition of the streets. They are in poor repair—poorer than the streets in a typical large city—and maintenance has not equaled the rate of wear in recent years. There is no demand, however, as there is in some nearby cities, for belt lines to take state highways around the city. Traffic is not heavy enough in Storville, and the main street was never a highway, as it often was or still is in small cities. The manager has recently convinced the council that it should pass an ordinance authorizing the council to install street paving, curbs, and gutters without first securing permission from a majority of the abutting property owners. This will give the manager much more flexibility in planning street improvements.

There is a serious shortage of parking spaces in downtown Storville, and the city government is trying to acquire a number of off-street parking lots. The weekly *Storville Star* has criticized this action by the city as adding a further burden to the overworked property tax. (The *Star*, unlike newspapers in many small cities, has been very critical of the mayor and the manager, irresponsibly so at times. The parking lots, for example, are to be paid for exclusively from parking-meter receipts, not from general taxes.) Parking meters were installed in 1948, and they blanket all of the commercial areas of the city. They have been profitable from the start. People no longer complain about them.

The parking situation, plus a need for more space and a desire for lower taxes and cheaper land, has led some merchants and small manufacturers to move outside the city limits. A grim headline in the *Star* warned, "Tax Loss to City Seen in Decentralization Trend." A fringe-area problem has resulted. Two adjacent townships have found it desirable to adopt zoning ordinances to control developments. Storville has been asked to supply water outside its limits. A slum area of dilapidated shacks has grown up on the fringe to the west, but a subdivision of expensive homes lies outside the taxing limits to the north. The fringe is growing along the main traffic arteries.

A new city plan and zoning ordinance was adopted a year ago to replace an outmoded one. It was prepared by a professional planner. But it was greatly altered by the council after hearings revealed the views of interested individuals.

THE SMALL TOWN: URBAN ANOMALY

Village and small-town life has been a traditional part of America, honored in memory and song and satirized in novel and poem. The town has its origins as a service center for a small rural area. Throughout much of the nation, towns were originally spaced close enough together to allow any farmer to reach one by horseback or buggy within a reasonable length of time, perhaps an hour. County seats were generally situated so that they were not more than a day's buggy ride from the farthest farmer. They were larger than ordinary trading places, since they contained the incipient bureaucracy of government, the offices of lawyers who dealt with that bureaucracy on behalf of clients, livery stables, hotels, and other establishments catering to the citizenry that found it necessary or desirable to visit the seat of government.

The ordinary town contained a general store, repair shops, a physician and a veterinarian, a weekly newspaper, a bank, a school, and a church or two. If the community was large enough, it also served as a market. With the coming of the automobile and telephone, this pattern began to change. By the 1950s, the general store had come more to resemble the corner grocery of the city or, in larger towns, had become a super-market (which is, in fact, a reconstitution of the old general store except that modern merchandising techniques have been added and the traditional function as a news and gossip center has declined). The physician found he could make more money and serve more people by moving into the nearby city. The weekly newspaper, in the face of high labor and newsprint costs, was beginning to disappear. The bank had become a branch of a city institution or had disappeared. The school now represented the consolidation of a great many formerly rural districts with an elaborate system of school bus routes. The churches continued to perform some, though not all, of their traditional functions. The population was made up of locally employed persons, a considerable number of retired farmers, and a new element—the commuters. Many persons, either because of a preference for the small-town life or because of shortages in low-cost housing in the cities, have taken up residence in the town but may drive up to 25 and more miles each day to their jobs in the city.

Small-town Politics. Politically, the villages and towns tend to be, throughout the nation, centers of conservatism. Most of them are one-party communities, whether Democratic or Republican, depending upon local traditions. Although their governments provide basic community services in the areas of water, sewage disposal and sewerage, police and fire protection, the small community remains a center of opposition to the social-service state. Lacking experience in the social problems of large cities or in living together with cultural groups having different values from their own, its citizens tend to be intolerant of proposed state or municipal legislation dealing with problems that do not exist or exist in minor ways in their communities. To them, the fact that such problems exist in large cities is taken to be evidence of the degeneracy or moral inferiority of urban life. This attitude cannot be ignored as quaint but harmless, however. Representatives from small towns dominate most state legislatures, which are the agencies that control the powers exercised by large city governments.

Yet the town is itself a political, economic, and social problem. Its difficulties stem from several things: the declining farm population which produces a declining market; the preference of many farmers for the more specialized and hence more expert services in the nearby city, now easily available by modern auto and good roads; the lack of opportunity in the town, while our culture emphasizes the desirability of opportunity, with the resultant draining off of the most able young people; extreme conservatism in a day when many attitudes which this produces do not fit into the value systems learned in the consolidated schools and on television by young people; and finally, current highway-department practices of bypassing practically all towns, thus cutting off the transient business that had earlier helped to sustain them. The small town is an urban place and its life style is no longer as different from that of the large city as it once was, but it is still different—and its governmental and social problems are different.[5]

Consensus and Inaction in Springdale. Springdale, a rural village in upstate New York, was studied by two sociologists who wanted to see how the villagers were accommodating to life in mass society. The community offers some not atypical examples of small-town life. Its politics differs radically from that of the metropolis. While the large city is often the scene of strident and undisguised political conflict, in the village: [6]

. . . politics is conducted on the principle of unanimity of decision. In two years of observation of village board meetings in Springdale, all decisions brought to a vote were passed unanimously. The dissent, disagreement and factionalism which exist in the community are not expressed at board meetings. Through a process of consultation prior to an official meeting and by extended discussion involving the entire group during the meeting itself, a point is reached when it seems reasonable to assume that everyone will go along with the proposed action. Only then, as a final parry, will someone suggest that a motion be made to propose the action.

While the large city is the scene of constant experimentation, the arena in which new social-service activities of government are launched,

[5] On town life in general, see H. P. Douglass, *The Little Town* (The Macmillan Company, New York, 1927); Granville Hicks, *Small Town* (The Macmillan Company, New York, 1947); W. J. Hayes, *The Small Community Looks Ahead* (Harcourt, Brace & World, Inc., New York, 1947); A. J. Vidich and J. Bensman, *Small Town in Mass Society* (Princeton University Press, Princeton, N.J., 1958).

[6] Vidich and Bensman, *op. cit.*, pp. 112–113. By permission of the Princeton University Press.

TABLE 1-1. DISSATISFACTION WITH LOCAL
GOVERNMENTAL SERVICES
(In per cent)

Number of services with which dissatisfied	Dayton	Suburban zone	Outer zone
None.............	45	20	32
One..............	26	24	20
Two.............	16	23	29
Three or more.......	13	33	14

Note that suburbanites and exurbanites desire the services that the core city already has.

SOURCE: John C. Bollens and others, *Metropolitan Challenge* (Metropolitan Community Studies, Inc., Dayton, Ohio, 1959), table 47. Used by permission.

and in which a highly professional bureaucracy administers complex programs, the pattern in the village is totally different:

Although the principle of unanimity of decision is almost a requirement in Springdale politics, few items of business outside of routine and legally required action ever reach the decision-making stage. It is an outstanding characteristic of village government that it does not initiate new undertakings and new projects. . . . It is a common complaint among all groups in the community that the village board does nothing.

Grand Plans and Grass Roots in Suburbia. Although great variety is the characteristic of urban politics in America, there are some common patterns. While the small-town dweller wishes to avoid decisions and opposes new or expanded programs, the suburbanite looks to his local government to provide many of life's amenities. (See Table 1-1.) While the person living in a large city has a feeling of isolation from the political process and tends to be apathetic, the surburbanite feels close to his government and is likely to believe that he and his neighbors can run it on a grass-roots basis. In fact, one characteristic of suburbia is the resident's [7]—

. . . acceptance of an obligation for extensive civic participation on the part of the lay constituency. . . . On the local level civic interest may express itself in the citizen's inclination to undertake the supervision of the local bureaucracy

[7] Robert C. Wood, *Suburbia—Its People and Their Politics* (Houghton Mifflin Company, Boston, 1959), pp. 156–157. By permission of the Houghton Mifflin Company.

directly, or in his suspicion of the role of the professional political leader. Here the image of resurrected grassroots democracy commits the citizen, theoretically, at least, to a do-it-yourself brand of politics, in which as many issues as possible, simple and complex, require his personal sanction, and the acceptable elected official is the part-time amateur, taking his term in office just as he once led the community chest drive.

Finally . . . there is a belief that the individual can and should arrive at his political convictions untutored and unled; an expectation that in the formal process of election and decision-making, a consensus will emerge through the process of right reason and by the higher call to the common good.

Closing Statement. The village, small city, metropolis, and suburb differ from one another in many ways. But they are all urban areas, and they share many characteristics, problems, and issues. This book will be concerned with their similarities and their differences.

THE COMING OF THE CITY

Meanings and Usages. Nothing much can be learned concerning the nature of an area simply because it is called a city. The term itself descends from the Latin *civis* (citizen) and was restricted in England to application to cathedral towns. (Other urban areas in England were known as boroughs—a term used today in the city of New York and to some extent in Connecticut, New Jersey, Minnesota, and Pennsylvania.) [8] A city in the United States is a *legal*, not a *sociological*, concept. City limits may be greater or smaller than the *de facto* urban area. In most states a city may or may not be larger than the largest villages in the state. Villages may be tiny rural trading centers, or they may be sizable urban areas, as in the case of several of Chicago's large suburbs. There may or may not be meaningful legal differences between cities and villages. In this text, what is said to apply to cities will also generally apply to villages as well. As a matter of fact, the smaller urbanized areas of a state may be legally called villages (as in Minnesota), or they may be called towns (as in Iowa). The smallest *rural* unit of government is usually the township—except in New England, where it is a unique institution and is called a town. To add to the confusion, however, townships do not exist at all in some states, especially in the South; in

[8] The word *town* is from the Anglo-Saxon *tun*, a homestead surrounded by a hedge or other fence (from Old High German, *zûn*, a hedge). *Borough* is from the Anglo-Saxon *burh*, a fortified town. Today, in the four states named above, it represents an incorporated area occupying a position between that of a city and a village. The five administrative subdivisions of New York are also called boroughs. *Village* is from the Italian and Latin *villa*, meaning originally a farm or country house. The term *municipality* is from the Latin *municipium*, which referred to certain Italian towns that enjoyed special privileges under Rome. In the United States today, the term is popularly (and in this book) used interchangeably with *city* or *village*.

Minnesota they are legally (although not popularly) known as towns; and around some of our cities they have become urbanized and constitute virtually another form of city government (for example, in Michigan and New Jersey).

The largest urban communities are often popularly (although not legally) known as metropolitan areas (from the Greek *mētēr*, mother, and *polis*, city-state). These "mother-cities" are ordinarily made up of an agglomeration of cities, villages, townships, special districts, and other units that may total several hundred in number. In the United States, these sociologically cohesive units are virtually never treated as legal units; the metropolitan area is almost never a single city.

The student should be warned, therefore, against any hasty conclusions concerning the meaning of the terms usually used in connection with urban areas. Without a standard terminology he must be prepared to adapt his understanding of terms to conditions prevailing locally. For purposes of this text, an urban area is conceived of as a sociological community wherein the individuals are engaged primarily in diversified nonagricultural pursuits and where distinctive, nonrural patterns of behavior prevail. A city, village, borough, or (sometimes) town is a legally described region which seldom coincides with the actual urban area.[9]

Urbanization of the Western World. The city in western civilization is primarily a product of the industrial revolution. To be sure, there were cities in Europe before 1770 (roughly the time of the beginning of the "revolution," which lasted for over a century thereafter), but they were chiefly capitals or trading centers.[10] In 1550, Paris, both a trading center and a great seat of government, was, according to W. B. Munro, the largest city in Europe, and its population did not exceed 300,000. Mighty London was a village during the Middle Ages, having only about 40,000 people as that period came to an end. It grew very rapidly in the sixteenth and seventeenth centuries as Britain became the trading center of the rising new economic world. By the time of the American Revolution, it had become the largest city in Europe, with a population of around three-quarters of a million people.

With the rise of a machine technology, steam power, and the factory

---

[9] It is neither realistic nor necessary to try to make a sharp break between rural and urban living, especially in present-day United States. For the difficulties involved in trying to define a city, see Noel P. Gist and L. A. Halbert, *Urban Society* (4th ed., Thomas Y. Crowell Company, New York, 1956), pp. 3–8; or Stuart A. Queen and David B. Carpenter, *The American City* (McGraw-Hill Book Company, Inc., New York, 1953), pp. 16–22.

[10] For a most interesting account of ancient and medieval cities, see W. B. Munro, *Municipal Government and Administration* [with subsequent revisions] (The Macmillan Company, New York, 1923), vol. 1, chaps. 1–4; or his article "City," in *Encyclopedia of the Social Sciences*, vol. 2, pp. 474–482. See also Lewis Mumford, *The Culture of Cities* (Harcourt, Brace & World, Inc., New York, 1938) and R. E. Dickinson, *The West European City* (Routledge & Kegan Paul, Ltd., London, 1950).

system, cities grew at phenomenal rates. Europe and America, predominantly rural from prehistoric times, rapidly became urbanized nations. In the United States, there were only small towns at the time of the Revolution. They were growing, however, and they continued to grow. From the turn of the nineteenth century, cities expanded at an ever increasing pace. Between 1820 and 1840 the number of people engaged in manufacturing increased by 127 per cent. Between 1840 and 1850 alone, America's urban population increased by nearly 50 per cent.[11]

After the construction of railroads, the heavy influx of foreign investment, and the War between the States (1861–1865), urban growth, which earlier had occurred on the East Coast and especially in New England, spread into the Middle West. The rise of the great corporations and the never-ending developments in technological knowledge continued to raise the American *standard* of living even as it changed the American *mode* of living. Immigrants who before had hurried to the rich clay loams of the Middle Western farm belt now remained in New York, or Cincinnati, or Chicago to become a commodity called "labor" in the factory, the steel mill, or the stockyard.[12] The children of country bumpkins yearned to become city slickers and hurried off at the earliest opportunity to what was often their disillusionment. And they continue to do so today.

The City Today. The population of cities doubled between the beginning of the War between the States and 1900. In the next quarter of a century, it doubled again. By 1920, over one half (51.2 per cent) of the American people were living in cities.[13] The percentage in 1960 was

[11] An account of the coming of industrial society to America is especially well done in Arthur M. Schlesinger, Jr., *The Age of Jackson* (Little, Brown & Company, Boston, 1945). More generally, see E. E. Lampard, "The History of Cities in the Economically Advanced Areas," *Economic Development and Cultural Change*, vol. 3 (January, 1955), pp. 81–136.

[12] See Arthur M. Schlesinger, *The Rise of the City* (The Macmillan Company, New York, 1933), and his "The City in American History," *Mississippi Valley Historical Review*, vol. 27 (June, 1940), pp. 43–66.

[13] For statistical purposes, the U.S. Bureau of the Census classifies cities as incorporated places with 2,500 or more inhabitants. Legal definitions differ from this in the various states.

In the census of 1960, the Bureau defined urban, as distinguished from rural, areas as (1) places of 2,500 inhabitants or more incorporated as cities, boroughs, or villages; (2) the densely settled urban fringe, whether incorporated or unincorporated, around cities of 25,000 or more (the limits of this area determined more or less arbitrarily, based upon physical features); (3) unincorporated areas of 2,500 inhabitants or more outside of the urban fringes; and (4) towns of 2,500 or more except in New England, New York, and Wisconsin.

The Bureau has also undertaken to define large urban places. "Standard metropolitan statistical areas" contain at least one city of 50,000 or more population. The nucleus of the area is the county or counties containing the core city or cities. Contiguous counties are included in the area if they are densely settled by nonagricultural workers and are socially and economically integrated with the core city. For technical criteria, see U.S. Bureau of the Budget, *Standard Metropolitan Statistical Areas* (1959).

around 70 and continues to climb. We live in an urban nation. The world today depends upon no man more than it depends upon the American farmer. But he is no longer a member of the dominant group in our society. And his cultural patterns and sets of values are rapidly being replaced by new ones more in keeping with our own, rather than our parents' or grandparents', world. (See Figure 1-2.)

In 1960, nearly two-thirds of the American population lived not merely in urban, but in *metropolitan* communities. Approximately one-fourth of it lived in the twelve largest metropolitan areas. About 220 counties hold over one-half of the nation's population. The other half is scattered over 2,800 essentially rural counties.

The population of the United States reached 179.3 million by census-count time in 1960. This represented an increase of more than 28 million in a ten-year period. All of that increase was urban, for the population that earns its livelihood from working the soil declines each year as it has—interrupted only by the years of the Great Depression—since shortly after the beginning of the century. The gain was high (about 24 per cent) in the 192 metropolitan areas, but it was highest of all in the suburbs. (See Figures 1-3 and 1-4.)

It was the very largest cities that generated the greatest suburban population increases, but the moderate-sized metropolitan areas (those between one-half a million and one million people) grew more rapidly than did any other size of community. The huge cities (except Los Angeles, which gained 24 per cent) generally lost population as people showed a preference for suburban life styles. New York remained the nation's largest city, with 7,781,984 people. However, New York lost 3 per cent in the preceding decade. So did Chicago. Of the huge cities, Detroit suffered the heaviest loss—nearly 10 per cent—though this merely repre-

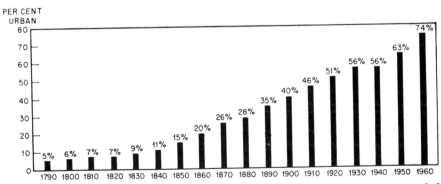

Figure 1-2. Percentage of population in urban areas. Figures have been rounded off. At the time of the first United States census in 1790, less than 5 per cent of the population lived in urban areas. Today, virtually three-fourths of all Americans are urbanites. SOURCE: U.S. Bureau of the Census, early preliminary figures.

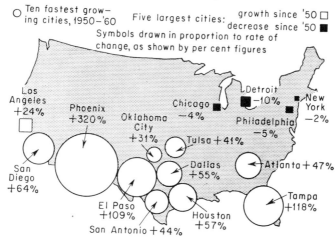

RATE OF CHANGE

○ Ten fastest grow-
   ing cities, 1950–'60   Five largest cities: growth since '50 □
                                                decrease since '50 ■
                Symbols drawn in proportion to rate of
                change, as shown by per cent figures

Los Angeles +24%
Phoenix +320%
Chicago −4%
Detroit −10%
New York −2%
Oklahoma City +31%
Philadelphia −5%
Tulsa +41%
San Diego +64%
Dallas +55%
Atlanta +47%
El Paso +109%
Houston +57%
Tampa +118%
San Antonio +44%

Figure 1-3. SOURCE: *The New York Times*, July 31, 1960.

sented a movement of its generally well-paid population to the suburbs, for its satellites gained 79 per cent. This rate was second, among cities of over one million, only to the 83 per cent in the burgeoning Los Angeles suburbs. The Los Angeles metropolitan area, in fact, became the second largest in the nation, passing the Chicago area during the decade. The greatest increases, as had been the case a decade earlier, took place along the Pacific and Gulf of Mexico Coasts, and in the areas near the Great Lakes. The nation, with nearly 70 per cent of its population crowded into only about 6 per cent of the area of the fifty states, had indeed become urban.

The Urban Region. Only seven of the fifty states contain no metropolitan areas. These are Alaska, Idaho, Montana, Nevada (which is, however, 70 per cent urban), North Dakota (the least urban state, with about 35 per cent), Vermont, and Wyoming. Elsewhere, of course, it is around the metropolises that the population continues to cluster. In fact, these areas are growing into one another, so that Charlton F. Chute has found it advantageous to define "urban regions." These consist of two or more contiguous standard metropolitan statistical areas. The greatest of these is the Eastern Seaboard region, which stretches for 600 miles from the vicinity of Haverhill, north of Boston near the New Hampshire border, to the southernmost suburbs of Washington, in Virginia. This vast region contained around 31.6 million people in 1957, or about 19 per cent of the total national population.[14] The Chicago and Cleveland urban

[14] For additional information on urban complexes, particularly that of the Eastern Seaboard, see *The New York Times*, Jan. 27 to Feb. 3, 1957.

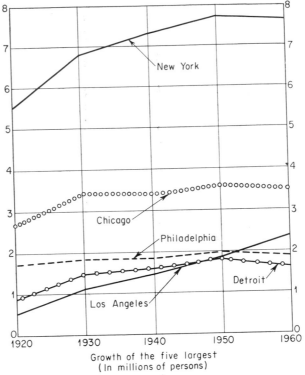

Growth of the five largest
(In millions of persons)

Figure 1-4. Except for cities with considerable vacant land within their legal boundaries (such as Los Angeles), 1950 marked a population peak. SOURCE: *The New York Times,* July 31, 1960.

regions are also huge—bigger, in fact, in the 1950s than the Los Angeles region, which stretches from the northwest suburbs of Los Angeles to the southern suburbs of San Diego, a distance of over 200 miles and is expected to become the second largest region in the nation in the 1960s.[15] In all, there are eighteen urban regions, containing about 40 per cent of the nation's population. Because the complexity as well as the cost of government increases disproportionately with density, it can be expected that these will be the areas where governmental problems will continue to make their greatest challenge.[16]

The Negro Leaves the Farm. American Negroes are descended from persons who were brought to the New World as slaves. Their ancestors labored on plantations in the South, and nearly all of them were rural

[15] See *U.S. News and World Report,* Sept. 16, 1955, pp. 47–66.
[16] See Charlton F. Chute, "Today's Urban Regions," *National Municipal Review,* vol. 45 (June and July, 1956). In this section, Chute's two separate regions, one centering around Boston and the other around New York, have been combined into a single region.

dwellers. After the War between the States, most Negroes remained in the deep South, becoming sharecroppers on land subdivided when the great plantations were broken up. Their number increased with each census, but a lower economic standard, leading to a higher death rate, combined with an almost all-white immigration, caused the percentage of the population, which had been nearly 20 per cent Negro in 1790, to drop to 14 per cent in 1860 and to about 10 per cent in 1930. The percentage has since remained at about this figure, rising slightly in 1960.

Even before slavery was abolished, some movement of Negroes out of the South took place. However, as late as 1900, only 10 per cent of the Negro population lived in the North. The big change, the one that brought economic opportunity to the poverty-ridden Negro sharecropper, was the demand for his labor in the urban factory. The first great demand for this purpose came during World War I, when a shortage of factory hands caused an imbalance in supply and demand of labor. It was the younger, more adventuresome who first made the long trek to Chicago, Detroit, or New York. The word they sent back was that one could make far more money in less time under better conditions of labor in a factory than in the almost hopeless atmosphere of the tenant farm. As early as 1914, Henry Ford created a sensation when he offered a $5-a-day minimum wage. He also established a quota for Negro employees.

The young man in a Chicago rooming house listening to the words of encouragement offered by the precinct worker for Mayor "Big Bill" Thompson's machine (Why, "Big Bill" would even let a Negro *vote* in Chicago!) did not write home about the terrible housing conditions, what would happen when employment dropped off, or the unscrupulous gougers who so often acted as real estate men or retail merchants in the burgeoning South Side "Black Belt." Nor did he emphasize the bitter loneliness of the culturally marginal man—the man who was reared according to the values of one culture, in this case, that of the Southern Negro tenant farmer, but who moves to an area applying a different set of cultural values, in this case, those of a Northern industrial urban community. To him, a job in the city meant, for the first time, the possibility of entering into the competitive struggle for upward mobility and an increase in status position that had long been a typical pattern of activity for other Americans.

Recent Developments. After World War I, only the Great Depression served temporarily to stop the urbanization of the Negro. Every other important economic and political consideration—the closing of the gates to immigrants (1924), World War II (1941–1945), and the prosperous years after 1945—encouraged the movement to cities. In the decade following 1940, 3 million Negroes made the rural-to-urban change. By 1950, 27.6 per cent of the Negro population lived in the North and nearly 60 per cent of the total was urban, for Southern Negroes also moved into Southern cities. This percentage has continued to climb.

In 1960, the percentage of the Negro population that was located in urban areas was very nearly as large as that of the white population. In the years following the beginning of war preparations about 1940, the nonwhite growth in urban population was far greater than that on the farm. In cities of over 50,000 the nonwhite population increased at a rate five times that of the white population (49.2 per cent as against 10.4 per cent) between 1940 and 1950. The Los Angeles and Detroit nonwhite populations doubled; that of San Francisco increased by 156 per cent. New York's Harlem became the largest Negro community in the world. (See Figure 1-5.)

By 1957, one person in five within the city limits of Chicago was a Negro; in Detroit the proportion had nearly reached one in four. But the growth of nonwhite suburban population has been very slow. Since Negroes, therefore, tend to concentrate in the core cities and since their rate of urbanization is much faster than that of the white population, we may expect that they will become the dominant racial or ethnic group in the core cities of many metropolitan areas in the coming decades. This

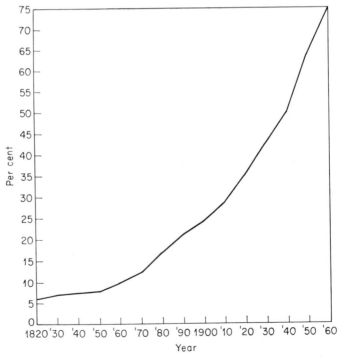

Figure 1-5. Negroes in urban areas, as per cent of Negro population. SOURCE: U.S. Bureau of the Census.

will likely mean dramatic changes in the political patterns of those cities, with Negro majorities on the council and a Negro mayor in city hall an eventual possibility in such cities as Chicago, Cleveland, Detroit, and St. Louis. It is a matter for speculation as to the effect that such developments will have upon metropolitan area government, intergovernmental relations, partisan conflicts in state legislatures, the suburban movement, interracial friction, and a host of other political and social matters.[17]

Population: In Summary. By 1959, America had become an industrial nation with over two-thirds of its population living in urban areas and chiefly in metropolitan communities. The large core cities had almost stopped growing: the great bulk of the population growth after 1950 was centered in the suburban areas. Small-town population continued to hold its own, and farm population, which had reached an all-time high of 32.4 million in 1915 and had been declining almost without interruption since, continued to drop.

In the metropolitan areas, the flight to the suburbs by the bulk of the middle-class and many working-class families was still being largely counterbalanced by the continuing arrival of migrants from rural and small-town areas. Negroes, in particular, were moving into the core cities from the rural South.

As the 1960s began, the high birth rate of the postwar years continued with no sign of letup, despite the fact that, before 1940, the long run American and European birth rates had been slowly declining. There was considerable evidence that the American attitude toward family size, early marriage, and economic opportunities had undergone a pronounced change from the time of the Great Depression. No slowdown in the long-run birth rate was in sight and no change in the general pattern of urbanization and suburbanization.[18] Each year 3 million additional Americans were demanding food, clothing, and shelter.

The Effects of Physical Mobility. Ours is a nation of seminomadic people. Opportunity for advancement, the necessity for going to the job that will not come to the individual, the practice of businesses and industries that operate over the entire nation or over even larger areas, to send men from assignment in one city to assignment in another while moving up the organizational ladder—all contribute to this mobility. As

[17] On the changing role of the Negro in America, see E. F. Frazier, *The Negro in the United States* (rev. ed.; The Macmillan Company, New York, 1957); on his rising political importance in metropolitan areas, E. C. Banfield and M. Grodzins, *Government and Housing* (McGraw-Hill Book Company, Inc., New York, 1958); on his increasing importance—along with that of another late-coming group of migrants—Oscar Handlin, *The Newcomers: Negroes and Puerto Ricans in a Changing Metropolis* (Harvard University Press, Cambridge, Mass., 1959).

[18] See T. J. Woofter, "Factors Sustaining the Birth Rate," *American Sociological Review,* vol. 14 (June, 1949), pp. 357–366.

William H. Whyte, Jr., has said, "The man who leaves home is not the exception in American society, but the key to it." [19] In the postwar years, one-fifth of the population has changed place of residence each year. Some people move more often than the average, of course, and there are still Americans who are born, live, and die in the same house; but it is estimated that in the five years after 1950, one-half of the people in the United States changed their places of residence.[20] Most of these moves are within the same county, although about 5 per cent of the total population annually moves to a different county within the same state and another 5 per cent moves to a different state.

Why Do People Move? To some extent, people move to escape unemployment. Some people shuttle back and forth between their old home town or farm and the city several times during a lifetime as it suits their momentary needs or whims. But, for the most part, moves are made as the result of, or in search of, economic advancement.[21]

This mobility of the American people has been criticized as undesirable. "Observers who would like to see less change argue that change breeds anxieties, tensions, and frustrations. This is true, and certainly the suburban [or core city] transients pay a great price for the up-rooting that has put them there. But how ideal for them would be the alternative?" [22]

America is and always has been an optimistic, changing nation with great emphasis upon meeting the needs of society as society sees these needs. This confidence is no doubt partly a result of a continuing conviction that "the routes to advancement are not closing down, our classes are not freezing; quite the opposite, there have never been so many people moving in so many different ways." [23] Whether it is the Southern sharecropper moving into the Northern city to become a factory worker or the son of a clerk becoming an "organization man" and a middle-class suburbanite, the result is viewed by the migrant as another step toward the fulfillment of the great American dream.

LOCATION OF CITIES AND FACTORS IN GROWTH

The Break-in-transportation Theory. One theory concerning the location and growth of cities is the break-in-transportation thesis, which

[19] William H. Whyte, Jr., *The Organization Man* (Doubleday Anchor Books, New York, 1956), p. 297.

[20] U.S. Housing and Home Finance Agency, *Housing in the United States* (1956), pp. 8–9.

[21] Noel P. Gist and L. A. Halbert, *Urban Society* (4th ed.; Thomas Y. Crowell Company, New York, 1956), pp. 354–365; and Whyte, *op. cit.*, chap. 21.

[22] Whyte, *op. cit.*, p. 309.

[23] *Ibid.*, p. 309.

holds that wherever the flow of goods is interrupted, either on the way to the manufacturer or from him, a city will grow up.[24] A snowball effect follows, with one institution creating the need for another, one business making it profitable for another to locate there, until a diversified city has been built up. The Wisconsin farmer ordinarily does not carry his dairy and poultry products to the ultimate consumer; he has neither the time nor the need to do so. He is a producer, not a middleman. Hence he wants a town nearby with a creamery and a produce dealer. He will transfer to these firms the responsibility for processing his products and sending them on to the urban consumer. He also wants a place where the finished products of others may be purchased. There is thus a need for the county seat and the smaller towns of rural America.

More obviously, goods destined for an inland city must be transshipped at excellent natural ocean ports such as New York and San Francisco. New York was at first a break between sea and river-canal transportation and later between sea and rail. Dodge City, Kansas, was the head of the old Chisholm Trail; St. Joseph, Missouri, served as an outfitting point for emigrants to the West and as the eastern terminus of the pony express; Omaha and Council Bluffs were ferry points across the Missouri River; New Orleans was located on the estuary of another great river; Chicago is at one of the western heads of the Great Lakes, Duluth at another.

Chicago is close to some of the world's richest farm land, to iron ore, and to coal. Cheap water transportation was essential in the utilization of these resources. With these advantages, with a relatively central location between East and West, and with Lake Michigan jutting deep into the Middle West, Chicago acted as a magnet in drawing railroads to it as a terminus, becoming perhaps the greatest rail center in the world. Duluth transships wheat sent by rail from the Red River Valley and iron ore from the nearby Mesabi iron range.

Of course, changes in transportation techniques may vitally affect cities. With the rise of the railroad some formerly important river towns and, especially, canal towns became stagnant. The rise of motor transportation in the twentieth century in the form of the auto and the semitrailer truck provided a previously unknown flexibility of movement. It was now possible for smaller cities to become more important industrially, and larger cities no longer had to have single "factory sections" on the waterfront or the rail spur. Inhabitants no longer had to crowd together, but could decentralize, as happened in the great suburban movement, depending

[24] See Charles H. Cooley, "The Theory of Transportation," in *Sociological Theory and Social Research* (Charles Scribners' Sons, New York, 1930); A. F. Weber, *The Growth of Cities in the Nineteenth Century* (Columbia University Press, New York, 1899); and H. W. Gilmore, *Transportation and the Growth of Cities* (The Free Press, Glencoe Ill., 1953).

upon the auto to get them downtown or to other business centers. The airplane has aided in freeing transportation from the rigidity of the stream and the rail, but has not had the great impact of the auto.

Proximity to Natural Resources and Other Factors. Wherever iron, coal, oil, and other raw materials are to be found, cities will arise to house and feed the workers. Manufacturers making use of these raw materials will also try to locate reasonably close by. Adequate transportation must be available or a possibility, however, and another prerequisite is a plentiful water supply. It costs much more to move water over great distances than it does to move electricity—and our estimated water needs within the next quarter century are double the present.

The accident of a rail-junction location may help produce a city, as in the case of Moberly, Missouri, or Wichita, Kansas. A capital city may be created primarily out of political considerations—even if it means building in an unhealthful humid swamp—as in the case of Washington and St. Petersburg (now Leningrad). Ancient cities were often located with a serious eye on the military defensibility of the site. Climate is worthy of consideration, but many American and foreign cities are located in areas affording physical discomfort. Pity the resident of New Orleans with its high summer humidity; the nigh-frozen dweller in Fargo, North Dakota, in February; the rain-drenched Seattle citizen in November or December.

War, with its modern emphasis upon assembly-line production of complex weapons and equipment, aids in bringing more people off the farms (where the continued increase in mechanization and other modern techniques and discoveries has been freeing manpower for the last two and one-half centuries) into the cities. World Wars I and II have aided in the rapid building up of such areas as Los Angeles, Detroit, Wichita, and Houston, to name a few. The future may see a dispersion of war industries as a protective measure, and hence the rise of new cities in inland areas away from the coast.

Proximity to Power. The city is chiefly a product of an industrial age, and industry requires power sources. At first, in America, this meant water power. It was available in New England, along the fall line, where this nation's manufacturing first developed. The same phenomenon was important elsewhere. For example, the Falls of St. Anthony located in the Mississippi River not far from rich grain fields helped account for Minneapolis, a milling center.

Later steam power became dominant, and this established a familiar pattern: steam required coal; coal could be moved most cheaply by water. Furthermore, disposal of industrial wastes from large plants required availability of water. Rail transportation also became vital once it was available, but only as a supplement and especially to haul away finished products. These conditions were usually fulfilled in an industrial town, and they dictated, for the most part, large industrial units. Today a new source of power—electricity—has allowed the old pattern to be modified somewhat. The trend today is toward the building of smaller plants in the suburbs rather than large plants on the waterfront, near the downtown section. Electrical power combined with modern motor transportation is also tending to make middle-sized cities more important in relation to the largest cities. While this trend is evident, there is no danger that Chicago and Philadelphia are about to become ghost towns. The differential advantages between Chicago and Kokomo to be found in lower wages, taxes, land values, and other costs in the smaller city only slightly offset the greater advantages in Chicago of a larger market immediately surrounding the factory and a ready supply of skilled and unskilled labor. Our cities will decentralize somewhat, but it will be chiefly in the well-established pattern of movement to the suburbs, where many of the advantages of the smaller city can be combined with those of the large city.[25]

A great new power source, atomic energy, if adapted to industrial use, may greatly alter the pattern of cities in the future. It may considerably accelerate decentralization.

Eclectic Factors as Causes of Growth. Cities are seldom created as the result of a single causal factor; and if they grow and become powerful, it is not necessarily for the same reasons as those of their founding. Break-in-transportation may provide the initial impetus, but subsequent growth may be a result of manufacturing and other diversified factors. Detroit was a quiet shipbuilding town in the nineteenth century, but it boomed with the rise of the auto industry. Hibbing, Minnesota, was a small trading center until the Mesabi range was discovered literally underneath it. Wichita, Kansas, was a rail junction that grew as an aircraft and diversified manufacturing center. Rochester, New York, was a tiny frontier trading post until the Erie Canal reached it. Innumerable other cities may also be cited.

A single city is not necessarily tied by destiny to a certain industry or function. Detroit had all of the prerequisites to make it an auto-manufacturing center—iron ore and limestone for steel to the northwest, the steel industry and coal fields around Pittsburgh and Youngstown to the southeast, the rubber industry at Akron, and the Great Lakes as a connecting link to bring in raw materials and to haul away finished products. Yet but for the accident of Henry Ford being born and reared in what is now suburban Detroit, and other early auto pioneers locating there, the in-

---

[25] W. C. Hallenbeck, *American Urban Communities* (Harper & Brothers, New York, 1951), a textbook, furnishes a collection of geographic, historical, governmental, economic, and social data on American cities.

dustry might well have centered (perhaps even more logically) in Cleveland, Toledo, Sandusky, or even Chicago or Milwaukee.

Many factors beyond mass-production techniques and rapid forms of transportation and communication have contributed to the growth of cities: The almost miraculous development of modern medical techniques, especially in the field of communicable-disease control, has permitted hordes of people to live healthfully in close proximity; the urban way of life itself has become a part of our cultural values, making the city symbolic of "excitement," a way out of the "dull" country life where "nothing ever happens," and hence a desirable place to live; the development of engineering techniques has made possible the skyscrapers so necessary to a concentration of business in a small, closely knit area and has overcome the technical difficulties of furnishing germ-free water and disposing safely of thousands of tons of sewage.

Cities are founded and grow—or languish—as the result, then, of an admixture of many factors—economic, political, technological, and cultural. In the next few decades we may expect a continuing trend toward urbanism in America, although the pattern will change somewhat: middle-sized cities will flourish, while large cities will "flatten out" to some extent, with a rush of dwelling areas, factories, and business and shopping areas toward the periphery.[26]

URBAN ECOLOGY

Theories of Urban Development. The term *ecology* refers to the study of the distribution of people and institutions in space. It is evident, of course, that cities have "sections" and "districts." The causes, effects, and interrelationships of these areas must be left to a course in urban sociology, but the fact of their existence is a matter of immediate concern in the politics and administration of cities. Urban areas are divided into several zones. There is a downtown or *central business district.* Next is a surrounding *zone of transition* where retreating higher-class residents have left an area now made up of rooming houses, cheap hotels, and business places that need not put up a good front for the public. Here live the casual laborers, the recent migrants from the rural South and other parts of America (for our cities depend upon rural America for much of their population as they once depended upon immigrants), the second-story men and other professional criminals, usually of the petty type, the prostitutes, gamblers, bootleggers, and, as a result of the social system rather than by fault of their own, many of the foreign-born and

---

[26] The present tendency toward the development of several nuclei in metropolitan areas rather than a single downtown sector is referred to by some sociologists by the term *polynucleation.*

the Negroes. This is the area of low home-ownership rates and high crime, death, insanity, suicide, juvenile delinquency, and public welfare dependency rates. This is the area in which the city must spend the greatest percentage of its budget and from which it receives its smallest contributions to the cost of government.

Next there may be a *zone of workingmen's homes* gradually improving into the lower-middle-class and finally the well-to-do living areas. The theory that these areas are to be found in *concentric circles* about the main business area was put forward by E. W. Burgess,[27] but it requires considerable modification to fit the facts of the automobile age.

To overcome some of the objections to the Burgess theory, Homer Hoyt has advanced the *sector theory,* which holds that the city and its suburban hinterland is sliced up to look somewhat like a pie, the wealthy sections to be found at the outer edge of one or more sectors and poor areas in another sector, with areas moving out along the radial spokes— the main arteries of transportation.[28] Other sociologists have held that no general theory of urban growth patterns can be hazarded. For the purposes of the political scientist, it is important to know that cities do have various sectors serving various clienteles.[29] The chapters on politics and public policy will make clear their political import.

SOME CHARACTERISTICS OF URBAN LIFE

The urban dweller, and especially the middle-class suburbanite, of today is motivated in the direction of pleasing others—particularly strangers and near strangers. He is afraid of the cold, impersonal world in which he finds himself. He desires power, prestige, and security. But these are hard to find in the metropolis. Yet they seem to be fundamental human needs. What is modern man to do?

The Lonely Escape. Erich Fromm, a social psychologist, has suggested that the contemporary urbanite seeks to avoid the isolation of modern life in "automaton conformity." [30] Man fears freedom and individuality. In an interdependent world, he is afraid to go it alone. He does not desire to emphasize creativity or opportunity for individual action. The person who deviates from the norm, even very slightly, is

[27] E. W. Burgess, "The Growth of the City," in R. E. Park, E. W. Burgess, and R. D. McKenzie, *The City* (University of Chicago Press, Chicago, 1925).

[28] Homer Hoyt, *The Structure and Growth of Residential Neighborhoods in American Cities* (Federal Housing Administration, 1939), chap. 6.

[29] If the student has not had a course in the sociology of urban areas, it would be profitable at this point for him to read Gist and Halbert, *op. cit.,* chaps. 6–10, or Queen and Carpenter, *op. cit.,* pt. 3.

[30] Erich Fromm, *Escape from Freedom* (Holt, Rinehart and Winston, Inc., New York, 1941); see also Margaret Mary Wood, *Paths of Loneliness: The Individual Isolated in Modern Society* (Columbia University Press, New York, 1953).

subject to immediate criticism from a mediocre, unimaginative, fearful society. It is *safer*—it is more conducive to security—if he conforms. No one will attack him, no one will persecute him, no one will single him out for criticism, no one will have a reason to exclude him from the children's play group, the country club, the Kiwanians, or a deaconship in the church if he loses his individuality in entire, uncritical conformity. He becomes *accepted*—and it is a deep-seated need for social acceptance that he feels.

David Riesman, building on the concepts presented by Fromm, has shown that until recent decades Americans sought security in conformity to parental, and particularly paternal, authority.[31] The middle-class urban American of today, however, seeks social approval, not from his family and close personal friends, but from his associates and, for the most part, from associates in secondary relationships. And this process begins before he, as a child, enters school and does not end until his funeral.

The individual seems doomed to frustration in Riesman's analysis, however, for he desires to come closer to other people by conforming to whatever they tell him to do, yet because almost all of his contacts with others are superficial rather than warm and personal, "he remains a lonely member of the crowd."

Between the security of the womb and that of the grave, the contemporary middle-class urbanite apparently wishes for little more than a few obscure years bending and swaying with the crowd.

Urban Classes. Although it has always been popular among tellers of the great American myth to say that this nation is lacking in classes, that all are equal, that anyone can do anything that his ability and determination dictate, less romantic sociologists point out that while we have a good deal of mobility between classes, the classes do, indeed, exist. Some sociologists would go further and say that, because of the inferior social position of the Negro, America has both a class and a caste system, although the rapid postwar changes in the status of Negroes has encouraged a trend away from a caste concept.[32]

A social class is a division of society in which individuals are recognized as belonging to a certain social-status group. These people have a sense of *belonging* to one another and of being separate from others. A social caste exists when the status position of the individual in society is determined by birth and cannot be changed by any personal efforts made by the individual. In the same sense just given, a class can be said to exist only in a given small or middle-sized community; on a nationwide basis, the middle class and working class are more statistical

[31] David Riesman, *The Lonely Crowd* (1950). See also *Faces in the Crowd* (1952). Both are published by the Yale University Press, New Haven, Conn.
[32] Gist and Halbert, *op. cit.*, chap. 14.

abstractions than self-conscious classes,[33] although some behavioral differences continue to exist.

America has no national class structure for several reasons, the three most important being (1) because the nation has always had a great deal of mobility, with much movement up and down the status ladder; (2) because the nation has until after World War I had a population made up largely of recent arrivals with widely varying national backgrounds; and (3) because of the egalitarian influence of the frontier which discouraged class-differentiated behavior for many decades. Under these circumstances, "the emergence of fairly uniform classes over an extended geographic area, such as are clearly discernible in England," never took place.[34]

Class systems, within a particular locality, are based upon relative wealth, occupations, education, manners, mode of life, and such things as membership in an "old family" or a recent-immigrant family. But migration and mobility and the distribution of material things throughout all except the lowest income tiers have tended to have a leveling effect upon American manners and way of life.[35]

Social Role and Social Status. The continuing trend in America—and this among many other things distinguishes the American from the European way of life—is away from status determined by class position, even within the local community, to status determined by occupation. In other words, one's social function has become more important than one's class position.

The structure of the American economy itself discourages the development of a clear-cut class system, and many social critics regard this as desirable. American business management, as compared with that of Belgium, France, or Italy, allows far more room for advancement in ranks and access to managerial status.[36] Decision making in business is more decentralized in America, and businessmen are much more conscious of *expanding* industry as against merely retaining control over it. Management of business in Europe tends to be concerned with security, which encourages working classes to look in the same direction, thus making business enterprise static. The European system does not, by its nature, work toward raising the standard of living and improving the health of the economy, as the American system does.[37] It does, however, tend to perpetuate existing class patterns.

[33] A. W. Green, *Sociology* (3d ed.; McGraw-Hill Book Company, Inc., New York, 1960), chap. 10.

[34] *Ibid.*, p. 181.

[35] *Ibid.*, chap. 12.

[36] See C. H. Coates and R. J. Pellegrin, "Executives and Supervisors," *Social Forces,* vol. 35 (December, 1956), pp. 121–126.

[37] See F. H. Harbison and E. W. Burgess, "Modern Management in Western Europe," *American Journal of Sociology,* vol. 60 (July, 1954), pp. 15–23.

Social Striving and Political Conflict. Sociologists find that social mobility remains high in America but that the prestige of white-collar work is diminishing. This will perhaps have a tendency to accentuate the traditional political struggle between the lower middle classes and the working classes. The former have long been the most insecure group in society, clinging desperately to identification with higher-status groups and seeking to differentiate themselves from workers. Yet, in their struggle, they have been faced with a continuing improvement in the lot of the workingman. This situation has made the lower-middle-class member a particularly sympathetic reactor to the nostrums of the demagogue. Current trends would seem to indicate possible increasing friction along the rough edge between the middle classes and the working classes.

Social striving in America is not along class lines alone. If it were, classes would be far more important and more identifiable. Instead, this type of behavior is related to three categories: social class, wherein the individual seeks to become identified with a particular group within his community; occupational success and prestige, wherein Americans tend to give recognition to individuals upon the basis of a culturally recognized hierarchy of jobs and the income and other perquisites connected with the job; and, finally, economic and political power which may exist in varying degree independently of class or occupation.[38]

Various public opinion polls have been conducted to show the rank order of jobs. These always show that certain positions involving responsibility for human life, such as those of physician or airline pilot, rate very high in prestige. Performing such a social role will gain the individual much social deference, regardless of his family background or of class behavior patterns. So far as power is concerned, it is often accompanied by a certain general type of occupational classification, and the economically powerful, in particular, tend to have high-class positions. But a Jewish merchant of great economic and political power in a community will be of lower class than a non-Jew in an equivalent position. A Negro politician may possess great power but low social prestige. The son of an Irish immigrant might become a city boss so powerful as to be able to hamstring the business activities of the economic chieftains, but he would not be received as a social equal in the very "best" homes of the city.[39]

Politics and Classes. Politically, a class or caste system is an important determinant of strategy or tactics of campaigning. Politicians appeal to Negroes, foreign-born, Jews, Puerto Ricans, Americanized Mexicans, homeowners, renters, and other socially or economically identifiable groups. These appeals may be basically harmless or they may arouse

[38] Green, *op. cit.*, chap. 11.
[39] See chap. 5 on power.

virulent intergroup prejudices.[40] Because of the prestige factor (which in turn has economic repercussions that affect, for example, property values), many political battles—in the city council chamber, in the mayor's office, on the campaign platform—are fought over the issue of what the sociologist calls *invasion*. "The process of invasion is a convenient name for what happens when a new type of people, institution, or activity enters an area previously occupied by a different type." [41] Much social, and hence political, tension is caused when a rapid increase in Negro population, as in Chicago and Detroit, forces rapid invasion. The question of intended policy, expressed or implied, toward invasion has been important in postwar mayoralty campaigns in Detroit, especially in 1945 at the height of the housing shortage, but also in the 1949 contest. The question sometimes takes the form of policy toward proposed public housing units. Should they be built only after tearing down existing slums, or should vacant areas be used where there may be alterations of the character (and hence the property values) of existing communities?

Tensions may also result from counterinvasions, as in the case of the re-expansion of Boston's Beacon Hill into the surrounding slums, or the white "colonial restoration" of the largely Negro Georgetown section of Washington, D.C., in the 1930s. Residential areas may be invaded by commerce and industry, which also causes resentment and political strife, because it, too, threatens property values. So-called "improvement associations" have been created in many neighborhoods of our cities, chiefly to protect property values. Many times these organizations exist primarily to keep "inferior" groups out of the area. In the past, they and subdivision developers have had legal assistance in the form of "restrictive covenants" in deeds to property. Such covenants prohibited conveyance of the land to specified groups of persons (e.g., Negroes, Jews, persons of the yellow race) for a certain number of years, or permanently. In 1948, however, the United States Supreme Court, taking note of the fact that the United States Constitution prohibits a state from denying "to any person within its jurisdiction the equal protection of the laws," declared all such provisions unenforceable.[42]

Many improvement associations have a broader interest. Nearly all of them concern themselves with all threats of commercial and industrial invasion and many of them spend much of their time on the little things (good street lighting, prompt repair of chuckholes, countless stop signs, etc.) that interest the people of the neighborhood. Chicago's Commission

[40] For examples of the latter, see Carl O. Smith and Stephen B. Sarasohn, "Hate Propaganda in Detroit," *Public Opinion Quarterly*, vol. 10 (Spring, 1946), pp. 24–52; Forest Frank, "Cincinnati Loses P.R.," *National Municipal Review* (now *National Civic Review*), vol. 46 (November, 1957), pp. 534–535.

[41] Queen and Carpenter, *op. cit.*, p. 109.

[42] *Shelly v. Kraemer*, 334 U.S. 1 (1948).

on Human Relations, the Commission on Community Relations in Detroit, and similar groups in other cities have encouraged a new type of improvement association designed to further tolerance and understanding and to help all groups in a neighborhood to seek to improve the area further.

Hearings before city councils or appeal boards on the rezoning of an area often conceal interclass or interracial conflicts behind ostensible arguments concerning property values. A public or cooperative multi-family housing project which is to be nonsegregated is likely to become a political issue. Opponents may not state their real objection but may advance other arguments, such as a complaint that the proposed project will destroy the single-family-homes character of the neighborhood. If the apartments were designed to rent to restricted clientele at $200 per month, the community attitude might be much different.

Invasion by a different class or caste may even cause the established residents of an area to encourage their own law-enforcement officers to violate the law. In the notorious Cicero riot of 1952, where a well-educated, middle-class Negro family attempted to move into a lower-middle-class all-white suburb of Chicago, not only did many members of the community encourage unlawfulness on the part of spectators, especially of impressionable teen-agers, but they actually encouraged the chief of police to refuse to extend the protection that the law grants to all peaceful persons. Refusal of the police to perform their duty when it involves the rights of members of minority groups is an old, though now a gradually more uncommon, story.

The problem of social prestige may appear in many different ways. In Park Forest, Illinois, for example, it arose in connection with the building of a swimming pool (in keeping with the requirements of suburban Americana, it was called an "Aquacenter," of course). A municipal pool was first discussed, but this might have required the admission of people from adjoining Chicago Heights, a community of less prestige and one, furthermore, that contains a large number of Negroes. The alternative, finally accepted, was a private pool. But this produced fears of a first step toward social stratification of the all-new suburb. Even though pool fees were set very low, many appeared to fear that their very existence was a move toward the creation of an unwanted country-club set.[43] In both Park Forest and Levittown, classlessness does not extend to the admission of Negroes, and in Levittown, Pennsylvania, there were open demonstrations during 1957 against a Negro family's moving in.[44]

[43] William H. Whyte, Jr., *The Organization Man* (Doubleday Anchor Books, New York, 1956), pp. 343–344.

[44] For case studies on social status, see the following: John Dollard, *Caste and Class in a Southern Town* (3d ed.; Doubleday and Company, Inc., New York, 1957); St. Clair Drake and H. R. Cayton, *Black Metropolis* (Harcourt, Brace & World,

Impersonalization of Life. Cities are based upon a money economy. Many business relationships are impersonal and devoid of sentiment, in contrast with these same activities in rural and small-town situations. In the apartment-house areas of the city, one is lost in anonymity, having casual contacts with many persons rather than intimate contacts with a relatively few. One is judged by what he can do, not by what he is—by his *reputation* rather than by his *character*. So relationships among people are brief and stylized. People are cool toward one another, quick to take unfair advantage, and, in the view of many ruralites, are callous and hardhearted.

In the small town and on the farm, society is subjected to social controls characterized by *primary,* that is to say, close and personal relationships. Some of these exist in crowded portions of cities, too, but to a much smaller degree. *Secondary* relationships and controls predominate there, and these are impersonal, fragmentary, and ephemeral. Social distance—the degree of relative lack of intimacy that one person has with another—is much greater. Urban society, therefore, becomes organized more formally, through more laws, than is the case in rural areas. The political process becomes more important in the city.

This book cannot examine the *why* of the characteristics of urban behavior, but it is important to note that this way of life has immediate effects upon the political institutions of the community. The rural society (and, to a considerable extent, suburbia) is policed largely by its system of primary social controls. Gossip and community opinion strongly discourage deviations from accepted values. The back-fence tattler may be a nuisance, but she is also a protectress. Crime rates are low, and there may not be a professional law-enforcement officer within 30 miles or more. In the heart of the city, things are not the same. The near absence of most primary controls means that the crime rate in cities is higher. It means that mores must be enforced by policemen and by more laws instead of by gossips and community opinion. It means that the courts

Inc., New York, 1945), Chicago's Negro community; O. D. Duncan and Beverly Duncan, *The Negro Population of Chicago* (University of Chicago Press, Chicago, 1957); R. S. Lynd and Helen M. Lynd, *Middletown in Transition* (Harcourt, Brace & World, Inc., New York, 1937), a study, in Muncie, Ind., that did pioneer work, although its findings are certainly atypical of contemporary Midwestern social-political structure; Kenneth MacLeish and Kimball Young, *Landaff, New Hampshire* (U.S. Bureau of Agricultural Economics, 1942); Henry W. Riecken, Jr. and N. L. Whetten, *Rural Social Organization in Litchfield County, Connecticut* (Storrs Agricultural Experimental Station, Storrs, Conn., 1948); W. Lloyd Warner and Paul S. Lunt, *The Social Life of a Modern Community* (Yale University Press, New Haven, Conn., 1941); W. Lloyd Warner and Paul S. Lunt, *The Status System of a Modern Community* (Yale University Press, New Haven, Conn., 1942); W. Lloyd Warner and others, *Social Class in America* (Science Research Associates, Inc., Chicago, 1949); Harvey Zorbaugh, *The Gold Coast and the Slum* (University of Chicago Press, Chicago, 1929).

are kept busier settling civil disputes. It means bigger government, reaching more people, in a more formalized, institutionalized manner.

Rootlessness. High physical and social mobility have been characteristics of American society from early colonial times. From the point of view of participation in democratic government, high mobility is of consequence in that large number of migrants fail to identify themselves with their adopted communities.[45] Their civic pride is likely to be nonexistent. There is no loyalty to the city as an institution or as "home." If the migrant happens to live in a suburb, he may not even know whether it is actually an independent unit of government. Politically, this means that appeals to community responsibility will fall on deaf ears. It means that elections will be ignored. Government will be left in the hands of others— and the others may be grossly unrepresentative of the interest of the newer arrivals.

The Transient as a Community Participant. Vast suburban growth has created special problems in the matter of rootlessness and a lack of belonging. The values of the middle class call for individual participation in political, social, and civic activities. Yet members of this group often lack the deep roots that at once command and, at the same time, clear the way for the assumption of local social responsibilities. Still, if nearly everyone in a community such as Levittown or Park Forest is a newcomer, some way must be found to get people to serve on city councils, on planning commissions, on united-community-fund boards. Thus, we come to the question: [46]

Are the transients a rootless people? If by roots we mean the complex of geographical and family ties that has historically knitted Americans to local society, these young transients are almost entirely rootless. They are very much aware of the fact; surprisingly often they will bring up the home town, and though they have no intention whatsoever of going back, they dwell on what they left behind. . . .

Whyte, in his examination of Park Forest, found that there was indeed a good deal of apathy toward community problems in a new town made up entirely of persons who are rootless in the traditional sense. But he

---

[45] See Robert C. Angell, "The Moral Integration of American Cities," *American Journal of Sociology,* vol. 57 (July, 1951), pt. 2; B. G. Zimmer, "Participation of Migrants in Urban Structures," *American Sociological Review,* vol. 20 (April, 1955), pp. 218–224; B. G. Zimmer, "Farm Backgrounds and Urban Participation," *American Journal of Sociology,* vol. 61 (March, 1956), pp. 470–475. A classic statement, though no longer fully accepted by social scientists, of urban living as contrasted with rural may be found in Louis Wirth, "Urbanism as a Way of Life," *American Journal of Sociology,* vol. 44 (July, 1938), pp. 1–24.

[46] Whyte, *op. cit.,* p. 318. There is a Levittown on Long Island and others in New Jersey and Pennsylvania, each built on a mass-production basis after World War II in an area which was previously open country. Park Forest is a similar suburb south of Chicago.

also found that many residents took up the real issues of providing for schools and public services because of a feeling of a need for "ties more meaningful than those of bridge and canasta and bowling." [47]

Trade Unionism. The factory worker, like the middle-class organization man, is also faced with the problem of establishing some kind of roots in lieu of the traditional type. He, too, is accommodating himself to the new American way of life. A study of Detroit automobile workers, for example, found that the great bulk of them (82 per cent) are American-born, in contrast to the factory worker in Andrew Carnegie's steel mills or to Jurgis Rudkus, the Lithuanian who slaved in the stockyards of Chicago at the beginning of the present century. [48] Over one-half of them (52 per cent) had immigrant fathers, however. Most automobile workers are living in towns where they did not grow up, and they are to some degree culturally marginal. The home-ownership level of 59 per cent is high, almost as high as that of Detroit in general (65 per cent), but much lower than that of the middle-class and upper-working-class suburban dwellers. (In Chicago, a preautomobile-age city of apartments, home ownership is only 30 per cent and would be lower than that for factory workers. Detroit, like many other industrial cities is, however, a postautomobile-age city consisting principally of one- and two-family homes. Home ownership in most types of suburbs runs around 90 per cent.)

One-fifth of Detroit automobile workers grew up on farms, another one-fourth in small towns. Only 44 per cent were raised in large cities. Two-thirds of them are the only breadwinners in their families. One-half of them are church members, but factory workers seem to be quite inactive in church groups, fraternal organizations, veterans groups, neighborhood associations, and parent-teacher associations—a matter of considerable importance so far as social and political representation of interests is concerned. [49]

In suburbia, neighbors are the mainstays of social relationships, since organization-man families are often forced to live far from any of their relatives. Residents of the core city, including factory workers, find that relatives are more important than are next-door neighbors. Unskilled workers probably migrate more to areas where relatives have already located than do middle-class persons. The latter have less of a choice of destination, being required to go where their skills are demanded. In Detroit, 89 per cent of core-city working-class couples have relatives living in the community; more than one-half of them have relatives in the

[47] *Ibid.*, pp. 325–327.

[48] In the novel by Upton Sinclair, *The Jungle* (The Viking Press, Inc., New York, 1906).

[49] See Arthur Kornhauser, H. L. Sheppard, and A. J. Mayer, *When Labor Votes* (University Books, Inc., New York, 1956), pp. 26–28.

same neighborhood. Two-thirds of the couples see their relatives once or twice a week at least, and over one-fourth see some relative nearly every day. Family gatherings at weddings, funerals, birthdays, and holidays are important. Of the people who see relatives once or twice a week, more than one-half see neighbors less than once a month.[50]

Core-city residents are thus less neighborhood-oriented than are suburbanites, though they seek to maintain primary relationships of some kind. When relatives live within driving distances, they are likely to concentrate their social activities upon them (and upon the impersonal aspects of urban recreational activities), thus emphasizing traditional family ties in preference to amalgamation into the impersonal community and its activities. This difference between core-city and suburban dwellers may have important effects upon the pattern of politics in the community and upon political participation. It should be noted, however, that persons with family ties are probably more likely to develop an interest in the community than are isolated persons.

Trade Unions in Politics. In contrast to the frantic, reformist periods of the 1930s, trade unionism became an accepted part of the American way of life after World War II. By no means are all members of unions enthusiastic over the necessity of membership, and collective security by way of the union runs counter to American values of individualism; but only the wistful consider it even remotely possible that unions will not remain a significant social and political force in America. The day when working-class people had no voice, or only the voice of the political machine, in local politics is gone.[51]

By 1960, union members and their immediate families made up one-third of all the eligible voters in the United States. In urban industrial centers, over one-half the potential voters were in this category.[52]

In municipal elections and in the consideration of legislation pending before city councils, the working class, represented by the highly professional bureaucracy of the trade union, will continue to make its position known and its votes felt.

Closing Statement. Some of the characteristics of American life and the values that guide our decisions concerning governmental policies have been presented in this chapter. Others will be discussed in the following two chapters. The issues of policy raised in connection with various functions of government will be developed in more detail in the appropriate later sections of the book.

[50] Survey Research Center, University of Michigan, 1955, report of the Detroit Area Study. See also Joel Smith and others, "Local Intimacy in a Middle-sized City," *American Journal of Sociology,* vol. 60 (November, 1954), pp. 276–284.

[51] See chap. 5.

[52] Kornhauser, *op. cit.,* p. 261.

Chapter 2

SUBURBIA

The American city today is much more than a legal entity existing within carefully described boundaries and headed by a single government. It is actually a sociological complex consisting of a downtown sector, a blighted and decaying older portion, newer sections of a principally residential character, and, beyond the legal limits but an intrinsic part of the community, the suburbs. A suburb may be defined as a community beyond the legal boundaries of the core city, but lying within its economic and sociological limits and with a population at least partially dependent for a livelihood upon the core city.

There are still sections within some core cities that are relatively undeveloped and assume some, but not all, of the characteristics of the suburb. The movement toward the urban fringe is overruning both types of areas.

THE MOVEMENT TOWARD THE SUBURBS

Why Move to the Suburbs? What is behind the centrifugal force that is pushing our urban population toward the periphery of the community? No doubt the increasing size of the urban population is itself a factor, for additional population is likely to require increasing area. But this alone is not a sufficient reason to explain the great suburban movement of the last thirty-odd years and especially that since the end of World War II.

Rather we should ask, what do most American people want out of life? Where and under what conditions can their desires best be fulfilled?

A summary of the findings of social-psychological research into these questions has been reported as follows: [1]

The goal which, if reached or reasonably approximated, will fulfill the basic needs of the urbanite is a community that will combine some qualities of both

---

[1] William L. Slayton and Richar Dewey, "Urban Redevelopment and the Urbanite," in Coleman Woodbury (ed.), *The Future of Cities and Urban Redevelopment* (University of Chicago Press, Chicago, 1953), p. 367. By permission of the University of Chicago Press.

small town and large city. Neither, in its present form and at the current stage of cultural development, satisfies all of the fundamental human requirements. The small town provides ample opportunity for companionship and friendship, for easy access to local services, and for certain forms of security. On the other hand, it may fall short of fulfilling man's need for recognition and variety of experience. The large city does provide insurance against boredom, affords wider opportunity for choice of occupation, freedom from unwanted interference with one's personal life, and permits one to identify himself with the city's greatness or, at least, bigness. Nevertheless, it may fail to meet other basic social needs of man. The city can be a very lonesome place. It can thwart natural human friendliness. It can breed suspicion and misunderstanding. It often has dissolved long-established values as to behavior while putting nothing comparable in their place.

The suburb, more and more urbanites believe, is the best available compromise, especially if the medium-sized city is not a possible choice. In addition to allowing the urbanite to keep *some* of the best of both the large city and the small town, there are other subjectively determined values held by Americans today that add to the attractiveness of the suburb. Studies show that people want to own their homes, that they want single-family dwellings, and that they want more space than is available within built-up cities at a cost they can afford. They want to avoid, or at least reduce, dirt, noise, congestion, traffic, and taxes. They want vegetable gardens and rosebushes. They want a private play yard for the children.

People want better government than they think they are getting in the core city. They want "services without politics." The suburbanite, as a good conformist, talks of the desirability of a council-manager government, which the large city, as a rule, does not have. A "better, more honest" government is something that many think is available in the suburb, although this is a much less important factor than are many others. Neighborliness, the re-establishment of some of the primary controls of the rural and small-town society, is something that many yearn for. A suburban address is also a symbol of higher prestige than the typical core-city address, and this fact does not escape many urbanites, for social climbing of this sort is very important as a source of recognition in an impersonal society.

The suburb keeps within hailing distance of the variety of scene and activity, of job opportunities, and of accessibility to multiple and specialized services that people want from the large city. Most people would like to have nearby a corner grocery for last-minute shopping (the supermarket for the large weekly shopping list may be some distance away), a drugstore, a playground, and a grade school. Other services, entertainment media, and places of work may be considerable distances away, for the automobile, people believe, will take them there within the limits of a tolerable amount of sacrifice. The commuting time and effort, within present value systems, is not too great a price to pay for the advantages of not living near the manufacturing or business districts.[2]

What Makes Suburban Living Possible? A brief answer might be simply this: modern techniques of transportation and communication. To the extent that a decentralization of industry is also a factor, the availability of highly mobile sources of *power* in the form of electricity has also been important. Together with prosperity after World War II, the Federal government's policy of aiding purchasers of new homes through a loan guarantee to the mortgage holder has been another important factor. The Veterans' Administration and the Federal Housing Authority have thus been substantial contributors to the suburban movement by making low-interest mortgages a possibility for large numbers of families who could not otherwise have afforded homes of their own.

World War I brought an acceleration in the rate of urbanization in the United States. People began to look for additional space to occupy. They found it outside of the city proper. They also found that a prewar novelty, the automobile, had now become commonplace. In fact, it had become a necessity for members of the middle class, and Henry Ford was building a "poor man's" car in the famous Model T. There were suburbanites and commuters before the 1920s, to be sure, for those were the days of the electrified interurban lines and there were commuter trains operated by the railroads out of the largest cities, but it was the coming of the automobile that made suburban living as it is known today a possibility.[3]

Modern methods of communication are also contributors to the suburban movement. Without the effective, inexpensive telephone service of today, few would isolate themselves from the core city. The telephone is used to obtain services rapidly, for the employer in town to contact his employee in his suburban home, for the husband at work downtown to "check on things back at the house," and for all to keep in contact with relatives and friends in other parts of the city even when many miles of crowded highways separate them.

Without the automobile and the telephone, it is possible that the present-day value patterns previously discussed would never have evolved. Even if they had, it is certain that few would have been able to take advantage of them.

[2] This section draws heavily upon Slayton and Dewey, *op. cit.*, pt. III. The empirical research justifying the above statements is there summarized and cited. See also William Dobriner (ed.), *The Suburban Community* (G. P. Putnam's Sons, New York, 1958).

[3] The early movement toward the fringe is discussed in H. P. Douglass, *The Suburban Trend* (Appleton-Century-Crofts, Inc., New York, 1925).

Rate of Suburban Growth.[4] During the ten years preceding 1960, suburban populations of metropolitan areas increased by 47 per cent, reaching a total of over 53 million persons, and accounting for two-thirds of the entire population increase of the nation. In addition, most cities of under 50,000 people—indeed, even very small communities —saw the bulk of their growth take place in the suburbs. It seems likely that nearly three-fourths of the population growth since 1950 has taken place in urban areas outside core cities of all sizes. This figure is up from about 50 per cent in the previous census, a reflection of the fact that core cities now are largely built up and—in most states—find it difficult to annex new territory.

Chicago, which has virtually no vacant land left within the legal city limits, lost 3.5 per cent in population between 1950 and 1960 (the previous decade, it had *gained* 7 per cent), while its suburbs increased by 71 per cent (as against only 32 per cent in the previous census). Minneapolis and St. Paul collectively lost 4.7 per cent, but the Twin City suburbs gained 114.7 per cent. Most core cities had some increases, although nearly all of the large ones did not. The most phenomenal gains took place in the California suburbs. Even the core cities in that state continued to gain considerably, partly through annexation, but also because not all of their land was yet fully built up.

Increases in suburban populations were not uniform throughout the country, of course. The greatest gains were made around the perimeter, and especially along the Great Lakes, the Gulf of Mexico, and the Pacific Ocean. Some areas lost population not only at the core, but for the metropolitan area as a whole. This happened particularly in regions having difficulties in readjusting their economic bases as the result of changing manufacturing or mining patterns. New England, which has lost some of its former economic base, particularly in textiles, to the South, and Pennsylvania's depression-ridden coal fields are examples. The Scranton, Pennsylvania, area as a whole lost almost 10 per cent of its people; New Bedford, Massachusetts, lost nearly 1 per cent, and Wheeling, West Virginia, 4 per cent. These results contrast sharply with increases for metropolitan areas of 124 per cent at Orlando, Florida, 120 per cent at San Jose, California, and 86 per cent at Tucson, Arizona. The story around the nation was typically somewhere between these extremes.

---

[4] For a discussion of theories of growth, see William Dobriner (ed.), *The Suburban Community* (G. P. Putnam's Sons, New York, 1958), pt. 1.

TYPES OF SUBURBS

Suburbs may be of many types. They are somewhat difficult to classify, and it is probable that most of them will include characteristics of more than one of the following types: first of all, the "dormitory" suburbs, especially built up on undeveloped land for the purpose of absorbing the overflow from the city; second, the industrial suburbs; third, suburbs, or *enclaves*, that have become completely surrounded by the core city; fourth, recreational suburbs; fifth, communities that were once independent, autonomous municipalities, probably serving as marketing towns, and that have been overrun by a metropolitan community; last, the heterogeneous suburbs that serve many purposes and for that reason cannot be classified readily.[5]

The Dormitory Suburbs. The residential suburbs are characterized by the fact that they are living places, primarily, for persons who earn their living within the core city or the industrial suburbs. The suburb may have a well-developed business district, but many of the newer ones have only a series of shopping areas along the main highways. There may be very little community spirit and almost nothing to give the area the appearance of a natural community. In fact, its boundaries may well be determined by following main traffic arteries.

Dormitory suburbs may be made up of very expensive subdivisions, or working-class areas with modest frame homes, or anything in between. Some of them allow only individual homes under the strictest zoning and subdivision regulations, while others will allow the more moderately priced mass-production projects of the Levittown type. In transitional zones, they may permit apartment houses. Some seek to exclude industry altogether, while others are of a mixed type, admitting industry in order to give some backbone to the tax base.

Industrial Suburbs. Industrial suburbs or satellite cities have been described by two sociologists as follows: [6]

These are usually built around one or a group of large manufacturing establishments. Frequently marked physiographic features cut them off from the rest of the metropolitan area. Sometimes they are larger, and usually they are more congested, than other suburbs. Satellite cities live more to themselves because their people dwell, shop, worship, play, educate their children, earn their living, and spend most of their time within their own communities. Their people read the metropolitan newspapers less than do the residents of other

[5] A more elaborate classification is described and developed in Stuart A. Queen and David B. Carpenter, *The American City* (McGraw-Hill Book Company, Inc., New York, 1953), pp. 119–130. Another is to be found in Grace K. Ohlson, "Economic Classification of Cities," *Municipal Year Book, 1946* (International City Managers' Association, Chicago, 1946), pp. 32–70.

[6] Queen and Carpenter, *op. cit.,* p. 120.

suburbs. However, the industries of the satellite city are dependent on the central city for financing, managing, sale of products, and extra labor supply, and the inhabitants go to the central city for some forms of recreation and for specialized shopping.

In addition to such long-established suburbs of heavy industry as Gary and Dearborn, there has been a strong postwar trend toward the building up of light and medium industrial plants in the suburbs. It would probably not be justified to make the flat statement that industries are decentralizing,[7] but it is certainly true that *some* industry is decentralizing. It appears that various groupings of industry are following different trends. Factories that do not need railroads, bodies or streams of water, or heavy power sources nearby, and particularly the supplier sections of large industries, seem to be looking to the suburbs.

From the turn of the century until World War II there was a slow, rather persistent diffusion of industry within the major areas of industrial concentration. It appears to be continuing, especially in the Middle Atlantic, East North Central, and Pacific industrial regions.[8]

Industries seem to be leaving the core cities not primarily because of being squeezed or pushed out, but rather in response to positive factors. Suburbs offer some hope of lower taxes; they offer cheaper land, a vital consideration since a properly laid out, healthful, physically attractive factory needs a good deal of room; they offer better parking facilities for workers; they bring the factory nearer the workers' homes; they eliminate the need to bring large semitrailer trucks into the heart of the city, for the factory can be located near important highway intersections; and they aid in reducing congestion on the commuter highways and in the central portion of the core city.

In addition to a pattern of diffusion for some industries in our larger manufacturing cities, there has also been a certain amount of dispersion of industry.[9] Smaller cities are acquiring more industries and becoming more important economic units. This pattern is especially to be noted in the South Atlantic states and in the South in general. These cities are expanding partly at the expense of the metropolitan areas and partly as the result of industrial emigration from New England's cities. The Department of Defense has encouraged dispersion as part of a pattern of protection against attack by thermonuclear weapons, but its efforts appear to have had little net effect.

[7] See Coleman Woodbury and Frank Cliffe, "Industrial Location and Urban Redevelopment," in Woodbury (ed.), *op. cit.*, chaps. 5 and 6.

[8] *Ibid.*, p. 209. *Diffusion* is defined as "the redistribution of industrial plants and facilities from a major area of concentration, such as a central city or metropolitan area, to a nearby or adjacent area."

[9] *Ibid.*, p. 209. *Dispersion* means a wider redistribution of industry than in the case of diffusion, "as from a major industrial concentration in a large city or metropolitan area to a number of smaller localities."

Gary and Hammond were deliberately set up as industrial suburbs of Chicago. Their favorable location on Lake Michigan was well suited to the needs of the steel industry. Kansas City's suburb Argentine is a semi-autonomous industrial suburb, and St. Louis has three heavy-industry suburbs: Granite City, Madison, and Venice, all in Illinois.

Enclaves. Some American cities have grown so rapidly that they have quite literally swallowed up their suburbs. A city that suddenly becomes economically more important and therefore creates a population vacuum as job opportunities increase may stretch its boundaries outward quite rapidly. Independent suburbs on the urban fringe may choose to remain approximately static in area while this is happening. The core city may then surround them on all sides, making something of a mockery out of their independent legal status and their suburban appellation. Los Angeles has about fourteen such enclaves, Cincinnati three, and Detroit two.

Recreational Suburbs. This type of suburb probably seldom exists by itself, and the term should be taken to mean places where people go to play, to escape. Sometimes there is a lake or the sea near the core city. Beaches, dance halls, and picnic places are built up, with perhaps a carnival or amusement-park area included. Excelsior in the greater Minneapolis area and Walled Lake, near Detroit, are examples of this type.

Some suburbs become havens of gambling establishments and houses of prostitution.[10] This is sometimes the result of advance knowledge that these localities will not enforce the law strictly. They may be across a county or state line and in the case of some, such as Tijuana and Windsor, across an international boundary. Race tracks, because they require a great deal of room for the physical plant and for parking space, and because they cause dust and a good deal of noise both day and night, are nearly always located in a suburban area which is (at least at first) not too heavily populated.

Formerly Autonomous Communities. Not only does the core city sometimes swallow up its suburbs, but it may sometimes draw into its economic and sociological (but rarely into its *political*) orbit communities that were once independent of it, that were created for and developed as the result of factors other than those that created the core city. Chicago has drawn many cities into its orbit, including Joliet and much of northern Indiana. The Minneapolis-St. Paul metropolitan area has come to include the county-seat town of Anoka, the prison and river town of Stillwater, and the resort towns around Lake Minnetonka.

[10] See James A. Maxwell, "Kentucky's Open City," *The Saturday Evening Post,* Mar. 26, 1960, pp. 22 ff. The story of Newport, Ky., recreational suburb to Cincinnati for three generations.

Detroit has expanded its magnetic field to include the county-seat and manufacturing city of Pontiac and the county-seat and resort town of Mt. Clemens, and is even beginning to encroach upon the county-seat and university town of Ann Arbor. The city of New York has socially annexed the old towns of southwestern Connecticut and dozens of others in New Jersey.

Heterogeneous Suburbs. It should not be assumed that suburbs are planned to perform a single function or that many will be found that would fit exclusively into any of the above categories. To illustrate from the Detroit metropolitan area: Livonia contains a race track, a large amount of medium industry, and some fairly heavy industry (including a tank arsenal), but it also has a great deal of living area and many of the residents of the community work in the core city. Furthermore, the homes are not of a homogeneous value pattern, for they vary from working-class sections to extremely expensive subdivisions. Dearborn, containing the mammoth River Rouge plant of the Ford Motor Company, is also to a large degree a dormitory suburb and contains some very wealthy areas. Hazel Park is basically a working-class dormitory town, but it also has a race-track industry.[11]

RESIDENTIAL SUBURBS

Among the residential suburbs, certain patterns have begun to emerge. Although the wealthy were generally the first to move out of the central city, they were rivaled by the working people of some communities. In any case, all income levels of people are suburbanites today, and collectively they behave somewhat differently in relationship to their governments than do their economic peers in the central city. We might note some of the types of residential suburbs here, keeping in mind, however, that a great many of them contain mixed groups. Although the goal of Americans seems to be to reduce social conflict by moving into a suburban area where people share one's income level, beliefs, and life styles, it is not always possible to achieve complete homogeneity among the various groups.

The Wealthy Suburb. Before the beginning of the present century, wealthy Americans began to move out to fringe-area "estates" where they built large homes that were manned by armies of servants. They reached their offices in the central city by using commuter trains. The early developments along the main line of the Pennsylvania Railroad outside of Philadelphia demonstrate this type of phenomenon. Today, the suburbs of the wealthy are likely to have smaller lots—perhaps half an acre—

[11] See Dobriner, *op. cit.*, pt. 1, and Leo F. Schnore, "The Functions of Metropolitan Suburbs," *American Journal of Sociology*, vol. 61 (March, 1956), pp. 453–458.

but 10-acre plots and larger are still to be found in many of them. The large size discourages efforts of lower-income people to move into the area and guarantees the pristine charm of quasi-rural living.

Here the homes are all individually designed by architects. Services may be of a luxury type—in one "estate" suburb of Cleveland, the police deliver the milk, many such suburbs have "city parks" that are exclusively for residents and are actually country clubs administered by the suburban government. In other cases, though, the wealthy do not want ordinary city services—street lights, curb and gutter, paved streets —because these things remind them of urban life, not of the gentlemanly country living they seek to imitate. Around the largest cities, many of the wealthy are seeking to locate on the outer fringe, far from the core, where open land is still available and where the leisure implied by great distance from the hub assures high status. These people even have a special term for themselves—the *exurbanites*.[12]

The government of these suburbs is often a triumph of amateurism of a sort that the business executives living there would never permit in their own firms. Some wealthy suburbs have professional city managers, but the key administrator—the clerk, or supervisor, or mayor—may be a local resident who lives in one of the several modest enclaves that are likely—perhaps through historical accident—to exist. The full-time non-professional, nonelective persons that are needed, such as clerical help and street-maintenance men, may not live in the suburb at all. The people in the city or town hall are likely to be obsequious in the extreme in their relationships with the great men for whose homes they provide services.

The elected council and school board will probably be made up of both men and women from among the wealthy residents. They will seek to establish policies that fit their objectives—no invasion of lower-status families or groups, a school system that will allow their children to gain admission to the most prestigeful preparatory schools and universities. Some of them will be concerned about metropolitan-area government generally, and about the pattern of change in the core city—after all, they are frequently landowners or members of the top bureaucracies of core-city business and manufacturing firms. As "organization men" of corporations, they have been told that they have a responsibility to take part in public affairs, to be concerned about "metropolitan-area problems," and to help make their organizations "good citizens." As a result: [13]

[12] For social criticism of the movement, see Max Shulman, *Rally Round the Flag, Boys!* (Doubleday & Company, Inc., New York, 1957) and A. C. Spectorsky, *The Exurbanites* (J. B. Lippincott Company, Philadelphia, 1955).

[13] Norton E. Long, "The Corporation, Its Satellites, and the Local Community," in E. E. Mason (ed.), *The Corporation in Modern Society* (Harvard University Press, Cambridge, Mass., 1960), p. 210.

An . . . executive will inveigh against the jurisdictional mess of his metropolitan area in a staff-ghosted speech that repeats uncomprehendingly the clichés of current municipal reform. This activity is good corporate citizenship, the more so as the executive hasn't the foggiest idea as to how the changes he advocates will help his company, though doubtless in all honesty he thinks they will. It is difficult for the corporation executive to avoid a kind of ritualistic do-gooding when he embarks on the unfamiliar role of city father.

The wealthy suburbanite is likely to play some kind of role in core-city politics as well as in the community where his home is situated. He is not so likely to be as concerned about surburban independence as are lower-income persons because he believes that he can probably influence core-city policy, should his area be annexed or a supergovernment created, while the more typical suburbanite fears that annexation means loss of influence over matters—school and land-use policies especially—that he considers really important. Yet the high income suburbanite—perhaps especially his wife—will not approve of metropolitan-area changes that may result in significantly lessened influence for him over the policies of the government that serves his place of residence.

The Typical Suburb. This is the home of the average-income person, the white-collar worker, the skilled blue-collar worker, the picture window, the charcoal grill, and the power mower. It is here that preoccupation with property values and with conformity has helped mold, in the postwar years, a distinctive American life style. (See Figure 2-1.) The homes here are all mass produced, the number of different models that

*"Congratulate me, dear. I hesitated a moment this morning
before I agreed with Mr. Wardmore."*

Figure 2-1. SOURCE: Drawing by Stan Hunt; © 1960 The New Yorker Magazine, Inc.

Figure 2-2. Suburbia, home of comfort and conformity, is the goal of millions of Americans. SOURCE: Courtesy of Levitt and Sons, Inc., Levittown, N.J.

the builder has to offer depending generally on the cost level of the area's homes (see Figure 2-2). The people in the mass-produced houses follow carefully the fashions in mass culture and mass leisure. They are not innovators; they do not want to solve the world's problems, or even those of their own metropolitan area. Social conflict is not, to them, a challenge to be met through the institutions of democratic government— they seek to avoid conflict in homogeneity by living with those who share their goals. There is no place in their lives for experimentation with the admission of lower-status ethnic or racial groups, with seeking meaning in life through a concentration on one's personal resources, for questioning the values imposed upon them by homes-and-gardens or weekly news-and-pictures magazines. The suburbanite "is attuned to others but never to himself." [14] In David Riesman's words, "he is other-directed, not inner-directed, as were his grandparents."

[14] Robert C. Wood, *Suburbia, Its People and Their Politics* (Houghton Mifflin Company, Boston, 1959), p. 6. This book offers a general theory of suburban politics. See also William Dobriner (ed.), *The Suburban Community* (G. P. Putnam's Sons, New York, 1958), pts. III and IV; David Riesman, "The Suburban Sadness," in *ibid.;* John R. Seeley and others, *Crestwood Heights: The Culture of Suburban Life* (Basic Books, New York, 1956); John Keats, *The Crack in the Picture Window* (Ballantine Books, Inc., New York, 1957); Frederick Lewis Allen, "The Big Change in Suburbia,"

These people—the statistically typical suburbanites—have helped bring back a revival of interest and confidence in local grass-roots government, an interest that rarely exists in rural communities which are governed by consensus, low-tax ideologies, and the avoidance of innovation; and a confidence that is not often to be found in the government of the core city, which is typically regarded with suspicion as being distant, run by an impersonal professional bureaucracy, and strife-ridden, if not also corrupt.

The suburbanites, then, have a life style with a special view, including a special view of politics: [15]

Deeply concerned with the quality of schools, conscious of their new status, suburbanites are inclined to "care" about local affairs—zoning regulations, recreational plans, garbage collection, school curricula, street paving—in an especially intense way. As the logical converse of their apathy toward strong party affiliations, suburbanites approach the politics of the community on the basis of individual preferences; they are, more and more frequently, nonpartisan, sharply distinguishing their local public preferences from their views of national and state affairs.

The Workingman's Suburb. The suburb of the hourly rated unskilled or semiskilled worker is, if built in the postwar years, made up of mass-produced single-family homes which have less variation than those of the middle-class types described above. They are built of siding that is less expensive than that of brick or stone, the lots are small—possibly no larger than the minimum established by state statute—and the traditional gridiron pattern of streets may be used rather than the loops, cul-de-sacs, and curves that typify the neighborhood of the organization man. Low cost, not aesthetics, is the concern of the developer. These are the homes that are often spoken of as America's next slums, but because of individual ownership (and a concern for resale value), they have generally been well cared for and have a satisfactory appearance after ten or twelve years of use.

There are other working-class suburbs, too, however. Many of these were first developed in the 1920s and were located at the end of the streetcar line. Some of them are built around amusement parks which the transit company built before World War I in order to attract customers and to give core-city dwellers somewhere to go on a summer Sunday. Others are built around a lake or stream, and consist largely of summer cottages that were converted for year-round living by desperate factory workers during the Great Depression. These tiny old

Harper's (June, 1954), pp. 21–28, and (July, 1954), pp. 47–53; and Harry Henderson, "The Mass-produced Suburbs," *Ibid.* (November, 1953), pp. 25–32, and (December, 1953), pp. 80–86.

[15] Wood, *op. cit.,* p. 153.

homes, on lots now below the state minimum size, create health and roadway problems. Many of them are occupied by retired factory workers. All of the residents want to enjoy the status of homeownership and they imitate some, but not all, of the patterns of Babbittville, which is nearby. One would find breezeways and charcoal grills, for example, but also an ancient car under repair in the backyard—a situation that would generate a call to the police or the planning commission in a middle-class suburb—and a tavern on the corner. (The organization man does his drinking at home or in a core-city nightclub.)

The working-class suburb is quite likely to be unincorporated. It is cheaper that way, and the residents must look for ways to save money so as to preserve their status as homeowners in time of economic difficulties—and in order to spend money on luxuries in imitation of the middle class. If the county or township administers the area, part of the cost of governmental protection and services may, through the property tax, be transferred to residents in wealthier areas, and there is less likelihood for demands for costly services to be made against a more distant government than against one's own municipal organization. If the area is incorporated as a separate municipality, there is likely to be less participation in government than is the case in the middle-class suburb. The residents are likely to be skeptical of the council-manager plan or other forms of professionalization, and they will expect taxes to be low. Services will be few: septic tanks are preferred to sewage disposal systems, state parks to municipal parks, inexpensive gravel to hard-surfaced roads, open ditches to curb and gutter. Building codes will place few limitations on the builder and will probably, in any case, not be rigidly enforced. The educational system will probably have a pronounced vocational cast to its curriculum. The area as a whole will view with hostility potential annexation to the core city, or the imposition of a metropolitan-area supergovernment. Both threaten to expand services, raise the caliber of the existing ones to a professional level (more expensive than what exists), and deprive the residents of such access to government as they may now have. These are marginal homeowners and they do not want to fall below the margin.

Racial and Ethnic Suburbs. Specialization is a characteristic of American culture and it is applied, as with almost every other aspect of our lives, to residential suburbs. The larger the metropolitan area, the more specialization there is of suburbs by racial, ethnic, and religious criteria. In a city of around 100,000, there are not enough Italian ethnics or Jews, say, to make possible separate suburbs, or even segregated neighborhoods, or to make economically feasible the ethnically specialized land developers, builders, and realtors one finds arcing the large cities. Negroes have had the least opportunity of all to move to the suburbs, not only because of the policies of realtors and home-sellers, but also because of their relatively low income position.[16]

How do people select a suburb in which to locate when they move from the core city or from some distant community? [17]

This out-movement follows what might be called the "homogeneity principle," that is, like kinds of people tend to segregate themselves: the rich, religious or ethnic groups, white-collar workers, etc. This tendency is reinforced by the practice of building houses in large blocs within a fairly narrow price range, which results in economic segregation.

Also, institutions locate or relocate in certain areas. For instance, the building of a synagogue in an already Jewish residential area multiplies the attraction of this area for more Jewish people. The suburban parish does the same for Catholics—even more so when the church buys up considerable residential land around its new church structure, and sells it largely to Catholic home builders.

The objective of minimizing conflict within the suburb threatens America's traditional emphasis upon a concept of fair play and the teachings of equality. How, then, do suburbanites rationalize their practices of segregation? They do so in two ways, principally (1) by arguing that nearly all persons are happier if they live among people like themselves and if there is as little friction as possible of the sort that results from a clash of values, and (2) by arguing that the "ghettoization" of the suburbs "protects property values."

A sensation was caused in 1960 when the attorney general of Michigan —with one eye on re-election prospects, perhaps—publicly revealed the techniques used in the wealthy Grosse Pointe suburbs of Detroit in order to control the land use, life styles, and ethnic composition of the area. For each person who wanted to buy in one of the suburbs involved, the local property-owners' association and the realty board had an investigation conducted by a private detective. The detective filled out a standard form; for most people, 50 per cent was a passing grade. The questions asked dealt with such things as level of education, place of birth, and church membership. But the realtors also inquired into whether the family's life style fitted that of the Grosse Pointes, or perhaps more closely resembled that of some cultural subgroup—in particular, whether the applicant spoke English without an accent, whether his friends were primarily from the main stream of American culture rather than from an

[16] See Edward C. Banfield and Morton Grodzins, *Government and Housing in Metropolitan Areas* (McGraw-Hill Book Company, Inc., New York, 1958), various passages; and Albert I. Gordon, *Jews in Suburbia* (The Beacon Press, Boston, 1959).

[17] Governor's Study Commission on Metropolitan Area Problems, State of Michigan, *Final Report* (State of Michigan, Lansing, Mich., 1960). The author served as chairman of the commission.

ethnic group, whether the men of the family dressed in conservative or flashy style, and whether they were swarthy or fair-skinned. Persons of, or descended from, certain cultural subgroups had to have more than 50 points: Italians, for example, had to have 65, and Jews 85. Negroes apparently could not qualify at all.

This technique for segregation is probably more formalized and elaborate than one would find in most suburbs, but the process takes place through one means or another. When asked how this system could be justified, one broker explained that the "fears and prejudices" of the *buyers* made the system necessary. He said they "prefer congenial neighborhoods where their investment is likely to be secure." [18]

The standard argument that homogeneity protects property values requires some examination, and it has received this in a study of 10,000 real estate sales in areas that were changing from all-white to mixed Negro and white.[19] The findings indicated that the odds were 4 to 1 against property values declining when Negroes began to buy into an area. Even when values did go down, as they did in 15 per cent of the cases studied, the decline was modest, nearly always less than 9 per cent. Thus we find that the real reason for restrictive land-use and realty practices is not to save property values, but rather to maintain the social homogeneity of the area—and for this purpose local control, that is, suburban rather than metropolitan-wide government, is a powerful aid.[20] But, regardless of the statistical facts, many a suburbanite would agree with the businessman in the Chicago suburb of Deerfield who said, "I've put everything I have into my home here and I don't want to lose it to a bunch of do-gooders," and with another man who complained, "We're all mortgaged up to here. And although we've got most of our money tied up in our homes, we don't expect to live in them really very long."

American suburbanites and their little governments which seek to preserve values and life styles on a parochial basis are hence a source of political conflict by the very techniques they use in seeking to minimize conflict. The Balkanized pattern of suburban America is not designed to help solve the racial and group conflicts that are a national problem.[21]

[18] This account borrows from various editions of the *Detroit Free Press* and *Detroit News* during April and May, 1960.

[19] Luigi Laurenti, *Property Values and Race* (University of California Press, Berkeley, Calif., 1960).

[20] See also Martin Meyerson and E. C. Banfield, *Politics, Planning and the Public Interest* (The Free Press, Glencoe, Ill., 1955), pp. 88–89. For a case study of proposed Negro invasion of Deerfield, Ill., see Wilma Dykeman and James Stokely, " 'The South' in the North," *The New York Times Magazine*, Apr. 17, 1960, pp. 8 ff.

[21] On this last point, see Wood, *op. cit.*, pt. III.

PROBLEMS OF THE CORE CITY

The centrifugal movement of population and industry to the periphery of the urban area has caused a multitude of problems for both the core city and the suburbs. Some of these problems are severe and are likely to prove to be chronic.

Loss of the Tax Base. While the cost of operating municipal governments has increased along with almost everything else in the postwar years, the movement toward the suburbs has seen the core cities lose more and more of their tax base. Industries have been moving out. Retail stores are following the shoppers. The large department stores of many core cities are expanding their facilities to meet the increases in population in the community—but they tend to build in the suburbs, where land is cheaper and more plentiful and where the customers are nearby.

The people who are moving to homes in the suburbs are the people best able to pay taxes, for the movement is dominated by members of the middle and upper-middle classes. They build their immodest expressions of consumption and leisure outside the taxing limits of the city. On the other hand, the great majority of the very poor continue to live within the core city. To heap trouble upon trouble, as the prosperous citizens move out, part of the population loss is made up by the rural-to-urban migration that supplies the extra manpower to cities—but the newcomers to the core city are likely to be a financial liability rather than an asset. The majority of migrants will settle first in the city, probably in the decaying zone of transition. Because they are culturally marginal people—that is to say, they live in the culture of a large city, but still have many of the values they earlier received from a quite different rural culture—they are likely to create police and juvenile problems. They are insecure and confused people. They are very unlikely to be homeowners, and those who own their blighted dwellings do not pay as much in taxes as the city must spend in the area.

Furthermore, as the density of population in the core city decreases, the value of homes also decreases, since demand for them becomes less. The eroding of the tax base is therefore a cumulative phenomenon.

One student of municipal finance has concluded that: [22]

. . . Under present and foreseeable circumstances . . . the per capita property tax base of our central cities in real terms is likely to decline. This suggestion follows, first, from the fact that a great deal of property is being and will continue to be removed from the tax rolls as space is taken for the pro-

[22] Harvey E. Brazer, "The Role of Major Metropolitan Centers in State and Local Finance," *American Economic Review*, vol. 48 (May, 1958), pp. 305–316. The quotation is from pp. 308–309. Used by permission.

vision of transportation facilities in the form of limited access and widened arterial highways and streets, public parking sites, and terminals.

A second factor that is suggestive of a decline in the property tax base is the less intensive use of urban land; that is, the reduction in the ratio of brick and mortar to land area. Contributing to this decline are the increasing need for private parking facilities closely adjacent to factories, office buildings, theaters, shops, churches, and so forth; plants designed so that they can be readily engineered for the horizontal movement of goods; and the increasing insistence on the part of architects and city planners upon the desirability of providing for "green spaces" if redeveloped areas are not to revert rapidly to slum and blight.

In addition, because major metropolitan centers may expect to lose substantial portions of their manufacturing activity while gaining in service employment, defined in the broadest sense, this must mean a continuing shift from the location in the cities of the more capital-intensive to more labor-intensive activities. This, then, provides a third major reason for expecting that the property tax base per person served, if not per person resident in the city, will decline.

Finally, if income levels of central city residents decline through population shifts, we may expect as well that the value of residential property occupied per person will fall.

Threats to the Central Business District. The traditional "downtown" area of cities, the central business district (CBD), has been undergoing a gradual decline in value and social usefulness in the years since 1945. Its streets are congested, it has inadequate parking facilities, it lacks off street loading facilities, it is not compactly organized for shopper convenience, its land remains highly valued—often, perhaps, overvalued —and is hence difficult to redevelop, it is usually owned by a great many persons—many of them nonresidents—who often cannot agree on policies of renovation. And the area is generally old in appearance, unattractive, and lacking in an architecturally integrated design.[23]

Yet the CBD is an area carrying an enormous investment. The Cleveland CBD, for example, is estimated to be worth at least 750 million dollars in land and buildings. Many of the "metropolitan area studies" that have been so popular in the postwar years have probably been inspired by those who fear the results of the pattern of decline that is evident in the CBD. They wish to put a stop to this trend and hope that an integrated government and area-wide land-use controls will lend them a hand. In many cases, city fathers have sought to correct the CBD situations that are making suburban living and trading alternatives so much more attractive. At best they can hope only to diminish the rate of decentralization. They cannot stop it.[24]

[23] *Horizons*, vol. 3 (June, 1956), p. 1.

[24] See "Can the Big Cities Come Back?" *U.S. News and World Report,* July 19, 1957, pp. 72–90; "Our Changing Cities," *Newsweek,* Sept. 2, 1957, pp. 61–68; John Rannels, *The Core of the City* (Columbia University Press, New York, 1956).

Just how much decline has there been in the CBD? Studies indicate that it varies by community and especially by economic function. The CBD remains a central area of finance, and the headquarters of specialists in the various fields of law, medicine, engineering, and advertising, among others. Decline is taking place, however.[25] In states without branch banking, less than 4 per cent of bank deposits have, on the average, been shifted from the CBD to outlying areas. The big commercial accounts remain with the downtown banks. But 40 per cent of the insurance business left the CBDs between 1946 and 1958. Privately owned utilities remain core-oriented; about 92 per cent of utilities headquarters are still located within CBDs. But retail sales per capita have declined, on the average, by 14 per cent in metropolitan areas of 100,000 and by 28 per cent in a sample area of 3 million people. And per capita office space downtown has decreased in average amounts of from about 2 per cent in areas of 200,000 to 12 per cent in an area of 3 million—total office space in the CBD is still increasing, but at much less than the rate of population increase. Central business districts are not dying, but they are undergoing transformations, and the changes that are taking place represent a threat to investors' incomes, and to the tax base of core cities.

Subsidization of the Suburbs. In addition to its decreasing tax base, the core city has been forced in most states, to subsidize the suburbs. As the tax base declines, the amount and number of subsidies increase. There are at least two ways in which the core city is forced to help the suburbanite pay for his governmental services: by furnishing services of the city free or below cost; and by paying a disproportionately large share of state and county taxes in return for a disproportionately small share of their services.

The core city furnishes services free to suburbanites in many ways. Whether it likes it or not, it builds strong, wide commuter highways to carry the load into the city each morning and back to the dormitory towns each evening. After the morning rush hour is over, it must be prepared to handle another miniature rush hour as the shoppers come into the city. The city pays for the repairs on the highways that deteriorate rapidly under the pounding of an ever increasing traffic load. The city hires extra policemen to handle the nonresident traffic.

Some cities subsidize their public transportation system from taxes but allow it to operate in the suburbs and to carry suburbanites without their sharing in the subsidy. Parks and recreational facilities of the core city are available to suburbanites, although quite a few suburbs restrict their own parks to residents. The city must expand its public health de-

[25] The data that follow are from E. M. Horwood and others, *Studies of the Central Business District and Urban Freeway Development* (University of Washington Press, Seattle, Wash., 1959).

partment in order to inspect the restaurants where the noontime hordes of suburbanites eat—blissfully unaware that it costs other people money to see to it that they are not poisoned. Many core cities make their tax-supported libraries available to nontaxpaying suburbanites, especially to those who are employed in the city.

Some core cities are required by state law—the rural legislature is likely to listen more sympathetically to suburban pressure groups than to those of the metropolis—to furnish fire protection, water, sewage disposal, or other facilities to the suburbs at less than cost. Because of the lesser density in population and in order to build up a protective reserve, most cities charge somewhat more to the suburbs to which they furnish water than they do to their own residents. (If rates to core-city residents prove to be too low, or depreciation reserves inadequate, the deficit can be made up from taxes. This is not true of suburban customers; hence the protective reserve.) Chicago, however, is prohibited by law from charging a higher rate to the suburbs. As a result, in 1951 Chicago sold water to forty-eight of its suburbs at twelve cents per thousand gallons. The suburbs in turn sold it to their residents at an average markup of 200 per cent. In the extreme case of Forest Park, the water purchased at twelve cents was being sold to residents at seventy-three cents.[26] To add insult to inequity, many suburbanites undoubtedly blamed Chicago for their high water bills. Chicago has tried unsuccessfully since 1904 to get permission from the legislature to charge a differential rate to suburbs.

The core city also subsidizes the urban fringe through the payment of a disproportionate share of the county taxes. The county is traditionally a rural unit of government. In many urban communities it performs almost no functions within the core city. There are some exceptions to this, but for the most part the county collects most of its taxes within the city and spends them outside, particularly in unincorporated areas. The inequity is increased by the fact that core-city properties are assessed at a higher rate than are those in most suburbs. Property in the core city, for example, may be assessed in practice at 60 per cent of market value, while that in some suburbs may be assessed at 40 per cent. In theory, such inequities are illegal and should be corrected by the board of equalization. In practice, they exist almost everywhere.

In Minneapolis in 1949, about 87 per cent of the Hennepin County taxes were paid by city taxpayers who received no benefits, or only very small benefits, from nine of the county functions, including some of the most expensive ones. Residents of Dallas pay twice as much per capita toward the city-county hospital as do suburban taxpayers. Detroiters pay not less than 75 per cent of Wayne County taxes, yet during some heavy

---

[26] For the political factors involved in this situation, see Illinois Legislative Council, *Chicago Sanitary District* (State of Illinois, Champaign, Ill., 1953), pp. 27–31.

snowstorms the residential streets in unincorporated suburbs are plowed by the county, while those in the city remain snowbound. Suburban roads are often maintained by the county, but few core cities receive such aid.

The large cities also pay most of the state taxes since, in spite of losses to the suburbs, they remain centers of concentration of wealth. Yet the state tends to spend most of its money in the rural and suburban areas, expecting the large cities to finance most of their functions themselves. The state police, for example, will often lend assistance to the amateurish efforts of suburban policemen but seldom operate within the core city. Health, education, highway, welfare, and other state functions may be provided more generously outside the large cities than inside them. Grants-in-aid by the state usually give preference to the lesser-populated local governments.

Some observers justify this general policy as one which helps to assess costs at least roughly on the basis of ability to pay. They argue that a man who lives in a tax-poor bedroom community, but who works for a large corporation housed in the core city, should gain some of the benefits of the tax base supplied by his employer. The distribution of costs just described does, in fact, help offset some of the alleged inequities in the property-tax system which would otherwise benefit only the community which is lucky (or foresighted) enough to have industry.

In America, we have traditionally developed an area, used it for individual and social profit, and then, as the efficiency of the area declined, we have abandoned it with its problems and moved on to newer, more promising places. Such, to a considerable degree, has been the fate of the core of our metropolitan areas. Yet, the core cities and the central business districts within them still serve a useful social purpose and therefore cannot be abandoned.

Problems of the Suburbs. The politically atomized pattern of contemporary American suburbia results from the fact that this was a rural nation in the days when laws of annexation and attitudes toward large cities were developing. Rural-dominated legislatures have for the most part kept the traditional legal situation unchanged. As a consequence, the boundaries of a city are almost always artificial and arbitrary and have nothing to do with economic and social realities.

The entire community is an organic whole, despite its artificial compartmentation, and most suburbs, if they were moved 50 miles away, would wither and die. The prevailing pattern produces independent suburbs that, because of their extravagant use of the resources of government, are expensive. Yet, most suburbanites wish to retain the present system. Some of their reasons are based upon important psychological factors; others stem from ignorance and misinformation.

The Demand for Independence. Not only has the population of the fringe area grown rapidly, but the number of suburbs has been increasing at a great pace. In 1911 there were eight incorporated municipalities in St. Louis County. In 1935 the number had increased to twenty-five. The postwar expansion raised the total to ninety-six by 1956.[27] Montgomery County, Ohio, of which Dayton is the core, had ten cities and villages in 1900, and nineteen six decades later. A similar pattern is to be found around most metropolitan areas. These figures would indicate not only that the population is expanding in many directions from the core cities, but also that there is a tendency toward a governmental fragmentation of the fringe area. As each group of subdivisions becomes partially populated, it tends to seek incorporation for itself rather than annexation to another suburb or to the core city.

Why do people want "their own" little suburb? A major reason is surely a desire to own their own homes, however heavily mortgaged. Because the cost of home ownership is increased by core-city taxes levied in order to provide urban services, suburbanites hope to be able to afford to own a home by keeping taxes low. Since many suburbanites may feel that they literally cannot continue to afford a home in the price category they are in if costs increase, they will fight anything that threatens higher costs, including taxes. This attitude, therefore, produces hostility toward annexation. It may also produce opposition to the incorporation of the suburb, for incorporation symbolizes increased taxes and the threat of being required to accept urban service costs.

Another significant reason deals with the common belief that the core city is run by professional politicians, is expensive to operate, and is strife-ridden. The first of these is regarded as bad because it violates the Jacksonian value of government by neighbors. The second runs counter to the citizen's use of his home as a status symbol which causes him to prefer a larger home to additional services. The last violates a desire for a sense of community, a consensus of values such as existed in rural areas of an earlier day. The core city is made up of many ethnic and racial groups, a variety of subcultures. The one-class, one-culture, one-group tendency in individual suburbs appeals to the desire of the citizen to minimize social tensions and conflicts.

Government in the suburb is also likely to be more personal. One may easily come to know the suburban officials personally or by reputation. The city hall is more personalized and humanized than in the core city. All of these features are regarded as desirable by the typical suburbanite.[28]

---

[27] John C. Bollens and others, *Background for Action* (St. Louis Metropolitan Survey, St. Louis, Mo., 1957), pp. 30–34; John C. Bollens and others, *Metropolitan Challenge* (Metropolitan Community Studies, Inc., Dayton, Ohio, 1959), table 16.

[28] On the general subject, see Wood, *Suburbia*.

The Desire for Access. A psychological factor that has contributed to the Balkanization of the suburbs is the desire of citizens to have access to the decision-making centers of local government. As urban life became more impersonal with the growth of population and as the old-fashioned political machine, which had served as an access point to great numbers of citizens, declined, the feeling of isolation and of frustration on the part of the urbanite must have increased. The reform-period practice of electing all councilmen at large contributed to the iron curtain that the ordinary citizen saw as being dropped between himself and those who decided things that mattered. But in the suburb, he found a re-establishment of the close relationships that symbolized democracy on the frontier. After he moved to the suburb, the citizen did not necessarily participate more by voting or attending meetings, and he did not make a greater effort to know his governmental officials, but he regained the comfortable feeling that goes with confidence in the thought of having influence over government decisions and of having officeholders who share one's social values.

To the urbanite of today, the concept of community is, in any case, a vague one. Certainly he feels only the most tangential loyalties to the metropolitan area as a whole. There are few regional institutions. To the typical citizen, the only reality is the family and the neighborhood, so "regional problems find no vehicle for their solution and the capacity to look ahead, to plan rationally, to awake a regional consciousness is lost." [29]

Because of his narrow scope of vision and narrow loyalties, the typical suburbanite knows little of the structure or physical limits of his local government, to say nothing of the metropolitan area as a whole. He does not know what legal powers it possesses, what it is prohibited from doing by state law, how services can be provided, what a reasonable cost for them would be, or why they cost what they do.[30] The local government to him is good, not because he has an emotional loyalty to it, but because through it he has influence and access in relation to governmental services while through any type of regional government he does not.

The Desire for Local Control. Over which governmental functions does the suburbanite wish to retain control for himself and his neighbors? In which service areas is diversity positively preferred to uniformity? An attitude survey would probably show that suburbanites feel that some

[29] Wood, "Metropolitan Government, 1957: An Extrapolation of Trends," *American Political Science Review,* vol. 52 (March, 1958), p. 111. On this section, see also his *Suburbia,* and E. C. Banfield and Morton Grodzins, *Government and Housing* (McGraw-Hill Book Company, Inc., New York, 1958).

[30] B. G. Zimmer and A. H. Hawley, "Local Government as Viewed by Fringe Residents," *Rural Sociology,* vol. 23 (December, 1958), pp. 363–370, provides partial verification.

services are more important than are others in terms of the way in which policies will affect the character of their neighborhoods. Among the areas where local retention of control is most wanted would probably be the following: land use, garbage and rubbish collection, maintenance of residential streets, and education.

Local wishes may call for luxury services, for minimal services, or for some level in between. Wealthy people do not want to be forced into a single mold by the creation of one legal entity for the whole area, for they can afford and often wish to have luxury services which core-city government would not be likely to provide. Paradoxically, wealthy suburbanites sometimes want fewer services than they might have to take from the core city. For example, as noted earlier, they may not want their streets paved or lighted.

In contrast, one finds in modest suburbs a violent dislike and fear of the core city. In these areas, residents can barely afford to own their homes. They want minimal services because they fear that even a small increase in costs through "unnecessary" services, for example, might force them out of the homeowning category with all of its prestige and psychological satisfaction. To these people, joining the core city would mean buying a package of services that they feel they can do without and

TABLE 2-1. CITIZEN PARTICIPATION AND ABILITY TO NAME
LEADERS
(In per cent)

Types of participants	Local leaders			
	None named		Two or more named	
	Dayton	Rest of county	Dayton	Rest of county
Actives........	40	40	31	23
Casuals........	38	52	18	10
Nonvoters.....	61	76	11	4

Note that suburbanites *do not* necessarily have a better knowledge of local leaders than do core-city dwellers. Similar findings have been reported from other metropolitan areas.

SOURCE: John C. Bollens and others, *Metropolitan Challenge* (Metropolitan Community Studies, Inc., Dayton, Ohio, 1959), table 46. Used by permission.

cannot afford. People in between these two extremes recognize that additional services are symbols of status and that they cost money. They are usually willing to pay extra taxes for extra services, but they generally believe that these services can be secured more cheaply by incorporating the area than by becoming annexed.[31]

It should be clear why residents of different types of suburban areas would want to control the above functions. Low-income neighborhoods may want to haul their own rubbish to the dump. Well-to-do people may prefer twice-a-week collection from the back door while the core city offers only once-a-week service from the front curb. Local control of educational services is desired because of the great expense of this item and because of the importance of the school plant as a status symbol. Parents want to control the social environment of their children in grammar school and high school, just as they later may want them to go to the "right" college and join the "right" fraternity. Low-income areas and areas of older people may want minimal services in education out of cost considerations. Higher-income areas use the school to indicate their relative status. The automobile and the wife's wardrobe are important devices for displaying "pecuniary emulation" (in Thorstein Veblen's terms), but the size and luxury of the school auditorium and, especially perhaps, of the swimming pool (if any) have become equally important symbols in contemporary suburbia. To have decisions about these policies left to the impersonal bureaucracy of a large-city school system would be undesirable to all suburbanites, of low and high income alike. Land-use policies, which by the logic of the planning profession are the most region-wide in character of all policies, are vitally important to the suburbanite. The ethnic, industrial, and commercial balance is of the greatest concern to him. He wants races, classes, and occupations segregated. He wants to be personally acquainted with, or to feel that he can influence, those who sit on the planning commission so that they will not change the land use in his area (except to his advantage). The professional bureaucracy of the core city with its impersonal dedication to the principles of planning does not spell an improved community to him; it spells loss of control and potential disaster for him as a homeowner.

The Control of Functions of Marginal Importance. In addition to the services named above, certain other services are regarded by the suburbanite as being important enough so that local retention of control over them is preferred. These include police, fire protection, mass trans-

[31] For partial verification of this paragraph, see three articles by B. G. Zimmer and A. H. Hawley: "Home Owners and Attitude toward Tax Increase," *Journal of the American Institute of Planners,* vol. 21 (Spring, 1956), pp. 65–74; "Property Taxes and Solutions to Fringe Problems," *Land Economics,* vol. 32 (November, 1956), pp. 369–376; "Approaches to the Solution of Fringe Problems," *Public Administration Review,* vol. 16 (Autumn, 1956), pp. 258–268.

portation, and public housing. To the suburbanite, police protection has a highly elastic demand curve.[32] He does not view it as being vitally important. In a suburb that has never had a case of murder, rape, or arson, arguments for a metropolitan police force make little sense indeed. If a difficult case should come along, the county sheriff or the state police, both heavily subsidized by the core city, would provide the needed extra help. Fire-protection costs can be reduced in the suburbs by using volunteer help—there is usually a waiting list of persons wanting to join the company—and people seem not to mind paying higher fire-insurance premiums than do core-city residents. Furthermore, by avoiding a metropolitan fire-protection system, the suburbanite can avoid helping to pay for the expensive equipment needed to guard the high-rise buildings and warehouse areas of the core city. Suburbanites, with one, two, or more cars in the family, would rather not help subsidize a public transportation system designed primarily for the lower-income residents of the core city. And to the suburban homeowner, public housing is regarded with suspicion and as something that might better not exist at all, especially in his part of the urban scene.

There are certain areas where the suburbanite might not object strongly to region-wide administration of services. These would probably include functions where professionals in the field make basic policy—and the average citizen therefore views the function as not involving policy making, or "politics," at all. Examples include public health and welfare, garbage and sewage disposal, and water supply. In these areas, the suburbanite feels no strong need to control policy, but he is not willing to spend more than a minimum amount, in the typical situation, for the service. With few multifamily dwellings, restaurants, or public assembly places, he is likely to think of health as a matter for the family physician (many suburbs spend nothing on public health); he will favor disposing of sewage in the raw state into the nearest stream if no one stops him; and he will insist that a well is cheaper than a municipal system, so long as the pump brings forth water.

Wasteful Duplication. The social waste of a legally atomized urban area is great. With the community broken up into a series of small units, it becomes difficult to make use of the advantages of specialization of personnel and mechanization of equipment. For example, sewage-disposal and water-filtration plants require such large capital investments that they are not economical unless they are in constant use. Small plants are expensive either because they are inefficient or because they do an inadequate job. Yet these plants are to be found in great numbers in any metropolitan area. Suburbanites may favor them through deliberate

[32] So it would seem from the figures in Seymour Sacks and others, *Metropolitan Cleveland: A Fiscal Profile* (Metropolitan Services Commission, Cleveland, Ohio, 1958).

choice ("We don't want to depend on the city for our water"), or through ignorance, or because the cost of the inefficiency is widely socialized (as when a suburb dumps partially treated sewage into a river which then flows through the core city).

Amateurism. In the midst of specialists of every type, many of the suburbs try to get along with untrained amateurs. On the other hand, the governmental operations of suburbs are simpler than are those of large cities, and fewer skills are required.

Lack of Services. "Taxes are lower in Perambulator Park," the real estate advertisements proclaim—they are less likely to mention that they are lower because almost no services are provided. The absence of many services which are usually thought to be characteristic of urban life may be accounted for in a variety of ways, some of which have been mentioned earlier in this chapter. Suburbanites may think they cannot afford the services and thus deliberately refuse to institute them. They may prefer to perform the service individually for themselves. They may regard the services as not worth the cost. Many services are more expensive in the suburbs than in the core city because of the lesser density of population. This applies particularly to sewage, storm drainage, street paving and maintenance, street lighting, water supply, garbage collection, and sewage disposal.

Lack of Cooperation. Suburbs tend to become intensively jealous of their independence, and—egged on by local officeholders—they attribute ulterior motives to all suggestions of cooperation with the core city or even with another suburb. This attitude is likely to increase the lack of coordination and of inefficient use of equipment.

Unequal Tax Bases. The accident of boundary lines contributes to the creation of suburbs with highly unequal financial facilities for supporting local government. There may be very wealthy suburbs alongside of a core city that is desperately in need of more taxable wealth to support its services—which are used by residents of that suburb. Other suburbs may be very poor, even though they are located in the heart of a prosperous urban area. This is true, for example, of middle- or lower-income suburbs with no industry. Often the suburbs most needing services are the least able to afford them.

There is some evidence that these inequities are being partly relieved by the transfer of some functions to special districts, the county, or the state; by increasing use of state and Federal grants-in-aid with built-in formulas to consider relative need; by state-shared taxes; by forcing the commuter to pay some of the cost of his use of services of other local units of government through the application of earnings taxes or through his payment of state and local taxes; and by a broadening out of the tax base so that even poor suburbs that have not attracted industry are having their property-tax income increased somewhat through the diversified location of offices, salesrooms, medical clinics, supermarkets, shopping centers, and other commercial establishments.[33] But these trends are being partially offset by the decline in the relative average value of new construction in suburbs as they become increasingly the home of all classes.

Rising Costs. Fringe-area taxes may start at what appears to be a much lower level than those of the core city, but the suburban buyer can be assured that they will increase at a rapid pace. The major portion of one's property-tax bill goes toward the support of schools, and in contemporary suburbia one school-bond issue has followed another with regularity. Each issue raises taxes. As population density increases, furthermore, the need for other urban services increases. Each new service must be paid for by additional taxes.

Water and sewage systems must be installed. Soon neighbors want to have their street paved and a storm sewer laid. Street lights become desirable. Fire and police service may have to be expanded. The sewage-disposal problem, enormously expensive and nearly always ignored as long as possible, must be solved.

All of these problems fall upon the mortgage- and debt-ridden suburbanite. Many of them were never faced by the subdivision developer. He has, in any case, long since disappeared from the area. In desperation, the citizens seek solutions through special districts, incorporation, new state legislation, or, more rarely, annexation to an existing municipality.

Problems of the Metropolitan Area. The problems listed above generally are those of either the core city or of the suburbs. But there are also matters of concern to the metropolitan area as a whole. Unsafe sewage-disposal practices in any part of the area may endanger health in another part. Economics may dictate a collective effort to secure additional water supplies from a distant lake or mountain stream. Traffic-flow patterns for the entire area are necessarily interrelated. Land-use practices in any one section will affect those in other sections. Smoke and noise nuisances pay no more attention to legal boundaries than do disease germs.

These are some of the collective problems. There is little agreement as to which are the most important, and they probably differ from one metropolitan area to another according to local values and existing service levels. The greatest problem of all, perhaps, is "the inability of metropolitan residents to reach any substantial degree of consensus as to what should be done . . . about the generally recognized issues of their common life—government organization, finance, blight and redevelopment, schools, race relations, land use control, and so on."[34]

[33] Wood, "Metropolitan Government, 1957," pp. 113–115.
[34] Coleman Woodbury, "Great Cities, Great Problems, Great Possibilities?" *Public Administration Review,* vol. 18 (Autumn, 1958), pp. 332–340. Quote from p. 339.

Chapter 3

IDEAS ABOUT LOCAL
SELF-GOVERNMENT IN AMERICA

Ideas make a difference in politics. So do emotions. The effective politician knows how to mix the two in the proper proportion. He seeks to find the ideas that will make the most effective type of appeal in a given situation. He knows, too, that the typical citizen often responds more readily to an emotional appeal than he does to a closely reasoned argument. Since this is the case, the politician becomes interested in ideas as *weapons*. They become devices through which people can be manipulated. Ideas are stated in terms that reflect existing value patterns of society. They are repeated with variations and elaborations; they are tied together with clichés that are already well established in their ability to produce a desired response, and through skillful reiteration, ideas are boiled down until they become slogans or proverbs that produce a conditioned response in the individual who is exposed to them. But it must be remembered that politicians, in seeking to influence people, are limited and restrained by the existing value structure, and they cannot move effectively except within that structure.

An understanding of ideas, attitudes, ideals as goals, and cultural values is important not just to the politician seeking to sway the minds of citizens, however. To know something about these concepts is vital to anyone who would wish to understand the political process. The materials in this chapter, then, are some of the most important analytical tools that are necessary for the citizen to make a meaningful analysis of the political events which take place about him and which affect him as a participant as well as an observer of politics.[1]

THE FRONTIER PRECEPTS OF JACKSONIAN DEMOCRACY

The British-colonial Background. It was an agricultural nation that declared its independence from the mother country in 1776. Only about

---

[1] For a more elaborate development of ideas and attitudes than is offered here, see Charles R. Adrian, *State and Local Governments* (McGraw-Hill Book Company, Inc., New York, 1960), chaps. 3 and 4.

70

3 per cent of the people lived in nonrural communities, and there were not more than twenty-four incorporated municipalities in all thirteen of the new states.[2] The city having the largest number of people living within its legally defined area was New York, which fourteen years later, in the first census of the United States, claimed a population of 33,131. The urban area, including suburbs, with the largest number of inhabitants was Philadelphia with 42,444. Today the United States possesses hundreds of cities of that size or larger, and an urban area in the 30,000 to 40,000 population class is often summarily dismissed as a "small city." In fact, a New Yorker of today would probably refer to it as "a wide place in the road."

These few statistics are cited to indicate that there was little *need* for Americans of the late eighteenth century to devote their time to the development of a theory of urban government. As a matter of fact, the cities and villages of the time used a governmental structure modeled upon a system that had been familiar to the colonists in their native England. There was no separation of powers between the legislative and executive branches. The council possessed virtually all power. It was headed by the *mayor,* who had no veto power and practically no executive power. His task was to preside over meetings of the council as one of its members and to perform the ceremonial functions of the city. He was appointed, usually for one year, by the colonial governor, by the council as a whole, or by the aldermen. In a very few instances he was elected under the complex suffrage rules then prevailing. Another appointed officer was the *recorder,* who held his post for an indefinite period. He was a member of the council and a member of the local court,[3] and served as the corporation counsel (city attorney). In addition to these two, the council was made up of *aldermen* (distinguished citizens of the community who were usually selected by the common councilmen from their own membership) and *councilmen.* The latter were the only members of the city government to be elected directly by the "people"—i.e., by the eligible electors.[4] Furthermore, nearly one-third of the boroughs (the English term

[2] In New England, urban and rural areas alike (including Boston) were ruled by the same unit of government, the *town.* In its pristine form, the town was a form of direct democracy, with the town meeting serving as the policy-making body. At this time, New England had no legally described villages or cities.

[3] The court was usually made up of the mayor, the recorder, and the aldermen (but not the common councilmen). Jurisdictions varied but usually covered misdemeanors in violation of state law and of municipal ordinances. Powers of a justice of the peace were also included. From this court came the term *recorder's court,* which we still find in North Carolina for minor courts, in the city of Detroit for the major criminal trial courts of the city, and in other places in the United States.

[4] To find out who was eligible in a rather complicated system, see K. H. Porter, *A History of Suffrage in the United States* (University of Chicago Press, Chicago, 1918). For more recent research indicating that voter eligibility was less restricted than was formerly believed, see R. E. Brown, *Middle-class Democracy and the Revolution in Massachusetts* (Cornell University Press, Ithaca, N.Y., 1955), chaps. 1–5.

for an incorporated municipality and the one generally used in the United States in the early years) were "close corporations" in which no popular elections at all were held. In these cities, the original charter named the members of the council, and vacancies were filled from time to time by surviving members of the body.

The city actually had a plural executive. Administrative supervision was exercised and minor appointments were made by the council as a whole, by committees of the council, or by the municipal court.

This plan, largely removed from the supervision or participation of the common citizen, remained in effect without basic change for the first few decades after independence. (In England, this same fundamental structure is in use today. It has been made operable under modern conditions by the installation of permanent, professionally trained department heads, a competent civil service, and an extension of voting privileges on the principle of universal suffrage.) That alterations might be expected was, however, presaged in one change that took place at the time of the Revolution. Under colonial rule, no charter could be made or amended without the consent of the city or village. With the cessation of British rule, control over charters passed from the Crown to the state legislatures rather than to the logical successor, the governor, for executives fell into disrepute during the Revolution. Since the legislatures appear to have assumed that their powers were plenary and unrestricted (excepting in a few cases of state constitutional limitations), the trail was opened for domination of the city government from the state capital—a phenomenon that characterized nineteenth-century American city government.

This potential for domination probably would never have been developed—the British tradition of local self-government being to the contrary—were it not for the evolution in the early decades of the nineteenth century of a genuinely American philosophy of government. This philosophy came out of the everyday experiences of the American frontiersman, and as such it was pragmatic rather than introspective, functional rather than universal; and it was applied to state, county, township, village, and city governments alike. We usually refer to its rather unsystematic precepts by the use of the term *Jacksonian democracy*.

Jacksonian Theories and City Government. The rustic idyl that was the America of the dreams of Thomas Jefferson began to disappear as an actual possibility well before that philosopher and statesman had completed his days on earth. Jefferson firmly believed that democracy, if it were to be successful, must find its strength in the individual farmer working in soil that he could call his own. Directly, he did not know very much about large cities (except for what he had seen in Paris), but he was an insatiable reader, and what he read about them did not please him. His opinion was stated trenchantly in *Notes on Virginia* (1782): "The mobs of great cities add just so much to the support of pure government, as sores do to the strength of the human body." So long as he lived, he urged that the United States remain an agricultural nation.

But the cities came anyway, and with them the urban proletariat that Jefferson thought spelled doom for democracy. With the rise of the city came also a philosophy for its proper government. That philosophy came via Jefferson and the frontier to the rising urban centers, where it was embraced by the workingman. It was an attitude toward government taken by those who labored on the farm and in the city alike; it was a philosophy of a rapidly growing nation, constantly pushing westward, founding new towns, building up old ones through the rise of a new industrialism; it was a viewpoint of a people constantly in debt, yet perennially optimistic as they realized, or at least hoped for, the unearned increment of increasing site value of land; and it was the thoughts of the common man about a nation that was now his own and that no longer belonged to an oligarchy of propertied aristocrats. Together it made up the political myth of Jacksonian democracy and it provided a rationalization for city government that survived nearly intact the remainder of the nineteenth century and is still important in our thinking today.[5] Its general principles are not difficult to summarize.

Jacksonian Principles. Probably antecedent to all others in importance was the concept of *government by the common man.* Government existed, not for a privileged class, but for the general citizen. Any one man was equal to any other man. Jefferson had said so in 1776, when the country was controlled by an aristocracy; now the words were to be taken quite literally.[6] If this were the case, then it followed that any man was as good as any other man *in a public office*—no special qualifications were needed, no special training, nothing other than status as a human being willing to serve the community.

Out of this concept came the principle of *universal manhood suffrage.* It followed logically from egalitarianism, it was necessary to the development of Jacksonian thought, and, furthermore, it was the natural result of the effect of inertia upon the already existing trend. There were property requirements to vote. These appear to have been quite easily met in rural areas—it is estimated that nearly 90 per cent of the adult white males of Massachusetts could vote at the time of the Revolution—but their continued existence might have created a disfranchised urban proletariat.

---

[5] For a background picture of the era in which the American industrial city was born and in which the ideas for governing it matured, see Arthur M. Schlesinger, Jr., *The Age of Jackson* (Little, Brown & Company, Boston, 1945), especially chaps. 2–4, 24, 26, 37.

[6] But only the visionary extended the concept beyond the *white* man in the 1820s.

With the Democrats seeking the support of urban workingmen, restrictions on the suffrage disappeared almost completely in the two decades following the first election of Andrew Jackson to the Presidency (1828).[7] From thenceforth, the general public possessed the potential for the control of government in its own interests.

Universal manhood suffrage made it possible for any man to run for office, to get support from all kinds of people, and to be elected. Jacksonians were not greatly concerned with the education, background of experience, or private calling of a candidate. It might be noted in passing that this viewpoint made a career as a professional politician or even as a political hack legitimate.[8]

Following from the above, Jacksonians believed that public officeholders, as servants of the people, should hold their mandates directly from the people. It was therefore held desirable to elect public officials rather than to appoint them. Gradually this came to mean the election of virtually all top-level officers, thus imposing upon Americans the unique institution of the long, or "bedsheet," ballot. To further ensure proximity to the people, a short term of one or two years in office and rapid turnover of personnel was advocated. In the small village or city, government could be *personal,* and the long ballot was therefore of little handicap to the casual voter, for he probably knew all or most of the candidates either personally or by reputation. Similarly, while rapid turnover of personnel meant inexperienced officeholders, this was no great problem where government was on a neighborly basis and administration was simple and nontechnical.

The movement toward the direct public oversight of officeholders through the use of the ballot was begun when the office of mayor was made elective. This was initiated in Boston and St. Louis in 1822 and spread rapidly throughout the nation. It was but a start, however. The Detroit charter of two years later not only made the office of mayor elective, but in true frontier spirit added the other city administrative offices to the list. This idea spread less rapidly than did that of the elective mayoralty, but gradually along the frontier the council was deprived of its power to appoint administrative officials. Some or all of the following became elective in various cities: the offices of tax collector or city treasurer, clerk, assessor, and city attorney, and, somewhat later, the

---

[7] See Brown, *op. cit.,* chaps. 1–5; and Walter Hugins, *Jacksonian Democracy and the Working Class* (Stanford University Press, Stanford, Calif., 1960).

[8] The frequently used term *political hack* may be said to refer to the individual who has never "made good" at anything else, who is a perennial office seeker, and who depends for a livelihood upon scraps from the political table. His competence and public faith in him are questionable. The term *professional politician* is here used to refer to a person who secures his livelihood from political jobs, but whose competence is assumed or has been demonstrated.

myriad posts on the various boards and commissions that became a part of city government.

The rise of the independent board or commission for administrative purposes came about gradually as a protest against inadequacies in the performances of council committees as administrative overseers. It also reflected the growing distrust of city government and the desire to take certain functions "out of politics" by setting up independent commissions —sometimes appointed by state officials—to administer them. The New York charter of 1830 replaced the committees with single officers or boards (still, however, appointed by the council). In 1849 New York made their offices elective, and a similar plan was applied in Cleveland in 1852. After the War between the States, the use of the independent board and commission gained headway rapidly, and throughout the remainder of the nineteenth century this was the general practice. While the use of multimember boards did not originate in the springtime of Jacksonianism, it was a direct and logical outgrowth of its tenets.

Deterioration of Responsible Self-government in the City. By the time of the War between the States, a system of city government based on Jacksonian principles had matured. It is usually referred to as the "weak-mayor" plan. It dominated the last half of the nineteenth century, and even now it is found in more cities and villages in America than is any other structural form.[9] Its characteristics included a mayor who usually had a veto power but who was very weak administratively; a large council that dominated the scene, performing both legislative and administrative functions; a long ballot with many elective administrative officials, each independent of the others; numerous elective or appointive (but almost unremovable) boards and commissions; many ex officio positions; and an extreme deconcentration of both legislative and executive responsibilities.

Legislative Domination. During this period there was a strong tendency for the state legislature to control the profitable or politically important aspects of city government. This it did in a variety of ways: by reserving for itself the power to grant public utility franchises for gas, water, electricity, and street railways; by granting special-act charters to specifically named cities, amendable only at the legislature's discretion; by removing many local powers from a city if it fell to the control of a party not in a majority in the state legislature; by direct state administration of particularly patronage-laden local functions through special commissions (so-called "ripper" legislation); and by many other techniques. After about 1850, special legislation (i.e., legislation affecting exclusively a specifically named city) became so common that in many states its consideration took up more of the legislature's

[9] A detailed examination of structures of city government will be made in chap. 8.

time than did legislation directed at the state as a whole. In many instances it had the effect of making the legislative delegation from each city a veritable supercouncil, far more powerful than the members of the formal council.

Political differences between the state legislative majority and the largest cities of the state led to reduction in the degree of local self-government in many cities. As early as 1861 Chicago was Democratic while the legislature was Republican; this resulted in a struggle for control of the city that has lasted intermittently for a century. Similar differences caused trouble between the city of New York and the state, between Boston and Massachusetts, and between St. Louis and Missouri. A feud within the party resulted in the temporary abolition of self-government for Pittsburgh and other Pennsylvania cities in 1901. In 1879, the Alabama legislature actually abolished Mobile, and Memphis suffered the same fate in Tennessee. In the latter case, the city had become bankrupt and the creditors applied pressure on the legislature to help them save their investments.

Special commissions controlled by the governor or legislature to take control of police, health, and other functions of cities became common after 1850. At various times, the police departments of New York, Chicago, Boston, Detroit, Baltimore, and St. Louis, among others, were removed from local control. It should not be assumed that the legislature was never motivated by any other desire than to secure control of luscious patronage pastures: often municipally controlled departments were so corrupt that citizens rushed to the legislature asking that certain functions be transferred to state control with the hope, at least, that a change might be effected.

Legislatures often were not beyond paying out the city taxpayers' money for the benefit of favored businessmen. Note, for example, the elaborate set of city buildings erected for Philadelphia in 1870 by the state legislature without consulting the citizens of the city—but with the uninvited bill being turned over to them. Individual legislators in those days were far more often guilty of questionable ethics and even of sheer venality than is the case today. Members were frequently in the pay of railroads, land speculators, liquor interests, and the like. Gas, electric, street railway, and other franchises were sometimes virtually auctioned off by legislators to the highest bidder. Public faith in the state legislature as the guiding authority for cities could not be great under such circumstances. The city boss and machine, a phenomenon of the new industrial city, operated under a value system similar to that of the legislators.[10]

[10] For the city boss and machine, see chap. 6.

Reaction to State Control. Protests and reactions to this situation could be expected, and they were not long in coming. However, reforms proved to be much easier to suggest than to make effective. As early as the 1820s specific provisions were written into constitutions granting voters in cities certain privileges, such as the power to choose their own principal officers. Special legislation—the most direct technique of state control—was prohibited by the Ohio constitution of 1851. Similar provisions are found today in most of the state constitutions. A further development in the effort to free the city from control by the state legislature came with the provision for constitutional home rule in the Missouri constitution of 1875. Home rule refers to the right of the voters of a city (or their representatives on a charter commission or city council) to frame, adopt, and amend their own city charters, as distinguished from the practice of having this done for them by the state legislature.[11]

These attempts often met with frustration. The courts commonly permitted legislatures to continue to enact special legislation so long as it was thinly disguised as general legislation. Constitutional home rule, likewise, did not of itself establish autonomous and effective self-government in cities.

While these experiments were failing to provide urban self-government, the unwieldy, uncoordinated, complicated, weak-mayor system was becoming increasingly ineffective as a form of government for America's rapidly growing cities. Something more was needed

THE INHERENT RIGHT OF LOCAL SELF-GOVERNMENT

A Romantic Legalism. Under the theory of "home rule," advanced in protest against legislative control of local affairs, the community has an inherent right to rule itself on local matters without interference by the state. The doctrine enjoyed but a brief life as a *legal* theory; yet overtones of the concept were felt in American thinking long before Judge Thomas M. Cooley of Michigan first expressed his often-cited dictum, and they are still felt today whenever the "rights" of city government as against state control are argued by citizens at civic-association, council, charter-commission, and other meetings of a similar nature.

The lay citizen, arguing for a "right" of the city to control local affairs, is not likely to give a closely reasoned argument for his view, but the crux of it is likely to hold that there are three levels of government in the United States and that each has certain areas of exclusive control. The legal argument is somewhat more sophisticated, but it comes to the same

[11] See chap. 7.

thing. In 1871, Judge Cooley, asserting that local self-government was a matter of "absolute right," gave a historical argument augmented by some concepts from the eighteenth-century natural-rights philosophers. The historical argument holds that local self-government was well established as an Anglo-American tradition long before an American state was created and that this practice was transferred to American municipalities through the common law. Unless the state constitution specifically turned over control of local government to the states, the argument ran, it remained as it had long been established. Writers sought to show that the principle of local self-government predated the establishment of the Kingdom of England, that it had, in fact, been the greatest contribution to government of the Angles and Saxons before William the Conqueror, and that its origins were to be found in the democracy of the ancient German tribes in the days before that part of Europe fell under the influence of Rome.

The argument as presented by Judge Cooley was actually an obiter dictum—that is to say, his remarks were not absolutely necessary, since he had already settled the case before him upon other, more conventional, grounds. His remarks suited the spirit of the times, however, and were used by judges at one time or another in California, Indiana, Iowa, Kentucky, Michigan, Nebraska, and Texas. The doctrine, however, never became established, for the courts generally followed the opposite principle, that the state is supreme and the city is its creature. This is hardly surprising, since the doctrine of the inherent right of cities to home rule was a wistful, fanciful notion based upon very weak legal reasoning and largely manufactured by judges who were sympathetic to local self-government.

Actually, local government in England is not, and probably never has been, independent of the central government. Since the days of William I there certainly has been no question but that any "rights" that cities may have are actually privileges extended by the Crown. Sovereignty over the former colonies passed from the British Crown to the American states, which have since retained such powers as were not relinquished to the national government. And as for any "rights" of cities existing under the common law, all judges, and most certainly the scholarly Thomas M. Cooley, knew that the unwritten common law is automatically superseded by any contrary provisions in statute or constitutional law. More important, there is no natural cleavage to separate local from state powers. Probably all "local" concerns have within them some element of state-wide interest, and state powers must often be administered, when it comes to detailed application, in specific local areas. The definition of "local" concerns is therefore not natural at all, but a fairly arbitrary legalism that has historically been determined in the United States by the state legislatures and the state courts.[12]

Short-lived as was the legal protest, a legacy remains in the widespread belief among Americans that the municipality has, or should have, a "right" to rule itself in local matters without detailed supervision by the state.

PREMISES OF THE MIDDLE-CLASS BUSINESSMAN: THE EFFICIENCY AND ECONOMY MOVEMENT

The Organization of Protest. Well-meaning but poorly organized amateurs began their efforts to reclaim city government from the boss and the political machine as early as the 1870s. They lacked experience and organizational skills and were often politically naïve. The movement, like its Jacksonian predecessor, was pragmatic, unsystematic, and loosely coordinated. It had no single intellectual leader and was not part of a general philosophy, although it did have definite Hamiltonian overtones. Its strength was centered in the middle-class businessman with additional aid coming from a handful of academicians. The businessmen had a particular motivation for action. They paid a large portion of the taxes to city governments that were not noted for cautious expenditure of public funds, and they lived under their own code of civic obligations.

The difficulties which confronted reformers were at first almost overpowering. Political machines, often headed by a well-known boss, resisted by using any technique that would destroy or discourage the neophytes. The machine was usually well organized, with an army of precinct workers and large numbers of voters who were obligated to it, and hence was generally able to defeat any attempts at reform. The minority of businessmen who turned reformers were in a particularly vulnerable position. A strong political machine in control of the city government had many weapons at hand to injure those who dared to oppose it, as, for example, increasing the assessment of their properties, refusing them permits and licenses, or harassing them through over-administration of fire, health, or other city codes.

Many industrialists and businessmen refused to cooperate with reformers because they followed a belief popular among their kind that it was cheaper to buy off the machine than to fight it. The reformers were

---

[12] The principal legal case is *People of Michigan ex rel. LeRoy v. Hurlbut,* 24 Mich. 44 (1871). A supporting argument is given in A. M. Eaton, "The Right of Local Self-government," *Harvard Law Review,* vol. 13, pp. 441 ff., 570 ff., 638 ff. The reasoning in the Cooley doctrine is effectively rebutted in H. L. McBain, "The Doctrine of an Inherent Right of Local Self-government," *Columbia Law Review,* vol. 16 (March and April, 1916), pp. 190 ff., 299 ff.

THE TAMMANY TIGER LOOSE—"What are you going to do about it?"

Figure 3-1. "What are you going to do about it?" In the early 1870s, Thomas Nast was offered $500,000 to stop drawing cartoons such as this one denouncing the Tweed ring of Tammany Hall.

also confronted by a public that was almost completely cynical regarding the possibilities for honesty in municipal government, and they had to fight that greatest of all opponents of change, public apathy.

Attitudes and Antidotes. Nevertheless, reforms took place. Some were the result of political accidents and compromises, such as the adoption of constitutional home rule in the Missouri constitutional convention of 1875. Others were the result of organized pressures upon the state legislatures, as in the case of the New York and Massachusetts acts of 1883 establishing civil service for all cities in those states. A nationwide organization, the National Civil Service Reform League, had been organized in 1877. In that same year, the report of a governor's commission

ELECTION TIME GIMMICKS

Figure 3-2. The Tammany tiger has been a target of cartoonists for over eighty years. During that time, however, the animal has been partly domesticated. SOURCE: Copyright, 1953, New York Post Corporation. Cartoon by John Pierotti from the *New York Post.* Used by permission.

in New York condemned the use of national political parties in municipal elections, giving an opening wedge to the concept of election without party designation, an idea that became a favorite of reformers.

In answer to demands for a more modern type of city government, a version of the *strong-mayor plan* was put into effect in Brooklyn in 1880 and Boston in 1885. This plan is one in which the council is restricted to a sharing of the legislative power with the mayor, while the entire administrative structure is integrated [13] under the control of the mayor, who is also a powerful policy maker. After about 1820 many cities imitated the American national government by adopting a bicameral (two-house) council and mayoralty appointments subject to council approval. This trend was later abandoned. The strong-mayor plan, however, was thought by reformers to be a much more workable, systematic approach to the problems of city government than was the weak-mayor plan, for the latter had not been conceived of for use in the larger cities of an industrial age. Although varying considerably in detail from one city to another, the strong-mayor plan met with the approval of an increasing number of state legislatures during the 1890s and today is the plan generally used in America's largest cities.

The reform movement developed through organizations on the local level. The Municipal Voters' League was formed in Chicago in 1896, and before long such groups, supported by and made up chiefly of local businessmen, began to appear in nearly all large and medium-sized cities, although they were, of course, not all of equal effectiveness. They were characteristically known as "voters' leagues," "citizens' leagues," "taxpayers' associations," "nonpartisan reform committees," "committees of 100," or by similar titles.

An important effort to coordinate these local groups was made through the National Municipal League, which was formed in 1894. This organization became the center, and a veritable symbol, of the movement. In its "model" charters and laws, its booklets and pamphlets, it made available to local groups ammunition that included all of the most recently developed reform favorites. It became an effective and respected leader of the struggle. [14]

Another key step toward effective organization was taken with the

[13] By an *integrated* administrative structure, political scientists mean one in which all administrative authority and responsibility is in the hands of a single individual or body. The administrative structure is arranged so that each employee or officer is in theory responsible to some one superior who in turn must answer to his superior, until ultimately department heads are each responsible to a single chief executive.

[14] The story of the League is told, largely from its own viewpoint, in Frank M. Stewart, *A Half Century of Municipal Reform* (University of California Press, Berkeley, Calif., 1950); see also Richard S. Childs, *Civic Victories* (Harper & Brothers, New York, 1952).

creation of a Bureau of Municipal Research in New York in 1906. Dozens of imitations appeared in other cities in the next decade and after.

The municipal research bureaus were often formed with the thought that attempts to elect reform administrations were doomed to failure and that the best way to secure improvement in the administration of cities would be to work with city officials, furnishing them with research data. The bureaus were privately financed. They concentrated upon problems of finance and administration.

More organizations followed: the Proportional Representation League (to further the plan designed to give every significant interest group or political party representation in proportion to its voting strength at the polls); the National Popular Government League (to secure the public ownership of local utilities [15] and to urge the adoption of the *initiative, referendum,* and *recall* [16]); the National Short Ballot Organization (to end the "bedsheet" ballot); taxpayers' leagues (sometimes chiefly to protect the interest of the largest taxpayers); local government committees of chambers of commerce; many different women's clubs; and the League of Women Voters (which does not confine its activities to reform or to local affairs). By the early years of the twentieth century, reform was still largely in the hands of amateurs, but it was now effectively organized and the amateurs were experienced in politics.

Institutions of Reform. Practical results of "reform" began to be made evident. The commission plan of city organization appeared in Galveston in 1901, shortly received the endorsement of many reformers, and in the next few years it spread rapidly throughout the nation wherever the movement was effective. This plan, which provides for elected "commissioners" (usually five) who serve collectively as the legislative body and individually as heads of administrative departments, was regarded as an improvement over the weak-mayor system, especially in providing for a shorter ballot and for some semblance of an integrated administrative structure, but it contained fatal defects which caused it to pass into eclipse after about 1917.[17] It was succeeded by the council-manager (or city-manager) plan, which got its start about 1908. It is characterized by a governmental structure that places legislative power in a small, preferably lay, council and administrative authority under a professional "manager" who is appointed by and responsible to the council.

The reform movement also generally included the initiative, referendum, and recall, although some conservatives at first feared that they

[15] Public ownership of public utilities was neither socialistic nor radical in concept. It was merely an attempt to get rid of racketeering or gouging private organizations in this area by adopting the standard European practice of public ownership.
[16] These terms are defined on pp. 109, 113.
[17] See chap. 8.

would serve the causes of radicals. The *initiative* (which allows the voters themselves to enact legislation or amend city charters without resort to the legislative body) was first authorized by city charter in San Francisco in 1898. This charter also provided for the *referendum* (which requires popular approval, under certain conditions, of acts of the legislative body before they become effective). The *recall* (removal of an elective public official from office by a vote of the people prior to the expiration of his term) seems to have been authorized first by the Los Angeles charter of 1903.[18] In an attempt to write a "model" reform charter and apparently under the assumption that if a little medicine is good, a lot of medicine is better, reformers in Des Moines combined the commission plan with the initiative, referendum, and recall (1907). For some years the "Des Moines plan" symbolized reform. (As a word of caution to the zealot who may be in the habit of devising an "ideal" solution and then dogmatically defending it as a permanent panacea, it might be noted that in 1949 Des Moines abandoned the "Des Moines plan" and adopted a council-manager form of government.)

During their heyday—the first and second decades of the present century—reformers sponsored other organizational and procedural changes: preferential voting, such as the Bucklin and Ware systems, which did not catch on; reapportionment of urban representation in state legislatures; "model" plans of budgeting, accounting, contract procedures, election procedures, and bond issuing; the direct primary election system of nomination for city offices and a shorter ballot. Underlying nearly all reform efforts were two basic assumptions: (1) that the political party and politicians in general were not to be trusted, and (2) that the principle of "efficient business management" could and should be applied to city government. The muckraker at the turn of the century had shown the low moral tone to which the professional politician of the day had descended, and the reforming businessman wanted no part of it in his city.[19] In contrast, he viewed the structure of the private corporation and the "business methods" of the nineteenth century with pride and respect. He made famous the assertion that "there is no Democratic way to lay a sewer and no Republican way to pave a street" and that running a city is simply a matter of applying the "principles of good business management."

An Appraisal. The reform movement made a real contribution to local self-government by recovering a certain amount of responsibility, by replacing the checks and balances of Jacksonian democracy with a more

18 See chap. 4 for more details.

19 The most famous muckraker was Lincoln Steffens. See his *The Shame of the Cities* (McClure, Phillips & Company, New York, 1904), which originally appeared as a series of magazine articles; and his *Autobiography of Lincoln Steffens* (Harcourt, Brace & World, Inc., New York, 1931).

modern system of centralized leadership, and by reestablishing at least a modicum of public respect and confidence in local government. However, it did some damage, too. It placed a misleading overemphasis upon *forms* and *structures* of government. It led people astray in its constant preaching to the effect that there are few, if any, partisan issues in city government—that it is a mere matter of "efficient business management." Not only was this concept false, it also did a great deal to discourage interest in local politics.

The reform movement failed, for the most part, to make local government in large cities more representative of a cross section of the community.[20] The old-style politician was rather thoroughly repudiated, true enough, but the balance of power in government was not fundamentally altered. The business community continued to dominate city government. Formerly it had had to do this indirectly, through the machine. Now a new type of control grew up. Businessmen began to participate directly in government. Control of the voter was now achieved, not through the traditional devices, but through control of the media of mass communication. Nonpartisan elections, in particular, made it easy for the conservative business interests to run the city government.

The movement—and especially what is left of it today—has in most places become closely associated in the minds of workingmen and labor leaders with the business community and its interests. Workingmen and labor leaders know that the reformers have produced a more efficient type of government, but they feel that it is often more concerned with saving taxpayers' money than with solving the problems of the community. This situation is partly responsible for the manner in which organized labor has turned to the national-government level for legislation.

Many of the "citizens' action" groups and bureaus of municipal research (there are exceptions) have changed a good deal from their original character and purpose. A quarter of a century ago these groups had life, ideas, and a set of goals planted in the future. Today many of them have become tools of large taxpayers who want attacks on municipal taxes and essentially on municipal government itself. In seeking to minimize city-government services and expenditures, they have in effect become organizations *opposing* municipal government.

CURRENT THEORIES OF CITY GOVERNMENT

The City and the New Deal. The worst depression in the history of the United States began in the autumn of 1929 and did not actually end

---

[20] The failure of the movement to include a "solid basis in mass support" was pointed out many years ago by John A. Vieg, "Advice for Municipal Reformers," *Public Opinion Quarterly,* vol. 1 (October, 1937), pp. 87–92.

until the country began preparing for war about a decade later. The election of 1932 produced a huge protest vote that resulted in (1) the election of Franklin D. Roosevelt and (2), as it proved, the New Deal. The New Deal attempted to do at least two things simultaneously: to combat the Depression and to effect social reforms. It developed programs for almost every area where extensive demands for improvement were heard: social security for the aged and dependent; farm-price supports; slum clearance; soil conservation; protection for organized labor; emergency "make-work"; and a host of others.

The farmer, worker, banker, small businessman—almost everyone, in fact—began turning to the national government for whatever aid they felt was needed. The states and cities were bypassed, either because their financial resources or their legal authority was hopelessly inadequate, because they were unwilling to tackle the problems, or because the scope of the problems was so broad that they could be handled adequately only by the national government.

However, some effort was made by the New Deal to utilize local agencies. PWA projects (such as new city halls, water standpipes, sewerage systems, bridges, even public housing units) were determined upon the approval of recommended plans submitted by local governments. Perhaps the most outstanding case of New Deal reliance upon municipalities came as a result of the United States Housing Act of 1937.[21]

Most people probably think of Franklin D. Roosevelt as the very symbol of centralized authority in Washington, yet one of his long-time advisers tells us that although he favored business regulation and credit control through the national government:[22]

Aside from this, he would be against the development of strong central government, would indeed be in favour of minimum Federal powers . . . and [would want] most governmental functions to be decentralized—carried on by the states and municipalities.

This was in fact the kind of programme President Roosevelt would have liked to carry out. It was the furniture of his mind down into 1932; and his mind was never entirely purged of these preferences. . . .

To some [projects], such as the building up of a Federal (central) relief organization, he gave only the most grudging consent and got rid of it at the earliest possible instant. . . .

And when a permanent social security system came to be worked out, he settled an internal argument in his official family by coming down on the side of state rather than Federal administration. This was a momentous and revealing choice; it showed what side he would like to be on if he could.

[21] See chap. 19 for a closer look at housing.

[22] R. G. Tugwell, "The Experimental Roosevelt," *Political Quarterly*, vol. 21 (1950), pp. 239–270. The quotation is from p. 241. By permission.

Perhaps this is overstating the case somewhat, or possibly circumstances soon forced these preferences to the back of Roosevelt's mind. In any case, the same writer ten pages later speaks of "the President's incorrigible tendency to think in terms of national rather than local administrative units. . . ."

Contemporary Theory. Municipal self-government faces a problem of finding a satisfactory mid-twentieth-century niche for itself. The preceding brief review of American theory indicates that the concepts of the Jacksonian frontiersman and the resulting institutions (such as the weak-mayor system and the city boss) are not appropriate for an industrialized, urbanized, specialized, technological society. The theory of an "inherent right" of local self-government is quite dead. The efficiency and economy movement did much to modernize local government. But its modernity was that of fifty years ago, before the advent of either powerful organized labor or the social-service state. The movement never had a strong base in mass support, and its institutions have not often included in their membership a cross section of the general public.

The trend has not been toward abandoning municipal government as meaningless, but rather toward blending its activities into those of the state and national governments. In the areas of health, highways, education, welfare, recreation, and others, the cities and villages have increasingly worked in cooperation with the higher levels of government. They have come closer together not only through the use of grants-in-aid, but also because modern means of transportation and communication have ended community isolation, and because much contemporary policy making tends to be dominated by the values and goals of professional administrators—professionals who increasingly man the bureaucracies at all three levels of government and who share the concepts of what constitutes "good" school administration, sanitation programs, highway plans, and the like. The municipality has not ceased to be a decision-making center, but it no longer makes its decisions alone, and the decisions that emerge are increasingly based on the policy goals of professional administrators rather than of amateur grass-roots leaders.

How do today's urbanites view city government? What do they consider to be the proper functions of their municipality? There are probably many images of local government. Few of them have been identified, but one study has tentatively isolated the following images: [23]

1. *The City as an Instrument of Community Growth.* Those who see the municipality in this guise believe that it has a duty to help the com-

[23] This material borrows from a forthcoming monograph by Oliver P. Williams and Charles R. Adrian tentatively titled, *Fighting City Hall: A Comparative Study of Politics in Four Middle-sized Cities.*

munity to expand in both population and wealth. This is the "booster-ism" that is traditional in America, stemming from the frontier notion that growth is progress, bigness is goodness, and that a community must expand or die. The merchant, banker, newspaper editor, chamber of commerce manager, and city bureaucrat all stand to gain from growth, and they are all likely to see the city government's highest duty as that of furthering it.

2. *The City as the Provider of Life's Amenities.* In a wealthy nation with a high standard of living, Americans are conscious of themselves as conspicuous consumers. Their status in an impersonal society is sym-bolized in large part by the consumption items they can afford. To an increasing extent—above all in suburbia—government is viewed as an agency for providing not merely the necessities of life, but for adding to the comforts of urban living. Supporters of this image of municipal government reject growth as the highest goal, or sometimes as any goal at all. They often prefer the smallness of the suburb to the growing metropolis, the expenditure of funds in residential neighborhoods to out-lays benefiting Main Street.

3. *The City Government as a Caretaker.* This is the view of the small-government, low-tax advocate—the conservative. He sees government at all levels as best when it survives at a minimal level, providing only those functions that are ancient or—from his viewpoint—essential. Municipali-ties may patrol the streets against thieves and purify the water supply, but they should not seek expansion of functions into new areas. The advocate of caretaker government believes that the private allocation of personal resources is invariably to be preferred to governmental alloca-tion. The caretaker philosophy appeals particularly, in addition to the person who prefers minimal government at all levels, to retired persons on fixed incomes, to the marginal homeowner who can barely afford to keep himself in that prestigeful category, and to the person whose neigh-borhood already has a full quota of local services and is better supplied than are the poorer neighborhoods or the newer areas of the com-munity.

4. *The City as Arbiter of Conflicting Interests.* Those who hold to this view do not see local government as having a single dominant mission, but rather they consider it an umpire with responsibility to allocate the scarce resources of the community in such a way that all interested groups get a share. The self-conscious minority-group leaders, seeing no prospect for controlling the local government by themselves or in an effective coalition, are likely to take this point of view, as did the tra-ditional political boss. The psychic or numerical majority can realistically advocate a concept of the "general good" or the "public interest," but a

permanent minority can seek only access, and a set of rules that will help to guarantee it for them.[24]

All of these images, and probably others, probably exist in any community simultaneously. Rarely would a community larger than a small town demonstrate such total agreement that a single type would stand in unrivaled control over the minds of policy makers. In most cases, a variety of images serve as frames of reference for officeholders and for citizens as they vote on referendum matters. These ideas about the proper role of municipal government serve to channel the kinds of decisions that are made and the way in which they are made in the contemporary American city.

[24] For an illustration of the community-growth theory, the reader might read almost any talk by a chamber of commerce manager. For the caretaker idea, see A. J. Vidich and Joseph Bensman, *Small Town in Mass Society* (Princeton University Press, Princeton, N.J., 1958). The interest in amenities in Park Forest, Ill., is described in William H. Whyte, Jr., *The Organization Man* (Doubleday Anchor Books, New York, 1956). The arbiter function in "Paper City" is outlined in K. W. Underwood, *Protestant and Catholic* (The Beacon Press, Boston, 1957).

Chapter 4

MUNICIPAL ELECTIONS

Probably the simplest, most common, and ultimately most important *direct* contact the typical citizen has with his city or village takes place when he steps into the booth and exercises his privilege of voting. Unlike voting in national-government elections, the local suffrage imposes a duty to vote for many offices (in most cities), in addition to numerous proposed charter amendments, bond issues, and referred and initiated municipal ordinances. While the simple *act* of voting is easy enough, its conscientious exercise requires serious efforts.

THE ELECTORATE

Who Is Eligible? Time was when more persons were eligible to vote in state than in municipal contests. As a matter of fact, some American cities in the colonial period were "close corporations" where no one at all, not even the wealthiest men, enjoyed the suffrage. Until after World War II (1945), Great Britain had one set of suffrage laws for parliamentary elections and another, less universal, set for municipal voting. In the case of the latter, occupancy as owner or tenant had traditionally been a prerequisite for voting in local contests. In Canada, voting restrictions for municipal elections are still generally greater than for other elections.

Today, with but a few exceptions, the right to vote in American municipal elections is determined by eligibility to participate in state elections. The usual prerequisites include American citizenship, a minimum age of twenty-one (less in four states), a minimum period of residence in the state, county, and polling district, and registration. Other requirements are sometimes added.[1]

[1] The basic historical reference is Kirk H. Porter, *A History of Suffrage in the United States* (University of Chicago Press, Chicago, 1918). Dudley O. McGovney, *The American Suffrage Medley* (University of Chicago Press, Chicago, 1949), discusses voting restrictions in the various states. He opposes "unnecessary disenfranchisements" and urges a uniform national suffrage law as a remedy. One may learn more about voter restrictions and qualifications from the current issue of the annual *Book*

Special Local Requirements. During the Great Depression, Arizona, Michigan, Montana, Nevada, Texas, and Utah provided that only property-tax payers could vote on questions of direct appropriation of public money or the issuance of bonds.[2] One study has indicated that the Michigan law prevented more than one-half of the Detroit electorate from voting on such issues during the Depression.[3] A very few states make, or are constitutionally permitted to make, an actual distinction between eligibility for municipal, as against general, elections. But all of these provisions are unusual, are seldom resorted to, and are far off the course being steered by contemporary democratic theory. The almost universal rule is that persons who are eligible to vote in national and state elections may also vote in municipal elections.

VOTING AND NONVOTING

Political scientists have been able to collect enough data concerning voter participation both in the United States and abroad to develop some fairly clear concepts as to the kinds of people who vote, those who do not, and why they do not. Some reasonably confident generalizations can be made.

Apathy on Election Day. In comparison with the people of such advanced democracies as Great Britain and the Scandinavian countries, Americans take their voting responsibilities lightly. Studies indicate that only about one-third of the eligible voters are in the habit of going to the polls regularly. Even in presidential elections, which regularly attract the greatest number of people, the record is not impressive. The turnout for state elections is ordinarily much smaller than when the nation chooses a chief executive, and the pattern for local elections can usually be expected to be the smallest of all. It is not uncommon for the vote in municipal elections to drop to less than one-fourth of the qualified voters. Even that lionized example of democracy, the New England town meeting, does not appear to inspire citizens to participation. In one study, a town meeting was analyzed in which 700 citizens were qualified to take part. Only 110 did so, a participation figure of 15.7 per cent.[4]

---

of the States, published by the Council of State Governments, Chicago, or by consulting the local official in charge of elections, usually the city or county clerk.

[2] By property-tax payers is meant property owners, of course. Contrary to popular misunderstanding, a renter pays just as much in property taxes as an owner, although it is hidden in the rent. While there may well be a *psychological* difference between owner and renter when it comes to taxation, there is no *economic* difference.

[3] Donald S. Hecock and Harry A. Trevelyan, *Detroit Voters and Recent Elections* (Detroit Bureau of Municipal Research, Detroit, 1938).

[4] From an article by Andrew Nuquist reported in Roscoe C. Martin, *Grass Roots* (University of Alabama Press, University, Ala., 1957), pp. 60–61.

The extent of voting varies in different sections of the country, and even between different governmental units in the same section. Each community has its own tradition of participation or nonparticipation. Sometimes a matter of particular interest will bring out a larger vote for a local election than was the case in the preceding presidential vote. The degree to which the electorate is organized or to which organized groups are active in campaigns influences the size of the turnout. In almost all jurisdictions and at all levels of government, the primary election is of considerably less interest than the general election. (Exceptions are to be found in one-party areas, such as the deep South and parts of New England.) [5]

An ambitious voter-participation study was conducted by the Bureau of Governmental Research at the University of California, Los Angeles, under the direction of Lawrence W. O'Rourke.[6] It found that in the average city of Los Angeles County between 1935 and 1952, voter turnout at the average state and national election amounted to 77.2 per cent of the registered voters. For the average municipal election, however, the figure was only 41.1 per cent of those registered.

The study indicated that participation did *not* vary inversely with the size of the municipality. The city of Los Angeles ranked twenty-sixth out of the forty-five cities in local elections, but ranked lower in state and national contests. Tiny Avalon had a very good record, but San Marino, only slightly larger, had the poorest of all records in local elections. Some cities had very good records in state and national elections, but very poor ones in local elections, and vice versa.

The study found that there was no correlation between distance from the core city and amount of voter participation. It was found, however, that predominantly Republican cities had better voting records than did those that were predominantly Democratic.[7] But wealthy communities

[5] On voter participation, see Angus Campbell and others, *The American Voter* (John Wiley & Sons, Inc., New York, 1960); Angus Campbell and others, *The Voter Decides* (Row, Peterson & Company, Evanston, Ill., 1954); Arthur Kornhauser and others, *When Labor Votes* (University Book, Inc., New York, 1956); J. K. Pollock, *Voting Behavior: A Case Study* (University of Michigan Press, Ann Arbor, Mich., 1939); E. B. Olds and D. W. Salmon, *St. Louis Voting Behavior* (mimeographed, 1948); L. W. O'Rourke, *Voting Behavior in the Forty-five Cities of Los Angeles County* (Bureau of Governmental Research, University of California, Los Angeles, 1953); *The Municipal Year Book, 1937* (International City Managers' Association, Chicago, 1937); H. Sharp, "Migration and Voting Behavior in a Metropolitan Community," *Public Opinion Quarterly*, vol. 19 (Summer, 1955); B. R. Berelson and others, *Voting* (University of Chicago Press, Chicago, 1954); and more generally, R. M. Scammon, *America Votes* (The Macmillan Company, New York, 1956); and Eugene Burdick and A. J. Brodbeck, *American Voting Behavior* (The Free Press, Glencoe, Ill., 1958).

[6] O'Rourke, *op. cit.*

[7] The municipal elections themselves are nonpartisan in California.

did not necessarily have good records in *local* elections. Beverly Hills, for example, had next to the poorest record.

Among the important conclusions of the study were these: [8]

1. . . . People tend to vote *against* candidates and propositions rather than for them. . . . People attend city council meetings more often to protest than to affirm some proposed action.

2. . . . Voter turnout is dependent upon the degree of *opposition* that can be generated in the minds of voters.

3. . . . There is a sizable number of citizens who consistently participate in state and national elections, but *never vote* in municipal elections.

4. . . . Percentages of the registered electorate remain fairly *constant* in each city for almost all municipal elections. This may be contrasted with the somewhat more erratic percentages found in voting for state and national offices. . . . *There is a small core of citizens in each city who sustain municipal government.*

Apathy and the Duty to Participate. Although the doctrine of grass roots democracy calls for vigorously active participation in the political process and in the assumption of public office as a duty to the community, the fact is that in America there is frequently a great deal of difficulty in getting public positions filled. Not only may there be no competition for the jobs, but there is sometimes no one who will even allow himself to be drafted.

The small town, the suburb, and the school district often present scenes, not of strident conflict, but of citizens putting pressure on other citizens to accept jobs that need to be done. These are positions that carry not a little prestige but involve the budgeting of a considerable amount of what would otherwise be leisure time for the individual.[9]

In the case of bond-issue referendums, genuine disagreement may be generated, and hence more interest, but even when money is involved, the community may be essentially agreed as to how it should be used. The principal reason for apathy in municipal elections, in fact, is likely to be a pervasive consensus, that is, there may be widespread agreement in the community as to the kinds of persons who are wanted in public office, as to expenditure levels, and as to public policies. Under such circumstances, there is little incentive for any but the most conscientious voter to go to the polls.

There are many other reasons, of course, for the absence of a contest in a local election, and hence for low-interest levels to exist. Some of them are included in the following list:

1. The incumbent is sometimes so popular that other potential candidates have little or no chance to unseat him. He is hence unopposed.

[8] O'Rourke, *op. cit.*, chap. 2. Italics added.
[9] See Martin, *op. cit.*, pp. 60–62.

2. In strongly one-party cities with partisan elections, there may be a contest in the primary election of the major party, but the second party can expect to have difficulty in getting candidates to run.

3. The formal political process may not be the effective process of decision making. That is, the important decisions affecting the community may be made outside of government, and public offices are therefore of little importance in the view of the ordinary citizen. There is a long tradition in America of keeping as many issues as possible "out of politics," because the political process is not trusted. Furthermore, community leaders may prefer to negotiate privately among the various interests centering around a controversy, keeping control out of public officials' hands—and outside the reach of the voter. Thus businessmen may agree among themselves on the amount of money that is to be devoted to port development and present a packaged plan to the council for its ratification. Land-use policies may be controlled in a similar way.

4. The ruling political group may be so strong (as in Chicago much of the time) that no one thinks it worthwhile to oppose it.

Lack of competition for office reduces the importance of both the primary election or other nominating device and the final election. Absence of genuine conflict is certain to contribute to apathy.

Futility and Nonvoting. Even so, we are justified in asking why voter turnout is so low. Why should 28 per cent of the interviewees in a representative sample in the 1952 presidential campaign—one in which interest was generally regarded as having been high by American standards—be willing to state openly that they were "not much interested" in the contest? [10] Why should 32 per cent of those interviewed say that it would make no difference whether the Democrats or Republicans won the election and another 40 per cent think it would make only a small difference? [11]

Part of the answer seems to be furnished by a study made in Detroit.[12] A representative sample of persons was asked these questions: Do you feel that there is anything you can do to improve the way the city is run? What do you feel you can do? *More than one-half the people declared that they can do nothing.* One-third could suggest only voting. Only one person in twelve believed that he could exert influence by means of personal criticism or by joining in group action.

In another study, one-third of the members of the United Automobile Workers agreed that "people like me don't have any say about what

[10] Campbell and others, *The Voter Decides*, p. 34.
[11] *Ibid.*, p. 38.
[12] Arthur Kornhauser, *Attitudes of Detroit People toward Detroit* (Wayne University Press, Detroit, Mich., 1952), p. 28.

government does." [13] These sentiments were especially strong among persons who had feelings of estrangement from society, or feelings of personal futility, or who were generally pessimistic. Persons who felt they could not influence governmental policy also, not surprisingly, tended to be nonvoters. On an authoritarian-democratic scale, they tended more toward the authoritarian position in personal values. A similar attitude of futility was to be found before the 1945 election in the city of New York when one-third of those eligible to vote told pollster Elmo Roper that "no matter which of the candidates is elected, the city will be run about the same." [14] Similar findings have been reported in Philadelphia and Boston.[15] In the latter city, the favorite in the 1959 mayoralty election apparently was defeated because he was perceived by many voters as the leader of a group of powerful politicians, businessmen, and others who wanted to run the city in their own interest. This reaction "was particularly strong because many voters in Boston felt politically powerless." [16] His opponent won, not for the positive qualities in his personality, record of experience, or campaign promises, but because people wanted to vote *against* the favorite. Furthermore, of those who helped elect John F. Collins as mayor, 57 per cent thought he would be "no better than his opponent." They could only *hope* that he would come closer to the wanted image. Furthermore, they did not expect Collins' policies to differ fundamentally from those of the man he defeated.

They may have been quite right. Elections do not usually decide issues in America; the interaction of interest groups do that, and the election is only one part—perhaps a relatively minor part—of the political process.

Just how serious is our high percentage of nonvoting anyway? The chances are that its dangers have been greatly exaggerated. Although feelings of voter "alienation"—of frustration and impotence—are reported in studies of large-city politics, these feelings seem much less common in middle-sized cities. Furthermore, even in large cities, the cynicism reported may be more of a culturally expected response—almost everybody by tradition damns the politics of large cities—than of an actual abandonment of faith in democracy. The person who says "both candi-

---

[13] Kornhauser and others, *When Labor Votes*, pp. 198–200.

[14] Elmo Roper, "New York Elects O'Dwyer," *Public Opinion Quarterly*, vol. 10 (Spring, 1946), pp. 53–56. For a later study reporting similar findings, see the impressionistic reporting in F. J. Cook and Gene Gleason, "The Shame of New York," *The Nation*, Oct. 31, 1959, entire issue.

[15] James Reichley, *The Art of Government: Reform and Organization Politics in Philadelphia* (The Fund for the Republic, New York, 1958); Murray B. Levin, *The Alienated Voter: Politics in Boston* (Holt, Rinehart and Winston, Inc., New York, 1960).

[16] Levin, *op. cit.*, p. 28.

dates were no good," or that "voting was a waste of time" may also give strong support for political action through interest groups, such as his union, trade association, neighborhood improvement association, or church. Elections may leave him unmoved, but he may see the interaction of groups in lobbying rather than elections as the key to policy making. An elaborate study of New York City politics found that "anyone can fight city hall," that most groups do, and that many are very successful.[17]

Most people who stay away from the polls do so deliberately and by their own choice. They are not interested, and they feel that voting in the particular instance will avail them nothing. Except where cynicism is pervasive, the important question is not whether people *do* vote but rather whether they *may* vote if they so choose. Studies made of why people do not vote show that, outside of illness or a broken fan belt on the way to the voting booth, most people stay home because of lack of interest.[18] To most people, choice of candidates is of marginal interest. When something they consider to be truly important comes up, they will appear at the polls. Americans are more interested in voting against candidates than for them.[19] They become excited about elections when they are determined to register a protest. The ballot box is the safety valve of democracy.

Political Participation. Not only do a large number of Americans not vote in elections, and particularly state and local elections, but another huge bloc of citizens does nothing politically except to vote. In the 1952 presidential contest, 27 per cent of the eligible voters said that they talked politics and tried to persuade others to vote for their candidates and 11 per cent engaged in some kind of organized party activity. In this category, 3 per cent said they did some party work such as stuffing envelopes; 7 per cent said they attended political meetings, rallies, picnics, and the like; only 4 per cent contributed money or bought fund-raising tickets. Some people, of course, were active in all three types of positive activity, and some did not vote either because of ineligibility or for some other reason.[20] In a postelection survey in the same year, 9

[17] Wallace S. Sayre and Herbert Kaufman, *Governing New York City* (Russell Sage Foundation, New York, 1960). Alienation studies to date do not show whether or not the alienated regard all possible roads to political influence as equally blockaded.

[18] For studies, see C. E. Merriam and H. F. Gosnell, *Non-voting* (University of Chicago Press, Chicago, 1924); Morris Rosenberg, "Some Determinants of Voter Apathy," *Public Opinion Quarterly*, vol. 181 (Winter, 1954–1955), pp. 349–366; P. F. Lazersfeld and others, *The People's Choice* (Columbia University Press, New York, 1948); J. K. Pollock, *Voting Behavior* (University of Michigan Press, Ann Arbor, Mich., 1939); and the Campbell and Kornhauser studies previously cited. These citations are also the basis for the following sections on "Political Participation" and "Who Goes to the Polls?"

[19] The Roper and O'Rourke studies, cited above, lend support to this statement.

[20] Campbell and others, *The Voter Decides*, p. 30.

per cent of the United Automobile Workers' membership claimed (in a sample study) to have been active in the campaign in such things as handing out leaflets, displaying posters, and the like. Another 17 per cent said they had talked politics during the campaign, and 73 per cent stated that they had done nothing active.[21]

Who Goes to the Polls? Certain generalizations can be hazarded concerning the qualitative make-up of our voting population. We know that in terms of percentages, more men vote than do women, more whites vote than do Negroes (there is some evidence to indicate that Negroes in some Northern urban areas vote in higher percentages than do whites in the same economic category),[22] more people who are property-tax payers vote than do those who are not, and more conservatives vote than do liberals. Except for persons who must stay at home because of the infirmities of old age, people vote in larger proportions as they grow older. Almost twice as many vote at the age of fifty-one as vote at twenty-one. This seems to support the general theory that people do not vote because they theoretically ought to or because they feel it is a duty or a great privilege, but rather they vote when they feel that they have a direct stake in the outcome.

It should further be noted that there is a direct relationship between size of income and participation in elections and between amount of education and participation. In the postwar years, at least, urbanites have voted in greater proportion than have farmers. The white-collar middle class votes in greater proportion than do nonunion members of the working class.

It is not known whether these state and national voting-population characteristics generally fit municipal voting, too. One study has addressed itself to the question.[23] In a Midwestern state, it found that the above characteristic patterns generally applied. There was one significant modification: the evidence indicated that, in municipal elections, voter turnout tended to be greatest among the groups that were normally most influential in controlling municipal politics. In three cities where Republican-conservative groups dominated, voters of these interests had the highest voter-turnout habits. In one other city, where Democratic-labor groups controlled, the wards dominated by Democratic labor-union members had the superior voting record. Apparently, the prospects for victory encouraged participation—and helped to ensure it.

All of these patterns affect the balance of forces in the political arena.

[21] Kornhauser and others, *When Labor Votes*, chap. 1.

[22] *Ibid.*, pp. 49–50.

[23] Oliver P. Williams and Charles R. Adrian, "The Insulation of Local Politics under the Nonpartisan Ballot," *American Political Science Review*, vol. 53 (December, 1959), pp. 1052–1063.

Apathy or a sense of futility within any given category can have the effect of further weakening the particular interest involved. Each group in society, therefore, has a stake in getting its supporters to the polls, for the vote may be a genuine force in affecting the content of public policy.

An alert public is probably a prerequisite to progress in the art of democratic government. But cheerful homilies about the obligations of the citizen will never serve to inspire the individual who believes that the outcome of the election will have no effect upon his condition of existence. Far more effective than sermons would be serious campaigns to remove the factors that have tended to create a sense of futility in the nonvoter, in other words, to make government more responsible and more representative of a cross section of the public.

BALLOTS, NOMINATIONS, AND ELECTIONS

American cities use both partisan and nonpartisan ballots in their municipal elections. In a few cases, a system called proportional representation is used. The ballot itself may take several forms.[24]

General Parties on the Local Scene. From necessity, the basic strength and organization of a political party is in the local community. Until nonpartisan elections came into use around 1910, municipal election campaigns were invariably conducted by the local party organizations. In that earlier day, many large cities were dominated by well-organized political machines, particularly of the majority party of the community. The minority party was usually less well organized and often had very little chance for success at the polls. In most cities the ward was, and is today, the basic unit of party organization. It was often subdivided into precincts.

Today few political machines remain, and partisan elections are used in only about 40 per cent of American cities. Despite the trend away from partisan municipal elections, many persons believe that such elections are desirable, at least for large cities, because the strength of our vitally necessary state and national parties depends upon effective local organization and because public policy today is executed simultaneously on all levels of government. The functions performed by cities are interdependent parts of the whole process of government. Politics and politicians on the local level do not differ fundamentally from their counterparts on the higher levels. Charles A. Beard once asserted that many

---

[24] Details concerning political parties and elections that cannot be further treated here may be found in a course in political parties or in any one of several good textbooks. See, for example, Hugh A. Bone, *American Politics and the Party System* (2d ed.; McGraw-Hill Book Company, Inc., New York, 1955); V. O. Key, Jr., *Politics, Parties and Pressure Groups* (4th ed.; Thomas Y. Crowell Company, New York, 1958).

local problems can be solved only by cooperation with either the state or the national government or both. Today this is surely true of such functions as public health, welfare, safety, housing, and unemployment. Since political parties serve as a liaison between politicians and since a party approach toward a public problem may include plans that require action at all levels of government, partisanship on the local scene may be definitely desirable.[25]

Opponents of partisanship, on the other hand, argue that running a city is not a matter of skillful politics, but rather one of efficient business management. The editors of the *National Civic Review,* for example, argue in the following vein: [26]

There is, after all, no valid reason for national and state parties to be involved and every reason why they should not.

It has been amply demonstrated that, to be effective and self-reliant cities must be emancipated from the tyranny of the national and state political parties. Good citizens who agree on vital local issues should not be divided by blind loyalties that serve only to confuse these issues.

The way to decency and honesty in national as well as local politics is to eliminate parties from the local scene and thus make all voters "independent."

The arguments on both sides are doubtless exaggerated. Many municipal officers elected on a nonpartisan ballot do cooperate successfully with partisan state and national officers. Our general parties have not proved to be very effective in a liaison role, neither do they stand on definite principles or policies.

Local organizations of the national and state parties, on the other hand, are often quite independent of the higher party structure, especially on local questions. The "blind loyalties" of party exist without doubt, especially in cities where the remnants of political machines are to be found, but this phenomenon may be exaggerated, too. Devoted members of a political party in national and state elections may well vote quite independently in municipal elections. This is especially true if city and general elections are held at different times.

Certainly party leaders often try to inject state or national issues into local campaigns. Sometimes they are successful, sometimes not. Surely, however, it is a fallacy in logic to say that local campaigns in which candidates run as Republicans or Democrats cannot be conducted on local issues.

Whatever the merits of the conflicting arguments presented, there remains one very serious obstacle to the effective use of national parties for

[25] See Charles A. Beard, "Politics and City Government," *National Municipal Review,* vol. 6 (March, 1917), pp. 201–205.

[26] Editorial, "Revolt of the 'Independents,'" *National Municipal Review,* vol. 40 (December, 1951), pp. 564–565. Now the *National Civic Review.*

city elections: most of our cities, instead of having two well-balanced parties where one stands ready at all times to take control away from the other, actually have only one strong party. This is highly undesirable, for our political system is conceived of as an in-party–out-party relationship. Where one party dominates almost to the total exclusion of the other, there is no effective criticism, there is no control of the party in power, and there is no real responsibility to the electorate. The city with a working two-party system is rare. The pattern in New York, where the Democratic party is rarely defeated except by its own dissidents, or in Philadelphia, where the Republicans once controlled the city government for over eighty consecutive years, is a common one. It is this situation, and not some of the more often cited objections, that forms the greatest weakness of partisanship in municipal affairs.

An Illustration. The type of interrelating of national and local politics which has often been criticized can be illustrated in the April, 1953, mayoralty election in St. Louis. The Democratic candidate was Raymond R. Tucker, Washington University Professor of Engineering. His Republican opponent was a little-known real estate dealer. On local issues, the Democrats sought to defend the record of their incumbent administration, while the Republicans argued that it had been a "defeatist" administration, lacking in any willingness to solve the city's acute financial problem. The national party organizations hailed the city election as a test of strength and presumably of the popularity of the newly inducted Eisenhower administration. The chairman of the Democratic National Committee came to town to speak, while Harold E. Stassen, then Mutual Security Administrator, spoke for the Republicans.

Tucker was elected by the greatest plurality in the history of the city. The Democrats also elected the controller and eleven of the thirteen ward aldermen, a gain of three seats. No one, however, appeared to be able to give a very confident estimate of the relative importance of the personalities of the candidates and of local and national factors in the outcome of the election.

Nonpartisan Elections: The Hope of the Reform Movement. Early in the twentieth century, many members of the reform movement began to advocate the use of nonpartisan elections. They argued that city government was a matter of efficient business administration and that state and national politics had nothing in common with local politics.

The nonpartisan ballot is used in over 60 per cent of the American cities of over 5,000 population. It is especially popular in council-manager cities, over 85 per cent of which use it. A nonpartisan ballot does not, of course, in itself eliminate party activity from local politics, though it certainly appears to encourage such a development. To the extent that partisanship is removed, the goals of the reformers of two or three generations ago are achieved.

Many patterns appear to result from a nonpartisan ballot. The principal ones are the following: [27]

1. A system of elections in which the only candidates who normally have any chance to win are those supported by a major political party organization. In these cities, a short ballot is used, candidates are easily identifiable by party, and the result is not much different from partisan elections. Chicago is an example of this type of "nonpartisan" city; Jersey City was another during the time of the powerful machine of Frank Hague.

2. A system of elections in which slates of candidates are supported by various groups, including political party organizations. Here the voters perceive nonpartisan elections as being a distinctive type, but the political party groups are able to compete against slates of candidates presented by nonparty groups. The politics of Albuquerque, Cincinnati, and Wichita, along with other cities, appear to fit this pattern.[28]

3. A system of elections in which slates of candidates are supported by various interest groups, but political party organizations have little or no part in campaigns. In these cities, candidates may have no party affiliation, or it may be unknown, or the voters may consider it to be irrelevant. This pattern appears to be far more common than the two listed above. Kansas City (since the fall of the Pendergast machine), Dallas, Fort Worth, and many California and Michigan cities appear to fit this category.[29]

4. A system of elections in which neither political parties nor slates of candidates are important. This type appears to be very common, possibly even more so than the third type. It is especially important in small cities, for in these communities what Eugene Lee has called the "politics of acquaintance" is often the decisive factor.[30] Under this system, according to Lee, the typical pattern is "the development of support, organization and funds by the individual candidate himself on an ad hoc basis.

[27] Charles R. Adrian, "A Typology for Nonpartisan Elections," *Western Political Quarterly*, vol. 12 (June, 1959), pp. 449–458, and citations.

[28] See Dorothy I. Cline, *Albuquerque and the City Manager Plan* (University of New Mexico Press, Albuquerque, N.M., 1951); Ralph A. Straetz, *PR Politics in Cincinnati* (New York University Press, New York, 1958); and, for Wichita, Marvin A. Harder, *Nonpartisan Election: A Political Illusion?* (Holt, Rinehart and Winston, Inc., New York, 1958).

[29] See Eugene C. Lee, *The Politics of Nonpartisanship: A Study of California City Elections* (University of California Press, Berkeley, Calif., 1960); Oliver P. Williams and Charles R. Adrian, "The Insulation of Local Politics under the Nonpartisan Ballot," *American Political Science Review*, vol. 53 (December, 1959), pp. 1052–1063.

[30] See Lee, *op. cit.*; and Richard S. Childs, *Civic Victories* (Harper & Brothers, New York, 1952), appendix C.

Rather than being recruited by a group and assuming its apparatus, the average candidate must build his own campaign from the ground up."

The Effects of Nonpartisanship. In small cities and villages, where government is largely on an informal personal basis, nonpartisanship has worked satisfactorily. In the largest cities, however, nonpartisanship has not aided in producing a satisfactory degree of representative and responsive government. Without a guiding label on the ballot, the large-city voter has difficulty in identifying candidates, especially for council. The most important thing for the candidate is therefore not to have a platform, but rather to have a name that rings a bell in the voter's mind. Publicity becomes all important and the election is normally won by those who can control the media of mass communication, the newspapers in particular. This has been largely the pattern, for example, in Dallas, Fort Worth, Los Angeles, San Francisco, San Diego, and Detroit.

In large cities, nonpartisanship makes it difficult for voters to cast a protest vote. The discontented will normally vote against the "in party" and for the "out party." They cannot do this under nonpartisanship. The incumbent is thus given an advantage in a campaign, for his name is often the best known to the voter. Nonpartisanship in large cities also has a definite tendency to benefit the cause of conservatism.[31]

Local Parties: The Exception.[32] Numerous examples of local parties exist in municipal politics, although they have in no way become an integral part of the American political system. Americans in overwhelming numbers have taken the attitude that efforts toward third parties are a waste of time, and this viewpoint probably spills over into local politics. Local parties for the most part fall into three classes: (1) the Socialist party; (2) small-town parties; and (3) reform parties.

Sewer Socialism. The Socialist party is, technically at least, not a local party at all, since it was conceived of as a national organization. Its success has been restricted almost entirely to the local level, however, and in several cities (especially in Milwaukee and in Bridgeport, Connecticut) the party has acted and has been pictured by the public as being largely a local party.

The rise of the Socialists came simultaneously with the rise of the middle-class reform movement. Their program of action, with perhaps

[31] See Charles R. Adrian, "Some General Characteristics of Nonpartisan Elections," *American Political Science Review*, vol. 46 (September, 1952), pp. 766–776. For examples of professional public relations work through the mass media of communication in communities with little political structure, see Irwin Ross, "The Supersalesmen of California Politics," *Harper's*, July, 1959, pp. 55–61, and more generally, Wilbur Schramm (ed.), *Mass Communications* (2d ed.; University of Illinois Press, Urbana, Ill., 1960).

[32] See J. Leiper Freeman, "Local Party Systems: Theoretical Considerations and a Case Analysis," *American Journal of Sociology*, vol. 64 (November, 1958), pp. 282–289.

a few exceptions, does not sound very radical or even surprising today. It stood for most of the principles of the reform movement plus much of what we would now call New Deal policies. The Socialists differed from the Republicans and Democrats in that they held to a series of platform planks that dealt with genuinely local matters. While the great parties straddled the fence on local issues or ignored them entirely, the Socialists of the second decade of this century came out strongly for such things as proportional representation, the initiative, referendum, and recall, relief of unemployment through public works, and the municipal ownership of all public utilities. In part their successes, such as they were, could be attributed to the fact that cities were, of course, centers of the working classes, to which socialism made its primary appeal.[33] The great majority of people who voted for Socialist candidates were, however, not Socialists or sympathetic to socialism. Voters no doubt often felt that Socialists could provide more competent, honest reforms in local government than could or would their opponents.

During the years before the conservative reaction of the twenties, several cities elected Socialist mayors or councilmen, including Reading, Schenectady, Minneapolis, Seattle, Milwaukee, Butte, and Bridgeport. A Socialist came within 1,600 votes of becoming mayor of Los Angeles in 1907. Daniel W. Hoan of Milwaukee, one of America's most famous mayors, was a Socialist.[34] Socialist mayors and councilmen have, for the most part, acted independently of party discipline, and many of the more idealistic members of the party have referred disdainfully to municipal reform activities as "sewer socialism."

Socialism was revived in a handful of cities during the Great Depression, and a very few cities continue to elect Socialists today. The relative success of the municipal reform movement and later of the New Deal largely eliminated the basis for the local Socialist party.

Local Parties for Small Towns. Local parties are to be found, secondly, in many villages and in small and even middle-sized cities where politics is on a personal basis, national parties are not desired, and yet for one reason or another (perhaps local custom, or state laws which do not permit nonpartisanship) a party label must be used. A small Iowa city, for example, may have a municipal contest between members of the People's party and the Citizen's party, or the Liberal party and the Temperance party, or the Progressive party and the Conservative party. These labels are most often nothing more than collective terms for slates of candidates which have no organization, platform, or treasury. Politics is on a personal basis, and the label is meaningless.

[33] See Ira Kipnis, *The American Socialist Movement* (Columbia University Press, New York, 1952).

[34] He tells his story in D. W. Hoan, *City Government: The Record of the Milwaukee Experiment* (Harcourt, Brace & World, Inc., New York, 1936).

Reform Parties. Reform parties have been organized from time to time in various cities chiefly for purposes of driving out existing machines or corrupt politicians, or for establishing some of the principles of "efficiency and economy." Most of these parties have been short-lived, and their general failure has caused most reform groups to organize themselves as *pressure groups* rather than political parties, endorsing candidates and policies, but not putting men of their own into the field. This is true today of the New York Citizens' Union, the Chicago Municipal Voters' League, and the Detroit Citizens' League, for example.

Some of these groups, such as the one in New York, began as local parties but found this impractical for one reason or another (the Citizens' Union was nearly taken over by a Tammany Hall fifth column). They then proceeded to work toward their goals on a bipartisan or nonpartisan basis.

New York City had a genuine local party created during the Great Depression in the form of the Fusion party with Fiorello H. La Guardia as its principal driving force. The organization was made up of Citizens' Unionists, many Republicans (including La Guardia), sundry persons not usually politically active, and antimachine Democrats. Although the party still exists, it was greatly weakened with the death of its able, imaginative, and colorful leader. It was quite unsuccessful when it ran Newbold Morris for mayor against Tammany Hall in 1945, the year that William O'Dwyer was elected. The party was, however, one of several groups backing the successful candidacy of Rudolph Halley, of Kefauver investigation fame, for council president in 1951.

There are two other local parties in the city of New York. Both of them are state-wide parties in form but draw nearly all of their support from within the city. The American Labor party was organized in 1936 chiefly by several labor leaders and some Socialists who had broken with their national party. It campaigned against Tammany Hall and proclaimed itself the "true" New Deal party of New York. It reached its greatest power in the city election of 1937, following a practice of endorsing other candidates or running its own, whichever might prove most advantageous in each individual case. The party became infiltrated with Communists, and a long fight ensued for control of the organization, culminating in 1944 with the withdrawal of the bulk of the non-Communists, who then formed the Liberal party.[35] Since that time, the Liberals (dominated by the Hatters and International Ladies Garment Workers unions) have usually preferred to endorse other candidates (generally Democrats on the state level and Republicans in city contests) rather than run their own, although they do run their own whenever they think it desirable. The American Labor party now serves as a Communist front in local

[35] The Amalgamated Clothing Workers of America did not withdraw until 1948.

politics. Since other candidates will no longer accept its endorsements, the party runs its own candidates or none at all, but with very little success.

The Charter Party. Perhaps the best-known and most successful local party in the United States is the City Charter Committee of Cincinnati, often referred to as the "Charter party." Although the organization does not formally call itself a party and although its name does not appear on the Cincinnati nonpartisan ballot following the names of its candidates, it is thoroughly organized in the general pattern of urban parties, and it functions very definitely as a local party.[36]

Cincinnati had long been controlled by a powerful Republican machine when, in 1924, a reform effort secured the adoption of the council-manager plan and proportional representation. It was in order to safeguard these achievements that the Charter party was formed immediately after the election. Its organization has come to equal the best of political machines of the old type: it not only has complete men's and women's ward and precinct organizations, but is actually built upon a broad base of the block worker. It has publicity, literature, and speaker's committees, poll watchers, telephone brigades, and all the other paraphernalia necessary to get out the vote. Perhaps most important of all, it has a permanent and effective organization for financing its efforts. The party differs from traditional machines in that it is interested in good government per se and makes no political promises in return for volunteered efforts. That is, it is not based on patronage, as are other political machines, but relies entirely on unpaid citizens.

From its inception, the Charter party has been opposed in elections by the regular Republican organization. About one-half of the time the Charterites have organized the city council. At other times, either the Republicans have taken control or there has been a 4-4-1 split, with an independent holding the balance of power. This spirited and closely balanced two-party system has forced the regular Republican organization to reform itself (a large number of Charterites are Republicans in state and national elections).

Groups in several smaller cities, especially with council-manager forms of government, have sought to imitate the Cincinnati type of local party with varying degrees of success. Generally they fail to solve the problem of how to establish themselves as a party if no labels are on the ballot, or of maintaining a permanent organization, or both. In many cities, however, reform or business groups put candidates into the field and help finance their campaigns. These groups often have the backing of the local press. They should perhaps be classified as pressure groups rather

[36] For detailed information see the pamphlet *Citizen Organization for Political Activity: The Cincinnati Plan* (3d ed.; National Municipal League, New York, 1949).

than local parties, although the line between the two is not easy to draw in this case.

Local Parties: An Appraisal. Local parties suffer from serious handicaps that make the Charter party or even the Fusion party rare successes in America. It is often argued that such parties would quickly become mere adjuncts of national parties—the same old parties under different names. While this does not necessarily follow and it would be quite possible to maintain these parties as separate entities, some very real problems do confront local parties.

In the first place, local parties require constant attention and interest from a large part of the public. This is difficult to secure, and the normal result is that shortly after "the rascals" are thrown out, the party begins to disintegrate. This has happened many times in the United States. A permanent organization with permanent electioneering on the Cincinnati model is imperative for longevity of local parties. Secondly, local parties are difficult to organize in any case. Political-party structures are complex and require much coordinated effort. It is virtually impossible to organize a successful local party except under unusual circumstances (a deep economic depression, a particularly corrupt administration), and even then it is not easy. Thirdly, attempts to organize local parties, as such, are likely to be resisted by the informal ruling group of businessmen who put up candidates, finance them, and—in lieu of having an organized party structure—control the media of communication. Lastly, local parties have a great deal of difficulty in securing enough funds for survival. People will not make contributions unless they believe in the cause to begin with and further believe that a particular organization is capable of advancing that cause. The Cincinnati Charter party has been successful because it has been able both to develop an effective money-raising organization and to get the confidence and support of businessmen who have funds that can be tapped. The American Labor and later the Liberal party could survive in New York because they had a firm financial base in labor-union support. A poorly financed party has no chance of survival.

Methods of Nomination. Before there can be an election, the individuals who are going to make the race must first be nominated. There are numerous ways of placing candidates in nomination. The overwhelming majority of nominations on the local (or any other) level made in the United States today are by way of either the partisan or the nonpartisan direct *primary* election. There are, or have been, however, numerous other techniques, including caucus or convention nomination, sponsorship, and petition.

Early Nomination Devices. The *caucus*, the oldest form of nomination in the United States, consisted originally of an informal meeting to choose candidates deserving of support for the various public offices becoming vacant. In America's early days the caucus members could print a ballot and distribute it themselves.

With the development of cities, the caucus system degenerated. A more formal method and one that would make known the desires of the common voter, rather than those of the organized few, was demanded. The *convention* method called for nominations at a formal gathering whose membership was chosen by caucus at the precinct level. With the organization of nineteenth-century political machines, both the caucus and the convention tended to be dominated by a few people, with the general public having little real choice in the nomination—and in most cities nomination by the dominant party was tantamount to election.

Reforms in Nomination. Beginning at the turn of the century, the reform movement produced a change in nomination procedure. The *direct primary election* was substituted for the caucus and convention. It is now almost universal in the United States, although a few states do not use it for important state offices and there are cities in such populous states as California, Texas, New Jersey, and Massachusetts that do not use it.

Strictly speaking, a primary election is nothing more than a *nonassembled* caucus. That is to say, in an earlier day every eligible voter was entitled to take part in the selection of candidates. Next, part of this job had to be turned over to what were theoretically his representatives acting at a convention. When the convention proved to be unrepresentative and boss-ridden, the primary election was devised to return nominations "to the people." The plan in large measure transfers control of the nomination machinery from the party to the state, all parties choosing their candidates on the same day under the supervision of public election officials, with ballots standardized and printed at public expense and with a secret ballot (in contrast with most caucus and convention systems).

The primary election has never been understood by the vast majority of American voters. They are annoyed by the fantastically long "bedsheet" ballot with which they are confronted; they bitterly resent the fact that they must usually reveal their party preference in order to vote, and even when the open primary is used, they become incensed when they discover that splitting the ticket is not permitted.

Types of Primaries. Primary elections are of two types, nonpartisan and partisan. The latter is subdivided into two classes, open and closed. In the *nonpartisan* primary, we have what is actually an elimination contest. Names appear on the ballot without party designation. The first election, popularly and sometimes legally called a primary, serves to eliminate all candidates except twice the number to be elected. Hence if seven file for the office of mayor, only two will survive the primary—the two with the highest number of votes. If seven councilmen are to be elected, the fourteen highest at the primary are nominated. In some cases, such as in many California cities and in elections for the Chicago council, if any candidate receives a majority of the vote cast in the primary he is declared elected, and the taxpayer is saved the cost of placing him on the final ballot.

In nonpartisan as well as partisan primaries, one gets on the ballot in the first place in one of three ways: by a simple formal declaration, by signature petition (in either of these two, a small filing fee to defray part of the expense of putting the name on the ballot may be charged), or by filing a forfeitable deposit.

The *partisan* primary may be open or closed. An open primary is open to any eligible voter regardless of which party may be his own, or whether he is a party member or a confirmed independent. He need not demonstrate or declare anything other than that he is a qualified voter in order to receive a ballot. A closed primary, on the other hand, is closed to everyone except members of the political party concerned.

Other Nomination Devices. Some cities in a number of states make use of nomination by *petition* directly onto the final ballot. This method saves the expense of a primary election, and usually has satisfactory results in small cities. But when the plan was used in Boston, the mayor was often a plurality rather than a majority choice, for there were nearly always more than two major candidates.[37] Boss James Michael Curley, as the best-known mayoralty candidate, sometimes found this plan of considerable help to him.

The *Model City Charter* of the National Municipal League recommends a plan, especially in connection with proportional representation, called the *sponsor system.* It has been used in some California cities for several years. It is similar to the British system of nomination, for it requires a petition signed by ten persons who are listed as "sponsors" of the candidate and the filing of a sum of money, to be returned under certain conditions.[38]

EXPERIMENTS IN DIRECT DEMOCRACY

The Initiative and Referendum.[39] With the decline in the prestige of governing bodies in the last half of the nineteenth century came also

[37] A *plurality* is more votes than any other candidate receives. A *majority* is at least one vote more than one-half of the number cast.

[38] *Model City Charter* (5th ed.; National Municipal League, New York, 1941).

[39] See W. B. Munro (ed.), *The Initiative, Referendum and Recall* (The Macmillan Company, New York, 1913). Studies of the initiative and referendum in individual states have been made by W. W. Crouch in California (1943 and 1950); the Colorado Legislative Reference Office in that state (1940); L. L. Pelletier in Maine (1952); J. K. Pollock in Michigan (1940); and J. G. LaPalombara in Oregon (1950).

a decline in citizen faith in representative democracy. As a consequence, reformers proposed what were then considered radical solutions. They renovated and reorganized some old American institutions, introduced some new ones, and hopefully presented us with techniques for direct democracy as a check upon excesses and incompetence. The *initiative* permits a legally defined number of voters to propose changes in the city charter or ordinances which are then accepted or rejected by the voters at the polls. This device permits legislation to be effected with no recourse at all to the legislative body. The *referendum* permits the voters to accept or reject at the polls council-proposed changes in the city charter or ordinances. The referendum differs from the initiative in that it *follows* favorable action by the legislative body, whereas such an institutional device as the initiative takes place independently of the legislative body.

The Procedure. An initiated proposal is normally drafted by the attorneys for the particular interest group seeking the legislation. Petitions to put the proposal on the ballot are then circulated, either by volunteers or by persons hired for the purpose, often at the price of a certain amount per signature. The total signatures required may be a specific number or a certain percentage of voters (registered, or voting for a certain office at the last general election, or some other formula). Where such a percentage is used, it is generally from 5 to 10 per cent but may be higher. In most instances the proposal is adopted if a majority of those voting on the proposal vote in its favor, although in some cases a majority of those voting *in the election* is required (this means that if a voter ignores the proposal he is in effect voting "no"), or some special formula may be used. It is often provided that an initiated ordinance may not be amended or repealed by the city council, at least within a certain prescribed time limit.

The initiative and referendum (I. and R.), particularly the latter, date from early times in America and elsewhere. Antecedents are to be found in the direct democracy of ancient Greece, the ancient tribal governments of Germany, the right to petition the king in medieval England, the town meeting of colonial New England, and the direct democracy of Switzerland.[40] As early as 1825, the Maryland legislature provided for a referendum on the question of establishing a public school system. It later became very common to hold referendums on liquor questions, charter amendments, public utility franchises, bond issues, and other matters. California, Iowa, and Nebraska in the late nineteenth century authorized municipal use of the initiative and referendum. The San Francisco home rule charter of 1898 was the first such document to pro-

[40] See Munro, *op. cit.*, chap. 1. Also R. M. Goldman, "The Advisory Referendum in America," *Public Opinion Quarterly*, vol. 14 (Summer, 1950), pp. 303–315.

vide for them. From then the movement spread rapidly, and it is today widely authorized for municipal governments.

Around the turn of the century, when many cities adopted the initiative and referendum, proponents made greatly exaggerated claims of their merits. Opponents were equally vociferous, viewing with alarm the potentiality for hamstringing of the governmental process by their use. The results have not borne out the claims of either side.

Arguments Concerning I. and R. Proponents of direct democracy argued that corrupt and low-quality city councils made it necessary for people to have a check upon the government. Reformers also took note of the trend toward a concentration of authority in government and a breakdown of the traditional check-and-balance system. The initiative and referendum could serve to replace some of these disappearing checks. It was argued that the use of these devices strengthened popular control over city government by giving the people "a gun behind the door" which could serve as a means of requiring greater alertness, honesty, and responsiveness on the part of council members.

It was believed that I. and R. would protect the people from political tricks and thefts from the public treasury. Some argued that it would encourage voters to become better informed on issues, since they would have to vote on so many of them directly and since they could now feel that they had a real chance to get things done in local affairs.

Opponents of the system argued that it confused legislative responsibility, lengthened an already overly long ballot, created a bad psychological effect upon the city council, expected more than was reasonable from an uninformed and uninterested electorate, would promote radicalism and a disrespect for property rights, was opposed to the best principles of Americanism (since the Constitution is based upon *representative*, and not direct, democracy), and would allow well-organized pressure groups representing a minority of the population to exercise an inordinate advantage.[41]

I. and R.: An Appraisal. The debate over the use of I. and R. has subsided in recent years, though the use of these devices is, if anything, increasing. Perhaps it is necessary here to make only two points without discussing the merits of the arguments briefly outlined above.

First, the I. and R. seem to carry the implicit assumption that the individual voter is always informed and rational in his choices. Actually, of course, this assumption is false. Furthermore, democracy as we know it does not require such an assumption. In an ordinary election, the voter is merely asked whether or not he is relatively satisfied with things as

[41] Extensive arguments on the pros and cons are presented in Munro, *op. cit.*, chaps. 1–11.

they are. According to the state of his satisfactions, he votes for those in power or he casts a protest vote. His reasons for his vote are his own, and they need not be rational, logical, or informed. He is not asked to rule, but merely to choose those who are to rule. But the I. and R. ask more than this of the voter. They ask him to help rule himself and to make policy decisions on questions that are often complex, technical, and minutely detailed.

It is not uncommon, for example, for the voter to be asked a question such as the following: [42]

GENERAL RETIREMENT SYSTEM AMENDMENT

Do you favor an amendment to Title IX, Chapter VI, General Retirement System, of the Charter of the City of Detroit, changing membership service pension from 1/120 of average final compensation to 1/100 average final compensation times years of membership service; to increase maximum city pension from $1,800 per annum to $2,400 per annum; to provide for optional benefit to widow or dependent husband for member who continues in service after becoming eligible to retire and to provide for increase of employees' annuity contributions from 5% on $3,600 to 5% on $7,200 or under per annum?

　　YES ☐
　　NO ☐

Where the law permits or requires complex questions to be submitted to the general public for direct action, the results are sometimes humorous—or would be if government were not such a serious business. In the November, 1952, election, the voters of Waldwick, New Jersey (1950 population: 3,963), on the edge of the New York metropolitan area, voted to establish a full-time police force, but on another question refused to appropriate the additional $10,000 a year to finance the project, and on a third question voted to retain the existing part-time system. And this all at the same election.

Second, opponents of the I. and R. are wont to overlook the fact that the American political structure is pluralistic and not neatly integrated, and that the American political process is typically based upon the interaction of pressure groups. American cities, for the most part, do not have responsible political-party structures, and few cities have a two-party system of any kind regularly competing for voter support. Furthermore, it is unlikely that this pattern will be changed much in the foreseeable future. Since this system may result in city councils that are neither re-

---

[42] Proposed Amendment E to the Detroit City Charter, election of Nov. 6, 1951. Incidentally, the proposal passed, 119,717 to 110,234, after city employees urged a favorable vote. Probably most voters did not know that they were raising city expenses by one-half million dollars a year.

SAMPLE

RECALL BALLOT

Special Election of July 22, 1930

INSTRUCTIONS: Make a cross (X) in the square to the right of the words YES or NO. Before leaving booth, fold ballot so initials of inspector will appear on the outside.

REASONS FOR DEMANDING RECALL

He has tolerated lawlessness by law enforcement agencies. Delegated to Frank Dohany, an attorney financially interested in claims against the Street Railway, control of the Street Railway's claims department. Gave Gillespie, professional lobbyist and bondsman, control of Detroit's Public Works programs with power to deal with contractors who had made him wealthy—and paving costs to the homebuilder increased twenty cents per yard in days of financial distress. Gave Gillespie official direction of public garbage disposal despite Gillespie's long private monopoly of this business. Destroyed efficient public service through dismissal of faithful employees. Threatened success of municipal ownership by attempted increase in car riders' fares and unwarranted discharge of Street Railway Commissioner Couzens. Made people fifteen pledges before election and again at inauguration; kept none. Directed that public records be kept secret. Seeks to weld street railway and other city employees into political machine by manipulation of patronage and public funds. Hindered the Police Commissioner, Harold H. Emmons, in his enforcement of the law by taking control of the Vice Squad from his jurisdiction and later discharged him for enforcing the law while the mayor was out of town.

OFFICER'S JUSTIFICATION OF HIS COURSE OF OFFICE

The law allows the mayor a 200 word defense against the reasons for his recall. It is enough to say that these accusations are malicious and untrue.

As mayor he has worked faithfully for the good of the City and has saved the taxpayers millions of dollars. He has succeeded in having the State pay $3,000,000 per year for our street widenings and remove 275 felons from the House of Correction. He has saved the City thousands of dollars in reduced interest charges and reduced taxes. Lowest tax rate in 11 years.

Detroit never had better law enforcement or a better Police Commissioner than Thomas C. Wilcox.

What the recall will actually decide is whether the people or the Detroit News and the Detroit Free Press shall govern the City. Everyone knows that the recall is a fraudulent conspiracy, backed by these papers and selfish, greedy interests. The mayor is not charged with one dishonest or questionable act. Their aim is to destroy him because he will not do their bidding.

The question is: Shall these newspapers or the people rule?

Every good citizen should vote "NO" in the cause of decency and independent government.

SHALL CHARLES BOWLES BE CALLED FROM THE OFFICE OF MAYOR OF THE CITY OF DETROIT?

YES ☐

NO ☐

If you want Bowles PUT OUT of office, make a cross (X) in the square after the YES.
If you want Bowles to REMAIN IN office, make a cross (X) in the square after the NO.

Figure 4-1. SOURCE: Reproduced in Carl O. Smith, *A Book of Ballots* (Bureau of Municipal Research, Detroit, 1938).

sponsible nor representative of a cross section of the population, the
I. and R. may well be used as a check, a "gun behind the door." [43]

The Recall. The third member of the triumvirate that was to produce
"popular control" of city government was the *recall*. This is a device
whereby any elective officer may be removed from office by a popular
vote prior to the expiration of his term. Although it is often popularly
mentioned in connection with the initiative and referendum, the recall
may exist independently of them. It was brought into extensive use by
the same people and for largely the same reasons. It was argued that a
faithless or incompetent public servant should not be inflicted upon the
people for the duration of his term—that he should be removed as soon
as his shortcomings are discovered. Again, Jacksonians who were none
too happy over the increasing popularity of the four-year term as against
the traditional two years found it easier to accept the longer term if
"continuous responsibility" were maintained through the availability of
the recall. The mechanism was probably first provided for in the Los
Angeles home rule charter of 1903; unlike its two sisters, it has no direct
precedents in American political practices.

The Procedure. In order to recall an official, a petition must be circulated. Since a large number of signatures are usually required—such as
15 to 25 or even as high as 51 per cent of the vote cast for the office of
mayor in the last election—an organized group with a good deal of motivation and a sizable treasury is usually required. After sufficient signatures are procured and certified by the city clerk or other appropriate
election official, an election becomes obligatory. There are several variants of the recall ballot, and its form may itself serve to either aid or
discourage the prospects for removal of the official.

Arguments pro and con. The principal argument for the recall is
that it provides for continuous responsibility (especially important with
the four-year term) so that the public need not wait in exasperation and
frustration until the term comes to an end. It is similarly argued that
with a sword constantly hanging over the head of the public official he
will feel a need to remain alert at all times.

Opponents of the recall point to its costliness: a *special* election is imperative for its use, since it would be grossly unfair to conduct such an
election in connection with other questions (although this is sometimes
done). A second objection to the recall is that it is not an attempt to
prove charges against an officeholder, but is merely an attempt to persuade the electorate, by whatever means, to remove the incumbent. A

---

[43] In this connection, see J. G. LaPalombara and C. B. Hagan, "Direct Legislation:
An Appraisal and a Suggestion," *American Political Science Review*, vol. 45 (June,
1951), pp. 400–421. On the use of professional public relations firms in I. and R.
contests, see Ross, *op. cit.*

third objection is that the recall is unnecessary. In all states, improper conduct by public officials is grounds for removal by other judicial, councilmanic, or sometimes gubernatorial action.[44]

A final objection to the recall centers in the assertion that it serves as a tool for well-organized pressure groups and for political recrimination. Similarly, it is said that the threat of the recall is a constant and perfectly legal means for intimidation of public officials who must therefore slavishly follow public whims and sentimentality. In many instances, a strong leader with a positive program will find that some interest group will stand in his path threatening him with a recall action if he seeks to carry out his plans—even if those plans represent the planks of the platform upon which he was elected.

There is a trend away from the recall, and it has never been widely used. Few new adoptions of it have taken place since 1920. The question of the use of the recall is no longer a very burning one, but it does seem as if the experiment has been of little success and as if this particular control device can, at best, be replaced by other, fairer methods and at worst can be a positive detriment to the effective operation of democratic society.

The Faceless Man: A Case Study in Irresponsibility.[45] Roger Dearborn Lapham was a businessman. He had been born in New York and educated at Harvard, and had then proceeded through a career in the shipping industry, ultimately becoming chairman of the board of the American-Hawaiian Steamship Company. In 1943, as he was approaching retirement age, he was prevailed upon to run for the office of mayor of San Francisco to succeed Angelo Rossi, a florist who had held that position for twelve years. Lapham had not run for political office before, but he was a bluff extrovert and enjoyed campaigning. As a long-time business administrator, he was in the habit of giving orders and expecting them to be carried out, and this lifetime habit he carried not only into the campaign but also into the mayor's office after his promises to take a "nonpolitical approach" and to run the city on a "businesslike" basis proved successful.

Lapham managed to get into difficulties almost immediately. He appointed two department heads from minority groups that had never before been represented in these positions. He dropped one of Rossi's park commissioners, who had served ten years in the office. He supported higher taxes for badly needed postwar developments of the sewerage

[44] See chap. 9.

[45] The material for this section is drawn from John M. Selig, "San Francisco Upholds Mayor," *National Municipal Review*, vol. 35 (October, 1946), pp. 465–470, now the *National Civic Review;* and *Time,* July 15, 1946.

system, city purchase of the public transit system, a fare increase to repair its dilapidated and overworked equipment, and in general launched into an ambitious plan for making up the time lost from public improvements because of World War II.

It took the opponents of an assertive municipal policy and of higher taxes, together with disgruntled politicians, three years to make use of a weapon that seemed to be begging for them to come after it. The recall petition was the work of a group led by the dismissed park commissioner, who was also the publisher of a daily throwaway and a municipal employees' magazine.

The recall petition and pamphlet (which in San Francisco is published at public expense, each side being allowed 300 words) asserted, among other things, that Lapham had:

1. Failed to reappoint a "good public servant"—the park commissioner
2. Raised trolley fares three cents in an "arrogant" manner (public hearings had been held)
3. Raised taxes
4. Refused to declare an emergency so that trolley operators could get wages boosted by edict
5. Refused to endorse a "Dimes for Manila" campaign—or for that matter any "days," "weeks," or "months" on the ground that they were inane
6. Failed to obtain the permanent United Nations headquarters for San Francisco
7. Acted like a dictator

Clearly none of the charges suggested that Lapham had acted in an illegal or immoral manner (unless the last name caller is taken seriously). Clearly, too, some people did not like his appointments and his policies—something that is true of any mayor, but especially true of one who tries to get things done.

It would not be part of Lapham's character not to fight back. Besides, under the San Francisco charter, an official against whom an unsuccessful recall attempt is made is entitled to reimbursement for campaign expenses within prescribed limits. He argued that no one had charged him with anything more serious than a difference in opinion; that a successful recall would disgrace the city and discourage office seeking; and—not giving the opposition a monopoly on the use of the cliché—that the recall was contrary to the principles of American democracy. He signed his own recall petition and urged that the election be gotten over with.

Lapham supporters bought space on signboards and showed pictures of a ghostlike creature and the admonition: "Don't surrender your city to the faceless man. Vote NO on recall." This was a reference to the fact that the board of supervisors [46] would choose his successor. Board members had made no statements, and so no one could know for certain who the next mayor would be.

The well-known "women's" novelist Kathleen Norris, sent a postcard to every registered voter in the city urging a "no" vote, and somehow *Time* magazine was prevailed upon to devote its cover story of the issue before the election to a defense of Lapham.

On July 16, 1946, the voters of San Francisco—actually only a modest turnout of them—decided that they had been right the first time. Roger D. Lapham was retained by a vote of 109,526 to 73,946.

The election had cost the taxpayers a great deal of money, and Lapham had been forced to save from ruin a reputation that he had spent a lifetime in establishing. And all this over an issue that would not have lasted five minutes before a court or an impeachment proceeding.

The Public Hearing. A few words should be said about another important American device for involving the citizen in decision making, the public hearing. This well-established institution is unusual in Europe but fits in perfectly with the American tradition, which calls for the general public to be consulted, or at least informed, about every significant decision affecting public policy. Public hearings generally involve a rather informal procedure at which every citizen present is allowed to speak if he cares to do so. They are commonly used prior to the making of decisions concerning such matters as the zoning of land, the location of taverns, the moving of highways, the changing of public utilities rates, the exempting of certain property from the tax rolls (as in the granting of a permit for a cemetery), the location of a new school, and for dozens of other purposes.

Political neophytes find the hearing procedure puzzling, because at a typical meeting nearly all persons expressing themselves are opposed to the proposal which is the subject of the hearing. The official or public body conducting the hearing does not, of course, take a vote at the time and dispose of the issue on that basis. Instead, the hearing is used as a safety-valve device for allowing persons disapproving to vent their feelings. These people thus gain a feeling of having had their "day in court," and they may succeed in having the proposed policy modified somewhat so as to meet at least partially some of their objections. The hearing also allows the responsible officials to judge in advance of decisions the political climate in which they will find themselves. They may also learn something that will suggest to them the language in which to couch the announcement of a decision so as to minimize the number and intensity of unfavorable responses.

[46] The city and county of San Francisco are consolidated, and the board of supervisors also acts as the city council.

PROPORTIONAL AND PREFERENTIAL VOTING SYSTEMS

The Hare System of Proportional Representation.[47] One of the schemes advocated by members of the reform movement was the Hare system of proportional representation by single transferable vote. P.R. reflected the untiring efforts of reformers to reduce the power of political machines and constituted a definite improvement over other attempts to remove objections to both the old ward system and the newer at-large system of councilmanic elections. The ward system encouraged parochialism in politics, while election at large could give 100 per cent control of the council to whatever group might receive a plurality in the voting.

Some cities experimented with the St. Louis practice of nominating by wards and electing at large; many others elected part of the council at large and part of it by wards. Some (including New York, Boston, and the present Philadelphia charter) tried *limited* voting, by which each elector was required to vote for less than the total number of councilmen to be elected. This gave the minority representation, as a rule, but not necessarily in any systematic proportion.

The Hare system, named for an Englishman, Thomas Hare, is designed to give representation upon a multimembered body in direct proportion to the numerical strength of the various interest groups in the community. Its whole object is to give each voter but one vote for the council (or such multimembered bodies as school, park, and library boards, if elective), but to make every effort to see that the vote is eventually used to help someone get into office.

P.R. has had little use in the United States, although several Massachusetts cities have used it, as did the city of New York between 1936 and 1947. Any chance it may have had for gaining popularity in this country seems to have died with its repeal in 1957 in Cincinnati, the city that had used it the longest. Opposition by the dominant political party in both New York and Cincinnati eventually proved fatal to the plan.[48]

Preferential Voting Systems.[49] While reformers were concerned, on the one hand, with ensuring extensive representation for minority groups

[47] See George H. Hallet, Jr., *Proportional Representation: The Key to Democracy* (2d ed.; National Municipal League, New York, 1940).

[48] See Belle Zeller and Hugh A. Bone, "The Repeal of P.R. in New York City: Ten Years in Retrospect," *American Political Science Review*, vol. 42 (December, 1948), pp. 1127–1148; Ralph A. Straetz, *PR Politics in Cincinnati* (New York University Press, New York, 1958).

[49] No contemporary studies have been made of preferential voting in the United States. For material from the hopeful days of the system, see R. G. Mott, "Preferential Voting and How It Works," *National Municipal Review* (now *National Civic Review*), vol. 1 (July, 1912), pp. 386–400; L. J. Johnson, "Preferential Voting," *ibid.*, vol. 3 (January, 1914), pp. 83–92.

through P.R., they also desired, on the other hand, to devise a system to prevent minorities from manipulating elections by promoting additional candidates designed to split the vote of the person who would otherwise be expected to win. Several mechanisms have been devised that seek to prevent a minority from gaining control by splitting the majority. In effect, these devices reassemble the atomized majority vote. All of them attempt to do so by allowing the voter to make more than one choice for each individual office. If his first choice will not help elect a candidate, the mechanism is designed to allow his second or later choice to aid in selecting the winner.

The earliest plan, the Bucklin system, was first used in Grand Junction, Colorado, in 1909 and eventually gained some fifty-five adoptions. All of these cities have since abandoned the plan. Three other preferential voting systems have had a total of only two adoptions among them. These systems have never been popular in the United States, little use has been made of them, and they are almost forgotten today, except for state elections in Maryland.

Chapter 5

INTERGROUP ACTIVITY AND POLITICAL POWER

Politics is not an evil thing. It is the catalysis that changes citizens into public officials and individual wishes into public policy. It is essential to democracy. On the local scene it operates largely in the same manner as it does for state and national governments. Only the emphasis and the relative balances of forces are changed.

THE NATURE OF THE POLITICAL PROCESS

Politics as Demand and Supply. In order to have an understanding of the nature of the political process, it is necessary to be able to picture it, not as the principal purpose of a certain type of human activity, but rather as a *by-product*. Human life in Western culture is a struggle for power, prestige, and security. Some people, in their search, turn to politics to secure this. They become the relatively small group of politically active people. The general public, politically passive though it may be, becomes a collection of clientele groups, seeking services from government in order to help themselves, in turn, achieve these same ends. Or, alternatively, they seek to *prevent* government from launching certain types of services if they feel that their goals can be reached by some alternative type of activity.[1]

The politician, then, is a person who seeks to determine what a considerable portion of the public is asking of government and to make this available to them if possible. (He may also seek to determine what the public potentially may want and seek to "sell" it to the voters.) Since the individual normally has a certain amount of actual choice in selecting public officers and is free to join various groups that exert pressure upon government, government is responsible to the people—the essential characteristic of a democracy.

In order to achieve his desired objectives in public policy, the indi-

[1] See the writings of Harold Lasswell, especially *Psychopathology and Politics* (University of Chicago Press, Chicago, 1930), and *Power and Personality* (W. W. Norton & Company, Inc., New York, 1948).

119

vidual may choose to work through a political party. If the party stands for a definite set of principles, this approach is worthwhile and is the common method used in European democracies. In the United States, however, political parties are loose coalitions, each covering a great variety of political viewpoints. This is true very often even at the local level. The individual belongs to a political party for a variety of reasons connected largely with economic status, geographic location, and family tradition. He can, however, seldom go to the polls and vote for a set of policies.

He may choose to become active in a political party, of course, and seek to influence its policies. But by the simple act of voting for the slate of a particular party, he will not be able to assure himself that he has selected a group of public officials who are philosophically in accord with himself. If he wishes to influence public policy, therefore, he will usually find it more expedient and fruitful to join forces with like-minded persons in a pressure group. In fact, the individual normally belongs to a number of such groups, not all of which have like views toward the same questions of policy. It is this overlapping of membership in groups which helps to mitigate their conflicts and to enable a workable system to develop.

What Is a Pressure Group? A pressure group differs from a political party chiefly in that it does not seek to capture offices for its members, but rather attempts to influence public policy. It also differs from most political parties in the United States in that it is made up of persons with basically the same interests and viewpoints—it is normally much more philosophically cohesive than is a political party in this country. Much has been said of the evil influences and dangers of pressure groups in politics. It has even been suggested by some critics that they be legally abolished or stringently controlled. Most such suggestions are, however, naïve. If we had a system of two or more political parties, each standing upon a definite platform of proposed action to which the parties could be held, pressure groups, or at least their lobbying activities,[2] could be greatly reduced. Such is not the case in the United States, however. Neither is it practical to say that a public official can determine the viewpoints of a cross section of the citizenry simply by noting the comments of those who contact him personally—not in any but the smallest villages, at any rate. And only the naïve or foolhardy would suggest that the officeholder should be elected with no promises to the public and then be entrusted to use his own free will and best judgment in doing as he

---

[2] *Lobbying,* often performed by professionals, consists of seeking to influence legislative and administrative officials in a variety of ways so that their actions will be favorable to the group doing the lobbying. Lobbyists are also frequently in charge of the dissemination of propaganda to the general public. In this book *propaganda* is used to mean any communication designed to create a desired effect, impression, or opinion.

sees best "for all the people" while in office. He must constantly be reminded of the nature of the shifting viewpoints of his constituents.

A pressure group is not only not an evil, it is an absolute necessity in a democracy lacking in disciplined political parties. It serves the purpose of marshaling individual opinions, organizing them, and presenting them in a skillful way to the proper governmental officials. While individual pressure groups no doubt do sometimes go beyond the bounds of the mores of society, do fail to give an accurate picture of the interests, desires, and aspirations of their individual members, and do act otherwise irresponsibly, most of them are kept in check quite automatically by the fact that for nearly every pressure group that comes before government, there is a counterpressure group. In this fashion, most of the potential dangers of the organized power of such a group are neutralized by the watchful eye of an opposing group. And each watcher is also watched. In fact, *public policy* might be defined as the end result of the interaction of the various interested pressure groups upon one another. It is the sum of the vector forces, where each vector represents the total force and direction of each group as determined by its age, respectability, size of membership, wealth, ability of leadership, skill at lobbying, inside connections, intensity of interests, and other pertinent factors.[3]

Characteristics of Groups. Several things should be kept in mind in classifying these interest or pressure groups. Some of them are especially created for the single purpose of lobbying, while to others lobbying is only a side line. Some are temporary organizations created for a special problem, while others are permanent groups. Some, in large cities and in state and nation at any rate, are always present and lobbying at the seat of government, while others do not lobby except when a matter of particular importance to the group is under consideration.

Pressure groups are forever realigning their forces as expediency de-

---

[3] For further analysis of pressure groups, see any good introductory textbook on American government or political parties. Probably the best reference on the nature of the political process is D. B. Truman, *The Governmental Process* (Alfred A. Knopf, Inc., New York, 1951). See his bibliography. Also H. E. Freeman and M. Showel, "Differential Political Influence of Voluntary Associations," *Public Opinion Quarterly,* vol. 15 (Winter, 1951–1952), pp. 703–714; D. C. Blaisdell, *American Democracy under Pressure* (The Ronald Press Company, New York, 1957); Earl Latham, "The Group Basis of Politics: Notes for a Theory," *American Political Science Review,* vol. 26 (June, 1952), pp. 376–379; N. E. Long, "The Local Community as an Ecology of Games," *American Journal of Sociology,* vol. 64 (November, 1958), pp. 251–261; R. E. Lane, *Political Life: How People Get Involved in Politics* (The Free Press, Glencoe, Ill., 1958); "Unofficial Government: Pressure Groups and Lobbies," *Annals of the American Academy of Political and Social Science,* vol. 319 (September, 1958), entire issue; W. J. MacKenzie, "Pressure Groups: The 'Conceptual Framework,'" *Political Studies,* vol. 3 (1955), pp. 247–255; S. M. Lipset, *Political Man: The Social Bases of Politics* (Doubleday & Company, Inc., New York, 1960).

mands. It should not be assumed that politics is simply business versus labor, or that businessmen always work together, or that various groups operate in fairly permanent alignments. The *fluidity* of the pressure-group system is one of its most prominent characteristics.

Businessmen often line up on opposite sides of an issue, for example. Downtown merchants might lobby before a city council for one-way streets, since this would help hurry traffic to the place where their stores are located, but neighborhood-shopping-area merchants oppose one-way streets, since they feel that they reduce accessibility to their locations. Downtown and neighborhood-shopping-area merchants alike may favor municipally owned parking lots, but realtors are quite likely to oppose them. Labor unions frequently come into conflict with one another before legislative or administrative bodies. Jurisdictional disputes and the long-standing conflict of interests between the railroad brotherhoods and the teamsters' (truckers') union are examples. Businessmen and labor leaders work together on many matters. Ours is a dynamic system. (See Figure 5-1.)

Organized and Unorganized Groups. If all groups in society were equally well organized and equally effective in presenting their sides of issues, the process of determining public policy through compromise among the various interests involved would be highly satisfactory, indeed, nearly as perfect a device for democratic policy making as human society could achieve. It happens, however, that not all groups have

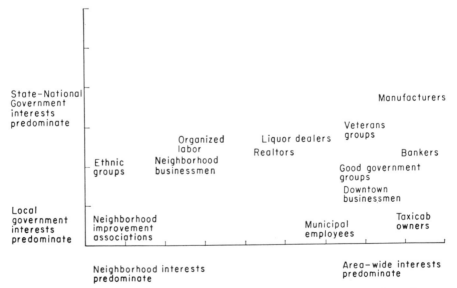

Figure. 5-1. Group interests are multidimensional. Two aspects are shown here.

their interests equally well protected. The less verbal members of the working class are not so likely to have their views expressed before councils as are members of the most prestigeful groups in society. They are certain to be accorded less deference when they speak. In terms of status, inside connections, funds for spreading propaganda, and other factors, there are vast differences in the relative power of groups.

It should not be assumed, however, that a group is necessarily strong because it is well organized or weak because it is unorganized. A well-organized and vigorously active group may, for example, have its relative strength reduced through the gerrymandering of the city council. Some unorganized groups are very weak politically (e.g., exconvicts); others are very strong (e.g., the elderly). In a democracy, virtually all groups are free to organize and to lobby, but the ability of the members of a group to understand the techniques of doing this vary greatly, and the result is a weakening of the representativeness of a politics based upon the summation of vector forces.

The Techniques and Motivation of Groups. Not only do groups vary according to their degree of organization, but they also vary according to the techniques they use and the level of motivation they have for political participation.

Techniques might be said to vary according to the way in which the groups fit into the system of cultural values. One group may be able to "get away" with something that would produce highly unfavorable publicity for another. The medical association feels impelled to act within the public image of dignity which it has created for itself; a labor union can safely be more free swinging in its behavior. A conservative group may be able to make recommendations concerning the election of non-partisan judges with newspaper approval; a liberal group may be criticized by the same newspaper for "interfering" if it does the same thing.

There are many bases for the political motivation of groups. Many organizations, for example, seek to use the sanctions of the state to support their own battles against other interests. Either labor or management can benefit in their struggles by having governmental officials or legal provisions supporting one side. In other cases, one might make the generalization that *the political activity of any group is proportionate to its stake in the marginal definition of legality and of law-enforcement levels.* Thus, the middle-management bureaucrat in private industry is not intensely involved in politics, except by choice, because his job and his way of life are well within the bounds of accepted behavior. He is not likely to be in trouble with the law, or his welfare especially dependent upon its decisions. Similarly, the professional bank robber is not politically active because his job is so far outside the law that he cannot possibly hope to secure governmental sanction for his activities. But those on the edge of legality, where economic survival depends on marginal definitions, are the ones with the greatest stake in political definitions and decisions, and they make the maximum investment in the political process. Thus, a race-track owner must be politically active because his business is just barely acceptable as legitimate by American values. The electric-utilities executive is similarly highly motivated, because his rate structure is determined through the governmental process. The corner druggist is deeply concerned over traffic-flow patterns. A decision to prohibit parking near his store may wipe out his margin of profit.

The pattern of marginality varies over time. Prostitutes and public servants holding office by political appointment were once highly active in politics. Neither group is apolitical today, but their activities have diminished as the prostitute has moved outside the pale, while the merit system, by extending protection to civil servants, has moved public employees away from the margin, toward stability and acceptance. On the other hand, Negroes who once thought they could not make economic or social progress through political action now find that they can. As a result, they have changed their behavior pattern from almost total political apathy to intense activity. Americans vote, lobby, issue propaganda, or otherwise take part in the process of politics according to their level of motivation. This, in turn, varies according to whether the individual's activities are well within the norms of society and of established public policy or whether decisions on public policy that may affect the individual are of a sort that are unpredictable but of immense importance to his social or economic welfare.

Groups and the Public Interest. When any group announces a policy position, it seeks explicitly or implicitly to associate its stand with the public interest. In fact, virtually every politically active individual or group claims—sincerely, no doubt—to be acting in the name of the public interest. Critics of the stand taken by a particular group, on the other hand, not uncommonly complain that pressure groups are selfish and that they ought to act in the public interest. With everyone thus borrowing the term, it becomes useless as an analytical tool. Yet it is a basic part of the myth of democracy to say that public policies as they are adopted are, or ought to be, in the public interest. As such, the concept may serve a useful function in encouraging compliance with the law, which in turn is an important device for achieving a stable society. It is also useful as a symbol to remind legislators and administrators that no matter how many groups they may have listened to before making a decision, other groups and citizens who are unrepresented or underrepresented before them will also be affected by the decision.

As one writer on the subject has said: [4]

Instead of being associated with substantive goals or policies, the public interest better survives identification with the process of group accommodation. The public interest rests not in some policy emerging from the settlement of conflict, but with the method of that settlement itself, with compromising in a peaceful, orderly, predictable way the demands put upon policy.

URBAN PRESSURE GROUPS

Pressure groups operate in basically the same pattern whether on the national, state, or local level. To be sure, there may be differences in the relative balance of power of the various groups. On the national and state level, for example, agricultural groups tend to be the most powerful of the lot. Liquor lobbyists tend to be more powerful before state and local bodies than before the national government. Real estate groups and downtown merchants tend to be extraordinarily powerful in city politics.

Good-government Groups. The so-called "good-government groups" are among the few who restrict most of their organized efforts to the local scene. These groups have been mentioned above in connection with the reform movement.[5] Examples of them include the Citizens League of Pawtucket, the Richmond Civic Association, the Municipal League of Spokane, the Cleveland Citizens League, the Citizens Union of New York City, Citizens Action of Grand Rapids, the New Boston Committee, the Worcester Citizens Plan "E" Association, and the Hartford Citizens Charter Committee.[6] While many of these groups date back to the reform era, new ones continue to be formed, just as old ones become inactive.

In general these groups lobby for the lowest possible taxes and the greatest possible value from each tax dollar. They often seek to promulgate the basic aims of the reform movement, such as the council-manager plan, a professional civil service, performance budgeting, municipal home rule, nonpartisan elections, and sometimes proportional representation.

[4] F. J. Sorauf, "The Public Interest Reconsidered," *Journal of Politics*, vol. 19 (November, 1957), pp. 616–639. Quotation from p. 638. See also Glendon A. Schubert, Jr., "The Public Interest in Administrative Decision-making," *American Political Science Review*, vol. 51 (June, 1957), pp. 346–368. E. P. Herring, *Public Administration and the Public Interest* (McGraw-Hill Book Company, Inc., New York, 1936). The way in which administrators view the public interest is discussed below, chap. 13.

[5] See above, pp. 82–83.

[6] The activities of good-government groups are reported in the "Citizen Action" section of each issue of the *National Civic Review*. The *Review* does an excellent job of collecting and reporting municipal-government activities that are otherwise not readily available outside of each immediate locality.

They are interested in "good government" as such, usually with no immediate personal benefits expected except in the belief that the changes they advocate will save taxpayer dollars. Some members belong to these groups as something of a hobby, while others consider it to be a civic obligation. The groups often work in close cooperation with municipal research bureaus (such as the Citizens' Research Bureau of Milwaukee, the St. Louis Governmental Research Institute, and the Cleveland Bureau of Governmental Research).

Because these groups are interested in keeping taxes low through keeping city expenses down, they often find themselves arraigned against labor unions in struggles for higher pay for city employees, the extension of old services, the assumption of responsibility for new services by the city, or a change or increase in the city tax structure. While these groups were considered "progressive" and forward-looking forty years ago during the reform movement, quite a few of them are today aligned with the largest taxpayers on the side of conservatism. Others, however, continue to be primarily interested in studying municipal issues and advancing rational attitudes toward them.

These "leagues" and "unions" often follow the practice of making recommendations concerning initiative and referendum propositions at each election and of endorsing a slate of candidates on a nonpartisan or bipartisan basis. These recommendations receive much newspaper publicity in many cities, including New York, Chicago, and Detroit, for the groups often enjoy the open support of at least some of the newspapers. The effect of these endorsements varies greatly, however, depending upon the degree of political organization, local traditions, and many other factors. The Detroit Citizens League is far more effective, for example, than the Municipal Voters League of Chicago. Some groups, such as the Seattle Municipal League, do not make recommendations for voting, but do give their opinions as to whether or not each candidate is qualified for the office he seeks.

Related to the above type of group are various other middle-class clubs and endeavors. Women's clubs, particularly the League of Women Voters, often work for good government per se. The League prepares a voter-information sheet in many cities. Being strictly nonpartisan, the League usually has a prepared set of questions on current issues which it submits to candidates. The questions are generally not "loaded" (the League *does* sometimes endorse certain policies—for example, perhaps, the council-manager plan, or a four-year term for elective officials), and the answers are printed verbatim (unless, of course, the candidate gets carried away too far). The Parent-Teachers Association (PTA) is also a powerful pressure group, much more interested in the affairs of the school board, of course, but where its interests overlap with those of the city, the PTA may be found lobbying before the council, or before the voters if a referendum is involved.

Improvement Associations. In many cities virtually every neighborhood shopping area has an association for the safeguarding and furthering of the interests of the businessmen operating in that community. Likewise, in many sections of the city, similar groups will be found for the various residential subdivisions. These groups serve many purposes. If the city is growing or shrinking in size, they fight to keep property values high. If the city or neighborhood is losing population, the slackening of demand for homes demands diligence in order to save as much as possible of the homeowners' investment. If the city is increasing in size, older neighborhoods are constantly undergoing transition in character. In this case the association fights—usually without ultimate success if there is real demand for space—to keep Jews or Negroes or Mexicans or some other socially unwanted group out of the area.

These groups often appear before the council or administrative officers of the city, for they have almost countless bases for making such contacts. They are interested in every proposed rezoning of the area, since this has a direct effect upon property values. They do not want commercial or industrial areas nearby, they want the factory eight blocks upwind to stop making all that smoke and noise, they want more stop signs in the neighborhood ("Trucks are using our street for a through street"), they want the chuckholes repaired immediately (though this must not result in a tax increase), they want the squad car to drive past the house more often at night (but "Look at all the money the police want to run that lousy department for next year!"), and they want only single-family dwellings in the neighborhood if such has been the previous character of the area.

The improvement associations also serve other functions. Americans seek to lessen insecurity by joining together with others who feel as they do, and the neighborhood civic association gives the individual another club to add to his list. There are also offices to be filled, and Americans like to be presidents or vice-presidents of almost anything. They will appoint a committee at the first excuse, and neighborhood associations present a multitude of reasons for appointing committees: to "investigate the situation of 81st Street," or to "see the police chief." The associations also help to satisfy the urban dweller's longing to restore the primary relationships characteristic of the small town and rural community, for most of these groups are limited to a fairly small, truly neighborly area. If the group is made up primarily of homeowners, as a suburban group is, or if it is a businessmen's association, the organization also affords an opportunity to identify oneself more closely with these socially honorific classes. Members of neighborhood associations are fond of talking about the rights and responsibilities of homeowners and taxpayers, while members of a businessmen's group remind one another that they are indeed businessmen and hence the mainstays of the American economy. In fulfilling these psychological needs for prestige, the improvement associations, like many other pressure groups, serve a useful social function beyond that of exerting political pressure alone.

Taxpayers Groups. As something of a cross between the good-government groups and the business groups in the community, there are often organized "taxpayers leagues" of one title or another. In general they stand for lower taxes and fewer government activities and services and have their support in the more conservative business community—the large taxpayers. They often publish propaganda based upon either real or pseudo research on taxation, budgeting, and borrowing policies. Their membership is normally not large, and their influence on government varies greatly from place to place. Some of these groups have broader interests, more in the nature of the good-government groups.

Business Groups. There are so many business groups exerting pressure upon government that they would probably overshadow and overpower all of the others if it were not that they spend so much of their time opposing one another. There is an organization equipped to lobby for every business interest in the city. To name only some of them: there is often an association of downtown merchants, representing the owners, or in a large city probably the managers, of the large, usually retail, stores downtown. That these people would have numerous interests is obvious. They pay much of the general property tax of the city and so have an interest in tax rates; they want ample parking spaces, paid for, if possible, from taxes and not from their own pockets; they want superhighways that will bring people downtown to shop and will discourage the development of competing neighborhood shopping areas.

The small businessman, especially in the village or small city, sees his gross income as fairly fixed. His prospects for expansion are poor. For this reason, he thinks in terms of cutting costs, and sees taxes as one of his fixed costs. To him, additional taxes will not produce commensurate benefits, but will only diminish his possible profits. He becomes, therefore, a supporter of a low-tax ideology.[7] In middle- and large-sized cities, the more prosperous, expansion-minded merchants of the central business district are likely to be advocates of boosterism—and of tax levies to support its aims of a bigger and better city—but the neighborhood small businessmen are likely to have views similar to those of the village mer-

[7] See A. J. Vidich and Joseph Bensman, *Small Town in Mass Society* (Princeton University Press, Princeton, N.J., 1958), chap. 5.

chant and to see the large downtown businessmen with their ideas of constant growth as a threat.

The large retailers have political problems, too. They must constantly be on the alert against all kinds of threats to their profits, many of which the ordinary citizen would not even think of as being political in character. For example, the mighty and prestigeful Fifth Avenue Association of New York City once took a large advertisement in the *New York Times* in order to urge the mayor to veto an ordinance which would permit a Loyalty Day parade on a regular business day. The city council was anxious to oblige the veterans groups, but the great shops along the Avenue pointed out that this particular expression of patriotism would cost them 1 million dollars in sales.[8]

The downtown merchants and property owners are of tremendous influence both in determining the outcome of elections and in setting policy afterward. In middle-sized cities without political machines they are often the dominant group, and even in large cities, they wield great power. In Detroit and Los Angeles, for example, their influence is pervasive, although it is kept unpublicized and *sub rosa* by choice.

If a political machine exists, these groups must use a somewhat different approach. The traditional arrangement, as it exists in Chicago, is described by John Gunther: [9]

Recently I asked an eminent Chicagoan what ran the city, and he answered "State Street and the Irish." The great merchants in the Loop have great influence, together with their allies such as the packers. . . . What the State Street oligarchy tries to stand for is civic and social leadership. The tycoons live in subdued beautiful estates along the Lake Shore or on the "Gold Coast" in town; it is they who sponsor such manifestations of civic energy as the Chicago Planning Commission and the like; their impregnable inner citadel is the Commercial Club. The Irish meantime, the most articulate of the great immigrant bodies that grew up under the layer of oligarchs, allied with other racial [and ethnic] groups, run the city politically. There is a kind of unspoken, unwritten deal. "We let the Irish have the government, if they let us do what we please," is one way I heard it put.

General Business Groups. The chamber of commerce is interested at the local level, as at the state and national, in tax rates, labor legislation, and other matters that affect business activity and costs. In quite a few cities, the chamber serves as the principal spokesman for business before the council and city officials. Often it acts in lieu of a downtown property association and exerts the same type of pressure.

[8] *The New York Times,* Apr. 22, 1958, p. 11.
[9] John Gunther, *Inside U.S.A.* (Harper & Brothers, New York, 1947), p. 372. By permission of Harper & Brothers.

The so-called "service clubs," the Rotarians, Lions, and Kiwanians, are basically for businessmen, but their interests are not primarily political and they are not likely to act in this capacity, except perhaps in connection with a summer playground program or some such community service project.

Banks. Banks and related financial institutions are important pressure groups for several reasons. In the first place, they are businesses and have the interests of the businessmen. In the second place, bankers being among the most respected of all businessmen, their views are likely to be taken into the bosom of other businessmen, who then present them as their own. Furthermore, because the banker decides who is to be able to borrow money and under what conditions, he may in dozens of subtle or open ways influence the thinking, or at least the behavior, of other businessmen. Thirdly, bankers have a direct stake in local legislation affecting public utilities, in which banks have a pecuniary interest, and in bond issues and sinking funds, since banks act as brokers in servicing these. Banks are also interested in public policies that may affect businesses to which they have loaned money; hence they are interested in such matters as business regulation, taxation, zoning, and housing.

Utilities. Public utility companies in a great majority of cities are today dependent upon a state body for determining rates and service, but they also have many local interests. They must guard against movements to place their utility under public ownership, they are often dependent upon the good will of the city administration in order to extend or restrict the area covered by their services; and since the city is responsible for the public safety, the city's interpretation of what is safe or adequate equipment is of vital interest.

Contractors. The city has the power of inspection over all sorts of construction. The building, plumbing, lighting, and other codes are hence of great interest to contractors, as is the manner in which these are enforced.

Businessmen who are particularly desirous of procuring public contracts are, of course, unusually interested in the political scene. Some businesses, such as road-grading and -surfacing companies, depend for most of their work upon public contracts, and they can be expected to seek to do their utmost to influence both elections and policy decisions.

Taxicabs. Taxicab owners (and their drivers' unions) also play an important role in municipal politics. The city council normally determines the number of taxi licenses to be issued and decides the question of who is to get them. The council can thus make or break any given company. Furthermore, both the owners and the drivers are interested in *restricting* the number of licenses below that of actual need—so that they may charge monopoly rates. The driver and his union are just as interested in keeping down competition as is the company itself.

In almost every American city, taxicab rates are high (especially if one includes the tip, which is really a hidden portion of the charge) and the number of cabs available is greatly restricted. This is a direct result of pressure-group activity upon the council and is a good illustration of the council acting in the interest of the organized few rather than the unorganized many.

Taxicab companies, and often their drivers, find it necessary to pick candidates and support them in municipal campaigns. Those who bet on the winning candidates will have the lion's share of the licenses for the next term of office, while those who are wrong will get the crumbs. Taxicab companies also seek ordinances against "jitneys" and strict enforcement of these ordinances.

The Professions. Professional organizations have a stake in government. Some of them, such as medical and dental groups, are more important as lobbyists before state and national governments, but others, and particularly the city or county bar association, are also active locally. The bar association is interested in city government for a variety of reasons. Lawyers make up a large portion of the candidates for public office and are likely to view this field as a private hunting ground. Lawyers and their organizations look upon themselves as singularly responsible for guarding the law and its traditions. They are particularly concerned over the modern tendency to use administrative tribunals rather than law courts in the settlement of many public matters, since the former need not always be made up of lawyers and do not necessarily use the traditional processes of the courts of law. Lawyers, furthermore, often consider themselves to be trained in the problems of public policy formulation and peculiarly qualified to comment upon them, even though the law is not a social science and most lawyers have had very little training in sociology, economics, psychology, or even political science.

Real Estate Groups. The local real estate board and other similar groups have a special interest in local government. The city zoning ordinance and building code are of the greatest interest to them; the city tax rate is important, since the general property tax is the major source of city revenue; the cost of paving streets is a factor in the selling of homes; public housing is anathema to them. Builders and real estate speculators are often among the most influential groups before a city government, and this is particularly true in suburban areas in a period of expansive home building. A builder may often contribute to the campaign funds of *all* candidates for office in a modest-sized suburb, especially if he is of the large, assembly-line type of "project" builder. There are often conflicts before the city council between project builders and improvement associations representing subdivisions of individually built homes and also between homeowners and large real estate companies interested in the development of commercial and industrial properties.

Liquor Interests. Time was, around the turn of the century, when the two most powerful pressure groups in most cities were the public utilities and the liquor interests. Since the turn of the century there has been a considerable decline in the power of the liquor and beer industry. Prior to prohibition, licensing of beer and liquor stores was largely a local function, making the interests of these occupations in city government obvious. Of course, there was also the question of the attitude the local police would take toward laws dealing with closing hours, selling to minors, selling on Sunday, engaging in such socially disapproved but financially profitable side lines as the narcotics trade and prostitution, and the like. During prohibition, the liquor industry continued (with public approval) quite unabated. In order to do so, it was necessary to buy off local governments whose officials were in a position to work an easy shakedown racket. Bootleggers in many instances virtually captured whole city governments, even in very large cities, as when the infamous Capone gang dominated Chicago in the twenties. Today liquor interests are less powerful in most cities, but they still exercise considerable influence, especially where the law and local mores are not in accord. The policing of the liquor industry, now largely in the hands of state government, has relieved city officials of some of the problems and temptations that existed before prohibition.

Illegal Occupations. The gambling, prostitution, and narcotics businesses are almost everywhere illegal, but they operate to some degree in most of our larger cities, as well as in many smaller places. They may be beset by peace officers from all three levels of government, but they persist because they are profitable; and they are profitable because of the highly inelastic character of the demand for their services. Because they are illegal, they must be particularly concerned with politics. Where they cannot purchase protection, they must seek to establish a pale wherein their operations are allowed by either tacit or explicit arrangement. Failing this, or as a preferable substitute, they may seek to operate in a suburb if the core-city administration is especially hostile. The narcotics trade is probably the least thriving of these businesses, for, despite the cruel cravings suffered by the drug addict that will make him go to any extreme in order to obtain supplies, Federal government officers have ruthlessly sought to exterminate the trade, usually, although not always, with the cooperation of state and local peace officers. On the other hand, gambling and prostitution are likely to be with us for some time to come.

Newspapers. As has often been pointed out, newspapers tend to be conservative influences in the community because big business is conservative and newspaper publishing, at least of the city dailies, is big business. It is also true that newspapers which are middle-of-the-road or responsibly conservative on national and international questions may well become much more conservative or even reactionary on matters of local politics. A daily which recognizes that labor unions are here to stay when discussing national labor law may speak of unions in the same terms it might have used in the nineteenth century when speaking of them in connection with local politics. Physical proximity and the immediacy of the economic interest involved may be factors in producing this phenomenon. There is the further consideration that businessmen are dependent on the city government for all types of permits, licenses, favors, and sympathies in order to operate freely and successfully. A government controlled by labor or by unsympathetic liberals is a frightening specter to most businessmen and hence to newspaper editors.

Newspapers often work together with good-government groups and give them much free publicity. They may even print their press releases on the front page as news stories and not mention that it is partisan propaganda of an interest group. In many cities, newspapers have been important forces in achieving honest, efficient, and modern government.

Reasons for the Importance of Newspapers. The over-all effect of the opinion of a newspaper editorial board would probably not be great if the publication's effect were limited to its editorial opinions. Probably only a tiny percentage of newspaper readers pay any attention to the editorials, and those who do for the most part agree with them already. Yet a newspaper can be very influential in a dozen different ways. It can influence individual opinion by playing up or burying an item; by distorting the relative importance of the various facts involved in a story; by choice of location of the story; by choice of adjectives and adverbs; by phrasing of headlines; by its use of cartoons (picture editorials that reach far more people than do the ordinary ones). A newspaper that would not permit the "loading" of a story on a national matter may make its stories during a local election into veritable editorials. It may play up the speeches and pictures of Candidate Twitingham and bury those of Candidate Torkelson on page 37. Individual newspapers vary greatly in their use of these available weapons. Some seek to give balanced attention to all events. Others, for example, the Hearst newspapers, normally pay relatively little attention to local issues, being more concerned with the national and international scene. A locally owned newspaper is more likely to play up local issues (and to take sides) than is one that is chain-owned or one whose editorial policy is determined by a person who lives elsewhere.

In many cities, especially large ones, limited-circulation weekly newspapers may be of more influence in elections than are the large down-town dailies. These newspapers are usually aimed at a definite clientele: residents of a suburb or of a neighborhood area in the core city, foreign-language-reading members of an ethnic group, members of a labor union, Negroes, Catholics, or Jews. Since they emphasize the interests of par-ticular groups, they are able to call specific candidates or issues to the attention of the voter and to discuss them in terms of his interests.

The suburban and neighborhood newspapers are especially influential since they are not viewed as "commercial" or "partisan." Because they reflect the interests and values of the neighborhood, they are thought of rather as agents of "community welfare and progress." [10]

Radio and TV. Radio and television are important media in large cities for reaching voters and people to be propagandized over local issues. In the days before television, radio was not too successful for conveying ideas concerning local matters. People would listen to the President, but not to the mayor, and almost certainly not to a local labor leader or the president of the local chamber of commerce, unless the issue were of the most unusual importance. There is reason to believe, however, that television, with a hypnotic quality lacking in radio, is able to catch the eye and thought of citizens where radio failed. Radio and television managers seldom attempt to influence voting or council-manic decisions.

Organized Labor. Probably no event in the last thirty or more years is likely to have so great an effect upon the future pattern of urban govern-ment as the coming to power of organized labor. Especially important as a long-range factor was the rise after 1937 of the Congress of Industrial Organizations (CIO) with its organization of the unskilled and semi-skilled workers and its fresh supply of imaginative, able, and ambitious leaders. The full effect of organized labor as a political-action group has not yet been felt, partly because the leaders have so far not succeeded in persuading the members to support the union position in local politics. While the leaders deliver the votes quite well on national and even state matters where they can convince members that they have a real and immediate stake, there has been less success in convincing them that local politics is of equal importance to the labor movement. Progress is undoubtedly being made in this direction, however, and this is why the political activities of organized labor seem to be destined to change the picture of municipal politics in the future.

At the present time, however, "unions have a long way to go before they achieve a community position equal to that of older and better

[10] Morris Janowitz, *The Community Press in an Urban Setting* (The Free Press, Glencoe, Ill., 1952).

established groups."[11] To date, they have not been willing to devote a major share of their political-action funds to the local level. In addition, labor efforts to win local elections are quickly criticized as "partisan" and "aimed at the advantage of a small minority" in the conservative press. This makes the task the more difficult.

Labor groups have always had some effect upon urban politics in the largest cities, but the coming of the CIO with its definite social philosophy made a great difference. The older craft unions of the AFL were interested primarily in what is called "business unionism"—the highest possible wages, best possible working conditions, shortest possible hours. Few of them, however, had developed a social philosophy. The AFL sought essentially to achieve a monopoly of skilled labor and to make its members better and more prosperous members of the middle class. The CIO, on the other hand, sought to inculcate into its members the idea that the working class has a set of interests to pursue that are different from those of the business-oriented middle class. It is therefore to be expected that they would seek to challenge the business community for control of city government. After the merger of the two great unions into the AFL-CIO in 1955 and the establishment of a political arm—the Committee on Political Education (COPE)—the CIO philosophy of political action came to dominate the new organization and vigorous action in municipal politics was made a part of its program.

The Goals of Labor. Organized labor has a whole list of wants it desires from government, and a large number of them result in a conflict with other interest groups. Labor expects that the many services it demands be financed on an ability-to-pay theory of taxation, rather than on a benefit theory. This brings labor into conflict with those who are expected to foot the bill. Labor is more interested in services than in the tax rate. Many workingmen feel that the burden of the general property tax is of no concern to them because they do not own homes. This assumption is, of course, fallacious, since the renter pays the property tax as part of his rent. It does, however, affect his attitude.

The considerable increase in the rate of ownership of homes by members of the working classes since the end of World War II as a result of liberal financing provisions of the Veterans Administration and the Federal Housing Authority is likely to change this attitude in time. Many workingmen, especially in the skilled trades, have today become mem-

[11] For a case study of one union local (of the United Steel Workers) in one city (probably Gary), see Joel Seidman, Jack London, and Bernard Karsh, "Political Consciousness of a Local Union," *Public Opinion Quarterly*, vol. 15 (Winter, 1952), pp. 692–702. The quotation is from this study. See also William Form, "Organized Labor's Place in the Community Power Structure," *Industrial and Labor Relations Review*, vol. 12 (July, 1959), pp. 526–539.

bers of a new middle class of suburbanites quite different from the traditional pattern. They are sometimes called the "blue-collar" class. While these people tend to be Democratic in state and national politics, they are likely to assume the conservative characteristics of homeowners on the local level.

Labor is also interested in such things as a subsidized public transportation system in contrast to the businessman's views on a pay-as-you-ride system, preferably privately owned. It wants public housing with low rentals, perhaps an FEPC ordinance, and high wages for city employees, all of which is likely to run it into various conflicts with business, good-government, and other middle-class groups. Labor also wants to control the city administration, if possible, partly in order to ensure a sympathetic police force in the event of strikes or other labor disturbances. It well remembers the time, not long ago, when the local police department was often considered available to any manufacturer for strike-breaking purposes.

The flight to the suburbs, led by members of the middle class, is changing the role of organized labor in core cities. In a larger and larger number of them, labor will elect mayors and a majority of the council in future years; in many it already does so. Labor is also serving a special role as the social institution that is bringing together members of various ethnic groups for unified action. In the Ohio steel-manufacturing city of Lorain, for example, the multiplicity of ethnic groups had long produced mutual jealousy and suspicion which prevented effective political action. As a result, middle-class residents controlled the town, though they were a small minority. After 1937 and the unionization of the steel mills, the United Steel Workers of America succeeded in bringing the ethnic groups together by superimposing a sense of labor identity upon the ethnic sense that had long prevailed. The result was political control of the community by the combined groups.[12]

Racial and Ethnic Groups. Although there is no logic from a theoretical standpoint in having democratic representation on the basis of racial or ethnic groups and no particular reason why such groups should be separated from one another in such a manner as to require them to act as pressure groups, such is nonetheless the case. Minority groups find that they are beleaguered and feel the need to protect themselves from further encroachment by an unsympathetic dominant group in society. Negroes, Jews, Mexican-Americans, and sometimes Poles, Italians, or Irish groups find that by banding together they can seek protection in the law.

Minority groups are interested in such things as FEPC, the protection

[12] James B. McKee, "Status and Power in the Industrial Community," *American Journal of Sociology,* vol. 58 (January, 1953), pp. 364–370.

of their equal right to civil-service jobs, equal police protection and treatment, and a fair share of housing. Minorities often vote in blocs in political campaigns, resulting in such situations as that in New York where the mayor, the controller, and the president of the council must always be of different ethnic or racial groups. For a well-balanced city-wide ticket, there must be an Italian, an Irishman, and a Jew, while a fourth important position could well be found for a Negro. A similar recognition of political realities may be found in many cities where identifiable groups are important.

For pressure purposes, there are many organizations for these people. Negroes, for example, will be represented at council hearings by the National Association for the Advancement of Colored People as well as by the local Urban League. The NAACP has been more active politically than has the League, which has been interested mainly in making more jobs, more economic opportunities, available to Negroes. Both are potent organizations, especially in large cities, even though they cannot by any means claim to speak for all Negroes.

Religious Groups. Virtually all religious and church-related organizations represent political forces. Perhaps the only exception would be those sects that are opposed to political action. Since a religion—any religion—is based upon some kind of faith or set of beliefs, it is to be expected that political and social questions will be interpreted in the light of these moral-value scales and viewpoints taken in accord with them.

In almost any important councilmanic hearing, ministers, priests, rabbis, or leaders of religious lay groups will be found testifying for their members. Because Catholics tend to be concentrated in cities and because the Church is disciplined and dogmatic, its views are often particularly powerful and effective. The Church has dozens of lay organizations that act as pressure groups. Protestants are less well organized, but may be equally active, especially through local ministerial associations. Methodist groups may work for a policy of restricting the number of retail liquor permits; Quakers may be interested in the humane treatment of prisoners in the local workhouse; a group of ministers may lobby for an FEPC ordinance.

Ministerial associations may be interested in matters related to public health, welfare, housing, and other matters. They are especially likely to be concerned with public policies relative to vice, race tracks, liquor sales, and juvenile delinquency. In Underwood's "Paper City," Catholic priests were concerned about policies that affected the parochial schools, religious practices in public schools, public health clinics if they provided birth-control information, gambling, and problems related to excessive drinking. The politicians, he found, "tend to look upon either

Roman Catholic or Protestant moral interests chiefly as those of one more organized group to be anticipated, managed, and met." [13]

Municipal Employees. Employees themselves are organized into pressure groups and can exert influence on the administration and council for matters that interest them, particularly wages, hours, and conditions of labor. Because many employees belong to labor unions that have close association with the other AFL and CIO unions of the city, they are in a position to bring up reinforcements from these other unions at important times.

There are professional organizations such as the International City Managers' Association, the Civil Service Assembly of the United States and Canada, and the American Society of Municipal Engineers. Others are regular labor unions, affiliated with the AFL-CIO. Purely local unions commonly exist, either because they are old, respected, and powerful, or because other types of unions are discouraged by local public policy. Examples include the Milwaukee Government Service League and the Detroit Police Officers Association.

In some cities, the municipal employees band together for political action, seeking to eliminate from the council members who will not support their demands regarding wages, hours, and conditions of labor. If they have the aid of the regular labor unions of the city, and if other organized political activity is not strong, municipal-employee unions may even succeed in electing a slate of councilmen that constitutes a majority of the council. [14]

Veterans. After each war, veterans—at least many of them—organize themselves into interest groups. They are particularly powerful because, unlike ordinary groups, they have no organized opposition, no counter-pressure group. It is not easy for a politician or another pressure group to oppose the interests and demands of a well-known veterans' group. In local politics, returned servicemen are interested in such things as tax exemptions, civil service preferences on job certification, "patriotism," taxicab licensing, and all other types of licensing with an eye toward privileges for veterans.

The largest and most powerful veterans' groups on the local as well as the national scene are the American Legion and the Veterans of Foreign Wars, both of which have members who served in the two world wars and in the Korean conflict. Products of World War II, such as the Amvets and the AVC, are smaller and less powerful. There are also groups that

[13] For more on churches and local politics, see K. W. Underwood, *Protestant and Catholic* (The Beacon Press, Boston, 1957), especially chaps. 18–20. Quotation is from pp. 319–320.

[14] For one example, see city Delta in Oliver P. Williams and Charles R. Adrian, *Fighting City Hall: A Comparative Study of Politics in Four Middle-sized Cities.* (Forthcoming monograph.)

represent two special interests simultaneously, such as the Catholic War Veterans
and the Jewish War Veterans.

THE POWER STRUCTURE AND
GROUP LEADERSHIP

"In all societies," a famous sociologist
once wrote, "two classes of people appear—
a class that rules and a class that is ruled.
The first class, always the less numerous,
performs all political functions, monopolizes
power and enjoys the advantage that power
brings, whereas the second, the more numerous class, is directed and controlled by
the first." [15]

Today, social scientists know that political organization is not so simple as all that.
The ruled do not accept uncritically the orders of a ruling class, at least not all of the
time. Group leadership is actually as vari-
egated, complex, and filled with cross cur-
rents as are the interactions of the groups
to which the leaders belong. The notion
that the exercise of power is a conspiracy

Figure 5-2. SOURCE: Drawing
by D. Fradon; © 1959 The
New Yorker Magazine, Inc.

against the common people is still to be found in some writings,[16] but it
is probably much more realistic to view political power as a tool of social
organization rather than a weapon of oppression.

To talk of "power relationships" is not to imply sinister evil-doing.
The term does not contain any value implications. The possession of power
—the ability to manipulate social institutions toward desired goals—is
vested in individuals and groups in society because, in practical terms,
power is necessary to perform the vital function of establishing and maintaining an ordered society. The particular type of political structure or
process through which social order is achieved is determined by the
values which are dominant in a particular society at a particular time.
Whether the exercise of power by specific individuals or groups is good or

[15] Hannah D. Kahn (trans.), Gaetano Mosca's *The Ruling Class* (McGraw-Hill
Book Company, Inc., New York, 1939), chap. 2.

[16] C. Wright Mills, *The Power Elite* (Oxford University Press, New York, 1956),
is an example, although Mills denies using a conspiracy theory. An implicit conspiracy hypothesis seems to underlie the work in Floyd Hunter, *Community Power
Structure* (University of North Carolina Press, Chapel Hill, N.C., 1953), and some
other writings in the field.

bad, therefore, is decided by the citizenry on the basis of whether or not individual actions are in accord or discord with the values of the society.[17]

The Power Structure. Not enough is as yet known about those who are discovered in studies to be the "leaders" of the community. It is possible, for example, that persons who appear to be policy leaders, even to the extent of seemingly dominating the decisions of those holding public office, are really only verbalizers. That is, they merely say, as symbolic leaders of the community, the things that are already widely believed in the community. If this is the case, the same policies might have resulted whether or not these persons had taken any action in seeking to have policies developed. Leading bankers, merchants, realtors, and chamber of commerce secretaries are certain, in small towns or middle-sized cities, to have their remarks given considerable publicity through newspapers, radio, and television and may thus seem to be real leaders. Merchant princes and bankers are sometimes listened to because they are natural leaders or because of the deference they receive as a result of their prestigeful positions. But their preferences as to public policy may be forestalled, for example, by implacable resistance from workingmen responding to a labor leader. This leader's own status position will probably be a modest one, and his technique not one of oppressive coercion but merely of pointing out to the union membership the consequences for them of a proposed line of action.

Yet leadership is an intrinsic part of group existence, and leaders make decisions. Furthermore, group action generates power. Those who take a positive interest in any problem are likely to have a considerable advantage over those who are passive and apathetic. And, of course, those who feel they have the most at stake are also likely to be the ones who become the most active in political decision making.

If leadership were absolute, there would probably be consensus and little community conflict—only a disgruntled few would resist. In most cases, however, leaders have to do more than to make a decision and launch a selling campaign. They must overcome opposition from competing leaders. A small amount of knowledge and drive—with a purpose—can sometimes project a relatively low-status person into a leadership position. He finds power in the community unused and seeks to ex-

---

[17] See Robert S. Lynd, "Power in American Society as Resource and Problem," in Arthur Kornhauser (ed.), *Problems of Power in American Democracy* (Wayne State University Press, Detroit, 1957), pp. 1–45; and Talcott Parsons, *Structure and Process in Modern Societies* (The Free Press, Glencoe, Ill., 1960), chap. 6. A good bibliography of power structure studies may be found in R. O. Schulze and L. U. Blumberg, "The Determination of Local Power Elites," *American Journal of Sociology,* vol. 63 (November, 1957), pp. 290–296, and P. Wasserman and F. S. Silander, *Decision-making: An Annotated Bibliography* (Graduate School of Business and Public Administration, Cornell University, Ithaca, N.Y., 1958).

ploit it. When he does so, his action spurs dominant leaders into counter-attack. A conflict ensues that may not only get out of control for the initiators of action, but may bring back memories of countless old (and often irrelevant) conflicts from the community's past.[18]

The following points might be kept in mind in regard to the political power structure as it exists or is supposed to exist:

1. Some economically powerful leaders, in particular the managers and top executives of local plants of nationwide corporations, may refuse to become involved in community activities of any kind not directly affecting the company, lest enemies are unnecessarily made. Thus some of the persons who, because of great economic power, might be expected to be important decision makers exert little or no influence on decisions regarding community public policy.[19] Heads of locally owned firms, on the other hand, are likely to be both active and powerful locally.[20]

2. Power structures may not necessarily be constructed in the shape of pyramids, although some studies have found such shapes.[21] It is quite possible to have power structures that do not lead to a few top leaders but instead have a polynucleated structure with various leaders, each of whom is powerful in some particular area of public policy but not in all such areas. In other words, there may be functional specialization, so that a man who is very influential in deciding questions dealing with, say, traffic-flow patterns, may have much less to say about housing policies and may not be consulted at all relative to the introduction of a new recreation program.

3. Some studies show that there are a few people who are very much interested in, and influential over, virtually all important decisions made in regard to public policy. These are the top members of the power elite. It is possible, even probable, that no such small clique of general leaders exists in the largest cities [22] simply because of the great complexity

---

[18] See J. S. Coleman, *Community Conflict* (The Free Press, Glencoe, Ill., 1957).

[19] See Peter H. Rossi, "Community Decision-making," *Administrative Science Quarterly*, vol. 1 (March, 1957), pp. 415–443; R. O. Schulze, *Economic Dominance and Public Leadership* (University Microfilms, Ann Arbor, Mich., 1956); R. O. Schulze, "The Role of Economic Dominants in Community Power Structure," *American Sociological Review*, vol. 23 (February, 1958), pp. 3–9; H. M. Scoble, "Leadership Hierarchies and Political Issues in a New England Town," in M. Janowitz (ed.), *Community Political Systems* (The Free Press, Glencoe, Ill., 1959). Middle, as distinguished from top, management is likely to be active, however, especially in the suburbs, according to William H. Whyte, Jr., *The Organization Man* (Simon and Schuster, Inc., New York, 1956). The activities of these men are less likely to be interpreted as official company policy.

[20] See city Alpha in Williams and Adrian, *op. cit.*, as an example.

[21] See the Mills and Hunter studies cited above.

[22] See, for example, Martin Meyerson and E. C. Banfield, *Politics, Planning and the Public Interest* (The Free Press, Glencoe, Ill., 1955), which is a case study of public housing policy formulation in Chicago in the years following World War II, or Long, *op. cit.*, on Boston.

of social organization that exists in such large governmental units. In such cities, the leaders in various areas of community policy making seek their own goals, with imperfect coordination of their efforts with those of other leaders seeking other goals. Communication—keeping other leaders and the public informed—becomes increasingly imperfect as the size of community increases. To the public, interest groups, as such, become more visible than the individual leaders as the size of the city increases.

4. Policy leadership should not be confused with policy invention. The studies made so far tend to show that leaders need not themselves be creative in finding solutions to social needs. Their job is to assess proposals as to their degree of adequacy as solutions and then to push for the adoption of those found most acceptable. New ideas in meeting problems are most likely to come from persons with exceptional technical knowledge of a particular subject, persons who may be in the bureaucracies of private business, government, the universities or elsewhere. Their names are commonly little known to the general public and sometimes even to the person who serves as symbolic leader for the promotion of the ideas they have put forth. Thus, when the headlines read "Banker Lauded in Presenting New Parking Plan" or "Mayor Torkelson Announces Plan to Renew Business District," the prestigeful persons mentioned in the stories are merely playing out their particular social roles. The anonymous men who actually thought up the plans in the first place will probably not even be mentioned in the story.[23]

5. Governmental officials may once have been tools of the economic leadership group, but they are becoming increasingly important centers of power in their own right; and this is especially true as government plays an ever greater role in the lives of citizens.[24] In earlier times, government was simple and performed few functions. With business institutions overwhelmingly important by comparison, business leaders sometimes used officeholders as their front men. This is less likely to happen today, and many important community leaders now themselves become councilmen and mayors. Local politicians today generate demand, mobilize support, and otherwise serve as leaders, as power centers.

6. The top members of the power structure may be powerful because they come from high-status families to whom deference has always been paid by other residents of the community or because they are newspaper editors. But they are most likely to be powerful because they are spokesmen for interest groups and have ability to bring some of the weight of the group to bear upon political institutions. One's place in the power structure reflects, except perhaps in small cities and towns where individ-

[23] See Peter H. Clark, *The Businessman as a Civic Leader* (The Free Press, Glencoe, Ill., 1960).

[24] See Parsons, *op. cit.,* on this point.

uality remains especially important, the relative over-all strength of the group for whom the leader is a spokesman.

Case Study: A Large Southern City. The local officials in a Southern city of about a half million people (perhaps Atlanta) were found to be the pawns of the principal policy makers in the community. A very few men made the important decisions on behalf of the whole community, and a few hundred carried them out. The top men conferred by telephone or by meeting in the home of one of the members of the group. After they reached a decision, the word was passed down to the next lower level of the pyramid for action—or inaction. In the study, no Negroes and no labor leaders were included in the inner circle, although they were growing in importance. All of the top decision makers were also the top leaders in the business community. Their power was greatest in relation to city government and grew progressively less at the higher levels of government.[25]

Case Study: A Small Oregon Town. In a small Oregon community of about 1,700 people, two political scientists found that the degree of political participation and leadership depended upon such things as the status position of the individual in a community where he was well known, upon his own perception of his duty to the community, and upon his awareness of the consequences of public policy for himself, his family, and their friends. The top leaders had in their minds an image of what the town should be like, and their behavior in decision making seemed to be conditioned by that image.

Three men were identified as being most influential in the community, and they were consulted in connection with every major decision made by either the city council or the school board. In many ways, this group resembled the top leaders in the Atlanta study, except that they operated on a far more modest level in the economic world and they were opposed to the booster spirit found in Atlanta and commonly associated with chambers of commerce throughout the country. A key paragraph in the study describes them as follows: [26]

The top trio of leaders shared a belief that the "good community" was a relatively small, semi-rural community of Jeffersonian virtues. To them business was a service function and not primarily a means to wealth. Their perspective

[25] Floyd Hunter, *Community Power Structure: A Study of Decision-makers* (University of North Carolina Press, Chapel Hill, N.C., 1953). The reading of this should perhaps be followed by that of an incisive criticism: Herbert Kaufman and Victor Jones, "The Mystery of Power," *Public Administration Review,* vol. 14 (Summer, 1954), pp. 205–212.

[26] Vincent Ostrom and R. E. Agger, "The Comparative Study of Politics in Local Communities" (Paper presented to the American Political Science Association meeting, 1955). See also R. E. Agger and Vincent Ostrom, "The Political Structure of a Small Community," *Public Opinion Quarterly,* vol. 20 (Spring, 1956), pp. 81–89. Used by permission.

was conservative but certainly not reactionary. They were not dedicated to freezing the status quo, but were almost scientific in their assessment of long-range, indirect consequences of policies with an interest in making as sure as possible that a policy change was either necessary to bridge an existing "cultural lag" or to take care of some "unanticipated consequences." They were aware of changes in the state and nation; they had better communication channels with the "outside world" than anyone else in the community. They accepted, even if they did not sympathize with, "inevitable" social forces.

Under the top leaders was a pyramidal power structure with the second echelon highly aware of the power of the leaders, but themselves important and active. Below them was a set of categories of persons of declining influence and activity. Slightly over one-half of the community consisted of nonparticipants who not only were inactive in policy making but who had a low record of voter participation. These people in general ranked below those higher in the power structure in terms of education and income. They paid little attention to the local newspaper, did not identify themselves strongly with the community, and were the least able to identify the top-power trio or, for that matter, anyone who was influential in policy making.

Case Study: A Middle-sized Midwestern City. In a Midwestern city of about fifty thousand people, it was found that a group of six or eight persons were the most influential in local policy making and that these individuals exerted general leadership, while those in the power structure beneath them tended much more to specialize by concentrating on certain types of problems (e.g., schools, traffic control). There was no unified leadership group as was reported in Atlanta, however, and different individuals were influential depending upon whether the problem dealt with local, state, or national levels of government. The holding of prestigeful positions in government, business, or industry rather than character or personality traits seemed to be the most important determinant of leadership, although such traits might, of course, have much to do with the reasons why the individual achieved the particular position which, in turn, gave him influence in government.

This study also reached the noteworthy conclusion that persons inactive in community affairs tend to point to *formal* leaders as people who are "most important" while persons active in community policy making name *informal* leaders more often.[27]

Case Study: A Monster Metropolis. Chicago is one of the ten largest cities in the world. It is so large and complex in its political, economic, and social structure that we could expect communication to be very

[27] See George Belknap and Ralph Smuckler, "Political Power Relations in a Midwest City," *Public Opinion Quarterly,* vol. 20 (Spring, 1956), pp. 73–80.

difficult, even among persons who in other communities would be extremely powerful and in close communication with one another. With so many important and powerful people we might expect there would be difficulty in fitting them into any kind of pyramidal structure of relative power. A case study dealing with the resolution of a public housing controversy in that city indicated that the above assumptions were valid and that, while some individuals had far more influence than others, they tended to specialize within a fairly narrow but complex field of interest. There were no over-all general leaders who had a veto over all basic issues of policy, and groups interacting upon one another seemed to be more important in the settlement of controversy than were conference and compromise among individual leaders.[28]

Public Awareness of the Political Power Structure. In both the small-town and middle-sized city cases mentioned above, there was evidence that many citizens were not aware of the identity of the most influential persons in the community when it came to policy leadership. The extent of this specific problem was inquired into in a study made in Detroit. (Keep in mind that the small Oregon town referred to above contained many people who could not identify the informal leaders—possibly size is not too important a factor in relation to this matter.)

Before answers are given to the question: Who runs Detroit? it should be pointed out that Detroit city government has been dominated almost without interruption from the time of World War I by the businessmen of the community, members of the board of commerce, the downtown merchants, and the real estate groups in particular. This is accomplished through a community of interests with the daily newspapers, whose control of the principal means of local communication is all-important in a system of nonpartisan elections. Detroit political parties are weak, and there are no political bosses in the traditional sense. The labor unions, despite the huge membership of the United Automobile Workers, have been weak in local politics. Jews and Negroes have had little representation in either the legislative or the administrative branch of city government. (The first Negro was elected to the council in 1957.) Organized racketeering has not been influential in Detroit government for many years.

The answers to the question: Who runs Detroit? were classified as follows: [29]

[28] See Meyerson and Banfield, *op. cit.*, especially p. 115, ftn. For a similar picture in Boston, see Long, *op. cit.*

[29] Arthur Kornhauser, *Attitudes of Detroit People toward Detroit* (Wayne State University Press, Detroit, 1952), pp. 13–15. This is a summary of a longer, more technical study, *Detroit as the People See It* (Wayne State University Press, Detroit, 1952). By permission of the Wayne State University Press.

Answer	*Per cent*
No special group: "the public," don't know, etc.	42
Special groups named:	
Businessmen, industrialists, the rich	18
Labor unions, organized labor	11
Politicians, political bosses	11
Jews	6
Negroes	5
Racketeers, gamblers, underworld	2
Others	5
Total	58

The survey showed interesting variations of response among different population groups. The better educated were most convinced that special groups "really run the city." Only 30 per cent of those who went beyond high school named no groups that had most influence, while 50 per cent of people with eighth-grade education or less named no particular groups. High school and college graduates and the upper socioeconomic groups almost never named Jews or Negroes. It is significant that the more education a person had, the more likely it was that he would be able to name the influential groups. Although this particular survey did not attempt to measure the ability of respondents to name specific individual leaders, it does give some idea of the relative ability of citizens in a large city to assess the actual power relationships that exist as against the tendency that exists in some personality types to ascribe power to those who are distrusted or feared.

Closing Statement. In this chapter, the concepts of power and of the intergroup political process have been introduced. Both are important parts in the drama of community decision making, and they will reappear in the later chapters on functions of government.

Chapter 6

URBAN POLITICAL ORGANIZATION

Basic election machinery was described in Chapter 4, pressure groups and power structure in Chapter 5. The task of putting the pieces together remains for this chapter.

At one time in American history, the political process in the city would have had to be explained in terms of the boss and the machine. Today that is no longer the case. This chapter will therefore briefly describe the cause of decline of bossism and then examine the political process that has replaced it.

THE CITY BOSS AND MACHINE: A PASSING PHENOMENON

The Function of the Boss and Machine. In American folklore, in newspaper editorials, in magazine articles, in political campaigns, and in suburban gossip, it has been all too common to picture the nineteenth-century city boss and machine as if they were a contemporary phenomenon. It is not uncommon even today to hear the phrase "boss-ridden cities." Actually, the boss and machine performed a necessary social function in their day, but they have outlived their usefulness and have been disappearing from the American scene. William Marcy Tweed of New York, "Ed" Flynn of the Bronx, "Big Bill" Thompson of Chicago, "Doc" Ames of Minneapolis, "Abe" Ruef of San Francisco, and a host of others have left the front pages of the newspapers and are taking their place in the history books, where they will become a romantic, if not exactly an honored, memory.[1]

There is probably no need to describe in detail the method of operation of the old-time machine. A few points should be made concerning it, however.

In the first place, the machine did not exist *in spite of* society. It existed because it filled a real need. It served as a highly effective, if inefficient, system of social welfare. To the poor in the slums of cities, the

[1] See Suggested Readings at the end of this book for a bibliography on bosses and machines in various cities.

machine provided needed services: it found jobs, or tided the family over during periods of unemployment; it buried the dead; it cared for widows and orphans; it organized youth activities; it provided a multitude of neighborhood social functions; it contributed to the churches of poor neighborhoods; it provided bail bonds and legal advice; it furnished assistance in finding housing and tried to help tenants talk their landlords out of rent increases. It provided literally hundreds of services, the need for which was not recognized by a callous society.

Secondly, the machine was a product of universal suffrage, perhaps its first important manifestation. The services provided were offered in the expectation that the recipients would cast their ballots in support of the machine. If the ordinary worker in the slum had not been enfranchised, as he was in the 1830s and 1840s, the pattern of urban politics during the remainder of the nineteenth century would have been quite different from what it was.

Thirdly, the machine raised the great amounts of money that were needed for the services it provided (and often for the personal profit of its leaders) by acting as a broker for the city's services. It raised most of its money from businessmen and industrialists; and owing to the then current belief that it was cheaper to buy off the machine than to fight it, the business community often worked hand in glove with the machine.

The organization raised its money in a great variety of ways. It made available, for a price, building permits, all types of licenses, utilities franchises, and ordinances that might be helpful to a business. Sometimes it resorted to simple blackmail, or the shakedown racket. Much money was made through contract rebates. Contracts were granted to a firm that was working closely with the machine with the understanding that part of the profit would be returned to the machine. Municipal employees were very commonly assessed part of their pay, and other funds could be raised by the purchase of land by inside members of the organization for resale to the city. It was this type of profiteering that was made famous as "honest graft" by George Washington Plunkitt of Tammany Hall. It was Plunkitt who stated the code of the more sincere organization worker when he said, "If my worst enemy was given the job of writin' my epitaph when I'm gone, he couldn't do more than write 'George W. Plunkitt. He Seen His Opportunities, and He Took 'Em'" [2] (see Figure 6-1).

The Decline of Bossism. Opportunities, as seen by Plunkitt, began to fade away as the effects of the reform movement came to be felt. The decline of the boss and machine began to accelerate after World War II in particular, and by 1950 the boss and machine in almost every American

[2] See the fascinating profile by W. L. Riordon, *Plunkitt of Tammany Hall* (Doubleday & Company, Inc., New York, 1905).

city had been either destroyed, badly mangled, or profoundly modified in its pattern of behavior.

There were many reasons for this. Since World War I, there has been a steady decline in the percentage of foreign-born in American cities, and it had been to the needs of this group that machines had particularly appealed. Negroes and other rural-to-urban migrants likewise became less subject to machine control after they became more sophisticated in urban ways. Another factor was the high employment after 1940, which allowed large numbers of people to escape the extreme poverty that had forced them to be partly dependent upon the machine.

The general adoption of the officially printed, secret ballot made it more difficult for the machine to stuff ballot boxes, falsify election returns, or conduct other election frauds. Lincoln Steffens tells us that the voting lists of Philadelphia at the turn of the century were padded "with the names of dead dogs, children and non-existent persons." Success in such practices has become increasingly difficult in recent years. Yet it

IT'S A BUSINESS LIKE ANYTHING ELSE
—Boss Pendergast.

Figure 6-1. SOURCE: By permission of Daniel R. Fitzpatrick and the *St. Louis Post-Dispatch.*

was not so very many years ago—in 1936—that the *St. Louis Post-Dispatch* won a Pulitzer Prize for uncovering 45,000 false registrations in that city. Charges that the candidate of the party or faction not in power has been "counted out" in close election contests because the in-group controlled the election machinery continue to be heard today, and it is reasonable to expect that not all of them are unfounded.

The reform movement in general damaged machine government by helping to arouse potential members of opposition groups and by rallying businessmen to fight the machine instead of buying it off. The stabilizing of the population of some of the older cities in the nation has helped produce a sense of identification with the city in its inhabitants. A stable population, one with a low physical-mobility rate, helps to develop a civic pride and political awareness that does great damage to machine control. The rise to power of organized labor has upset the traditional balance of control in many cities and has caused a shift in loyalty of the worker from the machine and its leadership to the trade union and its leadership.

Lastly, and perhaps of greatest importance, a modern and professionalized approach to the problems of social welfare has taken away from the political machine its principal means for achieving loyalty and support. The development of government control of such functions as workmen's compensation, unemployment compensation, old-age pension, and old-age insurance, and their administration by professionally trained civil servants rather than by political hacks, proved a mortal wound to the old-time machine.

Machines in Decay. Beginning with the reform movement around the turn of the century, an entire procession of machine defeats has paraded across the front pages of the newspapers of the nation. The one-time organizations in St. Louis, Minneapolis, and San Francisco are long dead. The once-powerful Republican machine in Cincinnati was defeated and permanently modified by reform efforts in the elections of 1924 and those that followed. The castle of Thomas J. Pendergast and his Democratic machine in Kansas City came crashing down in 1939 and today lies in ruins, nearly if not quite entirely destroyed.[3] Tammany Hall in New York has been losing ground since the 1932 Seabury investigation of the "Jimmie" Walker administration. It was greatly weakened during the long period when its enemy, Fiorello H. La Guardia, served as mayor.[4] Tammany has undergone considerable modification and today, despite the fact that reformers still denounce it in each campaign, operates with a far more modern concept of politics than it did in former years.

[3] Miniature portraits of some of the more recent city machines are painted in John Gunther, *Inside U.S.A.* (Harper & Brothers, New York, 1947).

[4] See the views of La Guardia in his article "Bosses Are Bunk," *The Atlantic Monthly*, vol. 180 (July, 1947), pp. 21–24. On New York, see Wallace S. Sayre and Herbert Kaufman, *Governing New York City* (Russell Sage Foundation, New York, 1960).

By the time of the coming World War II, bosses and machines were thoroughly outmoded. Nearly all of those that remained were liquidated during the period of postwar readjustment. The Republican machine of Philadelphia, which had enjoyed uninterrupted control of that city since shortly after the War between the States, lost important ground in the election of 1949 and was thoroughly routed in 1951, when it lost control of the mayor's office and of a majority of the council to a reform Democratic group.[5] The old Democratic Kelly-Nash machine, now under Mayor Richard J. Daley, still held control of the city of Chicago in 1961. Despite much criticism from many sources and a serious scandal in the police department in 1959, the Kelly-Nash organization is regarded as having brought Chicago politics closer to prevailing urban patterns in the years after World War II.

James Michael Curley of Boston long ruled that city by building up a Robin Hood legend about himself. He was known as a builder of schools, a provider of jobs, and a man who got things done. He was strongly supported by the great bulk of the minority ethnic groups in the city. He was so effective in personal contacts that as recently as 1945, 10 per cent of his supporters claimed to know him *personally*.[6] Yet in 1949 a reform group, called the New Boston Committee, defeated him, elected a mayor, and took control of the council. In the next election, Curley again lost.

In 1940, Dayton D. McKean wrote that the Hague machine in Jersey City "is so nearly perfect that other machines may be measured against it."[7] Yet Hague's candidate was defeated in 1950 and in succeeding elections, although the destruction of his machine did not signal the rise of a reform administration, as happened in many other cities. In Memphis, Edward H. Crump managed to keep an effective machine together until his death in 1954. But like so many who exercise power for a long time, he had made no adequate provision for a successor, and in the following year his heirs were not even able to field a candidate for mayor.

There can be no doubt that the nineteenth-century machine system has outlived its usefulness. Some of its techniques are being adopted by

[5] See James Reichley, *The Art of Government: Reform and Organization Politics in Philadelphia* (The Fund for the Republic, New York, 1959); Joseph D. Crumlish, *A City Finds Itself: The Philadelphia Home Rule Charter Movement* (Wayne State University Press, Detroit, Mich., 1959).

[6] J. S. Bruner and S. J. Korchin, "The Boss and the Vote," *Public Opinion Quarterly*, vol. 10 (Spring, 1946), pp. 1–23. See also J. M. Curley, *I'd Do It Again* (Prentice-Hall, Inc., Englewood Cliffs, N.J., 1957); Joseph Dinneen, *The Purple Shamrock* (W. W. Norton & Company, New York, 1949); and a fictionalized life of a Curley-like boss, Edward O'Connor, *The Last Hurrah* (Little, Brown & Company, Boston, 1956).

[7] D. D. McKean, *The Boss: The Hague Machine in Action* (Houghton Mifflin Company, Boston, 1940).

a few men and organizations of a new type of middle-class, twentieth-century development such as is discussed below in connection with the political structure of Dearborn, Michigan. Most American cities today, however, are based upon quite a different pattern of politics, characterized by an informal, loose political structure and with primary importance being placed, in large cities, upon control of the media of communication. This pattern is explained below.

TWO CASE STUDIES

The Depression Years: Kelly-Nash in Chicago.[8] Chicago proper had a population of 3,492,945 (by the 1960 census), yet it received its first charter, as a village, only in 1833. In a century and a quarter it has grown from sand dunes and prairie to the second largest city in the nation and one of the largest in the world. Its rapid growth has made it a natural target for machine rule and corruption. Even so, it has not, as popular belief would have it, always been one of the worst-ruled cities in the United States. As a matter of fact, during the periods of worst corruption in American cities, Chicago was relatively restrained and its government was far more effective and honest than that of most large cities. Under the two Carter H. Harrisons, Chicago had capable administration.[9] It has been since 1915 that it has most often blackened its own eyes.

"Big Bill" Thompson: Republican. While most Americans probably think of Chicago as a stronghold of Democratic strength, the colorful William Hale ("Big Bill") Thompson, who was mayor from 1915 to 1923 and again from 1927 until the Depression-year election of 1931, was a Republican. As a matter of fact, throughout the twentieth century, both major parties in Chicago have been divided into factions, and the

[8] The best sources on Chicago are C. E. Merriam, *Chicago: A More Intimate View of Urban Politics* (The Macmillan Company, New York, 1929); H. F. Gosnell, *Machine Politics: Chicago Model* (University of Chicago Press, Chicago, 1937); Lloyd Wendt and Herman Kogan, *Big Bill of Chicago* (The Bobbs-Merrill Company, Indianapolis, 1953); an entertaining, although essentially hostile, panorama painted by one of America's greatest reporters, A. J. Liebling, *Chicago: The Second City* (Alfred A. Knopf, Inc., New York, 1952); Gunther, *op. cit.*, chap. 23; Martin Meyerson and E. C. Banfield, *Politics, Planning and the Public Interest* (The Free Press, Glencoe, Ill., 1955); "Challenge for a Machine," *Life*, Feb. 21, 1955, pp. 53 ff.; and J. B. Martin, "Who Really Runs Chicago?" *The Saturday Evening Post*, Nov. 19 and Nov. 26, 1955.

[9] See C. O. Johnson, *Carter H. Harrison I, Political Leader* (University of Chicago Press, Chicago, 1928); and for the son, Carter H. Harrison, *Stormy Years: The Autobiography of Carter H. Harrison, Five Times Mayor of Chicago* (The Bobbs-Merrill Company, Indianapolis, 1935). The elder Harrison was mayor from 1879 to 1887 and for a few months in 1893; the younger, from 1897 to 1903 and from 1911 to 1915.

political picture has been made up most of the time of constantly changing alliances, with little regard to party membership.

It was under Thompson that Chicago descended into a "saturnalia of corruption, more disgraceful, if possible, than any that had preceded it. In this new outburst of municipal greed almost nothing escaped, beginning with the plunder of the schools [which most bosses were wise enough to avoid] and extending to almost all branches of the municipal service." [10]

Thompson had an organization "resting upon patronage and spoils, and flanked by the support of predatory business interests, with open defiance of the press and the independents. . . . The utility interests centering around Samuel Insull became the chief [financial] bulwark of the later flowering of the Thompson group." [11]

Thompson was born into wealth and social position. Unlike many politicians who had not chosen their parents with equal care, he had little interest in graft for personal gain. As Gosnell puts it, "He liked the game and the crowds." [12] He clowned before the public while his henchmen pillaged the city. He was a genius at showmanship. He campaigned to make Chicago the "wettest city in the country"; he believed in "America first" and campaigned against King George, Marshal Joffre, and the League of Nations. He would use such stunts as that of bringing two rats on the stage and carrying on a "conversation" with them, calling them by the names of his political opponents, or bringing his "opponent" on the stage in the form of a bridled donkey. The voters of the roaring twenties loved him. He had color and, behind him, Insull's money. Never before had people been more cheerfully plundered.

But Insull's pyramided empire of utility holding companies collapsed, an honest state's attorney began to bring indictments against some Thompson men, and the Great Depression brought on everywhere a demand for a change.

The Depression and Cermak. It was through these circumstances that the Democrats were able to build a political machine, after the greatest day of that social phenomenon had passed elsewhere, more powerful than any the city had previously known. They were not too well organized when the great day came. Roger Sullivan, the old-time boss, had passed the mantle on to George Brennan, but his death in 1928 had left the party temporarily leaderless and with a threatened struggle for

[10] Merriam, *op. cit.*, p. 22. Merriam, late University of Chicago professor of political science, was once a city alderman and, in 1911, was nearly elected mayor. This and the following quotation by permission of the Charles E. Merriam estate.

[11] *Ibid.*, pp. 185–186. Thompson was mayor during the heyday of the notorious "Scarface Al" Capone, and some of Thompson's lieutenants were friends of Capone and his gang.

[12] Gosnell, *op. cit.*, p. 11.

control. Leadership, and the successful 1931 mayoralty choice, passed, however, to the Czech-born president of the County Board of Supervisors, Anton J. Cermak.

Cermak had the social philosophy of a businessman and of an organization politician. In the 1931 campaign he did not talk about ameliorating the distress of the unemployed, but concentrated on promises for reducing the city budget and saving taxpayer money. Thompson replied with the accusation that "Saving Tony . . . saved six million out of a $10,000 salary" while on the County Board.[13]

Not only was Cermak lacking in a social philosophy with which to meet the city's Depression problems, but he quickly got into bad odor with Franklin D. Roosevelt and with James A. Farley, who became chairman of the Democratic National Committee, when he backed Alfred E. Smith for the 1932 Democratic presidential nomination. It was in February, 1933, that he went to Miami in order to talk over with Roosevelt the unhappy prospect of federal patronage control in Illinois being turned over to another Democrat. While he was conversing with the President-elect an assassin aimed his pistol at Roosevelt. The aim was bad and Cermak fell with a fatal wound.

Kelly and Nash: Democrats. Control of the organization now passed to the chairman of the Cook County Democratic Committee, aging Patrick A. Nash, who preferred to run things from the background. He had the Illinois General Assembly pass legislation permitting the city council to name the new mayor. The council, at Nash's "suggestion," named Edward J. Kelly, president of the South Park Board and chief engineer of the Chicago Sanitary District. Kelly was a personal friend of Colonel Robert R. McCormick, publisher of the *Chicago Tribune* (who had disliked Republican "Big Bill" Thompson), he was a trusted friend of Nash, and he was favorably known to many of Chicago's businessmen. He had the good wishes of the press and the general public.[14]

How did the Kelly-Nash machine operate in the depths of a pervasive depression? Gosnell tells us: [15]

Seven years of depression in the city of Chicago [he wrote in 1936] have made practically no changes in the fundamental character of party organization, methods and leadership. It is true that the fortunes of individual politicians and parties have been greatly altered, but the party system has remained about the same. The party which controlled only a minority of the local offices when the financial crash came was greatly benefited by its connection with the new national administration, but it did not change its outlook. *Jobs and spoils were the currency of Chicago politics in 1936 as well as in 1928, and not*

[13] *Ibid.,* pp. 13–14.
[14] *Ibid.,* pp. 15–16.
[15] *Ibid.,* pp. 24–26. Italics added. By permission of the University of Chicago Press.

issues which concerned the functions of municipal government in times of great economic stresses and strains.

The political bosses who found themselves in power in the great metropolis of the Middle West in the 'thirties were, for the most part, self-made men. Chicago, in contrast to New York, has been a center abounding in self-made men—industrialists, grain merchants, large department-store owners, and real estate speculators. . . . The self-made politicians understood the self-made business men, as they talked the same language. While the sources of revenue available for local governmental purposes were greatly reduced, the politicians were able to use what there was to consolidate their positions. They said, in effect, to the business men: "You leave us alone and we will leave you alone." *The economic crisis in Chicago was met not by the local governments but by the national government.* . . .

Economic hardships undoubtedly created feelings of discontent which might have been used to bring about political changes, but the city lacked the kind of leadership which was necessary to guide the inarticulate demands of the masses. The new Tammany which was created on the ruins of its opponents' machines was led by men who were thoroughly in sympathy with the philosophy of big business. The conservative political outlook of the political, industrial, and financial leaders and a lack of local constitutional powers prevented the city government from becoming a major instrumentality of the citizens in meeting their problems during the crisis.

The political machine had failed to meet the needs of modern society.

Mid-century Style: Hubbard in Dearborn.[16] Politics, to Orville L. Hubbard, is public relations. It is one long publicity stunt. It is neither graft nor corruption, nor is it service to the underprivileged or personal profit. For Hubbard represents a new, mid-twentieth-century style of political leader. He symbolizes the modern successor to the old boss and machine: the political leader of the middle-class suburbanite. Just as the old boss is moribund, so the new system of Hubbard or of J. Russel Sprague in Nassau County, Long Island, is in the ascendant.

The Suburb. Dearborn, Michigan (1960 population: 112,007), is a southwestern suburb of Detroit. With the exception of one slum area immediately adjacent to the mammoth River Rouge plant of the Ford Motor Company, it is made up of lower- and upper-middle-class residents, with several very expensive neighborhoods. It consists of single-family dwellings for the most part, although there are some expensive apartment buildings of the type known in the Detroit area as "terraces." Over 80 per cent of the families living in Dearborn are homeowners. The population of the city has grown rapidly during and since World War II.

[16] This section is based in large part upon personal interviews and observations by the author. Two newspaper feature serials are helpful: *The Detroit Free Press,* Nov. 16–17, 1949; *The Detroit News,* Apr. 17–19, 1950. See also *Time,* Aug. 21, 1950, and E. E. Malkin, "Dearborn's Madcap Mayor," *Coronet,* vol. 44 (September, 1958), pp. 66–70.

In 1941, three important things happened in Dearborn, things which were subsequently intertwined and confused in the minds of many of the voters. In the first place, the Ford Motor Company was unionized that year by the UAW after a long and at times bloody fight. In the second place, a grand-jury investigation uncovered officially the already well-known fact that Dearborn was a wide-open town for gambling and prostitution with little or no interference from the police, and the city was cleaned up. In the third place, Orville L. Hubbard, who had been a perennial candidate since 1933, was elected mayor. By 1960, he had been elected to his tenth consecutive term and had survived, in addition, a 1950 recall attempt. Almost from the beginning he has been called a "boss" or "dictator" by his many opponents. He is hated by many, yet he wins elections easily. How does he do it?

The Middle-class Appeal. Hubbard does not have a machine in the traditional sense. He has almost no patronage appointments. There are no ward or precinct organizations. Nor does he have the support of the regular party organizations, for Dearborn has a nonpartisan city ballot. Instead he depends upon personal contacts, professional public relations activities, municipal services of good quality, and trouble-shooting department heads. Each department head is assigned a district within the city. He is expected to cover that area constantly, looking for things to be done, anticipating complaints of residents, keeping the service departments on the alert.

Hubbard is aware of the continuing value of some of the techniques of the old-time machines. The personal touch is a good vote getter, he knows, and sometimes he will appear in person at the home of a complainer to say that the problem has been taken care of—and to the satisfaction of the resident, he hopes. He knows that the propaganda technique of *transfer* is especially useful in connection with religious activities. Hubbard attends many different churches within the city. Can he help it if the members of each congregation receive the impression that he is a member? Under his administration the city has erected two signs for each church in the city in locations selected by the pastor and pointing toward the church. Municipal parking lots are located with a mind to their use for free Sunday church parking.

Dearborn has some of the best municipal services in the Detroit metropolitan area. It is a policy of Hubbard to start at least one new service before each election. In 1953 sidewalk snow removal and sweeping was introduced—a service that is otherwise available only in the expensive Grosse Pointe suburbs. Camp Dearborn, a "private country club" for Dearborn residents and their guests only, was established in 1949.[17]

---

[17] It has lakes, over 500 acres of timber, picnic areas, camping areas, a trout brook, a large beach, 100 aluminum rowboats usable without charge, but no canoes—a drown-

Under Hubbard a "tot lot" has been established in every subdivision. He has provided for dozens of baseball diamonds, ice-skating rinks, hockey rinks, fireworks displays on the Fourth of July and Labor Day, thousands of trees and shrubs, and hundreds of new street lights and street signs.

All of this costs a great deal of money, for these services are normally available only in "millionaires'" suburbs. How does he do this without being driven from office as a spendthrift? Hubbard is fortunate, for he is mayor of an unusual city. It is tremendously wealthy, with most of its wealth held not by the homeowners who get the superior services, but rather by industry. Something like two-thirds of the assessed valuation of the area is in industrial property, about one-half of it in the hands of the Ford interests alone. Only this makes the unusual services budgetarily possible, but Hubbard gives the credit to Hubbard.

Techniques of Appeal. Hubbard is a great campaigner, and he loves campaigning. His electoral support at the polls varies inversely with the income of the voter. In the slums of south Dearborn he gets nearly all of the votes; in the Springwells Park section, made up largely of Ford executives and engineers, he can expect to be defeated by as much as ten to one. His greatest support, numerically, comes from the lower middle class, and his campaign platform contains three *implicit* planks: better services for a cleaner Dearborn; a firm stand against the Ford interests; and a preservation of property values especially by keeping Negroes out of the city. The platform is aimed directly at the hopes and fears, the aspirations and the insecurities, of the lower-middle-class property owner. It has proved greatly effective.

The better services have already been explained. He has delivered on his promises. When he talks of keeping Dearborn "clean," he means not only that he will keep the garbage and rubbish cleaned up and the alleys free of dead dogs, but that the area will be "spiritually clean," for he will not tolerate organized gambling or prostitution. If a policeman seeks to line his pockets from this source, he ceases to be a policeman. Hubbard understands how to appeal to middle-class values.

The feud with the Ford company and family is largely window dressing, but with a symbolic purpose. Dearborn contains many skilled and some unskilled workers from the great River Rouge plant which dominates the life of the whole community. In the old days, before the plant was unionized, it was a common thing for the Dearborn police to be used for strikebreaking purposes and for the prevention of labor disturbances. Hubbard asserts that he is an "unbossed mayor," which in Dearborn means that he is independent of the Ford company, something unusual in the history of that city. Many who remember the earlier days

---

ing would cause bad publicity and a loss of votes. Buses haul children the 35 miles to the camp, where they can stay at a charge far less than cost.

count on him to keep the city government from becoming "annexed" once again. (The Ford Motor Company operates under an entirely different philosophy today from that of 1939 so far as labor relations are concerned, but fear is a convenient tool for the politician.) He finds many ways to badger the company and family, sometimes with resulting gifts to the city. Yet he named his youngest son Henry Ford Hubbard, and once when accused of driving Ford gifts out of the city and into Detroit, he ordered "Home Town of Henry Ford" printed on all city stationery.

There are no Negroes in Dearborn, and no Japanese-Americans have moved in while Hubbard has been mayor. In an industrial area with an ever increasing Negro population, the lower middle class tends to become obsessed with a fear of Negro invasion and of "lowering property values." Because this is so, some politicians in Detroit and many of its suburbs find it politically profitable to exploit this fear. Hubbard has found ways of using this gimmick effectively in irrelevant situations. In 1948, the John Hancock Mutual Life Insurance Company sought to build a multimillion-dollar private housing development in the city. There seemed to be no objection to the proposal until Hubbard decided to oppose it, probably on the theory that his stand would be popular with owners of single-family homes. Once he had spoken it became necessary for him to win, since a defeat on a major issue can be disastrous for any politician. He called upon the voters to defend themselves against "an invasion of renters." He called the expensive units a "bunch of row houses" and a "*public* housing project" (which it was not). He attacked the Ford interests for selling the land for the project to the insurance company. But his trump card was played on the day of the referendum. He sent his department heads around to the polling places, distributing cards bearing the injunction: "Keep the Negroes out of Dearborn. Vote against the John Hancock Housing Project." [18] That did it. There had never been any intention of renting the homes and apartments in the project to Negroes, but that did not matter—Hubbard had won. In his 1951 campaign for re-election, he emphasized that he had stopped a proposed Wayne County park from extending into Dearborn since it would have "attracted all types of undesirables." One of the greatest attractions of Camp Dearborn to prejudiced whites is that it, unlike other public parks, is not open to Negroes. If you ask a Hubbard man about the administration's Negro policy, he will explain that the city does nothing to keep anyone out. It just so happens that there are no homes for sale if a Negro wishes to buy.

Politics as Showmanship. Like many of the bosses of old, Hubbard is an expert in public relations and is an excellent judge of public opinion.

[18] *The Detroit News,* Apr. 19, 1950.

For sheer color and campaigning skill, he is on a par with "Big Bill" Thompson of Chicago of the twenties. He keeps a dossier of his contacts with every constituent. He thus not only knows who is indebted to him, but can also give his correspondence a personal touch. He sends a letter or makes a personal call whenever there is a birth, death, wedding, house fire, or the arrival of a new resident in Dearborn. He signs his name in green ink with a special pen and in letters up to an inch high. His name and picture appear almost everywhere in the city. He was at the station to say good-by to every Dearborn inductee during the war and was there to greet him on his return as a civilian. He created the Dearborn Navy during World War II to protect the city from the German submarine menace. (When city employees began to use the boats for pleasure cruises, the navy was scuttled.) He takes the city directory with him on vacations and sends home hundreds of postcards to citizens—who are flattered by the mayor's thoughtfulness. He sees to it that some department head is a member of every club or organization of any size in the city. He himself belongs to as many as possible. (In the 1951 campaign he listed membership in twenty-five, including everything from the National Sojourners to the Michigan Academy of Science, Arts and Letters.) Like so many of his constituents, he started from the bottom of the social ladder, and, again like so many of them, he was born and raised on a farm before coming to the big city. (On this score, among many others, he differs from the traditional boss.) Like "Big Bill" Thompson, he is an expert at substituting irrelevancies for issues and in covering up embarrassing situations with confusion.

The final stage of an election campaign is completely professionalized. A meeting is likely to be held at Fordson High School, with a professional master of ceremonies, a professional show, and professional chorus girls. All of the good sign spots, parking places near voting booths, and auditoriums are taken up well in advance of the campaign and usually well in advance of the less alert opposition.

In 1945 a jealous council (often he elects enough members of his slate to control the council, but before the next election he is usually feuding with many of them) passed an ordinance prohibiting the mayor from talking business with his constituents either personally or by telephone. Through the newspapers he received national attention. After having milked the publicity possibilities dry, he had himself arrested for deliberately violating the ordinance (more publicity) and then had the whole thing declared unconstitutional. An embarrassed council repealed the ordinance.

In facing his enemies—and they are many—Hubbard can be as merciless as any old-time boss. His path is strewn with the political bodies of those who have opposed him. He will do whatever is necessary, his opponents say, to destroy a man whom he has turned against. He has triumphed over all opponents and has dismissed some of his department heads (including his own law partner) even though they had been instrumental in his own advancement. After the *Dearborn Press* turned against him, the publisher's personal property assessment was increased 50 per cent.[19] Hubbard's opponents do not think it a mere coincidence. They claim that other property assessments have taken sudden, unexplained dips and increases while Hubbard has been mayor. But there has been no graft or corruption. The worst charge that a one-man grand jury investigation into the Hubbard administration could levy was that after the 1950 tax assessments of a large Dearborn retail store were reduced by $120,000, Hubbard was offered and accepted a television set as a gift from the company.[20] But Hubbard, like many old-time bosses, has no interest in money. He wants power and publicity.

Interpretation. Hubbard seems to represent a new trend in urban political organization. He is a charismatic leader, appealing to the middle class of a metropolitan suburb with things they want to hear, in contrast to the older pattern of appeal to the working class in the slums of the core city; a leader with little interest in patronage or personal financial gain, but with a desire to give effective, professionalized services that the voters demand.

Allowing for local environmental and personality differences, this pattern is likely to become more and more in evidence. The Sprague Republican organization in Nassau County on Long Island is an efficient political machine. It receives its support from upper-middle-class New York commuters—businessmen, bankers, and lawyers. The county is organized with a county manager. J. Russel Sprague is both the manager and county Republican chairman. His department heads are also leaders in the machine. Sprague is a power in state politics and an ally of former Governor Thomas E. Dewey.

The Hubbard and Sprague organizations illustrate the adaptability of political institutions to changing environments. They and their kind will bear watching.[21]

THE MORE TYPICAL CITY

Cities without Machines. While a few cities have well-organized political machines which control the local government, others, especially large cities, tend to be controlled by pressure groups. Though organized

[19] *Time*, Aug. 21, 1950.

[20] Wayne County, Michigan, Circuit Court, Misc. 78616 (1953).

[21] Additional case studies may be found in R. S. Allen (ed.), *Our Fair City* (Vanguard Press, New York, 1947), which discusses seventeen cities.

labor is the largest of these, it is usually not this group, but the business community, which assumes control. If the downtown businessmen, the chamber of commerce, the real estate groups, and the newspapers can unite, they can normally control the city.

We have already seen that the big businessmen and manufacturers in the past often supported machines. Where there is no machine, they are likely to go along with the merchants or perhaps to ignore local politics in favor of the state and national scene. The motion-picture and aircraft industries do not dominate Los Angeles politics, for example. In fact, they have far less influence than do the large merchants. Contrary to what an outside observer might expect, the automobile industry does not control Detroit city government. In fact, it has almost nothing to do with it. (But in sharp contrast, the UAW is perhaps the dominant group in control of the Michigan Democratic party, while the automobile manufacturers tend to dominate the Michigan Republican party. Both groups look beyond city government for the protection of their positions in society.[22]

The Business Point of View. Wherever possible, and for the reasons discussed above,[23] businessmen seek to control nominations for the principal city offices. If the city has partisan elections but the party or parties are not organized effectively enough to be called a machine, business groups seek to back an acceptable candidate in the primary election in the party that is likely to win. Whether that party is Republican, Democratic, or a local party depends upon local circumstances. Sometimes they can get men with acceptable viewpoints nominated by all important parties.

If the city has nonpartisan elections, business groups (they do not always agree among themselves, however) seek out a likely person, or they choose one who has already entered the lists and back him. The principal opponent in either partisan or nonpartisan elections may be the candidate of another business group or, in an increasing number of cities, he may be the labor-backed candidate.[24]

The Rise of Labor. When the AFL was the only major organization of unions, it was either not active in local politics, or it tended to back business candidates and to participate in the political process in much the same way as another business pressure group, for the interests of its members did not differ much from those of the merchants and other businessmen. The rise of the CIO and more recently of the combined AFL-CIO, has made a great difference, however. The combined union

[22] Stephen B. Sarasohn and Vera H. Sarasohn, *Political Party Patterns in Michigan* (Wayne State University Press, Detroit, Mich., 1957).

[23] See pp. 128–130.

[24] For examples from four cities, see Oliver P. Williams and Charles R. Adrian, *Fighting City Hall.* (Forthcoming monograph.)

is more and more supporting policies sharply in contrast with those of the business community, although local leaders do not necessarily view local politics as a contest with management.[25]

The influence of the AFL-CIO and other unions that will join with it has not yet been fully felt. For several reasons, the union has not yet been greatly successful in selling its endorsees to the rank and file. The AFL-CIO and many of its member locals tend to look toward the larger units of government as the first areas to be conquered. Many union members have lived in the city where they are now located a comparatively short length of time and have not yet identified themselves closely with the community. There can be little question, however, but that the AFL-CIO is expanding its municipal area of political activity and that its increasing influence is changing and will continue to change the basic pattern of politics in large American cities.

Illustrations of Business-supported Mayors. The professional politician is sometimes supported by businessmen when he seeks city office, but businessmen often prefer, where practicable, to take one of their own kind. (Labor unions, in cities where they are strong enough, generally prefer a member of the union bureaucracy or a union attorney to a professional politician.)

Harley Knox of San Diego was the operator of a dairy business in the city until other businessmen drafted him for the city council in 1939.[26] In 1943 they were successful in putting him into the mayor's office, a position actually of president of council in a manager-type city. Roger D. Lapham of San Francisco was another business choice.[27] He was board chairman of the American-Hawaiian Steamship Company and had not run for public office until he was asked to run for mayor. Both of these cities have nonpartisan ballots. Since most large American cities are normally predominantly Democratic, while most non-Southern businessmen identify themselves with the Republican party, nonpartisanship is of considerable aid to large-city business groups in political action.

In Los Angeles, Fletcher Bowron became the choice of business and other reform forces to succeed Frank Shaw, who was recalled in 1938. (Shaw had been charged with running a wide-open town.) Bowron had been a Hearst reporter, secretary to the governor, and a superior court judge. He was sold to the public as "a decisive, aggressive, dynamic, politically courageous personality," [28] although much of his supposed

---

[25] W. H. Form and W. L. Sauer, "Organized Labor's Image of Community Power Structure," *Social Forces,* vol. 38 (May, 1960), pp. 332–341.

[26] See John Gunther, *Inside U.S.A.* (Harper & Brothers, New York, 1947), pp. 55–56.

[27] On Lapham, see pp. 114–116.

[28] Aldrich Blake, *You Wear the Big Shoe* (Privately printed, Los Angeles, 1945), p. 39.

character appears to have been manufactured by a public relations staff.

Bowron began to lose much of his business support after he backed a multimillion-dollar Federally aided public housing project and other business-disapproved policies. In May, 1953, Bowron tried for re-election depending upon his well-known name and the support of one newspaper and much of organized labor (because of his housing policy). His opponent, Congressman Norris Poulson, however, now commanded the support that mattered—the downtown merchants, the realty groups, the chamber of commerce, middle-class neighborhood improvement associations, and three of the newspapers. Poulson was able to defeat the man the business community had jettisoned.

These few sketches indicate the type of person who is likely to be elected mayor in a machineless city of medium or large size today. It should be noted that not one of the persons mentioned above has what politicians call "color." In fact, they are quite definitely colorless, in contrast to most machine mayors. Businessmen are not interested in color. They prefer a man with a fairly dependable business orientation, if possible with some business experience of his own, for that adds to his stability. These men are sturdy and honest, but they are not popular heroes.

THE POLITICS OF SUBURBIA

The Preservation of Property Values. The suburban movement of the years since World War I has produced a value pattern in which at least two things have been deified: conformity and property values. The suburbanite is nearly always a homeowner in a community where some of the primary relationships of the small town have been restored. Gossip is a factor in social control; contacts with people are likely to tend in the direction of meeting the whole person on a warm, personal basis; and politics is likely to revolve around property values, for the individual who holds title to property will, in local politics at least, tend to be conservative in his desire to protect his investment.

In a few suburbs organized labor is important, but not in most of them. Even the skilled machinist, die maker, or truck driver who graduates to the ranks of the "blue-collar class" is likely to be very conservative on local matters once he buys a suburban home, even though he may continue, for a time at least, to take labor's liberal view on state and national matters.

The Pattern of Suburban Politics. If the suburban community elects its officers on a partisan ballot, the Republican party will quite certainly dominate, for it is the party of middle-class respectability. We would find an exception, of course, in most Southern suburban communities.

Even though many suburban newcomers are, or recently were, Democrats, they will find themselves in the minority, and there will be great social pressure applied for them either to switch parties or at least to remain discreetly quiet. Women appear to succumb to this pressure even more readily than do their husbands. Suburban America is today the greatest stronghold of the Republican party.[29]

On the local scene, the national party may be well organized, with a disciplined group of active workers, as it is in Nassau County, New York. But it is much more likely, especially for local purposes, to be made up of a series of small cliques, like the pattern in suburbs having nonpartisan elections. These cliques may have a rapport established with the district and state organizations of a major party, or they may exist only to take part in local elections. They are made up, for the most part, of political amateurs who are in politics for a hobby or for prestige or, less frequently, for the sake of power and the ability to manipulate the process from behind the scenes. As in the core city, however, the vast majority of citizens are politically passive. This is the case even though, as David Reisman has suggested, we are entering upon a new era of leisure time in which suburban politics is becoming an avocation to be indulged in as we do golf or the amateur theater.

The women of suburbia, bored with dishes and diapers, are more likely than are the women of the core city to be active in the League of Women Voters and other women's clubs of varying degrees of political activity.[30] Neighborhood civic associations or city-wide community councils are particularly alive and of very considerable influence in community policy making. They frequently have lobbyists whose duty it is to represent the group at city or village council meetings and to report back to the group. Sometimes the associations endorse candidates in election campaigns. Local businessmen's groups are also important in the local political process.

Suburbia is especially the home of small political-action groups with such names as "The Taxpayers' Protective Association of Sequoia Grove," "The Azalea Park Citizens' League," and "The Nonpartisan Voters of Vertigo Heights." These are generally nothing more than small cliques which have assumed general (and often important- and neutral-sounding) names in an attempt to give their propaganda greater prestige and influence. They usually accept viewpoints on public policy that are already prominent in the community.

[29] See the comments of Stephen Mitchell as Chairman of the Democratic National Committee in *Time*, Oct. 26, 1953.

[30] The higher one's position on the class continuum, the greater one's participation in political and civic organizations. This is especially true of women. Mirra Komarovsky, "The Voluntary Associations of Urban Dwellers," *American Sociological Review*, vol. 11 (December, 1946), pp. 686–697; Carol Slater, "Class Differences in Definition of Role and Membership in Voluntary Associations among Urban Married Women," *American Journal of Sociology*, vol. 65 (May, 1960), pp. 616–619.

Issues in Suburban Politics. During an election campaign, the suburbanite will be assured by each politician in turn that the candidate is a "homeowner and taxpayer," or that he is a "local businessman." The voter will be urged to "elect candidates who will work for you and protect your property values."

There may be red-hot issues on preventing invasion by socially unwanted groups. There may be bitter debate over the question of whether to allow the development of industries within the community, and, if so, their proper location (which, so far as the individual voter is concerned, is usually on the opposite side of town from his home). There may be taking of sides on whether the community should become incorporated (a very common problem as the population increases in density), or whether a village should become a city, or whether the council-manager plan should be adopted in preference to the mayor-council. There is the question of how to solve the sewage-disposal problem, or the water-supply problem, or the problem of water in the basement every spring.

While violently fought campaigns may appear from time to time on such issues as the above, it is more likely that the platform of a slate of candidates for the city council in suburbia will look something like this:

THE ABOVE CANDIDATES ARE PLEDGED

1. Not to raise taxes. We believe that we can give you more services with no increase in taxes by achieving greater efficiency and economy.

2. To legislate only for the benefit of the entire community.

3. To protect your tax dollar through sound budgeting, controlled expenditures, and other scientific budgetary practices.

4. To protect homeowners' rights. We will insist upon strict and adequate zoning laws. There will be no duplexes, motels, or apartments illegally pushed on certain subdivisions. There will be no shanty towns and no faulty home construction below subdivision and zoning standards. We will oppose the rezoning of any residential area for light or heavy industrial use.

5. To provide adequate police protection for your home and your business and to ensure safety of school children.

6. To continue and enlarge your parks and recreation program.

7. To improve the condition of our neglected streets and to secure better and safer traffic control.

This, then, is the pattern of suburban politics. It may be a jumble of amateur politicians fighting for control and attention, or it may be an organization led by a strong leader such as J. Russel Sprague or Orville L. Hubbard, for the conditions exist for this type of system, too. Most of all, the suburbanite wants an "efficient," economical, honest, conservative government that gives him the services he wants, when he wants them, at less cost than he would have to pay in the core city.[31]

[31] See Robert C. Wood, *Suburbia* (Houghton Mifflin Company, Boston, 1959), chap. 5.

Chapter 7

THE LAW OF MUNICIPALITIES

Americans have a penchant for discussing problems of public policy in terms of constitutional law rather than in terms of public policy. This is particularly true in municipal affairs, for the legal position of the city is one of lowest priority: "The city is a political subdivision of the state, created as a convenient agency for the exercise of such of the governmental powers of the state as may be intrusted to it." [1]

May a city perform whatever functions a substantial proportion of its residents wants to have performed? Not at all. It may perform only those functions that the state legislature or the state courts allow it.

THE CITY AS A CORPORATION

The Problem of Sufficient Authority: A Case Study. Let us suppose that the city council wishes to eliminate a group of billboards that surround a city park. The council members believe that the billboards are destroying the natural beauty of the park and that people use the park in order to get away from the prosaic, hurried, commercialized world of everyday. The council has had numerous complaints about the billboards, and a majority of the members promised in their campaigns for election to vote them out of existence. Is this sufficient justification for council action? Certainly not.

Before any action can be taken effectively, these questions, and perhaps many more, might have to be answered: Does the city charter authorize regulation of billboards? And because the legal mind is razor-sharp and hence capable of splitting hairs, the further question, perhaps: Does the city charter authorize regulation of billboards *on the periphery of public parks?* If the city charter does authorize regulation, is there a contravening general act of the legislature? Is such regulation, in any case, *reasonable?* Would it somehow violate the state or Federal constitution? Would this particular regulation constitute, according to the

[1] *Trenton v. New Jersey,* 262 U.S. 182 (1923). This is the standard rule, and its substance may be found repeated in dozens of cases.

common law, an *abuse of discretion* by the council? And is the proposed ordinance for a *public purpose?* Before World War I, roughly speaking, regulation of billboards was considered by the courts an invasion of the rights of private property.[2] Then the courts began to allow regulation on the basis of the police power.[3]

In order for a city ordinance regulating billboards to be valid, it must be shown that such regulation is necessary to the safety and welfare of the people. The city must show that a rickety billboard might topple over on an unsuspecting pedestrian, or that a billboard might well be used as a place of ambush by a rapist, or that a billboard might serve to collect flammable newspapers and leaves.

It was not until 1935 that a high court was willing to allow regulation of billboards on a simple basis of aesthetics in the public interest. "Gran-deur and beauty of scenery," the Supreme Judicial Court of Massachusetts said, "contribute highly important factors to the public welfare." This concept, while gaining in recognition, has not become the generally accepted rule.[4] Note the skepticism of an Illinois judge: "Authorities in general agree to the essentials of a public health program, while the public view as to what is necessary for aesthetic progress greatly varies. Certain legislatures might consider that it was more important to culti-vate a taste for jazz than for Beethoven, for posters than for Rembrandt, and for limericks than for Keats. Successive city councils might never agree as to what the public needs from an aesthetic standpoint, and this fact makes the aesthetic standard impractical as a standard for use re-striction upon property." [5] The judge said, in effect, that he can deter-mine better than can the council the point at which the public interest becomes more important than the private interest.

If all the many questions that may be raised can be answered in a satisfactory manner, the city may, perhaps after paying expensive court costs, proceed with its drive to eliminate the offensive billboards. Such are the limitations of authority under which city government must operate.

[2] *Massachusetts v. Boston Advertising Company,* 188 Mass. 348 (1905); *New York ex rel. Wineburgh v. Murphy,* 195 N.Y. 126 (1909); and other cases. See also Illinois Legislative Council, *Regulation of Billboards* (State of Illinois, Springfield, Ill., 1953), pp. 17–20.

[3] The *police power* is usually defined as the power of the state to "protect the health, safety, and morals" of society. See *St. Louis Gunning Advertising Company v. St. Louis,* 235 Mo. 99 (1911) and nearly all subsequent cases where billboard regulation was upheld.

[4] *General Outdoor Advertising Company v. Massachusetts Department of Public Works,* 193 N.E. 799 (1935). A more recent supporting case is *Berman v. Parker,* 348 U.S. 26 (1954).

[5] *Forbes v. Hubbard,* 180 N.E. 767 (1932). In accord with this more common opinion, see *Youngstown v. Kahn Brothers Building Company,* 148 N.E. 842 (1925); and *Wondrak v. Kelley,* 195 N.E. 65 (1935).

The Nature of a Corporation.[6] The city, in lawyer's language, is a municipal corporation. A corporation, in turn, is an artificial *person* created by the state. In this sense, the city is something of a cross between the national or state governments on the one hand and the private corporation on the other. It differs from both, however. In theory, both the United States and the states are *sovereign*, or at least share sovereignty. A sovereign body is one possessing supreme temporal power, a state that owes allegiance to no one. Actually, of course, neither the United States nor any of the states possesses full and true sovereignty. The plenary powers of government are divided in a federal system in such a manner that the ancient concept becomes somewhat obscured. It is perfectly clear, however, that cities, villages, and other municipal corporations possess no sovereignty at all. They are children of the state, created usually by the action of the state legislature; and even in those states most dedicated to the principle of home rule, the *state* courts remain the final arbiters of what are local concerns.[7]

The municipality, like any other corporation, derives its powers from the state, and those powers granted to it are expressed in a *charter*. A charter is the fundamental law of a corporation which establishes (1) the structure or form of government, (2) the powers that may be exercised by it, and (3) the general manner in which the powers granted may be exercised. The charter is almost never a single document, but includes all state laws and judicial opinions that affect the structure, powers, or manner of exercising the powers of the corporation.

The city, in some respects, has a legal position not unlike that of a private corporation. In fact, it has been only in the last two centuries or so that a definite distinction has developed. The two are still similar in that each has an existence independent of the members of the corporation, may own property, may make contracts, may exist, normally, in perpetuity, and may sue and be sued. They possess very important differences, too. A private corporation is created entirely by the *voluntary* request of a group of people who wish to form a corporation. They know the corporation law in advance and hence know the conditions under which they will operate. Furthermore, once the corporation charter is granted it becomes a *contract* which cannot be altered or taken away (except under the rarest circumstances involving an overriding public

---

[6] The most current of the outstanding commentaries on municipal corporation law is Eugene McQuillin, *The Law of Municipal Corporations* (3d ed., Callaghan and Company, Chicago, 1949). Held in even higher esteem by legal authorities, but now partially outdated, is John F. Dillon, *Commentaries on the Law of Municipal Corporations* (5th ed., Little, Brown & Company, Boston, 1911). Much illustrated material may be found in J. B. Fordham, *Local Government Law—Text, Cases and Other Materials* (Foundation Press, Brooklyn, N.Y., 1949); and C. S. Rhyne, *Municipal Law* (National Institute of Municipal Law Officers, Washington, 1957).

[7] See section on home rule, pp. 180–187.

interest).[8] A public corporation, on the other hand, may be created with or without the consent of its membership (the persons living in the area), the terms of its charter may be quite different from what the people of the community desire, and, even more important, the charter is *not* a contract and is hence subject to constant, involuntary, and sometimes arbitrary changes. It can even be taken away without advance notice, unless the state constitution specifically prohibits this.

There are two other important differences between public and private corporations. A public corporation can act only in the *public* interest and for a public purpose. A private corporation must always have the public interest in mind (one could not long exist, for example, if it were organized for the purpose of robbing banks), but it may also have private interests (such as profit making for the individual owners). The two also differ in the amount of control the state exercises over them. A private corporation can carry on any activities it wishes, so long as it does not violate some law; a public corporation can do only those things that it is authorized to do. A corporation producing cigarettes, for example, could take on a side line of producing, say, plowshares, without seeking an amendment to its charter or any other kind of permission from the state. (It could not, however, put in a side line of marijuana cigarettes, since this would not be in the public interest and could be curbed by the state under its police powers.) A municipal, or public, corporation, on the other hand, could not decide to enter into such side lines as, say, municipal parking lots or a municipal theater or to adopt a new form of taxation without having first the specific authority to do so.

The Elements of a Corporation. What are the elements necessary in order to have a municipal corporation? Stated by McQuillin in the language of the law, they are: [9]

1. Incorporation as such pursuant to the constitution of the state or to a statute.

2. A charter.

3. A population and prescribed area within which the local civil government and corporate functions are exercised. However, the inhabitants of the municipality are not a separate legal entity and do not themselves constitute the municipality, and the common council or other governing body of the municipal officers does not constitute the corporation.

4. Consent of the inhabitants of the territory to the creation of the corporation, with certain exceptions [actually, the legislature in most states may act without consulting the local residents].

5. A corporate name.

6. The right of local self-government, although in most states this is held

---

[8] The contract could be altered or taken away, of course, if provision for this existed in the contract itself.

[9] McQuillin, *op. cit.*, vol. I, sec. 2.07. By permission of Callaghan and Company.

to be not an inherent right.[10] Unless otherwise provided by statute, a test as to whether an organization is a municipal corporation, using the term in its strict sense, is whether it has the power of local government as distinguished from merely possessing powers which are merely executive and administrative in their character. The characteristic feature of a municipal corporation beyond all others is the power and right of local self-government.

The Corporation and the Quasi Corporation. In the above passage, McQuillin suggests that there may be local units of government that are not in the strict sense municipal corporations. He is referring to a legal distinction that is made between corporations and quasi corporations. The former include cities, villages, and the relatively few *incorporated* (under a separate written charter) counties and school districts. The latter include most of the counties, townships, unincorporated New England towns, and the so-called special districts such as sewage-disposal, airport, drainage, mosquito-abatement, fire, and irrigation districts.[11]

So far as the lay citizen is concerned, the principal distinction between genuine corporations and quasi corporations is to be found in the fact that quasi corporations serve only as administrative agents of the state—while the true municipal corporation serves a dual purpose. It not only acts as a local agent for the state, but also performs certain local functions exclusively in the interests of the people living within the corporate boundaries of the city.

In theory, the city acts as an agent of the state whenever it performs a function in which the state as a whole has a certain interest; for example, when it enforces the law, or maintains public health standards, or collects taxes. On the other hand, the city may perform some tasks purely for the comfort and convenience of the local inhabitants, in theory at least. In this classification we find such things as the operation of a water-supply or public transportation system. Counties and school districts, in contrast, perform only such functions of state-wide interest as the maintenance of records, the prosecution of crimes, the maintenance of roads, and the education of children.

Since the city acts in a dual capacity, it is said that the city performs two types of functions, *governmental* (as an agent of the state) and *proprietary* (as an agent of the local inhabitants and for their comfort and convenience). This distinction is less important for laymen than it is for lawyers. As will be seen later, the line of demarcation is in any event difficult to draw, is an artificial legalism, and has probably created

[10] This is an example of the cautious legal mind. It is safe to say that in *no* state is the concept of local self-government as an inherent right legally acceptable. See above, chap. 3.

[11] The special districts are discussed in chap. 11.

more problems than it has solved. Property owned for carrying on governmental functions is in theory held for the state, which may dispose of it without consulting the city and without payment to it. On the other hand, property owned by the city for carrying on its proprietary functions cannot ordinarily be taken by the state without compensation, on the theory that constitutional guarantees of property rights extend to property held by the city in its proprietary capacity.[12] The same distinction is followed in the law of municipal-tort liability.[13]

Powers of the Corporation. The subordinate legal status of cities makes it necessary that the question of whether or not a particular city has the power to perform a particular function in a particular way be decided by the courts. Because the city is merely a creature of the state while the state itself is a sovereign body, the courts have established a rule of a narrow construction of municipal powers and a broad construction of state powers. To put it another way, the courts say that, if in doubt, the city does *not* have the power to do something it wishes to do. The authority that is almost invariably cited by courts in support of this interpretation is *Dillon's rule.* John F. Dillon, a renowned Iowa judge and author, summarized the legal position of cities in the following words: [14]

It is a general and undisputed proposition of law that a *municipal corporation possesses and can exercise the following powers, and no others:* First, those granted in *express words;* second, those *necessarily or fairly implied* in or *incident* to the powers expressly granted; third, those essential to the accomplishment of the declared objects and purposes of the corporation—not simply convenient, but indispensable. Any fair, reasonable, substantial doubt concerning the existence of power is resolved by the courts against the corporation, and the power is denied.

It is this rule that explains why a city might have to spend weeks of time and thousands of dollars in actions before the state courts seeking to justify its decision to finance a municipal parking lot from the parking-meter fund rather than from the general-revenue fund. Or seeking to find some theoretical justification for an FEPC or a smoke-abatement ordinance. That the community should demand them and that they should be adopted according to democratic procedures is not enough (see Figure 7-1).

It should be evident that Dillon's rule allows the courts a good deal of leeway in determining what a city may or may not do. What are necessarily or fairly implied powers? What powers are essential to "the accom-

---

[12] See McQuillin, *op. cit.,* vol. II, sec. 4.132. The United States Supreme Court makes no such distinction so far as the Federal Constitution is concerned. *Trenton v. New Jersey,* 262 U.S. 182 (1923).

[13] See below, pp. 192–195.

[14] Dillon, *op. cit.,* vol. I, sec. 237. By permission of Little, Brown & Company.

Ridiculous, Isn't It?

Figure 7-1. Most of America's wealth is to be found in its cities. Yet because they are creatures of the state, city governments can normally raise taxes only as the state permits. SOURCE: By permission of Frank Williams and the *Detroit Free Press*.

plishment of the declared objects and purposes" of the city? Only the judges know. They base their decisions as much as possible on the principle of *stare decisis*,[15] of course, but much is left to their discretion. It may be implied, for example, that a city may offer a reward for the arrest and conviction of an *ordinance*[16] violator, but not for the violator of a state

[15] *Stare decisis:* "let the decision stand." The basic principle of the common law under which a rule of law in one case becomes the basis for deciding subsequent cases that are the same in essence.

[16] Legally an ordinance has a lower priority rating than a law. Laws are enacted

law, even for the murderer of the city's chief of police.[17] An implied power may vary greatly from one state to another. For example, it *cannot* be implied from anything in the Cleveland charter that the city has the right to spend its money in order to send councilmen to the state capital as lobbyists,[18] but it *can* be implied from the Minneapolis charter that aldermen may be sent to attend meetings of the Rivers and Harbors Congress in Washington.[19]

Creation and Dissolution of the Corporation. Cities and villages are normally created upon the receipt of a *charter*. The charter may be granted in any one of several different ways.[20] It is also possible, however, for a municipality to be created in other ways. The people of a city might *think* that the community is incorporated and act accordingly over a long period of time, only to discover later—perhaps years later—that there was somehow a mistake made when it was "incorporated" and that the precise requirements of the law were not met. In such a case, it would be unreasonable to try to undo all of the presumed legal acts that the city had committed up to that time. The courts, therefore, provided that the legislature has in the meantime treated the supposed city as if it were indeed a city, will say that the area is a municipal corporation *de facto* (in fact), even though not *de jure* (in law).[21]

Some years ago, the Minnesota Supreme Court discovered that when the state constitution granted a city the power to "frame a charter for its own government," it meant that it could do so only once and that subsequent changes would have to be in the form of amendments and not in a completely new charter.[22] This bit of divination had the immediate effect of changing every home rule city not using an amended form of its original charter from a *de jure* to a *de facto* corporation. The people living in the affected cities were not seriously shaken by the development; in fact, they were hardly aware of any difference.[23]

Some cities and villages flourish, and others become "ghost towns." There are deserted shacks that once represented cities and villages in the mining areas of the mountain and Pacific states, in the timbering regions

---

by sovereign institutions. Ordinances, in theory, simply clarify or apply laws. City councils cannot enact laws, except where they have special constitutional authority to do so.

[17] Compare *Choice v. Dallas*, 210 S.W. 753 (1919), and *Madry v. Scotland Neck*, 199 S.E. 618 (1938).

[18] *Cleveland v. Artl*, 23 N.E. 2d 525 (1939).

[19] *Tousley v. Leach*, 230 N.W. 788 (1930).

[20] See below, pp. 174 ff.

[21] *Tulare Irrigation District v. Shepard*, 185 U.S. 1 (1901).

[22] *Leighton v. Abell*, 31 N.W. 2d 646 (1948). This highly technical decision destroyed the results of months of effort by the Minneapolis Charter Commission.

[23] Municipalities may also be created by implication or prescription. See McQuillin, *op. cit.*, vol. II, sec. 7.09.

of Minnesota, Wisconsin, and New England, and in the hill country of North Carolina and Tennessee. There are decaying crossroads trading centers throughout the nation—victims of the automobile, the telephone, and the migratory movement toward the large cities. It sometimes happens, therefore, that an incorporated municipality loses its original need for a charter. The question arises as to when a municipality ceases to be a corporation.

In actual practice, when a community becomes so depopulated as no longer to need a municipal government, it usually simply stops electing officers, collecting taxes, and functioning as a municipality. In legal theory, however, the corporation does not cease to exist merely because it is not functioning. It has simply gone into hibernation, from which it can reawaken at any time by resuming its activities. Permanent destruction of the creature that was created by the state can be accomplished only under the laws established by the state. Formal dissolution normally takes place after a petition by a sufficient number of residents, either to the municipal council or to a designated court. Depending upon the state, the council or court then either orders dissolution or provides for a popular referendum on the issue. It is also possible for a corporation to be dissolved by being wholly absorbed by another corporation or by a specific act of the state legislature. Whenever a corporation ceases to exist, its debts must be settled, its property disposed of, and other administrative details cleaned up. These minutiae are accomplished according to state law.

Charters: General and Special Act. While the concept of the city as a corporation dates back to Roman times, and noblemen granted charters of special privileges to unincorporated cities of Europe as early as the eleventh century, the modern practice of incorporating urban communities and prescribing their powers did not appear in England until the fourteenth century.[24] Often these charters merely legalized the informal situations that already existed. In any case, the Crown (or an important lord or colonial governor) began to grant special charters *wherein the specific city to be incorporated was named and its powers enumerated.* This plan became the standard practice in England, on the continent of Europe, and in the British colonies of North America.

It was not until the French Revolution that the *general charter* came into use. As one of the reforms of 1789, the French established *a general*

---

[24] A good general survey of the history of city charters may be found in W. B. Munro, *Municipal Government and Administration* (The Macmillan Company, New York, 1923), chap. 9. Further useful reading includes E. Griffith, *The History of American City Government: The Colonial Period* (Oxford University Press, New York, 1938); for Europe, H. Pirenne, *Medieval Cities* (Princeton University Press, Princeton, N.J., 1925), and C. Stephenson, *Borough and Town* (The Medieval Academy of America, Cambridge, Mass., 1933).

municipal code to apply to all communes, giving them equal status and powers. From that time on, the use of the general charter became standard in European democracies, although the pattern was somewhat modified in the United Kingdom, where the general laws were often supplemented by special laws and administrative ("provisional") orders granting special powers to particular municipalities.

The Special Act Charter. The special charter plan, inherited from the mother country, was standard practice in America from Colonial times and remained so until well past the middle of the nineteenth century. In 1851, Ohio, and a few months later, Indiana, outlawed special legislation, including special act charters of incorporation.[25] The following century produced a series of attempts to eliminate or modify the use of the special act charter. The major objection to it was to be found in the tendency of the legislature to substitute its own desires for those of a locally elected city council on important matters of public policy. In theory, there was nothing wrong with the special act: it provided a tailor-made charter to fit the special circumstances of the particular city. In actual practice, however, the legislature often refused to allow local governments to run their own affairs. Local urban dwellers, therefore, sought to find ways of retaining or recapturing local control.

Where special legislation was not completely outlawed, an attempt was made after about 1870 to allow it only after due notice had been given that the legislature was considering changes in the fundamental law of a city and after an open hearing at which interested persons and groups could testify. This plan was modeled on the British technique. It is in use in several states, but has met with considerable success only in Massachusetts. Legislators will usually not cooperate with devices that have the effect of restricting their powers, as this plan does.

In a few states, special legislation was permitted only if the proposed legislation received local approval. The New York constitution of 1894, for example, allowed special legislation if the proposal, after passage in the general assembly, was approved by the mayor in a first-class city (New York, Rochester, and Buffalo) or by the mayor and council in other cities. The bill would then go to the governor for his consideration in the usual manner. If disapproved either locally or by the governor, it could be repassed by the legislature and become law nonetheless. The New York plan appears to have given considerable protection to localities, although quite a few bills continued to be passed despite local disapproval.[26] The adoption of home rule in 1923 made the plan obsolete.

---

[25] State legislative control over cities, and attempts to curb these controls, are discussed in chap. 3 above.

[26] H. L. McBain, *The Law and the Practice of Municipal Home Rule* (Columbia University Press, New York, 1916), gives a detailed account.

An amendment to the Illinois constitution in 1904 sought to give Chicago some protection for its local self-rule. It provided for a referendum on all special legislation applying to Chicago. The plan had the effect of protecting Chicago from what it did not want, but it provided for no method by which the city could obtain what it did want.[27] As a result, the provision has had little use, and the Chicago charter is seldom amended.

Some states outlawed special acts only if it was possible for a general act to "be made to apply" to the situation. This rule contained a loophole that could be discovered by even the dullest legislator. Since the courts are normally inclined to resolve doubts in favor of the action of lawmakers, a pretense could almost always be found to argue that a given situation could not possibly be met by general legislation.

It should not be assumed that special legislation is used only to prevent local policy making. In Iowa, when special act charters were used, "the people of the local community not only had in many instances a considerable share in formulating their charters in accordance with local needs, but they also had in effect authority to amend their charters. Special charter cities had little difficulty in securing amendments from the legislature. . . . While such charters and their amendments were subject to legislative control, the records do not show the existence of a meddlesome attitude on the part of the General Assembly." [28] But the picture was, and is, different in other states, and it aroused considerable urban resentment.

Despite its unpopularity in urban communities, special legislation continues in use. It is to be found especially in New England and the South, particularly in Alabama, Florida, Maryland, North Carolina, Tennessee, and Georgia. In Maryland, for example, 70 per cent of the bills passed by the 1951 legislature were local in character. About one-half of the states are constitutionally authorized to grant special charters or special acts, and a number of the states still employ this system either exclusively or predominantly. In more than one-half of the states, there will be found old special act charters still in existence, but no new ones are being created, either as a matter of policy or as a result of subsequent constitutional prohibition. About twelve states provide, at least in some instances, for a local referendum on new special act charters.

The General Act Charter. The general act charter, designed to provide for uniform powers, privileges, and structures for every city in the state, has not met with much real success, except where it has been modified by home rule or local option. Since American towns vary from hamlets to empires of millions of people, it is unrealistic to expect that every city

[27] As has been pointed out in Munro, *op. cit.*, pp. 180–181.
[28] George F. Robeson, *The Government of Special Charter Cities in Iowa* (Iowa State Historical Society, Iowa City, 1923), p. 178.

government should be exactly like every other in powers and structure. There must be some variation. The failure of general acts to allow for an expansion of local autonomy is, however, more importantly attributable to the fact that legislators have been largely unwilling to vacate traditional areas of authority over local government. They have sought for loopholes of evasion and have met with a success that forces one to pause and admire their resourcefulness.

Constitutionally required use of general legislation has been circumvented by three techniques, principally by the passage of laws that purport to be general but are not in fact; by the erection of special districts other than cities; and by prostituting the classification device. If special legislation is prohibited, the question arises: What *is* special legislation? The answer, of course, must come from the courts. Following the general rule of a broad construction of legislative powers of the state, the courts have hesitated to rule against the legislature. Most of the state high courts have therefore been willing to allow as "general" any legislation that *on the surface* appears to be general, or any legislation that may *potentially* apply to another city, even though at the moment it affects only one. In one case, pointed out by Munro,[29] the Ohio legislature, despite a constitutional prohibition against special legislation, passed an act applying to "any city having within its limits an avenue more than 100 feet wide known as Lincoln Avenue." Is this special legislation? Not at all. Practically any city could qualify if it chose to build such a street. If, however, the legislators had added "on January 1, 1900," or some such prohibitive qualification, the supreme court would almost have been forced to void it. In point of fact, however, it has been easy to achieve special legislation without judicial proscription.

Another method of avoiding the ban on special legislation has been by establishing special districts: for parks and recreation, sewage disposal, police, and the like. This has been possible because the prohibition on special legislation applied only against "municipal corporations" or "cities."

Some state constitutions, while outlawing special legislation, did recognize that, say, the city of New York and the village of Au Sable Forks in the northern lakes country of the state could not be treated adequately with the same legislation, and therefore permitted the *classification* of cities. In some states the constitution set up the classifications, in others it authorized the legislature to do so, and in a third group of states, where the constitution was silent, the courts permitted the legislature to classify, holding this to be general legislation. Whatever the source of authority for classification, it was permitted because it was generally recognized

[29] Munro, *op. cit.*, p. 178.

that the equal treatment of all cities, large and small, was impractical. General acts did not allow for unique problems.

In some states, for example in Wisconsin, classification legislation has been used sparingly and for its intended purposes. In other states, however, the legislators have deliberately sought to use the classification device as a disguise for special legislation. Sometimes the courts have insisted that classifications be reasonable, but in most cases they have been tolerant when the legislators resorted to subterfuges. True, the courts did on occasion prohibit some types of classifications, especially those using a *geographical*, rather than a population, basis,[30] but the lawmakers usually had their way. Classification made it particularly easy to pass special legislation for the largest cities.

In Pennsylvania the three largest cities were each placed in a separate class, while in Ohio the *eleven* largest cities at one time stood each in its own class.[31] Although some classification is necessary because the problems and needs of large cities are not the same as those of small cities, state legislatures under the guise of classification have deprived the larger cities in many states of much of their powers of local self-government.

General Act Charters: Cafeteria Style. In those states without home rule or special act charters, it has been necessary to devise some way of meeting the particular needs of particular cities. Variations in needs occur in connection with both powers and forms of government. A large city might want the strong-mayor form, a middle-sized city the council-manager, and a village the traditional weak-mayor. In order to meet these variants, some states have adopted *optional charter laws*. More than one-half of them make use of this device, with about one-third using it as the principal source of city charters.

Under this plan, upon petition of a prescribed number of voters, or by resolution of the council, the council or the voters of a city may decide which *form* of government they wish to adopt. They are limited in choice, of course, to the type of options the legislature provides. There may be two or three basic charters, or five, as in Massachusetts, or as many as fourteen, as in New Jersey. The people of the city may go through the cafeteria line, picking from among the offerings set out by the state. They may take only those things offered, however, and without variations or alterations. There can be no special orders to the kitchen. This plan is

[30] The *form of government* (commission, council-manager, home rule charter, etc.) is sometimes used as a basis, as are other criteria.

[31] After classification had been reduced to an absurdity in Ohio, the Supreme Court belatedly outlawed *all* classification in *State of Ohio ex rel. Knisely v. Jones*, 64 N.E. 424 (1902). The legislature then unsuccessfully attempted to treat all cases alike. The dilemma was resolved in 1912 with the introduction into the state of municipal home rule.

convenient for the state, and it offers some real local choices as to type of government, although the *powers* that the city is authorized are normally much less variable. The plan is gaining in popularity in the United States. Of course, the legislature still determines the structure of government for each city, and *all* amendments to charters must still be obtained from the state,[32] but the local population can determine whether it prefers to abandon the weak-mayor form, for example, or perhaps whether it wants the council-manager form with or without ward elections for council.[33] A liberal optional charter plan, such as that of New Jersey, may, to local residents, be a very satisfactory method of bestowing charters.

Appraisal. Efforts to prevent or reduce legislative domination over local government have been made through such devices as the constitutional control of classification of cities, and the use of the optional charter plan. These efforts have met with only limited success. The legislature remains paramount, and its members have found it relatively easy to legislate for specific cities whenever they have desired to do so.

But in seeking to grant independence to cities, advocates of general legislation tended to minimize the fact that cities do have unique requirements that must be met by specific legislation. As a matter of fact, no state today has a single general act to cover the powers, functions, and structure of all of its cities.

While legal restrictions on legislative control were circumvented by imaginative legislators, often with the cooperation of the courts, and while legislative participation is still common in several states, notably in the South, the legislatures of an increasing number of states have, as a matter of public policy, given the people of cities a good deal of autonomy in local affairs. In some states, home rule has helped provide con-

---

[32] In several home rule states, charters originally granted by general (or special) acts of the legislature may subsequently be amended by the home rule process.

[33] Because variations are so great from one state to another, each student will have to do some independent research in order to get a picture of the situation in his own state. At this point, it might be well for the student to attempt to answer the following questions: Does *your* state have a constitutional provision seeking to control special legislation? If so, what limits does it attempt to set? What has been its *practical* effect upon legislative action measured in terms of judicial decisions? Are there any cities in your state operating under special act charters? Does the legislature create or amend special act charters by special acts (either openly or by subterfuge)? Does your state have a system for *classification* of cities? If so, is it established by constitutional provision or legislative policy? Is the *number* of permitted classes determined in the constitution? Are the specific classifications themselves set out in the constitution (as they are, for example, in Kentucky)? How many classes are there? If there are more than four, can the large number of them be reasonably justified? Does your state have both a classification system and municipal home rule? If so, what is the purpose of this arrangement? Does the state have an optional charter law? If so, what are the options? Are some options preferred more often than others? Why? Is there a *pattern* of adoptions (by size of cities, location, or other criteria)?

siderable local autonomy. This is especially true in California, Michigan, and Wisconsin, as well as perhaps Minnesota and Texas. Optional laws in many states enable cities to modify their forms of government as to details, and sometimes such laws establish permissive, as distinguished from mandatory, legislation which each locality may avail itself of as it sees fit. This is especially true in Wisconsin, Washington, and Nevada.

It should also be noted that some types of state control and supervision have been helpful to cities and not pre-emptive of local policy making. Furthermore, in many cases city officials, instead of chafing under the existing degree of state controls, approve of this control or are unconcerned with it.[34] Cities will inevitably be subject to a great deal of legislative control. Nearly every function performed by them affects the people of the state as a whole. In a day of large economic units and rapid means of transportation and communication, it is impossible for the cities to isolate themselves. Furthermore, there is no natural cleavage between state and local interests and functions. Because one tends to grow out of the other gradually, the state and its cities must of necessity work together.

Charters: Municipal Home Rule.[35] As towns were founded in colonial Rhode Island, "the local communities . . . organized and managed their own local affairs and services. Each town retained its own individuality and functioned to a great degree without reference to any higher authority, except for those few laws which were commonly accepted by all communities." [36] It was not until after the Revolutionary War that the general assembly of Rhode Island, together with the legislatures of other states, began to enforce claims of sovereign and plenary powers over matters of local concern. In the new United States, the earlier idea that local communities should be left alone as much as possible all but dis-

---

[34] On the general topic of legislative control over cities, the standard reference is still H. L. McBain, *The Law and the Practice of Municipal Home Rule* (Columbia University Press, New York, 1916). A recent discussion is *State-local Relations* (Council of State Governments, Chicago, 1946).

An old article, still useful, is Harry Hubbard, "Special Legislation for Cities," *Harvard Law Review*, vol. 18 (June, 1905), pp. 588–604. For Nebraska as a case study, A. C. Breckenridge, "The Mockery of Classification," *National Municipal Review*, vol. 36 (November, 1947), pp. 571–573.

[35] The two basic reference books on municipal home rule are H. L. McBain, *The Law and the Practice of Municipal Home Rule* (Columbia University Press, New York, 1916); and J. D. McGoldrick, *Law and Practice of Municipal Home Rule, 1916–1930* (Columbia University Press, New York, 1933).

A more recent argument for home rule is found in Rodney L. Mott, *Home Rule for America's Cities* (American Municipal Association, Chicago, 1949), which summarizes developments to that time. Students should also read the skeptical appraisal by Harvey Walker, "Let Cities Manage Themselves," *National Municipal Review* (now *National Civic Review*), vol. 36 (December, 1946), pp. 625–630. The title of this article is misleading.

[36] Robert J. M. O'Hare, "Cities Rush Home Rule Gate," *National Municipal Review* (now *National Civic Review*), vol. 42 (February, 1953), pp. 73–77.

appeared. Municipal home rule charters represent a somewhat romantic attempt to return to an earlier situation that is often pictured as ideal. The home rule movement was another device that won the support of early-twentieth-century reformers in their drive to free the local community from the all-powerful grasp of the state legislature.

Municipal home rule, which is a genuinely indigenous Americanism, may be defined as the power granted to municipal corporations to frame, adopt, and amend a charter for their government and to exercise all powers of local self-government, subject to the constitution and general laws of the state.[37] Home rule may be provided for in the state constitution or simply by enabling acts of the state legislature. It may be available to all cities and villages (e.g., Oregon and Wisconsin), or only those of over a certain population (e.g., California and Colorado), or to a very limited number of cities (e.g., eleven in Washington, one in Pennsylvania). It may be a self-executing provision of the state constitution (e.g., Arizona and Nebraska), or it may require legislation before a city can avail itself of the authorization (e.g., Texas and Wisconsin).[38] It may be used by many municipalities in the state (e.g., in Oregon and Michigan), or by relatively few of them (e.g., in Ohio, Missouri, and West Virginia).

The coming of home rule produced a very important difference in the procedure for securing charters and subsequent amendments to them. Under the older system of special and general act charters, a charter is secured through the process of lobbying before the legislature, and *every amendment* to the charter requires the sending of city officials and other interested persons to the state capital to harangue, threaten, and bargain with legislators. Under home rule, this is not necessary: the amendment is proposed (usually) by the council and is voted upon by the eligible voters. Under general act charters of either the classification or optional charter type, a city that lobbies for an amendment may find itself in the peculiar position of being opposed by another city in the same class or using the same option. This never happens under home rule.

Framing a Charter. The procedural rules for drawing up a new charter or making major revisions in an old one vary, of course, from state to state. In states having self-executing constitutional home rule, the procedures are outlined in the constitution itself. About one-half of them do not go into these extensive details, however, but simply authorize the

---

[37] This definition is based upon the home rule provisions of the constitution of Ohio, art. 18. The term *general laws* does not apply in a few home rule states.

[38] For the preference of the American Municipal Association, Chicago, see their Committee on Home Rule, *Model Constitutional Provisions for Municipal Home Rule* (1953); and the National Municipal League, New York, *Model State Constitution* (1941). The former is not self-executing; the latter is.

legislature to make the rules. The constitution of Wisconsin, for example, provides simply that "the method . . . shall be prescribed by the legislature." [39] All states operating under legislative home rule, of course, use procedures established by the legislature.

The common procedure is for the people of the city to elect a charter commission. In Minnesota, the commission is appointed by the local district judge, while in Oregon the city council acts as the charter commission, or a charter may be presented through the procedure of the initiative. The commission is usually given a certain length of time in which to draft a charter for submission to the voters, who must then approve (usually by a simple majority vote). It may sometimes be necessary to elect a second or third commission if the first cannot agree upon a charter or if its proposed charter is defeated at the polls. Sometimes (see Table 7-1), state approval is required in addition to that of the voters.

Once a home rule charter is adopted, it may be amended from time to time. In some states the charter commission is a permanent body that can propose amendments at any time (e.g., Minnesota and West Virginia), but the most common system is to have the proposals for amendment come from the city council, or through the use of the initiative. Ratification is normally by popular vote.[40]

Because of the practical effects of Dillon's rule, city charters must be lengthy, complex, and technical in some sections. (The index to the Los Angeles charter alone contains more words than does the United States Constitution.) The result is that in many home rule cities the voters are constantly being called upon to consider amendments to the charter, often many of them at a single election. Furthermore, many of the proposed amendments are of minor importance, while others are highly technical. The public is often either apathetic or confused, or both. In order to overcome this handicap to the effective operation of home rule, the New York constitution allows the local council to draft and *adopt* all charter amendments of a minor character without submitting them to a popular vote. If, however, there is organized opposition to the action of the council, a referendum can still force a public vote, and for certain types of amendments involving important questions of public policy the conventional type of referendum is always required. A similar rule applies in Wisconsin, while Oregon and West Virginia (for third-class cities) allow charter amendment without popular vote under certain conditions. These methods reduce the length of the already crowded ballot and remove some of the technical amendments from decision by the voters.

[39] Constitution of Wisconsin, art. 11.

[40] Much technical detail on home rule procedures in the various states may be found in E. B. Schulz, *American City Government* (Stackpole & Hack, Pittsburgh, 1949), chap. 7.

TABLE 7-1. STATES WITH CONSTITUTIONAL HOME RULE

State	Year adopted	Cities eligible	Cities with home rule*	Self-executing	State approval
Alaska	1958	First-class cities	0	No	None
Arizona	1910	Over 3,500	5	Yes	Governor
California	1879	Over 3,500	68	Yes	Legislature
Colorado	1902	Over 2,000	14	Yes	None
Connecticut	1953	Any city, town, borough	0	No	—
Louisiana	1947	Any municipality	3	Partly	Governor
Maryland	1915	Baltimore	1	Yes	None
Michigan	1908	Each city and village	211	No	Governor
Minnesota	1896	Any city or village	84	No	None
Missouri	1875	Over 10,000	8	Yes	None
Nebraska	1912	Over 5,000	3	Yes	None
New York	1923	Every city	8 †	No	None
Ohio	1912	Any municipality	40	Yes	None
Oklahoma	1907	Over 2,000	55	Yes	Governor
Oregon	1906	Every city or town	167 †	Yes	None
Pennsylvania	1922	Over 10,000	1	No	None
Rhode Island	1951	All cities and towns	6	Yes	None
Tennessee	1953	Any municipality	7	Yes	None
Texas	1909	Over 5,000	135	No	None
Utah	1932	Any city or town	2	Partly	None
Washington	1889	Over 20,000	9	No	None
West Virginia	1936	Over 2,000	7	No	Attorney general
Wisconsin	1924	Cities and villages	175 †	No	None

* Data on number of cities with home rule are approximate.

† Numerous amendments to existing charters by home rule.

SOURCE: Adapted from Rodney L. Mott, *Home Rule for America's Cities* (American Municipal Association, Chicago, 1949), pp. 58–61, by permission of the American Municipal Association, Chicago; various issues of the *National Municipal Review;* and J. R. Kerstetter, "Home Rule Cities," *Municipal Year Book, 1956* (International City Manager's Association, Chicago, 1946), p. 258.

The Origin and Spread of Home Rule. Like so many American political institutions, including the United States Constitution itself, municipal home rule had its origins in the expedient actions of practical politicians. The first state to establish a version of it was Iowa, which did so under an 1851 act of the legislature. After operating since territorial days under the special act charter system, the legislature in that year established a single method of charter adoption for newly incorporated communities or for towns desiring to become cities. If the inhabitants decided to incorporate, the law provided that an election would be held to choose persons to prepare a charter. The legislature provided the general limits of authority that could be granted by the charter, but these were broad. The charter, once written, was submitted to the voters for approval or disapproval.[41]

This unique and liberal law was not given a full opportunity to show its merit and hence was not actually the beginning of the home rule movement. Few uses seem to have been made of it. Most of Iowa's municipalities had already been established by earlier special charters. In 1858 the law was repealed, for the new Iowa constitution adopted the preceding year followed the contemporary fashion and required the use of a general incorporation act. However, the new law allowed the already existing city charters to be amended locally, and the four remaining cities to which this applies still exercise this privilege.[42]

The Missouri constitutional convention of 1875 furnished the stage for the first provision for *constitutional* home rule. The people and politicians of St. Louis had long been dissatisfied with legislative oversight of the city government and the need to secure the approval of the legislature to any changes in the fundamental law of the city. The St. Louis delegation, therefore, came to the convention with a set of proposals for the government of the city, including one for what is now known as home rule. This plan was included in the constitution and was adopted by the voters of the state, although home rule was restricted to St. Louis at that time. The reform period that followed helped to spread the idea of home rule throughout much of the nation.

Home Rule Today. In 1960, home rule was provided for in the constitutions of twenty-three states, and was actually in use in some cities of all but two of these.[43] Of the cities of the United States with populations of over 200,000, some two-thirds have home rule. It is in these larger cities, of course, that home rule charters to meet unique situations are most important. Of the ten largest cities in the nation, only Chicago, Boston, and Pittsburgh do not have home rule. The movement, which appeared to have spent itself with the decline of the reform spirit after World War I, enjoyed a revival after World War II with the granting of home rule for the first time to Philadelphia,[44] the first-class cities of

---

[41] State of Iowa, *Code of 1851,* chap. 42. For even earlier antecedents for home rule, especially in New York, see H. L. McBain, *American City Progress and the Law* (Columbia University Press, New York, 1918), pp. 22–29.

[42] Robeson, *op. cit.,* pp. 178–180.

[43] Based upon Mott, *op. cit.,* and, since 1949, reports in the *National Civic Review.* See Table 7-1.

[44] J. D. Crumlish, *A City Finds Itself: The Philadelphia Home Rule Charter Movement* (Wayne State University Press, Detroit, Mich., 1959).

Alaska,[45] and potentially to all municipalities in Connecticut, Louisiana, Rhode Island, and Tennessee. Local politicians, good-government groups, chambers of commerce, and other interests over the nation continue to press for home rule, although they are no longer as sure of its advantages to them as they once were. The change in viewpoint is coming about as a result of the advantages that home rule gives to suburban fringe residents. It encourages the idea that citizens have a "right" to form and maintain their own governments and hence conflicts with the metropolitan-wide interests of some of the groups mentioned above, groups which favor area-wide consolidation or a metropolitan super-government.

The Practical Meaning of Home Rule. Some reformers have assumed that municipal home rule results in the granting of greater powers to cities, with more independence from the state legislature. Students should not make the same mistake. That the granting of home rule makes for changes in several aspects of the political scene is not to be questioned, but does it grant more power or greater independence to cities? The question cannot be answered categorically, but a 1938 study suggested that home rule had been "helpful but not of great importance in enlarging the zone of municipal activity." [46] A commentary upon that study found that home rule gives cities their greatest freedom in choosing the *form* of government they are to employ and in exercising routine housekeeping functions (civil-service rules, the fixing of salaries, the establishment of pension systems, etc.). In these areas, non-home rule cities must nearly always secure enabling legislation from the state. Home rule cities may *possibly* be freer on matters that are fairly definitely *local* in interest (the establishment of parks, zoos, the control of building regulations), but "their freedom is not measurably greater in matters of education, general police control and utility rates and services (except in Colorado)." [47] On financial matters, in which the state can always claim an interest, home rule cities have virtually no advantage at all over special and general act charter cities, except in California.

In many states, home rule has helped to give municipalities greater power of discretion in solving their day-to-day problems. Cities without home rule must often go to the legislature in order to get authorization to perform some minor function or to exercise some power that most laymen would consider to be obviously a local responsibility. For example,

[45] Paul C. Bartholomew, "The Constitution of the State of Alaska," *Southwestern Social Science Quarterly,* vol. 40 (June, 1959), pp. 40–53.

[46] George C. S. Benson, "Sources of Municipal Powers," *Municipal Year Book, 1938* (International City Managers' Association, Chicago, 1938), pp. 149–165.

[47] *State-local Relations* (Council of State Governments, Chicago, 1946), pp. 164–166.

in recent years a North Carolina town had to have the legislature pass an act in order that the council might declare it a misdemeanor to use roller skates on the public sidewalks. A Maryland city had to get special permission to increase the salary of a stenographer by $300 a year. A Nevada city had to get legislative permission in order to purchase a rotary pump for the fire department. An Iowa town discovered that it lacked power to purchase uniforms for the members of its police force.[48] Home rule is not a guarantee against such municipal impotence, but it has been helpful in overcoming it.

While home rule cities often, in fact, enjoy greater powers than do non-home rule cities, most of them are *potentially* just as subject to state control over their affairs. In most home rule states, the legislature enjoys concurrent or superior power to the city government in matters of local concern. And the legislature is, of course, supreme in those areas that the courts deem to be of state, rather than of local, concern. In most states, general acts of the legislature, or what purport to be general acts, take precedence over ordinances or charter provisions. Under these circumstances, the question of whether municipal home rule will promote greater local discretion, and the extent to which it will do so, is a question not of law, but of *public policy* determined by the legislature, at whose sufferance home rule actually exists.[49] To be sure, the enactment of a constitutional amendment providing for home rule places an implied moral obligation upon the legislature to carry out the spirit of its provisions, and this moral pressure appears to have had an effect upon the legislatures of several states.

A somewhat different, more autonomous kind of home rule is to be found in California, Colorado, Ohio, Oklahoma, and perhaps Arizona and Nebraska. In these states, a distinction is made either by the courts, or by the constitution plus the courts, between matters of local and of state concern. The legislature has definitely less power over localities, and general laws do not supersede local ordinances or charter provisions.

In some of these states, the constitution attempts to define some, at least, of the powers that are properly those of the municipality, but it cannot define them all, nor can it attempt detailed definitions of powers so as to explain where they end and state-wide interests begin. Because this is so, this type tends to *transfer* control from the state legislature to the state courts (Ohio offers the clearest example). The courts, in most cases, strongly tend to resolve doubts in favor of the state. A leading authority has pointed out that "after all, it seems clear that the determina-

---

[48] Examples from among those cited in *Home Rule in Nevada* (Legislative Counsel Bureau, Carson City, Nev., 1952).

[49] An interesting attempt to classify home rule cities according to the extent to which they remain subject to legislative control is made in Schulz, *op. cit.*, pp. 130–131.

tion of the actual extent of power to be exercised is wholly a question of policy and not at all a question of law." [50] The task, under the theory of American government, belongs to the legislature.

Home Rule: An Appraisal. Home rule allows charters to be tailor-made to suit the needs of the particular community and permits them to be more flexible than the types provided by the legislature in allowing for changing exigencies and in taking advantage of new developments in administrative techniques. Home rule probably makes it easier to experiment with charter provisions, since the amendments are locally proposed and adopted.

Perhaps the greatest effect of home rule lies in its psychological value. To those interested in local government, it gives the impression of granting more independence to the city than is often the actual case. This gives encouragement and incentive to those who would be active in local government and thus gives the reformer the feeling that if he fails, he has only himself to blame. The psychological effect upon legislators is also significant. Most legislators have been willing to accept the mandate of the voters when a home rule provision is written into a constitution and to permit home rule to operate even where legal authority to commit sabotage lies with the legislature. This is not always the case, but it usually is. In home rule states, bills which would deal with local matters are sometimes opposed by legislators who wonder if they would not "interfere with the rights of local self-government" or "violate the principle of home rule." Home rule is hence more often an *attitude* toward local government than it is a legal injunction against legislative action.

Multiple Charter Systems in Nebraska: An Illustration.[51] City charters, as has been indicated, may be provided for in general acts, special acts, classification systems, optional charter acts, or home rule. Rather than use one of these devices to the exclusion of all others, it is common for the state to allow charters under several of them. Nebraska offers a good illustration of this.

The basic law of the state provides for a *general act charter* of the mayor-council type. It applies to all cities of from 1,000 to 40,000 population and applies automatically to all cities that do not specifically adopt some other kind of charter. Since there are provisions for minor structural differences between first- and second-class cities, the plan might be called a classification-type charter rather than a simple general act charter.

The state also has a provision for two *optional* forms of local govern-

[50] McBain, *American City Progress and the Law,* p. 7.
[51] This section is based on a note by A. C. Breckenridge in the *National Municipal Review* (now *National Civic Review*), vol. 42 (February, 1953), pp. 84–85.

ment. One establishes a commission structure for which all cities of over 2,000 population are eligible. The other permits municipalities of 1,000 people or more to adopt a specified council-manager plan. A third system is provided for in the Nebraska constitution, which permits *home rule charters* to be adopted by all cities of over 5,000 population.

In 1960, only one city was operating under the commission option. Nine were using the council-manager option. Three cities had home rule charters, under which it is of course possible to adopt any governmental structure. The two largest cities, characteristically, had taken advantage of the home rule provision. The majority of Nebraska cities, it should be added, operate under the general act charter.

THE CITY AND THE STATE

It should be clear by now that the city is a child of the state. It has been noted that the state has been most unwilling to allow its child to grow up. A theory of perpetual infancy was adopted by nineteenth-century legislatures in their attitudes toward their offspring. Efforts at achieving independence for municipalities through the legal device of constitutional limitations were largely unsuccessful. Cities in most states did achieve more independence and less legislative supervision of their affairs after the first decade or so of the twentieth century, but the change seems to have been produced principally by a changing climate of opinion toward cities that accompanied the urbanization of the nation, together with a slight increase of public trust in the politician, both state and local.

Legislative oversight of local government declined in the twentieth century for another reason: government got to be too complicated to be sufficiently understood by amateur legislators meeting for a few weeks annually or biannually as an interlude away from other occupations that took the whole of their time. City government became professionalized and technical; its complex details came to be understandable only to the professional, full-time technician. Flexibility, which legislatures did not possess, was needed. So was continuous, rather than sporadic, oversight. It could therefore be said that the twentieth century represented a period during which state legislators were somewhat reluctantly, but inexorably, forced to transfer increasing amounts of supervision over local government to the professional bureaucracies of the administrative branch of the state government.

It is perhaps desirable to postpone an examination of the details of state-local administrative relationships until a more appropriate place is reached.[52] In addition to legislative and administrative oversight of cities,

[52] See chap. 12 on intergovernmental administrative relationships.

the judicial branch also acts in a supervisory capacity, and some facets of this control require development.

State Judicial Oversight of Cities.[53] Standing behind every city official, looking over his shoulder as the baseball umpire looks over the shoulder of the catcher, is a judge. He is the individual who settles all disputes between the city and the state, a taxpayer and the city, one local government and another. He is the umpire. While he makes a determination only when asked to do so and then upon the basis of laws and ordinances made by other people, he is himself in a real sense a lawmaker, for the judge decides ultimately what the law *means* and hence what the city can and cannot do.

Because the city is not a sovereign body, its standing at law is approximately the same as the standing of a private corporation, except when it is acting in the name of the sovereign (the state). Because of this legal position and because it enjoys only those powers granted to it under the principle of Dillon's rule, the city is constantly faced with the task of proving in court that it has the power to do what it seeks to do.

The Taxpayer's Action. The court actions in which the municipality constantly finds itself embroiled may in some cases be brought by a state official, but most of them are brought by a taxpayer resident in the city, or by a corporation that is a taxpayer, since a corporation is an artificial person at law.

It is a well-known principle of ancient Anglo-Saxon common law that "the King is the fountainhead of all power" and that therefore "the King can do no wrong" and likewise that "the King cannot be sued without his own consent." This principle was transferred to the American republic, where the word "people" was substituted for "King" in the first quotation, but "state" was used in the last two. The United States Supreme Court has consistently held that status as a taxpayer does not give one sufficient interest in the matter to test the legality of an act of Congress in a judicial action,[54] and this rule also applies in most of the states. The same protection does not extend to municipalities, however, for they are normally subject under the common law to taxpayers' suits even when there has been no statutory grant of the right.

Taxpayers' suits may be brought for three purposes: (1) to enjoin acts of the municipality that are unauthorized, unlawful, or *ultra vires;* [55] (2)

---

[53] In addition to the great commentaries on municipal law by Dillon and McQuillin, *op. cit.*, contemporary developments are reported in an annual volume by the National Institute of Municipal Law Officers. Prior to the 1953 edition, it was called *Municipalities and the Law in Action*, since then, the *NIMLO Municipal Law Review*.

[54] *Massachusetts v. Mellon*, 262 U.S. 447 (1923).

[55] *Ultra vires* actions are actions legally beyond the power of the municipal corporation or its officers.

to compel unfaithful officers, or even third persons, to repay into the treasury sums illegally paid out; and (3) to protect the interests of the municipality where its officers wrongfully refuse or neglect to perform their duties. This third type may involve legal actions by the taxpayer in the name of the city to protect municipal powers and rights that the officers of the city fail to protect.

In theory, taxpayer actions are analogous to the actions that a stock-holder may bring against the officials of a private corporation (who are legally acting as his agents). The purpose of the action is to stop acts that are allegedly illegal, or to stop or remedy situations that give evidence of fraud, corruption, or other wrongdoing. The taxpayer suit has sometimes prevented the granting of fraudulent contracts, the issuing of improvident bonds, or the granting of illegal franchises.

The taxpayer action is often used as a weapon by interests that disagree with proposed municipal policies. Theoretically, an action cannot be brought simply because the taxpayer dislikes the judgment or doubts the wisdom of the city officials, or because their policies might damage the profits of his business. In practice, however, these are often the real reasons behind suits. Almost any public policy that deviates even slightly from traditional municipal behavior will result in an action in which the policy is claimed to be *ultra vires*. The individual or corporation in such a case may be seeking to protect his own economic interests or to impose his own personal philosophy upon local policy making. The courts are often the last resort of the obstructionist, and state-court judges have often lent a sympathetic ear. City-government proposals have again and again been delayed by expensive, time-consuming legal actions.

A parking-lot owner may have a right to bring action to prevent a city from going into the parking-lot business on the seriocomic ground that it is *ultra vires* to use money from the general-revenue fund (rather than the parking-meter fund) for this purpose. A home builder may be permitted legal action to stop a public housing project on the ground that such a project is not for a public purpose. A television-station owner may be permitted legal action to prevent the city from operating a municipal television station on the ground that the city charter permits only a radio station. In such cases, the interests opposing the action are able to use the machinery of the law to support their positions, for the burden of proof is on the city government.

Taxpayer actions cause so much delay—and are so nearly inevitable— that many cities, especially the larger ones, commonly arrange for a "friendly suit" to be instigated in order to clear away the legal cobwebs before launching into a new program, or attempting to issue bonds under an untried procedure. Such actions not only save time and avoid the wasting of money in preparations that might otherwise later have to be abandoned, but they sometimes lead to the discovery of possible legal alternatives even when the original proposal does not survive the legal process. Middle-sized and small cities tend to allow the large municipalities to break legal ground; they are often slower in moving into a new area of activity and by the time they do so, the court rulings may already be established.

THE CITY AND THE CITIZEN

Because cities are corporations and not sovereignties, they are responsible for contract violations and torts.[56] They become answerable before the courts in much the same way as do private corporations. The basic rules of municipal liability are established in the common law, but they are subject, as is any part of the common law, to statutory variations in the individual states.

Municipal-contract Liability. Cities, as would appear obvious, enter into countless contracts with individuals and corporations. In general, cities must be answerable for these contracts in the same manner as private corporations. Even where there is no question of good faith involved in the carrying out of a contract, many other problems may arise —problems of interpretation of the contract, of determining when its conditions have been completed, of making settlement when performance of the conditions of the contract becomes impossible. Cities may therefore find themselves in court in the normal course of carrying out their activities.

The principal problem that faces the courts in the interpretation of contracts to which the city is a party is that of determining the conditions under which a contract is either valid or invalid. In general, a valid contract is one that the city is authorized to make, that is made by the proper officer according to law, and that has been adopted according to proper procedures (for example, the law may require that certain contracts be let only after advertising for bids, and then only to the lowest responsible bidder). An *ultra vires* contract is normally invalid, but the courts of the various states sometimes order monetary settlements where the city has benefited from the contract. Similarly, a contract made by the wrong officer or without following proper procedures may sometimes be validated, but at other times it may not be, and the other party to the contract

---

[56] Almost every culture, even the most primitive, distinguishes between a *tort*, or wrong against an individual, and a *crime*, or wrong against society. A tort is a violation of a personal right established and protected by law. A violation of a contract is the violation of a personal right established by mutual agreement and protected by law. For purposes of this text, a tort is an injury to a person that is neither a crime nor a violation of a contract.

may have to assume any loss. Court practices vary from one state to another.[57]

Municipal-tort Liability. In a large American city a few years ago, an elderly lady tripped over a loose floor board at the head of the stairs in a city-owned building, fell down the stairs, and was seriously injured. Was the city liable for damages for maintaining a defective stairway, as a private business firm would be? It may well come as a surprise to the layman to discover that the law would make the answer depend, in most states, upon the *use* to which the building was put by the city. If it was used as the offices of the city-owned water supply system, the injured person could recover damages, but if it was used as a police station, no claim would be allowed against the city.

If a university student walking down Main Street is struck by a runaway bus belonging to the city-owned transit system, he will not be in the same legal position as he would have been if the vehicle had been a fire truck. A broken leg or a caved-in chest hurts as badly in either case and is just as costly to repair, yet in most states the student could collect if he were hit by the bus, but could not if hit by the fire truck.

Why should this be? The answer is to be found largely in historical accident and in a failure to change the municipal-tort liability law. There is a legal argument to justify the arrangement, but it is not likely to impress the layman.

It will be recalled that the city was earlier described as performing two different types of functions: those which it does involuntarily as an agent of the state, and those done at local option as a service to the immediate community. In performing the former type of activity, the city becomes a veritable department of the state government and as such becomes cloaked in the state's mantle of sovereignty. It is said to be performing a *governmental* (or public) function. In performing services of comfort and convenience to the immediate community, however, the city acts very much as if it were simply a private corporation doing the same job. It is said to be performing a *proprietary* (or corporate, or sometimes private) function.

Clearly a theoretical line could well be drawn between those functions where the city directly represents the sovereign, and hence cannot be sued without its own consent, as is the rule with the sovereign power, and where the city acts as an ordinary corporation and hence could reasonably be expected to assume the same responsibilities as other corporations. The difficulty with such a legal fiction arises when an attempt is made to classify the multitudinous activities of a modern city. The theory requires a perfect bifurcation, with every function being

---

[57] Details of municipal-contract liability are developed by McQuillin, *op. cit.*, vol. 10, secs. 29.01–29.04.

either governmental or proprietary, and with no messy edges or leftover pieces. The functions themselves, however, are not very cooperative when a classification is attempted.

Is the parks and recreation function, for example, carried on only for the comfort and convenience of the community, or is it part of the sovereign's responsibility to protect the health, safety, and welfare of the inhabitants of the state? How about airports, hospitals, or garbage disposal? The answers to these questions are not easy to find. Furthermore, the law of municipal-tort liability is not the same in any two states of the union.

The classification of functions is done in the various states either by legislative statute or, in its absence, by the judges. The legislature is free to overrule the judges and can, if it chooses, make functions that are the most clearly governmental in character subject to tort action. The whole law of tort liability is based upon the judge-made common law, however, and most legislatures have been content to allow the judges to work their way through the problem on their own.

What criteria do the judges use in trying to determine whether a function is governmental or proprietary? Even on this question, there is no agreement. There are three principal criteria, but they are not given the same weight or precedence in the various states. First, the judges sometimes use a historical test. Since the whole question has been one that has gradually developed over time, it is felt that the historical usage or treatment of the function should be given weighty consideration. The difficulty with this approach is to be found in the tendency of the judges to call "old" functions—those long performed by municipalities—governmental and newer ones proprietary. But there is no logic in denying suability because the function has been performed by governments for too many decades or centuries.

A second criterion sometimes used is based upon the question of whether the function is performed involuntarily by the city at the insistence of the state or is voluntarily assumed at the option of the local community. But the degree of compulsion imposed upon the city varies greatly from state to state, and it is not often easy to determine the meaning of the term *voluntary*.

A final criterion is one based upon the question of whether or not the function is revenue-producing. A function that does, or may, return a profit resembles the functions of private corporations, it is argued, and is therefore more likely to be proprietary in nature. But how about a profit from, say, garbage collection that is incidental to the operation of the function? Or profit from the operation of a miniature railroad at a park that represents only one small segment of the whole function of parks and recreation? None of the criteria are consistently or systematically applied.

They vary from state to state, and none of them can mark a satisfactory trail through the wilderness of tort liability.

The courts almost invariably place certain functions in the governmental category, for which the city may not be sued. These include police, fire, education, libraries, traffic signals (they act in lieu of policemen), and public health. Functions that are nearly always held to be proprietary include city-owned public utilities, such as water, public transportation, gas, and electricity. There are many functions that vary considerably from state to state in their classification: parks and recreation (which tend to be governmental), hospitals (likewise), airports (which tend to be proprietary), street lighting, street cleaning, garbage collection and disposal, and the construction and maintenance of sewers.[58]

There are certain functions which are generally recognized as being essentially governmental, but for which the municipalities must nonetheless maintain responsibility for torts. These are functions dealing with the *public ways*. Historically, the state has expected the municipal corporation to be responsible for torts committed in the maintenance (but usually not in the construction) of streets, sidewalks, bridges, culverts, and the like. The citizen has a right to expect that a bridge will not collapse under him or that he will not walk into an open manhole in the sidewalk. Even in these cases, however, doubts are resolved against the individual. It is always held, for example, that the city must be given a reasonable time in which to correct a fault or post a warning.

The Rule on Discretion. Regardless of whether a function is claimed to be governmental or proprietary, most courts will ask another question before deciding whether tort liability exists. That question deals with whether the action in litigation involved a *discretionary* or a *ministerial* act. That is to say, is damage claimed because the city decided to do or not to do something, or is it claimed because of the manner in which city officials or employees carried out established policy? Discretionary acts involve the making of public policy decisions, and they are *not* subject to tort action. Ministerial acts involve the carrying out of established policy, and they are normally the only type of acts that will allow for a legal action. For example, if the city council decides not to extend a water main or not to build a bridge across a stream, or if a police officer (acting in good faith and upon probable cause) decides to arrest a person who subsequently proves to be innocent of any crime, there could be no maintainable action, since these all involve decision making. On the other hand, once a bridge is built, the public has a right to expect the min-

---

[58] In the absence of statutes to the contrary, quasi corporations such as school districts, counties, and townships are not responsible for *any* torts. The theoretical reasoning holds that all of the functions of a quasi corporation are involuntarily performed as an agent of the state.

isterial function of maintaining it to be carried out, and once the city decides to operate a bus line, the public has a right to expect that individuals will not be injured while riding on the buses.

The Rule of Respondeat Superior. According to the common law, the master is responsible for the actions of his servant, providing that those actions may reasonably be said to follow from the orders given to the servant. This is the rule of *respondeat superior.* In municipal-tort liability, it means that the city must answer for the action of its officers and employees, providing that the city is suable for the particular function involved and that the officer or employee was acting in general compliance with the requirements of his job.

If a city official or employee does something not called for in the performance of his duty, his actions are *ultra vires* and the city bears no responsibility for them. Since an individual is responsible for his own actions where there is no master-servant-relationship to protect him, this means that the citizen who is wronged may sometimes be able to sue the *individual* city official or employee when he cannot sue the city itself. This may sometimes protect the injured person when he is wronged in the course of the city's performing a governmental function. But the individual, it must be remembered, is not responsible when the city cannot be sued unless his actions are *ultra vires.* If a city policeman arrests an innocent man against whom he holds a grudge, or if a fire-truck driver operates his vehicle in a grossly negligent manner, or if a public health officer quarantines a hotel while drunk, the individual who is harmed may be able to collect from the officer or employee as an individual. The chances are excellent, however, that even if he gets a court judgment, the city employee will not earn enough from his job to pay for such damages.

Recapitulation. A tort is an injury to a person that is neither a crime nor a violation of a contract. Cities and villages are responsible for torts committed by their officers and employees (generally speaking) when the tort was committed in the performance of a ministerial act, by an employee who was not acting in an *ultra vires* fashion, in connection with a municipal function of a proprietary character, or in connection with the public ways, and not one of a government character. In most states, if any one of these conditions is not met, the city is not responsible in tort action.[59]

Closing Comment. The question of whether the municipality is or is not liable in tort action is controlled by state legislatures, which can overrule court decisions when they choose to do so. Legislatures do not act on the basis of equity or logic but rather, as with other legislation, on the basis of the balance of the pressures upon the membership. City

[59] The basic material on municipal-tort liability is to be found, of course, in the treatises by McQuillin and Dillon.

attorneys, mayors, and managers, who must be concerned about their budgets, generally oppose expanding the city's responsibility. Lawyers who specialize in tort cases, persons who want to try making easy money through spurious suits, persons who have been injured on or by city property, logicians, and others would like to see municipal liability expanded. In contrast, some persons who are especially concerned about governmental expenditure levels would prefer that the municipality be made as immune as is the state.

The balance of interests seems to be such that the *status quo* is maintained, by and large. In most cities, it remains less costly to the individual to be struck by a water-department truck than by a police-department patrol car.[60]

[60] On the tort-liability problems of one city, New York, see Rufus Jarman, "Let's Sue the City," *The Saturday Evening Post,* Apr. 22, 1950, pp. 31 ff. On the general legal principles, see Leon T. David, *The Tort Liability of Public Officers* (Public Administration Service, Chicago, 1940); and for the argument in favor of expanding liability, George A. Warp, "Can The 'King' Do No Wrong?" *National Municipal Review,* vol. 21 (June, 1942), pp. 311–315, and K. C. Davis, "Administrative Officers' Tort Liability," *Michigan Law Review,* vol. 55 (December, 1956), pp. 232–236.

Chapter 8

FORMS OF GOVERNMENT

A Minneapolis alderman once told this writer that forms of government have nothing at all to do with the effectiveness or honesty of government. He felt that Minneapolis, which has a nineteenth-century form, operates under a government as good as could be had under any of the newer forms which are so often advocated by supporters of reform. The viewpoint was scarcely new with him, however; similar expressions have come from Alexander Pope, Edmund Burke, and Lincoln Steffens.

It is true that Americans have been rather obsessed in recent decades, with the idea of a relationship between structure and effectiveness of government. Many advocates of reform have been guilty of overstatement in this direction. Much literature may be found urging the commission or council-manager plan, for example, on the ground that these plans follow the organization form of the business world, the corporation. The implication is that the success of the one should ensure the success of the other.

The truth of the matter, it would seem, is that structural arrangements do have an effect upon the quality of government, but they neither guarantee good government nor prevent it. The forms of government are important because they affect the pattern of influence of various groups upon policy making. The specific structure in any given case helps to establish behavior patterns and attitudes toward power and the exercise of power that definitely affect the process whereby decisions are made.

A study of St. Louis government found that structure "plays an important role in determining the scope and intensity of political conflict in the community." [1] The mayor of that city is the dominant policy-making figure and, as such, groups interested in policy seek to influence his election and to secure access to him. Business leaders look to him for the development of programs affecting the location of industry, tax rates, adequate city services, and "the social climate of the community necessary

[1] See Robert H. Salisbury, "St. Louis Politics: Relationships among Interests, Parties, and Governmental Structure," *Western Political Quarterly*, vol. 13 (June, 1960), pp. 498–506.

to attract technical personnel for their businesses." If the mayor were not as effective a policy leader as he is, these groups might be disadvantaged.

Another set of interests, those of low-income people—of the small merchants and businessmen, and of the Negro minority—seek to have their interests protected by the elective "county" officers (St. Louis is a city-county) and by the ward aldermen. These groups are interested, not in broad policy, but in such things as patronage jobs and individual favors of all kinds, such as the location of stop signs, parking regulations, help in getting an apartment in a public housing unit, and the other traditional types of political assistance to individuals. If the county officers were subject to the same rules as city officers—as could happen by elimination of the formal structural distinction—most of the patronage would disappear. If the councilmen were elected at large, they would have far less interest in doing favors for individuals than is the case under a ward system.

In another study of four Midwestern cities with about 50,000 population,[2] structural differences also seemed to be significantly related to the pattern of politics in the cities. The nonpartisan ballot, for example, appeared to help destroy the potential influence of national parties in municipal elections. The level of education of councilmen was lower and the degree to which ethnic groups were represented was higher in cities using the ward system as compared with those using at-large elections. The absence of a primary election in one city appeared to favor organized groups, or groups that had achieved a high degree of consensus on goals, as compared with independent candidates. The ward system militated against an aggressive annexation policy such as existed in the at-large cities. Why? Because aldermen feared that annexed territory might be added to their particular wards, thus upsetting the balance of forces that had, in the past, permitted them to secure election.

In 1954, Indiana mayors, acting through the state municipal league, succeeded in killing a proposed home rule amendment to the state constitution. They feared that its passage might result in a spate of adoptions of the council-manager plan, which was not permitted in that state under existing law. The unwanted plan represented a threat to the mayors, both in terms of political power and of compensation. In Indiana, St. Louis, and the four middle-sized cities, formal structure of government *did* make a difference in the making of policy and in determining which individuals and groups would be most influential in the process of making decisions.

The Basic Forms. There are three basic forms of city government in the United States, the mayor-council, commission, and council-manager

---

[2] Oliver P. Williams and Charles R. Adrian, *Fighting City Hall: A Comparative Study of Politics in Four Middle-sized Cities.* (Forthcoming monograph.)

plans. To this must be added the New England town meeting and its accommodation to modern urban conditions, the representative town meeting. There are many variations of these plans, and especially of the mayor-council plan.

A word of caution should be given at the outset in examining forms of government: there are probably no two cities in the United States that have *exactly* the same structure of government. There are very few that fit the theoretical ideal of the general plan they follow. Nearly every charter commission or state legislature, in considering structure, finds it politically expedient to add its own improvisations on the given theme. For example, the strong-mayor–council system calls for the appointment of department heads by the mayor, yet many such cities have elective clerks and treasurers.

Boston and Cleveland are the only large mayor-council cities that do not elect any administrative officers other than the mayor. New York, Baltimore, Buffalo, and Houston elect the controller. Los Angeles elects the controller and city attorney. San Francisco elects not only the city attorney and treasurer, but the assessor as well.

The mayor of New York has many administrative powers, a characteristic of strong-mayor cities, but the chief fiscal officer of the city reports to the Board of Estimate, rather than the mayor. Detroit clearly has a strong-mayor government, yet its organization chart is cluttered with a series of advisory boards and commissions that are vestiges of the old weak-mayor *administrative* boards and commissions.

The manager plan calls for the manager to appoint all department heads, yet in most cities with this form, some administrative officers are either elective or selected by the council. The variations are quite endless, and the structural descriptions that follow must be thought of as models which city charters tend to imitate. The difference between the weak- and strong-mayor systems, in particular, is a relative one. The models of each are at opposite ends of a continuum, and the various mayor-council cities must be thought of as being located somewhere along the continuum—rarely, if ever, at one of the extremities.

CITIES WITH A SEPARATION OF POWERS

The general historical context in which the structures of American city government developed has already been discussed.[3] During nearly all of the nineteenth century, American cities were operated under the weak-mayor–council (or weak-mayor) system. Near the end of that century, what is now called the strong-mayor system gradually evolved. In recent

[3] See above, chap. 3.

years a third principal derivative of the plan, a result of efforts to strengthen administratively the strong-mayor system in large cities, has evolved. For purposes of this text, it will be called the strong-mayor–council plan with chief administrative officer (or strong-mayor with CAO). This plan will be described later.

The various types of mayor-council cities taken collectively make up one-half of all cities of the nation under any form of government.[4] Most smaller cities use this form, too, except in New England, where the town-meeting form is common. All but one of America's seventeen largest cities use the mayor-council plan, usually of a strong-mayor type. Over one-half of the small cities of 5,000 to 10,000 people have the mayor-council form, usually of a weak-mayor type.

The Weak-mayor–Council Plan. In the early decades of the nineteenth century, America's budding cities borrowed from rural government certain essential concepts. Today we call it the weak-mayor–council plan (see Figures 8-1 and 8-2).

Characteristics. The weak-mayor plan is a product of Jacksonian democracy. It reflects the spirit of the frontier, with a skepticism both of politicians and of government itself. It grew out of a time when the functions of city government were few, when the need for a single executive was not recognized, and when people were afraid to give powers to a single executive. Implicit in the weak-mayor plan is the belief that if a politician has few powers and many checks upon him, he can do relatively little damage and that if one politician becomes corrupt, he will not necessarily corrupt the whole city government.

The council is both a legislative and an executive organization under the weak-mayor plan. In small cities today, the council is small—five or seven members—but in larger cities it is usually a fairly large body of perhaps eleven to fifty members. At one time councils might be as large as two hundred. Members are (except in small cities) ordinarily elected by wards on a partisan ballot.

In addition to making policy, the council appoints several administrative officers, such as the city engineer and the city attorney. Councilmen (often called aldermen if they represent wards) may serve on several ex officio boards and commissions.[5] A committee of the council usually prepares the budget and may even appoint the controller, who administers the expenditure of the budget.[6]

---

[4] *Municipal Year Book, 1960* (International City Managers' Association, Chicago, 1960), p. 82.

[5] Ex officio boards and commissions have a membership of persons who hold office by right of holding another office. For example, the airports commission might be made up of the mayor, the clerk, the treasurer, and two aldermen.

[6] See chap. 16 on fiscal administration.

The mayor is not "weak" because he lacks policy-making power—he normally has a veto, can recommend legislation, and may even preside over the council. He is "weak" because he lacks administrative power. There is, in fact, no single individual charged with the responsibility of seeing to it that the laws and ordinances are properly carried out, or that the city administration proceeds in accord with an over-all plan. The mayor has very restricted appointive powers; even when he is allowed to make appointments, he may not be able to remove those he places in office, so that he is deprived of any real control over them or responsibility for them.

Ordinarily several of the principal city offices are filled by direct election—the long ballot is a characteristic of the weak-mayor plan. (See

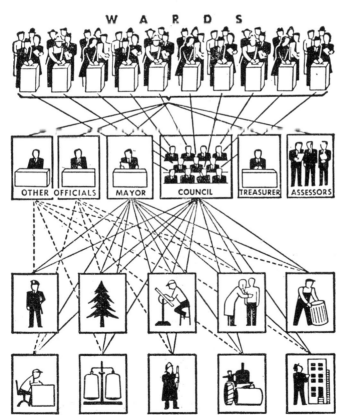

Figure 8-1. Weak-mayor–council form. SOURCE: Used by permission of the National Municipal League, New York.

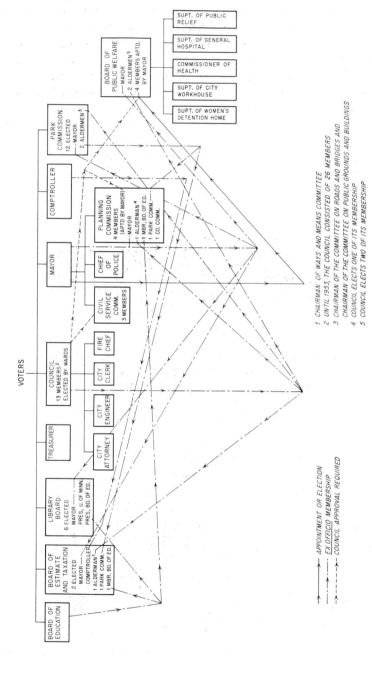

VOTERS

BOARD OF EDUCATION

BOARD OF ESTIMATE AND TAXATION
2 ELECTED
MAYOR
COMPTROLLER
1 ALDERMAN [1]
1 PARK COMM.
1 MBR. BD. OF ED.

LIBRARY BOARD
6 ELECTED
MAYOR
PRES. U. OF MINN.
PRES. BD. OF ED.

TREASURER

CITY ATTORNEY

CITY ENGINEER

CITY CLERK

FIRE CHIEF

COUNCIL
13 MEMBERS [2]
ELECTED BY WARDS

CIVIL SERVICE COMM.
3 MEMBERS

CHIEF OF POLICE

MAYOR

PLANNING COMMISSION
4 MEMBERS
(APTD BY MAYOR)
MAYOR
1 ALDERMAN [4]
1 MBR. BD. OF ED.
1 PARK COMM.
1 CO. COMM.

COMPTROLLER

PARK COMMISSION
12 ELECTED
MAYOR
2 ALDERMEN [3]

BOARD OF PUBLIC WELFARE
MAYOR
2 ALDERMEN [5]
4 MEMBERS APTD.
BY MAYOR

SUPT. OF PUBLIC RELIEF

SUPT. OF GENERAL HOSPITAL

COMMISSIONER OF HEALTH

SUPT. OF CITY WORKHOUSE

SUPT. OF WOMEN'S DETENTION HOME

1   CHAIRMAN OF WAYS AND MEANS COMMITTEE
2   UNTIL 1953, THE COUNCIL CONSISTED OF 26 MEMBERS
3   CHAIRMAN OF THE COMMITTEE ON ROADS AND BRIDGES AND
      CHAIRMAN OF THE COMMITTEE ON PUBLIC GROUNDS AND BUILDINGS
4   COUNCIL ELECTS ONE OF ITS MEMBERSHIP
5   COUNCIL ELECTS TWO OF ITS MEMBERSHIP

→   APPOINTMENT OR ELECTION
—·→   EX OFFICIO MEMBERSHIP
--→   COUNCIL APPROVAL REQUIRED

Figure 8-2. An actual weak-mayor–council city: Minneapolis, Minnesota. Note: There are many other appointive and ex officio boards and commissions which are not shown. Departmental subdivisions are also not shown.

202

Table 8-1). Other offices, in addition to those filled by election and the council, may be of the ex officio type. Even the governor or some other state official may make some appointments, such as that of the police chief. Without a chief executive, the weak-mayor system is likely to be one in which the various departments are independent of one another and without coordinated effort.

The weak-mayor system requires the voters of the municipality to choose members of sundry boards plus such administrators as, perhaps, the clerk, treasurer, assessor, controller, and attorney. Two candidates for the park board might well offer differing platforms of policy (one might want a new park on the west side, while the other might prefer a new swimming pool on the east side), but will the voter have the time and energy to look past the mayoralty contest as far as the councilmanic contests, much less to that for the park board?

In electing a clerk, treasurer, or assessor, the voter is even more sorely beset. Most of the voters will not know which candidate is best qualified to be the assessor, and they will not even know what functions are exercised by the clerk, treasurer, or, especially, the controller. In most cities, the clerk is a glorified file clerk, keeping the records of the city, while the treasurer is a bookkeeper, maintaining the financial records

TABLE 8-1. MUNICIPAL ELECTIVE OFFICES IN CITIES OVER 5,000, EXCLUSIVE OF THE MAYOR AND COUNCIL

Title of office	Per cent of cities electing*	Number of cities electing
Treasurer	33.3	839
Clerk	25.1	633
Assessor	14.2	360
Auditor	12.0	302
Attorney	8.1	205
Controller	3.9	98
Police chief	3.1	77
Public works director	1.3	34
None of the above elective	49.3	1,242

* There were 43 cities not reporting that are not included in the above statistics. The above list includes *all* forms of government. Percentages for mayor-council cities alone would be higher.

SOURCE: *Municipal Year Book, 1960* (International City Managers' Association, Chicago, 1960), p. 88.

of the city. Both officers are important, but they are ministerial rather than policy making. Theirs are normally routine jobs of an office-manager type that could well be performed by either appointive or civil service personnel. The voter, unacquainted with criteria usable in selecting persons to serve in offices such as these, is likely, in a large city, to vote for the person whose name is best known to him—usually the incumbent—regardless of the candidate's qualifications. In small cities, the voter is likely to support a candidate on the basis of sympathy. A qualified person may be passed over in favor of his opponent who is a veteran, or a handicapped person, or one with a large family who needs the pay, but who is not qualified.

The number of elective offices in American cities, even under the weak-mayor plan, has been declining for many decades. In 1936, 70 per cent of the cities of over 5,000 population elected one or more administrative officers other than the mayor. By 1960, this figure had dropped to 49 per cent. In 1936, 240 cities elected their police chiefs. Despite a great increase in the number of cities since then, only 77 elected the chief in 1960.[7]

Appraisal. The arguments for the weak-mayor plan are based upon the precepts of Jacksonianism. Many of these ideas are still popular with a large number of American people. For example, Americans may not know which officers are elected and which are appointed, but they are likely to insist that those who are elected should continue to be elected. They may not know what tasks are performed by a particular officer or what the criteria are for choosing an officer for the post, but they want him elected.[8] The weak-mayor system encourages this frontier type of concept.

The weak-mayor plan was a product of a different world from that which Americans occupy today. It was never intended to serve large, impersonal urban communities. The plan does not encourage modern methods of housekeeping—budgeting, personnel, purchasing, and the like. In fact, it fosters the use of the spoils plan, with its resort to performance by amateurs acting without coordinated leadership. For example, the city engineer (in charge of maintenance of public ways) may well be appointed by the council in a weak-mayor city. If this is the case, the ward aldermen on the council may personally direct the activities of the engineer's office within each of their wards and will probably have considerable control over selection of the employees of the office. Street maintenance becomes not a matter of professional judgment and per-

[7] See the current issue of the *Municipal Year Book* (International City Managers' Association, Chicago).

[8] Donald S. Hecock, "Too Many Elective Officials?" *National Municipal Review* (now *National Civic Review*), vol. 41 (October, 1952), pp. 449–454, offers a case study of this phenomenon on the state level.

formance, but one of doing repairs where they will be of the most help in the next election. The mending of political fences rather than of public ways becomes the first order of business.

Most of the great nineteenth-century machines operated under this plan, for it encourages the boss by its very clumsiness and lack of co-ordination. Under this plan, the voter can scarcely determine, after the most conscientious effort, who is responsible for what, or even what functions are being performed by whom. With no clear-cut locus of answerability to the voter, the boss has a real advantage. To be sure, bosses have existed under every form of city government: under the strong-mayor plan (Boston under Curley), the commission plan (Jersey City under Hague), and the council-manager plan (Kansas City under Pendergast). Even so, the weak-mayor plan is the most easily corrupted and bossed because of the confusing pattern of organization.

Probably the greatest criticism levied against the weak-mayor plan concerns its lack of provision for administrative leadership. The mayor, with very limited appointing powers and even more limited removal powers, is not a true chief executive. There is no officer to coordinate the various activities of the city. The mayor may not even make up the budget, which would serve at least to give an over-all picture of the needs of the city and of someone's rank-ordering of relative importance of the proposed expenditures of departments. Suppose, for example, that the city is short of funds (and all cities are short of funds). In a form of city government in which one person is legally responsible for all administration, it would be possible for this person to determine that the parks and recreation department should spend less for the coming year so that more streets could be repaired. Under the weak-mayor plan, however, the park board is a law unto itself, not answerable to either the mayor or the council, especially if it has its own tax levy and hence funds independent of the council, as might well be the case. Each department is likely to gallop off in its own direction with no one empowered to co-ordinate. The effect of all of these independent agencies is to make city government into a series of many little governments rather than one. There is one city government for parks, another for libraries, another for airports, another for sewage disposal, and so on.

Despite the great amount of criticism that has been levied against the weak-mayor plan, modifications of it remain the most common form of municipal government in the United States today. This is so in large part because the traditional form of village government throughout the United States is that of the weak mayor. Of course, the form of govern-ment is less important in the smaller municipality because government is more personal, performs fewer functions, and has less elaborate machinery. It has therefore been less important for smaller cities to experiment with newer forms of government, and there has been less agitation for them to do so.

While the weak-mayor system is characteristically found in small cities and villages, there are still quite a few cities of considerable size with relatively weak mayors, especially in the South. Atlanta (1960 population: 485,425) is the largest city in the United States with what is clearly a weak-mayor system. Large cities outside of the South using the plan include Minneapolis and Providence. Chicago, with its huge council of fifty members elected by wards, retains many of the characteristics of the weak-mayor system, as does Los Angeles, where administrative boards and commissions are extensively used.

Rather extreme examples of the weak-mayor system may still be found in many places. Stevens Point, Wisconsin (1960 population: about 17,000), is an excellent example. The voters select directly a mayor, a controller, a clerk, a treasurer, an assessor, a city engineer, a health officer, a street superintendent, a park superintendent, a city attorney, and ward aldermen, in addition to school officials. The pattern is even more complicated, for control of the police and fire departments is vested in a commission separate from the council.

The structure of the weak-mayor–council plan is not regarded as being satisfactory for modern government. It is clumsy, uncoordinated, and has, for a long time, been declining in use for all but the smallest cities.

The Strong-mayor–Council Plan. The development of a strong-mayor system of government in the last two decades of the nineteenth century was a gradual one. The new plan differed only in degree from that of the weak mayor. It was not conceived of as a distinctly new form of government, nor was it one. Actually, the weak-mayor form resembled the structure of most state governments of that day and this. The strong-mayor system, on the other hand, was modeled on the national government, with its integrated administrative structure [9] under the control of the President.

Of course, there are few, if any, cities that meet exactly all of the conditions of the theoretical model of the strong-mayor system as it is described below and in Figure 8-3. Most mayor-council cities represent a compromise between the very weak and the very strong mayor plan. The typical one is actually difficult to classify.

Characteristics. In the strong-mayor–council city, administrative responsibility is concentrated in the hands of the mayor, while policy making is a joint function of the mayor and the council.[10] The plan calls for a

[9] For a definition of *integration,* see p. 82.

[10] The strong-mayor plan is sometimes called the "federal" plan, because it follows roughly the plan of the Federal government, but this term is confusing and will not be used in this text.

short ballot with the mayor as the only elected administrative officer. He in turn appoints and dismisses department heads, often without councilmanic approval. The mayor thus becomes the officer responsible for the carrying out of established policy and for coordinating the efforts of the various departments. The mayor also prepares the annual budget and controls its administration once it is adopted by the council. This allows the whole financial picture and the claims of the various departments to be compared in financial policy making, in contrast to the piecemeal methods by which these things are approached under the weak-mayor plan.

The mayor's legal position allows him to exert very strong political leadership. Not only does he have the veto power and the right to recommend legislative policy to the council, as is the case under the weak-mayor system, but his wide control over administration gives him great power which can be used in many ways as weapons to overcome opposition, and furnishes a vantage point from which to recommend policy. Furthermore, his strong administrative position encourages the newspapers to give him credit or blame for events that take place within city government. The resultant publicity makes the public keenly aware of his activities and of his recommendations to the council. As in the case of the President of the United States, when a strong mayor speaks, he receives far

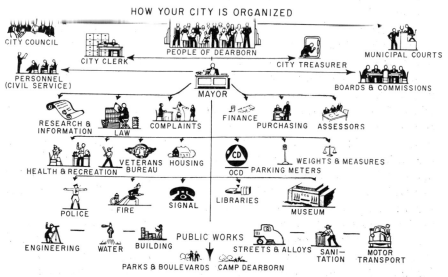

Figure 8-3. An actual strong-mayor–council city: Dearborn, Michigan. Note: There are twenty boards and commissions. A few of them perform staff functions (e.g., Board of Assessors, Civil Service Board); others are for appeal purposes (e.g., Plumbing Board of Appeals, Zoning Board of Appeals); the remainder are advisory (e.g., Plan Commission, Recreation Commission). SOURCE: *A Diary of Service, 1950–51* (City of Dearborn, Mich., 1951).

more attention than does even the most experienced or most respected member of the legislative branch. The fact that the mayor presents a comprehensive budget to the council for consideration also adds to his dominant political position, for by this very act public attention is focused on the mayor and the burden of proof for any changes in the budget is placed upon the council.

The council plays a highly subordinate role in a strong-mayor city. It does not, as in the weak-mayor city, share in the performance of administrative duties. Its functions are limited to the exercise of legislative policy making, and even this role must be shared with the mayor. If there is an aggressive member of the council, this body may seek to make policy for itself. But it is more likely that the mayor's recommendations, backed as they are by the greater public attention focused on him, by his constant oversight of the city administration, and by his veto power, will be dutifully enacted by the council, perhaps after insignificant changes or after a symbolic show of independence. The average citizen is not likely to have much knowledge of council activities in a strong-mayor city. In a large city he is unlikely even to know the names of more than one or two of the councilmen, especially if the council is elected at large, as is often the case.

Because the council is exclusively a policy-making body for the city as a whole, it is likely to be small (typically seven or nine members) and elected at large on either a partisan or a nonpartisan ballot. Unless the city is very large, members serve on a part-time basis, since they have no administrative duties to perform and are not expected, as they are in the weak-mayor system, to be errand boys for residents of their wards. When council members serve only part time, the effect is to give the mayor even greater powers, since he has the advantage of spending the whole of his day studying the needs of the city. This may tend to place the council in an even more subordinate position. It will certainly put its members at a disadvantage in obtaining and evaluating information from the various departments and will place an even greater burden of proof upon the council when it disagrees with the proposed policies of the mayor. Terms of office for both mayor and council are likely to be four years in length. This is the result of the reform-movement attitude that public officials should be given time enough in office to prove themselves.

In addition to performing part of the legislative function, the council is also entrusted with the important task of serving as critic. This is a function of all legislative bodies, of course, but it becomes unusually important where vast administrative power is vested in one official. The council is usually given full power to conduct investigations into any department or any phase of administration. In addition, an officer, usually called the auditor and responsible to the council, checks upon the way in which the administrative branch of the city has spent the moneys appropriated by the council.[11]

Appraisal. Because of its provision for vigorous political leadership, the strong-mayor plan is especially desirable in large cities, where the complexities of government require someone to give firm leadership and direction. No other form of government in use in American cities makes an equal provision for leadership. Nearly all of the nation's largest cities have some version of the strong-mayor plan. In smaller cities, where the functions performed are fewer and simpler and where government is more personal, the need for this type of leadership is somewhat less.

The strong-mayor plan has several distinct merits in comparison with the weak-mayor–council plan: it allows for the placement of responsibility by the voters; it allows for modern methods of budgeting and of handling personnel; it permits the coordination of administration; and it allows for over-all policy planning.

It has some problems, too. Perhaps the major one is that it expects too much of the mayor. In addition to serving as ceremonial head of the city, he is supposed to be both an adroit politician and an expert administrator. This combination is not easy to find. The able politician is likely to be either inexperienced with administration or bored by it, or both. The person whose training and interest are in administration or some specialized phase of it is very possibly a colorless campaigner or one who finds politics personally distasteful. While the popular view that all politicians are extroverts and all public bureaucrats are introverts is not correct, it is true that skill in campaigning and administrative leadership are not often combined in the same person. The strong-mayor system expects that it will be.

Another problem in the strong-mayor system is that of getting persons of the required qualifications to run for office. A person who can do all of the things expected of a strong mayor is usually highly successful in business and industry and is ordinarily unwilling to give up a position which pays a high salary and in which he has reasonable security to conduct a political campaign for a position which carries far less salary and no security.

In selecting a mayor, many voters would no doubt like to consider the qualifications of each candidate as a capable administrator, but they are necessarily unable to do so. Judging whether or not a person is a good administrator is very difficult—more difficult than judging whether a person is technically qualified as an engineer or a physician. The candidates themselves are not of much help to the voter; the one who makes the greatest claims of administrative ability may be the one least qualified.

It has sometimes been said that the strong-mayor plan is undesirable

[11] See chap. 16 on fiscal administration.

because it "mixes politics with administration," but this is not a valid argument. As a matter of fact, this could be offered as an argument *for* the plan. The mayor is able to place administrative problems in their political context—where they must eventually be placed in a democracy. He can compromise between these two inseparable aspects of government.

A final problem must be mentioned. Because it is based upon that American favorite, the separation of powers, in combination with its obverse, the checks-and-balances system, the possibility of a deadlock between the mayor and the council on the formulation of policy is always present. On the national level, where the same system exists, most students are aware of serious deadlocks that have taken place—during the last two years of Wilson's administration, the last two of Hoover's, and almost the whole of Truman's after 1946. It is perhaps less common on the local level than on the national, however, because the strong mayor so often tends to dominate the political scene and is in a position to keep the council in line. The threat is, however, inherent in the system.

The Strong-mayor–Council Plan with Chief Administrative Officer. The chief executive in a strong-mayor city may well recognize his own shortcomings as an administrator and attempt to do something about it. The most common method of buttressing his position is to appoint an able, professionally experienced administrator to the position of chief fiscal officer, usually called the controller. He may act as something of a deputy mayor and attend to many details of administration.

The typical politician-mayor is not always willing to choose professional deputies, however. In order to provide some legal incentive for him to do so, a recent trend has been toward establishing by charter or ordinance an official known by various titles and here called a chief administrative officer (CAO). (See Figure 8-4.) His powers vary considerably from one city to another, and sometimes he can scarcely be differentiated from the chief budget or fiscal officer, but according to the theory of the position, he should be appointed by the mayor and should perform, in general, such functions as the supervision of heads of various departments, preparation of the budget (or supervision over the budget director), and personnel direction. It is his task to correlate the various departments in the important routines of day-to-day administration, to give technical and professional advice to the mayor, and hence to free the mayor for his other two major jobs of serving as ceremonial head of the city (greeting the governor, laying cornerstones, and crowning the latest beauty queen) and of proposing and launching broad over-all policy.

The origins of the CAO are somewhat obscure, since the position grew out of the garden-variety mayor-council plans, but the city and county of San Francisco appointed one in 1931 who must have been one of the

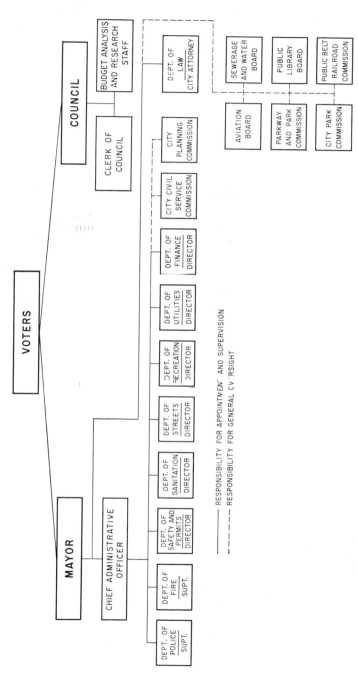

Figure 8-4. An actual strong-mayor–council city with chief administrative officer: New Orleans, Louisiana. Note: Not all agencies are shown. SOURCE: Adapted from *Annual Report of the Mayor* (City of New Orleans, La., 1953).

211

earliest.[12] Many CAOs have been appointed in California in the postwar years, but these all appear to be *managers* with reduced administrative authority. These so-called CAOs are appointed by the council, as is a manager, rather than by the mayor. In California, only San Francisco has a CAO in the sense defined in this book, and even in that city he heads up a group of city offices dealing with public works. He does not make up the budget or coordinate city departments.[13]

Some authorities believe that the CAO plan should be classified as a variation of the manager plan, rather than of the mayor-council plan. It combines some of the characteristics of each, and its classification is probably not too important. It is listed here in this book because it is a plan that continues the use of the separation-of-powers theory and places ultimate responsibility for administration in the hands of the mayor, rather than the council as is the case with the manager plan. In states where there are broad home rule powers, many of the advantages of the council-manager plan can be incorporated under the strong-mayor form. As a result, there is no rigid dividing line between the two forms.

The Current Trend. Large-city interest in the strong-mayor plan with CAO has been definitely on the increase since the end of World War II. The Philadelphia charter of 1951 provides for a CAO, as does the 1952 model of the New Orleans charter. Both are home rule cities. The New Orleans charter, for example, calls for a council of seven, five elected by districts and two elected at large, for four-year terms. The mayor has the usual powers in policy making and in addition appoints a CAO, who serves at his pleasure. The CAO, with the approval of the mayor, appoints the heads of departments, except for those whose positions are filled according to state law. The CAO, of course, has supervisory and coordinative powers over the departments whose heads he appoints.[14]

A CAO established by ordinance has served in Louisville under two mayors. St. Cloud, Minnesota, adopted the CAO plan in its 1952 charter. A director of administrative services, with some of the powers of a CAO, has been established in Boston. A 1951 charter amendment provides for an administrative officer for Los Angeles. He is appointed by the mayor

---

[12] John C. Bollens, *Appointed Executive Local Government: The California Experience* (University of California Press, Berkeley, Calif., 1952), pp. 12–14; John M. Selig, "The San Francisco Idea," *National Municipal Review* (now *National Civic Review*), vol. 46 (June, 1957), pp. 290–295. See Lent D. Upson, "A Proposal for an Administrative Assistant to the Mayor," reported in *The American City*, vol. 44 (June, 1931), p. 93; or, more generally, Wallace S. Sayre, "The General Manager Idea for Large Cities," *Public Administration Review*, vol. 14 (Autumn, 1954), pp. 253–257, and, for an argument that the council-manager plan may be more appropriate, even for large cities, John E. Bebout, "Management for Large Cities," *ibid.*, vol. 15 (Summer, 1955), pp. 188–195.

[13] See Bollens, *op. cit.*, pp. 9–11, 119–123; and Selig, *op. cit.*

[14] See *National Municipal Review* (now *National Civic Review*), vol. 41 (May, 1952), p. 250; vol. 41 (December, 1952), p. 570.

with majority confirmation by the council and is removable by the same process or by a two-thirds vote in the council. This officer cannot properly be called a CAO, since Los Angeles is basically a weak-mayor city and the administrative officer at present is principally the mayor's budget officer. In that city the council has numerous administrative duties, and there are a score of departments controlled by five-man commissions appointed by the mayor with the check of councilmanic approval and with a limited removal power. The city attorney and controller are elected officials.

The 1950 Faulkner Act in New Jersey provides for optional charters that are adopted in the various cities after a local charter commission decides to present one of the options to the voters for approval. It makes the strong-mayor plan with CAO one of the options.

Adoption in New York. In 1953, two study groups recommended the CAO plan for use in the city of New York. After a three-year study (it cost $2,200,000) the Mayor's Commission on Management Survey in its final report recommended against a general overhaul of the city's organizational structure and suggested the creation of a new office, that of a CAO to be called a director of administration. It was also suggested that a "management cabinet," to consist of seven ex officio members, be appointed to aid the mayor. The director of administration would perform supervisory and coordinative functions over most of the city's departments and agencies. The deputy mayor would be assigned nearly all of the ceremonial duties of the city.

Immediately after his election as mayor of the city in November, 1953, Robert F. Wagner, Jr., announced that he would appoint a CAO to the new post of City Administrator. For this task he selected a widely known student and practitioner of public administration, Luther H. Gulick.

Although the Administrator had to engage in a fight for survival against jealous and older city agencies, he and his office have "become the most fully realized assets of the Mayor's office. They have become the Mayor's most active problem-solvers, especially in matters requiring interdepartmental agreements or departmental reorganization." [15]

Appraisal. The strong-mayor plan with chief administrative officer seeks to free the mayor for policy making, and give the city a professionally competent man to head administration. This new variation on the old theme would appear to be especially acceptable in large cities, and these are the ones that, in fact, seem most interested in the development. The use of the strong-mayor plan with this modification would, however, leave that system still with at least one major potential defect: the continuing threat of a legislative-executive deadlock. It would appear, too,

[15] Wallace S. Sayre and Herbert Kaufman, *Governing New York City* (Russell Sage Foundation, New York, 1960), pp. 665–666.

that there would be a great potential for jealous rivalry between the mayor and the CAO or for an uncooperative mayor to appropriate for himself the powers and functions of the appointive CAO.

CITIES WITHOUT A SEPARATION OF POWERS

The Commission Plan. A hurricane in September, 1900, almost completely destroyed the city of Galveston, Texas, and in doing so created the conditions under which the commission plan was produced. Actually, as Richard S. Childs has pointed out, the commission structure was not planned; it was the result of an accident.[16] During the period of rebuilding Galveston, the legislature suspended local self-government in the city and substituted a temporary government of five local businessmen—the Galveston *commission*, hence the name for the system. The commission, working with great zeal under extraordinary conditions, accomplished much more at less cost than had its almost bankrupt predecessor. A new charter in 1903 tried to retain the system that had been working well and provided for a continuation of the commission, with three of its members appointed by the governor and two to be elected within the city. The courts held this unconstitutional, since an emergency no longer existed. The legislature then made all five commissioners elective.[17]

The success of the commission plan in Galveston soon attracted wide attention. Other Texas cities adopted the plan, and it quickly became popular in many parts of the nation. A Des Moines attorney, visiting Galveston, was impressed with the new "businessman's government" and proceeded to persuade the Iowa legislature to permit his city to adopt the plan. The legislature added other reform devices to the new charter—nonpartisan elections, and the initiative, referendum, and recall. It then became the "Des Moines plan."

The commission plan was adopted in Houston in 1905 and in Des Moines in 1907, and by 1910 it had spread to some 108 cities. In 1917 at least 500 cities were using the plan. Then a reversal took place. The number of commission-governed cities stopped increasing and then began to diminish. Municipal reformers lost interest in the commission plan and began to advocate the council-manager plan as the true embodiment of a business form of organization. There have been almost no new adoption since the 1930s, and the total number of commission cities has declined steadily since World War I.

[16] Richard S. Childs, *Civic Victories* (Harper & Brothers, New York, 1952), pp. 134–136. Earlier precedents for the commission idea are cited in E. B. Schulz, *American City Government* (Stackpole & Heck, Pittsburgh, 1949), pp. 319–321.

[17] Many state constitutions guarantee municipalities the right to elect their own officers.

Characteristics. The commission plan's outstanding feature is the dual role of the commissioners. Each of them serves individually as the head of one of the city's administrative departments, while collectively they serve as the policy-making council for the city. In this plan, unlike the various mayor-council structures, there is no separation of powers. The commission performs both legislative and executive functions (see Figure 8-5).

The commission is always small, usually consisting of five members, as did the original Galveston model. Some cities, especially small ones, have only three members, and quite a number have seven. There is a mayor, but in the theoretical model he has no powers beyond those of the other commissioners, except that he performs the ceremonial duties for the city and presides over the council. He has no veto power. In most cities the office of mayor is specifically named on the ballot and is hence filled by popular vote. In some cities, however, the council chooses one

COMMISSION FORM

Figure 8-5. SOURCE: Used by permission of the National Municipal League, New York.

of its own members to serve as mayor, and in a few places the person who happens to receive the highest number of votes among all candidates becomes mayor.

Because the plan is a product of the reform movement, the commissioners are usually elected on a nonpartisan ticket. This is the case in about three-quarters of the municipalities. The commissioners are usually expected to serve as full-time public servants, even in fairly small cities; and in the original plan it was hoped that they would possess business or engineering experience and not be "mere politicians." They are nearly always elected at large, and four-year terms are most common.

There is a short ballot. According to the original plan, only the commissioners are elected. Often staggered terms are used so that only two or three members of a five-member commission are elected at one time.

Appraisal. The commission plan was a radical departure from the prevailing weak-mayor systems of the turn of the century. It concentrated responsibility in the hands of a few men so that the general public could assess credit or blame for municipal activities. It greatly shortened the ballot from that which existed under the weak-mayor, or even most strong-mayor, systems. This gave the average voter a chance to know something about the character and qualifications of the candidates. Furthermore, only commissioners were chosen. Voters were not asked to select persons to fill routine offices (such as clerk or treasurer) or technical offices (such as controller or assessor). Since the separation-of-powers theory was not followed, there was no problem of the deadlock between the legislative and executive branches that is always a threat in any mayor-council city.

The commission plan had, however, too many disadvantages to make it workable. It was supposed to provide for a city policy-making body on which businessmen on leave from their ordinary pursuits would be willing to serve. Sometimes this was the case—for a few years. Actually, as a regular practice, it was not possible to select commissioners from among successful businessmen, or successful persons from any walk of life, for they were unwilling to give up their own businesses and run for an office that paid a low salary.

Responsibility to the public was not definitely fixed; it was divided among the several commissioners. The plan did not eliminate amateur administrators as department heads. In this respect the situation was not changed much from the weak-mayor plan. A local citizen might well be able to help make basic policy for the police department or for public ways, but he would be able to serve capably as *administrative* head of either department only as the result of political accident.

The commission was often too small to provide for the function of *criticism.* It is essential in a democracy that the actions of public officials are constantly subjected to critical evaluation. While the mayor-council system might lead to deadlocks, it at least provided a mechanism of criticism. This was not true of the commission plan. There was no separation of powers, so that only the commission members were left to criticize one another. In theory they could do so, but three to seven people seeing one another day after day put their relationships on a personal basis. As politicians they are certain to desire to avoid criticism. The commission very often, therefore, became a fraternity of tolerance.

Instead of watching one another, the commissioners would agree that "if you stay out of my department, I will stay out of yours." Criticism came to an end. There was no minority party to watch the majority. There were no "backbenchers" eagerly awaiting the chance to replace a member of the cabinet, as there is in the parliamentary system of government. There was no mayor with policy message and veto ready. The mutual hands-off policy went even further. In many cities it meant that there were really several different city governments, each operating independently of the others, but with an occasional five-power conference being held to satisfy the demands of the charter.

There were two further serious weaknesses of the commission device, both of them dealing with a lack of leadership. The plan did not provide for a chief executive. The strong-mayor and manager forms provide for administrative integration with a top official ultimately answerable to the council for all administrative operations. No such person existed in the formal structure of the commission plan. And jealousy of the rights of independence of one's department was likely to keep it from existing in actual practice. The top of the administrative pyramid was sawed off. Each department ran off in its own administrative direction with no coordination at the top. This might be true to a degree even exceeding that found in the weak-mayor system.

There was no provision for top-policy leadership either, except fortuitously. The commissioners were equals and were likely to guard their equality with great zeal. There was no top policy maker, as under the strong-mayor system. An individual commissioner might by personality, experience, or skill at political organization come to dominate the council, but this was not the rule.

The plan attracted a great deal of attention for a brief period, but it was quickly outmoded by the invention of the manager plan and the development of a modern strong mayor. The inherent weaknesses of the commission plan then rapidly became manifest.

Present Status. A large number of commission-governed cities remain in the United States today (309 in 1960), although all of the many Canadian cities that once used it have by now abandoned it. The total number of cities under the plan has been on the decline since about

TABLE 8-2. LARGEST COMMISSION CITIES IN THE UNITED STATES

City	1960 population	Size of council	No. at large	Type of election*	Term, years	Salary, 1960	Other elective officers
Memphis........	491,691	5	5	NP	4	$12,000	
Portland, Ore....	370,339	5	5	NP-s	4	10,080	Auditor
Birmingham.....	338,569	3	3	NP	4	7,000	
St. Paul........	313,209	7	7	NP	2	9,000	Controller
Jersey City......	269,621	5	5	NP	4	12,000	

*Under "Type of Election," "NP" refers to nonpartisan elections, while "-s" following means that commission terms are staggered so that all do not expire at once. "Salary" refers to that of commission members.

SOURCE: *Municipal Year Book, 1960* (International City Managers' Association, Chicago, 1960), pp. 92–93.

1917, and the drop has been especially sharp since 1946. Even so, about 12 per cent of the cities with a population of more than 5,000 still use it, the largest city in 1960 being Memphis (see Table 8-2).

Abandonments, especially in larger cities, have come at a rapid rate in the postwar world. The "Des Moines plan" was abandoned in Des Moines in 1949 in favor of the council-manager form. San Antonio, after thirty-seven years as a commission city, switched to the manager plan in 1951. The Hoboken, New Jersey, charter commission denounced the commission plan in that city as having been "a complete failure," and the city changed in 1952 to the strong-mayor plan with CAO. So did New Orleans. Inadequacy of policy leadership is felt most in the largest cities. Medium-sized and small cities, however, are also abandoning the commission plan.

Outmoded structures of government live beyond the time when they are needed, as do all human institutions which suffer the rigidity of being organized on a formal basis. There is no future for the commission structure of government.[18] Those commission cities that remain do so as a result of apathy or because officeholders have a vested interest in the *status quo*.

The Council-Manager Plan. The origin of the idea for the council-manager plan is not known with certainty. It seems that one of the first

[18] The view of reformers toward the plan during its most popular years is expressed in E. S. Bradford, *Commission Government in American Cities* (The Macmillan Company, New York, 1911). The failure of the plan is expressed in C. M. Fassett, "The Weakness of Commission Government," *National Municipal Review* (now *National Civic Review*), vol. 9 (October, 1920), pp. 642–647.

instances in which it was urged was in an editorial in the August, 1899, issue of *California Municipalities*. Haven A. Mason, editor of the magazine, urged that there should be "a distinct profession of municipal managers." He listed desirable qualifications, saying that a manager should know something about engineering, street construction, sewers, building construction, water and lighting systems, personnel, accounting, municipal law, fire protection, and library management. "Every city that receives or expends $50,000 annually," he said, "ought to have a salaried business manager." He even went so far as to say that "when we require adepts to run our cities, our universities will establish a department to specially fit our young men to enter the new profession of conducting municipal business." [19]

The claim for having the first council-manager city is sometimes disputed between Staunton, Virginia, and Sumter, South Carolina. In 1908, Staunton, with a weak mayor and a bicameral council, sought a different form of city government. Getting a new charter from the legislature would not have been easy. It was decided, therefore, to hire a "general manager" for the city on the basis of an ordinance. He was to be a full-time employee in charge of administration, was to be hired by the council, and could be dismissed by it at any time.

While the Staunton experiment did not produce a neat organization chart and was not based upon a carefully calculated theory, it may correctly be said to have become a manager-plan city in that year. Richard S. Childs, a businessman who was at that time secretary of the National Short Ballot Organization and who later was to become president of the National Municipal League, took a leading part in the development and popularizing of the plan. In 1911 he drew up a proposed city charter which was endorsed by the Board of Trade (chamber of commerce) of Lockport, New York. As it happened, the state general assembly refused to allow the city to use this model manager charter, but the charter attracted a good bit of attention and was adopted by Sumter, South Carolina, in the following year.

The manager-plan idea spread with great speed. During 1913, several small cities and towns adopted the Childs charter. At the same time, the Chamber of Commerce of Dayton appointed a committee to study the need for a new charter in that city, for the state of Ohio had just granted to its municipalities the power of home rule. The committee, which was headed by John M. Patterson, president of the National Cash Register Company, came to favor the manager plan. While the group was pursuing its efforts, the Miami River, which passes through the city, overflowed its banks in spring flood. The ineptitude of the existing city government in meeting the problems that followed gave unexpectedly

[19] The editorial is reprinted in Bollens, *op. cit.*, appendix III.

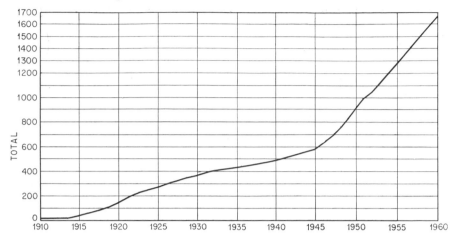

Figure 8-6. The growth of the council-manager plan. The table is based only upon adoptions still in effect Jan. 1, 1960, and includes only municipal corporations, towns, and townships in the United States. Note the post-World War II spurt and contrast it with the Depression years (1929–1939). SOURCE: "The City Manager Profession and Directory," *Municipal Year Book, 1960* (International City Managers' Association, Chicago, 1960), pp. 497–528.

dramatic support to the efforts of the charter-study committee. The voters adopted the proposed new charter in August. It went into effect on January 1, 1914, and the new council promptly hired the city engineer of Cincinnati as manager, thus setting a precedent for the type of person that is still very commonly preferred for the position.

The Dayton episode, partly because it occurred in a large city, partly because of the personal publicity efforts of Patterson, and partly because of the extraordinary drama connected with it, gave a tremendous boost to the council-manager plan. By 1915, there were 49 manager cities. Five years later there were 158. The number has increased uninterruptedly ever since. On January 1, 1960, there were 1,682 manager cities and other local governments in the United States and Canada. Over 36 per cent of the cities of over 5,000 population had managers. (See Figure 8-6.)

Only Hawaii, Indiana, and Louisiana had no manager cities of any kind in 1960. The manager plan has enjoyed a rapid expansion in the period following World War II. Its growth has closely paralleled that of suburbia. It seems to be especially suited to the politics of consensus and the acceptance of professionalism that we find there.[20]

Characteristics.[21] The outstanding identifying marks of the council-

[20] See Robert C. Wood, *Suburbia* (Houghton Mifflin Company, Boston, 1959), pp. 183–186.

[21] The National Municipal League, New York, has issued several pamphlets in popular form. See especially *Forms of Municipal Government* (revised, 1958), and *The Story of the Council-Manager Plan* (revised, 1959).

COUNCIL-MANAGER FORM

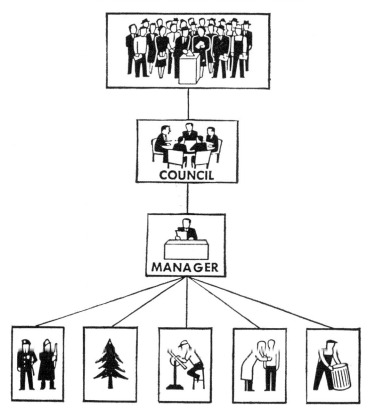

Figure 8-7. SOURCE: By permission of the National Municipal League, New York.

manager-plan model include a council of laymen responsible for policy making and a professional administration under a chief administrator responsible to the council. The theoretical structure rivals that of the British parliamentary system in its simplicity (see Figures 8-7 and 8-8).

The council is small, five to nine members, and is commonly elected at large, on a nonpartisan ballot, often for four-year staggered terms. It is responsible to the public for all policy making and ultimately for the over-all character of administration. Under the model charter,[22] members of the council are the only officers who are popularly elected. The intended purpose of the short ballot is to concentrate responsibility upon these people and to ask the voters to fill only important policy-making positions in which they can reasonably be expected to take an interest.

There is no separation of powers or checks and balances. There is a

[22] See the *Model City Charter* (revised, 1941) of the National Municipal League, New York. The manager plan has been endorsed by the League since 1916.

mayor or president of the city or village, but he normally performs only ceremonial functions and presides over the council. He has no administrative powers, except in the case of an emergency, and has no veto. In more than one-half of the manager cities over 5,000 population (51 per cent in 1960), the council chooses the mayor from among its own membership. In most other cities he is directly elected, although a few give the post to the person with the most votes in the councilmanic race.

The administration of the city is integrated under the control of a professional manager, who is hired by the council. He serves, in the model plan, for no definite term of office, but rather at the pleasure of a majority of the council. He is not subject to recall by the voters, for they did not hire him, and furthermore, ultimate responsibility for the quality of the administration belongs to the council. No manager may serve effectively if he does not enjoy the confidence of a majority of the council, and therefore the credit or blame for what he does rests with the council.

Not only is the manager a professional person, but he is expected to hire

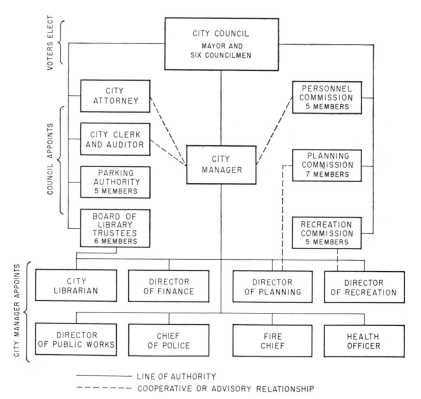

Figure 8-8. An actual council-manager city: Modesto, California. SOURCE: Adapted from *A Report of Progress* (City of Modesto, Calif., 1952).

professionally competent technicians to run the various departments of the city. The lower administrative positions, roughly those below the department heads, are also filled with persons who are technically competent. They are usually chosen by civil service merit examination.

Appraisal. Municipal reformers have tended to accord to this plan inordinate praise, often attributing to it miraculous powers to bring about efficient and economical city administration regardless of the traditions of city government, the kind of personnel which it employs, and whether the public understands and supports the basic principles of the plan. These exaggerated claims for the plan, as well as some of the specious arguments used against it, should be discounted by the sophisticated student of municipal affairs.

The council-manager plan calls for lay citizens, commonly political amateurs, to serve on the council and make public policy as representatives of the community. There are no professional politicians seeking to make a living from the position, for the councilmanic jobs normally pay only a very nominal salary or only a per meeting allowance under the theory of the plan, the execution of policy as approved by the council is in the hands of a professional staff of administrators headed by the manager. All administrators and technicians are especially qualified for their jobs—an important fact in a day when government performs many complicated and technical functions. The chief administrator can be selected by the council, not from among local politicians of one party, as would be the case if it were a patronage appointment, but rather from among trained persons from anywhere in the nation. The choice is limited only by what the council believes it can afford to pay.

But while the manager plan emphasizes professional administration, the theory does not turn the city over to the whims of an independent bureaucracy. The manager and his subordinates are constantly responsible for their actions to the political branch of the government. They normally attend council sessions, where they are expected to answer questions, report on progress of various projects, and explain any of their actions that involve matters in which the council is interested. And there are none of the legislative-executive conflicts that arise from time to time in the mayor-council city, since, as in the parliamentary system, those who carry out policy serve at the pleasure of the legislative branch.

In contrast to the commission plan, however, there is a provision for criticism. There is no dividing up of the administrative spoils among the council members, and hence there is less of a need for a collusion against criticism. The legislative branch remains free to oversee the operation of administration, and it is especially important to note that the people who appropriate the funds are not the people who spend them. The council votes the funds and then checks upon the manager and his staff, both through their own supervision and through the receipt of auditors' reports.

Although the manager plan is a simple mechanism, it is not always understood by the general public. An important factor contributing to this is the carry-over to the present day of many elements of Jacksonian philosophy. For example, the plan is sometimes challenged as "dictatorial" or "un-American" because the chief administrator is not elected. To be sure, this fact violates an almost sacred precept of Jacksonianism. But the argument is invalid, since there is full responsibility for administration. The absence of a check-and-balance system also troubles those dedicated to Jacksonian tradition.

Some people argue that the manager plan costs too much for small cities, because the position of manager must command enough pay to attract competent personnel. It is also argued that the manager would not have enough work to keep him busy in a small city. These arguments would seem invalid for most small places, however, for the plan is in operation in a large number of municipalities of under 5,000 population.[23]

There are more serious objections to the plan, however. The number of cities needing managers and professional department heads has increased so rapidly in the postwar era that there is a shortage of able managers. The numerous positions in private business for administrators and engineers has also helped to reduce the number of persons available to cities. Some cities have tried the plan, only to complain bitterly that the manager was incompetent. In many cases the complaint is undoubtedly justified.

Managers are sometimes criticized on another ground. Many of them are engineers who have had no training in the social sciences. As such, some of them may tend to view issues of public policy as a series of engineering or budgeting problems rather than as matters of economics and sociology.

Some advocates of the manager plan have made the erroneous assumption that a sharp distinction can be made between politics and administration. No such line exists. One shades off into the other. Their theory holds that the manager is a nonelective employee who should not make policy but should concern himself only with the details of administration. Actually, it is almost a necessity for the lay, part-time council to look to the professional, full-time manager for recommendations concerning policy. If harmonious relations exist and the manager and the council are competent, the council will ordinarily not act on any policy matter without first getting the recommendations and a state-

[23] The pattern of managership in these cities is described in W. C. Busby, "The Small Council-Manager City," *Public Management*, vol. 35 (July, 1953), pp. 154–156.

ment of the pertinent facts from the manager.[24] On some types of highly controversial issues a manager, if he is prudent, will avoid taking a stand, but apart from these, it is his job to make recommendations and, in fact, to initiate policy recommendations. He is nearly always in a better position to interpret policy demands than is the council. If the council accepts the recommendations of the manager with regularity, it does not necessarily mean that it is a rubber stamp; it may mean merely that the council has hired a competent manager, and that his recommendations accord nicely with the consensus of values in the community.

Among managers themselves there are two philosophies (perhaps it is more a matter of two personality types) which deal with the proper relationship of the manager to the council. Some managers center their attention on administrative operations and routine matters, carefully avoiding taking a stand on any city issue; others center their attention on policy matters and the development of the city. In some instances—Berkeley and East Cleveland at one time were examples—a well-entrenched manager, long in office, may completely dominate a council. He may not only make it into a rubber stamp, but may even have considerable influence in determining who is elected to the council.

While the manager may tend to dominate the council in some cases, it is also true that the policy-making arm may tend to invade the area theoretically reserved for professional administrators. If the manager is weak, or if several members of the council do not accept the spirit of the manager plan, there may be a good deal of "political" interference in administration. Councilmen may bypass the manager and deal directly with members of departments or seek to influence administrative decisions on the basis of short-range constituency considerations rather than professional standards and values.[25] Hostile councilmen may even appoint a local politician to the post of manager. In cases such as these, the manager plan cannot operate according to the model plan.

It is not uncommon to find, especially where a modified manager plan

[24] See Charles R. Adrian, "Leadership and Decision-making in Manager Cities: A Study of Three Communities," *Public Administration Review*, vol. 18 (Summer, 1958), pp. 208–213; K. A. Bosworth, "The Manager *Is* a Politician," *ibid.*, pp. 216–222; C. A. Harrell and D. G. Weiford, "The City Manager and the Policy Process," *ibid.*, vol. 19 (Spring, 1959), pp. 101–107.

[25] For a case study of a city where several of the phenomena discussed in this section were found, see Dorothy I. Cline, *Albuquerque and the City Manager Plan, 1917–1948* (University of New Mexico Press, Albuquerque, N.M., 1951). Only about 4 per cent of the cities adopting the manager plan have later abandoned it. See A. W. Bromage, *Manager Plan Abandonments* (5th ed.; National Municipal League, New York, 1959); E. O. Stene and G. K. Floro, *Abandonments of the Manager Plan: A Study of Four Small Cities* (University of Kansas Press, Lawrence, Kan., 1953); and B. B. Mason, "What's Back of Opposition to Council-Manager Government?" *American City*, vol. 75 (March, 1960), pp. 177–181.

leaves some administrative powers with the mayor, a disrupting power struggle between the mayor and the manager. This is also true in cities where the mayor does not understand or accept his role under the manager plan. If the public does not understand the principles of the plan, it is likely to support the mayor in such a fight, for the title of his office implies to many people that he ought to be the chief administrator. In some cities, certain officials, such as the city attorney, the city engineer, or the police chief, may be appointed by the mayor rather than by the manager. In such a case, there may in effect be two managers, one amateur and the other professional. It often follows that the council members are eventually forced to "choose up sides" if either the mayor or the manager launches into a policy of aggrandizement. The results are usually a dead, or at least badly wounded, manager plan.

Perhaps the greatest potential weakness in the plan is to be found in connection with the problem of policy leadership. No adequate provision for it is made in the model plan. The council is a body of equals. One of the members may emerge as a leader in policy making, but if this is so, it is the result of accident. It is more likely that the council will flounder about or turn to the manager. This problem is not so important in middle-sized cities, for these places do not usually contain as complex a set of groups in conflict and the solving of issues of policy is normally not as complicated as it is in larger cities. San Antonio is the only really large city to adopt and retain the plan since the Depression years. Ten cities of over 250,000 were employing managers in 1960, however, and with apparent satisfaction.[26] (See Table 8-3.)

There is some evidence to indicate that the operation of the manager plan in a style somewhat approximating that of the model is dependent upon the existence of a fairly high degree of consensus in the community. When a city's politics produces a line-up of two fairly well-balanced groups and each, when it comes to power, dismisses the manager hired by the opposition and finds one loyal to itself—as sometimes happens—the plan is in difficulties. Similarly, it apparently does not operate effectively in communities where the function of city government is viewed by a large number of citizens as that of an arbiter,[27] for this implies the need for a strong elective leader. If the fragmentary evidence supporting these statements is correct, the plan should be more effective in suburbia than in large core cities.[28] And, indeed, that appears to be the case.

The lack of a chief policy maker causes another problem from a different angle. In large cities, especially, it is difficult for the general public

[26] See Bebout, *op. cit.*
[27] See above, pp. 88–89.
[28] See Oliver P. Williams and Charles R. Adrian, *Fighting City Hall.* (Forthcoming monograph.)

TABLE 8-3. LARGEST COUNCIL-MANAGER CITIES IN THE UNITED STATES

City	1960 popula- tion	Date in effect	Size of council	No. at large	Type of elec- tion*	Term, years	Other elective officers
Dallas...........	672,117	1931	9	9	NP	2	
San Antonio.....	584,471	1952	9	9	NP	2	
San Diego.......	547,294	1932	7	7	NP-s	4	Attorney
Cincinnati.......	502,550	1926	9	9	NP	2	
Kansas City.....	468,325	1926	9	5	NP	4	
Oakland.........	361,082	1931	8	8	NP-s	4	Auditor
Ft. Worth.......	353,388	1925	9	9	NP	2	
Long Beach......	323,996	1921	9	9	NP	3	Auditor
Rochester.......	316,074	1928	9	5	P-s	4	
Toledo..........	315,643	1936	9	9	NP	2	

* Under "Type of Election," "NP" refers to nonpartisan and "P" to partisan elections, while "-s" following means that council terms are staggered so that all do not expire at once.

SOURCE: *Municipal Year Book, 1960* (International City Managers' Association, Chicago, 1960), pp. 91–93.

to know much about the various candidates for the council or about the voting records of incumbents. The problem is especially great when the council is elected at large on a nonpartisan ballot, as is often the case. It is therefore not necessarily true that concentration of responsibility in the council will result in informed voting. In cities small enough for candidates to be known by reputation, this is not likely to be as serious a problem, if indeed it is a problem at all.

Actual Results.[29] In considering typical results, we find that the adoption of the council-manager plan has led to increased prestige for the council and in greater control by it over municipal affairs. Managers have generally been appointed by the council without regard to political affiliation, and tenure for the manager has, in most cases, not been interrupted by considerations other than administrative competence. Most managers have provided administration based upon professional values and standards, and have brought far more coordination to the activities of their governments than had existed before. They have furthered long-range policy planning and have encouraged the employment of specialists for advice on technical problems. They have emphasized the merit principal

[29] This section is based upon the findings reported in H. A. Stone, D. K. Price, and K. H. Stone, *City Manager Government in the United States* (Public Administration Service, Chicago, 1940), which is a report on a three-year survey of 50 cities.

in personnel administration, and have increased the interest of employees in their jobs. Managers have promoted coordinated, executive budgeting methods and have provided more financial information and better financial management than was afforded under the older forms of government.

The adoption of the council-manager form has not reduced the size of the total budget in most cities, but it has increased the public's confidence in municipal government. While the plan has not reduced the *total* cost of city government, it has sometimes reduced *unit* costs by eliminating graft and waste and by utilizing personnel and methods of greater efficiency. There is some evidence that any competent manager, regardless of the size of the city, can save his own salary many times over each year and that the plan has therefore been a practical one, even for very small cities.

The council-manager plan, then, suffers from some weaknesses, as do all human institutions. It has, however, so satisfied the bulk of the voters in cities using it that, once adopted, abandonments are rare.

Proponents and Opponents: The Politics of Reform.[30] The council-manager plan is often launched and supported by good-government and business groups, chambers of commerce, property owners' associations, taxpayers' associations, civic associations, citizens' action groups, women's clubs, and, very often, newspapers. Opposition to proposals for adoption frequently comes from organized labor, politicians in office (especially mayors who stand to lose considerable power in their offices by the employment of a manager), and political parties. Political leaders often dislike the manager plan, both because it offers little in the way of patronage and because it is so often coupled with nonpartisan elections.

In many cities, the two leading contenders in campaigns over manager charters have been the local chamber of commerce and local organized labor. The impression that the plan is antithetical to the best interests of organized labor is held by many, though not all, labor leaders in various parts of the country.

In contrast, the plan has been accepted with enthusiasm by business groups. There are many reasons for this. It was the Board of Trade of Lockport that first endorsed the Childs plan, and it was the Chamber of Commerce in Dayton that was responsible for the first large-city adoption. The plan is often lauded as a "businesslike government" in imitation of the corporate form of private business.

The upper-middle-class suburbs which are the homes of metropolitan

[30] For case studies on the adoption of council-manager government in various cities, see H. A. Stone, D. K. Price, and K. H. Stone, *City Manager Government in Nine Cities* (Public Administration Service, Chicago, 1940); F. C. Mosher and others, *City Manager Government in Seven Cities* (Public Administration Service, Chicago, 1940); Harold Stein (ed.), *Public Administration and Policy Development* (Harcourt, Brace & World, Inc., New York, 1952).

businessmen are characteristically administered by a manager. Very many managers are engineers, and some are trained in schools of business administration. This means that they received much of their education in the most conservative colleges of our universities. They are likely to be personally conservative in political views. They are business-oriented in their social values. Many of them have had experience in private business before becoming managers; others may hope to move into good positions in private business after serving for a number of years in city government.

Labor leaders often fear that the council-manager plan requires them to take an all-or-nothing plunge into local politics. The risk in this is especially great if elections are at large. Under such circumstances, the labor leaders are faced with getting a majority on the council that is not hostile to their interests. Failing this, the entire administration of the city may fall into opposition, or at least (from their viewpoint) undependable and unpredictable hands. In most core cities, the AFL-CIO works closely with the Democratic party which is likely to dominate partisan elections. The council-manager plan advocates nearly always favor nonpartisan elections, however, and this is a device that favors conservatives and weakens the effectiveness of the labor-Democratic coalition.

There are other reasons for labor's skepticism of the plan, too. While business leaders and chamber of commerce managers may be concerned with large issues of policy, the typical workingman thinks of the machinery of government as something to be used for personal favors, to help him in an emergency. For this purpose, the ward aldermanic system is far more effective than are the at-large elections which are the rule under the manager plan. Furthermore, at-large elections tend to produce councilmen out of middle-class ranks, men who often have had little experience with the problems of low-income persons or the members of unions. Not only may they be unfamiliar with the concerns of these people, but they may be overtly hostile to unionism, especially if they are small businessmen. In cities where labor leaders have been active in municipal politics, workingmen are especially likely to be dissatisfied with the manager plan.[31]

In contrast to the general pattern, some unions have taken the lead in urging the manager plan. Furthermore, it would appear that labor usually supports the plan once it is well established in a city.

The manager plan enjoys labor support in Cincinnati, Kansas City, and Toledo. The AFL-CIO takes no national stand on forms of local government; it allows local organizations to decide positions in local campaigns for themselves. In 1950, union leaders in eighty cities where the plan

[31] See Kenneth E. Beasley, *Attitudes of Labor toward City Government* (Governmental Research Center, University of Kansas, Lawrence, Kan., 1954).

had been in effect for twenty years or longer overwhelmingly approved of the plan. In only three of the cities was definite opposition expressed.[32] Labor is being somewhat reassured concerning the motives of those who favor the manager plan. It is likely, however, that the device will remain especially the favorite of chambers of commerce and middle-class good-government groups.[33]

OTHER FORMS OF GOVERNMENT

The New England Town. The direct democracy of the town meeting characterized local government in New England until the urbanization of that area began to force the acceptance of modifications. In some urban areas, the town-government feature has been abandoned, while in others it has been made into a representative form.

The town makes no distinction between rural and urban places. As an area becomes more and more urbanized, it continues under the town system, sharing the same government with the neighboring rural area. The town is governed by a meeting of all the qualified voters, who choose officers and make basic policy. There is an annual meeting, traditionally in March, with as many other meetings as may be necessary. After making basic policy, the people choose a board of selectmen, usually three but in some places as many as nine, and a fairly large number of other officers. The selectmen and elective officers are then entrusted with carrying out the basic policies established by community action.

The urbanization of many towns has been accompanied by a sharp decrease in attendance at town meetings and a consequent decline in the effectiveness of this form of government. In many areas of New England, therefore, a *representative* town meeting plan has been developed. Under this plan, the voters choose a large number of citizens, perhaps a hundred or more, to attend the meeting, represent them, and vote. Any citizen can attend and take part in debates, but he no longer has a direct vote. This plan is used in such large urban places as Brookline, Massachusetts (1960 population: 54,044).

Town government, outside of the meeting feature, resembles the weak-mayor or, more particularly, the American village form, except that there is no mayor at all, only a president of the council, and no one has a veto power. It is becoming more and more common for the selectmen to choose

[32] See the pamphlet *Labor Unions and the Council-Manager Plan* (1950), issued by the National Municipal League, New York, and designed to be read by workingmen.

[33] In addition to material already cited on the manager plan, see C. E. Ridley and O. F. Nolting, *The City-manager Profession* (University of Chicago Press, Chicago, 1934), and R. S. Childs, *Civic Victories* (Harper & Brothers, New York, 1952). Contemporary developments in the field are reported annually in the *Municipal Year Book* from 1934 on, and before then in the *City Manager Year Book*. The yearbooks are publications of the International City Managers' Association, Chicago.

a manager and turn actual administration over to him. This is particularly the case in Maine and Vermont and is to be found in all New England states.

The New England legislatures have been under constant pressure to alter the traditional town government in order to help meet contemporary needs. They have created new offices and commissions such as those of aviation commissioner, planning boards, civil service commissions, library trustees, and finance committees, the last in order to help provide for better planning in budget making so that this document is not pieced together in haphazard fashion at the public meeting. (Titles vary by states and even towns, of course.) [34]

Closing Statement. Structures of government are tools. They make a difference as to how a community is governed and as to which groups and interests in the community are most influential. Local cultural circumstances will determine the type of structure that is wanted by the politically dominant, and the type of government that will be produced under any chosen form. Structure is significant, but it is only one of the factors that make up the particular characteristics of politics and community decision making in a city.

[34] For more on New England towns, see Lane W. Lancaster, *Government in Rural America* (2d ed.; D. Van Nostrand Company, Inc., New York, 1952), pp. 34–36.

Chapter 9

EXECUTIVE OFFICERS

The mayor of today's American small town is commonly a moderately successful small businessman, long active in local politics and civic affairs and well liked by his neighbors. In the large city of an earlier day, the mayor was often corrupt and incompetent—although there were outstanding exceptions. Today our large cities seem to be producing an increasingly large number of capable chief executives. Still, many contemporary mayors are amiable mediocrities, lacking in ability and imagination and under obligation to a few pressure groups that put them in office.

An impressive list of public servants can be made up from among the names of men who have served as mayors of American cities, especially since the early 1900s. Samuel M. ("Golden Rule") Jones, Mayor of Toledo at the turn of the present century, was a great humanitarian and fighter against domination of cities by public utility interests. He was succeeded by one of the most famous of all mayors, Brand Whitlock, an exponent of the principles of municipal reform. There were several other reform mayors at the turn of the century and during the second decade, among them Joseph W. Folk of St. Louis, Patrick Collins of Boston, and Mark Fagan of Jersey City.

The Socialists offered America several mayors who had both imagination in meeting problems and administrative ability in carrying them out. Emil Seidel, the first Socialist to be elected mayor of Milwaukee (1910), and later Daniel W. Hoan were at the top of this list. New York has had many mayors of doubtful ethical standards and many who were mere voices for the hidden machine, but it also had flamboyant, honest, energetic, and imaginative Fiorello H. La Guardia. Earlier in the century, the nation's largest city also had mayors of considerable administrative ability in Seth Low and John P. Mitchel.

Murray Seasongood, a prominent attorney and law professor, demonstrated in Cincinnati that a mayor-councilman under the manager plan can offer political leadership without seriously clashing with members of the administration. Frank Murphy, Detroit's Depression mayor had

enough ability and sufficient political acumen to move on to higher political office. He later served in several high positions and finally was
appointed to the United States Supreme Court. Many members of Congress were at one time mayors of their home towns.

Cleveland, with a strong mayor elected on a partisan basis,[1] has been
an exceptional city so far as chief executives are concerned. It has not
only had able reformers, but has sent several men on to more important
positions in state and national government. Tom L. Johnson (1901), a
prominent businessman, became famous for fighting the "special interests." His campaigns were carried on by his successor, Newton D. Baker
(1909), who was chosen a few years later to be President Wilson's Secretary of War. In 1935, Harold H. Burton was elected mayor of Cleveland.
After being re-elected for two more terms, he was promoted to the
United States Senate and finally became a member of the United States
Supreme Court. While he was not outstanding in these positions, his
record is an indication that the mayor's office can be used as a step
toward more important jobs. Burton was succeeded as mayor in 1941 by
Frank J. Lausche, a man of little administrative ability but with a great
deal of political skill and ambition, as well as a special reputation for
honesty.[2] He was re-elected in 1943 in an election in which he received
almost three-quarters of the votes cast, before moving on to become
Governor of Ohio and then United States Senator. In 1953, Lausche appointed his successor, Thomas A. Burke, to fill a vacancy in the United
States Senate. But the Cleveland system of consistent promotion to
higher office is not typical.[3]

The problem of securing able men as mayors of large cities is particularly complicated, however, by the fact that men who seek these
offices are likely to have to place themselves under obligation to interest
groups with specific political goals. This is so because someone must
furnish the money for the expensive large-city campaign. While a mayor
so obligated could be, in theory, representative of a substantial portion
of the population, could be imaginative and aggressive in meeting prob-

[1] Cleveland uses a nonpartisan ballot for council, but since all councilmen are
elected by wards and the mayor and president of the council are the only other
persons elected, the resulting short ballot has produced elections which are, in effect,
partisan in character. Since 1958, the mayor's election has been on a partisan ballot.

[2] Lausche attributes his decision to run for mayor to dramatic and mystical circumstances; see John Gunther, *Inside U.S.A.* (Harper & Brothers, New York, 1947),
p. 425.

[3] There are some interesting autobiographical works that may be examined profit-
ably. See especially Tom L. Johnson, *My Story* (B. W. Huebsch, Inc., New York,
1911); Brand Whitlock, *Forty Years of It* (Appleton-Century-Crofts, Inc., New
York, 1925); and Daniel W. Hoan, *City Government, the Record of the Milwaukee
Experiment* (Harcourt, Brace & World, Inc., New York, 1936). A series on eighteen
mayors of all types is to be found in the *National Municipal Review* (now *National
Civic Review*), vols. 15–18, various issues from 1926 through 1929.

lems, and could be responsive to changing demands of the people of the city—in practice, it appears that often he is not.

The need for forceful, imaginative leadership from the mayor has been emphasized in large cities as a result of concerns about potential deterioration of property, and economic obsolescence resulting from the flight of people, business, and industry to the suburbs. Concerning the triumph of competence over other considerations in choosing mayors, a journalist has noted: [4]

This has not been a victory for "good government." To most people, good government is primarily honest and efficient administration, and they believe that the sure way for the city to get it is to tighten civil service, eliminate patronage, and accept all the other artifacts of "scientific" government, including the council-city manager plan. But today's big-city mayor is not a good-government man, at least in these terms, and if he ever was, he got over it a long time ago. He is a tough-minded, soft-spoken politician who often outrages good-government people, or, as the politicians have called them, the Goo-Goos.

One of the biggest threats to his leadership, indeed, is too much "good government." The big problem at City Hall is no longer honesty, or even simple efficiency. The fight for these virtues is a continuous one, of course, and Lucifer is always lurking in the hall, but most big-city governments have become reasonably honest and efficient. Today, the big problem is not good housekeeping: it is whether the mayor can provide the aggressive leadership and the positive programs without which no big city has a prayer. What is to get priority? Industrial redevelopment? More housing? (And for whom?) There is only so much money, and if hard policy decisions are not made, the city's energies will be diffused in programs "broad" but not bold.

The mayor is hemmed in. As he strives to exercise policy leadership, his power is challenged on all sides. In his own house the staff experts and the

[4] Seymour Freedgood, "New Strength in City Hall," in Editors of Fortune, *The Exploding Metropolis* (Doubleday Anchor Books, New York, 1958), pp. 63–64. For examples of mayors as aggressive leaders, see Sally O. Shames, *David L. Lawrence, Mayor of Pittsburgh* (University Microfilms, Ann Arbor, Mich., 1958) and, on Joseph S. Clark and Richardson Dilworth of Philadelphia, see James Reichley, *The Art of Government: Reform and Organization Politics in Philadelphia* (The Fund for the Republic, New York, 1959). On others whose place in history cannot yet be predicted, see the following: on William O'Dwyer of New York, Philip Hamburger, "That Great Big New York Up There," *The New Yorker*, Sept. 28, 1957, pp. 47–82; on Robert F. Wagner of the same city, Philip Hamburger, "The Mayor: Profile of Robert F. Wagner," *ibid.*, Jan. 26, 1957, pp. 39–67 and Feb. 2, 1957, pp. 39–69; Seymour Freedgood, "The Vacuum at City Hall," *Fortune*, February, 1960, pp. 124 ff. Bibliography on other New York mayors is listed in Wallace S. Sayre and Herbert Kaufman, *Governing New York City* (Russell Sage Foundation, New York, 1960), pp. 701–706. On Chicago mayors, see ftn. p. 152 above. On Mayor Thomas D'Alesandro of Baltimore, see Harold H. Martin, "The Case of the Bouncing Mayor," *The Saturday Evening Post*, Sept. 24, 1955, pp. 19 ff. On the post-Curley mayors of Boston, see George Blackwood, "Boston Politics and Boston Politicians," in Murray B. Levin, *The Alienated Voter: Politics in Boston* (Holt, Rinehart and Winston, Inc., New York, 1960), chap. 1.

civil-service bureaucrats threaten to nibble him to death in their efforts to increase their own authority. Then there are the public "authorities." Some are single-purpose authorities—like the city housing authorities, and the sewer districts; some, like the Port of New York Authority, handle a whole range of functions. They are eminently useful institutions, but however efficient they may be, they are virtually laws unto themselves and they have severely limited the mayor's ability to rule in his own house and, more important, his ability to plan for long-range development.

The power struggle also goes on between the mayor and the state legislature, which has a controlling voice in the city's fiscal affairs, but whose membership is apportioned in favor of the rural areas. It is the rare mayor who need not make frequent trips to the state capital for additional funds, and the legislature is usually unsympathetic. Colorado's, for example, gives Denver a niggardly $2,300,000 a year in state aid for a school system of 90,000 children; right next to it, semi-rural Jefferson County, with 18,000 pupils, gets $2,400,000.

There is the continuing struggle between the mayor and the suburbs, whose people, the big city firmly believes, are welshing on their obligations to the city. The mayor must win the cooperation of his suburban counterparts if he is to do anything at all about the city's most pressing problems—e.g., the traffic mess—and the going is grim. No one is against "saving our cities," but in this seemingly antiseptic cause there are fierce conflicts of interests and the power struggle is getting more intense.

The strong mayor—the policy leader of today's large city—has great powers and many sanctions which he can apply in order to clear the path for the things he wants to do. But he is also hemmed in by restrictions— he works in a glass house, a prisoner to a considerable extent of those who serve him. The house is heavily mortgaged to the state and the fence around it is a barricade manned by earnest defenders of suburban independence.

POWERS OF THE MAYOR

The powers exercised by the mayor vary widely throughout the United States. The person called the mayor in a commission or council-manager city normally has few powers other than those of presiding over the council and performing the ceremonial role for the city. The mayor in a mayor-council city may have a great many powers, or he may be merely one of many virtually coordinate members of the city administration, as is the case in a very weak mayor city.

Legislative Powers. It will be recalled from the preceding chapter that there is no necessary difference between weak and strong mayors so far as their legislative powers are concerned. In virtually all instances, the mayor has the right to submit messages to the council and hence to recommend policy. These messages carry with them the prestige and the publicity potential of the mayor's office and must be considered by the council in light of this. Some mayors have the right to attend council sessions and to introduce measures. In those municipalities that have remained closest to English precedents, the mayor is actually a member of the council and presides over it. This is true in a very common form of village government and is also the case in nearly all commission and council-manager cities.

Most mayors in mayor-council cities have a veto power (see Table 9-1). This is, of course, a substantial supporting weapon when the mayor recommends policy. The greatest power of the veto, in the hands of a mayor as of a president, is measured by its threatened use rather than by the number of times it is actually invoked. A veto may be overridden either by a simple majority or by some extraordinary vote such as two-thirds or three-fourths. In a few cities, notably Boston, a veto is absolute. This does not, however, appear to be truly compatible with the checks-and-balance theory and would seem almost to turn the policy-making function over to the mayor.

In strong-mayor cities, it is not uncommon to find that the mayor is so powerful that the council does not attempt to make policy independently of him. Under such circumstances, he need rarely use the veto. The use to which the veto is put will depend, of course, on local custom, prevailing circumstances, and the personal philosophy and political strategy of the incumbent mayor.

In some cities the mayor has the power of casting a vote in case of a

TABLE 9-1. VETO POWER OF MAYORS IN CITIES OVER 5,000

Form of government	Per cent of mayors who may			
	Veto all measures	Veto budget only	Veto selected items	Not veto anything
Mayor-council.......	43.7	0.8	22.5	33.0
Commission.........	5.5	0.5	0.0	94.0
Council-manager.....	7.5	0.2	16.5	75.8
Town meeting.......	0.0	0.0	0.0	100.0
Rep. town meeting...	0.0	0.0	0.0	100.0
All cities over 5,000...	39.0	0.6	18.1	52.3

SOURCE: *Municipal Year Book, 1960* (International City Managers' Association, Chicago, 1960), p. 84.

tie, even though he may not be a member of the council. If he presides over the council, he is quite certain to have this power (see Table 9-2). When the mayor is an actual member of the council, he, of course, has a vote.

Powers over Administration. The characteristic differences between the weak and strong mayors of America are to be found in connection with their powers over administration. The strong mayor, unlike the weak mayor, is given powers to make him the chief administrative officer. He has supervisory and coordinative powers over the activities of the various departments and is in charge of the preparation and administration of the budget. In a few cities he has so much power in budget preparation that the council is empowered to do no more than decrease or strike out items in the budget. The controller, who supervises expenditures by the operational departments, is normally an appointee of the chief executive in a strong-mayor city. At the opposite extreme, the budget is sometimes prepared by a committee of the council well out of the hands of the mayor, and the controller may be an elective official or a council appointee. When the mayor has control over the preparation and expenditure of the budget, he has great powers which he can use to reach into agencies that might otherwise be totally independent. For example, he can use this power to influence policies within agencies otherwise controlled by an elective board (e.g., parks in many cities), or by the bureaucracy (e.g., public health).

TABLE 9-2. VOTING POWER OF MAYORS IN CITIES OVER
5,000 POPULATION, BY FORM OF GOVERNMENT *

Form of government	Per cent of mayors who may vote	
	On all issues	In case of tie only
Mayor-council........	10.0	67.2
Commission..........	97.6	2.4
Council-manager......	48.7	46.1
Town meeting........	33.3	0.0
Rep. town meeting....	80.0	20.0
All cities over 5,000...	29.9	54.3

* Statistics include only mayors directly elected by the people.

SOURCE: *Municipal Year Book, 1960* (International City Managers' Association, 1960), p. 83.

Law Enforcement. Most city charters impose upon the mayor the executive function of seeing to it that the laws and ordinances are enforced and that peace and order are maintained. Actual power to do this is not always granted. It is significant, however, that because this is a traditional power, it is common to give the mayor control over the police department. If he has no other exclusive power of appointment, he is usually given the right to hire and dismiss the police chief or commissioner. Sometimes, however, the mayor is given the responsibility of enforcement of laws and ordinances, but is at the same time deprived of any control over the law-enforcement agency. St. Louis and Kansas City have police heads appointed by the state. A few cities elect the police chief; in some he is responsible to the council, and in others he is chosen by a semi-independent police board.

Appointments. In order to have effective power over administration and to coordinate its activities, the mayor must have the power both of unrestricted appointment and of removal. Weak-mayor cities are likely to have several administrative officers elected by the people and others selected by the council. In a strong-mayor city, these officers are appointed by the mayor. In some cities, such as New York and Detroit, his powers extend to virtually all of the department heads in the administrative branch and he need not consult the council or anyone else in making appointments. He is in full charge of administration. He may appoint the heads of the major subdivisions within the departments, or this power may go to the department heads. In actual practice, it does not make much difference which method is used, since a serious conflict between mayor and department head over any matter would mean the resignation or dismissal of the recalcitrant department head.

In many cities the mayor must have the approval of the council in making appointments. This is the more common pattern and is in keeping with the system of checks and balances upon which the mayor-council plan is based. It is in accord with American traditions, but it confuses responsibility for administration; the public cannot directly fix the blame, since several persons have a hand in each appointment. In addition, it provides a gratuitous system of patronage to council members. The mayor must, in practice, consult the council to a degree in making appointments, and as in the case of the President in relation to the United States Senate, in practice, many or perhaps most of the appointments become patronage items for the council members. Councilmen are not elected in order to make appointments, of course, and placating their patronage demands is not likely to provide a good system for procuring able administrators in the city government. The mayor, clearly answerable for administration to the public, will more probably pick persons of ability. He is likely to combine patronage and competence considerations in making choices, while councilmen will consider only patronage. There is no pressure upon them to do otherwise.

Removals. At least as important as the power to appoint is the power to remove. In the strong-mayor city, the chief executive can remove any member of his administration in whom he has lost confidence. Only by the possession of this power can he be responsible to the people for the acts of his subordinates. In New York and Detroit, the mayor can remove almost all of his appointees at pleasure, even those who are nominally appointed for a specific term of years.

Because of the frontiersman's distrust of government, however, it is more common to find restraints on the removal power. Unlike the President of the United States, who commonly must have the approval of the Senate in order to make appointments but may remove all except members of the independent regulatory establishments at pleasure, the mayor often must have councilmanic approval for both appointments and removals. This pattern is found, for example, in Los Angeles. It is subject to the same criticism as is approval for appointment. The mayor cannot control the acts of those nominally subordinate to him where this system exists.

It is also common to restrict the mayor's removal power by providing that he may make removals only "for cause." This means, usually, removal only after notice and hearing, and the action of the mayor is in such cases normally subject to review by the courts. The operation of the city cannot be smooth if the mayor's appointees may defy him or if he loses prestige in the eyes of officials and employees by being forced into a court fight over a dismissal. If a mayor loses such a fight, morale problems are especially likely to become acute. In practice, however, the notice-and-hearing requirement frequently does not seriously impair the removal power of the mayor. It does discourage him from making hasty decisions in a fit of temper.

It should be noted that in most cities, department heads are usually civil service employees. Despite this, however, the mayor usually has the right to choose his department heads and to remove them if he thinks they are not doing a good job. In the event of the removal of a department head who has civil service tenure, he is reduced in status and given other assignments, but is not dismissed from the service.

Ceremonial Functions. In every city there are beauty queens to be crowned, conventions to be greeted, presidents to be introduced, parks to be dedicated, cornerstones to be laid, baseball seasons to be opened, parades to be led, and charity drives to be launched. The mayor is expected to do all of these things. In fact, it is partly because he must do them that the office of mayor is retained under the commission and council-manager forms. He is the symbol for the whole city.

Probably the typical mayor enjoys the attention that is his at these occasions. He is surely aware of the free publicity attendant upon them. In smaller cities, this duty of the mayor is not burdensome or time-consuming, as it is in larger cities. In the very largest cities, the ceremonial function becomes a real burden, taking up valuable time that could be spent upon the pressing problems of administration or policy making. It is partly for this reason that a deputy mayor is appointed in New York.

Whatever the size of the municipality, Americans are always likely to "try to get the mayor to be there" whenever a committee plans some function, modest or mammoth. If the mayor is interested in his political future, he will usually be on hand.

Duties as a Lobbyist. Since cities are largely at the mercy of the state legislature, their officials necessarily follow closely the course of proposed legislation which affects them. The cities are collectively protected in most states by the lobbying activities of the state league of municipalities, just as their interests on the national level are looked after by the American Municipal Association and the United States Conference of Mayors. The largest cities have paid lobbyists who are at the state capital throughout legislative sessions.

At times, when legislation of particular importance to a certain city or group of cities is being considered, the mayors of the affected cities may be called to the state capital by the secretary of the league of municipalities so that they may use the prestige of their offices in an attempt to protect the interests of their cities. Political skill is most important at such times.

Judicial Powers. In early America the mayor exercised minor *judicial* powers as well as having a seat in the *legislative* body and serving as chief *executive*. For example, a provision of the 1851 special act charter of Davenport, Iowa, provided that the mayor "shall by virtue of his office be a justice of the peace, and as such shall be a conservator of the peace."

Some cities still have a "mayor's court," and legally the mayor of New York is such a judge, but in practice the use of this power is disappearing. Also, since the mayor is in a position analogous to that of the governor and the President, he usually possesses power to grant pardons for violations of city ordinances (but not of state law). The exercise of this power is today comparatively rare.

THE OFFICE OF MAYOR

Selection of the Mayor. The way in which the mayor is chosen varies a good deal according to the form of government. In all but a few mayor-

Table 9-3. Method of Selection of Mayors in Cities over 5,000 Population, by Form of Government

Form of government	Per cent directly elected	Per cent selected by council	Highest no. votes in council election
Mayor-council...........	96	4	1
Commission.............	69	30	1
Council-manager.........	48	51	1
Town meeting...........	67	33	0
Rep. town meeting........	51	47	2
All cities over 5,000.....	74	25	1

SOURCE: *Municipal Year Book, 1960* (International City Managers' Association, Chicago, 1960), p. 83.

council cities, he is elected directly by the voters. He is chosen in this fashion in about 69 per cent of the commission-plan cities, but in somewhat less than one-half of the council-manager cities.[5] (See Table 9-3.) In such large municipalities as Kansas City, Dallas, and San Diego, however, he is elected directly.

The public is accustomed to electing the mayor and probably feels more comfortable with a charter that gives it that privilege. The popular election of the mayor tends to elevate him in public prestige and to provide him with high status, which he finds useful if he seeks to be a legislative leader.

The mayor may also be selected by the council. This is the method used in over one-half of the council-manager cities, and in many commission cities. But it is used in only 4 per cent of the mayor-council cities of over 5,000 population. These appear to be chiefly in places in which the government has evolved from the village or township structure.

In a few cities, the man who receives the highest number of votes for council becomes mayor. This is uncommon, but can be found, for example, in Hartford and Kalamazoo, both manager cities, and in a very few commission cities. Strangely enough, a few mayor-council cities also make the person with the highest number of votes for council the mayor. This is true, however, only where the structure has grown from the old village type of government, based upon English traditions and without a clear separation of powers.

[5] Statistics on the method of selection of the mayor are available in the current issue of the *Municipal Year Book* (International City Managers' Association, Chicago).

Salary. The pay of the mayor varies according to both the size of the city and the structure of its government. In general, the salary varies directly with the size of the city, as might be expected. Small cities are likely to pay only a token salary, something less than $1,000 a year. New York, at the opposite extreme, pays $45,000.

In a commission-plan city, the mayor usually receives the same pay as the other commissioners or a few hundred dollars additional. There are some exceptions where he may receive quite an appreciable amount more. In manager cities, the same general rule applies.

It is not uncommon for the mayor to be paid less than some of his subordinates.[6] The city engineer, the health officer, the attorney, and especially the superintendent of schools, are likely to be paid more than he is, except in the very largest cities.

The average length of service of a mayor is approximately four years and in running for and accepting the office he takes a grave risk of damaging his personal reputation. Clearly, persons with administrative and leadership ability can make more money, with a longer professional life, in private endeavor. Yet few arguments presented to the voters are greeted more coldly than those suggesting a higher salary for the mayor.

Term of Office. The Jacksonians insisted upon terms of not over two years, for they believed in keeping government "close to the people." The traditional term of office in New England was one year—from one town meeting until the next.

The term of office of the American mayor today depends to some extent upon the type of city-government structure in the particular city. The two-year term was still dominant in mayor-council cities in 1960, especially in those of the weak-mayor type. Most council-manager cities had two-year terms, too. Commission-governed cities, on the other hand, are likely to have four-year terms. (See Table 9-4.)

Terms of less than four years allow the mayor little time to establish a record or to devote to his job. With a two-year term he begins his campaign for re-election almost as soon as the results of his first campaign are in. Some cities cling to the cynical rule prohibiting the mayor from succeeding himself. During the palmy days of the Republican machine in Philadelphia (until 1951), the charter of that city had such a rule. However, such a rule did not appear to weaken the machine in the least.

Removals. The mayor who is incompetent, unrepresentative, or callous of the wants of the dominant public may be removed by allowing his term to expire or by securing his defeat at the next election. There are times,

---

[6] Extensive data on salaries of various municipal officials are reported in the current issue of the *Municipal Year Book* (International City Managers' Association).

TABLE 9-4. TERM OF OFFICE OF MAYOR IN CITIES
OVER 5,000 POPULATION

Form of government	Per cent of reporting cities					
	One year	Two years	Three years	Four years	Five years	Six years
Mayor-council..........	2	56	1	41	0	0
Commission...........	6	24	10	57	2	1
Council-manager *.....	20	53	2	25	0	0
Town meeting.........	31	38	31	0	0	0
Rep. town meeting.....	33	33	33	0	0	0
All cities over 5,000..	10	51	3	36	—	—

* The large number of one- and two-year terms for mayor in council-manager cities is partly a result of town-meeting communities adopting this form while retaining the New England traditional short term of office for elective officials. In other cases, the short terms stem from the practice of rotating the essentially honorary office among the councilmen.

SOURCE: *Municipal Year Book, 1960* (International City Managers' Association, Chicago, 1960), p. 84.

however, when the public may wish to terminate the authority of a chief executive before his regular term expires. This is particularly true when he is thought to be guilty of what the lawyers call non-, mis-, or malfeasance in office. That is to say, if he fails to perform his duties, or does them in an unlawful manner, or does illegal things under the mantle of office. There are several remedies at law in such cases.

First of all, there is the *recall*. As has already been noted, it is unlikely, under this device, that the case will be decided on its merits.[7] But several other (and incidentally older) remedies are available.

In most cities, the mayor may be removed by action of the council—an ancient common-law power. Most charters require a vote of something more than a simple majority to effect a removal, however. It is also possible for the mayor to be removed by a court order for certain causes as prescribed by law. In Michigan, New York, North Dakota, and Ohio, the mayor may be removed by the governor. All three of these removal techniques are "for cause" only. The courts have regularly held this to mean that there must be a presentation of specific charges, due notice to the official whose removal is sought, and a hearing, usually public. It also

[7] See above, pp. 113 ff.

means that the official may appeal to the courts if he feels that the procedural safeguards to which he is entitled have not been followed.

Vacancies. If a mayor dies, resigns, or is removed from office, the law or charter provides for his immediate replacement. It is quite important that there always be someone to serve as mayor. Since the mayor leaves the city from time to time for a vacation, a conference, or a convention, it is also necessary for someone to act in his temporary absence.

The succession may pass to the presiding officer of the council or to some administrative officer, most commonly the controller. In some cities if the office is vacated, the council is allowed to choose the new mayor, not necessarily from its own membership. If the next election is some time off, say more than six months or a year, the law may provide for an acting mayor and a special election to choose a person to serve out the term.

Legal Qualifications. In virtually every city, there are charter provisions requiring the mayor to be a United States citizen, to be of a certain minimum age, and to have lived in the city for a certain minimum number of years. It might be required, for example, that the mayor must be at least thirty years old and have been a city resident for three years. These rules are probably largely in imitation of the requirements in the United States Constitution for the presidency. Clearly they are of little practical meaning and could well be left out of the charter, even the citizenship requirement—for no alien could be elected to a mayoralty position in any American city today.

THE CITY MANAGER

The city manager is a man of importance in most cities where his office exists. He is also a man of great power. But the power he possesses is, in most cases, used in a different manner and toward different ends from that of the old-fashioned machine leader.

Qualifications of the Manager. It is a basic part of the theory of council-manager government that the entire administration of the city be professionalized. Managers are supposed to be trained to use the tools of administration and, especially in smaller cities, to possess a technical skill, such as engineering, as well. The manager needs to be a diplomat, for his job is dependent upon his ability to get along with the council. He is supposed to be a politician of a special sort, too, for his job calls upon him to give advice on matters of public policy without becoming ensnared in the political process when these problems become campaign issues. Are managers actually able to do all of these things? What sort of people are they? One study concludes: "The average city manager in office is a college graduate, entered the profession between the age of 30 and 44, is still serving in his first city, has received salary increases averaging $366 per year, spends 52 hours per week on his job, gets two weeks vacation a year, and is covered in a retirement system." [8]

In the early days of the plan, managers were most often engineers, and in smaller cities this profession is still preferred, the manager also serving as the city engineer. The trend in medium- and larger-sized cities is away from hiring engineers and persons trained in business administration as managers. More and more universities are offering special training in public administration designed to prepare students for the city-manager profession. After graduation, these trainees advance through the administrative hierarchy of city governments until they become managers, many of them later moving on to larger cities with higher pay and greater prestige. This training provides the future manager with more of a background in the social and economic character of the city than was formerly the case.

Only 13 per cent of the managers appointed in 1959 came from non-governmental jobs; over 61 per cent had been employed in other manager cities—as the manager, as his administrative assistant, or as an intern. Managers are thus receiving better on-the-job training today. In 1939, only 23 per cent of those hired came from administrative positions in other cities. (See Table 9-5.)

The profession of manager appears to carry enough salary and prestige to make it a sufficiently worthwhile occupation for many to spend a lifetime in it. In 1959, only 8.7 per cent of the managers left the field, a number which included those who died and retired.[9]

Selection and Tenure of the Manager. Perhaps the most important task faced by a council is the selection of the manager. How does the council go about doing this? Councilmen, encountering the problem relatively seldom, may not know how to approach it. They may know that there are qualified persons about the country who might be interested in the position, but they may not know their names or how to go about discovering them. The International City Managers' Association has published a helpful pamphlet for cities, *The Selection of a City Manager* (revised, 1957). The Chicago headquarters of the Association often assists cities on request in securing qualified applicants and publishes notices of available openings. Similar assistance may also be secured from the state leagues of cities and departments of political science in nearby universities.

The council may consider one of the city's department heads for pro-

---

[8] "An Analysis of City Managers," *Public Management,* vol. 36 (January, 1954), p. 5.

[9] See the *Municipal Year Book, 1960* (International City Managers' Association, 1960), pp. 498–499.

motion to manager. Leading managers whose names and reputations are known to the councilmen will probably be asked to offer names of possible candidates. From such a list the council can then proceed to invite interested persons to apply. (Some unsolicited applications will be received.) The council may next reduce further the size of the list and then invite those still being considered to appear, if possible for personal interviews, before finally choosing the person to whom the job is to be offered. The process is thus similar to the selection of other *professional* staff members in government. The procedures described here are favored by the managers' professional organization, for they tend to discourage the selection of a nonprofessional.

The manager is normally selected by the council by majority vote and is dismissable by the council at any time by the same method. For the plan to work according to the model, it is essential that the council be allowed to remove the manager at any time, and for any reason that

TABLE 9-5. COMPARISON OF CITY-MANAGER APPOINTMENTS

Background of appointees	Ten-year period 1940–49 incl.		For 1958		For 1959	
	No.	Per cent	No.	Per cent	No.	Per cent
Governmental:						
Manager promotions from other cities	277	18	99	33	93	32
Former managers accepting appointments . . .	177	11	23	8	26	9
Administrative assistants and asst. managers	69	4	58	19	58	20
Public administration specialists.	13	1	10	3	6	2
Other public administrative positions:						
Engineers	168	11	15	5	24	8
Finance Officers and Clerks	109	7	16	5	22	8
Other city department heads	86	5	23	7	12	4
Federal, state, and county	171	11	9	3	7	2
Miscellaneous	71	5	10	3	2	1
Nongovernmental:						
Business and industry	152	10	25	8	21	7
Engineering	51	3	2	1	4	1
Miscellaneous	34	2	8	3	15	5
Appointments from outside city	803	58	233	78	220	75

SOURCE: *Municipal Year Book, 1960* (International City Managers' Association, Chicago, 1960), p. 497.

the council majority thinks sufficient. Otherwise the administration of the city becomes autonomous and irresponsible, uncontrolled by the machinery of democracy. Since ultimate responsibility for all that takes place in city government rests with the council, this body is assigned to the job of overseeing the activities of the manager.

In some cities, a practice has developed whereby each new council majority chooses "its own" manager, but this is not the general rule. The manager is supposed to be a professional administrator. If this is how he is perceived by councilmen, there is no reason why he should not be continued on in his job despite transient council majorities. It is significant to note that the average tenure of a manager in a city today is about seven years and that it would be longer except for the shortage of managers, which has encouraged, in the postwar era, their promotion to larger cities.

A few charters permit the removal of the manager through the use of the recall. According to the model, this is highly undesirable, not only because the recall under any circumstances is of questionable value, but also because it allows the council to shirk its responsibility for the manager and because it almost of necessity embroils the manager in politics—he becomes something of an appointive mayor instead of a manager and must play the political waves to prevent his own removal. Political rather than professional motivations become, of necessity, paramount to him.

The Jacksonian influence dies slowly in American politics, and it is still to be found affecting the hand that writes the council-manager charter. The extraordinary majority, such as two-thirds or three-fourths of the council, sometimes appears in the rules governing the removal of the manager. Charters also may permit dismissal only "for cause." Such a rule has the effect of putting final discretion in the hands of the courts rather than the council. Some charters require advance notice of one or more months to the manager if he is to be removed. This creates lame-duck managers and a stalemated government.

Both theory and practice call for the council to have full power over hiring and dismissing the manager. No argument for limiting the powers of the council can circumvent the fact that the manager plan can work effectively only if a majority of the councilmen have confidence in the manager.

Place of Residence. Most council-manager charters logically provide that the manager need not be a resident of the city at the time of his appointment, for the council is not looking for a deserving local politician, it is looking for a professionally competent administrator. In earlier years it was quite common to hire a person from outside the city. Until 1929, about one-half of the managers hired were nonresidents. With the coming of the Depression there was a reversal of trend, and in 1933 only 17 per cent of those appointed came from outside the city. This was probably the result of two considerations: (1) a desire of local politicians to keep scarce Depression jobs "at home"; and (2) the possibility of hiring local persons at a lower salary.

During World War II and since, there has been high employment combined with a rapid expansion in the number of manager cities, resulting in a definite shortage of qualified managers. Cities have turned to other cities in order to get chief administrators. The number of appointments from outside the city has accordingly risen to all-time highs. In 1959, 75 per cent of new managers hired were from outside the city. These figures probably also reflect a growing emphasis upon securing trained and experienced persons, persons who may not be available locally. Furthermore, the percentage of nonresidents hired as the first manager of a city adopting this form has always been high, and the rate of new adoptions has been unusually high in recent years.

Salaries. Obviously, if managership is to become a real profession with persons willing to make a lifetime career of it, the pay opportunities must be sufficient to attract able persons. The statistics shown in Table 9-6 indicate that managership affords fairly good salaries. It ranks well above teaching, for example, in pay opportunities.

There has been some opposition to the manager plan because salaries are thought to be *too* high. Public opinion in this country is often not sophisticated on this matter and may sometimes oppose the payment of salaries necessary to attract the talent wanted. This tendency is one of the common causes of disillusionment in the manager plan. This writer has been told that "we tried the plan, but we're giving it up—the manager was a nice fellow, but he was incompetent." In the postwar period of high employment and inflation plus a shortage of trained managers,

TABLE 9-6. SALARIES OF CITY MANAGERS, 1960

Cities of a population range	Mean	Lowest	Median	High
250,000–500,000	$23,901	$18,300	$23,703	$30,000
100,000–250,000	20,684	15,750	20,000	27,168
50,000–100,000	16,476	10,000	16,900	24,432
25,000– 50,000	14,142	8,000	13,500	24,000
10,000– 25,000	10,993	4,500	10,800	22,000

SOURCE: *Municipal Year Book, 1960* (International City Managers' Association, Chicago, 1960), pp. 156–158.

many of those hired were incompetent—and a city may expect that its manager will not be capable of doing a satisfactory job unless a sufficient salary is offered.

The Duties of the Manager. While charters vary widely and none conform in all details to the provisions of the *Model City Charter* of the National Municipal League, a manager, in both theory and practice, has all or most of the following responsibilities:

1. Overseeing enforcement of all laws and ordinances
2. Controlling all departments, with power to appoint, supervise, and remove department heads and bureau chiefs
3. Making recommendations to the council on such matters as he thinks desirable
4. Keeping the council advised of the financial condition of the city and concerning future needs and trends
5. Preparing and submitting to the council the annual budget
6. Preparing and submitting to the council reports and memoranda such as are requested
7. Keeping the council, and indirectly the public, informed concerning the operations of all aspects of the city government
8. Performing such other duties as the council may legally assign to him.

In a sentence, the manager has full responsibility to the council for the conduct of the administration of the city.

The Manager and the Council. When a city adopts the manager plan, the function of the council undergoes a considerable change, even if the city has previously operated under the strong-mayor form. The study by Stone, Price, and Stone [10] found that the council was relieved of most of its task of hiring department heads and subordinate employees. In all but a few cities the mayor and council were relieved of the duties of supervising the employees. Because of provisions of charters and state laws, however, councils were not relieved of the great mass of minor details that have historically been handled by that body. Even though the volume of work performed by the council could not be reduced, "the point of view and the approach of the council to municipal policy was different." [11] The difference resulted from reliance upon the manager for many things that could not be furnished in the same fashion by the mayor or a council committee.

In most cities, the manager presents significant matters to the council for consideration. Since they are not initiated by councilmen, these men are normally free to consider such items on the merits of the question,

[10] H. A. Stone, D. K. Price, and K. H. Stone, *City Manager Government in the United States* (Public Administration Service, Chicago, 1940), chap. 8.
[11] *Ibid.*, p. 174.

having no vested interest in them. New business coming before the council is normally first referred to the manager for a report at a future meeting. The manager, in making his report, is in a position to consider the effect of possible forms of action upon all departments of the city. No councilman making the report could do this, at least not as well. Furthermore, by leaving the report to the manager, the councilmen remain free to criticize it and to judge it without prejudice.

Most managers prefer to make their reports in writing. Of course, they are also quizzed orally by councilmen concerning various aspects and implications of the report at council meetings. Most managers also make recommendations for action in connection with a report.[12] Some managers present only one recommended line of action, the one they consider the professionally sound solution. Other managers present two or more possible approaches, thus affording the council opportunity to choose. The council may not always choose as the manager would prefer, but the latter knows that the council may be the best judge of what is most acceptable under prevailing local conditions.

In practice, although the manager plays a public role of "the expert" who is available only to answer questions and to administer, in fact, he or his subordinates are the principal sources of policy innovation in cities today. Ideas, if the manager or his staff do not think of them in the first place, are likely, in most cities, to come from interest groups rather than from council members. Once an idea is placed upon the community agenda, the manager becomes a major leader in securing its adoption, although he is usually discreet concerning his own views until the council has given formal approval.

The Manager and Elections. The manager performs many functions of community leadership similar to those performed by councilmen or the mayor. He is often active in service clubs, charitable organizations, churches, and the like.[13] He may make public speeches in which he seeks to explain a new policy which has been approved by the council (and which he may have originated). He may speak on the positive side of a proposed referendum on a bond issue (as frequently does the school superintendent who holds a parallel position with the school board), but he is prudent not to do so if the question involves partisan or factional issues.

In neither theory nor practice, however, does a manager engage in direct political activities. He does not appeal to the voters over the heads of the councilmen, or campaign against councilmen who have

[12] See Clarence E. Ridley, *The Role of the City Manager in Policy Formulation* (International City Managers' Association, Chicago, 1958); C. R. Adrian, "Leadership and Decision-making in Manager Cities: A Study of Three Communities," *Public Administration Review,* vol. 18 (Summer, 1958), pp. 208–213.

[13] Stone, Price, and Stone, *op. cit.,* pp. 243–244.

frequently opposed his policy recommendations, or support candidates or policies for personal or factional reasons. He can fulfill his almost inevitable role as a policy leader without himself becoming a political issue, by making sure that his recommendations are always "controlled by his expert knowledge and professional interest, never by selfish considerations or political friendships." [14]

The manager who does not observe this rule will eventually lose his job, and his reputation—and hence his employability elsewhere—will likely suffer. Sometimes a manager does offer assistance to one faction in a campaign, as the Cincinnati manager did in 1953, but under those circumstances he ceases to be a professional manager, becomes a politician, and will keep his post only so long as his faction has a majority on the council.

The Manager and Public Relations. Unlike the government of any other type of city, the city with a manager has a nonelective person serving in the position upon which chief public interest and attention is focused. Whether he likes it or not, to the manager falls the greatest responsibility for "selling" the manager plan, for making citizens satisfied with their government, and, often, for popularizing policies which the council has decided to undertake. The manager and his assistants meet the public daily, and the nature of these contacts has a great deal to do with the popularity of the manager, of the councilmen by whose leave he holds his job, and of city government itself.

All managers are necessarily aware of the importance of public relations, but they are not all equally adept in handling them. The Stone, Price, and Stone study found that some managers "had the knack of speaking and acting in a way that won confidence and brought about harmonious relations; others, no matter how hard they tried, never seemed to say in the right way what they wanted to say or to do in the right way what they wanted to do. How the manager spoke, acted, and conducted himself was often more important than what he said or accomplished." [15]

Some managers, like other chief executives, have assumed that the services of the city speak for themselves and have paid little attention to municipal reports to the public, have disliked making speeches, and have sought to avoid newspaper publicity. Most of them have recognized, however, the importance of informing the public about the functions performed by city government and the manner in which they are performed.

The Manager as a Professional. The International City Managers' Association (ICMA) is the professional organization to which most managers belong. The Association seeks to encourage high standards. It has

[14] *Ibid.*, p. 244.
[15] *Ibid.*, p. 159.

a code of ethics and a committee on professional conduct. There would probably be legal complications if a city attempted to require formally that the manager be a member of the ICMA, but such a rule seems unnecessary, since the council is always answerable to the voters for the manager and since it might be considered improper for a private organization to determine qualifications for a public position. State licenses are less necessary than in, say, law or medicine, since managers do not practice directly before a relatively helpless and uninformed public, but rather before a council with complete power over the professional life of the manager.

The Stone, Price, and Stone study found that: [16]

Perhaps the strongest support for the position the city managers took in regarding themselves as professional men lay in their attitude and in their conduct. Many city managers thought of themselves as professional executives devoting themselves to a job which required technical skill and a high sense of moral obligation. Many felt that they were selected as managers because they possessed special qualifications for the position and that political and private connections played no part in their appointment. With a large majority of managers, the job was the thing. Because city managers generally lived up to the ideals which they had set for themselves through the International City Managers' Association, they were quite widely recognized as professional men.

LESSER EXECUTIVE OFFICERS

Most cities elect at least one administrative officer in addition to the mayor. Some elect as many as five others. For the most part, such officers are likely to be the clerk (or recorder), the city attorney (or corporation counsel), and various fiscal officers. In addition, certain department heads who are nearly always appointed are important persons in the policy-making process. Of these, the treasurer, controller, auditor, and assessor are discussed in Chapter 16. The police chief, still sometimes elected, is discussed in Chapter 17, the city engineer in Chapter 18, and the planner in Chapter 20. The duties of two other officers will be mentioned here.[17]

The clerk is, in form, only the records keeper of the city. He also usu-

---

[16] *Ibid.*, pp. 67–68. By permission of the Public Administration Service. On managers as professionals, see also two articles by George K. Floro: "Continuity in City-manager Careers," *American Journal of Sociology*, vol. 61 (November, 1955), pp. 240–246; and "Types of City Managers," *Public Management*, vol. 36 (October, 1954), pp. 221–225.

[17] Special districts also sometimes have elective officers, or they may have elective governing boards which appoint professional managers as chief administrators. For the example of the school superintendent in this role, see Thomas H. Eliot, "Toward an Understanding of Public School Politics," *American Political Science Review*, vol. 53 (December, 1959), pp. 1032–1951.

ally serves as secretary to the council and keeps the formal minutes of its meetings. In practice, however, the clerk may become much more than an office manager. Indeed, he may become a virtual manager in small cities and villages. One reason for this is that he often serves a long time in the job. The public prefers to keep the position elective, but it also regards the clerk as being essentially noncontroversial in character. Thus, in municipalities of all sizes, the clerk is likely to be a person of modest ability who makes the job a career. Because he gradually comes to know more about the minutiae of government perhaps than any one else, he is relied upon for background details. From this responsibility, it is often a short step to giving advice when asked, and then to initiating suggestions. Because the consequences of any action this advice may generate will be attributed to others—the councilmen, the mayor, or the manager—the clerk goes on his bland way toward retirement, calmly riding above the storms of controversy that confront his colleagues.

One study has indicated that, in cities of under 10,000 population, a clerk has a great deal to do with policy formulation—that he does do, in a great many cases, the things suggested here. The study also indicated that certain factors reduced the importance of the clerk in a policy-making role, however. A part-time clerk was generally less effective than one who was constantly on duty. Women clerks were not usually effective as policy leaders. And clerks in council-manager cities were more likely to be restricted to ministerial (routine) duties than was the case in other cities.[18]

Cities today are not likely to elect the city attorney (see Table 8-1). He remains, however, an important policy-making officer, as he was a few generations ago when the voters expected to be allowed to select him directly. In larger cities, in strong-mayor, and in council-manager cities, the attorney is usually selected by the chief administrative officer and reports directly to him. In such cases, the attorney is influential as a policy maker, but he is subject to general oversight and direction by his chief, and this gives him a fairly definite policy framework within which to work. In other cities, and particularly in small communities, the council may select the attorney and rely heavily on his advice, since he has a near monopoly on the legal skills that are essential for effective municipal management.[19] The attorney and the clerk are the two most likely policy leaders in places of under, say, 10,000 people.

[18] Walter D. De Vries, "The Role of the Fourth Class Michigan City Clerk in Municipal Decision-making" (Unpublished master's thesis, Michigan State University, East Lansing, Mich., 1955).

[19] For a case study of an upstate New York village, see A. J. Vidich and Joseph Bensman, *Small Town in Mass Society* (Princeton University Press, Princeton, N.J., 1958), pp. 127–129. For the clerk in the town surrounding the village, pp. 144–146.

Regardless of size of community, the city attorney is important for other reasons: (1) Dillon's rule makes both councilmen and administrators dependent upon him for opinions as to what the city is legally authorized to do. Because he must be consulted constantly in this regard, he has great opportunities for becoming a general policy advisor. (2) To a considerable extent, he decides upon enforcement levels, though he may not be permitted to do so unilaterally, especially if he is not elected directly. The attorney has much to say about which laws are to be enforced, and how sternly they are to be enforced. He does not have the great power of the elective state's attorney in this connection as a rule, but he may be able to make great changes in the original intent of city ordinances and state laws in the way in which he administers them.[20]

The lesser executive officers of the city, whether elected or appointed, are important to citizens because, despite their low visibility level, they significantly affect policy making. Though the citizen may not know it, when the headlines proclaim "Mayor Zilch Announces New Bonding Program," or "Councilman Announces Tax-free Parking Scheme," the men given the credit are only acting out their roles in the play. The playwright probably will not even be mentioned in the news story. His is merely one of those "unimportant routine" offices of the city.

[20] On the policy-making powers of the state's attorney (or county prosecutor), see Charles R. Adrian, *State and Local Governments* (McGraw-Hill Book Company, Inc., 1960), pp. 282–284

Chapter 10

THE CITY COUNCIL

The historic functions of legislative bodies in Western civilization have been those of debate, criticism, and investigation. In recent centuries, the popular assemblies have also been accorded the task of declaring and thus legitimatizing the law—a function once performed by the courts.[1]

City councils, as local legislatures, have generally performed the historic role of assemblies. Under colonial frontier influence, however, American councils became somewhat more positive instruments of policy leadership. The weak-mayor–council arrangement of frontier days placed the council in center stage and Americans became accustomed to thinking of the councilmen as community leaders and as policy innovators. With the rise of the strong-mayor and council-manager plans, however, the council retreated to its traditional, essentially negative and symbolic functions—debate, criticism, investigation, and the formal declaration of the rules through resolutions and ordinances.

Reformers of several decades ago distrusted councilmen, or the role of the ward alderman, at any rate. Aldermen, by and large, were interested in the daily, short-range considerations of neighborhood constituents, in favors to beset individuals, and in jobs—but not in over-all policy development or in middle-class morality. Those who wrote the modern charters of cities, therefore, concentrated power in the chief executive—the mayor or manager—where they could expect policy leadership without the beclouding influence of errand running, patronage considerations before program content, or neighborhood concerns before community-wide interests. As a result, the council's role is now somewhat less that of leadership and innovation than it was a century go.

The pattern of councilmanic functions varies with the forms of city government, however. The duties of councilmen vary from the situation in weak-mayor cities, where each alderman, in addition to sharing in policy-making duties, serves very often as a ward foreman supervising administrative functions, to the council-manager city, where he usually

[1] See Charles R. Adrian, *State and Local Governments* (McGraw-Hill Book Company, Inc., New York, 1960), pp. 286–288.

has only policy-making duties. The type of person who serves on the council also varies considerably from place to place, but the differences are based upon the size of the city as well as the forms of government.

LEADERSHIP AND CONFLICT

Varying Functions of the Council. In cities in which councilmen are elected by wards, the popular assembly of the community is most likely to perform the role it did during the nineteenth century. In one study, of a city of about 50,000 population, the ward aldermen controlled patronage in their wards, carefully divided up the allocation of money for street repair, and were generally much more concerned with caring for the special wants of constituents than they were with over-all policy development. In a city largely untouched by reform, the councilmen from all except the upper-middle-class wards had not finished high school. They were neither very articulate nor capable of conducting public deliberations in an effective fashion. As a result, they sought protection from outside criticism through collective action. The majority faction (made up of aldermen from the working-class wards) spoke, to a considerable extent, as a single voice. There were no outstanding policy leaders on the council. The minority could not even exploit the weaknesses of the dominant faction.[2]

Three other cities with strong managers, on the other hand, had councils made up of men with considerable education and business or professional experience. The members were elected at large and generally did not want to be bothered with errand running for constituents—in one city it was customary practice to refuse to do so under all conditions. In these cities, members "did not emerge as either general policy innovators or as general policy leaders. The individual councilman, rather, was likely to assume leadership in connection with a specific issue or function of government. He developed pet interests or came to know one area of municipal activity especially well and concentrated upon that."[3]

A larger study—of eighty-eight council-manager cities—found that "while the number of policies initiated by councilmen in any one city is not large, they usually are on issues of considerable importance." Also it was found that:[4]

[2] Oliver P. Williams and Charles R. Adrian, *Fighting City Hall: A Comparative Study of Politics in Four Middle-sized Cities* (forthcoming monograph), chap. 11. For aldermanic politics in Chicago, see Martin Meyerson and E. C. Banfield, *Politics, Planning and the Public Interest* (The Free Press, Glencoe, Ill., 1957).

[3] Charles R. Adrian, "Leadership and Decision-making in Manager Cities: A Study of Three Communities," *Public Administration Review*, vol. 18 (Summer, 1958), p. 211.

[4] Clarence E. Ridley, *The Role of the City Manager in Policy Formulation* (International City Managers' Association, Chicago, 1958), pp. 17, 52.

Although the prestige of the council has not diminished in council-manager cities, the character of council action has changed as the city manager and others in the administrative organization make more of the recommendations for council consideration. The council naturally depends on the manager and his staff to study the problems and recommend solutions.

Conflict and Consensus. In general, the larger the city, the less is there likely to be consensus. Conflict becomes a part of daily public life in the large city and public policies that are hammered out are likely to represent uneasy compromises, not supported by a stable majority of either citizens or councilmen. In these cities, conflict among the citizens is normally reflected by conflict on the council—and this in turn leads to factionalism on the governing board.

Of fifty-one Los Angeles County cities in one study, 36 per cent (eighteen cities) reported the existence of factions on the council. In addition, many other cities had councils which divided occasionally over a basic issue of policy. The councils split most often over zoning matters, but it was policies concerning personnel and capital improvements that were most likely to create enduring splits.[5]

Factions may be organized, or they may be made up of the majority group which was elected through endorsement of some recruiting organization against the unorganized minority. They may exist primarily along liberal-conservative lines, as in the Minneapolis council for a long time, or they may divide according to neighborhood versus more general interests, or city boosters versus low-tax advocates, or on some other basis. The dominant faction may have a strong majority or, because city councils are usually small, a majority of one. In the latter case, of course, any tendency of majority-faction members to defect on certain issues is crucial, for such a defection reverses the majority and minority situations. In one study—of a Massachusetts city of 50,000—such defections were most likely to occur when a councilman was faced with supporting the particular demands—for improved water supply, sidewalks, or for street repairs—of his own constituents. The sanctions of his colleagues as a group were powerful, but not as powerful as the sounds coming from those who would, at the next election, support him—or turn him out.[6]

In contrast to the large and middle-sized cities is the small town. In populous communities, those who disagree are expected to say so, even at the final vote on a measure, if necessary. But the picture is quite different in the village where a consensus of values reduces political disagree-

[5] R. J. Huckshorn and C. E. Young, "A Study of Voting Splits on City Councils in Los Angeles County," *Western Political Quarterly,* vol. 13 (June, 1960), pp. 479–497.

[6] J. Leiper Freeman, "A Case Study of the Legislative Process in Municipal Government," in John C. Wahlke and Heinz Eulau, *Legislative Behavior* (The Free Press, Glencoe, Ill., 1959), pp. 228–237.

ments to a discussion of jots and where society may expect councilmen to agree unanimously: [7]

Within the formally constituted governing agency of the village, the village board, politics is conducted on the principle of unanimity of decision. In two years of observation of village board meetings in Springdale, all decisions brought to a vote were passed unanimously. The dissent, disagreement and factionalism which exist in the community are not expressed at board meetings. Through a process of consultation prior to an official meeting and by extended discussion involving the entire group during the meeting itself, a point is reached when it seems reasonable to assume that everyone will go along with the proposed action. Only then, as a final parry, will someone suggest that a motion be made to propose the action. After a short period of silence which provides a last opportunity for further discussion prior to the motion, the motion is made. Whereupon it is assumed that the motion is passed, or, if brought to a vote, as occasionally happens, it passes unanimously.

THE PEOPLE WHO SIT ON COUNCILS

Council Types. Councilmen have many impressions of their own role. Some of them are frankly concerned with representing a particular interest, perhaps Negroes or realtors. Others want to create a "city beautiful." Still others regard themselves as caretakers, guardians of the taxpayers' pocketbooks. Most commonly—according to one study—councilmen held one of two self-perceptions: [8]

. . . Some drew an analogy between the functions of the councilmen and the member of the corporation board of directors. Others viewed themselves as a vehicle through which the wishes of the public could be translated into public action.

The first view implies that the public interest is both ascertainable and indivisible. The good of the city, like the good of the corporation, must be stated in all-encompassing terms. This requires the councilman to view himself not as a delegate, but as a person possessing a mandate to use his own judgment in solving the problems presented to him. This judgment is shaped not only by his personal values, but by the exchange of views on the council. Thus the councilman is a participant in a dialogue which "serves the interests of all the people."

The second view asserts instead that the job of the legislator is to do what the people, both individually and collectively, want. The councilman is a public servant who should entertain the requests and grievances of citizens and attempt to accommodate their desires, if it is possible within the framework of the law. The public interest is articulated by the adjustment of indi-

[7] A. J. Vidich and Joseph Bensman, *Small Town in Mass Society* (Princeton University Press, Princeton, N.J., 1958), p. 110.
[8] Williams and Adrian, *op. cit.*, chap. 11.

vidual claims expressed through the representatives. Each councilman is an advocate of what he believes to be his constituents' desires.[9]

The City Hall Club. Because councils are generally small—the national average size is six members—the councilman is not merely the impersonal spokesman for his conscience or his constituency. He is also a member of a small group. The council is a club which tends to band together against outsiders. It also has certain rules concerning what a member can say about another member without being ostracized. The intimate knowledge that members gain of one another's idiosyncrasies modifies their behavior.

As one study has noted: [10]

. . . Once elected to the council, the legislator became part of an organization in which members had different roles to play and the different degrees of prestige, participation, and authority he enjoyed depended in considerable measure upon the committee posts assigned him. As in most other legislative bodies in the United States, the criterion of seniority was a traditional basis . . . for determining committee assignments.

Occupations. In the vast majority of American cities, the typical council member is a local businessman, well respected in the community, active in civic organizations, and often a college graduate. He runs for the council because of the prestige and power the position affords. He may consider the fact that the prominence of the position will help his business, but often he is merely acting out of sense of community responsibility. He is not likely to be among the top businessmen in his earnings and standing, but generally he is prosperous. He is usually above average in intelligence, but it is not necessary for the council to consist of a group of intellectual giants or the leading men of the community.

In one of the few systematic studies of a group of councilmen—those of Los Angeles county in 1957—the average age was forty-nine years; they ranged from twenty-five to seventy-six. Only 18 of 283 (6.7 per cent) were women. In an area of rapid change, 39 per cent had served two years or less. Communities with greater population stability probably have much less turnover.[11]

Outside of the very largest cities, the pay for councilmanic positions is very nominal and the job is thought of as being a community service. An exception to this is to be found in commission-governed cities, where the council (commission) is supposed to be made up, not simply of representative citizens of the community, but specifically of persons with

[9] For more on the concept of the public interest, see chap. 13.
[10] Freeman, *op. cit.,* p. 231.
[11] Huckshorn and Young, *op. cit.*

executive or engineering experience. Relatively low salaries, however, have tended to attract ordinary office seekers instead. Topeka, for example, once had a commission made up of a barber, a house mover, and a cub reporter—hardly logical occupations for training in public administration.

In general, the smaller the city, the more likely it will be that council members are the really leading citizens of the community. As cities increase in size, the professional prominence of councilmen, in general, tends to decrease. In the largest cities, the councilmen may well devote full time to work at the city hall and may have run for the office partly because of the salary involved. Although venal and corrupt councilmen were once commonly found in these large cities, they are now a rarity. The greatest sins of the councilmen of the metropolis today are likely to be in their allegiance to particular pressure groups—a real estate board, a labor union, a group of builders, the liquor dealers, the downtown merchants. They are likely to view their function as that of protecting these particular pressure groups, although they invariably pretend to act "for all the people." [12]

The difference between the council in a middle-sized and a large city can be demonstrated by contrasting Davenport with Detroit.

Davenport, Iowa (1960 population: 74,549), might be called a not untypical middle-sized Middle Western city. It has a mayor-council form of government tending toward the weak category. Councilmen receive a $900 annual salary. In 1953, there were fifteen candidates for the eight positions on the council. Among these, there were four insurance salesmen and three real estate dealers or agents. There was one retired minister and one career woman. The remaining candidates were small businessmen or white-collar workers. There were a barber, a bookkeeper, a filling station operator, a baker, a retired grocer, and a tax consultant. It is likely that in a middle-sized city with the council-manager plan and at-large elections, the candidates would have been drawn more from professional and executive categories.

Detroit (1960 population: 1,672,574) has a strong-mayor–council form of government. The council is elected at large and members receive a salary of $12,000 a year. In 1954, the council consisted of four persons

---

[12] The old-time ward alderman was a little mayor in his own bailiwick and was sometimes, for example in Chicago, quite independent of the party organization. For brief sketches of colorful Chicago aldermen such as "Bathhouse" John Coughlin, "Hinky Dink Mike" Kenna and "Foxy Ed" Cullerton, see Charles E. Merriam, *Chicago* (The Macmillan Company, New York, 1929), pp. 223–225. Lloyd Wendt and Herman Kogan, *Lords of the Levee* (The Bobbs-Merrill Company, Indianapolis, 1943), is the biography of Coughlin and Kenna, who ran the "levee"–Chicago's First Ward. A more recent ward alderman, Mathias J. ("Paddy") Bauler, is portrayed in A. J. Liebling, *Chicago: The Second City* (Alfred A. Knopf, Inc., New York, 1952), pp. 116–125.

who could best be called professional politicians: three lawyers, an automobile saleswoman, and a retired baseball player. Because a council position is ostensibly a full-time job and because long tenure is typical, it is not easy to distinguish clearly between professional and amateur politicians among its membership.

Minority Groups. In small cities, minority-group representation is not likely to be a major problem. In larger cities, the number of minority-group representatives on the city council tends to vary according to whether or not the council is elected at large. Where the council is fairly large and elected by wards, the ethnic groups that include political-activity patterns as part of their subculture tend to dominate, while in the case of a small council elected at large, the groups that are usually deemed "minorities" tend to be excluded.

There are other factors involved, too. Where political parties play a prominent part in local elections, minority-group representation is likely to be greater, since parties have historically sought the support of these groups in large cities. In cities with nonpartisan elections and a political process dominated by the business community, minority groups are usually quite badly underrepresented on city councils. The only exception to this seems to be in the case of the Irish, an ethnic group that has made political participation a part of its way of life. Other racial groups appear to be too poorly organized or too little interested in local politics to be effective, or at least proportionately effective, in the larger cities.

No Negro or Jew was elected to the Los Angeles council between the time of the adoption of the present charter (1925) and 1953. Only one person of Italian descent had served, and Protestants had dominated the council in a city in which a majority of the inhabitants were and still are Catholic. Precisely the same comments could be made concerning the Detroit council between 1919 and 1953. In the latter city, the large Polish ethnic group has also been greatly underrepresented.

Negroes, lacking in a cultural tradition of political participation and hence often poorly organized politically, have not yet learned to use their ever increasing political strength effectively in most cities. Oscar Stanton DePriest (1871–1951) was the first Negro to serve on the Chicago city council, beginning in 1915. Because that city elects its councilmen by wards, the "black belt" is assured of some representation.[13] There is always Negro representation on the New York council today. As the Negro migration from the southern sharecropper farm to the northern city continues, more and more Negro representation will no doubt appear on councils.

[13] On Negro councilmen in Chicago, see Martin Meyerson and E. C. Banfield, *Politics, Planning and the Public Interest* (The Free Press, Glencoe, Ill., 1957).

In the South, the increasing enfranchisement of the Negro since about 1944 has taken place largely in the cities, with the result that the political influence of Negroes is beginning to be felt there, too. Negroes have long been influential in San Antonio politics in the Southwest. In 1947, a Negro was elected an alderman in one ward of Winston-Salem, defeating a white opponent. The nine-member-at-large council that was first elected in Richmond in 1948 after that city adopted the manager plan included a Negro as one of its members.[14] Cleveland's council sometimes has as many as three Negro members, and there is almost always one in Cincinnati. Indianapolis, St. Louis, Philadelphia, Louisville, and New Haven have elected Negro councilmen in recent years. Nashville has had two (elected by wards) serving since 1947.

Women on the Council. It is quite common to find women serving on school boards throughout the nation. They also often serve on park boards, library boards, and other special-purpose bodies. Their numbers on councils have been smaller, however, although some cities have a tradition of always having at least one woman on the city council. Peoria and Los Angeles did not elect a woman to the council until 1953. In Milwaukee, the first woman was elected in 1956. Portland, Oregon, elected a woman mayor-commissioner in 1948, but this is rare in so large a city. The occasional "skirt slates" that appear in small-city clean-up campaigns are reported in the newspapers throughout the land for the very reason that they are so unusual. Although the pattern is changing, American men and women both still tend to think of politics as being male territory.

Qualifications. As in the case of the mayor, the city charter commonly provides for certain minimum qualifications in age, residence, and citizenship. Other requirements that may be found include such things as required residence in the ward from which elected or disqualification of persons holding contracts with the city.

Most observers believe that the quality of councilmen has improved in the last fifty years. There are no measurements for this, of course, and the degree to which it may be attributed to an improvement in the forms of government, to a decrease in the size of the council, to a change from ward to at-large elections and from partisan to nonpartisan elections, or to other causes is not known.

THE STRUCTURE OF THE COUNCIL

Salary. In the British tradition, councilmanic salaries are deliberately fixed at a low rate in most small and medium-sized cities to discourage

[14] Maurice R. Davie, *Negroes in American Society* (McGraw-Hill Book Company, Inc., New York, 1949), pp. 274–282.

TABLE 10-1. TERMS OF OFFICE, MEMBERS OF COUNCIL, IN
ALL MUNICIPALITIES OF OVER 5,000
(In per cent)

Type of city government	Two years	Four years	Other
Mayor-council..........	48	44	8
Commission.............	17	64	19
Council-manager........	36	53	11
Town meeting...........	27	0	73
Rep. town meeting.......	23	0	77

SOURCE: *Municipal Year Book, 1960* (International City Managers'
Association, Chicago, 1960), p. 87.

candidates who are interested in the salary and to make the job one in
which the prestige and honor of it are the decisive elements. For this
reason, membership on school and park boards and some others, including city councils, carries no salary at all in many communities.

In larger cities—say of over 50,000—the task of being a councilman
requires a good deal of time, even under the manager plan, and those
who serve are required to make a considerable sacrifice. High salaries for
councilmen in these cities often attract candidates who would make a
profession of officeholding.

Salaries tend to be highest in commission-plan cities for here the
councilmen are also being paid as administrative heads of departments.
Council-manager cities tend to have the lowest salaries, since under this
form the council is a part-time body even in large cities and is restricted
to legislative functions alone. In 1960, for example, the councilmen in
Austin and Hartford received no pay at all, in Des Moines they were paid
$500 a year, and in Berkeley $75. There are some exceptions in manager cities: Niagara Falls, New York, for example, paid $3,000 a year,
and Medford, Massachusetts, $4,000, which is more than was paid in
St. Louis, a mayor-council city.[15]

Term of Office. Councilmanic terms range from one year to six years.
One-year terms are found in cities with the town-meeting form. The six-
year term is found mostly in a few commission cities, but a very few
manager cities also use it.

In recent years, the four-year term has become the most common in
American cities (see Table 10-1). In general, the larger the city, the more
likely it is to have a four-year term. In about 40 per cent of the cities, the

[15] Councilmanic salaries are reported in the current issue of the *Municipal Year
Book* (International City Managers' Association).

terms of all councilmen expire at the same time. The larger the city, the more likely this is to be true. Overlapping, or staggered, terms are most likely to be found in manager and commission cities, where the emphasis has traditionally been upon imitating the business corporation and in playing down the political aspects of city government. There is an argument that staggered terms provide desirable continuity in a council, but this is achieved in any case by the almost universal habit Americans have of giving long tenure in office to councilmen.

Size of Council. Councils range in size from two members in several cities to Chicago's fifty. In the case of the former, the mayor practically becomes a councilman, for he must break any tie. In an earlier day, councils sometimes ranged in size to above two hundred members. Something of a dilemma is encountered in trying to determine the most effective size for a council. A large council is cumbersome and tends to obscure responsibility by working through committees. A small council is sometimes said to lack representativeness and raises some questions concerning the function of criticism. A small council becomes involved in personal relationships that make it difficult for members to criticize other members freely. It is generally held, however, that the small council has not been proved bad, while the large one has. In any case, the trend in recent years has been toward smaller councils.

Very roughly speaking, the size of the council increases as the size of the city increases. A more important variable, however, is to be found in the type of structural form. In commission cities, the size of the commission tends to remain the same regardless of the size of the city. The commission is made up of five members in a preponderant number of cases. (See Table 10-2.) Council-manager cities tend to increase from five to nine members as the size of the city increases, but there are many exceptions to this. In the case of mayor-council cities, it is not possible to find very much of a correlation between size of city and size of council.

Unicameralism. At the turn of the century, about one-third of the cities of over 25,000 population had bicameral (two-house) councils. The figure had once been higher, but never included one-half of the cities. From the days of the reform movement of that period until the present, the number of these imitations of Congress and the state legislatures has diminished. There is no logical basis for a two-house municipal council. To the extent that bicameralism on the state level makes sense, it is based on the need to compromise the rural-urban split. In the city, it has no justification, and only a few communities still use it.

The city of New York has a council elected by wards and a Board of Estimate with an ex officio membership. The board is made up of the mayor, the controller, the president of the council, and the president of each of the five boroughs. However, a system of weighing the votes of

TABLE 10-2. SIZE OF COUNCIL

Population of city	Mayor-council		Commission		Council-manager	
	Range *	Median	Range *	Median	Range *	Median
Over 500,000	7–50	15				
250,000–500,000	7–16	9	3–7	5	7–9	9
100,000–250,000	4–33	11	3–5	5	5–13	7
All over 5,000	2–50	7	2–7	5	2–20	5

* "Range" refers to the largest and smallest number of council members within each class.

SOURCE: *Municipal Year Book, 1960* (International City Managers' Association, Chicago, 1960), p. 85.

each of these elective officers gives control to the first three. The board had the power to make up the New York budget before 1933. Since that time, the board has the budgets of the city submitted to it first. It holds hearings and may alter the budgets in any way it sees fit. After it has passed them, they are sent to the council, which has powers only to reduce or delete. The council "has no important power in adopting local laws which the Board does not share on equal terms; the Board is, in effect, the upper chamber in a bicameral city legislature." [16]

Election by Wards. There is a strong tendency today to elect members of the council at large, except in cities of over 500,000. Well over one-half of the cities of more than 5,000 population now elect at large, and a much greater percentage of the smaller cities do so. Again, the pattern that prevails depends to a large extent upon the structural form that is used (see Table 10-3). Nearly all commission cities, for example, elect their members at large, since each member of the commission is a department head and almost necessarily is chosen by all the voters. The towns of New England almost always elect at large, since most of these places are quite small and all of them grew out of a rural tradition. The manager plan strongly leans toward election at large. Weak-mayor cities tend to use a ward system, which they have inherited from the nineteenth century. A few cities nominate by wards and elect at large in an attempt to secure better geographical distribution.

The great size of cities such as New York and Chicago seems to suggest

[16] Wallace S. Sayre and Herbert Kaufman, *Governing New York City* (Russell Sage Foundation, New York, 1960), p. 627.

TABLE 10-3. METHOD OF ELECTING MEMBERS OF COUNCIL IN
ALL MUNICIPALITIES OF OVER 5,000
(In per cent)

Type of city government	Elected at large	Elected by wards	Elected by combination *	Staggered terms
Mayor-council........	37	38	25	56
Commission..........	96	2	2	44
Council-manager......	74	16	10	76
Town meeting........	94	3	3	33
Rep. town meeting....	92	7	0	44
All over 500,000....	30	35	35	23
All over 5,000......	59	24	17	61

* "Elected by combination" refers to the election of some councilmen by wards and others at large within the same city.

SOURCE: *Municipal Year Book, 1960* (International City Managers' Association, Chicago, 1960), p. 86.

the use of ward representation, and this has been traditional in America. It is argued that election by wards provides a short ballot and gives representation on the council to the various ethnic, racial, and economic areas of the city. On the other hand, aldermen selected from small wards tend to become local errand boys. They are unable safely to consider the needs of the whole city lest they be quickly told by their constituents that they were sent to the city hall to protect the interests of their own ward. Attempts at "statesmanship" only produce candidates who say, "If Torkelson can't look after this ward and its interests, I can." Furthermore, city populations are constantly shifting—in general toward the periphery. This means that a ward system, especially one written into the charter, eventually becomes gerrymandered. The slums and the periphery become underrepresented to the profit of the intermediate areas.

Minority groups sometimes make strong arguments for ward election on the ground that this is the only way for them to get a voice on the council. Negro groups are likely to feel especially strongly about this. Yet it is not difficult for white politicians to gerrymander ward boundaries to keep Negroes off the council. Los Angeles and Detroit each have great Negro populations made up largely of recent arrivals (since 1940). Los

Angeles elects all councilmen by wards. Detroit elects all at large. Until the mid-1950s, neither city elected a Negro to the council.

Election at large lengthens the ballot, forces the establishment of a council so small that it may not be representative in a large city, and gives the election to the candidates who can find financial backers able to pay the expense of a city-wide campaign. Because large and medium-sized cities encounter a dilemma in seeking to choose between ward and at-large elections, compromises are common. Houston elects three members at large and five by wards. Buffalo chooses nine councilmen by wards for two-year terms and six at large for four-year staggered terms. Nearly one-fourth of the mayor-council cities use some sort of combination of the two devices.

Type of Ballot. Far more than half of the city councils in the United States in places of over 5,000 population are elected on a ballot without party designation (see Table 10-4). The nonpartisan ballot is found most commonly in manager cities, since both nonpartisanship and the manager plan grew out of the reform movement. Because the representative town meeting is a recent development in New England, it, too, is usually non-partisan. The commission plan, also a product of the early reform-movement years, is predominantly nonpartisan, but to a lesser extent. Its popularity declined before it received the full impact of the nonpartisan movement.

This leaves only the mayor-council city and the traditional New England town as the centers of partisan municipal activity. City and town governments that have not been reconstructed tend to retain the partisan ballot, and some cities are required by state law to use it.

TABLE 10-4. TYPE OF BALLOT, MEMBERS OF COUNCIL, IN ALL MUNICIPALITIES OF OVER 5,000
(In per cent)

Type of city government	Partisan	Nonpartisan
Mayor-council............	56	44
Commission..............	39	61
Council-manager.........	16	84
Town meeting...........	55	45
Rep. town meeting.......	23	77
All over 5,000..........	39	61

SOURCE: *Municipal Year Book, 1960* (International City Managers' Association, Chicago, 1960), p. 86.

Large cities might be said to tend to use the partisan ballot for the council, but such a statement would have to be made with caution. Two cities of over 1 million people, Los Angeles and Detroit, use nonpartisan ballots. Chicago has nonpartisan elections, but this is true only in a formal sense. All offices other than those of the aldermen are on a partisan ballot. All of the aldermen are elected in single-member wards. This makes it so easy for the parties to give direct support to an aldermanic candidate and to have this support made known to the voters that Chicago does not fit into the pattern of most cities with a nonpartisan ballot.[17]

ORGANIZATION AND PROCEDURE

The Presiding Officer. The mayor may preside over the council, or a member of the council may serve as its presiding officer. In the latter case, he may be selected either by direct popular vote, by the council members from among their own membership, or by making the person who receives the highest number of votes for council the president. When the president is elected separately for that specific office, as is the case in several cities, including the city of New York, he is sometimes not considered a true member of the council and often cannot vote except in case of a tie. The function of the presiding officer is in keeping with the usual powers and duties assigned to this officer in American legislative bodies. The council may also select other officers, including a secretary or clerk, although the city clerk usually serves in this capacity.

Committees. Because city governments tend to imitate those of the state and nation, the use of committees for the preliminary work on ordinances was customary in the nineteenth century. Even today almost all city councils make some use of committees. Reformers have generally frowned on this device, since it obscures the nature of the work of the council, confuses responsibility to the public, and allows a majority of a committee (a minority of the council) frequently to determine policy by minority rule. Standing committees also tend to take over administrative functions and for this reason are opposed by advocates of the reform-movement principles.

Standing committees are generally used in mayor-council governments, particularly of the weak-mayor type, but they are less common in council-manager governments. In manager cities, the council as a whole looks to the manager to do the preliminary work on ordinances, making committees less necessary. Because such committees tend to interfere in administration, they are especially disapproved of by experts on the manager form. Special committees are frequently utilized, however.

[17] The effect of nonpartisanship upon the political process is discussed in chap. 4.

ALDERMEN WANT BETTER
FREE SEATS AT ARENA
— *NEWS ITEM*

COUNCIL
SECRET
CAUCUS

KEEP OUT!

Figure 10-1. The use of some sort of presession secret caucus, with the result that the regular public meeting of the council is a mere formality, has produced criticism in several American cities in postwar years. SOURCE: From the *Milwaukee Journal,* with its permission and that of Ross Lewis.

In those cities making extensive use of committees, the system works largely in the same manner as does the committee system of Congress or the state legislatures: the council as a whole becomes chiefly a ratifying body for the actions of the committees. Even if the council has authority to override a committee recommendation or relieve the committee of further consideration of a bill, these things are not likely to happen, since each councilman—like each Congressman—will tacitly agree to allow other councilmen to be supreme in their committee areas if they will extend the same privilege to him.[18]

Some cities with small councils make frequent use of the committee of the whole, which is not a committee at all, but simply a convenient method for considering legislation in an informal atmosphere. Other

[18] A description of a large, machine-controlled council working through committees is given in C. E. Merriam, *Chicago: A More Intimate View of Urban Politics* (The Macmillan Company, New York, 1929).

cities hold an informal executive "conference session" before each meeting. If the city has a manager, he will probably attend. These sessions may be used to decide in advance the manner in which each item on the agenda will be disposed of. The formal session then becomes a hollow ritual, having given way to an informal, extralegal committee. This device is criticized as creating a "hidden government." Secret council sessions were an issue in Milwaukee in 1953, and Akron banned secret meetings of all city boards and commissions in 1954, indicating that the problem is not confined to the council alone (see Figure 10-1).

Meetings. The frequency of council meetings depends upon the size of the city, local custom, and the complexity of current issues in the community. In cities with part-time, lay councils, meetings are likely to be at night. In small towns the meetings may be only once a month. In the largest cities the councilmen will probably meet almost daily in committee or committee-of-the-whole sessions, with one formal meeting each week, perhaps at night in order to allow interested citizens to attend.

POWERS OF THE COUNCIL

The functions, and hence powers, of the council are basically the same in mayor-council and council-manager cities. In places operating under the commission plan, the council is also the multiple-executive administrative body. For purposes of this section, this special function of the commission will be ignored.

Determination of Public Policy. The most important task of the council, of course, is to pass ordinances and resolutions formally establishing public policy for the community. The council passes on public improvements and exercises such portions of the state police power to regulate and control the health, safety, and morals of the community as it is authorized to do. City plans are passed upon by the council, as well as modifications of the land-use control ordinances. The council makes policy for the municipally owned utilities and exercises control over those that are privately owned to the extent allowed by state law.

Taxation and Appropriation. While the current trend is toward executive preparation of the budget, the council must still vote the funds. Changes in the city tax structure are also made by the council, subject to the rules of the charter. The council also buys and sells city property. In most cities, the council has the power to pass upon all contracts, or at least upon the large ones. This is really an administrative function, but the power traditionally belongs to the council. Its action of approval or disapproval is a symbolic act on behalf of the citizenry.

Supervision of Administration. In a manager city, the administration is directly answerable to the council through the manager. In other forms of government, the council has an obligation to check upon the activities of the administration. It does this by receiving auditor's reports, by appointing investigating committees, by requiring testimony or reports from department heads and others, and by reviewing the activities of the various departments at budget hearings. Depending on the provisions of the charter, the council may be able to shuffle functions and bureaus to suit itself and to establish many rules of procedure of the departments.

In weak-mayor cities of the past and present, and especially where aldermen represent wards, the council has carried its oversight of administration to great extremes. Each committee of the council may engage in constant and detailed oversight of the department heads, creating problems of morale and confusion as to who is boss. Each alderman may tend to supervise functions operating within his own ward, concerning himself with details essentially administrative in character.

Other Powers. The council in many cities serves as the city board of equalization or review, hearing appeals from taxpayers on their property assessments. The council often has the power to pass on the appointments of the mayor, and in many cities it makes a goodly number of appointments of its own. In addition, it has the power to remove the mayor and other officials under certain conditions. Many other minor functions are assigned to the council. Their nature varies considerably from one city to another.[19]

PRACTICAL PROBLEMS FACING THE COUNCILMAN

Certain problems confront the councilman in any city of any size: metropolis, suburb, county seat, or small town. M. Nelson McGeary, a political scientist, while serving as president of the State College, Pennsylvania, borough council made the observations summarized in the following section.

[19] A comprehensive study of the American city council in action is badly needed. Some of the studies of individual city governments and of the manager and commission plans discuss the function of the council. Much organizational detail may be obtained from the annual issues of the *Municipal Year Book* (International City Managers' Association).

Several issues of the *National Municipal Review* (now *National Civic Review*) for 1924 to 1926 have articles discussing the councils of those days in some of the larger cities. There is also a series of articles in *Public Management* for 1935 dealing with the organization, procedure, and powers of the council. Arthur W. Bromage has written articles for several professional publications dealing with his experiences on the Ann Arbor city council. Some of these are reprinted in two booklets, *On the City Council* (Wahr Publishing Company, Ann Arbor, Mich., 1950), and *A Councilman Speaks* (Wahr Publishing Company, Ann Arbor, Mich., 1951).

Difficulties in Determining Public Opinion. The councilman always has difficulty in determining the prevailing views of the public. This is the case in cities of all sizes, not just in the large ones. McGeary, for example, found that it was very true in his modest-sized borough of about 9,500. A few people are always vociferous. The great majority are silent most of the time. Because this is so, a councilman quickly learns (or should quickly learn) that he cannot determine public opinion simply by counting the pros and cons expressed by office visitors or in letters to him or to the editor. (Letters to the editor in the local newspaper may have been written by the editor himself.) The councilman also soon learns that he will hear from his constituents more quickly if they disapprove of one of his acts than if they approve.

McGeary found that even when a person expresses himself, he may not state his true opinion. He writes of one case in which a man wrote a lengthy letter to the local newspaper on some current issue. When the councilman said he was glad to know where the citizen stood, the letter writer astounded everyone by explaining that his comments in the newspaper did not express his "real feelings." [20]

Difficulties in Adjusting to Criticism. A citizen is accustomed to the elaborate ritual of criticism by circumlocution found in everyday life. If he is elected to the local council, he finds that his actions now become subjected to a different, more open, more straightforward, and more vigorous criticism. Some of it is informed and responsible. Some of it is uninformed and irresponsible. The councilman must learn to hide his feelings and to accept these comments without undue sensitivity. But he must not become so immune as to ignore the warning flags of changing public opinion, at least not if he wants to be re-elected.

Difficulties in Learning to Trust Expert Advisers. The councilman is usually a lay citizen serving only part time at his job. Even in fairly small cities, and especially in large ones, he must learn to trust the advice given by experts, and to rely upon this in making public policy decisions. If the shade-tree expert says that extensive trimming will help preserve the trees, the councilman must overcome his preference for trimming the budget and instead vote the money for trimming the trees—if any is available. Of course, the councilman cannot simply accept the advice of experts, enact it into an ordinance, and go home. It is not that simple. McGeary points to difficulties that the councilman must face when (1) the experts present, as they often do, original estimates of the costs of large projects that are unrealistically low; and (2) the experts disagree among themselves as to the best solution to a problem. Many a councilman has voted for a sewage-disposal plant only to discover later that it

[20] M. Nelson McGeary, "The Councilman Learns His Job," *National Municipal Review* (now *National Civic Review*), vol. 43 (June, 1954), pp. 284–287.

cost 50 per cent more than the original estimates. And disagreeing experts can keep a councilman awake nights. After all, the councilman must choose among their conflicting suggestions—and they may all be wrong.

Difficulties of Informing the Public. The councilman must let the people know what he is doing and why he is doing it. Communication with a preoccupied and often apathetic public is difficult.

Difficulties in Making the Right Decision at the Right Time. An inexperienced or impetuous councilman is sometimes guilty of making a decision too rapidly for it to represent informed behavior. All of the arguments pro and con may not appear in the first few discussions of an issue. Facts that arise later may make the councilman who has already committed himself look ridiculous. Of course, the man who will not make up his mind, or who always follows the lead of someone else, is of limited value, but "a councilman seems to command respect, and may save himself considerable embarrassment if he takes a definite position only after the facts are in." [21]

Concluding Statement. McGeary has summarized his experiences by saying that "serving on the council is a headache. But democracy is based on the supposition that some citizens will be willing to endure headaches. Actually the travail is not unbearable. And sometimes, for brief periods, it is forgotten—believe it or not—in the knowledge that some little service is being offered." [22]

[21] *Ibid.*, p. 287.
[22] *Ibid.*

Chapter 11

GOVERNMENT IN METROPOLITAN AREAS

Nowhere in the United States today does the sociological and economic metropolitan area coincide with a single governmental unit that includes the entire area. Many of the problems that result from this have been mentioned in Chapter 2 (see Figure 11-1). There is a great deal of inertia, not to mention much overt opposition, to the reorganization of urban government. Why is a change advocated by students of "metropology"? Victor Jones, a leading authority, has put it this way: [1]

A metropolitan government is desirable (1) when coordination of a function over the whole area is essential to effective service or control in any part of the area; (2) when it is desired to apply the ability to pay theory of taxation to the area as a whole, instead of allowing each part to support its own activities at whatever level its own economic base will allow; (3) when services can be supplied more efficiently through large-scale operations; and (4) when it is necessary in order to assure citizens a voice in decisions that effect them at their places of work and recreation as well as at their places of residence.

The strange picture that is presented by the metropolitan-area situation has been demonstrated by one writer: [2]

Within ten miles of the Los Angeles city hall are ten other cities, each with more than 25,000 inhabitants. Within the county are 33 "county islands," territory entirely surrounded by some one of the 45 cities within the county. In addition, there are seven "city islands," surrounded, or nearly surrounded, by other cities; 14 "shoestrings," comprising annexed land a few hundred feet or rods wide and a few blocks or miles long; 13 small cities whose boundaries adjoin, and scores of other boundary irregularities—"peninsulas" and "isthmuses"—which multiply administrative costs, perplex officialdom, baffle students of government, and give people locomotor ataxia.

[1] Victor Jones, "Local Government Organization in Metropolitan Areas," in Coleman Woodbury (ed.), *The Future of Cities and Urban Redevelopment* (University of Chicago Press, Chicago, 1953), pt. IV, p. 508. This is probably the best current work on the subject. See also Jones's earlier study, *Metropolitan Government* (University of Chicago Press, Chicago, 1942). Quotation by permission.

[2] Aldrich Blake, *You Wear the Big Shoe* (Privately printed, Los Angeles, 1945), pp. 15–16. By permission of the author.

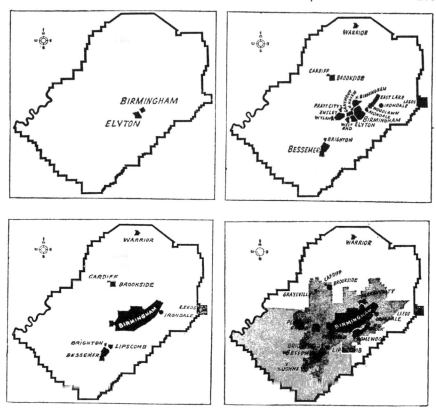

Figure 11-1. The growth of metropolitan Birmingham, Alabama, produced the typical atomization of local government. SOURCE: *Birmingham News,* Mar. 2, 1947; reproduced in Weldon Cooper, *Metropolitan County* (University of Alabama, Bureau of Public Administration, University, Ala., 1949), p. 5.

The outer boundaries of Los Angeles city proper look like a half completed jig-saw puzzle. Competent draftsmen, able to draw the borders of the inner 15 councilmanic districts, find it impossible to describe most of them. Assembly, congressional, supervisorial, and councilmanic lines cross each other everywhere in wild profusion and confusion.

And, superimposed upon the whole, are some 450 other districts, mostly with irregular lines, such as school districts, lighting districts, fire protection districts, flood control districts, sanitation districts and what not. . . .

There are even mosquito abatement districts. For in Los Angeles city and county, the citizen who is rendered sleepless by the buzz and sting of this pestiferous creature, has no means to combat his enemy without first creating a district, electing trustees, and voting the money necessary to spray the ditch or pond on his neighbor's privately owned acres. It's all because neither the city nor county health departments may legally appropriate funds for that purpose unless the victim, or his survivors, are able to prove that the bite caused malaria or yellow fever. The catch here is that the mosquito may escape to new breeding grounds, making the organization of still another district, with still more boundary lines, necessary.

Numerous proposals have been made over the years in seeking solutions for metropolitan government. Up to the present time, however, each of these has nearly always proved to be either unsuccessful as a permanent solution, or politically inexpedient.[3] At present there is no trend toward the adoption of a particular governmental arrangement, nor has anyone been able to devise a plan that would be both practical and successful. Some isolated exceptions are to be found, however, some makeshift and temporary devices have been put to use in various places, and the past efforts are worth studying, in any case, so that the reasons for their lack of success may be seen.

PROPOSED SOLUTIONS TO METROPOLITAN-AREA GOVERNMENT

Annexation. Superficially, the most obvious method of keeping the sociological and legal cities identical would seem to be for the core city to annex fringe areas as they become urbanized. Formerly this method was widely used to expand the city's legal boundaries to keep pace with the actual urban growth, but it has become increasingly unsatisfactory. Although a considerable number of annexations take place each year in both large and small cities, they seldom succeed in equating the political with the sociological city. Milwaukee, as a not untypical example, has annexed a good deal of territory over the years, but it has not produced metropolitan-wide government. The reason for this is quite simple: the laws in nearly all states provide that outlying areas may be annexed only after a referendum has been held and the annexation is approved by the

[3] For details of various proposals and places where they have been tried, see Jones, *op. cit.;* J. C. Bollens, *The States and the Metropolitan Problem* (Public Administration Service, Chicago, 1956); Martin Meyerson (ed.), "Metropolis in Ferment," *Annals,* vol. 314, November, 1957; Government Affairs Foundation, *Metropolitan Communities: A Bibliography* (Public Administration Service, Chicago, 1956); Barbara J. Hudson, *The Urban Fringe Problem: A Bibliography* (Bureau of Public Administration, University of California, Berkeley, Calif., 1952); W. M. Dobriner (ed.), *The Suburban Community* (G. P. Putnam's Sons, New York, 1958); W. H. Whyte, Jr., and others, *The Exploding Metropolis* (Doubleday & Company, Inc., New York, 1958); Betty Tableman, *Governmental Organization in Metropolitan Areas* (University of Michigan Press, Ann Arbor, Mich., 1951); H. A. Simon, *Fiscal Aspects of Metropolitan Consolidation* (Bureau of Public Administration, University of California, Berkeley, Calif., 1943). Current developments are covered in the *National Civil Review* and in *Metropolitan Area Problems: News and Digest,* published bimonthly by the Conference on Metropolitan Area Problems since 1957, and in the professional journals of political science, sociology, urban planning, and other fields. A critical history of metropolitan-area research may be found in Robert C. Wood, *Suburbia* (Houghton Mifflin Company, Boston, 1959), chap. 3.

voters of the outlying area as well as those of the core city. Only in a few states, notably in Virginia, is the core city relatively free to expand its boundaries as the surrounding area becomes urbanized.

Annexation is nearly always unpopular in the fringe areas. This is a reflection both of local pride and of the persistent belief that taxes will be higher within the core city, as well as of various other values of suburbanites discussed in Chapter 2. After 1890, there were few large annexations in the United States until after World War II, when several took place, especially in Texas. Even so, most recent annexations have been of only a few acres, and the larger cities in particular have not annexed much territory.[4]

Large cities usually cannot annex because they are surrounded, or nearly surrounded, by incorporated territory. When this is the case, the political community can be integrated only through *consolidation* of municipalities, and this normally involves even more difficult legal procedures than those of annexation of unincorporated territory. In 1951, Atlanta annexed 82 square miles of territory, some of it incorporated, but it did so by fiat of the Georgia Legislature and without a vote in the areas affected.

Perhaps more annexation would take place if it were not that cities seldom seek to propagandize outlying areas concerning annexation. In 1952, only one city in five where annexation was an issue tried to explain the core city's side of the case to the fringe-area dwellers.[5] Easily the most important factors encouraging fringe areas to want to become annexed are the sewerage and water-supply services. All other services furnished by cities are of far less interest. Sewerage—and especially sewage-disposal—facilities are very expensive and inefficient if used by small units of government. An adequate *source* of water supply is often a serious problem too.

A 1952 study indicated that officials in cities annexing territory felt, in more than four-fifths of the cases, that the new areas in the years immediately ahead would not pay as much in taxes as the city would spend on them. But about the same proportion believed that in the long run the areas would pay for themselves.[6]

Most state laws on annexation are unsuited as a means for securing an integrated government. The requirement of permission of all areas concerned, combined with the fact that suburban dwellers are likely to take a short view, heavily overlaid with concerns about access, representativeness, and the maintenance of life styles, carefully cultivated by

---

[4] Bollens, *op. cit.*, pp. 25–52; Wood, *op. cit.*, pp. 76–78.
[5] John C. Bollens, "Metropolitan and Fringe Area Developments in 1952," *Municipal Year Book, 1953* (International City Managers' Association, 1953), pp. 33–48.
[6] *Ibid.*

fringe-area officeholders protecting their own jobs, all help make this approach a slow-moving one. It is significant that the large annexations usually take place where state laws do not require the direct approval of fringe dwellers.

Texas, California, and Virginia lead in annexations in the postwar period. Texas and Missouri allow annexation of unincorporated territory by amendment of home rule charters without a popular vote. Texas also permits annexation simply by an ordinance of the core city, if the home rule charter so provides.[7] This was the technique used in San Antonio in 1952.

Virginia has an unusual annexation procedure whose origins are hidden in colonial obscurity. In that state, whenever a fringe area begins to become urbanized, the core city seeks control over the outlying land through a judicial proceeding before a three-judge court. The city is permitted to present the rational case for annexation, and the court is obligated to decide the question on the basis of its interpretation of the interests of the entire community—not on the basis of the pecuniary interests of the suburban dwellers versus those of the city taxpayers. Under these circumstances, the city usually wins its case. Limited possibilities for judicial annexation also exist in five other states.[8]

Jones, while viewing the Virginia method as more productive than that in nearly all other states, has suggested that annexation questions might best be handled by a state administrative body on the order of the postwar Local Government Boundary Commission in England.[9] It is not easy for a court to settle annexation questions on facts alone or to separate facts from values and interests. These distinctions need not be made by an administrative body which could also be more reflective of changes in public policy, could initiate action rather than wait for cases to come before it, and could settle problems on bases other than those proposed by the parties at issue.

It seems unlikely, however, that annexation to the core city will be the approach used in many metropolitan areas in the foreseeable future. There is no trend toward change in existing laws.

Special Districts. If annexation becomes impossible, the next approach that might suggest itself would be to take those functions for which a particularly evident need for metropolitan-wide administration is seen

---

[7] See A. O. Spain, "Politics of Recent Municipal Annexation in Texas," *Southwestern Social Science Quarterly*, vol. 30 (June, 1949), pp. 18–28.

[8] Victor Jones gives details, *op. cit.*, pt. IV, pp. 564–566. The Virginia plan is evaluated in two articles by Chester W. Bain, "Annexation: Virginia's Not-so-judicial System," *Public Administration Review*, vol. 15 (Autumn, 1955), pp. 251–262; and "Terms and Conditions of Annexation under the 1952 Statute," *Virginia Law Review*, vol. 41 (December, 1955), pp. 1129–1158.

[9] *Ibid.*, pp. 568–572.

and create one or more special districts to administer them. Hence, covering all or part of a metropolitan area, there might be park, sewerage, water, parking, airport, planning, or other districts.

"Special districts," one student of the phenomenon has noted,[10] "are the least known and least understood units of government in the United States. Yet, paradoxically, there are some 27,000 more special-district governments in the nation than all other units of government combined."

A special district is an organized unit of government, having substantial autonomy from other governments, its own taxing and—usually—its own bonding authority.[11] In particular, since it has its own fiscal authority and a governing body, it exists as a separate unit of government performing some public service. Districts exist for such varied purposes as recreation, sewage disposal, airports, planning, parking, and mosquito abatement. They may have boundaries coterminous with another unit of government, such as a city or county, or they may overlap other units. They exist in both rural and urban areas and are to be found in every state in the union, though 60 per cent of the national total are located in nine states: California, Illinois, Kansas, Missouri, Nebraska, New York, Oregon, Texas, and Washington.[12]

Growth of Special Districts. The general trend of special districts has been one of an increase in numbers since the end of World War II. This is true even though the most common form of special district, the school district, *decreased* by 53 per cent between 1942 and 1957. This countertrend was the result of special factors, however, and nonschool special districts increased by 74 per cent over the same period. In 1957, there were almost five times as many nonschool special districts as there were counties. The total of such special districts nearly equalled the total of municipalities in the nation. These same districts had nearly twice as much debt as counties and one-half as much as the state governments. Despite all the vast amount of school construction that has taken place in the postwar years, special districts other than for schools have debts 73 per cent the size of those for schools—a reflection of the fact that the functions generally assigned to special districts are of a high-cost, capital-outlay type.

Most nonschool special districts are in rural areas, particularly those for fire protection, soil conservation, and drainage, which together make

[10] W. G. Thrombley, "Texas Special Districts," *Public Affairs Comment,* vol. 4 (March, 1958), p. 1.

[11] U.S. Bureau of the Census, *Governments in the United States* (1957), p. 9.

[12] The basic reference on structure and powers is J. C. Bollens, *Special District Governments in the United States* (University of California Press, Berkeley, Calif., 1957); see his bibliography. For an early description of this peculiar political phenomenon, see K. H. Porter, "A Plague of Special Districts," *National Municipal Review* (now *National Civic Review*), vol. 22 (November, 1933), pp. 344–347.

up about one-half the total districts. But quite a few of these are in urban areas, especially fringe areas, as are many cemetery districts and most housing authorities. These five types taken together make up about two-thirds of the number of special districts.

Ad hoc districts may be governed by a body appointed by the state, one appointed by officials from the local governments overlaid by the district, with members being either appointed especially for the position or in ex officio capacities, one appointed by a judge, or, sometimes, one elected by the voters of the area. The variety is almost endless, but since the last possibility is not the usual one, special-purpose districts ordinarily do not come within the direct oversight of the voting public.

Reasons for Postwar Trend. The need for an area-wide approach to problems exists in rural areas, as in the case of drains that cross township and county lines, and in urban areas. Problems requiring such an approach have especially increased as urban populations have increased. Other solutions failing or seeming to be politically impossible, the special district has been turned to. It has been very popular in many rapidly urbanizing states and has, as in California, served as a substitute for incorporation or for a fringe government of less area than the county.

Often districts are the only means by which essential services can be supplied in a metropolitan area. The pattern of use for the special district is a strange one, however, seeming to depend upon local customs and perhaps upon the accident of the gradual accumulation of rigid constitutional and statutory restrictions controlling general governments and discouraging the use of the existing units for newer services. For ex-

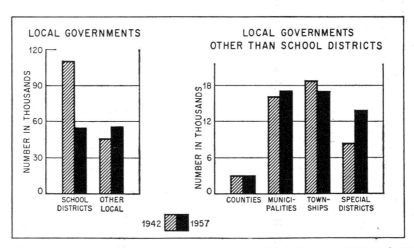

Figure 11-2. Number of local governments in the United States, 1942 and 1957. Note the sharp increase in the number of special districts. SOURCE: U.S. Bureau of the Census.

ample, one might expect special districts to be used especially in states not having townships, but six of the ten states with the most special districts also have townships in all or part of the state. Special districts are very popular in the West, where they are especially used for the procurement, distribution, and allocation of scarce water supplies. But they are found in every part of the land.

There are several reasons for the trend toward special districts. Citizens learn that their state or other states authorize districts to perform certain services. The approach usually has strong appeal. Citizens do not resist it as they do attempts at governmental consolidation, since they expect that it will be less expensive and that it will preserve the independence of their local government. Interest groups that may want services performed by government (amateur pilots wanting an airport, physicians wanting a hospital), together with the professional administrators of particular functions, characteristically want their special problems handled in a special way by a special organization.[13] School administrators have long ago convinced the American public that they should be independent of the rest of local government, and the school district is at once the most common and the best-known special district. Others have followed the lead of the educators and the pressure groups supporting them. The special district has also had great appeal to the wistful who would take their pet governmental function "out of politics."

Pros and Cons of Districts. The advantages of special districts are said to be several. Special districts make possible the provision of governmental services when and where they are most needed and limit the financial burden to residents most directly benefited, while at the same time they skip lightly over the myriad local-government boundaries which otherwise stand in the way of making these services available. Other units of government frequently cannot or will not supply these services. Consolidating local units is often politically unfeasible. By leaving the political *status quo* undisturbed, the social need is met with a minimum of resistance; political loyalties are not disturbed; jobs are not threatened; property-tax payers need have little fear of being assessed for someone else's benefit. Usually, the debts and costs of special districts do not count in determining debt and tax limits of regular local governments, and the bonds of such districts are sometimes more easily marketed than are those of other local governments.

Disadvantages of special districts, it is argued, include the fact that the behind-the-scenes way in which they generally operate helps to make them especially profitable for lawyers, engineers, bankers, bonding houses, and salesmen of equipment, services, and real estate. They are

[13] As Victor Jones has pointed out, *op. cit.*, pp. 527–528.

often designed to meet short-range needs and not only do not consider more permanent approaches, but, by taking the urgency out of the situation for at least a considerable portion of a community, serve to forestall efforts toward long-range, rational governmental organization.[14]

Special districts have often done very good jobs in construction and engineering and sometimes in management. They do not necessarily eliminate political patronage, however, do not guarantee professional administration of functions, and do not remove from the arena of politics governmental functions that involve issues of policy. Special districts often result in increased costs of local government because of the duplication of personnel, the inefficient utilization of equipment, and inability to save through centralized purchasing and other centralized housekeeping activities. They do not balance the various needs for services of a community, do not recognize the interdependence of various functions, and are not usually provided with a method for coordinating their activities and budgets with those of the other governments in the area in which they exist. If the governing board is elective, the ballot is made longer and voters are asked to fill offices in which they have little interest or competence to choose. If the governing board is indirectly chosen, as is usually the case, there is no real responsibility to the public for the function performed. Victor Jones has concluded: [15]

A corporate form of metropolitan government in which the selection of the authority or district commission members is once or more removed from the electoral controls may give us efficient and effective government but it cannot give us good government. It is not necessary, nor is it desirable, for all policy-making officials to be directly elected by popular vote. They should, however, be subject to the budgetary control of popularly elected legislators and their policies should be subject to debate and discussion.

Of course, any legislative body, whether it have jurisdiction over the matter or not, may debate anything it wishes. The object, however, is not futile and irresponsible talk. Our uneasiness should not be allayed by saying that the ordinary municipal governments are frequently corrupt, irresponsible, ineffective, and inefficient. Our job is to make them responsible and efficient. This cannot be done by slicing off the most important functions of local government and handing them over to one or several autonomous bodies.

---

[14] *Ibid.* See also Thrombley, *op. cit.*; Oregon Legislative Interim Committee on Local Government, *Findings and Recommendations* (State of Oregon, Eugene, Ore., 1956); California Assembly Interim Committee on Municipal and County Government, *Final Report* (State of California, Sacramento, Calif., 1957); York Willbern, "Administration in State Governments," in The American Assembly, *The Forty-eight States: Their Tasks as Policy Makers and Administrators* (Graduate School of Business, Columbia University, New York, 1955).

[15] Jones, "Local Government Organization in Metropolitan Areas," pp. 585–586. By permission of the publisher.

Multipurpose Special Districts. Most *ad hoc* districts serve a single purpose, such as the Sanitary District of Chicago, which handles sewerage for over 95 per cent of Cook County's population,[16] the Metropolitan Airports Commission of Minneapolis–St. Paul, and the Metropolitan Water District of Southern California, which brings water some 300 miles from the Colorado River to serve many communities in the Los Angeles area. There are some multipurpose districts in use and some states, such as Michigan, authorize them where they do not exist. Perhaps the most famous is the Port of New York Authority, which handles many aspects of water, highway, and air transportation. It is, however, a joint agent of the states of New York and New Jersey rather than a unit of local government.

Some observers of local government have supported the use of single-purpose special districts partly on the assumption that they will lead to general-purpose districts for metropolitan government. Such expansion has usually not occurred, however. It has not happened in the Boston, Chicago, Los Angeles, Minneapolis, and Seattle areas. Jones illustrates this failure by pointing to the history of the Massachusetts Metropolitan District Commission. This district is controlled by a commission appointed by the Governor of Massachusetts and is not in any way directly responsible to the local community. It was created in 1919 by the consolidation of three districts which furnished sewerage, water, and park services. In 1923, regional planning was added to its functions (but this has since been transferred to the state), and in 1952 refuse disposal was added. In 1929, however, a separate Boston Metropolitan District was created for rapid transit, and in 1947 a Metropolitan Transit Authority was established to take over the previously privately operated elevated railway system.[17] There appears to be no trend toward making super-governments out of the special districts.

City-county Consolidation. Until recent years, reformers have felt that consolidating the city with the metropolitan county was a desirability second only to annexation and a truer and more permanent solution than the use of the special district. This plan (there are dozens of possible variations of it) calls for an integration of the functions of the core city with the county. The county retains a partial identity, and incorporated municipalities remain independent for local purposes. City and county police, attorneys, clerks, treasurers, and health, welfare, and other de-

[16] Unifunctional districts normally carry on incidental functions. The Chicago district produces electric power and fertilizer, and its channels are used for navigation. Illinois Legislative Council, *Chicago Sanitary District* (State of Illinois, Springfield, Ill., 1953), pp. 22–27; Ward Walker, *The Story of the Metropolitan Sanitary District of Greater Chicago* (Metropolitan Sanitary District, Chicago, 1956).

[17] Victor Jones, "Local Government in Metropolitan Areas," pt. IV, pp. 582–583.

partments can be combined to save the core-city taxpayer from paying for county services that he does not use and that in any event duplicate those he is already paying the city to do.

At least fifteen attempts at city-county consolidation have been made in the twentieth century, and only the combination of Baton Rouge with East Baton Rouge parish in 1947 has succeeded. Attempts of this type usually require state-wide approval on a constitutional-amendment referendum, or legislative approval, or a majority vote on referendum both in the core city and in the portions of the county outside. Such approval is not easy to secure.

In Baton Rouge, one of the chronic obstacles to approval was overcome by setting up three taxing districts so that taxes were paid at one rate in urban areas, at another in rural portions of the parish where fewer services were provided or needed, and a third, lowest, one in some industrial areas where no services were provided. Representation, another difficult knot to untie before consolidation can be consummated, was solved by adding two persons elected from the portions of the parish outside of Baton Rouge to the city council whenever that body sits as the parish council.[18]

Not only is city-county consolidation almost impossible politically, but it does not guarantee that the city-county will have sufficient powers to meet all metropolitan problems, and it causes even greater political difficulties if the metropolitan area expands beyond the county limits. Despite the successful development in the Baton Rouge area, this approach to metropolitan government is not likely to bear fruit in many areas of the nation.

City-County Separation. Core-city dwellers, watching the county snowplows at work in the unincorporated reaches of suburbia and remembering that the core city bears most of the cost of county government while securing few services from it, are likely to be intrigued with the idea of separating the city from the rest of the county. This plan is not far different from the preceding one, except that instead of integrating the offices and leaving the county boundaries as they are, separation would create a city-county of the core city and create a new county of the outlying areas.

San Francisco, Baltimore, St. Louis, Denver, and all cities of over 10,000 in Virginia are separate city-counties and have been for a long time. Except in Virginia, there have been no separations in nearly half a century. The plan encounters much the same problems as does city-

---

[18] See T. H. Reed, "Progress in Metropolitan Integration," *Public Administration Review*, vol. 9 (Winter, 1949), pp. 1–10. See also R. G. Kean, "Consolidation that Works," *National Municipal Review* (now *National Civic Review*), vol. 45 (November, 1956), pp. 478–485. *Parish* is the Louisiana term for *county*.

county consolidation and is no more practical politically. Outlying sections of the county desire to control the county government, as they would under separation, but they also wish to retain the benefits of county services paid for mostly by core-city taxpayers. Furthermore, this is not really an approach to metropolitan government at all, since it traps the city within its own walls (except in Virginia) and instead of treating metropolitan problems on an area-wide basis, it serves as something of a parochialism, with the core city retreating in a huff to its own enclosure.[19]

Metropolitan Federation. There are strong arguments, based upon efficiency, economy, and equity, that call for functions of government to be integrated throughout the metropolitan area. At the same time there is merit in keeping government as close to the people as possible and a psychological value in retaining the community spirit of the smaller suburb as against the impersonality of the core city. Because of the dilemma thus created, some specialists have suggested that a federal plan of government be applied to the metropolitan area with two tiers of government, one area-wide to perform functions fitting into that classification and another for the local community to handle functions of a more parochial interest. It is sometimes suggested, for example, that such things as sewage disposal, water supply, police protection, and planning should be area-wide, while perhaps garbage collection and local street maintenance would be appropriate for the lower-tier government. This plan has been used in London, England, and Toronto, Ontario. Perhaps half a dozen American communities have considered it, but all such attempts up to this writing have been defeated.[20]

The Municipality of Metropolitan Toronto. The only example of the federal plan of urban government on the North American continent was established by unilateral action of the Ontario Legislature in 1953. Without a referendum vote in the areas affected, but after extensive public hearings, the Legislature created a federal plan with a metropolitan government over the thirteen municipalities of the Toronto area. In addition, the area was disconnected from the county which had had control over it and county functions were assigned to the metropolitan government.

---

[19] In 1951, the functions and offices of the coterminous city and county of Philadelphia were joined. A partial integration had taken place as early as 1854. It is difficult to classify this as separation or consolidation, since no boundary changes took place, as happens in separation, and there was no hinterland to provide for, as is the case in consolidation.

[20] See Eric Hardy, "Progress in Toronto," *National Municipal Review,* vol. 47 (October, 1958), pp. 445 ff.; W. W. Crouch, "Metropolitan Government in Toronto," *Public Administration Review,* vol. 14 (Spring, 1954), pp. 85–95; Bollens, *op. cit.,* pp. 86–104; John G. Grumm, *Metropolitan Area Government: The Toronto Experience* (Governmental Research Center, University of Kansas, Lawrence, Kan., 1959); and on problems with representation plans under federation, A. W. Bromage, "Political Representation in Metropolitan Areas," *American Political Science Review,* vol. 52 (June, 1958), pp. 406–418.

The action established a supergovernment six times the area of Toronto proper. The metropolitan council of twenty-five consists of the twelve suburban mayors of the cities or reeves (supervisors) of the townships, plus twelve representatives from Toronto proper. The chairman is appointed by the provincial government. The Toronto members are the mayor, two of the four elective members of the board of control, and one of the two aldermen from each of the nine city wards.

Not only is this representation ex officio and indirect, but it is malapportioned. The city has twelve councilmen for 687,000 people, the suburbs twelve for 467,000. The city population is static, however, and the suburban rapidly expanding, so this gap may be rather quickly closed. Each suburb, regardless of size, has one vote. Two of them have nearly 100,000 population, while three have under 10,000.

The assignment of powers to the metropolitan and to the local units is somewhat arbitrary. The metropolis controls assessment, water supply and distribution, sewerage and sewage treatment, main highways, public transportation, administration of justice, some welfare functions, land-use planning, and supervision of local zoning. It also has concurrent powers with the local municipalities on public housing and redevelopment, and parks and recreation. Other powers are left to the units, including some that are often thought of as being metropolitan-wide in scope: fire protection, libraries, public health, building codes, and direct public relief. No provision is made in the enabling act for a later redistribution of functions.

The Municipality of Metropolitan Toronto represents a major step toward an integrated approach to metropolitan government. There are some apparent weaknesses in the model established at Toronto, however. The dual responsibility of the metropolitan council to the voters is bound to be confusing. All but two of the council members must be elected annually when the "chief goal of the federation is to undertake and implement long-range planning." [21] The two may prove conflicting. Furthermore, the representation is inequitable when measured by a population standard.

The Municipality, as it has been established, does not include quite all of the metropolitan area. There is some duplication of personnel and equipment because the metropolitan government and the municipalities have concurrent jurisdiction over most functions of government.

Whether American metropolitan areas will follow the lines established by the Ontario Legislature will probably depend upon the desire of American state legislatures to use direct and drastic action. They are not likely to do this so long as they are rural-dominated. Most legislatures today are hostile to large cities and tend to be sympathetic to the

[21] Hardy, *op. cit.*, p. 329.

views of the satellites. It would seem that the fringe dwellers, in their fear of the core city, are unlikely to assist in the reapportionment of legislatures. In Northern states, where the core city is usually dominated by the Democratic party and the state legislature by the Republican, conservative suburbanites are torn between favoring a legislature dominated by rural Republicans and supporting one dominated by urban Democrats. Being largely urban Republicans, they are confronted by a dilemma. Because suburbanites are likely to hold, in the future, the balance of power in the politics of many states, the horn of the dilemma which they ultimately choose may indirectly determine whether or not sweeping experiments in metropolitan government will be attempted.[22]

The County as a Metropolitan Unit. Since about two-thirds of the standard metropolitan areas are located in single counties, it is sometimes suggested that the already existing county governments might be used as a basis for forming supergovernments. There are, however, several handicaps to such a plan. In the first place, the county may be a poor profile of the metropolitan area. The core city may be tucked off in the corner of a county that is in large part basically rural, or the metropolitan area may extend over several counties. Second, in most states, there are many legal obstacles to the county acting as a municipality. Third, the traditional structure of county government, under either the supervisor or commissioner system, is unsatisfactory for urban government, especially because of the absence of a chief executive officer.

A very few urban counties have been given powers and governmental structures that enable them to act as supergovernments.[23] One example is Los Angeles County, which has a chief administrative officer and furnishes many urban services to unincorporated areas as well as, by contract, to incorporated municipalities. Westchester County in New York has, in effect, the strong-mayor plan of government with an elective chief executive. Several counties have the council-manager form. Dade County (Miami), Florida, has adopted it, although the "Miami plan" absorbed some of the features of the federated plan, with twenty-six municipalities retaining their identities and some powers.[24]

Because of the various factors militating against the use of the county as a senior unit of government, the trend has been toward functional consolidation. Either a single function at a time is turned over to the county, or *ad hoc* arrangements are made for a function to be operated

---

[22] This paragraph is suggested by remarks in G. S. Birkhead, "Metropolitan Areas Demand Attention," *National Municipal Review* (now *National Civic Review*), vol. 42 (July, 1953), p. 366.

[23] Jones has a list in "Local Government in Metropolitan Areas," pp. 597–601.

[24] Gustave Serino, *Miami's Metropolitan Experiment* (Public Administration Clearing Service, University of Florida, Gainesville, Fla., 1958).

jointly by the county and the core city. This trend in metropolitain areas is perhaps supported by the fact that many officials of large cities, unlike their counterparts in smaller communities, find acceptable such transfers of power.[25]

An increasing number of city-county hospitals are being established, especially in Texas. City-county health units, such as that of Pueblo and Pueblo County, Colorado, are becoming more common. Savannah and Chatham County, Georgia, have a joint traffic commission. Many core cities combine with the county to build a city-county building. Newton and Catawba County, North Carolina, have a joint fingerprinting and photography laboratory. Buffalo and Erie County, New York, have consolidated their library facilities. Charlotte and Mecklenburg County, North Carolina, have a city-county animal shelter, while Dallas and Dallas County, Texas, have a joint intoximeter and have conducted a joint tuberculosis survey. Planning, zoning, parks, welfare, and correction are among the other functions being turned over to counties or being jointly administered with counties.

Other than in Los Angeles and Dade Counties, there has been a slow piecemeal movement toward a greater use of the county.

Extraterritorial Jurisdiction. Under certain conditions, a city may own and control land outside of its own boundaries. It may do this either under its governmental powers if state law permits, or it may own land in the same manner as a private corporation, in which case its powers are limited to those of the ordinary property owner.

About thirty states authorize some municipal control over the subdivision of land outside of the city limits.[26] The areas of jurisdiction vary from 1 to 5 miles. This type of control sometimes enables the core city to require the building up of land within the city before further plots are offered for sale on the periphery. Usually, however, it helps to prevent the uncontrolled growth of suburban slums by requiring suitable standards for new subdivisions. Many heavily urban states, including Massachusetts, Michigan, Missouri, New Jersey, and New York, have no such control.

Extraterritorial powers are sometimes given a city for such functions as controlling roadhouses, securing a water supply, abatement of nuisances, providing for parks (this need is often forgotten until the city is built up and no land within the city limits is left), stone quarries, airports, hospitals for contagious cases, and many others. Many California cities have summer camps and recreational centers in the Sierra Nevada and elsewhere.

[25] Edward W. Weidner, *Intergovernmental Relations as Seen by Public Officials* (University of Minnesota Press, Minneapolis, Minn., 1960), pp. 110–113.

[26] R. W. Maddox. *Extraterritorial Powers of Municipalities in the United States* (The College Press, Corvallis, Oreg., 1955).

The suburbs often resent extraterritorial powers of the core city. Airports may be unpopular in one's neighborhood; yet they are necessary, and there is rarely space within the core city to build one. A careless suburb cannot expect to be left alone if it allows a health menace to exist along the boundary between itself and the core city. If the core city constructs a park in the suburbs, there will be resentment over the city folk coming in droves into the area each Sunday. Yet the suburbanites flood into the core city each workday. Somehow, the suburbanite is not likely to feel that the one counterbalances the other. Clearly, the dispute over extraterritorial powers is a reflection of uncoordinated independent municipalities in the metropolitan area.

Voluntary Cooperation.[27] The lack of an over-all government in the metropolitan area can be compensated for to a degree through the use of informal or contractual agreements between one or more cities in the area. Agreements may be made by one suburb with other suburbs, or by a suburb with the core city.

It is becoming increasingly common for such intergovernmental arrangements to be made for the disposal of sewage, garbage, and rubbish, to share police radio networks, or to have the core-city police radio supply the suburban departments. Formal agreements or informal understandings concerning emergency stand-by assistance in the case of unusual police or fire problems are also common. (See Figure 11-3.) A large number of core cities sell water to the suburbs on a contractual basis. Baltimore and Cleveland, for the most part, sell the water directly to the suburbanite, but most cities sell it to the suburb itself at a master meter. Many cities have understandings of an informal type concerning traffic-flow patterns, including such necessities as the establishment of one-way streets through two or more communities. Thousands of other cooperative arrangements have been worked out in various parts of the nation.

Voluntary agreements are edged with a coloration of the haphazard. They represent an unsystematic approach, but they ease some of the strains encountered in furnishing services to urbanites.

Metropolitan-area Studies. As of 1961, a vast literature had been accumulated concerning metropolitan areas and the difficulties of supplying urban services in those areas. Over 100 surveys had been conducted.[28] Yet, despite the reams of paper devoted to the subject, most of the proposed solutions had been based upon a priori reasoning rather than

[27] G. W. Rutherford, *Administrative Problems in a Metropolitan Area: The National Capital Region* (Public Administration Service, Chicago, 1952), stresses that cooperative approaches, rather than the integration discussed above, offer the best solution to metropolitan government.

[28] See two publications of the Public Administration Service, Chicago: *Metropolitan Communities: A Bibliography* (1957), and *Metropolitan Surveys: A Digest* (1958).

upon empirical data; virtually no studies had been made concerning the climate of opinion existing in metropolitan areas or of the limits of tolerance within which proposed approaches might be feasible; [29] hardly any work had been done concerning the levels of awareness which metropolitan residents had of their community and its problems; no rank order of values had been worked out; few studies had been made as to why integration proposals had failed. In truth, little was known about the politics of metropolitan-area organizational changes.[30]

The Failure of Integration. The value patterns of those who support plans for metropolitan supergovernments are not the dominant ones in the total community, and the leaders of integration movements characteristically do not give adequate consideration to other values. The result is that proposals for reorganization of metropolitan governments are rarely implemented.

Suburban officeholders and the entrenched bureaucracy of the area will almost always oppose metropolitan government and reformers seldom pay enough attention to their values and interests or show any imagination in compromising with them. They fail to recognize that *representativeness* of government and *access* to the decision makers are likely to be more important considerations for the typical citizen than are questions of efficiency and economy. Rarely does a metropolitan-area study even mention these two psychologically important factors, to say nothing of adequately providing for them.

The reformers tend to forget that the symbols—efficiency, a bigger and better Zilchville, and the like—that they respond to with enthusiasm ring no bells for the *hoi polloi*. It is the latter, of course, which dominates the decision when a proposal is put to a popular referendum. The ordinary citizen is characteristically apathetic. If water flows from the tap and the toilet flushes today, he is not likely to ask if it will do so tomorrow. Communicating a concept of future needs on a realistic basis is seldom done by groups organized to support metropolitan governmental reorganization. Furthermore, reformers tend to put their arguments on a theoretical plane, discussing efficiency ("We have sixteen different fire departments in the metropolitan area!") without translating it into concrete terms as it affects the ordinary citizen. Examples are often not made meaningful. It makes little impression on the suburbanite to be told that his police force is amateurish and inferior if, in practice, his community has little crime and the state police take care of the arterial highway traffic.

Concluding Statement. It seems fairly evident that each device so far tried for the government of metropolitan areas either is basically un-

[29] One exception is John C. Bollens and others, *Metropolitan Challenge* (Metropolitan Community Studies, Inc., Dayton, Ohio, 1959). See pt. III.

[30] See Wood, *op. cit.*, chap. 5, and S. B. Sweeney (ed.), *Metropolitan Analysis* (University of Pennsylvania Press, Philadelphia, 1958).

MUTUAL AID CONTRACTS FOR FIRE PROTECTION,
MONTGOMERY COUNTY LOCAL GOVERNMENTS, 1958

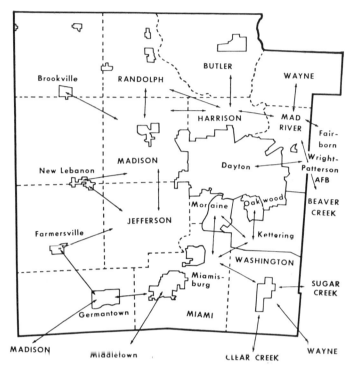

Figure 11-3. Americans are seeking to meet the problems of multiunit urban areas with their traditional empiricism. Here is one of dozens of examples of functional cooperation in the Dayton, Ohio, area. SOURCE: John C. Bollens and others, *Metropolitan Challenge* (Metropolitan Community Studies, Inc., Dayton, Ohio, 1959), fig. 20.

acceptable politically to groups powerful enough to block adoption or has proved to be inadequate as a solution. Any proposal that does not meet the requirement of responsibility and responsiveness to the general public must be dismissed—as it will be by the electorate—as lacking accord with our basic concepts of democratic theory.

Referring back to the Aristotelian mode of analysis, Norton Long has noted that "the search for metropolitan government is the search for a potential metropolitan governing class, the institutions through which it can function and a set of ideal goals which it can embody and which will render its leadership legitimate in the eyes of the people." [31] Here

[31] Norton E. Long, "Recent Theories and Problems of Local Government," in Carl J. Friedrich and Seymour E. Harris (eds.), *Public Policy* (Graduate School of Public Administration, Harvard University, Cambridge, Mass., 1958), pp. 285–295. Quote is from p. 295.

we find the reasons for slow progress in metropolitan-area government. The institutions for such government have not evolved because there is no consensus on goals and no acceptable governing group. The proposals put forth by self-appointed community leaders diverge so widely from the wants of a great portion of the citizenry that these volunteers for a leadership class are not accepted as legitimate spokesmen. Their offerings are rejected when the voters are polled and no trend toward consensus on the three Aristotelian components can now be discerned.

Chapter 12

INTERGOVERNMENTAL RELATIONS

The city in the metropolitan area must learn to live with its incorporated and unincorporated neighbors, and all municipalities must cooperate regularly with special districts, school districts, and the county. In addition, they must make satisfactory adjustments with both state and national governments.

The state government, as a parent, occupies a special relationship to the city. It has sought to oversee many of the activities of cities through its administrative agencies. The national government, which has no control over cities as such, has nonetheless forged many connecting links between its own administrative structure and that of the cities. Especially since 1933 has the number of national government–city administrative contacts become numerous.

STATE ADMINISTRATIVE RELATIONS WITH CITIES

State Administrative Oversight of Cities.[1] The administrative branch of state government follows the typical frontier pattern of decentralization. Because of the influence of this philosophy, departments of local government, such as the Ministry of the Interior in France or the Ministry of Local Government in Great Britain, are not to be found in the United States. Administrative contacts between the city and the state are characteristically on a *functional* basis. That is, members of the state department of education oversee the activities of the local school dis-

---

[1] On this subject, the standard references are S. C. Wallace, *State Administrative Supervision over Cities in the United States* (Columbia University Press, New York, 1928), and *Report of the Committee on State-Local Relations* (Council of State Governments, Chicago, 1946). There are numerous articles in the professional journals and many studies of specific functions. See the series of monographs on *Research in Intergovernmental Relations* (University of Minnesota Press, Minneapolis, Minn.), under the general editorship of William Anderson and Edward W. Weidner, 1950–1960; Dale Pontius, *State Supervision of Local Government: Its Development in Massachusetts* (Public Affairs Press, Washington, 1942); for a general bibliography, see W. Brooke Graves, *Intergovernmental Relations in the United States* (Legislative Reference Service, Library of Congress, 1956).

trict, the state department of health watches the activities of the local department of health, and so on. Canadian provinces, on the other hand, follow British and continental practices of consolidation for the most part, and perhaps six American states have made some move toward centralized supervision.[2]

Areas of Supervision. What local government functions are subject to state oversight today? Most of them, might be a brief answer. In particular, the state is especially watchful of municipal activities that involve (1) the expenditure of state grants-in-aid (e.g., in education, the building of expressways within cities); (2) those areas of national grants-in-aid which are administered through the states, but under conditions requiring state supervision of the expenditures (e.g., the building of airports in some states); and (3) those activities in which the state as a whole has a particular interest (e.g., the spread of communicable diseases, law enforcement, finances). The principal areas of control are those of education, finance, health, highways, and welfare, but to these must be added airports, fire prevention, libraries, housing, personnel, planning, police administration, and even control of municipally owned public utilities, among others.[3]

Techniques of Supervision. From all that has been said in this book and elsewhere about the tendency for the state to step in and take over much of the independence of local government, it might be assumed that the above-mentioned activities are controlled by heavy-handed bureaucrats from the state capital, armed with court decrees and administrative orders. While these devices do play a part, it has been the practice of most of the state agencies to try persuasion, education, and other noncoercive techniques wherever possible. The big stick is brought into play principally whenever the state overseers find evidence of incompetence, irresponsibility, or corruption.

State agencies exercising supervision usually start by requiring *reports* from local communities. This serves the purpose of warning the state when and where trouble spots begin to appear, and it tends to channel local activity, since the reporting official, knowing that he will be judged by his professional peers, will want to "look good." The state agency can furnish *advice and information*. This is especially important for the smaller communities, where amateurs may be floundering about seeking to do an adequate job with little experience, or where overworked professionals may not have time to keep up with the latest techniques in their fields. The relationship between the state and the large-city technical specialist may sometimes become strained when the city functionary thinks he is (or in fact is) professionally more competent than is his

---

[2] See below, pp. 297–298.

[3] Control over some of these functions will be discussed further in chaps. 17–21.

nominal supervisor on the state level. Is the manager of a large-city airport able to get along without advice from the state airports commissioner? He is likely to think so. It is by no means unheard of for a running feud of many years' duration to color the relationships between a department of a large city and the corresponding agency of the state. Usually, however, relations are friendly and cooperative. The smaller cities and villages have technicians who are likely to recognize the genuine need for advice and to seek it. To simplify requests for such help, Tennessee has established a clearinghouse for information—the Municipal Technical Advisory Service—in connection with the state university, and some other states have municipal research bureaus which may or may not be connected with a state school.

One step beyond advice is *technical aid*. The state agencies, with (perhaps) a relatively larger budget and with more specialized equipment and personnel, are particularly in a position to help out the local amateur or semiprofessional. How effective can the chief of police in a village of 1,500 people be against the professional criminal? And how much experience or scientific equipment can be put to use if the rare event of a murder should take place in his town? What would his colleague, the water commissioner, know about the technical problems of drilling a new deep well for the town? And how much does the overworked local general practitioner really know about public health, even though he may bear the title of health officer? How much special equipment can the town afford when it is needed? The state agencies in these and in dozens of other circumstances and activities stand ready to offer technical information, advice, and equipment.

Other approaches failing, the state may also make use of its *coercive power*. Among other things, its agencies can *grant or withhold permits* for certain things (e.g., to dump raw sewage into a stream under prescribed conditions); or *issue orders* (e.g., to build a sewage-treatment plant); or *issue rules and regulations* which are technically called ordinances (e.g., to prescribe the technical standards for water-supply purification); or *withhold grants-in-aid* if standards prescribed by state, or sometimes Federal, law are not complied with; or *review decisions* of local agencies (e.g., the power of the state tax-equalization board to review the determination of local boards and perhaps to order reassessment in extreme situations); or require *prior permission* from a state agency (e.g., the power of some state health departments to pass on the qualifications of local health-officer nominees); or *appoint certain local officials or remove them* (e.g., the local police chief). It is even possible in most states, as a last resort, to apply *substitute administration*. That is to say, in extreme cases the state may suspend local self-government altogether for some or all functions and allow state officials to govern instead. This is particularly true in the fields of finance, public health, and education.[4]

Organization for Supervision. The increasing tendency in recent years to turn over state supervision to the administrative rather than to the legislative branch of government has probably changed the pattern of state-local relationships to a considerable degree. Local professional technicians feel more at ease and have less of a feeling that they will be exploited when they deal with state professionals rather than with the politicians of the state legislature. A smoother, more confident relationship is the result. The community is likely to gain, too, for the *motivation* of the professional administrator is different from that of the politician and this is likely to have an important effect upon the eventual solution of local problems. The professional administrator has a pride and reputation at stake in everything he does, and his success is measured in terms of acceptance of his work by his professional peers, not only within the state, but also within the professional organizations to which he belongs. The politician has his job at stake in everything that he does, and his success is measured in terms of the number of votes he can get in comparison with those of his opponents. The administrator is hence interested in doing the best possible job in accord with the latest professional standards and techniques. The politician will meet the same problem with one thought in mind: What approach will produce the most votes? If he wishes to stay in office he has little choice but to appeal to the popular mind. The administrator's approach will likely result in an effective solution, while the politician's will only accidentally produce the same result.

The Balance between State and Local Government. The changing levels of services and evolving administrative patterns of government make it desirable to inquire into the question of what has been happening to the relative balance between the states and their subdivisions. The picture is quite clear: the states have expanded their role in society at a greater rate than have local governments. Local governments have come to depend more and more upon the states for financial assistance, and the states have generally seemed to prefer to give this assistance through grants-in-aid or shared taxes rather than through expanding the tax base of local government. Furthermore, certain functions that were once principally the responsibility of some local unit of government have been or are being transferred to the states. Thus, the states are financing (with the Federal government) most of the cost of public welfare, once exclusively a local function. Furthermore, increasing highway mileage is being turned over to the states from counties and cities,

[4] This section borrows from Pontius, *op. cit.*, and *Report of the Committee on State-Local Relations*, pt. 2.

and the states are rapidly expanding their contributions to primary and secondary education, once financed entirely out of local property taxes paid to the local school district.

State expenditures totaled only 12 per cent of all state-local expenditures in 1902, but by 1956 they equaled just over 50 per cent; state revenues in 1902 represented 17 per cent of total state-local revenues, but this figure had climbed to over 53 per cent in 1956.[5]

All of these figures indicate an increasing financial superiority on the part of states in relation to their local subdivisions. They indicate that we can expect an increasing amount of lobbying by local government officials before state legislatures and that the state government will become more and more the political battleground for the resolution of many financial problems relative to local services. Whether the increasing trend toward state financing of services will also be reflected in increasing state domination over policy making in these areas is a matter for speculation and for research which has, up to now, not been attempted. To date, state aid has been chiefly in the nature of shared revenues with no strings attached.

Functional Relationships or a Single State Agency? Because city-state relations have experienced a gradual unplanned growth on a piece-meal, function-by-function basis and because there have been few systematic overhauls of municipal government in this country of the type that have taken place in England, city-state relations are for the most part uncoordinated and subject to duplications and omissions. New Jersey, with a Division of Local Government in the state Department of Finance and Taxation, has gone the furthest toward an integrated bureau to direct state contacts with local governments.

The New Jersey division has the duty of investigating on a continuous basis the needs of local government and hence has information available for the legislature that does not exist in most states. The principal action of the division has been in the fiscal area. It has power to regulate local methods of budgeting and financial procedure. It makes certain that localities provide enough funds to service their debts and can even require local levies to reduce deficits. It supervises regular audits of the cities. Annual fiscal reports must be made by the cities on state-prepared forms. The Local Government Board, which sets policies for the division, may even take over control of a municipality if it falls into an "unsound financial condition," as defined by law.

While the board has been active primarily in the field of finance, it has become a general overseer of local government to a degree. It has

[5] U.S. Bureau of the Census, *Historical Statistics on State and Local Government Finances* (1955), table 3; U.S. Bureau of the Census, *Summary of Governmental Finances in 1956*, table 1.

made some investigations into conservation, public health, education, housing, planning, and metropolitan consolidation.[6]

Indiana has centralized fiscal control under the state Board of Tax Commissioners, but this agency does not act as a local government office otherwise. It has the power to review local budgets and reduce appropriations, tax levies, and bond issues. It may prohibit the issuance of bonds. The commission has a wide range of discretion under the law.[7]

Alaska has a Department of Local Affairs. Without resorting to the use of an integrated agency for the supervision of local government, other states control some aspects of local finance. A Local Government Commission in North Carolina has wide powers in controlling local bond issues, and Iowa and New Mexico exercise more direct fiscal supervision than does the typical state.

Some states prescribe uniform systems of accounts for municipalities. Most states have some degree of state jurisdiction over auditing of municipal accounts. About twenty-two states require municipalities to submit financial reports to the state periodically. Many states provide budget forms for municipalities, and the state form is compulsory in thirteen states. Nearly one-half of the states supervise municipal debt to one degree or another, often passing upon the legality of an issue before it is sold. A few states actually inquire into the necessity and wisdom of municipal bond issues. North Carolina and sometimes Virginia handle the sale of bonds to private investors on behalf of municipalities.[8] In most cases, however, these state activities are carried on in the time-honored decentralized manner.

A Comment on State Supervision. There are two basic issues concerning the relationship of the state to local administration. One is that of the use of a single state agency over local affairs versus the use of functional relationships;[9] the other centers in the question of the desirable degree of state coercive supervision over cities, whatever the method of organization. It is not likely that an integrated department of municipal affairs is desirable in American states. Plans such as those in New Jersey, North Carolina, and Indiana appear to be reasonably

[6] *Report of the Committee on State-Local Relations*, pp. 37–38, 48–50.

[7] State-local fiscal relations are covered in Wylie Kilpatrick, *State Supervision of Local Budgeting* (National Municipal League, New York, 1939); also his *State Supervision of Local Finance* (Public Administration Service, Chicago, 1941); T. E. McMillan, Jr., *State Supervision of Municipal Finance* (Institute of Public Affairs, University of Texas, Austin, Tex., 1953); and W. M. Griffin, *State Supervision of Local Assessments* (Bureau of Governmental Research and Service, Florida State University, Tallahassee, Fla., 1957).

[8] McMillan, *op. cit.*, provides details and has several charts showing the practice in various states.

[9] See *Report of the Committee on State-Local Relations;* and Joseph E. McLean, "Threat to Responsible Rule," *National Municipal Review*, vol. 40 (September, 1951), pp. 411–417.

successful, but they do not fit into the general trend. The over-all supervision of local government by a single central department, as in France, results in a high degree of central control, not only over techniques, but over programs and policies. One of the strengths of municipal government in this country lies in the initiative and autonomy exercised by local officials, in contrast with the French municipal officer, who must get approval of even small decisions from the prefect who represents the Minister of the Interior. Over-all supervision leads to uniformity, which in turn destroys the opportunity for experimentation. It is likely that in most states, improved administrative methods have more often originated in the city hall than in the state capitol. It is also important to note that state services to municipalities often tend to be mediocre in quality and that state departments sometimes have no real interest in rendering services to local government.

In general, technical assistance and advice rather than supervision and control are the ideal sought for in this country by both state and local officials. Although state supervision and control is sometimes used, the extent of state dictation to local officials has been relatively slight, and state officials have applied these sanctions only very reluctantly. In most cases, political expediency dictates this practice even when it is not called for by good administrative procedure, as it usually is. Local officials are powerful and well organized for political action and lobbying. The state agency that seeks to apply pressure thoughtlessly may find its appropriation reduced for enforcement purposes for the next year. The advancement of standards and techniques is being achieved, in any case, more through voluntary associations of local officials and professional technicians in the same field than through central tutelage of local officers.

NATIONAL ADMINISTRATIVE RELATIONS WITH CITIES

National Government Advice and Assistance to Cities.[10] There are more than 100 Federal government agencies that supply more than 500

[10] See P. V. Betters, J. K. Williams, and S. L. Reeder, *Recent Federal-City Relations* (United States Conference of Mayors, Washington, 1936); Committee on Intergovernmental Fiscal Relations, *Federal, State and Local Government Fiscal Relations* (Council of State Governments, Chicago, 1943); *Federal-City Relations* (National Institute of Municipal Law Officers, Washington, 1953); D. W. Hanks, "Neglected Cities Turn to U.S.," *National Municipal Review*, vol. 35 (April, 1946), pp. 172–176; J. K. Williams, "Federal Aid Due to Continue," *ibid.*, vol. 37 (February, 1948), pp. 86–90; J. P. Harris, "The Future of Federal Grants-in-aid," *The Annals of the American Academy of Political and Social Science*, vol. 207 (January, 1940), pp. 14–26. Detailed descriptions of Federal-city relations are given in the Anderson and Weidner series previously cited; and in United States Commission on Intergovernmental Relations, *A Report to the President* (1955).

services to cities in the United States. They range all the way from the well-known cooperation given to local police officers by the FBI to thousands of technical pamphlets on every subject from adequate specifications for firemen's gas masks to techniques for estimating land values.[11]

The U.S. Civil Service Commission furnishes local personnel agencies with information on examination techniques and will furnish testing materials. The Bureau of Standards makes a great deal of technical information available to cities concerning commodity specifications, a valuable service, since not many cities can operate adequate testing bureaus. The bureau will make performance tests on all kinds of material and equipment at cost. It also provides cities with model building, fire, plumbing, elevator, and other codes.

The Bureau of Mines gives technical advice on air-pollution problems. The Civil Aeronautics Administration tells city officials about the uses to which they might put airplanes, or furnishes them with a model airport-zoning ordinance, and may even give them a surplus Federal airport. The General Services Administration sells surplus Federal buildings to cities at "50 per cent off."

The U.S. Public Health Service furnishes a host of things: advice on sanitation problems; technical assistance, grants for planning and loans for constructing, sewage-treatment plants to overcome water pollution; advice on organizing and staffing a municipal health department; and cash grants through the state for research on heart disease.

FBI agents not only arrest local law violators who have left the state, but they testify without charge as experts in handwriting, tire treads, hairs and fibers, and shoe prints. The local police can find out from them without charge the marks made by a certain German typewriter, 1926 model, or the kind of headlight glass used in a 1930 Essex. The FBI academy trains city police officers to serve as instructors in local police academies, while the Bureau of Narcotics instructs uniformed policemen in drug identification and enforcement methods at the bureau's training school.

Many other Federal agencies cooperate with local officials from time to time, giving advice or assistance upon request. Local administrators can go to the Housing and Home Finance Agency for advice on problems of race relations in unsegregated public housing; to the Bureau of Prisons for methods of designing, building, and operating a jail; to the Bureau of Public Roads for help in making a parking survey; to the Bureau of Ships for help in learning how to fight a harbor fire; to the Fish and Wildlife Service for surplus bison and elk for the local zoo; and to the

---

[11] See R. H. Blundred and D. W. Hanks, *Federal Services to Cities and Towns* (American Municipal Association, Chicago, 1950), from which the following illustrations are drawn. Some of them may have since been discontinued.

Curator of the Navy for a list showing the shipping weights and handling charges on obsolete warships for the city park. But these are only a few of the total number of services available.

Federal Approval of Municipal Activities. The city, in its proprietary capacity, often acts as an ordinary corporation; and when it does so, it must get Federal approval wherever such approval would be necessary in the case of a private corporation. When Federal grants-in-aid are involved, the city must often get approval from the appropriate Federal agency for governmental functions, too. As examples, if a city operates a radio station, it must get a Federal Communications Commission license; if it builds an expressway with the aid of Federal funds, it must have the proposed route approved by the Federal Bureau of Public Roads; if it builds a bridge, it must have the plans approved by the Corps of Engineers. Municipal administrators thus have frequent and varied contacts with Federal agencies.

Federal Grants-in-aid to Cities.[12] Beginning in the early 1930s, the national government began a policy of extending aid through loans and subsidies to municipalities, either directly or through redistribution of grants made to the states. The beginning of Federal-city direct relations came with the Emergency Relief and Construction Act of 1932 in the closing days of the Hoover Administration. The act permitted the newly created Reconstruction Finance Corporation (a Federal agency) to make loans to municipalities in order to finance self-liquidating projects. The act was notable in that it established not only the first Federal-city fiscal relationship, but also provided the beginnings of *conditional* grants to municipalities by establishing certain standards of labor that must prevail in any project receiving a grant. The act was not a success, for it in effect required interest rates higher than the cities would accept and the conditions of repayment were overly stringent. But it was a beginning.

The New Deal provided for a host of Federal-city financial arrangements. It began by tiding over the nearly bankrupt cities and states by making grants to the states to care for the unemployed under the Federal Emergency Relief Act of 1933. The Federal government later began to deal directly with the cities through projects financed by the Civil Works Administration and the Works Progress Administration, and sponsored and supervised by municipal and other local governments. It also made grants and loans to municipalities and school districts to construct athletic fields, water standpipes, hospitals, sewerage systems, and other permanent improvements through the Public Works Administration.

The Federal government began to offer grants-in-aid for highways in 1916, but streets within municipal boundaries were specifically excluded

[12] For an introduction to grants-in-aid, see Charles R. Adrian, *State and Local Governments* (McGraw-Hill Book Company, Inc., 1960), chap. 5 and citations there.

from the program. In the early days of the automobile, the problem was to build hard-surfaced highways between cities. Once these were built, the new problem of bringing the streams of traffic from the city limits into the downtown area arose. Funds became available for municipalities beginning in 1932, and the Federal Aid Highway Act of 1944 specifically provided that one-fourth of the aid funds were to be used for the extension of U.S. highways within cities.[13] All of this money, however, is channeled through the state highway departments.

Legislation during the Great Depression and also under the War Mobilization and Reconversion Act of 1944 permitted cities to receive Federal aid for planning public works, such as city halls, and water and sewerage systems. In the field of low-rent housing, the United States Housing Act of 1937 authorized the making of contracts with municipal, county, or state housing authorities to supply most of the money on long-term credit for building housing projects. The act also authorized Federal contributions to these authorities as a subsidy to keep rents low. Where these authorities are county or municipal organizations, the Federal Public Housing Authority deals directly with the local government unless state law prohibits it.

President Roosevelt's recommendation for a postwar Federal aid program to cities for several activities was lost in the conservative trend in politics after 1945. Most of the existing aids were continued, however, and in support of the popular belief that the airplane and helicopter would replace the automobile in the best of all possible postwar worlds, the Federal Airport Act of 1946 provided for Federal grants to cities (directly if state law allows) to buy sites and build airports.

The Small Business Administration, established in 1953 to replace the RFC, was authorized, among other things, to continue the RFC practice of making loans to municipalities in the event of emergencies and disaster. The Federal government also provided, in the postwar era, matching funds for hospital construction by states and municipalities. Some housing subsidies were continued. Aid for the control of communicable and venereal diseases was made available to cities via the states. Federal aid was offered for civil defense. Special aid was also provided for communities which may suddenly be overwhelmed by the influx of new people into a defense area. Another law provided that some Federal surplus properties could be made available to states for distribution to municipalities in the event of major disasters, such as floods or tornadoes.

The list of Federal supervisory controls is almost endless. However, it would be an error to reach the easy conclusion that the Federal government makes all of the rules in modern American society. The areas of

[13] R. A. Gomez, *Intergovernmental Relations in Highways* (University of Minnesota Press, Minneapolis, Minn., 1950), chaps. 1, 4, and 9; Adrian, *op. cit.*, chap. 21.

Federal control are relatively few and it is not politically expedient for Congress or Federal administrators to seek to impose many effective policy controls upon the states or their subdivisions. In fact, many—perhaps most—administrators do not even want to be in possession of coercive powers of this kind.[14] But where they exist, Federal controls are often absolutely necessary. State and local radio stations, for example, could not operate effectively without being coordinated with commercial stations. Other rules are not viewed with alarm by state and local administrators because their sense of professional standards agrees with the sense of professional standards of the Federal employees with whom they deal. They therefore see themselves as being involved in a cooperative venture to apply professional standards and do not feel coerced. This was the finding, for example, of the Michigan "Little Hoover" Commission study in 1950. Furthermore, despite the impression often created, Federal administrators usually try to be reasonable in administering the law and seek to work out problems jointly rather than by fiat. Still, in the event of an unresolved difference between a Federal agency and the state or local government with which it is dealing, the Federal requirements must be met if the state or local government wishes to qualify for Federal aid.

Federal-City Relations and Postwar Problems. The trend, established in the thirties, toward closer and more direct Federal-city relations and increased financial aid to cities seems destined to continue and eventually to expand. This is so for several reasons: (1) Federal agencies have a great potential for assisting cities because they have both specialized personnel and equipment which the cities need but cannot afford and often cannot get from the state; (2) rural-dominated legislatures have often closed their eyes to the financial problems of the cities and wished them away, while the national government has met the call, at least to a degree—and if the national government has helped a few times when the states have failed, it is likely to be asked for help again; (3) the present level of taxes and the nature of the tax structure leave both the municipalities and the states in a position which will put them in financial distress in the event of even a moderate depression, and it is therefore likely that, in "bad times," cities will ask for increased Federal government assistance.

The principal postwar issues are two: (1) Is it proper or desirable for the national government to deal directly with the cities, bypassing the parent state government? (2) What can or should the national government do to improve the financial condition of cities? Concerning the former, what damage is done by direct dealing? Does the state perform

[14] Edward W. Weidner, *Intergovernmental Relations as Seen by Public Officials* (University of Minnesota Press, Minneapolis, Minn., 1960), chap. 4.

a function other than to provide another desk with an "in" and "out" box? Does direct relationship encourage greater Federal control of cities? Might Washington one day seize the state's children and adopt them forcibly? If the cities refuse Federal aid, or the states refuse to let them have Federal aid (as has happened in some cases involving urban planning, housing, and airports aid), how long must the cities wait before the states provide what their leaders consider to be adequate substitute legislation?

Concerning the financial needs of cities and Federal government power, there are several questions. Since Federal instrumentalities are not taxable by the states, are present Federal payments in lieu of taxes to cities equitable? Is the Federal subsidy to cities in the form of tax exemption for income from municipal bonds a rational basis for aid? If not, what should be substituted? What tax areas should the national government stay out of and leave to the cities? What kind of grants-in-aid and of what size should the national government provide for cities beyond those already provided for? How much of the fiddler's bill is the national government willing to pay while still allowing the city governments to call the tune? Shortly after President Eisenhower took office he named a Commission on Intergovernmental Relations to make a study of national-state-local interrelationships. It discussed these questions.[15] But Congress and the state legislatures will have to make policy. As a step toward an institutionalized approach to cooperation, Congress in 1959 established an Advisory Commission on Intergovernmental Relations.[16]

A Closing Note. Increasingly it is true that the major functions of government can be performed only through the joint activity and cooperation of national, state, and local governments. It is not a question of which level is to carry on these functions, but rather how all three may effectively aid and participate. This is true in education, highways, health, welfare, housing, airports, law enforcement, and perhaps other functions. The pattern of the future will inevitably see more, rather than less, cooperation among the three levels of government in the United States.

[15] Commission on Intergovernmental Relations, *op. cit.*

[16] For a summary of Federal-local relationships and a discussion of the important issues involved, see Robert H. Connery and Richard H. Leach, *The Federal Government and Metropolitan Areas* (Harvard University Press, Cambridge, Mass., 1960); and Daniel R. Grant, "Federal-Municipal Relationships and Metropolitan Integration," *Public Administration Review,* vol. 14 (Autumn, 1954), pp. 259–267.

Chapter 13

ADMINISTRATION

Administration is a part of the political process. The term generally applies to that process of government that is involved in the application of general policies to specific cases. One specialist in the field, after much effort, has produced the following summary of what administration is: [1]

Administration is cooperative human action with a high degree of rationality. . . .

The distinguishing characteristics of an administrative system, seen in the customary perspective of administrative students, are best subsumed under two concepts, organization and management, thought of as analogous to anatomy and physiology in a biological system. *Organization* is the structure of authoritative and habitual personal interrelations in an administrative system. *Management* is action intended to achieve rational cooperation in an administrative system.

DEVELOPMENTS IN ADMINISTRATION

The Growth of Administration. To have an understanding of the great size and influence of modern public management, it is necessary to compare the functions of local government today with those of, say, two generations ago. Local units spent 1,960 million dollars in 1913, most of it for schools. In 1957, they spent 30,710 million dollars. Even allowing for the declining value of the dollar, expenditures increased nearly sixfold in two generations.

In 1913, local governments provided much of the education of the day through the one-room school, offering minimal programs taught by poorly trained and largely inexperienced teachers who received low pay. Roads, another major expenditure program today, were largely cared for by the local unit two generations ago. They were often unsurfaced and required little care in that preautomobile age. Most states had little to

[1] Dwight Waldo, *The Study of Public Administration* (Random House, Inc., New York, 1955), pp. 11–12. By permission of the publisher, Random House, Inc., New York. Copyright 1955.

do with highways before the beginnings of the good-roads movement and the adoption of the first Federal-aid Highway Act. The mentally ill received no rehabilitative treatment in those days. They were given custodial care in ramshackle asylums run by untrained persons who received patronage appointments from the city, county, or state. Some patients were housed in the local jail. Welfare was a local function provided reluctantly and at the bare subsistence level; the states kept out of the field except for some institutional care. In general, state government was distant and had few direct contacts with the ordinary citizen. Local government was more active and spent more—about 6.6 times as much as state government—but it was a thin shadow of its present-day self as a supplier of services to the citizen. The growth in the activities of state governments has been the more spectacular, but both the state and local governments have become vitally important social institutions affecting the lives of each citizen each day. There were more than 4.2 million local employees in 1957. These people perform functions vastly more complicated and technical than those handled by the public bureaucracy of their grandparents' day.

The Historical Trend. Some of the developments in administrative organization have been noted earlier in this book.[2] We have seen that the legislatures at first dominated government at both the state and local levels. As legislative bodies and city councils declined in prestige and importance during the nineteenth century, they were replaced both by the direct democracy of the initiative and referendum and by a large number of elective administrative officials. Both of these trends contributed to the development of the long ballot.

As the number of governmental functions increased, the number of governmental agencies increased, too. Each new function tended to be established as a separate agency, usually in order to give it protection against the competing fiscal demands of the older, better-established functions. The interest groups which secured the adoption of new programs and policies generally preferred this arrangement. The more populous cities were once highly departmentalized, though reorganizations resulting from the adoption of the strong-mayor, council-manager, or commission forms have generally decreased the number of separate municipal agencies.[3] The rising number of agencies resulted after a while in a problem of accountability. It became highly difficult for the chief

[2] See chaps. 3 and 8. A fine summary of the subject, past and present, may be found in York Willbern, "Administration in State Governments," *The American Assembly, The Forty-eight States: Their Tasks as Policy Makers and Administrators* (Graduate School of Business, Columbia University, New York, 1955), chap. 5, from which this account borrows.

[3] See chap. 8.

executive, the councilman, or the citizen to know what was being done in the agencies or who was responsible for their activities.

Administrative Developments. The municipal-reorganization movement began in the 1890s and, to a degree, even earlier. It was concerned with both the eradication of corruption and the stopping of administrative sprawl. Administrative reorganization of states, counties, and other nonschool local units followed along at a much slower pace.

The Assumptions of the Reform Movement. Nearly all the reform efforts at the state and local levels have concentrated upon making administrative changes that have been based upon the following assumptions: [4]

1. Authority and responsibility should be concentrated in the chief executive officer by placing the heads of agencies under his authority and subject to his appointment, removal, and control. This was perhaps the most basic assumption and proved to be the most difficult to achieve. Pressure groups wishing to dominate the governmental administration of their interests have feared, probably with justification, that executive unity would increase the executive's power at the expense of their own. In cities, the dominant groups were more unified than at the county or state levels, and they wanted what they considered businesslike efficiency. As a result, strong mayors and city managers generally were given wide (but rarely complete) administrative powers, but governors were not; and counties remained without a chief executive of any kind.

2. Related functions should be integrated into single departments and the number of departments should be few enough to permit the executive to require direct accountability from the department head. Reformers complained that there were often many agencies performing functions in the same general field with little coordination, effective planning, or responsibility.

3. Boards and commissions might properly be used for advisory, but not for administrative, purposes. Boards sometimes serve as quasi-legislative or quasi-judicial bodies; that is, they act much as legislative or judicial bodies. This type of activity arose, for example, in the case of public service commissions which had to establish rates for public utilities, and were considered acceptable. In weak-mayor cities, these boards were and still are common devices for administration.

4. Budget control should be centralized under the direction of the chief executive with auditing under the legislative body. Some characteristics of the executive budget are discussed in Chapter 16. This ad-

[4] A. E. Buck, *The Reorganization of State Governments in the United States* (Columbia University Press, New York, 1938), gives a complete statement of the orthodox view.

ministrative device has had widespread acceptance in principle and has had perhaps the greatest effect of any single development upon executive control over agencies. Budget staffs, in the larger cities at least, have become the general-management arm of the chief executive, not only reviewing the budget estimates of the agencies, but also aiding in co-ordinating their activities. Budget offices have become important agencies for administrative supervision, though they generally have only a limited amount of control over expenditures by the departments. They apportion funds over the fiscal year and exercise certain minor controls, but they are not usually in a legal or political position to claim sweeping jurisdiction over detailed expenditures. The check-and-balance tradition has been maintained through the establishment of an independent audit—independent, that is, of the executive branch.

5. The staff services of administration should be coordinated, usually through central agencies, to serve all of the operating departments. This "principle" has received more acceptance than the others. The reason is to be found in the fact that the centralizing of housekeeping functions has been thought to be a means of saving money without the loss of policy control by the interest groups watching over the individual agency. As a result there has been a strong trend toward the central purchasing of materials and supplies (large-volume buying brings lower prices); the operation of central warehouses, records archives, motor pools, and mailing and telephone services; and the central maintenance of buildings and grounds. Personnel recruitment has also been centralized to a considerable degree.

6. An executive cabinet should be established as a device for the coordination of governmental agencies. Cabinet members should be appointed by the chief executive, rather than elected, so that he might hold them responsible for their acts.

Forces for Separatism. There are many forces at work that have discouraged reorganization. Some of these include the following:

1. Agencies prefer a maximum of autonomy. A department head feels that he will lose status if his agency becomes merely one of many bureaus in a larger department. He is likely to argue, often from conviction, that his agency is unique both as to function and as to the process by which it performs its service. He may claim, with interest-group representatives shouting "Amen" in the background, that the integration of his agency with another will result in a lower level of service to its clientele groups.

2. There is a strong tradition of separate responsibility to the electorate for many functions of government. Generally the public prefers to elect an officer who has traditionally been elected, even when the functions of the officer are obscure. The public believes that direct election

is more democratic than appointment by the chief executive. Political leaders like to have several elective offices on the ballot, since this enables them to develop a slate with widespread racial-ethnic or geographic appeal.

3. The clean-up campaigns that follow scandals often result in recommendations that encourage separatism. The usual suggestion is that the tainted function should be separated from the rest of government, given autonomous status, and "taken out of politics."

4. Clientele and interest groups normally prefer to have the function of their special concern separated from the rest of government. This preference also encourages the use of separate or "dedicated" funds. Pilots prefer a separate airport commission to a vast parks and recreation agency or public works agency involved in a dozen different activities. Their interest groups can more easily dominate policy under the former structure, while the department head or the chief executive is more likely to do so under the latter. Citizens are often in favor of the principle of "improved administration" but opposed to specific proposals that would alter the existing pattern of operation of governmental functions in which they have interests.

5. Professional groups prefer separate organization for the functions that they regard as being a part of their profession. These groups have "organized bodies of knowledge, generally available only to members; group standards of training and performance; codes of ethical conduct and, particularly, close group ties and associations." [5] Under these circumstances, they believe that their goals, procedures, and knowledge can best be organized to benefit their clientele groups if their function is not commingled with others. Librarians do not want libraries to be administered by the school board; penologists do not want the local jail administered by the same agency that handles social welfare.

6. The strings attached to Federal grants-in-aid encourage a link between Federal and state and local administrators of functions, but they discourage the association of various state and local programs into a single agency. In some cases, Federal-grant conditions require the establishment of earmarked or dedicated funds, which in turn encourages separate organization.

7. Citizens and legislators often believe that certain special programs should be placed "above politics" and hence in a separate agency. This has been true of fair-employment-practices activities, liquor control, and education, among others.

8. Legislators are reluctant to give greater power to the chief executive. They are jealous of his glamour, political power, and policy-leader-

[5] Willbern, *op. cit.*, p. 116.

ship potential. Urban chief executives have been less subjected than governors to this kind of suspicion, partly because councilmen in cities where the reform movement has been influential, many of them busy businessmen, do not want to be involved in the details of administration, and partly because of the widespread use of the council-manager plan, which keeps the manager always potentially subject to control by the council, since he is not an independent agent with a direct popular mandate.

9. Americans have generally been suspicious of strong administrative leaders and have been more concerned with specific functions than with the abstract principle of efficient, well-coordinated government in general. Many people believe that mayors are not usually elected on the basis of issues and that turning full administrative power over to them is as uncomfortable as signing a blank check. Managers have always been viewed with suspicion because of their great power, though this feeling is, in most cities, confined to a minority of voters.

Separatism of agencies remains the rule in state and county government because of the diversity of interests and forces involved in the political arena. In cities, the dominant groups have generally preferred integration and, with some qualifications, have been able to achieve it through the strong-mayor and council-manager plans. Groups for separatism have seldom been strong enough to prevail.

The Arguments for Integration. Persons supporting reorganization movements have used two principal arguments to support their cause: (1) Integration will produce coordinated governmental activities; and (2) responsibility to the public will be increased. It is sometimes held that there is really not much to coordinate in government. How much coordination, it is asked, is needed between those who work in the department of streets and those who work in the department of public health? The concept of coordination, it is held, goes beyond this, however. It involves more than the bringing about of cooperation between, say, the psychiatric social workers in the public welfare department and the psychiatric social workers in the juvenile section of the probate court. Coordination also makes possible the economies of joint housekeeping activities and of the balancing off, in the executive budget, of the relative priorities of various functions of government. The chief executive is the only feasible person available to perform the role of coordinator.

The argument on responsibility is based upon the assumption that there should be but a single legitimate source of authority, the chief executive, and that his lieutenants should receive their authority from him. If this is the case, authority and accountability are equal to one another. Authority cannot be exercised, in the words of the Hoover Commission, unless there is a "clear line of command from the top to the bottom and a return line of responsibility and accountability from the bottom to the top." [6]

Government, its services, and its many clientele groups are all too complicated for a simple, single line of responsibility, of course. Most of those who would reorganize government recognize this, but they argue that "a general responsibility to the general public interest may be better achieved through the main line of political responsibility . . . than through the limited, specific, hidden responsibilities involved in some of the other relationships." Government, it is held, becomes more visible, and hence more subject to public scrutiny, if there is a single chief executive to be held accountable.

The Middle Ground. Once again, things are never completely black or completely white in politics. Total integration is probably never possible, and not even the most enthusiastic reorganizer could argue that separatism is the equivalent of anarchy. As York Willbern has said: [7]

Separatism and integration are not opposites without middle ground. Neither is every absolute. Even with an agency that appears completely independent, the [chief executive] may have much influence simply because he has produced a majority of the popular votes, has influence with the legislature, and has public prestige and constitutional responsibilities. And even in an agency over which the [chief executive] appears to have complete control, the influence of a special clientele, of the group connections and thought habits of employees, of interested [councilmen], and of intergovernmental relationships all will be of incalculable importance. Agencies will be grouped all along the spectrum from nearly complete independence to nearly complete subordination to central political control.

The precise details of agency organization differ according to such things as historical accident, the wants and needs of the clientele of a particular agency, the desires of interested pressure groups, and the personal idiosyncrasies of transient administrators, chief executives, and legislators. Because differing points of view are often held by the various interested parties, questions as to whether an agency will be headed by a board or by a single administrator, the manner in which board appointments, if any, are to be made, who is to be represented on the board, the internal structure of the agency, and other such considerations are a matter not so much of deliberate planning as of negotiation among the interested parties. [8] The politics of the organization of an

[6] Quoted in Willbern, *op. cit.*, p. 120.

[7] *Ibid.*, p. 121. Willbern was discussing state government, but the comment applies equally to municipalities.

[8] On this point, see R. A. Dahl and C. E. Lindblom, *Politics, Economics and Welfare* (Harper & Brothers, New York, 1953).

agency in other words, follows the same pattern as that by which the policies of the agency are determined.[9]

ADMINISTRATION AND CULTURE

Administration cannot be wholly scientific or neutral. It must be related to the values of the culture in which it exists. The manner in which a social-welfare, police, or educational system is administered will depend upon cultural values of the contemporary society. There is no "one best way" to care for people on welfare, for example. The level of assistance they get, whether the needs of children or of old people are emphasized, the amount of outside income that is permitted by overlooking the precise requirements of the law, the amount of training which social workers are expected to have, the philosophy of social workers toward society, government, and, in particular, toward those at the lower end of the social scale—all of these things will be conditioned by the culture in which the program exists.

The Administrative Process. Administration is a part of the political process, not an activity fundamentally different from it. The determination of policy in the legislative body will at the same time inevitably involve questions of the means of carrying out policy. Similarly, the execution of policy always involves modification of the policy and its selective application to actual circumstances as they arise.

It should not be assumed that the degree of specialization of equipment, training of personnel, or types of organizational structure employed in a governmental unit are irrelevant. They are important variables in determining the level and cost of services, no doubt, but the kinds of equipment used, the training expected of personnel, the organizational structure, and the level of service itself that exists in connection with a given governmental function are a result of a balancing off of public attitudes, the values of those who are involved in the decision making within the legislature, the city council, and the administrative organization, and the expectations and goals of interested pressure groups. It will probably never be possible to eliminate these political considerations and to replace them with objective criteria as to how an agency should be organized and operated.

[9] On the reorganization movement, see Waldo, *op. cit.*; W. S. Sayre, "Premises of Public Administration: Past and Emerging," *Public Administration Review*, vol. 18 (Spring, 1958), pp. 102–105; J. W. Fesler, "Administrative Literature and the Second Hoover Commission Reports," *American Political Science Review*, vol. 51 (March, 1957), pp. 135–144; Herbert Kaufman, "Emerging Conflicts in the Doctrines of Public Administration," *American Political Science Review*, vol. 50 (December, 1956), pp. 1057–1073; *The National Civic Review* gives current information for individual cities.

Efficiency as a Point of View. There is no one best way to administer a program or a governmental unit. This is so because the best way to one individual may be the worst way to another. It is a matter of a point of view. For example, a management consultant might be asked to inspect a city health department and make recommendations as to its proper administrative structure and processes. Because, in private business, he is expected to look for ways of reducing costs and strengthening the hand of management, he may see a "one best way" to organize the agency. But his recommendations, if adopted, might not only upset established lines of communication and operation—thus threatening to damage the *esprit de corps* of the agency—they might also threaten to weaken the influence that an important interest group (in this case, the state or local medical society) might have over the agency. This threat would certainly result in damage-control operations on the part of the interest group. It would take its case to the council or the legislature.

Who would be right in this case—the management consultant or the medical society? Who can say? If the medical society refuses to cooperate with the agency, its whole program may founder. The medical society might claim that the proposal would discourage young men from going into the medical profession. The society might be right or it might be wrong in making the claim. It might be sincere in advancing the claim, or it might simply be seeking to retain its traditional monopolistic control over medical practice and programs. Suppose that it is right and does really mean what it says. Are the few dollars that the management consultant would save for the reorganized agency—assuming that he is right in saying that his proposal would save money—worth more to society than the social cost of a decreased supply of medical manpower?

There might well be other potential effects of the proposal by the management consultant, too. For dozens of reasons that cannot be examined in detail here, the proposal, if adopted, might have the ultimate effect of reducing the scope or effectiveness of the end program of the agency, the actual services it provides for society and its members, individually and collectively. Thus, what is said to be saving money may really be a downgrading of the program, either as an intended result or as an unanticipated result. The latter may come about because of changes in training requirements or pay levels or prospects for advancement or other factors involving recruiting potential and employee morale.

This example should not be taken to mean that the concept of efficiency is meaningless or that a review of administrative structure and practice could not result in improvements. To use an exaggerated illustration, it might be found that a health department is using physicians in laboratory work that could readily be done by technicians. It is doubtful if many undesirable results would follow a reclassification of such positions. Yet one could not say this for certain without an extensive examination of the whole environment in which the circumstance is found.[10]

ORGANIZATION

Municipal-government agencies may be organized in a great variety of ways. Some of them are headed by an elective officer. Some have a single administrator appointed by and responsible to the chief executive. In other cases, the administrator may be chosen by the chief executive but may be removable only by a complicated process involving perhaps the civil service commission or the courts. In a fourth category are the agencies headed by boards or commissions. (The two terms mean the same.) Board members are usually appointed for long, staggered terms, and the chief executive may find members to be irremovable for practical purposes. When a board controls, an agency may be administered in a variety of ways. The chairman of the board may also serve as the chief administrator of the agency; the board may choose an executive secretary or a director, with its own powers reserved in law or practice to board policy making; the commission may be advisory only, with the chief executive appointing the administrative head; but the most common arrangement has been for the board to divide up its work among its members, each exercising considerable autonomy. Each of these structures of the boards is likely to produce a different pattern of administration.

The Administrative Code of the City. The administrative organization of cities in the past was established in state law. Changes could be made only by the legislature. Functions assigned to a particular department could not be changed to another department by order of the mayor or council, no matter how much of an improvement in municipal services might result from the proposed change. This is still the case in some states. Even in home rule cities, administrative structure can often be changed only by the local charter-amending procedures.

Modern charters, however, do not attempt to establish a rigid depart-

---

[10] The interested reader will find the following especially worthwhile for purposes of further development of ideas gently touched in this chapter: P. H. Appleby, *Policy and Administration* (University of Alabama Press, University, Ala., 1949), which emphasizes administration as part of the political process; Harold Stein (ed.), *Public Administration and Policy Development* (Harcourt, Brace and Company, Inc., New York, 1952), a collection of cases, including some from local government, dealing with policy making in administration; Dwight Waldo, *The Administrative State* (The Ronald Press Company, New York, 1948), which shows how cultural values affect administration; Herbert Simon, *Administrative Behavior* (2d ed.; The Macmillan Company, New York, 1957), which should be read in connection with an important commentary, E. C. Banfield, "The Decision-making Schema," *Public Administration Review,* vol. 17 (Autumn, 1957), pp. 278–285.

mental structure, but rather authorize the council to adopt an *administrative code* for the city establishing a plan of organization. The council is then able to rearrange departments, bureaus, and lesser agencies as changing requirements dictate. This practice is not yet the rule, however. Often city officials must go to the state legislature with a request for authority to transfer garbage collection, for example, from the public health department to the public works department. Even in home rule cities, the public is often expected to decide on referendum such things as whether there should be a separate department of traffic engineering or whether central purchasing should be consolidated with the controller's office. Some specialists believe that many decisions on administrative organization might well be left to the chief executive himself, without even councilmanic action being required.

A complete administrative code or manual is useful in all except perhaps small cities not only to describe basic structure, but for another reason: it explains the responsibilities and authority of the various departments and their principal officers. The need for this is illustrated in an example cited in the Stone, Price, and Stone study.[11] Some years ago in Austin, Texas:

> . . . there was a complete lack of agreement between the manager and several department heads about the responsibilities of each. The manager assumed, and it was clear in his own mind, that one department was composed of the water, the electric, and the sewage divisions, but the superintendent of one of these divisions had no such idea. He reported directly to the manager instead of to the supposed head of the department, whom he did not recognize as his superior. The manager and the division head never got together to reach a common understanding. Similarly, the health officer in Austin had the notion that he should report directly to the council, which appointed him, rather than to the manager. On the other hand, the manager believed that it was his job to supervise the health officer. No written record of the council's desire was available to the manager and the health officer for guidance.

Clearly such a situation does not aid in the development of effective organization. But confusion as to administrative responsibility is quite a common thing in cities, and Stone, Price, and Stone found that many managers did not seem to know what an administrative code was or how it operated. They found that in one city, officials paid no attention to the code and "most of them were unaware of its existence."[12] As municipal management becomes more professionalized, however, the flexible and complete administrative code becomes more important.

---

[11] H. A. Stone, D. K. Price, and K. H. Stone, *City Manager Government in the United States* (Public Administration Service, Chicago, 1940), p. 84. By permission of the Public Administration Service.

[12] *Ibid.*, p. 85.

The Choice of Organization: A Problem. It is not only difficult to determine the best organizational structure, it is equally a problem to determine the allocation of functions within agencies or the best place to assign new functions. For example, in the 1950s, many local officials became interested in the establishment of programs dealing with the problems of the aged. These programs cut across traditional department lines, since they deal with housing, welfare, health, employment, and many other things. How should the program be established in order to minimize conflict with existing programs and organizational patterns? What organizational pattern would best fit the needs of the aged and be most acceptable to their interest groups? The answer is not easy to find, but there is a strong tendency to establish new programs as separate organizations. This usually best suits the interests involved and seems to give the new program its best chance for survival.

Single Agency Head. As compared with other types of organizations, where an individual serves as head of an agency and is appointed by the chief executive, the agency programs are likely to be more diversified, more related to the over-all balance of needs in the annual budget, less able to avoid cuts during an economy drive, more involved in the decisions that are important to the political future of the mayor or councilmen, less dominated by a single-interest group, and more easily shaken out of bureaucratic lethargy by a chief executive who is necessarily concerned with public reactions to governmental programs.

Independent Head. When the head of an agency is independent of the chief executive because he is elected to office, because he cannot easily be removed, or because he is a civil servant, the agency is likely to develop a strong in-group sense against the rest of the government, professional standards are likely to be the criteria used as an important measuring stick in making decisions, and bureaucratic inertia, if it becomes very great, cannot easily be overcome because of the difficulty of exerting pressure from outside. The agency becomes largely insulated from ordinary controls, although it will usually have to seek to maintain good relations with the legislative body unless it can find some means of obtaining an independent budget. Agencies with independent heads often include parks, police, social-welfare, or public health departments, although other examples also exist.

Boards and Commissions. The use of boards and commissions became widespread after the War between the States. This marked a transition from control of departments by council committees to control by the chief executive—a transition more nearly completed in cities than in other state or local units of government. It also reflected a desire to take government "out of politics." Boards were either bipartisan or, later, nonpartisan in structure, members were usually appointed for long and overlapping terms, and their removal from office was normally extremely difficult.

Librarians, educators, and other professional people strongly favor independent boards over their departments. Powerful and vociferous pressure groups often wish to take functions under their wings and protect them as infants that should not be exposed to the rigorous and competitive circumstances of the ordinary governmental agency. An attempt to make the agency autonomous almost always exists in the case of functions involving special-interest groups or special-clientele groups. Other instances of this sort of thing may be found in connection with public health, public transportation, airports, parks and recreation, art galleries, and museums.

Boards and commissions seem quite inappropriate for the direct administration of any agency, and the tendency to organize in this fashion is declining. On the other hand, a board chairman, if he possesses administrative skill, can sometimes serve adequately as the agency head. It is not uncommon, in agencies which have boards as policy-making bodies, for most of the policies ultimately adopted to be generated within the bureaucracy of the agency and to be "sold" to the commission by the administrative head. In some cases, as in public health, the board views its principal job as being that of preserving orthodoxy and preventing the administrative head, who may be a layman, from doing something the profession would not approve of.

Many boards and commissions are established by law in such a way as to require interest-group representation upon them. In other cases, it is a firmly established custom for certain groups to be included in the membership. The idea of group representation seems antithetical to the traditional American skepticism about "the interests" and "special privilege," but it is very much in harmony with the concept of a pluralistic society that is a basic part of our culture and one which is accepted by most Americans.[13]

An Evaluation of Boards. Millions of man-hours are probably spent in the United States each year by unpaid citizens serving on advisory and policy-controlling boards at the state and local levels of government. What do they accomplish? These were the findings of a study in Pennsylvania: [14]

1. Boards "study complex problems to which the elected body cannot devote enough time."

2. They insulate the legislative body and executive from certain types of political pressures. Since the members are (usually) nonelective, they

---

[13] See Alfred de Grazia, *Public and Republic* (Alfred A. Knopf, Inc., New York, 1951).

[14] *Horizons*, vol. 5 (April, 1958), p. 1.

can more easily do things that are thought necessary and desirable but which, in the short run at least, might be politically unpopular.

3. They do not "take politics out of important areas" of government.

4. The effectiveness of the boards depends upon the quality of the members "and not upon the advisory commission device itself."

5. They provide, especially at the local level, a great amount of staff work which, if paid for, would be very expensive. They, in other words, serve to socialize some of the cost of government.

6. Members perceive their jobs rather narrowly, tending to avoid performing a function about which they are in doubt. That is, they do not engage in "empire building."

7. Members often feel that they are not consulted frequently enough, that their advice is too freely ignored, and that they are not informed of the disposition made of their recommendations.

8. For things requiring decisive action and, outside of the work done by boards of adjustment, civil service commissions, and planning commissions, the professional administrative staff of a department works more "efficiently" than can boards.

9. "Citizens boards and commissions can still offer effective and useful aid to officials and the community."

The larger a city is, the more likely it is to use boards and commissions.[15] This is probably also generally true of other local units. In weak-mayor cities, they are especially likely to have formal policy-making powers that exceed mere advisory status.

The reason for the existence of advisory boards in the structure of the more populous units of government stems from the old problem of citizens having less opportunity to know their officials personally when population density is high. There is, at the same time, less opportunity to participate directly in policy making. The citizens group serves in lieu of the direct consultation between officeholder and constituent that is typical in the small suburb or the rural township. It provides a measuring stick by which public reactions to programs can be gotten and a more gentle stick it is than the one that may otherwise rap the politician's knuckles at the next election. A cross section of ideas and of opinion can be furnished to those whose political life depends upon a proper assessment of community attitudes.

Boards and commissions are extremely useful to the chief executive, whether he is an elective mayor or appointed manager. For one thing, boards allow pressure groups that are interested in a function to give positive advice to the administration through their appointed members. They might otherwise carp from the side lines or complain at public

[15] R. B. Richert, "How Michigan Cities Make Use of Lay Citizens in Government," *Michigan Municipal Review*, vol. 26 (February, 1953), pp. 33 ff.

hearings. For another, the use of boards involves a number of citizens in such a manner as to give them a stake in the success of an administration. This is a device that helps develop support for other programs of the chief executive in addition to the one in which the citizen is active as a member of a board. It also provides a built-in shock absorber so that the chief executive is protected from the full force of criticism against policy in a particular field. The chief executive can point out that, after all, "it was developed by the citizens on the committee," even though it may really have been a product of the fertile minds of the municipal bureaucracy, and the advisory commission may merely have given its stamp of approval. And, of course, unpaid boards provide a socially acceptable form of patronage which adds to the number of persons who become obligated to defend the administration—a situation useful to the mayor if he becomes a candidate for re-election, or to the manager if he should run into difficulties with his council.

Mr. Inside, Mr. Outside. In small communities, administrative structure is likely to be simple and rather informal. Precise departmentalization is not necessary. In such communities, the success of governmental operations may depend upon having two key administrators, one an "outside" man and the other an "inside" man. The former may have such a title as "director of public works" but may handle many matters including roads, parks, building inspection, water supply, and planning. The latter may be called the "clerk" or perhaps the "director of finance" and may handle finance, personnel, purchasing, and routine office duties. Of course, the greater the population, the more specialization is indicated.

THE CONCEPT OF ADEQUATE STANDARDS

The political process would be much simpler if we had objective criteria for measuring adequate standards both of service and of performance levels in government. But we do not. These standards are culturally determined and as such vary over time and geographic location. The people of a small village may not—probably do not—expect the civil servants in the city hall to be selected by a merit system, and they probably do not expect them to have a great deal of training for their jobs. In most cases, public employees probably meet community expectations as to standards. Similarly, the level of services wanted or expected will vary according to the economic conditions, local value patterns, density of population, and other considerations.

Professional Standards. Because of their vested interest, professional organizations set standards for their areas of governmental activity. These standards are often spoken of as being "optimum"—a word that somehow has come to be used in newspaper editorials and political speeches as if it meant "minimum acceptable" instead of "best." Physicians prescribe standards both for service levels and for administrative organization of public health departments; educators, for public schools; social workers, for public welfare; and so on. The goal is usually set so high that few governmental units can claim to meet them. Thus in the postwar era, public health administrators established standards for a health unit that could operate effectively in furnishing primary services. Yet in 1948, a survey showed that only forty-seven counties and seventeen cities in the entire United States met the standards.[16] The citizen might well wonder how realistic they were and what reasonable standards might be.

Politicians often use the optimum goals of professional organizations for their own political propaganda. So do nonelective administrators, who are often themselves members of such groups. Legislators and councilmen frequently find it difficult to defend themselves if they do not provide a full program or meet the standards, since neither the politicians nor the public can judge the fairness of the criteria used or whether they provide for minimal or ultimate goals. Furthermore, of course, each professional organization deals only with goals in its own area of governmental service while the beleaguered legislator must balance off one such demand against another, and all of them against what the public is willing to pay.

THE CONCEPT OF THE PUBLIC INTEREST

Theorists writing about administrative behavior have used a great many words in seeking to develop a notion of what would be accepted as "the public interest" in the decision-making process.[17] This is understandable, since public administrators are supposed by citizens to be serving the public broadly and not a minor portion of it. The typical citizen no doubt thinks that the duty of the government is to serve the public interest. He does not define it further. Certainly he is not likely to view government, as political scientists tend to, as serving a large number of clientele groups rather than a single public at large.

Administrators themselves probably are not much interested in, or aware of, what philosophers say about the public interest. To the extent that they consider the concept consciously or subconsciously, their

[16] National Health Assembly, *America's Health* (Harper & Brothers, New York, 1949), p. 61.

[17] A summary is provided in Glendon A. Schubert, Jr., "'The Public Interest' in Administrative Decision-making," *American Political Science Review*, vol. 51 (June. 1957), pp. 346–368.

implicit assumptions concerning its nature seem to include such items as the following: [18]

1. The administrator tends to identify the public interest with the expectations of his professional peers. If he is a physician, a social work administrator, a school superintendent, or other professional person, he is likely to think that the standards established and the administrative methods approved by his profession are both right and in the public interest.

2. He tends to accept the expectations of his administrative superiors and to view them as representative of the public interest. This is the road to both convenience and security. It is a simple and effective rationalization.

3. He identifies his personal value system with the public interest through the process psychologists call "projection." His views quite surely are held by a large number of persons in the general public, but he has no way of knowing what proportion of the public. In any case, this approach minimizes personal psychological strain. Of course, an administrator is often called upon to do things that do not fit his personal values; in such cases, the more easily he can accept his superior's position as the public interest, the easier it is for him.

4. He tends to reach a decision—as do elective politicians—that will minimize interest-group pressures upon himself and his agency. It is not difficult to identify in one's mind the views of the most interested persons or groups in relation to a particular policy or program with the general good. The tendency is in this respect to identify the public interest with the wishes of the interested publics.[19]

RED TAPE

Red tape—strict adherence to the forms and routine of office—is to be found in private and public bureaucracies everywhere. In part, it is a result of the desire of the members of a large, impersonal organization to protect themselves by making sure that their actions are in accord with established policy. If in doubt, the safest course is to apply as literal an interpretation of the rules as is possible and to keep a written record of every move. One is less likely to get into trouble that way and it provides a framework within which to make decisions.

Certain other factors contribute to governmental red tape. One is that in a democracy there is a need to account ultimately to the people for

[18] Based upon the author's observations while serving as administrative assistant to the Governor of Michigan.

[19] On this, see Avery Leiserson, *Administrative Regulation* (University of Chicago Press, Chicago, 1942), p. 14.

governmental actions. This accounting may be clumsy and at times obscure, but the requirement that bureaucrats follow the law as closely as
possible stems from the notion that government cannot do that which
it is not authorized to do. Furthermore, Americans have never trusted
their governments very far, and state constitutions, statutes, and city
charters have long been filled with minute detail designed to limit the
freedom of action of administrators. The result is an increase in the
amount of red tape.

One other factor should be mentioned. The seemingly absurd examples
of red tape that are sometimes produced may merely be by-products of
the necessary work of carrying out the requirements of the law. The
Indiana Unemployment Compensation Bureau at Gary, for example,
once ruled that out-of-work prostitutes were not eligible for unemployment compensation, holding that they were "independent contractors." [20]
The ruling was lampooned as an example of the excesses of bureaucracy.
Actually, of course, the bureau in this case had an application before it
and had, therefore, to rule on the citizen's rights. It really had no choice
in the matter but to take some kind of action. That the application was
a bit unusual was surely not the fault of the bureau.[21]

THE CHIEF EXECUTIVE

The chief executive is important in the administrative process, not
alone because he may have the power to hire and fire department heads,
but also because he is the coordinator of a variety of different programs
and interests, the principal architect of policy, and the liaison between
the agencies that provide services and the clientele groups that receive
them. His role is so crucial that a portion of Chapter 9 is devoted to it.

The Chief Executive's Personal Staff. In addition to major advisers,
such as the budget officer, the city attorney (if appointed by the chief
executive), and the planning director, and such advisory commissions as
may exist, the chief executive usually, except in small cities, chooses a
staff of personal advisers and assistants. These may include an administrative assistant or two, or sometimes, especially in manager cities, an
intern trainee just graduated from a university training program. In
larger cities, the chief executive may have a personal, confidential secretary and a number of stenographers and office assistants.

The staff of the chief executive has the task of helping him keep abreast
of the functions for which he is responsible. Needless to say, these per-

[20] *Time*, Mar. 28, 1949.

[21] On the general subject, see A. W. Gouldner, "Red Tape as a Social Problem," in
H. D. Stein and R. A. Cloward, *Social Perspectives on Behavior* (The Free Press,
Glencoe, Ill., 1957); and Peter McGlade, "Initiative and Bureaucracy," *Public Ad-
ministration Review*, vol. 20 (Winter, 1960), pp. 41–45.

sons must have his complete confidence, for they are often more closely associated with his success or failure in office than are his department heads.[22]

THE DEPARTMENT HEAD

Beneath the chief executive but above middle management and the clerical and minor employees is the principal administrator—the agency head or head of a large division. He plays a vital role in policy formulation because he is likely to know his particular governmental activity better than the chief executive and the councilmen do. If he does not, he has easy access to those who do. He advises the chief executive, who wants ideas on a program; he testifies before the legislative body or its committees, telling them what he wants them to know and often demonstrating great skill at withholding information unfavorable to his point of view.

The Agency Head as a Symbol. The agency head, like the chief executive and members of the legislative body, spends a great deal of time in symbolic activities. While matters requiring his decision pile up on his desk, he trudges from one meeting to another, often spending an afternoon in the mayor's or manager's office, or in an interdepartmental meeting, or as an ex officio member of some board, or at a convention of a professional group with which his agency has important relations, making a comment here and there or perhaps a platitudinous speech of welcome. In this way his activities follow much the same pattern as do those of principal executives in large private corporations.

From a rational or "efficiency" point of view, this activity may seem enormously wasteful. Yet it is most important, for at the top level, the administrator (often he has worked his way up and knows the tasks of the lesser positions within his agency) leaves to trusted aides much of the actual work that goes out over his signature. He spends most of his own time in molding the agency members into an effective working unit, reassuring them of their importance by expressing their values in public speeches and by awarding a pin to the clerk-steno who has just completed thirty years of service; and in seeking to maintain smooth relationships between the agency and its clientele groups, its pressure-group support, the chief executive, the council, the state legislature, and potential friends and enemies of all kinds. His principal job is to understand and to communicate to others the values, loyalties, and goals of his organization.[23]

[22] For an elaboration of the importance of staff, see Charles R. Adrian, *State and Local Governments* (McGraw-Hill Book Company, Inc., New York, 1960), chap. 13.

[23] In this connection, see Philip Selznick, *Leadership in Administration* (Row, Peterson & Company, Evanston, Ill., 1957).

The informed citizen should understand, too, that in the process of seeking to placate their various publics, the personnel in the various departments often come into conflict with one another. They compete over budgetary matters and in seeking status in the community. Some department heads feud publicly with other department heads—with resultant damage to all of government, since the citizen is likely to believe the worst that each official says about other officials.

Because the status and even the survival of a government agency may depend upon the way it is perceived by the public, large local agencies maintain their own public relations staffs. Often these may not be large—the council will generally see to that—but they are important.[24]

BUREAUCRACY AND DEMOCRATIC GOVERNMENT

The problem of bureaucracy in contemporary America is essentially this: Citizens want many services from their governments, but the values of the culture imply that there is a danger of losing democratic control over policy making if professional bureaucracies grow large.

Not all citizens are in favor of the expansion in the size and number of governmental services that has taken place since the beginning of the Great Depression (1929). Probably no citizen favors having his government furnish all of the services it does. But many citizens give support to each of the services. At the same time, regardless of whether a bureaucracy is developed and selected through merit-system examinations or purely on the basis of patronage appointments, today's jobs are technical and complicated. They, by their nature, indicate the necessity for the use of qualified specialists. And qualified specialists do not speak lay language. The result is a desire for service, coupled with a popular suspicion of bureaucracy, and no little fear of the implications for democracy in its growth. People like the product of government; they do not like the means that seem necessary in order to deliver the product.

Bureaucracy as Antithesis. Keeping in mind the political beliefs that have guided Americans in evaluating politics,[25] it is understandable that bureaucracy should come to be regarded as the antithesis of democracy. When the proponents of a professional bureaucracy, several decades ago, also gave support to the concept of integrated administrative control under the chief executive, they reinforced one popular fear with another. There has also been a tendency, both in folk philosophy and in some academic writing, to romanticize the representative character of

---

[24] On the attitudes, role perceptions, and problems of high-level administrators, see C. H. Coates and R. J. Pellegrin, "Executives and Supervisors," *American Sociological Review,* vol. 22 (April, 1957), pp. 217–220.

[25] See chap. 3.

legislative bodies, national, state, and local. Furthermore, this same combination of forces has been lined up at times in support of the idea that "whatever the people want is right, and they should have it." Hence, if the people want a chaotic pattern of government, it must be right; if they prefer amateur legislative opinion to that of professional bureaucratic opinion, the former must be better. This type of idea seems to stem from Rousseau's romantic notion of the "general will" and is reflected in the Latin inscription found somewhere in many a council chamber, though usually beyond the ken of tourists and councilmen alike: *vox populi, vox Dei*—the voice of the people is the voice of God. The difficulty with this self-congratulatory notion is that the *vox populi* can be interpreted in a great many ways by legislators, bureaucrats, chief

"Your question, sir, reveals a lack of faith not only in the officers and directors of Globe Steel but in the entire American free-enterprise system."

Figure 13-1. Bureaucracy, public and private, is endemic in contemporary American society. Bureaucrats have available many tactical techniques by which to maintain control over their organizations. This cartoon demonstrates several such techniques.
SOURCE: Drawing by Lorenz; © 1960 The New Yorker Magazine, Inc.

executives, and editors. And what seems to be the voice of the people today is viewed by those same people as all a horrible mistake tomorrow. The councilmen who must perforce take the short view and the bureaucrat who is sometimes permitted the luxury of the long view may both speak the voice of the people—if the problem is viewed from the vantage of the historian.

We may assume that it is difficult at times to turn the bureaucratic troops around or to divert their path; that red tape and literal interpretations of the rules are endemic to bureaucracy; that mature bureaucracies tend to resist innovation and lack initiative; and that trained specialists are sometimes impatient with unknowing laymen. We do not need to assume at the same time that bureaucrats wish to destroy the system in which, as citizens, they too live. (See Figure 13-1.)

Americans probably have reason to be on guard against an irresponsible, autocratic, muscle-bound bureaucracy. But there is no evidence to indicate that the danger from this direction is any greater than is the danger from an irresponsible legislative body, an autocratic chief executive, or a muscle-bound court system. Each contains its dangers; each must in turn be watched.[26]

ADMINISTRATION AND THE PUBLIC

Public Relations in City Government. Much of the activity of everyday administration goes along with little or no notice taken of it by the average citizen. His knowledge of the services that are available to him, or of the nature of bureaucrats or of the administrative process, is likely to be very skimpy indeed. But the average citizen does not automatically come by an understanding of these things. He must be told what his government is doing, and why.

It has already been noted that the political process involves not just

---

[26] Much has been written on the implications for democracy of a large and growing bureaucracy. C. S. Hyneman, *Bureaucracy in a Democracy* (Harper & Brothers, New York, 1950), emphasizes the view that the bureaucracy must be kept firmly subordinate to the legislature. The bureaucrats receive more gentle treatment in two books by Paul Appleby, *Big Democracy* (Alfred A. Knopf, Inc., New York, 1945) and *Morality and Administration in Democratic Government* (University of Louisiana Press, Baton Rouge, La., 1952) and in a series of lectures by E. S. Redford, *Ideal and Practice in Public Administration* (University of Alabama Press, University, Ala., 1958). The entire issue of *Annals,* vol. 292 (March, 1954), is devoted to "Bureaucracy and Democratic Government." Many fine novels deal with the problems of bureaucracy from one angle or another. See Rowland Egger, "The Administrative Novel," *American Political Science Review,* vol. 53 (June, 1959), pp. 448–455. Examples include J. G. Cozzens, *Guard of Honor* (Harcourt, Brace & World, Inc., New York, 1949); Pat Frank, *Mr. Adam* (J. B. Lippincott Company, Philadelphia, 1946); and John Hersey, *A Bell for Adano* (Alfred A. Knopf, Inc., New York, 1944). Bureaucracy is caricatured in C. N. Parkinson, *Parkinson's Law and Other Studies in Administration* (Houghton Mifflin Company, Boston, 1957).

one monolithic "public," but a series of publics each demanding satisfactions.[27] Citizens are rarely unanimous in their attitudes toward public matters. If they were, government officials would have few problems in public relations. Given the nature of the political process as involving the interaction of conflicting groups, public relations must normally be directed toward one or more of the interested groups in the community. Groups may be interested in municipal government because of their physical location within the community, their businesses, their tax bills, their income, their (high or low) status positions within the community, or for other reasons. Each individual belongs to several publics and can become displeased with city government in connection with any one of them. He can also be informed about the activities of his city by being reached as a member of any one of these publics.

Municipal departments often have peculiar publics of their own, and each of them must therefore be conscious of the importance of public relations. Departments dealing with particular professional or clientele groups are especially likely to have uniquely identifiable publics. The welfare department, for example, must please (1) welfare recipients; (2) the pillars of the community who take an interest in welfare as an avocation; (3) taxpayers who pay the bills; (4) editors, who may want to take the occasional welfare cheat and make a headline case out of him; (5) grocers and other businessmen who have welfare recipients as customers; (6) professional social workers, who may want the department to be established as an autonomous agency; (7) ordinary citizens, who are likely to believe that people on public relief are lazy, shiftless, and of a category akin to the criminal. The manager of the local airport must cope with publics that include passengers, pilots, airline officials, and people who live near airports or proposed airports; the health department must reach an understanding with the medical profession, with the Parent-Teachers Association and other pressure groups interested in the schools, with social reformers who want expanded public health services; and so on.

Gauging Public Attitudes. The public official who would keep his publics informed through an active public relations program must first of all be acquainted with the attitudes existing in the community. This is no easy task to accomplish.

How can the public official go about gauging attitudes? He may employ one of the so-called public opinion polling organizations, or alternatively establish a polling unit within, say, the city complaint department. But public opinion polling is quite a technical task and therefore requires specially trained personnel. It is also too expensive for most cities to

---

[27] Whenever the term *public opinion* has been used in this text, it has been meant in the sense of "the attitudes of interested publics."

finance. It is time-consuming, and the information is therefore often not available when it is needed. Perhaps most difficult of all, poll results that are unfavorable serve as ammunition for opponents of the administration, and this discourages their use.

The official is therefore likely to turn to older methods of measurement, most of which are of doubtful reliability. All persons in the political arena, for example, engage in *informal polling* by noting the views expressed by visitors and letter writers. But these views may be highly unrepresentative, and are of uncertain value at all times. *Advisory bodies* are often used as a means of measuring the attitudes and the intensity of attitudes of the important pressure group interested in a particular activity. *Letters, petitions,* and *resolutions* from groups are expressions of group attitudes and are useful as such. Usually they express protests rather than offer positive suggestions such as advisory bodies often make. *Elections,* of course, may serve as a final public opinion poll at which to measure important controversies. Municipal election campaigns, in theory, should be conducted primarily over important policy issues, but this is often not the case. Candidates usually prefer to deal in glittering generalities and indulge in name calling and other propaganda techniques rather than to take a stand on specific issues which may lose votes, and the citizen has not usually strongly objected to this practice.

Contacts with Citizens. Every public official has an obligation to inform the public of what government is doing, what it has done, and what it plans to do. Groundwork for future plans must be especially well laid if a city is to approach its problems on the basis of long-range planning. The public wants to know what services are available from each agency of government, what it is costing, and why it is costing what it is. On the other hand, most Americans would say that no official has a moral right to use taxpayer money in a public relations program that is simply a defense of incumbent officeholders, although this is sometimes done.

Public employees who daily meet the ordinary citizen in the course of their work are probably the most important persons in helping to determine whether a public relations program is to be successful. Many public works employees are in a position to make city government either popular or unpopular. Refuse collectors, for example, meet the public daily. If they are efficient in their work and courteous in receiving complaints or informing citizens of ordinance violations, they can create much good will. So can public works foremen in replying to "sidewalk superintendents" who want to know what is being done, why, and what the cost will be.

Policemen are perhaps the most important public relations men the city government has. Their uniform makes them conspicuous. Policemen are indoctrinated in the rules of courtesy and taught while in recruit training to be living city directories, for their responses to requests for information become in effect measurements of the efficiency of the force so far as the typical citizen is concerned. And, of course, one police officer seen in uniform in a bar or caught in some wrongdoing does untold harm. He may represent a tiny fraction of 1 per cent of the force, but he can do more damage than can be repaired by a dozen fancy annual reports.

Firemen have some special advantages in public relations. Fire fighting is dramatic and a public relations activity in itself. Firemen also gain good will by rescuing rat terriers from culverts and young boys from trees, and by making and repairing toys in their spare time for distribution to needy children at Christmas time. On the other hand, they must overcome the popular notion that firemen chop down doors, smash windows, and spill chemicals on the living-room rug with malicious glee. Fire fighting is a good example of the value in public relations of dramatic activities. Americans are quite generous in permitting the purchase of expensive fire equipment, although they are not very much interested in fire prevention, which would make the equipment less necessary. Lectures on fire prevention are normally not dramatic.

Departments vary a good deal in the nature of their public relations problems. Some of them must work hard to satisfy their clientele, but they do not often attract general public attention (e.g., recreation); some of them are vital but work largely in a manner that seldom attracts general public notice (e.g., public health); some perform functions that are generally approved of, but are potential public relations dynamite (e.g., public housing); some of them are constantly under public surveillance (especially police and public works). All of them have a good deal to do with the status position of public employees in the community and the general repute of local government. (See Figure 13-2.)

City Officials and the Newspapers. Nothing is more important to the reputation that city government enjoys in the community than the relationship city officials have with the local newspapers. These publications, reflecting the varied views of their editors and publishers, take many different attitudes toward local governments. Many of them are responsible in their criticism. Others believe that criticism of any sort is good for circulation building. Some of them encourage the continued existence of popular superstitions, prejudices, and misconceptions concerning the nature of government. Some of them are ably edited; others are headed by men who run the newspaper as a profitable business, but who have no concept of social, economic, or administrative realities.

The department head may find the reporter or editor informed, responsible, and intelligent, in which case their relationship is likely to be

Figure 13-2. In large cities, police often find it desirable to build public support through seeking to gain the confidence of children. This photograph, featuring Phil Rizzuto, once a great shortstop for the New York Yankees, and an idealized Howard Chandler Christy painting of a policeman illustrates some of the techniques used by the New York Police Athletic League. SOURCE: Courtesy of the New York Police Athletic League.

happy and easy. On the other hand, he may consider the reporter or editor to be uninformed or stupid. But, whether responsible or not, the newspaperman controls the most important medium of communication in the city. Newspapers are normally of special influence in the formulation of *local* attitudes, as distinguished from attitudes on national or international matters.

Of course, the problem may be that the newspapers are represented by able men seeking to keep the public informed, while the councilman or department head has developed a confused notion of what the press is entitled to know. Arthur W. Bromage, a councilman–political scientist, has pointed out to public officials that: [28]

[28] A. W. Bromage, *On the City Council* (Wahr Publishing Company, Ann Arbor, Mich., 1950), p. 73. This section has borrowed from E. D. Woolpert, *Municipal Public Relations* (Public Administration Service, Chicago, 1940). See also H. A. Simon, D. W. Smithburg, and V. A. Thompson, *Public Administration* (Alfred A. Knopf, Inc., New York, 1950), pp. 415–421. Several of the books in the municipal-management series published by the International City Managers' Association and cited throughout this text devote a chapter to public relations. One of the most important areas demanding effective public relations is that of police protection. See

The only attitude appropriate to press and radio relations is one of open frankness. When a newspaper or radio representative calls, there is no use pretending that you don't know something which you actually know. If you do not wish to be quoted, you can always say so. One must keep constantly in mind that public office is not private business. The press and radio operate to convey news, and you are a source of local news.

Public Reports. Outside of direct contacts between public officials and employees and the citizen, and information distributed through the press, local governments inform their publics in a variety of ways: through the use of annual reports, leaflets, radio and television programs, movies, "open-house" days, and talks before clubs and groups. Cities have long been required to issue some sort of annual statement of finances for public consumption. Out of this background, some cities have come to issue general annual municipal reports aimed at the citizens of the community. Often these are in traditional form—dull, formal, and understandable only to persons having some knowledge of accounting. Other cities have produced clever abbreviated annual reports, with dramatic graphs, pictures, cartoons, and other eye-catching devices that still manage to convey a great deal of information.

An increasing number of cities have adopted the practice of preparing leaflets in lieu of the more expensive report. Radio and television are used by some communities. A few have brought these media into the council chamber, but most meetings are so routine in nature that it is doubtful if they appeal to many listeners and viewers, except on very special occasions. A handful of cities have produced movies to be shown to various groups about town, and other techniques have been resorted to, both by mayors anxious to defend their actions prior to an election, and by managers who want continued public support for their budget requests.

In a day of intensely competitive commercial advertising, city governments have difficulty in competing. The public has been conditioned to expect representatives of all institutions to come to the individual and explain in a clear, firm voice and simple style the wares they have to sell. Many city administrations scarcely try; those that do find the task a challenging one.

---

the chapter on the subject in O. W. Wilson, *Police Administration* (McGraw-Hill Book Company, Inc., New York, 1950).

Chapter 14

THE MUNICIPAL BUREAUCRACY

Issues of policy abound in the area of municipal employee-employer relations. Many of these are submitted from time to time directly to the voters of the city. Some of them become campaign issues. All of them relate to the effectiveness of city government.

Should public employees be allowed to join regular trade unions? Should they be allowed to join any kind of union at all? Should public employees have a right to strike? What sort of job security should they have? Are public employees' salaries adequate, or are they too high? These are some of the questions that the citizen may be expected to know something about.

MODERN PERSONNEL PRACTICES

It seems likely that most urban citizens do not realize the degree of professionalization that has taken place in the municipal civil service in recent decades. Over 2 million people are employed in local government service in the United States (not counting school employees). Most of them are employed by municipalities, and most of them are performing specialized jobs that require training of one degree or another. While the number of Federal employees has had a general downward trend since 1945, municipalities continue to expand their services, the total number of employees, and the total size of the payroll.

A great many people still believe, as they believed in the mid-1930s, according to a survey, and as Andrew Jackson believed well over a century ago, that government jobs are so "simple that men of intelligence may readily qualify themselves for their performance." [1] Of course, a moment's reflection leads to the conclusion that this is no longer the case. Government now performs a great many, rather than a few, functions. In the last century or so, the performance of most of man's activi-

---

[1] See Commission of Inquiry on Public Service Personnel, *Better Government Personnel* (McGraw-Hill Book Company, Inc., New York, 1935); and Andrew Jackson's first message to Congress (1829).

ties has become specialized and mechanized. Governmental activities are no exception. Since the turn of the century, government employment has become increasingly specialized and increasingly performed by professionally trained personnel with professional attitudes toward their work.

The public, although it still has reservations about the worth of employment by government, seems to be giving ground in recognition of the changing role of government in our society. The prestige value of public jobs has increased markedly since before the Great Depression, and this is especially true among working-class, lesser-educated persons, that is, among the persons most benefiting from the availability of governmental services and from the increased security that they provide.[2]

Civil Service and the Merit System. The term *civil service* refers to civilian employees of government. In practice it is often used interchangeably with *merit system*. The latter properly refers to a method of choosing government employees on the basis of examinations demonstrating the technical or professional competence of the applicant. The beginnings of a municipal civil service based upon the merit principle appeared in 1884, but, as in the case of the states, the principle did not become widely accepted until the 1930s. The national government, through its insistence upon professional competence of administrators for some programs receiving Federal grants-in-aid, prodded many cities and states along in this direction.

The Civil Service Commission. The acts establishing civil service merit systems in 1883 (Federal) and 1884 (New York and Massachusetts) established a semi-independent civil service commission and began a pattern that is still typical in cities as well as higher units of government. It is common to have a three-member civil service commission appointed (usually by the mayor) for overlapping terms, not more than two of the members being of the same political party. An executive secretary is normally hired to handle the actual administration of its activities.

The commission makes rules respecting examinations, classifies positions, conducts examinations, and keeps a list of eligible appointees.[3] It establishes uniform wages, hours, and conditions of labor (so that two clerks doing about the same job, but in different departments, will receive the same pay). It makes rules on transfers and promotions. It may, especially in large cities, conduct training programs. It certifies the payrolls so as to discourage payroll padding. It may have other functions, too.

---

[2] See Morris Janowitz and Deil Wright, "The Prestige of Public Employment: 1929 and 1954," *Public Administration Review*, vol. 16 (Winter, 1954), pp. 15–21.

[3] See T. H. Reed, *Municipal Management* (McGraw-Hill Book Company, Inc., New York, 1941), chap. 12.

The Personnel Director. In recent years, students of public administration have often criticized the use of the civil service commission to head personnel recruitment. It is now argued that the commission competes with the mayor or manager for control over city employees. The resultant conflict is considered harmful to administration and to morale. It is argued further that personnel control is inherently a function of management and hence should be handled as a part of the chief executive's office—as it is in patronage systems.

It is probable that the commission system was preferred in the early days of civil service reform because the administrative branch of government was corrupt and was opposed to the merit principle. Today, however, a chief executive who wants to run a smooth, effective administration desires competent personnel. He dare not resort to spoilsmanship; if he tried to do so, he would in any case be detected immediately.

There is a trend, therefore, toward the establishment of a personnel department under a single head, the personnel director, who is responsible to the mayor or manager. Personnel then becomes an executive function and responsibility.[4] This form of organization has been used most often in manager cities, where it began. It is more easily accepted in such cities because the manager is himself a professional careerist.[5]

The old-fashioned, independent civil service commission, usually consisting of three members selected on a bipartisan or nonpartisan basis, has had much criticism. It has encouraged hostility between the personnel agency and the chief executive. Its very existence has implied that the chief executive was standing by, eager to return city employment to a patronage status at the first opportunity. Sometimes the commissions have actually been less anxious than the chief executive to establish a true merit principle of employment. Some commissions have sought to administer their policies themselves, but have been lacking in the technical qualifications that a personnel director would possess. Others, as independent agencies, have been unable to get funds in order to hire a technical staff capable of preparing and administering valid and reliable examinations—and neither the council nor the chief executive has had much incentive to go to bat for the independent commission at budget hearings.

Today it is widely believed that personnel administration needs to be a part of management, as it invariably is in private enterprise. Under

[4] Many cities use an *advisory* civil service commission or have the commission make policy, but with all administration of policy left to the personnel director.

[5] See Reed, *op. cit.*, pp. 253–256, and the *Model City Charter* of the National Municipal League. The argument for a single personnel director has been restated in W. S. Carpenter, *The Unfinished Business of Civil Service Reform* (Princeton University Press, Princeton, N.J., 1952).

the leadership of a director whose professional interest is in the improvement of personnel and the methods of selecting personnel, the chief executive is given one of his most effective tools for a successful administrative record.

The Merit System and the Culture. Many artificial safeguards have been established in the past in attempts to require use of the merit system. These have included the independent commission, elaborate rules concerning tenure and dismissal, detailed examinations, complex position-classification systems, and the like. All are inadequate protection, and many devices exist for evasion of the merit principle if that is the officeholder's desire. Yet, the professional career approach to personnel administration does work in many communities because it has become a part of the political-cultural pattern. And in England, where there are no formal safeguards at all against making every appointment a political one, the system works very well indeed. The voters would not allow it to be otherwise.

The spirit, rather than the letter, of the merit system is the important thing. Many small and middle-sized municipalities cannot afford to employ professional personnel directors and staffs. The mayor, manager, clerk, or some other official may act as personnel officer. Yet in many cities that have no organized merit system, there are no spoils, and existing policy is to get the best available man for the job. The personnel methods used in any city, incidentally, are not likely to be more modern in character than are those used in private enterprise in that community, and the major personnel problem in municipal government today is likely to be, not spoils, but low pay, particularly in smaller communities.

Position Classification. In the establishment of a merit system of civil service, the various jobs of the municipality are categorized. Position classification consists of determining the duties and responsibilities of each individual job, whether occupied or vacant, and the assignment of that position to a class together with other positions of similar or related duties and responsibilities. Thus positions may be classified, for example, as junior clerk-typist, senior budget analyst, patrolman, chauffeur, or personnel director. Accurate and meaningful classification of positions is a technical and difficult job and can be done properly only by persons with training in personnel-administration techniques. Once the duties of each position have been described, the number and type of classes needed for the particular city must be determined, classes must be given a descriptive title, and positions must be assigned to classes. This last activity may create a good deal of controversy. Since it is part of a supervisor's duty to look after the welfare of his subordinates, a bureau chief may well engage in a bitter controversy with the personnel agency over whether his best stenographer fits the job description of intermediate stenographer or senior stenographer.

Although a position-classification plan may be greeted as "red tape and bureaucracy" by the general public and municipal employees alike, it performs many useful functions. Classification raises employee morale by standardizing job titles. Employees in the public works department who are referred to on the payroll as "bookkeepers" are not happy if persons doing the same job in the department of water supply are called "accountants." Morale drops if the mayor lists his favorite stenographer as an "office manager." Classification of positions prevents this sort of thing.

Classification permits the use of a uniform pay plan so that all persons doing approximately the same work receive the same pay. In an earlier day, the pay of employees depended largely upon the ability of the department head as a lobbyist before the mayor, the controller, or the council. Even today, of course, much pressure may be brought to bear against standardization of salaries, and city councils may refuse to base salaries upon the position classifications established by the personnel agency. Established procedure, however, calls for the coordination of classifications and salary scales.

If salaries are standardized, classification permits the use of a system of periodic pay raises. These may be based on the employee's increased value and faithful service over a period of time, or on his receiving additional training. Often, however, they are based almost purely on the length of employment. Since the opportunities for promotion are necessarily limited, it is important to the morale of employees that they may be advanced in pay up to a maximum limit while continuing to perform the same type of duties. Such a policy may be systematically incorporated into a classification plan.

Classification allows for the transfer of employees among departments on the basis of their job descriptions. It simplifies recruitment, since a single standard examination may be given for a class, even though many positions in that class are to be filled.[6]

Training for the Municipal Service. Increasingly, public servants are receiving formal training for their jobs, both before and after entry into service. Some municipal positions require, as they always have, professional training. This is true of attorneys, accountants, and physicians, for example, although these persons are often untrained in the specialized aspects of their professions that deal with the public service.

For many routine positions only a general high-school education is necessary, or perhaps a business-school course. Training for these jobs involves no special difficulties. Many universities today offer general

---

[6] Ismar Baruch, *Position-classification in the Public Service* (Civil Service Assembly, Chicago, 1942), is a standard reference.

programs of training as preparation for administrative positions such as those of city manager, finance officer, and personnel officer. Several schools now offer courses in police administration, health administration, and other special technical-professional areas.

Many positions in municipal government require, or are aided by, in-service training programs. A clerk-typist or an elevator operator does the same job in public as in private employment. On the other hand, police and fire departments, especially, have found it desirable to establish training academies. There are few opportunities to learn the technical aspects of these jobs in preservice training or in private employment.

Many state leagues of municipalities have sponsored training programs for various jobs, and they often provide technical manuals or booklets. The International City Managers' Association and other professional organizations offer correspondence courses for training in various fields. Quite a few universities offer professional in-service training courses for policemen, firemen, public health workers, and other municipal employees.

Types of Examinations. Unlike the civil service examinations in most other countries, those in the United States tend to be specific, technical, and designed to test a person only for one single position. The practice of the national government in this regard has been copied by most of the cities and states. In recent years, however, there has been somewhat of a change in the type of examination used. Newer ones follow some of the elements of the British system and some taken from American business practices. Education is given more importance. So is the record of previous employment. Intelligence tests and adaptability or aptitude tests are used to a greater extent, as are personal interviews to determine personality traits.

The object of the new type of testing, of course, is to select persons who may be able to improve their job status over time—who will be able to move up into higher positions of responsibility. It is also designed to secure persons with enough flexibility so that they may switch from one job to another without too much inconvenience. The opportunity for promotion through the ranks is an important one for morale in the public service.

The Requirement of Local Residence. Except for teachers and city managers, it is a common rule established by state law, the city charter, or the civil service commission that a city employee be a resident of the city—and often for a specified length of time, such as one year, before employment. This rule is an anomaly in a contemporary personnel system. It is based upon a *spoils*, rather than a *merit*, concept. It is a vestige of Jacksonian thinking, that government jobs should be reserved for home-town persons. A merit system assumes that employees are chosen for demonstrated competence. Clearly if that is the true criterion, then it matters not where the person may live or how long he has lived there. A residence requirement sometimes works a hardship upon the city administration by requiring the employment of a mediocre person when a superior one may live a few miles away outside the city limits. This problem may be especially acute in metropolitan areas with their numerous independent suburbs. Out of necessity, cities are increasingly waiving residence requirements in recruiting persons for positions demanding technical and administrative training and experience.

The Method of Dismissal. Much controversy may appear from time to time in local newspapers over the discharge of a particular municipal employee. The public's attitude concerning these widely publicized dismissals is often one of ambivalence. Nearly everyone today works for someone else—has a supervisory superior. Through the process of identification, therefore, the individual is likely to have an initial reaction of sympathy for someone who is dismissed from his job. ("After all, the same thing might have happened to me!") But on the other hand, the lay citizen is likely to complain that—according to hearsay—no one is ever dismissed from a government job, that an incompetent may be transferred, or retired, or given nothing to do, but that he is never dismissed. Some will add that the law does not permit dismissal once the status of civil service tenure is given.

This ambivalence has its counterpart among public administrators in the conflict over the "open back door" versus the "closed back door" methods of dismissal from the service. Should a supervisor have the authority to discharge an unwanted employee summarily? Or should he have to serve a notice and accord a hearing before removal, and then discharge the employee only for "cause" as described in the law? And should the decision be left to the department head, or should it be made by the civil service commission? [7]

In the early days of merit practice, it was believed that department heads—political appointees—would dismiss employees of the "wrong" political faith if there were no safeguards, and so the back door was often closed. This was essentially a negative view of administration, of course. Today the emphasis is upon executive responsibility. This means that department heads must be given wide latitude of discretionary power in running their departments so that they may show they can produce worthwhile results. If they fail, or if they abuse the responsibility, they must be prepared to answer for it.

Yet many city charters provide that civil service employees may be

---

[7] On the related question of whether the supervisor or the civil service commission is to control promotions, see Chester B. Earle and Valerie A. Earle, *The Promotion of Lem Merrill* (University of Alabama Press, University, Ala., 1953).

discharged only for cause, and give the employee the right to appeal the decision to the independent civil service commission, which may order his reinstatement. The results have not been an aid to effective administration, as a rule. Independent civil service commissions often order the employee reinstated if they think that dismissal is too severe a penalty for the charges made against him. Sometimes the employee engages a skillful attorney to represent him at the hearings before the commission, and his attorney succeeds in turning the hearings into a trial of the head of the department, instead of an appraisal of the charges against the employee. After such an experience, the department head may decide that it is better to put up with employees who are incompetent, lazy, and even insubordinate rather than to go through the ordeal required to discharge them.

On the other hand, municipal civil service employees expect to be accorded reasonable protection against arbitrary dismissal, or discharge for political reasons. This can be provided in one of several ways. The personnel director is sometimes given, as one of his duties, the investigation of any cases involving suspension or discharge of employees, which will have a restraining influence on arbitrary actions by department heads. Similarly, in cities where the personnel board is advisory rather than administrative, it may be authorized to investigate dismissals and to make recommendations to the manager or the mayor, who exercises final decision. This arrangement provides safeguards against abuse, without the problems that may result from an independent review by a civil service commission with power to reinstate the employee.

THE PUBLIC ATTITUDE

Community Status and Municipal Employment. The Jacksonian frontiersman taught us to be skeptical of those who would "feed at the public trough." The lesson was taught so well that Americans are habitually infected with the notion that public employees are loafers, far less efficient than those in private employment. Some citizens believe that the *nature* of public employment itself makes people lazy and inefficient.

While students and practitioners of municipal government are in virtually universal agreement that this viewpoint is completely false, it is difficult to present conclusive evidence to that effect because there is no certain basis for comparing public and private employment. In the field of private endeavor, the test of profit exists. Cities, however, operate few services that are expected to be revenue-producing. Even when they do—such as in public transportation—the service is often one in which profit opportunities are too doubtful for most businessmen to be interested. The effectiveness of most city services—its recreation, welfare, highways, fire fighting, and other functions—can be given only a subjective evaluation. Where one person may think the city recreation program, for example, is inefficient and a waste of the taxpayers' money, another may think it excellent. There is no clear standard of measurement, and the recreation program certainly cannot be compared in efficiency with the method by which some local manufacturer makes motorboats.

Analogies with Private Business. There is a tendency in the United States to deify "business efficiency." In the light of the rapid development of industrialization and the commensurate rise in the standard of living that have taken place in this country since the War between the States, it is understandable that the businessman and his methods should be greatly admired. But we should guard against exaggeration.

It is well to remember that a great deal of business is conducted today by large corporations, and that these corporations are operated for the most part by self-perpetuating bureaucracies. These bureaucracies enjoy the same advantages and suffer the same disadvantages, for the most part, as do public bureaucracies.

Like their sisters in the city hall, clerk-typists in private industry will start putting on their coats fifteen minutes before quitting time if the supervisor permits it. And he often does. The public employee has no monopoly on morning and afternoon coffee breaks. In many cities today, the stenographers would quit if a private company tried to stop this type of "loafing." Magazines are not read during working hours in the street commissioner's office alone. Minor forms of bribery—tickets to next Saturday's football game, a turkey at Christmas—are not limited to councilmanic recipients: they are standard operating procedure in business. Bureaucratic maneuvering for advantage and struggles for power exist in the city hall, in the corporation offices, and wherever else bureaucracies exist.

Obscure, ritualistic, and technical language—gobbledygook—exists in business and in government. Red tape—a necessary means of maintaining and identifying responsibility in a large, impersonal organization—exists in big business as well as big government. The mimeograph machine, the typewriter, and the ream of paper are everywhere today. Almost everyone, when he thinks about it, recalls incidents of excessive delays and excessive filling out of forms in connection with a business matter involving a private company, especially a large company.

Private endeavor may be more efficient than public endeavor. We do not know. We do know that they have much in common. We do know that each is dependent upon professional, technical specialists in a day of mechanization and specialization.

MUNICIPAL EMPLOYMENT AND ORGANIZED LABOR

At least some employees in all of the largest cities in the United States are members of labor unions. The smaller the city, the less likely the employees are to be organized, but nearly one-half of the cities in the 10,000 to 25,000 class have employees belonging to national unions (see Table 14-1).

The AFL-CIO has two unions for municipal employees, the American Federation of State, County and Municipal Employees (AFSCME) and the International Association of Fire Fighters (IAFF). In addition, many city employees, such as truck drivers, belong to their own craft unions just as do persons in private industry plying the same trade. The United Public Workers of America (UPWA) is an independent union. There are also many local, unaffiliated unions. Some of them are "company unions," which are illegal under the National Labor Relations Act, but the provisions of that act do not apply to municipal corporations.

Several large cities, chiefly in the South, do not encourage organization of employees. Dallas employees, in 1955, were told that they would

TABLE 14-1. ORGANIZATIONS OF LOCAL EMPLOYEES IN CITIES
OVER 10,000

Population group	No. of cities reporting	Cities with employees in one or more national unions	
		No.	Per cent
Cities over 500,000......	17	17	100.0
250,000 to 500,000........	23	23	100.0
100,000 to 250,000.......	59	55	93.2
50,000 to 100,000........	116	93	80.1
25,000 to 50,000 *.......	176	175	99.4
10,000 to 25,000........	553	244	44.1
All cities over 10,000...	944	607	61.1

* Note the sharp decline in unionization in cities of under 25,000. This corresponds to the lesser importance of organized labor generally in these cities.

SOURCE: *Municipal Year Book, 1960* (International City Managers' Association, Chicago, 1960), p. 168.

be dismissed if they joined a union.[8] This policy was later modified, however, and unionization developed rapidly in the 1950s, even in the South.

Should Municipal Employees Be Unionized? In 1960, the city of New York had 238,978 employees; Chicago, 37,408; and Richmond, Providence, and El Paso over 5,000 each. Nearly all city employees have relatives and friends. Taken together, they constitute quite a pressure group and voting bloc. Fear of political power like this is certain to influence a city council when it determines wages and conditions of labor.

Many people argue that such political power, plus civil service protection, gives public servants adequate security. They hold that if unionization is added to the employees' weapons, they have a bargaining position that is disproportionate in comparison with employees in private business.

Certainly there is some merit to these arguments. In many cities, and especially in large cities, municipal employees with jobs comparable to those in private business sometimes receive a salary above the going market price. A New York study has indicated that in that city, salaries of public workers lag behind in times of inflation, but forge ahead in times of depression.[9] In 1960, Chicago and Philadelphia employees worked a 37½-hour week. A work week of less than 40 hours is not uncommon even in cities of less than 50,000. New Orleans employees received 18 days paid vacation in 1960; those in St. Louis received 15, and dozens of medium- and small-sized cities allowed over 10 days. Sick-leave days may accumulate to 300 in Buffalo and St. Paul. Pension plans are often generous.

While laborers, clerk-typists, draftsmen, and junior accountants may receive somewhat more than the market price for their services, this is often not the case with members of the semimilitary departments of the municipality, the policemen and firemen. Of course, there is no direct means of measuring the social value of a policeman or fireman, and he has few counterparts in private employment. Judging, however, by the quality of recruits and the success, or lack of it, that cities have in filling their quotas for these jobs, one finds that the salaries are not attracting men of sufficient ability in sufficient numbers. Quite a few cities have found it necessary in the postwar years to reduce physical and intelligence requirements in an attempt to get enough men on the force. Quality has been sacrificed.

[8] Associated Press dispatch, Aug. 30, 1955.

[9] Mayor's Committee on Management Survey, *Modern Management for the City of New York* (Bureau of the Budget, City of New York, 1953), vol. 1, pp. 69–73. For the bureaucracy in politics, see Wallace S. Sayre and Herbert Kaufman, *Governing New York City* (Russell Sage Foundation, New York, 1960), chap. 11.

The semimilitary services are barred from striking by one rule or another. This, plus the fact that the public will tolerate less "labor agitation" from them, has sometimes resulted in their salaries falling behind the trend of other employees. On the other hand, they often enjoy a pension plan that is more liberal than that of the other municipal employees. Firemen are commonly on duty for many hours consecutively, after which they have a long period off duty. In many cities, therefore, firemen take outside employment on their off days. Some policemen do too, although this is specifically prohibited in some cities because it might interfere with the policeman's duty to enforce the law impartially and for other reasons.

Labor unions are undoubtedly here to stay in cities, as in private industry. But public employee unions are subject to the same weaknesses as are all unions. They may be controlled by a small bureaucracy rather than by the general membership. Ambitious men struggle for their control. Unions may emphasize seniority and tenure rather than initiative and efficient management. They may resist mechanical improvements that they regard as speed-ups or that cause technological unemployment.

Some writers have argued—from a theoretical standpoint—that there should be no organizations of municipal employees because "the civil service commission is their union." But to the rank-and-file worker, the civil service commission and its executive secretary or the personnel director are the *employer*—and hence the opposition when it comes to bargaining. The commission cannot serve simultaneously as employer and as employee representative. At least it cannot do so in the mind of the employee.

Collective Bargaining. When it comes to differences of opinion between employees and supervisors, the employees are likely to demand collective protection. Many of their complaints lie outside the provisions of civil service law. William S. Carpenter has made the point that "few genuine grievances arise as a result of violations of civil service laws and regulations." [10] Other machinery is needed—the same machinery that is used to settle these grievances in private employment. To a great many employees, the labor union is a basic part of that machinery. [11]

Negotiations between labor unions and private management normally reach their consummation in a formal written contract. To this extent, practice there varies from that in the field of public employment, for in the case of the latter, formal written contracts are very exceptional. The

[10] Carpenter, *op. cit.*, p. 125. On grievance machinery, see R. B. Posey, "Handling City Employee Grievances," *Public Management*, vol. 35 (March, 1953), pp. 54–58.
[11] British local government settles disputes with its civil servants through the use of the Whitley Councils. See C. J. Schneider, "The Revival of Whitleyism in British Local Government," *Public Administration Review*, vol. 13 (Spring, 1953), pp. 97–105.

end result of negotiations is almost always either a gentleman's agreement or a unilateral statement of intended policy on the part of the civil service commission or the city council.

The Cincinnati Common Council, for example, passed a resolution in 1951 resolving "that it shall be the policy of the council of the city of Cincinnati through the City Manager and his designated assistants, to bargain collectively with city employees, their Unions, or other authorized representatives, on all matters pertaining to wages and working conditions before any final determination is made by City Council."

It is an established rule of law that a legislative body cannot contract away its powers and that it cannot bind future legislative bodies. Because of this, nearly all courts have held that, in the absence of express enabling law, a contract binding the city to certain wages, hours, and conditions of labor for a certain period of time is illegal and void.[12] Even given legislative permission, such agreements may be held to violate the state constitution. The gentleman's agreement or the statement of policy has usually served as a substitute. There is, however, some trend toward the increased use of contracts.[13]

An extensive study by Louis L. Friedland concludes that "the trend in personnel relations is away from unilateral dealings on the part of management with its employees."[14] He feels that "negotiated agreements whether formal or informal do not develop abstract rights destructive of management prerogatives"; and that "the end product is to provide employee associations a constructive place in the continuous improvement of the public service. The public and its government officials must establish democratic machinery for the adjustment of differences and provide for the synthesis of executive leadership and employee participation in public personnel administration."

The Right to Strike. The constitutions of some public employee unions contain a clause denying the strike as a weapon. State laws sometimes prohibit public employees from striking, as do city ordinances. A few judges have even found a similar prohibition in the common law. Policemen, firemen, employees of public hospitals, and others who perform services closely connected with the public health and safety are often prohibited from striking. Certainly the public itself is intolerant of strikes in these areas.

But strikes occur anyway. They are the one really powerful weapon of organized labor, and under certain conditions strikes will occur even in

---

[12] See C. S. Rhyne, *Labor Unions and Municipal Employee Law* (National Institute of Municipal Law Officers, Washington, 1946), which cites leading cases.

[13] A list and illustrations of various types of policy statements and agreements will be found in Louis L. Friedland, "The Role of Collective Bargaining in the Public Service," *Papers of the Michigan Academy of Science, Arts and Letters* (1953).

[14] *Ibid.*

the face of a law to the contrary. Even policemen and firemen will on occasion become frustrated or desperate enough to strike. Laws will not prevent strikes where the employees consider themselves seriously wronged.[15]

Those who hold that no public employee should be allowed to strike make use of several arguments. The principal ones are two. First of all, it is said that public service is so closely connected with the health and welfare of society that it is dangerous to permit strikes. Secondly, it is said that the government is the people, that a strike against "the government" is therefore a strike against oneself, that governmental employment is therefore substantially different in character from private employment and that a strike against the government is a disloyal act.

The Need for Equality with Private Employees. Public service is certainly closely allied with the health and safety of society. So are coal mining, the operation of the railroads, and many other private activities. Yet strikes occur in these fields. A strike is never a pretty thing. It is nearly always a last resort. Where the weapon does not exist and where no substitute is provided for it, employee caliber is likely to deteriorate. A minority of scholars have argued, therefore, that even policemen and firemen should have the nominal right to strike. These people have a sense of responsibility and of loyalty to the city—otherwise they would not readily go into these services. The threat of a strike, if used responsibly, may be a necessary and permissible weapon. And a threat is meaningless unless it is an actual possibility.

Public employees do not strike because they are seditious. They strike because they want an additional 10 cents an hour in pay. It may be sound legally to say that striking public employees are striking against themselves or the state. It is unsound psychologically. The bus driver or city-hall janitor has no such thought in mind. He is striking against the boss—just as is his fellow worker in private employment. His last thought is to destroy the government, for that would destroy his job as well as his way of life.

If it is deemed to be wise public policy to forbid strikes, the laws must be carefully drawn to avoid gross inequities. Michigan law, for example, permits Dearborn bus drivers to strike, but prohibits Detroit bus drivers from doing so. Each performs the same service for society. But the one system is privately owned, the other publicly.[16]

---

[15] See R. B. Posey, "Analysis of City Employee Strikes," *Public Management,* vol. 34 (June, 1952), pp. 122–127.

[16] On strikes and the public service, see three articles debating the issue in the *National Municipal Review,* vol. 30 (September, 1941), pp. 515–528; S. D. Spero, *Government as Employer* (Remsen Press, New York, 1948); David Ziskind, *One Thousand Strikes of Government Employees* (Columbia University Press, New York, 1940).

PAY SCALES AND POLITICS

Salaries in Public Employment. The total monthly payroll for municipal employees in October, 1959, was $548 million. This equalled roughly 45 per cent of municipal budgets. Obviously wage and salary levels are major factors in determining government costs.

The lesser-skilled and unskilled employees in large cities receive pay that tends to run somewhat above the average for comparable private employment. In smaller cities, pay is likely to be no better or less than private employment, although there is considerable variation. The higher pay in larger cities probably reflects in part the generally higher cost of living in those areas. It also reflects to some extent the trend toward the organization of public employees into trade unions and employee associations for collective bargaining, and the greater power of organized labor in large-city politics generally. Whether trade unions exist or not, however, the sheer numbers of governmental employees, their families, relatives, and friends are enough to exert considerable pressure upon councils to provide pay scales at a high level.

If salaries at the lower levels tend to be fairly good, pay for top government technicians and administrators is usually below the average paid similar employees in private industry. There is no labor union to look after the salary needs of the city attorney or the chief engineer at the city power station. Furthermore, persons in positions like these have, because of fewer numbers, far less political influence in getting pay increases.

When the rank-and-file workers in the mass transit or public works departments of a city ask for a raise, councilmen will consider the possible repercussions in the next election if they are refused. No such fears need sway the councilmen when it is suggested that $7,000 is an inadequate salary for the city attorney in a city of 150,000 people. Quite to the contrary, the Jacksonian tradition lends public support in opposition to an increase. Since the average citizen is making less than the present salary of the attorney, psychologically he is unsympathetic to arguments for an increase. A suggestion of $10,000 or $11,000 as being a necessary salary to get an able man will be greeted with jeers, for even today that is an income beyond the aspirations of the average citizen. Councilmen and other legislators can thus make friends by refusing a raise to chief administrators and technicians. In the years after World War II, however, there has been a trend toward paying salaries at the higher levels that are equal to those on private payrolls. Only the very top positions have not been included in this trend. (See Figure 14-1.)

The Escalator Clause. In the sharp inflationary period following World War II, several labor unions effected contracts with management calling for a sliding pay scale to be related to the cost-of-living index of the Bu-

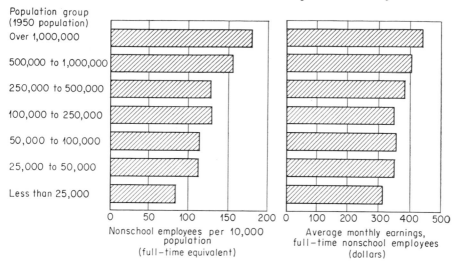

Figure 14-1. SOURCE: *Municipal Year Book, 1960* (International City Managers' Association, Chicago, 1960), p. 162.

reau of Labor Statistics. Under these plans, an increase of a certain amount in the index would mean an additional cent an hour in pay, and an equivalent decrease would mean a reduction in pay. The plan proved popular in a period of seemingly endless inflation.

In the early 1920s, St. Paul made use of the escalator clause for its own employees, and an increasing number of cities have adopted it recently. Needless to say, its popularity will decline in periods of declining prices.

Retirement System. As a part of the total remuneration for public employment, municipal retirement systems are commonly provided. Nearly all cities of over 10,000 and many smaller municipalities provide old-age insurance for all of their employees. Many cities operate their own local systems, often with the police and fire services under a separate plan, but about one-half of them are members of state-administered systems. Smaller cities, in particular, are aided in maintaining solvency by being banded together with other cities in a state system. Since 1951 there has been a sharp trend toward the covering of municipal employees in the Federal old-age and survivor's insurance program ("social security"). Amendments to the Social Security Act in 1954 aided in bringing more local governments into the Federal program, which often provides more liberal benefits than do local systems.

Most retirement systems are "contributing" plans, that is, both the city and the employee contribute part of the cost. Many systems are not on an actuarial basis and are hence financially unsound, although this is not true of an increasing number of them. Retirement boards, often with employee representation on them, commonly administer the investment of the funds that accumulate as the system develops. Retirement plans also provide for payments to persons who are permanently disabled before retirement, for payment to survivors if the employee dies before retirement, and for the return of funds invested in the system by the employee who is separated from the service before retirement.

Municipal retirement plans of today are merely a parallel to the general pattern of old-age-security plans that have developed throughout private enterprise in recent decades. It is likely that they will become virtually universal phenomena for cities of all sizes in the near future. Smaller cities will have their employees covered in state or Federal systems.

Concluding Statement. In recent decades, Americans have expected more and more services from city government. As a result of this, the public employee has perforce become a technical specialist, skilled in his task. In order to obtain such persons for the public service, the elaborate art of modern personnel administration and management has been applied to our cities. The day has long since passed when city employment could serve as a reward for faithful political effort.

To those who work for the city, their positions are not far different from similar positions in private employment. As a result, the same problems of labor-management relations arise in the city hall and in the offices of the business corporation.

The labor union is a basic institution in American life today, and public employees usually desire to share in its benefits. The principle of unionism does not conflict with that of the merit system. This is true even of the union shop under which employees might be *required* to join a union after employment. The union sometimes is, in fact, the only collective method of settling employee-employer disputes.

There may be some areas of union interest that conflict with the merit system. A strict emphasis upon seniority, often a union goal, is not in harmony with the principle. The closed shop is not permitted in public employment, since it would require one to be a union member *before* employment, and this would enable the union to supplant the personnel director or commission. In general, however, city governments must learn to live with the labor union. While the two will have occasional conflicts, they can also work together toward the common goal of a better personnel system and a more satisfied group of employees.[17]

[17] On the general subject of municipal personnel practices, see the many publications of the Public Personnel Association dealing with specific practical problems of personnel administration. See also *Municipal Personnel Administration* (5th ed.; International City Managers' Association, Chicago, 1950); R. L. Thorndike, *Personnel Selection Test and Measurement Techniques* (John Wiley & Sons, New York, 1949); C. S. Rhyne, *Labor Unions and Municipal Employee Law* (National Institute of Municipal Law Officers, Washington, 1946). The *Municipal Year Book* annually reports new personnel developments, prevailing wages, hours, and conditions of labor, and other information. It also contains a good bibliography.

Chapter 15

REVENUES AND EXPENDITURES

Municipal expenditures have expanded enormously in the last three generations. In the period following World War II, they have increased with almost every fiscal year. In 1958, for example, city revenues, expenditures, indebtedness, and financial holdings all reached new highs.[1]

Where Does the Money Go? In a period of rising costs and increasing urban populations, the demands for local government services have been regularly increasing. At the same time, however, revenue sources have remained relatively unchanged. The result is that local-government debt continues each year to reach all-time highs. In 1958, it stood at 20.3 billion dollars (see Figure 15-1, page 350).

A sharp expansion of services and of their costs cannot be met without a considerable amount of effort. Part of the cost has been offset by a great increase in the standard of living and consequent ability to pay. But the development has also helped to incite a desperate search for new revenue sources. The property tax remains the most important local tax, but local governments have sought to broaden their tax bases, looking to sales, excise, and income taxes.

Why Taxes? The typical citizen probably has little understanding of the relationships that exist between government revenues and expenditures. The traditional practice of politicians is one of promising to perform more services in a better fashion and at lower cost than can or will the opposition. This behavior has probably helped preserve the citizen's habit of making no association between service levels and costs. Each person, of course, has some knowledge about taxes. Every homeowner understands his property tax; at least he is able to determine how much he must pay, and he is likely to know whether it is more or less than the preceding year. The sales tax is known to most people because of the general practice of adding it to the marked price of goods in making a sale. The income tax cannot escape the attention of the employed person in any jurisdiction which levies it, especially since most states do not use the withholding system but require payment in one or two install-

[1] *Municipal Year Book, 1960* (International City Managers' Association, Chicago, 1960), p. 212.

YOUR GOVERNMENT DOLLAR

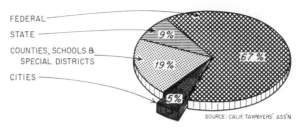

FEDERAL
STATE
COUNTIES, SCHOOLS &
    SPECIAL DISTRICTS
CITIES

9%
19%
67%
5%

SOURCE: CALIF. TAXPAYERS' ASS'N

Figure 15-1.

ments—each of which produces anguish on the part of the citizen. (Cities levying a payroll tax do use the withholding method.) Yet the economic merits of particular taxes are unknown to the typical citizen. He knows little more about the services that his taxes buy (except that he may associate the property tax with schools), and he certainly does not attempt to find his way through a wonderland of double taxation, grants-in-aid, shared taxes, dedicated funds, joint financing, and service charges.

It is easy for the citizen to agree with the politician or commentator who tells him that taxes are too high, since he has no criterion against which to measure them. He balks from time to time when major tax increases are submitted to him on referendum, and his reluctance to pay taxes which he does not associate with services has encouraged the extensive use in America of dedicated funds, so that a new or increased tax is pledged to a specific purpose. This helps the citizen understand why it is being asked for and helps persuade him to vote for it. Thus, an additional cent on the gasoline tax is pledged for road building; extra millage on the property tax may be exclusively for a library; most of the state sales tax may be pledged for grants to aid school operations. The use of dedicated funds has long been denounced by specialists in financial administration because of the rigidity it produces in the system. It leaves less room for the executive or legislative branches to make adjustments for changing demands. But the practice undoubtedly makes new taxes or service charges more palatable to the typical citizen.

EXPENDITURE PATTERNS

New functions of government have been added, and there have been some basic changes in the pattern of municipal expenditures over the years since the beginning of the century.[2] Among them are these:

[2] See U.S. Bureau of the Census, *Historical Statistics on State and Local Government Finances* (1955).

1. New functions of government have appeared and have begun to challenge the old functions for importance. Some that might be mentioned include urban redevelopment, public housing, smoke abatement, airports, and parking lots.

2. Old functions have been greatly expanded and changed in concept. This applies to recreation, highways, health, and welfare programs.

3. State governments have assumed an increasingly important role at the state-local levels. In 1902, state expenditures accounted for only 12 per cent of total state-local expenditures. By the late 1950s, they accounted for over 35 per cent of the total. The states have enormously expanded the number, and increased the quality, of their direct services to the public in the present century.

4. The states have gradually been becoming more and more collection agencies for local governments. In the late 1950s, about two-thirds of state government education expenditures were actually in the form of payments to local governments. The same disposition was made of about 20 per cent of state highway fund expenditures and over 40 per cent of state welfare expenditures.[3] Shared taxes and grants-in-aid were also important parts of other state budget items. This pattern represents, in part, the result of legislative recognition of the need for additional revenues at the local level combined with an unwillingness to delegate adequate taxing powers to local governments. So the states collect the money and then disburse it to their local governments.

5. State and local expenditures have represented an increasingly large proportion of society's earnings, as measured by the gross national product (GNP). This increase has not been enormous, but it has been significant. In the 1920s, expenditures ran around 8 per cent of the GNP; in the late 1950s, they had increased to 11 per cent. (See Figure 15-2.)

Reasonable Expenditure Levels. The question often arises: What are reasonable expenditure levels for state and local governments? The citizen is bombarded with propaganda, much of it conflicting in nature, which tells him of the unfinished business of government in providing highways, health programs, recreation for increasing leisure time, and so forth, but also of increasing debt burdens, of the need for increased taxes if current service levels are to be maintained, and of "all-encroaching government." The citizen wonders whether a new or increased tax is fair or whether he is being taken advantage of.

The question the citizen raises cannot easily be answered. Essentially, expenditure levels are culturally determined. In the 1920s, Americans would not permit elaborate welfare or unemployment-compensation programs, to say nothing of public housing or limited-access highways. But

[3] *The Financial Challenge to the States* (Tax Foundation, Inc., New York, 1958), p. 12.

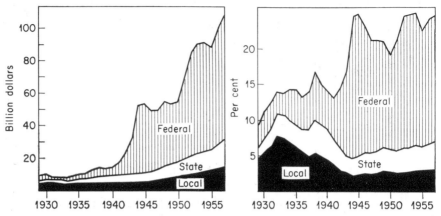

Figure 15-2. SOURCE: A. E. Lutz, "Talk about Taxes," *Public Policy* (New York State College of Agriculture, Ithaca, N.Y., 1960), p. 1.

since the Great Depression, Americans have come to expect government to provide a measure of security that is not otherwise available in an interdependent society, and they trust government further and are now willing to allow it to experiment with new programs where needs are felt to exist.

The relative ease with which money can be raised is also important in determining expenditure levels. Congress agrees more readily than a state legislature to add a new grant-in-aid program because it is relatively easy for Congress to raise the additional billions. A city or state that cannot increase services without also raising taxes or adding new taxes will be very slow to do so and will demand impressive proof before acting. But if a local unit of government is relatively prosperous, it is also likely to be relatively generous in expanding its budget. Services not now performed are often wanted; the problem comes in making the marginal sacrifice necessary in order to pay them.

Item: A study of municipal costs and tax rates has indicated that local expenditures vary according to the income of local residents. In other words, as income of residents increased, the marginal sacrifice involved in meeting higher budgets was less and people did not resist as much as they did in lower-income communities.[4]

Item: Because citizens want more governmental services than they are willing to afford and because they do not clearly associate tax levels

[4] Walter Isard and Robert Coughlin, *Municipal Costs and Revenues Resulting from Community Growth* (Chandler-Davis Publishing Co., Wellesley, Mass., 1957). See also Stanley Scott and E. L. Feder, *Factors Associated with Variations in Municipal Expenditure Levels* (Institute of Public Administration, University of California, Berkeley, Calif., 1957).

with specific services, governments tend to seize all available revenue possibilities and nearly always spend all funds available.

Item: Conservatives—individuals or groups who want government expenditures kept to a lower portion of gross national product than do most of the people—try to keep governments from making maximum use of their taxing and spending powers. They seek to restrict spending, not so much through counterpressures upon governing bodies (though that is an important technique for them) as through the adoption of restrictive constitutional and charter provisions. Once nestled in this protective armor, restrictions cannot usually be dislodged except by an extraordinary-majority vote or a complicated procedure or both. The fact that most state constitutions have such restrictions built into them, commonly by an accumulation of amendments, makes the conservative an opponent of constitutional revision. Thus, the Citizens Public Expenditure Survey of New York opposed a 1957 proposal for a constitutional convention in that state, pointing out that "had the convention proposition been approved . . . there would have been many pressures upon the delegates to enlarge government functions and open the door to increased spending on both state and local levels." [5]

REVENUE FOR PRESENT-DAY CITIES

All taxes are ultimately derived from either of two sources: property or income. Taxes are theoretically based upon some criterion of *ability to pay,* although the criteria used in various periods of history have not been the same, and a tax created in one period and logical and equitable at that time may live on into another time when its justification becomes less apparent. In some instances, payments to the government are based upon a *benefit theory* rather than on ability to pay, but such payments are more in the nature of service charges than taxes. The benefit theory is applied, for example, in cases of special assessments for street, sidewalk, street lighting, and similar improvements. It is also applied in determining water and light charges and, to a degree, in motor-vehicle license fees.

State Limits on Taxing and Spending. Cities have only those powers of taxation which are granted to them by the state. The only exceptions to this rule are to be found in a few home rule states, notably California and Wisconsin, where court interpretations of the constitutional home rule clause have given cities a general grant of powers to levy taxes. (Even in Wisconsin a general act limiting municipal taxing powers in particular areas at the discretion of the legislature is valid.) States, either

[5] *New York State Taxpayer,* vol. 18 (November, 1957), p. 1.

TABLE 15-1. SUMMARY OF CITY FINANCES: 1958

Item	Amount (in millions) 1958	Per cent change 1957–1958
Revenue and borrowing:		
Total revenue and borrowing...............	$15,454	4.6
Total borrowing.........................	2,622	−3.9
Total revenue.........................	12,832	6.5
General revenue, total.................	9,895	6.6
Taxes, total........................	6,242	5.7
Property........................	4,570	6.4
Sales and gross receipts............	972	4.1
Other........................	700	3.6
Intergovernmental revenue..............	1,953	11.2
Charges and miscellaneous..............	1,700	4.9
Utility revenue........................	2,525	6.2
Liquor stores revenue...................	61	1.7
Insurance-trust revenue.................	352	9.0
Expenditure and debt redemption:		
Total expenditure and debt redemption.....	15,029	6.9
Total debt redemption...................	1,254	3.3
Total expenditure by character and object..	13,775	7.3
Direct expenditure.....................	13,643	8.6
Current operation...................	8,763	8.2
Capital outlay......................	3,571	9.8
Assistance and subsidies..............	368	7.0
Interest on debt....................	558	8.1
Insurance, benefits and repayments.....	383	8.8
Intergovernmental expenditure..........	132	−51.8
Total expenditure by function.............	13,775	7.3
General expenditure....................	10,442	7.7
Police.............................	1,130	8.5
Fire...............................	774	9.2
Highways...........................	1,455	9.6
Sanitation..........................	1,248	8.0
Public welfare.......................	530	6.9
Education...........................	1,636	11.0
Libraries...........................	158	9.0
Health and hospitals.................	713	1.4
Recreation..........................	501	9.2
Housing and redevelopment...........	323	30.8
Nonhighway transportation...........	288	20.0
General control.....................	554	8.2
Public buildings.....................	161	2.5
Interest on general debt..............	334	8.1
Other..............................	637	−10.9
Utility expenditure......................	2,898	5.5
Liquor-stores expenditure..............	52	4.0
Insurance-trust expenditure............	383	8.8

SOURCE: *Municipal Year Book, 1960* (International City Managers' Association, Chicago, 1960), p. 214.

through the constitution or through statutes, will normally place limitations upon the taxing power of cities. The law usually states a maximum tax rate in terms of so many dollars per capita, or allows an increase of only a certain small percentage over the previous year's rate, or permits the city to levy a tax of only a certain percentage of the assessed value of the taxable property within the city. The last restriction is by far the most common. States also often impose conditions and regulations on the administration of municipal finances.[6]

Cities are limited in other ways, too. As a result of the famous case of *McCulloch v. Maryland,* Federal properties within the city are not taxable. The state may exempt many other categories, such as private educational and religious properties. Beginning in the days of the Great Depression, a large number of states have adopted "homestead exemption" laws, which exclude part or even all of the value of owner-occupied homes from the general property tax.

Limitations on Subjects of Taxation. The subjects that may be taxed by the municipality are normally strictly controlled by the state. Nearly all of the states tell their cities which taxes they may levy, for what period of time they may be levied, and under what conditions. A city that finds its property tax consistently inadequate may not, for example, decide to levy a payroll or a sales tax. The state must first authorize such a levy on a new subject.

Only a few states have been willing to permit cities to choose from a wide variety of tax sources by adopting broad enabling acts. California and Wisconsin cities have wide taxing powers as a result of judicial interpretation of constitutional home rule clauses. Pennsylvania and New York have given their cities broad taxing powers through legislation.

Limitations on Borrowing Power. In addition to limitations upon taxation, the state normally also seeks to protect the public credit by limiting the *borrowing* powers of cities. Such a limitation may be written into the city charter or into state law or the constitution. The limit is usually expressed in terms of a percentage of the assessed value of the taxable property within the city, but it may also be a specific number of dollars, or the debt may be limited to a figure equal to the annual tax revenue of the city.[7]

These debt limits may be unrealistic and bear no necessary relationship to the wants of the city. The artificial limitations are, therefore, sometimes circumvented. Many techniques have been devised for doing this. For example, bonds issued for certain purposes, especially public

[6] Control over spending is described in T. E. McMillan, Jr., *State Supervision of Municipal Finance* (Institute of Public Affairs, University of Texas, Austin, Tex., 1953). See also chap. 12 above.

[7] McMillan, *op. cit.*, appendix E.

utilities, may not be included under the limitation if they may theoretically be retired through revenue from the proposed project. Bonds to build a stadium, an auditorium, or a toll bridge might be paid out of revenues, and hence the courts or the legislature will sometimes exempt them from the limitation. In some states, the voters (in a few states, the property-tax payers) of a city may vote to raise the debt limit.

If either the debt or the tax limit is expressed in terms of a percentage of the assessed evaluation, the city can nearly always—and frequently does—resort to raising the assessed value of property in order to raise both the debt and tax limits. In the days before the Great Depression, when many states depended heavily upon the general property tax, a serious inequity resulted when large cities, encountering increasing costs, had to assess property at or above full value in order to get around debt and tax limits. Suburbs, country towns, and rural areas might at the same time be at one-third or one-fourth of market value. Obviously, this meant that the city, with a higher evaluation criterion, would pay a much larger proportionate share of the state tax. Few state governments today utilize the general property tax as a source of revenue, most of them leaving the field for local taxation. Large cities, however, still pay a disproportionate share of the *county* property tax wherever proper equalization of local assessing unit evaluations is not made. This is also sometimes a problem when rural and urban areas are combined in a school district.

Limitations on Use of Dedicated Funds. The income of cities, instead of being channeled into the general fund to be used as the council sees fit, is sometimes diverted into a series of special funds, each dedicated to a particular use. This may be required by either the city charter or state law. It is common, for example, to provide that the city's portion of a state-shared gasoline tax is to be placed in a special fund for highway use only. Or 1 mill of the property-tax levy may go to the library fund, for library use only.

Some sinking funds represent money that has been set aside to pay off bonds that will become due in the future. Others are not really funds at all, but merely appropriations from the general fund, but titled "funds" in the auditor's reports.

The General Property Tax.[8] It was stated earlier that all taxes must ultimately come from either income or property. A tax must produce adequate revenue, but a long-range tax policy is often discussed in terms of equity, too. *Equity* is usually thought of as meaning *ability to pay.* In

[8] On the sources of local government revenue, see A. M. Hillhouse and Muriel Magelsson, *Where Cities Get Their Money* (Municipal Finance Officers' Association, Chicago, 1946). There is a 1947 supplement by Hillhouse, and others in 1949 and 1951 by M. B. Phillipps. The *Municipal Year Book* also furnishes data on trends.

colonial America, ability to pay could best be measured in terms of property, or total wealth. Today, when most people receive a regular pay check (unlike the situation in the predominantly agricultural colonies), income is generally considered to be a better criterion.

The income tax takes into consideration the fact that not all property is equally able to pay taxes. A home, most Americans would agree, is less suitable for taxation than is a factory. A factory that is losing money is less a subject for taxation than one that is making a profit (although it might be expected to pay some taxes). The property tax makes them pay equally, the income tax does not. Saxophones, to an amateur musician, are as much a consumer good as are rutabagas, yet the former are (theoretically) taxable in many states as property. The income tax, in a complicated modern world, can be much more equitably administered and is less subject to evasion than is the property tax.

Yet in colonial America, the property tax was a fairly good measure of ability to pay. There was then a much closer relationship between property owned and income received than is the case today. Despite the fact, however, that the property tax has been bitterly attacked in more recent years as being unsuitable for a modern world, and especially for urban society, it remains by far the most important source of revenue for local government. It furnished 74 per cent of all city *tax* revenues in 1958.

The great authority on the property tax, E. R. A. Seligman, once suggested that there is nothing the matter with the general property tax except that it is wrong in theory and does not work in practice. What are the objections to the tax?

It has already been suggested that the property tax is no longer a very good measurement of ability to pay. Today, when very large incomes are sometimes possible from relatively small investments, it seems inappropriate for the city to derive a major portion of its income from a tax upon homes, many of which are owned by relatively low-income persons.

The general property tax has often been poorly administered. A large proportion of property today is intangible: stocks, bonds, mortgages, and the like. These are easily hidden from the assessor. So are much jewelry and other small tangible valuables. Depreciation allowances on automobiles, furniture, and other properties far in excess of what is reasonable by market conditions are claimed by taxpayers—and are frequently allowed by assessors.

The arbitrariness of property assessment and the failure to relate it to market value is indicated in a study conducted by the Oregon state tax commission. It found that local assessments in one county ranged from 6.5 per cent to 187.5 per cent of the commission's figures on residential properties. Such extremes are no longer typical, however. (See also Figure 15-3.)

Assessors are often elected even though theirs is a job requiring technical competence. Others are appointed on the basis of political considerations other than those of competence. Most assessors are honest, but many are not trained for their jobs. In the largest cities, trends toward professionalization have encouraged the development of a trained staff. Assessment in large cities is usually technically superior to the job done in small places.

Some attempts have been made to modify the general property tax in recent years. The withdrawal of the state from the scene has reduced or eliminated the old evils of competitive underassessment to reduce the burden of the state tax. Some states have classified property, taxing some of it at lower rates. Others have exempted intangibles or provided for the taxation of some of them at a low rate. An increasing number of them have virtually or completely exempted personal, as distinguished from real, property. The general property tax is not so inequitable or so

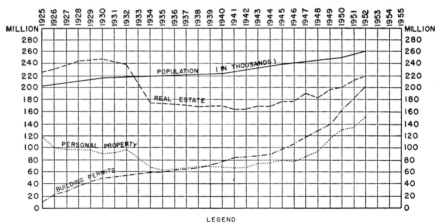

CITY OF OMAHA, NEBRASKA

GRAPH SHOWING POPULATION AND BUILDING GROWTH IN CONTRAST TO VALUATIONS
FOR THE YEARS FROM 1925 TO 1952

LEGEND
REAL ESTATE PROPERTY ASSESSED VALUATIONS ———
PERSONAL PROPERTY ASSESSED VALUATIONS ···········
BUILDING PERMITS ISSUED (CUMULATIVE) —·—·—
POPULATION, BY U S. CENSUS TO 1950 ————————

Figure 15-3. Note that assessed valuations bear little relationship to market prices, but are rather fictional values. Despite a transition from a depression to a wartime boom, real estate and personal property assessment totals remained almost constant between 1934 and 1946. Omaha's population increased by 25 per cent, and over 200 million dollars in building permits were issued from 1925 to 1952. However, at the close of 1952, assessed real estate valuations were still about the same as in 1925. SOURCE: *A Financial Report for the Year 1952* (City of Omaha, Neb., 1952).

poorly administered as it once was, but it is still not a uniformly applied tax.

Why Is the Property Tax Retained? If there are so many objections to the general property tax, why does it remain as the core of financial support of the local government? For one thing, inertia itself helps to preserve the tax. It would seem that taxpayers generally do not support improved property-tax assessments. In Wisconsin, for example, they have repeatedly turned down referendum proposals to place assessors on a professional basis and have rejected the efforts of governing bodies to provide a reassessment of all property within some municipalities. Hence inertia works against either elimination or modification of the tax and its administration.

A second reason is to be found in the venerable argument holding that any old tax is a good tax and any new tax is a bad tax. The argument, to the extent that it is accurate, is based upon the fact that society has accommodated itself to the old tax. Property values are adjusted to the property tax. When a person buys a home, he considers the annual tax levy as a maintenance cost, and its relative size is a factor in determining the price he is willing to pay.

A third reason for the continued use of the property tax is to be found in the fact that the subjects of local-government taxation must necessarily be things that will "stay put"—and most real property (if not personal property) is not easily moved out of the city the day the assessor comes around. Sales taxes on the local level tend to drive shoppers and buyers out of the city. Taxes upon income tend to cause political complications if levied upon nonresidents and if not, tend to drive people into the suburbs. On the other hand, the real property tax does not stay perfectly put, either. High property taxes tend to drive homeowners, businesses, and industry outside the municipal limits and thus undermine the tax base.

A fourth reason for retaining the tax is that it produces a very high yield, except in severe depressions. It probably meets the test of *adequacy* better than does any other tax with the exception of the retail sales tax, which is collected a bit at a time and often upon the necessities of life.

Lastly, the general property tax is retained because cities need money and no one has suggested a substitute satisfactory enough to replace the tax.

The Search for Municipal-tax Variety. In looking for likely subjects of local taxation, it is necessary to consider whether or not a subject will stay in one place long enough to be taxed there and whether or not the field has already been completely pre-empted by the national or state government. These considerations are in addition, of course, to the "requirements" for a tax system stated by Adam Smith—certainty, equity, economy, and convenience.

The *sales tax* became popular during the Great Depression because it yielded well even in such times. It became the backbone of many state tax systems and has had limited use as a secondary tax for city governments. The city of New York adopted it in 1934 as a "temporary" expedient. As is the fate of most "temporary" taxes, it has become a permanent fixture in that city, varying over time from 1 to 3 per cent. New Orleans, Denver, and other cities have adopted sales taxes. It has become especially popular in postwar California, where most cities have adopted such a tax ranging up to 1 per cent, but with most of them at 0.5 per cent. The yield from municipal sales taxes increased by 125 per cent during the decade of the 1950s. In California cities and in most others, the regressive tendency [9] of the tax has been ameliorated to a degree by exempting foods and other necessities.

The *income tax* supplanted the tariff as the principal source of revenue for the Federal government during World War I and has become increasingly important since that time. In recent years, many states have turned to this tax. Cities have, therefore, found the field largely preempted. Philadelphia, however, adopted an income tax in 1939 which has come to produce about one-fourth of the city's revenue. Many municipalities in Pennsylvania and Ohio and St. Louis, Louisville, and other cities levy an income tax. The use of the municipal income tax expanded by 200 per cent during the decade preceding 1960. Most city income taxes might more accurately be called "payroll taxes," for they normally do not permit any deductions, but are simply a certain percentage of the total amount of money earned by individuals, and sometimes corporations, within a city. The payroll tax has the great advantage to the core city of forcing suburbanites to help bear the cost of maintaining the city in which they earn their living and whose facilities they use daily. It is in effect regressive, however, if it allows no deductions or exemptions.[10] In many cities, the tax, moreover, applies only to earned income and not income from stocks, bonds, and rents.

Organized labor has tended to oppose the payroll tax because of its regressivity. In 1954, for example, a Cincinnati councilman who was also a CIO official resigned from the Charter party after that organization helped adopt a payroll tax in that city.[11]

Cities secure some revenue from *business taxes*. These may be primarily

[9] A regressive tax is one the burden of which is lessened as ability to pay increases. A sales tax on necessities is considered regressive, since low-income people spend a larger percentage of their income on necessities than do high-income people.

[10] See R. A. Sigafoos, *The Municipal Income Tax: Its History and Problems* (Public Administration Service, Chicago, 1954).

[11] *The New York Times*, Feb. 28, 1954.

levies to pay the cost of supervising a business directly affecting the public health, but some of them are higher levies and are designed to produce revenue beyond the cost of inspections. A city may, for example, levy a modest tax in the form of restaurant licenses, most of which must be spent upon health inspections of eating places. But other taxes may be levied upon businesses in which there are no regulatory activities under the police power.

Public utilities often, and other businesses sometimes, are taxed upon gross earnings. One version of this tax, called an "occupational tax" (usually upon gross earned income, but excluding unearned income), is becoming widely used, especially in the South and West. Because it is difficult to determine the value of inventory and other personal property for tax purposes, experts in public finance sometimes advocate the use of such a tax on business in lieu of the personal property tax. It is often used in addition to other taxes, however.

Several cities levy a local cigarette tax. Some resort and vacation cities, such as New York and Atlantic City, tax hotel-room occupancy. Mount Clemens, Michigan, another resort center, levies a tax upon every mineral bath taken within the city limits. Tourists and transients are favorite objects of taxation: they cannot vote in local elections.

It has often been argued in recent years that admissions taxes upon theatrical, motion-picture, and sports events would be a desirable subject for taxation—if the national government would but vacate the field. This tax has the advantage of "staying put," since theaters and stadiums are relatively immovable. It also would spread the tax over a large number of persons, including many from outside the city limits. The councilmen of Ann Arbor looked hungrily a few years ago at the mammoth University of Michigan stadium which seats more than 100,000 potential taxpayers. They stood ready to place a price upon the head of every fan attending football games, and the plan was popular—most of the stadium being filled each Saturday by Detroiters—until the state attorney general held that such a tax would actually be levied upon an instrumentality of the state, that is to say, the university.

In a search for taxes other than that on general property, cities have often followed the practice of using any subject that will yield well and will not be moved away. Equity is a secondary consideration, and taxes are added piecemeal rather than combined into a system. Paul E. Malone has said that "local financial practices are becoming more a process of scrounging than of revenue administration."[12] (See Figures 15-4 and 15-5.)

Nontax Revenues. Cities receive some money annually from fines and fees. The fines are paid for violating city ordinances and state laws. The

[12] *Wall Street Journal*, Nov. 10, 1953 (Chicago ed.).

fees are charges for certain services such as issuing marriage licenses and transferring the title of real estate.

Rather than pay for many services from general taxes, an increasing number of municipalities are levying service charges. These have traditionally been used for water supply. In recent years, they have also been levied in the form of charges on sewerage, garbage collection, street lighting and cleaning, snow removal, weed cutting, and others. Various formulas are used in determining these charges, but in general they are based upon the concept of payment according to benefits received.

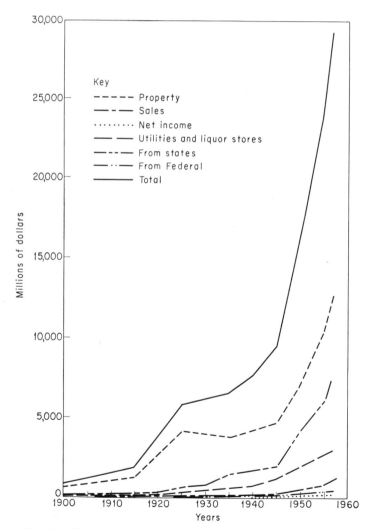

Figure 15-4. Local revenues, total, 1900 to 1957. Includes counties, school districts, and other local units. SOURCE: U.S. Bureau of the Census.

Often service charges are levied as a means of avoiding a raise in the general tax rate. It is a means of making the tax level appear to be lower than it actually is. This can be done effectively, for example, if the sewerage charge is a flat rate or a percentage of the water bill and is added to the periodic water bill. On the other hand, service charges may serve as a means of promoting equity in local taxation. Sewerage charges, for example, may be used as a method of charging tax-exempt property, of which there is a good deal in some cities, so that the cost of this service does not fall upon the rest of the public. Such charges are also useful where some industries contribute disproportionate amounts of sewage to the system while others contribute nothing, and where cities are close to their tax limit (service charges are not usually counted as taxes for limitation purposes).

Some cities make a small profit from the operation of utilities. This is seldom an important source of revenue. Few transportation systems meet operating expenses today. Water departments and other utilities generally charge only enough to meet costs and to permit a reasonable

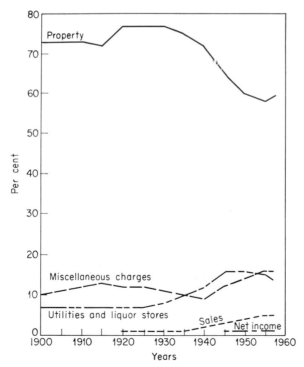

Figure 15-5. Local revenues as percentage of own source, 1900 to 1957. SOURCE: U.S. Bureau of the Census.

allowance for depreciation and potential expansion. Sometimes, however, a surplus will be turned in to the city treasury.

Some villages and cities own and operate municipal liquor stores. These may be package stores or ordinary liquor-by-the-drink bars. Where these have been permitted by state law they have often proved immensely profitable. Needless to say, powerful pressure groups oppose enabling legislation for such stores.

Grants-in-aid. Grants-in-aid are payments made by voluntary appropriation from one level of government to a lower level of government. The amount of a grant is generally independent of the yield from any particular tax or other source of income.[13]

Specific grants are normally made with conditions attached. These conditions may require, for example, the putting up of matching funds, the use of technically trained personnel in administering them, the maintenance of technical standards of equipment and material, or the use of the money only for certain very specific purposes.

Three principal objections are usually levied against the use of grants-in-aid.[14] First, it is said that they may stimulate extravagant expenditures because the locality is spending funds which are not an immediate and obvious burden upon local taxpayers. It is said that if local officials spend money that they need not solicit from the voters, they may feel no need to spend it wisely or on necessities. Second, grants are considered a threat to local self-government and local responsibility. Since the state or national government provides the funds only if certain conditions are met, they may come to supplant local government in the making of policies in these areas. Last, grants are held, potentially at least, to lead toward disproportionate expenditures in favor of those functions receiving grants. In other words, regardless of the merits or need of the various functions performed, some will always have a plentiful budgetary appropriation because of the grants, while others, perhaps more needy and deserving (by local value standards), may be skimped. Grants for venereal-disease and tuberculosis control may promote these services nicely while other functions of the health department shrivel for lack of funds. Although these objections arise virtually every time grant-in-

[13] On grants, see J. R. McKinley, *Local Revenue Problems and Trends* (Bureau of Public Administration, University of California, Berkeley, Calif., 1949), and the various state and local revenue studies that have been made.

[14] Robert S. Ford, "State and Local Finance," *The Annals of the American Academy of Political and Social Science*, vol. 266 (November, 1949), pp. 15–23. See also J. P. Harris, "The Future of Grants-in-aid," *Annals*, vol. 207 (January, 1940), pp. 14–26; *Federal Grants-in-aid* (Council of State Governments, Chicago, 1949); E. J. Sady, *Research in Federal-State Relations* (Brookings Institution, Washington, 1957); and the Commission on Intergovernmental Relations, *A Report to the President* (1955), chap. 5. A vigorous attack on grants is made in Alfred E. Driscoll, "The Biggest Con Game in Politics," *Reader's Digest*, December, 1956, pp. 33–38, and January, 1957, pp. 63–67.

aid problems are discussed, there appears to be little empirical study to support their validity. They may well be proper objections, but further research is needed on the matter of the effects of grants-in-aid.

Shared Taxes. A shared tax is one imposed by one unit of government but shared with other governments according to a formula. The amount sent to each receiving unit is sometimes intended to be representative of the portion of the tax produced within the area of that unit, but shared taxes may be distributed on any basis the collector chooses. Unlike the grant-in-aid, a shared tax delivers no fixed amount; rather, receipts are entirely dependent upon the yield of the tax.[15]

Shared taxes have become increasingly popular in recent decades, and they seem to be preferred by local officials to either grants-in-aid or an enlargement of the taxing powers of local governments. Part of the reason for this is to be found in the fact that fewer strings are normally attached to shared taxes than to grants. Shared taxes also bring less criticism from local citizens than does the enactment of additional local taxes.

Taxes that are most often shared by the state with local units of government include those on motor fuel, motor vehicles, liquor sales, and income. Shared taxes are sometimes defended as being less in the nature of charity than the grant-in-aid, for although they are state-imposed and state-collected, they are levied upon local wealth and hence are not a largess. Since they are viewed as a local tax with the state acting as a collecting agent, local units are usually more free in using the revenue as they see fit than they are in the case of grants.

Many criticisms are made of shared taxes, however. New York State commissions, both in 1936 and again in 1946, discouraged their use.[16] These study groups pointed out that shared taxes cannot be adjusted to local needs. Some areas with little need receive more from such taxes than they can spend, while others receive much less than their greater needs require. Grants-in-aid are better adjustable to need. Shared taxes, further, do not help to stabilize local revenues. They yield well in prosperous times but tend to be withdrawn by the state during depressions, when local need for funds is most critical. Last, the manner in which shared taxes are used is less subject to control than are grants. From a philosophical viewpoint this may be argued as either an advantage or a disadvantage. But from the viewpoint of imposing standards, the state cannot be as effective through shared taxes as it can be through grants. Whatever the arguments, a long look into the future will no doubt reveal the shared tax still with us.

---

[15] McKinley, *op. cit.*, pp. 22–27.

[16] See *Report of the New York Commission on State Aid to Municipal Subdivisions* (State of New York, Albany, N.Y., 1936); *Report of the New York State Commission on Municipal Revenues* (State of New York, Albany, N.Y., 1946).

Postwar Trends. Intergovernmental financial payments exist between the Federal government and the states; to a much smaller extent, between the Federal government and local units; between the states and their political subdivisions; and even between units of local governments. The amounts spent for each of these has been increasing in recent years, and the principal way in which most local governments have diversified their revenue sources and relieved the pressure on the property tax has been through the receipt of grants and shared taxes.[17]

In the postwar years, municipal expenditures, taken collectively, have increased so rapidly that the intergovernmental-payments portion of total revenues has changed hardly at all. In both 1948 and 1956, local governments received about 25 per cent of their revenues from the states (some of it money being handed on that had originated as Federal appropriations). In addition, just over 1 per cent of local revenues came directly from the Federal government.

Patterns vary greatly from state to state on policies for intergovernmental payments. A very low percentage of total state expenditures are for local-government aid in New England (except for Massachusetts), Montana, and South Dakota; a very high percentage in Wisconsin, California, and Colorado. In 1956, over one-half of the state appropriations in Wisconsin went for local aid.[18] The pattern of state payments to political subdivisions seems to be a function more of the balances among existing local pressures than of anything else. The national pattern does not appear to show a high correlation with any factors whether one considers geography (except for the New England situation), rural-urban balances, or ranking by personal income as a measure of relative wealth. New York, an urban Eastern state, had an elaborate and generous program of state payments to local units in 1956.[19] Pennsylvania, also an urban Eastern state, ranked forty-second in percentage of state budget devoted to payments to local units. Pennsylvania's state aid for public health amounted to 1 cent per capita, New York's to $1.00.

Most state payments to local governments are in the areas of education, welfare, and highways. Collectively, these make up about 85 per cent of the total, though practice varies by states. Payments are also made for public safety, health, hospitals, nonhighway transportation, housing, urban redevelopment, and natural resources, among others, and some are lump-sum, or block, grants for no prescribed purpose. Intergovernmental payments are important parts of the revenues of all local units of government, and they seem destined to continue.

[17] See Rowland Egger, "Nature over Art: No More Local Finance," *American Political Science Review,* vol. 47 (June, 1955), pp. 461–477; U.S. Bureau of the Census, *Historical Statistics on State and Local Government Finances* (1955).

[18] U.S. Bureau of the Census, *State Government Finances in 1956,* table 17.

[19] *Ibid.*

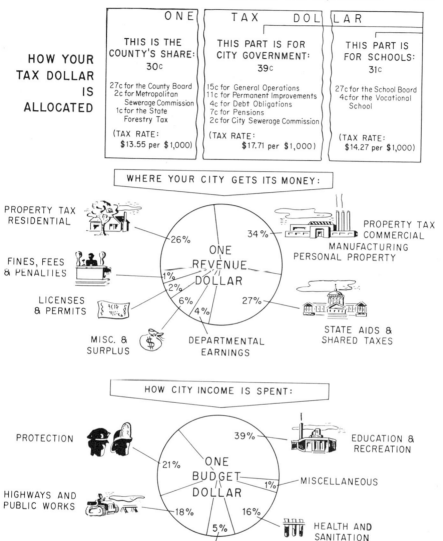

Figure 15-6. SOURCE: *The Milwaukee Way* (City of Milwaukee, Wis., 1952).

The Future Pattern. A conclusion on municipal taxation might hold that the general property tax will remain the backbone of the system. There are several possible supplementary taxes, the use of which is being considered, but none of them can replace the tax that has held the center of the stage for so long.[20]

[20] See F. L. Bird, *The General Property Tax: Findings of the 1957 Census of Governments* (Public Administration Service, Chicago, 1960).

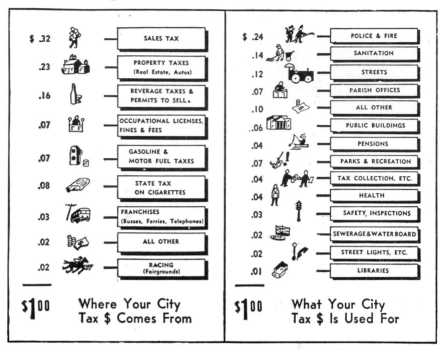

$ .32	SALES TAX
.23	PROPERTY TAXES (Real Estate, Autos)
.16	BEVERAGE TAXES & PERMITS TO SELL
.07	OCCUPATIONAL LICENSES, FINES & FEES
.07	GASOLINE & MOTOR FUEL TAXES
.08	STATE TAX ON CIGARETTES
.03	FRANCHISES (Busses, Ferries, Telephones)
.02	ALL OTHER
.02	RACING (Fairgrounds)

$1 00 **Where Your City Tax $ Comes From**

$ .24	POLICE & FIRE
.14	SANITATION
.12	STREETS
.07	PARISH OFFICES
.10	ALL OTHER
.06	PUBLIC BUILDINGS
.04	PENSIONS
.07	PARKS & RECREATION
.04	TAX COLLECTION, ETC.
.04	HEALTH
.03	SAFETY, INSPECTIONS
.02	SEWERAGE & WATER BOARD
.02	STREET LIGHTS, ETC.
.01	LIBRARIES

$1 00 **What Your City Tax $ Is Used For**

Figure 15-7. Note: The Milwaukee chart includes expenditures for schools, while that of New Orleans does not. The two are hence not directly comparable. Note, however, that Milwaukee revenue sources are traditional, with 60 per cent coming from property taxes. The New Orleans tax base is more diversified, particularly by the addition of a municipal sales tax. SOURCE: *Annual Report of the Mayor* (City of New Orleans, La., 1953).

Special Assessments.[21] Special assessments have become relatively less important since the Great Depression than they were before that time, but they are still used to a considerable extent, especially in rapidly expanding suburbs with their gross lack of services and conveniences. Special assessments are extra levies upon specific pieces of property designed to defray the costs of services or conveniences of particular value to that property.

By far the most common use of special assessments is to pay all or part of the cost of new street paving, installation of water lines, construction of off-street parking areas, and street lighting. In the last case, special assessments are most commonly levied only for ornamental lighting and not for the ordinary type. In smaller suburbs, however, and especially in unincorporated places, special-assessment "districts" may be

[21] See W. O. Winter, *The Special Assessment Today* (Institute of Public Administration, University of Michigan, Ann Arbor, Mich., 1952); and W. O. Winter and R. W. Rickey, *The Special Assessment in Illinois* (Public Affairs Research Bureau, Southern Illinois University, Carbondale, Ill., 1959).

created for all street lighting. Some cities defray part of the cost of developing new parks and playgrounds by special assessment.

The theory behind the special assessment is that certain neighborhood improvements installed by the city are of greater value to the nearby property owners than they are to the citizenry at large. On the other hand, they are not of *exclusive* interest to the nearby property owners, and the citizenry at large profit, as does perhaps the city government itself. Because of special benefit, special charges are levied. Yet it is difficult to determine a formula.

Obviously, you benefit greatly if the street in front of your home is paved. You might be expected to pay for this benefit and not enjoy this advantage at the expense of the general taxpayers of the city. Should you pay *all* of the cost, however? The neighbor on the next street now finds your street a handy short cut when he wants to get to the arterial highway.[22] Should he pay, too? How about the Torkelsons, who are your best friends? They live miles away, but they use the street almost every day. And how about Cousin Alfreda, who comes to visit once a year? Or the department store that delivers parcels on the street? Obviously the cost cannot be apportioned directly and precisely in relation to benefit. The problem is even greater in connection with the construction of boulevards, parks, and playgrounds. Cities do not often try to determine the economic benefits from such improvements. They may assess owners other than those whose property is immediately abutting, but the formula is likely to be rather arbitrary.

In trying to determine actual benefit, cities generally use a rule of thumb, assessing part of the cost to the local property owner, and having the general taxpayers of the city pay the rest. Oakland, California, for example, shares the cost of assessments for new street paving and curbs and gutters, but not for sewers or sidewalks. Syracuse helps pay for sewers, but not for other special assessments. Where the city does share the cost, there seems to be no predictable basis for the percentage of the cost that it will accept. Some cities pay 25 per cent of the cost; others pay 50, 80, or almost any other percentage one might name.

There is also no general agreement as to when the special assessment should be used. Cleveland, Ohio, and Alhambra, California, use it very extensively, for example. But Cranston, Rhode Island, uses it only for water lines; Albuquerque only for new street paving; and Fall River, Massachusetts, only for sidewalks.[23]

In newly developed urban areas, the older residents are likely to feel that special assessments should be used for nearly all capital improve-

---

[22] Special assessments are sometimes used for arterial streets and highways, but traffic on these streets may actually depreciate the value of homes along them.

[23] The *Municipal Year Book* annually reports extensive data on special assessments.

ments and that approximately 100 per cent of the cost of improvements should be paid by the benefited property owner. Older residents often contend that they have already met all the costs of their own improvements and they do not think they should be required to help pay for those of the newcomers. This type of controversy is likely to be a part of the fringe-area problem.

There is always the problem on the part of the property owner of paying for the special assessment. Four principal methods of financing are used. One is to demand advance payments from property owners. This requires them to be prosperous or to borrow the money from a private source. The use of this method is not uncommon. Secondly, the city may make temporary loans from a revolving fund. The property owners must repay these within a relatively short length of time. Thirdly, a few cities still issue property liens to the contractor who did the work, with the contractor then selling the liens to a local bank at a discount. These liens must usually be paid off in a time period of less than a year. They are lucrative for the bank, but are not very satisfactory for the property owner. Lastly, and most commonly, cities issue special-assessment bonds in order to get cash to pay the contractor. The bonds, with interest charged on the unpaid portion, must then be paid off over a period of time, usually several years. This is simply another application of that popular institution, the installment plan. In Chicago, bonds must be paid in five years, in New York in fifteen. At one time these bonds were commonly nothing but liens against property and hence could be sold to investors only if they bore a rather high rate of interest. Today, about two-thirds of the cities over 10,000 pledge the full faith and credit of the city as a guarantee that the bonds will be paid. This serves to safeguard the money of the investor and the good standing of the public credit and to make special improvements available to more property owners by reducing their interest costs.

Pay Cash or Issue Bonds? A debate that arises in every city from time to time centers in the alternatives of paying for capital improvements by issuing bonds or by increasing taxes and paying cash. The principles of borrowing on the municipal level are far different from those on the national level. The national government itself is the principal institution for the establishment of credit-creating institutions, chiefly the banks. If the national government borrows from banks, it is borrowing credit made possible largely by its own rules. Furthermore, the internally held national debt is not passed on to other generations. The credit of the United States is psychologically intertwined with nearly all that is held worthwhile by most Americans. Its borrowing power is limited only by the faith the American people have in their government, and that faith is enormous.

Municipalities enjoy none of these advantages of the national government when it comes to borrowing. Cities cannot create credit. Municipal debt can be, and is, passed on to future generations. When it is paid off, it is not a matter of taxing Americans to pay other Americans, as is the case with the national government. The debt of Nashville is held in many parts of the nation. If it is paid off in later years, Nashvillians must pay increased taxes, the proceeds of which are then distributed throughout the nation to bondholders. The result is a lower standard of living for the people of Nashville. The public faith in any given city is also immensely less than the public faith in the United States. Municipal borrowing power is accordingly greatly limited. Except for the nontax feature, municipal bonds are treated with no more respect on the open market than are the bonds of private corporations.

When should a city borrow money? Almost everyone is agreed that it should never be in a position of having to borrow to meet current operating expenses. In the past this has happened, either because a depression has dried up the revenue sources and the city was desperate, or because local officials desired to keep taxes low as a vote-gathering technique for the next election. Borrowing to pay for permanent improvements is another matter, at least if the bonds are to be paid off before the improvement becomes obsolescent or dilapidated. Borrowing to cover a period greater than the life of the improvement is never *economically* sound, although city councilmen find that it is often *politically* sound to postpone payment as long as possible. Cities sometimes borrow in anticipation of receipts that are scheduled to come in later in the fiscal year. They also borrow sometimes in the face of unanticipated emergencies.

Some people have argued that municipal-bond rates are so low that cities cannot afford *not* to borrow; others argue that cities should not borrow at all and should use a pay-as-you-go approach. It is sometimes said that cities should always pay cash because in this way they avoid the decades of interest payments that are often involved in borrowing, payments that may total several times the original cost of the improvement. There is also no chance of default or of bankruptcy if the city pays cash. And the city is less likely to be extravagant and buy more than its taxpayers are willing to afford.

Operating a city on a strict cash basis is impossible so long as the general property tax is the basic form of revenue. A cash basis means that the expenditures of the city will vary greatly from year to year, for one does not build a municipal auditorium, a new sewer system, or an expressway every year. If expenditures vary, the tax levy will also vary, and this creates problems in the property tax. This tax tends to become capitalized, affecting the value of the property directly. A varying tax would add a great element of uncertainty to the real estate market.

People also prefer to know in advance what to expect in the way of taxes.

Some municipalities attempt to reduce the need for borrowing by the use of reserve funds which may be built up in anticipation of expenditures on capital improvements. Through the use of this device, tax rates can be kept stable and yet interest need not be paid on money used for many improvements. If the municipal government can determine the normal amount of annual capital outlay, the tax rate can be set high enough to provide funds for this purpose. Often, however, cities do not plan this well, or the money on hand is used for other than capital-development purposes. Political pressures often prevent the stockpiling of funds. Bonds, then, appear to be necessary or at least the most practical approach, politically, in many communities.[24]

Characteristics of Municipal Bonds. Traditionally, municipal bonds were paid off by the establishment of a *sinking fund* which would, in theory, provide sufficient funds to retire the bonds when they came due. Most of the bonds of this type would be issued so that all of them would fall due at the same time. The sinking-fund method has proved to be seriously defective in several respects, particularly because (1) the council often failed to make adequate appropriations to the fund, which must be built up regularly and systematically, or the fund was otherwise tampered with for "political" reasons; and (2) the sinking fund could come to disaster in depression times if its investments failed.

More recently, most cities have tended to favor the use of *serial bonds*. These bonds mature gradually, a certain percentage of them each year. The council then, instead of appropriating money into a sinking fund, appropriates the amount for the direct retirement of part of the debt. This is the same plan that is so popular in bank loans to private individuals today: part of the principal is paid back each month, simplifying the planning for retiring the debt.

Another development is the inclusion of a call provision in municipal bonds. This is a feature, long included in many private bond issues, whereby the bonds can be paid off at any time prior to the date of maturity at the option of the debtor. Of course, exercising such a privilege must be offset by paying a premium—a higher price—for the bonds than would otherwise be necessary. The call provision is nevertheless likely to be profitable for a sharp drop in interest rates, or a suddenly increased income of the city might make it desirable to pay off debts ahead of maturity dates.

Types of Municipal Bonds. In addition to the special-assessment bonds already mentioned above, cities commonly issue three types of bonds: general obligation, mortgage, and revenue. General-obligation bonds are

[24] See C. H. Chatters and A. M. Hillhouse, *Local Government Debt Administration* (Prentice-Hall, Inc., Englewood Cliffs, N.J., 1939).

secured through a pledge that the full faith and credit of the local unit of government is available to pay them off. The community thus agrees to levy whatever tax is necessary in order to pay the interest and eventually to retire the bonds. Unless constitutional tax limits threaten to make this pledge meaningless, general-obligation bonds normally bear a relatively low rate of interest.

Mortgage bonds are normally used in connection with the purchase or construction of utilities, and they offer a mortgage on the utility as security. This type of bond has usually required a higher rate of interest than bonds of general obligation and as a result has been less popular. Sometimes mortgage bonds also involve a pledge of full faith and credit.

Revenue bonds have become increasingly popular in the years since the Great Depression. These bonds are secured by a pledge of the revenue from some self-liquidating project. Toll bridges, tunnels, and electric-light and water-supply systems may be financed in this way. Municipalities must agree to set rates high enough to pay the debt charges. Sometimes the bondholders are also given a mortgage on the utilities. Revenue bonds have several advantages for the municipality. These bonds are often not counted as part of the debt where a statutory or constitutional limitation

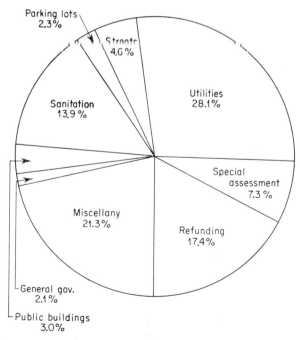

Figure 15-8. source: Michigan Municipal Finance Commission records, and Alfred L. Edwards, *A Study of Local Government Debt in Michigan* (Institute for Community Development, Michigan State University, East Lansing, Mich., 1960), chart 5.

exists. The ease with which their provisions can be enforced has made them very attractive to bond buyers.

Bond Prices and National-government Policies. The monetary policies of the national government are a major factor in determining the interest rates that must be paid by cities on their bonds. This is not the only factor: the credit standing of the city, the amount of existing debt, state restrictions upon taxing powers of the city, and other items are included in credit ratings. But when the United States Treasury and Federal Reserve System follow an easy-credit policy, state and local governments are encouraged to borrow; possibly they are encouraged beyond what they may later consider to have been prudent. When the Federal government follows a hard-credit policy, state and local governments will find it more expensive to borrow money in order to make improvements they believe to be needed. In a time of expanding school-age populations, for example, it may be necessary to build schools regardless of the current cost of borrowing money. Federal policies are tied to political philosophies or to the business cycle; they do not consider current state and local needs and may work hardships on these units of government.

A second national-government money policy of importance to state and local governments is that of exempting the income from their bonds from taxation by the national government. A series of nineteenth-century Supreme Court decisions established the principle of intergovernmental tax immunity, according to which one government cannot tax the instrumentalities of another. This principle was, in effect, set aside by the Supreme Court around 1940, but Congress has not taxed the yield of state and local bonds because of opposition from those units of governments, from bond houses, and from holders of the bonds.

The advantage of tax exemption to the city is clear. With no taxes to be paid on interest income, the city can sell the bonds at a lower rate of interest and thus, in effect, receive a subsidy from the national government. Municipal bonds are purchased in large part by persons of high income who are seeking to avoid being placed in a still higher income tax bracket. The exemption feature thus, in effect, subsidizes individuals who least need subsidization. It is possible that this results in a greater loss in Federal revenue than the amount that it saves the cities.

Some students of taxation have urged that municipal bonds be made taxable by the Federal government and that the cities receive a Federal grant-in-aid to replace their lost interest-rate advantage. There are many complications involved in such a proposal, however, and municipal finance officers undoubtedly prefer to keep the present system rather than to experiment with something new and unknown.[25]

[25] See Lyle C. Fitch, *Taxing Municipal Bond Income* (University of California Press, Berkeley, Calif., 1950).

Municipal Tax Exemption for Industries.[26] For a long time some of the states have authorized, sometimes even required, cities to exempt from property taxation for a certain number of years the manufacturing establishments of new industries in the city. The aim, obviously, is to attract industry to a city and thus provide greater wealth for the community. In some cases, tax exemption of a negative sort has been granted, too: an industry will threaten to leave the city and the state unless it is granted special tax consideration.

Beginning in 1936, the state of Mississippi went one step further with its "Balance Agriculture with Industry" program. It authorized cities to borrow money and to spend that money to buy or build industrial plants which would, in turn, be rented at a low rate to newly arrived industries. The bonds were to be retired from the rentals. Since 1951, a number of other states have adopted similar laws. These programs, like ordinary tax exemption, have been used particularly in the South in attempts to attract manufacturing. The textile industry has been most often enticed by them.

How effective has tax exemption been in attracting wealth-producing industries to a community? Studies that have been made offer some evidence to show that industries consider other factors as more important in determining situs, especially the availability of ample nonunion labor, and that cities offering special inducements gain little by such activity. In contrast, the risk is considerable, for the local tax base is undermined, and this produces serious problems in the event of a depression. When bonds have to be issued in order to build factories, a depression will find the community saddled with both the bonds and a "white elephant" factory. The Investment Bankers Association of the United States has condemned the practice for these reasons.

Tax exemptions are inequitable, too, for they are unfair to businesses and private homeowners that do not receive exemptions. They are demoralizing to those who pay taxes faithfully. Tax exemptions assume that all in the community gain enough to warrant charging the cost to all the other taxpayers. Such is not necessarily the case, however. The system is also likely to attract unstable, fly-by-night industries that are the least likely to permanently strengthen the tax base.

Most students of taxation and of general economics condemn tax exemption or the use of public credit to attract industry. If economic conditions are favorable, if the city is well run, and if local groups such as the chamber of commerce are active, these authorities argue, there is no need to resort to inequitable and unsafe subsidies.[27]

[26] See *Factors Affecting Industrial Location: A Bibliography* (Tax Foundation, Inc., New York, 1956); J. A. Larson, *Taxes and Plant Location in Michigan* (University of Michigan Press, Ann Arbor, Mich., 1957). Larson cites other studies.

[27] The contrary argument is given in W. E. Barksdale, "Mississippi's BAWI Program," *State Government,* vol. 25 (July, 1952), pp. 151–152.

The Politics of Industrial Recruitment. In previous generations, local government was not concerned with providing jobs in private industry for its citizens. The great business tycoons of those days were in possession of the image of the job giver. John D. Rockefeller, Henry Ford, and others like them were honored, in part, because they were seen as creators of work. As business became less personal and the heads of giant firms less dominating of total society, this image became blurred. Today, the role of the job giver is shared by many, but particularly by the secretary-manager of the local chamber of commerce and by the mayor or manager of the city. Seeking to attract new industry is seen as a duty of the chief executive, and sometimes of the council members, too. This activity is in part ritual—it fits nicely into the image of the city as an instrument of economic growth—but it is in part in dead earnest. With American industry constantly expanding and decentralizing, there are many opportunities for cities to ensnare new plants. These opportunities differ according to the specific location of the community, of course, and the efforts made by the chief executive and the chamber of commerce representative tend to be canceled out by the almost identical efforts being made in the next town down the road, but local "civic leaders" are likely to feel that the effort must be made—if for no other reason than to try to keep up with the Jonesvilles.

As with other public policy matters, there are interests involved that both favor and oppose city-government activity in industrial recruitment efforts. Generally speaking, local merchants and public utilities executives favor expanding the local work force because to do so offers them potentially more customers. The same interest exists for the local editor. The city manager can expect his pay to vary somewhat with the size of city, so in-migration of people or annexation of new territory may be profitable to him personally.

There are opponents of expansion, too. Marginal homeowners may fear that a policy of wooing new firms will mean generous tax allowances or the extension of municipally owned utilities to new locations at less than full cost. The person who can barely afford to own his home, and especially the retired person on relatively fixed income, is likely to see no benefit to him in the coming of another plant. He may see it as a threatened increase in the water bill and property tax. Industry already existing in the community may also oppose boosterism unless the firms that might be attracted could also become customers. If they could not, however, they are likely to be seen as competitors for the existing labor force. This means that new industry might bring pressure for higher wages. Or, especially if it is a national firm, it may bring into town a strong, active trade union. The union may represent a threat to the local balance of political as well as economic forces. Citizens, even some who may benefit financially from an increase in the local retail market size, sometimes oppose industrial expansion if it threatens to bring into the community new racial or ethnic groups or to alter substantially the existing ethnic balance.

The specific policies that a city may pursue as part of a program of boosterism vary with local conditions. Typical activities include the rezoning of land for industrial use, the extension of sewer and water lines to factory sites, efforts at annexation designed to bring potential industrial areas into the city, and a tax policy favorable to vacant land zoned industrial and to new plants. There may be a variety of other activities, too, such as a general program of beautification and of subtle or open advertising of the city as a "center of culture" and a nice place to live. (Wives of branch managers are said to sometimes have considerable influence over the precise location of plants. They are likely to reject grim, undistinguished, "uncultured" communities.)

Chapter 16

FINANCIAL ADMINISTRATION

To most of the public, the city treasurer seems to be a very important person indeed, while the controller is an obscure bureaucrat who might do almost anything—or nothing. The auditor performs functions but hazily conceived of, but there is no doubt as to the duties of the tax collector. It is well, at this point, to examine the functions of the top fiscal administrators (see Figure 16-1).

The Council. The city council formalizes basic financial policy for the city. It determines the tax rate, adopts the budget, and demands an accounting of the funds subsequently spent by the city. The budget is so much thought of as an administration document today that it is easy to overlook the fact that the council always must perform the final symbolic act of ratification on behalf of the people.

The Chief Administrator. The mayor or manager (in commission cities, the finance commissioner) acts as the chief fiscal officer of the city. Not only is he responsible for administration, but he often takes the lead in determining policies both of raising and of spending money.

The Treasurer. The office held by this person is one of the oldest in local government. As a traditional office, it was one that Jacksonians insisted upon making elective. As a result, most Americans probably think of the treasurer as being a very important person entrusted with major policy-making responsibilities. Actually, such is almost never the case. The treasurer is really a glorified bookkeeper. He receives moneys according to law, the amounts of which have been determined by others. He is custodian of the city funds, although these are normally actually deposited in local banks. He must be able to account for each cent received. He pays out moneys only on orders from the controller. In none of these acts does he exercise any discretion, and he is not often called upon to advise the mayor or council on fiscal policies since, as an elected official, he is independent of them. His is a ministerial office, yet one-third of the cities still do elect him.

The Tax Collector. At one time, especially in New England, an officer of this title commonly existed. Today tax collection is merely one of the

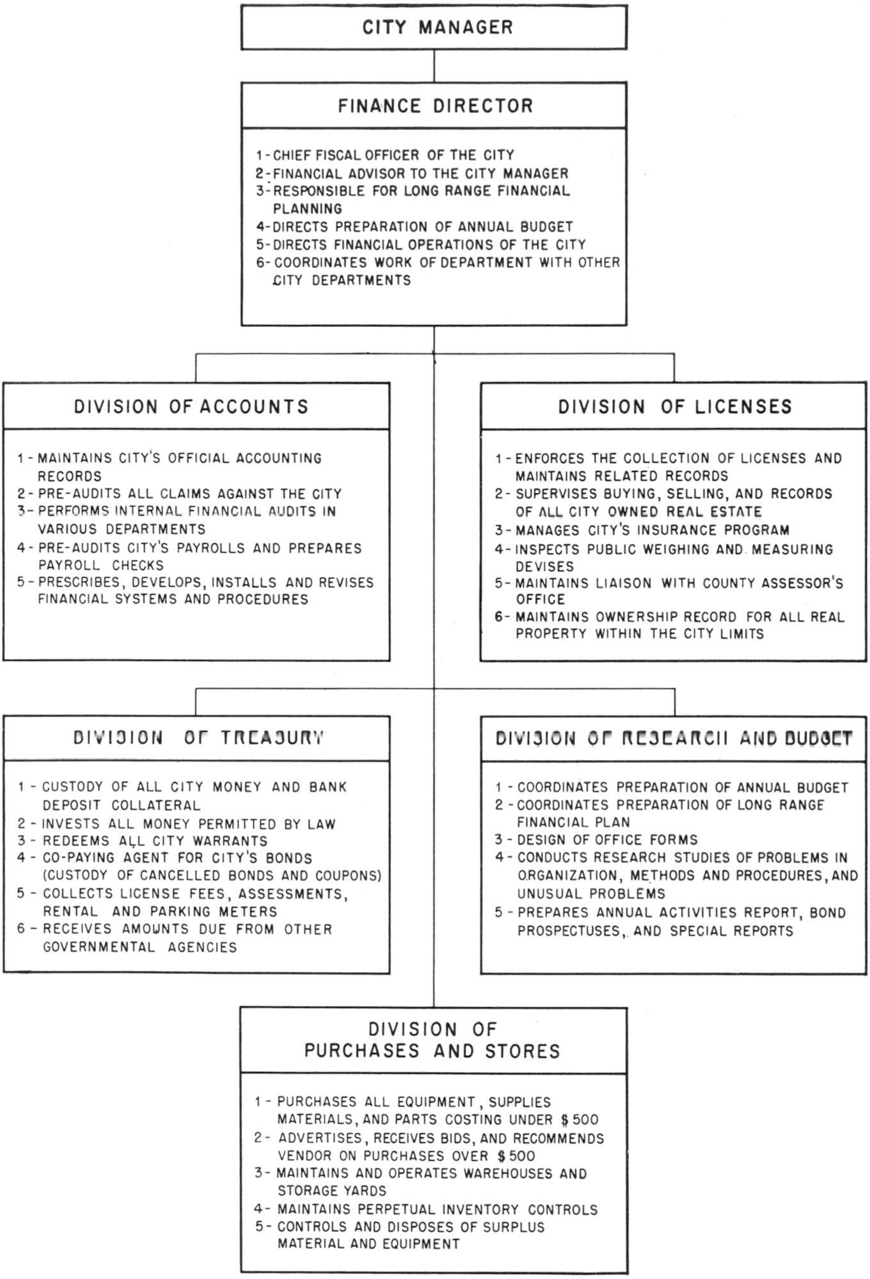

```
┌─────────────────────────────────────┐
│            CITY MANAGER             │
└─────────────────────────────────────┘
┌─────────────────────────────────────┐
│          FINANCE DIRECTOR           │
├─────────────────────────────────────┤
│ 1 - CHIEF FISCAL OFFICER OF THE CITY│
│ 2 - FINANCIAL ADVISOR TO THE CITY MANAGER
│ 3 - RESPONSIBLE FOR LONG RANGE FINANCIAL
│     PLANNING                        │
│ 4 - DIRECTS PREPARATION OF ANNUAL BUDGET
│ 5 - DIRECTS FINANCIAL OPERATIONS OF THE CITY
│ 6 - COORDINATES WORK OF DEPARTMENT WITH OTHER
│     CITY DEPARTMENTS                │
└─────────────────────────────────────┘
```

DIVISION OF ACCOUNTS

1 - MAINTAINS CITY'S OFFICIAL ACCOUNTING RECORDS
2 - PRE-AUDITS ALL CLAIMS AGAINST THE CITY
3 - PERFORMS INTERNAL FINANCIAL AUDITS IN VARIOUS DEPARTMENTS
4 - PRE-AUDITS CITY'S PAYROLLS AND PREPARES PAYROLL CHECKS
5 - PRESCRIBES, DEVELOPS, INSTALLS AND REVISES FINANCIAL SYSTEMS AND PROCEDURES

DIVISION OF LICENSES

1 - ENFORCES THE COLLECTION OF LICENSES AND MAINTAINS RELATED RECORDS
2 - SUPERVISES BUYING, SELLING, AND RECORDS OF ALL CITY OWNED REAL ESTATE
3 - MANAGES CITY'S INSURANCE PROGRAM
4 - INSPECTS PUBLIC WEIGHING AND MEASURING DEVISES
5 - MAINTAINS LIAISON WITH COUNTY ASSESSOR'S OFFICE
6 - MAINTAINS OWNERSHIP RECORD FOR ALL REAL PROPERTY WITHIN THE CITY LIMITS

DIVISION OF TREASURY

1 - CUSTODY OF ALL CITY MONEY AND BANK DEPOSIT COLLATERAL
2 - INVESTS ALL MONEY PERMITTED BY LAW
3 - REDEEMS ALL CITY WARRANTS
4 - CO-PAYING AGENT FOR CITY'S BONDS (CUSTODY OF CANCELLED BONDS AND COUPONS)
5 - COLLECTS LICENSE FEES, ASSESSMENTS, RENTAL AND PARKING METERS
6 - RECEIVES AMOUNTS DUE FROM OTHER GOVERNMENTAL AGENCIES

DIVISION OF RESEARCH AND BUDGET

1 - COORDINATES PREPARATION OF ANNUAL BUDGET
2 - COORDINATES PREPARATION OF LONG RANGE FINANCIAL PLAN
3 - DESIGN OF OFFICE FORMS
4 - CONDUCTS RESEARCH STUDIES OF PROBLEMS IN ORGANIZATION, METHODS AND PROCEDURES, AND UNUSUAL PROBLEMS
5 - PREPARES ANNUAL ACTIVITIES REPORT, BOND PROSPECTUSES, AND SPECIAL REPORTS

DIVISION OF PURCHASES AND STORES

1 - PURCHASES ALL EQUIPMENT, SUPPLIES MATERIALS, AND PARTS COSTING UNDER $500
2 - ADVERTISES, RECEIVES BIDS, AND RECOMMENDS VENDOR ON PURCHASES OVER $500
3 - MAINTAINS AND OPERATES WAREHOUSES AND STORAGE YARDS
4 - MAINTAINS PERPETUAL INVENTORY CONTROLS
5 - CONTROLS AND DISPOSES OF SURPLUS MATERIAL AND EQUIPMENT

Figure 16-1. Functional chart of finance department, City of Phoenix, Arizona. SOURCE: *Annual Financial Report* (City of Phoenix, Ariz., 1953).

jobs of the treasurer in nearly all cities. In a few places, the job is retained as a separate one from that of the treasurer, who keeps and disburses the funds.

The Controller. The controller, or comptroller (pronounced "controller" in either case), is an obscure officer so far as the general public is concerned, but he is actually the chief fiscal assistant to the mayor or manager.[1] He is thus the person who performs the functions that the public often attributes to the treasurer. In about one hundred cities, the controller is elected, but in over 95 per cent of the cities in which the office exists he is appointed.

The budget is often assembled, in the name of the mayor or manager and under his direction, by the controller or the budget officer in the controller's office. After the budget is assembled, it is reviewed and revised by the mayor or manager, and is then submitted to the council, which usually may alter it in any way it sees fit. After the council has adopted the budget for the ensuing year, the controller assumes the task of administering it. He must see to it that no department spends more than is authorized, that no department spends all of its appropriation in the first quarter and is then without funds for the rest of the year, that all expenditures are legally authorized in every way, and that the departments have permission to spend *before* they proceed to make purchases. He must sign every payment voucher, and normally the treasurer can pay no claim against the city without the approval of the controller. He also serves constantly as the chief adviser to the mayor or manager on financial and frequently on other matters. In some cities he serves as deputy mayor.

In small cities, and often in larger ones, the functions of the controller are performed wholly or in part by the council itself. Many a council session is devoted principally to the approval of routine bills. In some cases, state law requires the council to perform this ministerial function.

The Assessor.[2] The assessor (or board of assessors) is responsible for the valuation of property to serve as a basis for determining the general property tax. He is sometimes located within the department of finance, but often he has a separate office. And not all municipalities serve as assessing units. It was once common to elect the assessor, and about 15 per cent of the municipalities in the country still do so, even though the job requires technical training.

[1] There is no standard terminology for the office. He may be called "the director of finance," "the finance commissioner," "the budget director" (only one of his jobs, really), or by some other title. In many cities, no single officer enjoys all of the powers of a controller.

[2] Many technical pamphlets and monographs on desirable assessing practices are published by the National Association of Assessing Officers, Chicago.

Assessment, in theory, does not involve policy making, but only the application of state and local rules to the evaluation of property. In practice, however, assessors are often important policy makers. They may have considerable latitude in deciding on the relative percentage of market value that they will assess homes as against businesses, or in rating the worth of one subdivision against another in terms of site value, or in granting favoritism to certain individuals or groups.

The assessor's office, once it has prepared the tax rolls after assessment, may send out tax bills, although this is more commonly the job of the treasurer and many tax jurisdictions do not send a bill to the taxpayer at all—it saves money not to do so. The assessor may also handle condemnation proceedings.

Boards of Tax Appeal. Because of the potential incompetence, carelessness, or arbitrariness of the assessor, machinery for appeal and review of assessments exists in every taxing jurisdiction. The board of tax appeal (it has many different names around the country) may be a special body, or it may be the city council. In either case, its work is difficult and its members are not likely to gain many friends through the decisions that are made. The board is ordinarily subjected to great pressures from the large taxpayers of the community, and individual householders who bring in appeals are likely to present their cases in highly emotional fashion.

Beyond the local board, appeals in theory lie to higher authority, sometimes to a county board, usually to the state tax commission, and always to the courts. But these procedures are costly, time-consuming, and, unless the local assessor is vastly incompetent, usually unavailing. Only the largest taxpayers are likely to have enough influence and find the stakes large enough to expend the effort that is required.

The Purchasing Agent. Finance departments today often contain a division of purchasing. Through it most of the city's needs for supplies, materials, and equipment are procured so that savings of large-scale purchasing may be achieved. In large cities the purchasing division contains experts who understand differences in quality and who are acquainted with the technical advice available from the U.S. Bureau of Standards and other Federal and state agencies.

The division reduces the possibility of agency purchases beyond needs. It is also often given responsibility for handling the details of contract procedure for commodities, services, land purchase, and construction projects.

The purchasing officer may be a civil servant with special training. Often, however, he is an appointee of the mayor or controller.[3]

[3] See S. F. Heinritz, *Purchasing: Principles and Applications* (Prentice-Hall, Inc., Englewood Cliffs, N.J., 1951).

The Department of Finance. In some cities all of the above officers are grouped together into a department of finance headed by a director. Authorities on financial administration believe that this is a desirable organization, since it provides for direction and coordination of these several financial activities. Council-manager cities, especially smaller ones, are likely to have an integrated department of this type. But in many cities each of the finance officers is independent and may be popularly elected.

The Auditor. The auditor is the agent for the *legislative* branch of government. His job is to check upon the executive branch to determine if expenditures it has made were according to appropriation and were otherwise legal. In a few cities the auditor also makes recommendations to the council concerning the effectiveness of operation of the administrative agencies. Because the job is an old one, one auditor in eight is still elected, even though the position requires a knowledge of accounting. The auditor sometimes performs some of the functions described in this chapter as those of the controller.

Where the auditor is not elected, he may be chosen by the council, he may be sent to the city periodically from the state auditor's office, or the council may hire a private accounting firm to do a periodic audit. Large cities are likely to have their own auditing officers, smaller cities to use private firms or be subjected to a check by the state office, or both.

The important characteristic of the auditor is that he is independent of the chief executive officer. If this were not the case, the executive would simply be checking on himself. The independent auditor, however, is likely to be free to investigate and report as he sees fit. And he usually has a professional interest in doing so.

FINANCIAL PLANNING

The Executive Budget. During the enterprising years of municipal reform, "efficiency" and "economy" pressures were so great that many city councils were forced to surrender part of their traditional power of control over the purse. This permitted the establishment of all or part of the executive-budget system which divided up the financial process so that the chief executive makes a recommendation for revenues and expenditures in the form of a systematic, comprehensive statement of income and outgo. The council then adopts this budget, nearly always with some, and perhaps with many, modifications. The executive next oversees the expenditure of the appropriations by the various departments, requiring them to spend at a rate that will not exhaust their appropriations prematurely and will keep expenditures within the requirements of the law. Finally, the council, through its auditors, checks to ascertain whether or not its instructions have been carried out and whether or not appropriate provisions of the state law have been followed by the executive. The power of the chief executive, through his budget officer, is potentially very great, both in preparing the budget itself—the document is, of course, a major policy statement, explaining how he would spend moneys —and in controlling its expenditure after the council votes the funds. The budget officer is, therefore, one of the chief executive's top aides today. He and his budget examiners serve to advise both the executive and the councilmen, reviewing appropriations requests and preparing evidence in support of policy positions. He often controls the conditions under which appropriations may be spent.

The trend toward centralized administration, the increasing number of functions of government, and the increasing complexity of those functions have contributed to the rapid rise in the use of the executive budget in the United States since the turn of the century. As a result of the change, responsibility—except in cities of the weak-mayor and commission types—for the innovation of taxation and appropriation proposals is placed in the hands of the executive, but with the council continuing to perform its ancient functions of criticism, review, modification, and, sometimes, rejection.

Until recent years, every budget dealt with all of the minutiae that are needed to operate an office or function of government. Often the budget consisted of "line items" specifying the exact amount to be spent on a particular aspect of a function, and the funds were commonly not transferable from one line in the budget to another, even within the same department. The emphasis was upon the things to be acquired—paper clips, snow shovels, wheelbarrows—rather than upon the services to be rendered. This was necessary when public funds had to be guarded at all times against ingenious attempts at fraud. It encouraged, however, the citizen's habit of dissociating taxes from services provided. Many specialists in the field of fiscal administration have long urged that the budget should propose appropriations on a lump-sum basis. Under this plan, each agency or major subdivision would receive a single sum of money which the responsible administrator would then spend as he thought best—within generally established policies of the chief executive and the legislative body. Flexibility to meet unexpected emergencies and changes in service demands would result.

Since the original Hoover Commission reports in the late 1940s, a trend has been established toward a "performance" budget. This is a method of classifying expenditures so that each agency receives a lump sum for the operation of each of its different activities; so much for snow removal, so much for purchase of new park land, so much for public welfare programs. Although the method has its faults, it is designed to help make clear to both legislators and the public what funds are being used for; it makes it easier to compare past performances with future requests; and it may encourage agencies to do a better job of thinking through their needs in making requests. The budget is designed to reduce the tendency under the older budget method (appropriation by objects) to stockpile materials and accelerate the purchase of services in order to exhaust appropriations. Legislators are sometimes cool toward the performance-budget idea, feeling that it has the effect of transferring still more fiscal power to the chief executive and the bureaucracy.[4] The most rapid adoption of the performance budget has come in council-manager cities. It is used in other cities, some as large as Los Angeles, too.

The Budget as Policy. The budgeting function "is a specialized way of looking at problems in decision-making."[5] It is something of a negative view in the sense that after the agencies and interest groups have made known their positions, the budget examiners, and ultimately the chief executive, must balance off the various interests against one another and against a plausible estimate of income, often reducing requests. Budget making is also positive in the sense that a public budget is a basic statement of program and policy by the chief executive. He explains in it how he would evaluate the various demands upon the public funds, gives reasons for taking the stand that he does on the more controversial aspects of the program, and necessarily must stand willing to defend the explicit and implicit policies proposed in the budget. Many governments require agencies to estimate capital-outlay needs for several years—perhaps five years—in advance, thus making this part of the budget a long-range planning instrument, since capital needs cannot be considered apart from program needs. The budget, in this way, becomes to each agency a means for promoting both fiscal and program planning.

Contemporary budget practices have given state and local chief executives:[6]

. . . an opportunity to take the initiative in the most encompassing set of policy decisions that a legislative session makes. Budget decisions are in detail decisions to continue, discontinue, extend, or diminish existing programs and to initiate new programs and at a particular scale. They are also de-

[4] On performance budgeting, see Jesse Burkhead, *Government Budgeting* (John Wiley & Sons, Inc., New York, 1956), chap. 6, or a symposium, "Performance Budgeting: Has the Theory Worked?" *Public Administration Review,* vol. 20 (Spring, 1960), pp. 63–85.

[5] Paul Appleby, "The Role of the Budget Division," *Public Administration Review,* vol. 17 (Summer, 1957), pp. 156–158.

[6] K. A. Bosworth, "Lawmaking in State Governments," in The American Assembly, *The Forty-eight States* (Graduate School of Business, Columbia University, New York, 1955), p. 106.

cisions about proposed buildings and other construction and capital outlay. Budget decisions are, on a more general level, decisions on tax rates and tax policy and on the general scale of [governmental] activity. How much money agencies "need" depends upon the premises entertained by the estimator, and the estimates can vary substantially.

The Parts of a Budget. A budget consists of many parts. It usually begins with a message from the chief executive which may say simply, in effect, "Here is the budget for the next fiscal year," or it may explain proposed new expenditures, tell why tax changes are requested, and otherwise explain policy positions. A brief summary of the budget for the benefit of citizens and reporters usually follows. Next comes the detailed breakdown. It may start with a statement of anticipated revenues from all taxes and other sources. This will be followed by the expenditures section, often broken down by funds: the general fund plus a small or large number of others, such as a streets and highway fund, sometimes even a municipal-bond fund. A capital-outlay budget for new streets, buildings, and other structures will usually be presented separately from the operations budget, and the same may be true of utilities budgets, such as that of a municipal water-supply system. Provision must also often be made for governmental debt service. The budget may conclude with a statement concerning new taxes needed, or the property-tax levy necessary to bring the budget into balance.

Preparing the Budget. In municipalities operating under the executive budget plan, the document is prepared by a budget officer or controller under the chief executive. In a few cases, the budget is prepared by an independent, elected controller, or an ex officio board. In weak-mayor cities, a council committee often prepares the budgets.

The process begins with the collection of estimates for the following year's needs prepared by the various agencies. In all but small cities, these are gone over by budget analysts who look for padding, inaccuracies, and inconsistencies. There may be conferences between the agencies and members of the budget division when differences arise. Such differences are likely to result from differing premises. The chief executive's own philosophy, and perhaps his evaluation of his own political strategy requirements, will affect his own view of how "needs" should be interpreted in each agency. The agency will, however, probably use different criteria in arriving at "needs." It may base these on professional concepts of standards, or upon the pet interests of the agency head, or on the pressures it feels most from its clientele groups, or upon other considerations.

When detailed estimates of the needs of each department for the coming year are available, they are set out in parallel columns with statements of the estimated expenditures for the same items in the current year and the actual expenditures for those items in the fiscal year just completed. The budget officer must next go over the document in detail with the chief executive so that proposed changes in policy may be incorporated in the estimates.

The completely assembled budget is then ready to be sent to the council. Enclosed with it may also be the political future of the mayor, the career prospects of the young city manager, the hopes of the chief executive's critics for new ammunition in their fight, and the welfare of all the publics that reside within the boundaries of the city.

Enacting the Budget. The council has the responsibility for adopting the budget, nearly always with some, more commonly with many, modifications. It will usually hold budget hearings, either before the full body or before the tax and appropriations committees, the chairmen of which are normally senior legislators of great power. These hearings do not often give the councilmen information they do not already have, but they serve to allow groups and individuals to vent their annoyances, bitterness, or frustrations. They are an important part of the democratic process. A budget hearing is more likely to be attended by representatives of pressure groups, however, than by a representative cross section of the general public. Some department heads may lobby at this time to get a bigger share of the pie than was given to them in the budget division. If the chief executive is weak administratively, this may be done quite openly. If he is strong, however, it must be done more subtly, for a dissident department head may risk his job by going over the head of the executive. Pressure groups will at this time try to get favorable hearings, and those that find the legislative climate more receptive than was the executive may succeed in getting an increase in the department budgets in which they are interested. Other groups will have to fight to retain the level of funds recommended in the executive budget as legislators strive to re-establish a balance between income and outgo. Public employees may take the opportunity to try to improve their working conditions and pay, and the newspapers may use the occasion to view with alarm the ever increasing cost of government.

Usually the council is free to add, reduce, delete, or modify any part of the budget, although in some cases it may only reduce items or leave them unchanged, and cannot introduce new items. In mayor-council cities the chief executive has the final word for he usually has the power of the item veto.

Administering the Budget. In cities with the executive budget, the head of each department must submit a work program to the chief executive (or often, in practice, to the controller) before the beginning of a new fiscal year. This program will show how much of the total appropriation for that department is desired in each month or quarter of the coming fiscal year. This is known as the "allotment system." After approval, the allotments are turned over to the accounting division of the controller's office, which will then refuse to allow any money to be spent by that department unless it is both authorized by the appropriations ordinance or statute and falls within the time provided in the allotment schedule. In cases where budget administration is less well organized, no allotment system may exist, and the auditor may be the only one to check for the legality of expenditure. In small cities, the governing body may itself exercise the control function by passing directly on individual bills presented for payment.

After the moneys have been spent, the auditor checks to ascertain the legality of all expenditures and reports his findings to the council and sometimes also to the state auditor. Even as the money is being spent throughout the year, however, the budget officer is surveying the scene for possible alterations in the next budget, for the governmental process is an unending one.[7]

[7] See the bibliography in the current *Municipal Year Book* (International City Managers' Association); *Municipal Finance Administration* (rev. ed.; International City Managers' Association, Chicago, 1955); Burkhead, *op. cit.;* and *Research Bibliography: Financing Municipal Government* (Tax Foundation, Inc., New York, 1960).

Chapter 17

PUBLIC SAFETY

A great many of the functions of municipal government are related to the safety of the public. In this chapter, fire protection, smoke abatement, traffic engineering, civil defense, and, in particular, police functions will be discussed. Except in a relatively few cities, these functions are not grouped together into a single department. Their methods of operation and their technical requirements are so different that most cities assign police and fire to separate departments.

A PUBLIC ATTITUDE OF *LAISSEZ FAIRE*

An Old Story. In 1951, American televiewers were fascinated by the unsystematic but overwhelming collection of evidence concerning organized crime activities in the United States gathered by the staff of a Senate committee and presented, largely through the interrogation of witnesses, to the public. The Special Committee to Investigate Organized Crime in Interstate Commerce, headed first by Senator Estes Kefauver of Tennessee and later by Senator Herbert O'Conor of Maryland, amazed even the more cynical Americans. It frightened some local officials, if no professional gamblers. It made Senator Kefauver a hero to many Americans and made him a formidable presidential candidate at the 1952 Democratic National Convention. The investigation did considerable damage to the already shaky reputation of local-government officials and reinforced many misconceptions of long standing concerning public officials.[1] But whether any permanent diminution in the activities of or-

[1] The Kefauver hearings and reports include some twenty-five volumes. See *Hearings before the Special Committee to Investigate Organized Crime in Interstate Commerce* (1951). There were also three *Interim Reports* and a *Final Report* of the Special Committee (1951), cited hereafter as Kefauver committee, *Third Interim Report,* etc. Other useful investigations and studies include those of the California Crime Commission, *Combined Reports of the California Crime Commission* (1950); and the *Reports of the New York State Crime Commission* (1953). There are earlier studies, too, such as the report of the Lexow committee: *Report and Proceedings* of the Senate Committee Appointed to Investigate the Police Department of the City of New York (5 vols.; State of New York, Albany, N.Y., 1895); and the Illinois Asso-

ganized criminals resulted is doubtful. With the exception of a few communities, the ordinary citizen did not rise up in wrath at the reports. The problem of a policy toward the social functions performed traditionally by organized crime is yet to be met, or even faced frankly. Certainly it was not much considered in the Kefauver reports.

The situations uncovered by the Kefauver committee are not new or different: they are a restatement of long-existing practices. In fact, they may be viewed as one aspect of old-time machine politics that has not been eradicated.

The professional criminal is sometimes strictly predatory—the bank robber and the pickpocket, for example—but those who are organized into crime syndicates are normally providers of services to the general public. These services differ from those of the butcher, physician, or insurance salesman chiefly in that they are illegal and are usually considered immoral or detrimental to health. It was concerning these services that the Kefauver committee made the flat statement that "these operations could not continue without the protection of police and without the connivance of local authorities." [2]

What Makes Crime Possible? Part of our difficulty in suppressing crime stems from an ambivalent attitude. We have inherited certain puritanical values which condemn gambling and purely pleasurable activity. On the other hand, we live in a culture that is dynamic, complex, impersonal, and materialistic. Our whole economic and cultural pattern is based upon competition and "getting ahead." [3] Gambling and crime against property, therefore, are partly a result of a *hope for gain*, a desperate need to succeed. Establishments for performing abortions—another illegal occupation—exist because women have a great fear of loss of status through the bearing of an illegitimate child. Loss of status comes easily in our culture and symbolizes failure.

In our competitive society, it is often difficult to distinguish the criminal from the noncriminal. Many business activities verge on the classification of racketeering; certainly they often violate the moral values of many individuals. "Anything's fair in business that you can get away with." If so, how does one distinguish legitimate and illegitimate businesses? Many Americans believe that you cannot do so. Americans have never strongly believed that *all* laws should be obeyed. [4] A multimillion-

ciation for Criminal Justice, Chicago, *Illinois Crime Survey* (1929). On the Lexow committee, see M. R. Werner, "Dr. Parkhurst's Crusade," *The New Yorker*, Nov. 19, 1955, pp. 189–210, and Nov. 26, 1955, pp. 93–129.

[2] Kefauver committee, *Second Interim Report*, p. 3.

[3] D. R. Taft, *Criminology* (3d ed.; The Macmillan Company, New York, 1956), chap. 15. On crime as a ladder of social mobility, see Daniel Bell, *The End of Ideology* (The Free Press, Glencoe, Ill., 1960), chaps. 7–8.

[4] Taft, *op. cit.*, p. 236.

aire once told a Senate committee that it was morally right for an individual to avoid paying all taxes that he could possibly shirk. "Anything is legal that you can get away with" and "Everyone has his racket." So why should we condemn the gamblers, prostitutes, abortionists, or bootleggers?

An additional complication arises as a result of the fact that we are a heterogeneous population consisting of many subcultures, each with a variant set of values. There is no general agreement as to what is right and what is wrong. So the individual follows his own value pattern. He does not agree with the views of his neighbor, but he tolerates them. ("I wouldn't do that myself, but every man to his own way!")

The *Uniform Crime Reports* of the Federal Bureau of Investigation year after year indicate that of all crimes, murder is the one most likely to be solved. This is partly because solution is aided by a strong and obvious motive which is usually present whenever this crime is committed. But it is also partly because the public *wants* murderers to be apprehended. The punishment for the crime is likely to be severe. This is largely a result of the fact that what the public *says* is its attitude toward murder agrees with what the public actually *does* hold as its attitude toward murder. Social mores and criminal law do not always agree so nicely.

Prostitution and the sale or use of narcotics are everywhere illegal. Gambling, with certain exceptions, is illegal in all states except Nevada. (Several lotteries are legal in Alaska.) Yet it is safe to say that in every large city and in a great many medium- and small-sized cities, one may find gamblers, prostitutes, and narcotics peddlers engaging in their occupations. The fact of the matter is that there is a very sizable demand for these services, and hence there are those who will supply them in spite of almost all hazards. Unlike murder, gambling is not accorded identical viewpoints by the citizen in his public and his private opinions. For the sake of social appearances, the individual is likely to condemn it publicly regardless of his real views. The same thing is true, in lessening degrees, of prostitution and narcotics peddling.

Laws in serious conflict with the mores of society become unenforceable. The public, or at least a large segment of it, does not want the laws on gambling rigidly enforced. An even larger segment is indifferent to the question of how they are enforced. Many people do not gamble, but they do not object if their neighbors do.[5] Likewise, there are some cultural

[5] Virgil W. Peterson, "Obstacles to Enforcement of Gambling Laws," *The Annals of the American Academy of Political and Social Science*, vol. 269 (May, 1950), pp. 9–20, holds that "self-interest, personal conveniences, and expediency" are the principal motivating factors in law evasion and in the public attitude toward law enforcement. But this does not fully explain the tolerance of nonparticipants of some types of law evasion and intolerance of others.

groups in our society that accept the existence of the prostitute as an ordinary part of life. And a large number of persons who would themselves never enter what was once called a "house of ill fame" are not incensed at the thought that such places exist in their city. (A 1958 study of the American Social Hygiene Association found that prostitution was commonplace in thirty-eight out of one hundred and twenty-five communities studied. In the other eighty-seven, it was at an "irreducible minimum." [6]

A relatively few persons are the slaves of narcotics. The use of narcotics produces so many physical, psychological, and social problems that it is indeed fortunate that in this case society actually does not approve of its sale or use. Yet the cravings of the addict are so powerful—the demand for the product is so inelastic—that this risky business remains alive if for no other reason than that it is greatly profitable.

Psychological Factors. In our society, gambling, either in the casino, or in taking a chance on not being caught in illegal activity, often serves to fill important psychological needs. To some it is an escape from a troublesome, or unsuccessful, or dull world. To others it is, like liquor, a crutch, and hence something highly necessary. To others it is simply enjoyment, but one strangely exhilarating. To others, it is excitement and the vicarious conquering of worlds that will not lend themselves readily to conquering outside the gaming casino. Millions of Americans—psychopaths and normal people—spend greater or lesser amounts of time gambling.[7]

The psychological factors behind such other illegal occupations as prostitution and narcotic-drug sales are complex and beyond the scope of this text. It must be borne in mind that psychological factors are stimulated and conditioned by their sociological environment. There is, for example, almost certainly no inherent desire or need to gamble. But there is a need for security, and this psychological desire may be directed toward gambling as a possible means of fulfillment.

Legal Factors. Americans, especially of the middle classes, have a rather naïve faith in law and punishment as solutions for social problems.[8] As a result, the superficial action of making an occupation illegal is mistaken for a move toward the abolition of the occupation. Psychological and sociological phenomena cannot be legislated away, for their causes are complex and deep-seated. Since demand is not eliminated by

[6] *Social Hygiene News*, vol. 34 (February, 1959), p. 1.

[7] On the pathological aspects of gambling, see Robert M. Lindner, "The Psychodynamics of Gambling," *The Annals of the American Academy of Political and Social Science*, vol. 269 (May, 1950), pp. 93–107. On people of normal personality who gamble, see David D. Allen, *The Nature of Gambling* (Coward-McCann, Inc., New York, 1952), pp. 30–32.

[8] Taft, *op. cit.*, p. 235.

making the occupation illegal, such action merely has the effect of creating racketeering and gangsterism as well as an increased disrespect for the law.

The Pattern of Corruption. It should not be assumed, because a certain number of houses of prostitution are known to exist in the city, or because rumors have it that there are some narcotics peddlers about, or because the numbers racket is still in business, that the officer on the beat is being bribed, or that the city administration is necessarily corrupt. It is true that none of these things could take place without the knowledge of the city administration and police officials. That does not always mean that they *want* or *like* it that way.

In a large city, it is almost inevitable that at least a small amount of prostitution exists. The administration may want to eliminate all of it, but it will find this to be an impossibility, practically speaking. The administration may decide upon a compromise with the strict letter of the law, permitting prostitution within narrowly defined areas of the city and with the stipulation that it not attract unfavorable publicity. A policy such as this does not necessarily indicate corruption, and the administrators who establish it would defend it as "practical."

While quite a few city administrations may cooperate with gambling and some with prostitution, few will make an alliance with purveyors of narcotics. Even if they should want to, state and Federal law-enforcement officers are particularly alert and active in seeking out these persons. Yet large cities are quite certain to have dope peddlers. There is no simple formula for destroying the elaborate and extensive narcotics rings that are organized to carry on this profitable business.

Gambling. Gambling, which is an ancient type of human activity, is very widespread, and it takes many forms: the policy racket or numbers game; the bookmakers who take bets on horse races, athletic events, and even the outcome of presidential elections; the casinos with a great variety of card and dice games; the slot machines, which add mechanical ingenuity to the pattern. There are others, too.

The police can never escape knowing of the existence of gambling, but they may not be able to eliminate it even when they wish to do so. Often, of course, they have no such wish. The attitude of a city administration toward gambling can be determined to some degree simply by observing the type of gambling that is tolerated. The policy racket, for example, probably could not be completely eliminated in large cities. Convictions are difficult, the evidence is easily hidden, and the operators are highly mobile. On the other hand, gaudy casinos in the Monte Carlo tradition, or heavy, bulky slot machines, cannot be operated except with the passive cooperation of the police (see Figure 17-1).

Figure 17-1. SOURCE: By permission of Daniel R. Fitzpatrick and the *St. Louis Post-Dispatch.*

Gambling is big business in many American cities. Rough estimates by Kefauver staff workers found that nationwide illegal off-track betting on horse racing totaled from 3 to 5 *billion* dollars annually. This was in addition to some 2 billion dollars legally bet each year at the race tracks. It was estimated that the net profit on 3 billion dollars to illegal bookmakers would be not less than 600 million dollars each year.

Similarly, "In Chicago some $10,000,000 is spent annually on policy playing alone; no other business in the Negro community is so large or so influential. As elsewhere in Negro communities, the policy racket in Harlem is the most widespread form of lawbreaking." [9]

The Kefauver committee concluded that at least 20 billion dollars changed hands each year in organized illegal gambling of all kinds. No estimate was attempted as to the amount of this that was paid in protection money, except to state that it must amount to millions of dollars annually.[10]

Police Graft. Where illegal occupations take place with the permission of the police, graft may be collected at either the top or the bottom of the hierarchy. The cop on the beat may receive petty bribes. If payments are at the top, however, the money is not likely to be passed along downward. But in that event, the effect upon the morale of the ordinary patrolmen cannot be anything but unhappy. A policeman under these circumstances will meet with nothing but futility and frustration. He will find that, even if he is not personally bribed, there is no point in his attempting to enforce laws which it is not the policy of the department to have enforced. He will not secure convictions—or promotions for himself—if he does. He may become cynical and resort to picking up graft on his own. The knowledge of rookie officers that the top administration does not respect the law will lead to low morale that will reflect itself in poor law enforcement in all fields, not in just the "protected" areas.

The Kefauver investigations demonstrated some of the methods of graft payments to top police administrators and to members of the city administration.[11] The hearings and the summaries of conditions in various cities in the reports show that traditional techniques are still being used: [12]

In some cases, the protection is obtained by the payment of bribes to public officials, often on a regular basis pursuant to a carefully conceived system. In other cases, the racketeering elements make substantial contributions to political campaigns of officials who can be relied upon to tolerate their activities. Sometimes these contributors will support a whole slate of officers in more than one political party, giving racketeers virtual control of the governing body.

The interests of those who favor lax enforcement may be powerful and highly effective. The city council of Camden, New Jersey, stripped the mayor of control over the police department and took away other powers in 1960, after he tried to eradicate organized gambling in the

[9] Maurice R. Davis, *Negroes in American Society* (McGraw-Hill Book Company, Inc., New York, 1949), p. 254.

[10] Kefauver committee, *Second Interim Report,* pp. 13–14.

[11] A history of the relationship of crime and politics in Chicago is given in Virgil W. Peterson, *Barbarians in Our Midst* (Little, Brown & Company, Boston, 1952).

[12] Kefauver committee, *Final Report,* p. 5.

city. The mayor had been elected a year earlier on a reform platform, ousting an incumbent who had held office nearly a quarter of a century.

The Vice-squad Pattern. Where a city government, or only the top police leadership of a city, has been corrupted by organized crime, it is necessary to find a method of making certain that promised protection is actually afforded. A police commissioner and his chief lieutenants will not wish to share their payments with ordinary policemen, yet the rank and file of the departments are sworn to enforce the law. To circumvent the ordinary policeman—who may, after all, be a completely honest individual who took his job thinking that it was the task of policemen to enforce laws—police heads commonly resort to what the Kefauver investigators called the "vice-squad pattern": [13]

> This device is used in many cities where the rackets thrive. The political department bosses set up a vice squad composed of a chosen few directly accountable to them. They instruct the remaining law enforcement officers to stay away from gambling and vice and to channel any complaints to the vice squad for action or, in most cases, inaction. By this device a small clique frequently controls the collection of the protection pay-off.

The person who observes the existence of corruption in some particular city should not assume that the cop on the beat is lining his pockets with illegal payments or that he is callously unconcerned with the law. His hands are tied.[14]

Crime and the Culture. Gambling, prostitution, and predatory crimes against property, as well as (in a modified way) crimes against the person, are a product of the culture. Our own values, goals, and behavior patterns to a large extent determine the extent of their existence. Certain kinds of overt behavior can be punished by the judicial system, but the behavior itself cannot be legislated away. Organized criminal gangs as a means toward recognition, wealth, and power; gambling by the respectable businessman; embezzlement as means toward quick cash; even the sex-crime rate—none of these will deviate from their present statistical trends unless society's values and life patterns change. They are, whether the individual may want them or not, part of our way of life, and they are the daily bread and butter of the policeman and the judge.

[13] Kefauver committee, *Third Interim Report*, pp. 95–96. Most police departments have vice squads. It should not be inferred that the existence of such a group implies corruption.

[14] It is sometimes argued that gambling, if not prostitution, could be better controlled if it were legalized. For arguments, see Kefauver committee, *Final Report;* the entire issue titled "Gambling," *The Annals of the American Academy of Political and Social Science,* vol. 269 (May, 1950); and Allen, *op. cit.*

POLICE PROTECTION [15]

While vice and organized crime are not the major police problems of today, they are among the most difficult to combat. In the typical city, these occupations exist in spite of the efforts of the police department, if they exist at all. Most departments, it should be understood, enforce the law to the extent that they are permitted by public opinion as reflected in the political process. Two of the major problems in connection with police work in recent years have been the continuing increase in the crime rate in postwar America and the increasing cost of police protection (see Figure 17-2).

The insecurities of continued international tensions have added a new psychological factor to the many other reasons for a high American crime rate.[16] The number of serious crimes committed in the United States, according to the *Uniform Crime Reports* of the FBI, increases every year almost without exception.

The Crime Rate. The crime rate increased at four times the rate of the population in the years 1950 to 1958, and the conviction rate declined. Significant increases have taken place in all types of crimes, except murder and manslaughter, the rates of which have remained near their prewar levels. One reason for this, perhaps, is that the odds are in favor of the robber, auto thief, or burglar each time he commits a crime (unless he resorts to violence). The police catch relatively few thieves—only in about three cases in ten is anyone even charged with the offense. The public does not tolerate a similar lack of success where a person loses his life.

The American crime rate is several times as high as that of any European nation; yet as in the case of the fire department, the police are the best equipped in the world. An outstanding police chief has said: "Despite the technology that has been acquired through no small effort and expense, the police service today fulfills its task with no greater success than it did a quarter- or half-century ago." [17]

---

[15] This section draws extensively from O. W. Wilson, *Police Administration* (Mc-Graw-Hill Book Company, Inc., New York, 1950). See also the detailed manual on administration, *Municipal Police Administration* (4th ed.; International City Managers' Association, Chicago, 1951); W. C. Reckless, *The Crime Problem* (Appleton-Century-Crofts, Inc., New York, 1950); "New Goals in Police Management," *The Annals of the American Academy of Political and Social Science*, vol. 291 (January, 1954), entire issue; and Bruce Smith, *Police Systems in the United States* (rev. ed.; Harper & Brothers, New York, 1949).

[16] See Taft, *op. cit.*, or one of the other textbooks in that field. For a view that crime is not increasing, that the contrary impression is a result of newspaper exploitation and statistical anomalies, see Bell, *op. cit.*, chap. 8.

[17] W. H. Parker, "The Police Challenge in Our Great Cities," *The Annals of the American Academy of Political and Social Science*, vol. 291 (January, 1954), pp. 5–13.

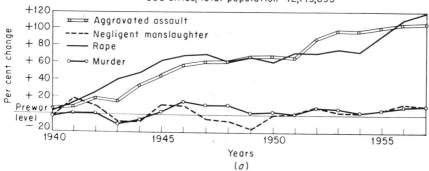

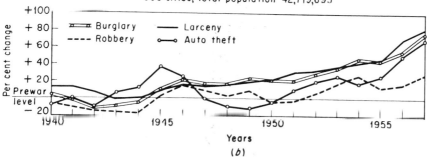

Figure 17-2. Crimes against property, per cent change in relation to prewar levels; offenses known to the police. SOURCE: Adapted from Federal Bureau of Investigation, *Uniform Crime Reports* (1958).

Americans tend to be careless of property losses resulting from robbery just as they tend to be careless of fire losses. The poor record of American police is, therefore, in large part a result of public apathy. Furthermore, "the individual police officer operates with a remarkable lack of public support, cooperation or trust."[18] The police are sometimes hampered partly by efforts on the part of public officials or the citizenry at large to "save" tax money. American police forces are small by comparison with European forces.

Police Organization. Police and fire departments, by tradition, are organized along quasi-military lines. The head of the police department is commonly a professional policeman called the chief.[19] In some cities, especially in the largest cities, the highest-ranking uniformed officer may

[18] *Ibid.*, p. 5.
[19] Terminology for various ranks is not standardized. The most common titles will be used in this section.

be subordinate to a lay department head, called the commissioner, director, or in a few cities, the chief. The lay department head usually does not perform details of departmental administration. His job is to serve as liaison officer between the force and the chief executive. At one time a council committee administered the police department, and in the last half of the nineteenth century it was common for the department to be operated by a semiautonomous board. This is still the case in about seventy cities,[20] but is increasingly giving way to control of the department by the chief executive.

When the head of the department is a professional policeman, he usually serves the chief executive at his pleasure. Under this arrangement, if the appointing chief executive or his successor wishes to appoint a new chief, the incumbent is not dismissed from the service, but is dropped back to a lower position in the departmental hierarchy.

Under the chief, and depending largely upon the size of the city, are numerous supervisory officers arranged in a hierarchy. They are traditionally given military titles. Under the chief, there may be assistant chiefs, then majors or inspectors (especially if the city is large enough to have precinct or district stations), captains, lieutenants, and sergeants. The patrolmen make up the broad base of the pyramid. Detectives may outrank patrolmen, or they may merely be patrolmen with a special position classification.

The force is organized according to the nature of the tasks performed (e.g., patrol and traffic divisions). Larger cities are divided into geographical districts, or precincts, especially for administering the patrol force. In some cities, some of the specialized divisions may also be decentralized so that they operate out of the district stations. Since police work, especially that of the patrol division, is continuous, the force is also divided into platoons, or shifts.

Specialized Units. Even fairly small departments have some degree of specialization, and most departments of more than about 100 men have all of the following operational divisions: [21]

Patrol—to repress criminal activity, regulate conduct, and perform a number of services to the public

Detective—to apprehend criminals, recover stolen property, and gather and prepare evidence for the prosecution of criminals

Traffic control—to prevent accidents and congestion

Vice control—to eliminate commercialized vice and safeguard the morals of the community

---

[20] See the current edition of the *Municipal Year Book* (International City Managers' Association, Chicago) for statistics. The department head is still appointed by the council in about eighty cities.

[21] Wilson, *op. cit.*, pp. 22–24.

Juvenile—to prevent the development of delinquent tendencies in children and to aid in the correction of such tendencies when they do develop

Women's—to perform police duties that can be done best by policewomen

Only a few cities have separate women's divisions. In other places, policewomen are often assigned to the juvenile division and are made available to other divisions as needed.

Police departments, except small ones, are also organized with several staff, or service, divisions to aid the operational divisions. The common ones are:

Records—to record, classify, index, file, and tabulate facts relating to crime, criminals, and other police matters

Communications—to receive and transmit police information and orders, using the telephone, teletype, radio, and other communications devices

Crime laboratory—to identify or establish other facts relating to physical evidence by examining it scientifically

Jail duties—to provide suitable custodial care of prisoners

Property management—to care for department-owned property and property temporarily in police custody

Maintenance—to service, repair, and maintain police buildings, vehicles, and other property

The Patrol Division. The largest division, and the core of police-department operations, is the patrol division. Patrol attempts to eliminate the opportunities or desire for misconduct, investigates offenses, apprehends offenders, recovers lost or stolen property, aids lost or distressed persons, and performs dozens of other tasks.

In an earlier day, the patrolman followed his established beat alone. He could call for assistance by using a whistle, but he was largely on his own. Later, telephone call boxes with signal lights were established so that the patrolman could call in to his supervisor or be called. But today the foot patrol is being used less and less, and the motor patrol has become the standard operation. Most cities still use the former for the business district, however.

In an effort to explain the high rate of crime to their own satisfaction, some laymen have in recent years come to the conclusion that one fault is to be found in this trend in patrol usage. They argue that the cop on the beat is more effective in *preventing* crime than is the patrol car, since the latter can arrive on the scene only *after* the report of a crime or a suspicious person. The foot patrolman, it is argued, may surprise a burglar at work, and his very presence on the sidewalk is a deterrent to potential lawbreakers. Experts in police administration point out that actual experience does not support this viewpoint. In fact, the motor patrol with its constant communication, speed, range, and other advantages is not only the least expensive form of patrol, but it is for most purposes far more effective than is the old-fashioned foot patrol.[22]

Partly as a result of attempts to reduce the wage bill and partly because some authorities on police administration believe them to be more efficient, a trend has developed toward the use of one- rather than two-man patrol cars. About 90 per cent of the municipalities over 10,000 now use the one-man patrol for some shifts. O. W. Wilson, an authority on police administration, has urged the use of one-man cars because "a patrolman who is able to perform his duty satisfactorily while alone on foot should not find it necessary to have a brother officer accompany him when he is equipped with the most modern means of transportation and communication. Actually he works more efficiently, effectively, and safely when alone." Wilson believes that this system provides more patrol units, with each officer giving his job undivided attention with no visiting, swapping of stories, or neglect of safety precautions.[23]

Bicycles were once used for patrol by many police forces, and they have not completely passed from use today. Horses were once common, especially for controlling crowds and traffic, and for mobility and range before the auto. Today, departments that retain a mounted division do so as a luxury. The beautiful animals are impressive at parades, but they have been supplanted for useful purposes. The three-wheeled motorcycle is used a good deal for chalk marking and ticketing parked autos and is apparently the best piece of equipment for this purpose. The two-wheeled motorcycle is still used a good deal, especially in large cities, because of its high maneuverability and acceleration rate, but it has little to recommend it over patrol cars and its operation is extremely hazardous.[24] Cities as large as Boston and Cincinnati have virtually abandoned its use.

The Detective Division. Laymen may be surprised to learn that until recent years detectives had no greater training or education than uniformed patrolmen. In fact, the two classifications were commonly interchangeable. This situation still exists in many cities, but it is now generally recognized that detectives should be specialists. O. W. Wilson says: [25]

[22] O. W. Wilson, "Put the Cop Back on the Beat," *Public Management*, vol. 35 (June, 1953), pp. 122–125; S. R. Schrotel, "Changing Patrol Methods," *The Annals of the American Academy of Political and Social Science*, vol. 291 (January, 1954), pp. 46–53.

[23] Wilson, *Police Administration*, pp. 101–102.

[24] *Ibid.*, pp. 95–96.

[25] *Ibid.*, pp. 124–125. See also P. L. Kirk, "Progress in Criminal Investigation," *The Annals of the American Academy of Political and Social Science*, vol. 291 (January, 1954), pp. 54–62.

Routine patrol service with its manifold problems and experience in preliminary investigations provides invaluable training for future detectives. The qualities of a good detective are an abundance of physical and nervous energy, considerably more-than-ordinary persistence, imagination, and ingenuity with the initiative and force to apply them, and a broad background of experience with special reference to information sources. Psychological and physical tests may one day be developed to measure these qualities, but at present the best method of discovering latent investigative talents is to observe preliminary investigations by patrolmen for the purpose of selecting those who give evidence of investigative ability for trial service in the detective division.

The detective, although he is experienced in investigation and interrogation, today leaves much of the work that he himself once attempted to specialists in the records and crime-laboratory divisions of the department. Examinations for physical evidence and measurements, diagrams, and photographs at crime scenes, for example, have been turned over in larger cities to specialists from the laboratory who are assistants to the expert criminalist.

It is quite common, especially in larger cities, for detectives to work in pairs. Some police authorities believe, however, that cities can economize while at the same time improving service by using them singly. It is argued that detectives operate better alone for the same reasons that patrolmen do, and therefore should do so except when making a dangerous investigation or arrest.[26]

The Traffic Division. In handling traffic, the department is concerned with many problems that are not police problems within a narrow sense. It also deals with law violators who are not usually criminals in the popular sense. Because this type of police work is specialized, traffic divisions were organized in a great many cities beginning in the late twenties and early thirties, when the increasing number of automobiles created congestions, hazards, and accidents against which the public rebelled.[27]

More than any other police division perhaps, traffic control is forced to tread a narrow path between public indignation over law violations that lead to hazards and accidents on the one hand, and public objection to vigorous enforcement programs on the other. Almost every citizen is directly and constantly affected by the activities of the traffic division. As is the American habit, driver-citizens are quick to criticize no matter

[26] Wilson, *Police Administration,* p. 127.

[27] See F. M. Kreml, "The Specialized Traffic Division," *The Annals of the American Academy of Political and Social Science,* vol. 291 (January, 1954), pp. 63–72; and W. S. Smith, "Widening the Traffic Enforcement Front," *The Annals of the American Academy of Political and Social Science,* vol. 291 (January, 1954), pp. 73–77.

how lacking in technical knowledge of traffic enforcement they may be, and they often expect miracles from those entrusted with solving the traffic problem.

The traffic division is made up of policemen using specially equipped vehicles who are specially trained to investigate accidents and record data and evidence. Traffic policemen sometimes help handle the enforcement of parking regulations, the regulation of moving traffic, and intersection and crosswalk duty in addition to their principal functions. The division also records and analyzes accident and traffic-flow data so as to be able to judge enforcement effectiveness and to plan changes in the traffic pattern. For this function, the division requires the help of traffic engineers, who may be inside or outside the police department. In policing traffic and accidents, the division is partly dependent upon support and cooperation from other divisions, especially patrol, and in investigations, the detective division as well. Furthermore, traffic officers have a responsibility to aid other divisions in ordinary law enforcement in the course of their regular duties.

Since the police cannot issue warning or citation tickets for every violation, a policy of *selective enforcement* must be followed. Under these circumstances, the traffic division has an important responsibility in safety education. It attempts to educate not only school children but the adult public to be better drivers. Seeking to do this, the division tries to develop safe driver attitudes and habits. (There is a well-known tendency for the motorist to use his auto as a weapon for working off aggressive and rebellious feelings and thus to act selfishly and differently from the way he does when not behind the wheel.) It cooperates with schools, safety patrols, safety councils, radio and television stations, and other agencies in seeking to inform the public and to get a better public understanding of police problems.

There are three principal methods of enforcing traffic regulations, other than through a general-education campaign: through use of the warning, the traffic-violator school, and the citation. The warning is relatively inexpensive both as to administrative costs and as to costs in public good will. It is successful in controlling a very large part of the driver population. The traffic-violator school is a product of Depression days, when few people could afford to pay traffic fines. It is the most effective treatment, according to studies, although violators resent the time they must spend at traffic school.[28] The citation, ordinarily followed by fine or jail, is the traditional treatment for traffic violators, but its effectiveness is more limited than the lay public realizes. Criminologists know that the threat of punishment, including that of incarceration, is of limited value

[28] See Wilson, *Police Administration*, pp. 158–166 and 171–177.

as a deterrent to law violation. In the case of traffic violation, punishment is even less effective because the public is often unsympathetic to police efforts toward rigid enforcement. While the police can, through education, build up traffic "enforcement tolerance," it is not high in any American community.

The Vice Division. [29] Enforcement of laws dealing with the moral code is the duty of the vice division. The term *vice* includes gambling, prostitution, and the illegal use of narcotics and intoxicants. Because this task involves problems and techniques differing from those of ordinary criminal investigation, a separate division handles vice in larger cities, and even in middle-sized cities a squad or a detective or two will normally be assigned exclusively to vice control.

Contrary to what much of the public believes, the professional policeman is ready, willing, and able to suppress organized vice whenever the public demands that he do so. In the typical middle-sized or small community, little or no organized vice exists. Despite this, however, and as a result of public tolerance, vice operations are active in many cities, and the need for their suppression is everywhere continuous for reasons discussed above.

Although police officers, especially those in command positions, are not infrequently corrupted by organized crime, this cannot happen if the city administration is opposed to it; and it will never happen if the dominant opinion among citizens indicates a desire to have the law enforced. While an element of selective enforcement of vice laws must always exist (it would be immensely expensive, for example, for the police to attempt to eliminate all private, small-stakes gambling), professional law-enforcement officers are able to enforce the laws, and they do not consider vice control a hopeless, uncontrollable problem as the layman often does.

The Juvenile Division. Police administrators view the juvenile division as being in the same class as preventive medicine and fire prevention—it deals with the prevention of crime "by correcting conditions that induce criminality and by rehabilitating the delinquent." [30] In seeking to do this, the police cooperate with schools, probation officers, social agencies, recreation departments, and public welfare agencies. Sometimes they attempt to duplicate or usurp the functions of these agencies and conflicts or power struggles ensue.

[29] Above, the term *vice squad* was used because it was found in the Kefauver reports. In this section, "division" is used as the principal subdivision of a department. Vice control may be invested in a division, bureau, squad, unit, or a subdivision with some other designation.

[30] See Wilson, *Police Administration*, chap. 11, and Jane E. Rinck, "Supervising the Juvenile Delinquent," *The Annals of the American Academy of Political and Social Science*, vol. 291 (January, 1954), pp. 78–86.

According to O. W. Wilson, a well-rounded program should include the following activities: [31]

1. The eradication, by patrol, inspection, supervision, and investigation, of elements that induce criminal tendencies and of conditions that promote criminal activities, especially among children;

2. The discovery of delinquents, near delinquents, and those exposed to high-risk situations, and the treatment of the poorly adjusted;

3. The planning, promotion, and direction of recreation, character building, and other group activities that provide wholesome influences.

The Staff Services. Serving all af the operating divisions are the specialists in the staff divisions. A small city or village cannot afford specialists, has only a rudimentary police laboratory, and must depend on state detective bureaus and the FBI for technical assistance. Larger cities have elaborate crime laboratories under the direction of a criminalist trained in chemistry, biology, and related fields. The advantages of scientific crime detection have caught the public's imagination and interest. The polygraph, or lie detector, is also operated by special personnel at headquarters. The police department needs a records division providing classified, indexed, and filed records of complaints and arrests, together with property-control and identification records, the latter including fingerprint, photograph, and *modus operandi* ("M.O.") files. In large departments these cards may be sorted by electrical automatic data-processing equipment to narrow down the search for a criminal.

Recruitment. American policemen, although improving in ability, are generally considered by authorities to be of inferior quality when compared with European policemen. A part of the cause of this may be traced to our salary schedules. New York, in 1960, expected to attract adequate personnel while paying an entrance salary of $4,800. San Francisco was paying the best beginning salary, $6,228. These offers, in inflationary times, were not very attractive, especially when one considers the qualifications required of competent police officers. Furthermore, the prospects for better pay are not at all good. In 1960, Philadelphia patrolmen could not earn more than about $5,200 even at maximum salaries unless they were promoted to higher jobs. Because policemen are usually prohibited from holding a second job, low pay is probably a particularly important inhibition against recruitment. (In New York in 1955, seventy-two policemen became firemen; probably many of them wanted to take side jobs, which was permitted in the fire department.)

The earliest salaried policemen in America were political appointees. Gradually applicants came to be subjected to physical, mental, and moral examinations or scrutiny. In many cities of all sizes, the recruitment and disciplining of police are under the control of the municipal personnel

[31] Wilson, *Police Administration,* pp. 210–211.

agency. Police administrators in general disapprove of this practice and desire independent control over personnel.[32]

Local-residence requirements are contrary to the merit principle, yet they remain common. According to police authorities, a desirable candidate is one in his early twenties who has a high-school education or better, is above average in size, is in very good health, is psychologically stable, and is above average in intelligence. Police recruits must be of unimpeachable character and should have a suitable personality as determined by psychological tests and interviews. One of the problems of recruiting in an earlier day was that sadists, overly aggressive persons, and other psychologically unstable persons often chose to become policemen, and there was no process for weeding them out.

Promotions are based upon a variety of considerations, depending on local conditions. No reliable written examination has yet been developed to test leadership potential. In the actual practices of many departments, promotions are often made because the officer has been an excellent patrolman, has strong political support, is regarded by his superiors as having leadership ability, has given faithful service for many years, has a large family and needs the money, or has committed acts of heroism. Effective leadership, however, does not result from sentimentality in the promotion process.

Training.[33] Police departments usually encourage some preservice training in the form of useful high school and college courses, but the superintendent of the Cincinnati Police Academy believes that correspondence courses, cram courses to pass the entrance examinations, and preservice college courses in police administration are of little or no value. Concerning the last of these, he believes that a person should not be prepared for a high police administrative post before he has had field experience as a policeman.[34]

In recent years, efforts to raise the caliber of personnel has led to the establishment of police academies in most larger cities and the operation of hundreds of police institutes for smaller cities under the sponsorship of the FBI. In Los Angeles, for example, the recruit is put through a

[32] Police administrators, like members of other professions, desire autonomy for their function of government. Because of the unique nature of their task, they often succeed in securing independence from central municipal staff services in budgeting, personnel, purchasing, and maintenance, and from traffic engineering. On police personnel, see R. A. Lothian, "The Operation of a Police Merit System," *The Annals of the American Academy of Political and Social Science,* vol. 291 (January, 1954), pp. 97–106; and Wilson, *Police Administration,* chaps. 19–20.

[33] See R. E. Clift, "Police Training," *The Annals of the American Academy of Political and Social Science,* vol. 291 (January, 1954), pp. 113–118; Wilson, *Police Administration,* chap. 21; "Police in the Making," *The New York Times Magazine,* May 15, 1960, pp. 43–44.

[34] Clift, *op. cit.,* p. 114.

thirteen-week training course in police law and procedures, first aid, self-defense, physical conditioning, and discipline. Emotionally unstable men and others who should not have passed the entrance examinations are eliminated at this time. Patrolmen undergo periodic retraining during their years on the force. Other training takes place constantly on the job, of course, as supervisors correct the mistakes of subordinates.

The Jail. The city jail is usually administered by the police department. The local prison is likely to be primarily of the congregate type of design with a large bull pen to house most prisoners. There may be a few cells to segregate notoriously tough prisoners and the violently insane. Jails are seldom constructed to meet the multifunctional demands placed upon them. They house a great variety of persons: major offenders awaiting trial; habitual misdemeanants, many of them psychopaths; elderly degenerates; youthful minor offenders; traffic violators; drunks locked up for a single night; vagrants; material witnesses; and others.[35]

At least 1 million persons spend some time in jail each year. It is doubtful if many profit from the experience. The general public has never regarded jails as being of much importance and does not approve of the expenditure of large amounts of money "to make things comfortable for crooks and drunks." Police administrators of jails, in the great majority of cases, are concerned with custody, and little effort is made in most cities to identify the personal problems which helped cause incarceration. Even less effort goes toward rehabilitation or preventive activities.

MUNICIPAL COURTS

Courts are essentially state institutions. Outside of cities, the justice of the peace has traditionally handled minor civil and criminal cases, with county, district, superior, or other trial courts of record handling the major cases. Within cities, where a large number of misdemeanors, especially by traffic violators, take place, it is common to provide so-called "municipal" courts, although major civil and criminal cases are usually handled by the regular court system. In the largest cities, however, special courts often exist for each type of case.[36]

The Concept of Justice. Justice is a relative thing. And in the individual case it depends upon the philosophy, attitude, diligence, interest, and other considerations of the police officer, the prosecutor, the judge, the jurors, the defense attorney, the probation officer, and every other

[35] U.S. Bureau of Prisons, *Handbook of Correctional Institution Design and Construction* (1949), p. 168.

[36] For more detail on the judiciary, see Charles R. Adrian, *State and Local Governments* (McGraw-Hill Book Company, Inc., 1960), chap. 17.

person who comes in contact with the case. A generation ago, union organizers, upon entering many a community, were beaten up and driven from town by the very police who were supposedly entrusted with the protection of their civil rights. Whether a sex offender is given a long sentence but no psychiatric treatment, or is put on probation with treatment made a condition, may depend largely upon the personal view of the judge. The United States Supreme Court can hand down impressive opinions concerning freedom of speech, but the actual freedom one enjoys is likely to depend upon the policies of the local mayor or manager and police chief. After all, it takes years to appeal cases and a decision by the high court against the local police may sometimes be met by the simple expedient of ignoring the ruling when the next related case comes up. Of course, the appeal of the second case may take years, too. The United States Supreme Court has sought to retain the ancient concept of freedom from unreasonable searches and seizures. But for every formal ruling that takes place, the local police make thousands of searches and seizures. One's individual rights in most of these cases are a hostage of the standard procedures of the police department and of the judgment of the individual policeman. The cop on the beat does not read Supreme Court decisions. He uses what he considers to be common sense, heavily overlaid, no doubt, with his personal sense of values and his own estimates of what will gain him a promotion and what will bring down censure from his superior

The justice one receives also depends partly upon one's status and one's connections in the community. A police officer may take a different view toward a man in greasy overalls who stumbles out of a working-class tavern than he will toward a man dressed in a well-tailored suit who stumbles out of the bar of the most expensive hotel in town. The former may spend the night in the "drunk tank"; the latter may be helped to his room.

Differential justice of this type should not be confused, however, with a tendency of a jury to apply cultural values or the popular sentiment of the moment to a particular case. A jury will often refuse to convict a woman who kills her unfaithful husband, for example. In the South, the mores may prevent a jury from finding a white man guilty of a crime against a Negro. If the jurors believe the penalty prescribed by law is too severe for a particular crime, they will not convict regardless of the evidence, and the result sometimes is that the state legislature must modify the law to suit the jurors' concept of justice.

Justice is slow and costly. Newspaper editors turn some cases into Roman holidays. The laws of evidence do not maintain pace with the advance of scientific knowledge. The people who have the most difficulty with the law are also least likely to have the social and economic resources with which to defend themselves; those who possess these resources, should they require use of them, therefore have disproportionate influence.

Law and the judicial process, then, are parts of the total culture in which they exist and are subjected to the same kinds of pressures that affect our other institutions. They change, as do our other political institutions, but because they are widely expected to maintain stability in society, they change rather slowly, and they give advantage to those who favor the *status quo* and obedience to the existing law.

The Justice of the Peace. The traditional institution for community justice is that of the justice court. This court originated in England and has existed in this country almost without change since colonial times. The justice of the peace (JP) need not be an attorney and probably knows little law, but he is authorized to hear and settle civil actions involving small amounts of money (up to a limit of, say, $500), hold preliminary hearings for felonies, and try minor criminal cases. The JP was once a man of considerable prestige in his neighborhood, but this is not likely to be the case today. Instead of being a country squire whose "father image" allowed him to dispense a rule-of-thumb justice in neighborhood disputes in an agrarian society with a relatively simple legal system, he is now likely to be some minor local politician of modest social standing.

Normally, JPs are paid through fees and so do not receive salaries. The justice thus profits from each case that comes before him, and he may engage in advertising and in agreements with local peace officers in order to increase his volume of business.

The office of the justice of the peace has been criticized a great deal in recent decades. The fact that the JP is elected by a small constituency gives him an opportunity to profit from nonresidents who come before his court, and he may do so with no fear of electoral recrimination. Although appeal lies from all justice court decisions to the major trial court of the area, in practice the delay and cost involved in appeals usually leave the citizen at the mercy of the justice. Yet this officer is commonly untrained in the law, responsible to no one for his acts (the professional lawyer-judge is embarrassed if he is criticized or overruled by a higher court, but not the typical justice), and has a financial interest in the outcome of each case.

Efforts have been made to eliminate the justice court, but its presiding officer is normally influential in local politics, especially in those states where he sits as a member of the county or township governing board, and the justices frequently have powerful state-wide organizations to protect their interests before the legislature. Despite this, in recent years the character of the office has been changing. In some states, it has lost some of its powers. In many parts of the country, justices are largely inactive and many do not even bother to qualify for office once elected. In 1957, Ohio abolished the office of justice of the peace, substituting for it a system of county courts and municipal courts with expanded jurisdiction.[37]

Other Minor Courts. Although justice courts continue to exist in urban and especially suburban communities, the tendency is for cities to have their own court systems, generally under names such as "magistrate's court," "traffic court," "court of common pleas," or "police court."

In some cases, these courts are little more than renamed justice courts and have generally the same powers and characteristics.[38] Others, however, are headed by salaried judges who have legal training and devote full time to the job. The pay is likely to be poor, however, the courts undignified, and the judges not of high quality, though there are probably many exceptions to this generalization. The person of influence is usually treated far differently from a low-status person.

These courts deal particularly with traffic cases but also handle such things as lawsuits or contract-violation claims involving a few hundred dollars, violations of building codes, and landlord-and-tenant statutes; family disputes, alcoholics, prostitutes, and feuding neighbors; or complaints from mentally disturbed persons who fancy that they have been wronged. In some cases, the judge's ability to serve as a counsellor or lay psychiatrist may be more important than his knowledge of the law.[39]

Item: The Texas Courts.[40] A study made of the Texas municipal courts offers some examples that suggest the particular characteristics of these institutions. More people come before the so-called "corporation courts" of that state each year than before all other courts of the state combined. The power of the judge is enormous and in his hands is held the fate of the citizen who appears charged as a misdemeanant—his judgment is final in 99 per cent of the cases handled by the court. Proceedings are highly informal:

[37] On the justice of the peace, see L. W. Lancaster, *Government in Rural America* (2d ed.; D. Van Nostrand Company, Inc., Princeton, N.J., 1952), pp. 175–180; C. F. Snider, *Local Government in Rural America* (Appleton-Century-Crofts, Inc., New York, 1957), pp. 305–317; and the citations from both works.

[38] Forrest Talbott, *Intergovernmental Relations and the Courts* (University of Minnesota Press, Minneapolis, Minn., 1950), pp. 53–61; James M. Cook, "The Metropolitan Traffic Problem and the Corporation Court," *Public Affairs Comment,* vol. 6 (July, 1960), pp. 1–4.

[39] See George Warren, *Traffic Courts* (Little, Brown & Company, Boston, 1942); Morris Ploscowe, "The Inferior Criminal Courts in Action," *Annals,* vol. 287 (May, 1953), pp. 8–12, and other articles in the same volume; H. H. Curran, *Magistrates Courts* (Charles Scribner's Sons, New York, 1942); and Maxine B. Virtue, *Survey of Metropolitan Courts, Detroit Area* (University of Michigan Press, Ann Arbor, Mich., 1950).

[40] Cook, *op. cit.*

A constant procession of defendants and witnesses stream before the judge, and the judge has only a limited amount of time to consider each case before pronouncing judgment. Although the defendant is entitled to a jury trial in the corporation court, only a small percentage of cases are actually tried before a jury. The great majority of persons appearing before the court do so without benefit of legal counsel.

Under such circumstances, the question of whether the defendant gets what society would consider a fair trial depends almost entirely upon the sense of duty of the judge and prosecutor, upon the inhibiting influences of the ethos of the law which affect every actor in the courtroom.

The system offers considerable advantage to the person who has a general knowledge of politics and the law, who is verbally skilled, and who can afford to hire an attorney. For example, such a person might know, or could learn from his lawyer, that he might well escape penalty by appeal to the county court. Under Texas law (and the law in most states), appeal from the minor court results in retrial starting over again from the beginning (tried *de novo*, as the lawyers say). But the busy county judges tend to postpone the trials of these cases, for they consider them to be less important than the murder charges and major lawsuits that await hearing. In the meantime witnesses die or move away. Perhaps the case never is scheduled for trial. Even cases that are, in some of the county courts, are dismissed by the harried and overworked judge on technical grounds simply in order to clear the docket. But the typical defendant does not know this, or believes that he cannot afford appeal. He is convicted and fined, or jailed.[41]

FIRE PROTECTION

Color, Drama—and Carelessness.[42] American cities have the finest fire equipment in the world, but they also have the greatest annual fire losses. Such losses in the United States exceed 1,000 million dollars annually— most of it in cities. Americans are not very economy-conscious. Europeans, endowed with fewer of nature's gifts, must be conservationists. Americans, for example, are seldom prosecuted for contributory negligence

[41] For the local courts of a large city, see Virtue, *op. cit.*, and Wallace S. Sayre and Herbert Kaufman, *Governing New York City* (Russell Sage Foundation, New York, 1960), chap. 14.

[42] A detailed manual of administration is *Municipal Fire Administration* (6th ed.; International City Managers' Association, 1956), from which the author has borrowed for this section. See also President's Conference on Fire Prevention, *Reports of Committees* (1947); an urban case study by J. K. Trump, Morton Kroll, and J. R. Donoghue, *Metropolitan Los Angeles: A Study in Integration*. VI. *Fire Protection* (The Haynes Foundation, Los Angeles, 1952), and Frank P. Sherwood and Beatrice Markey, *The Mayor and the Fire Chief* (University of Alabama Press, University, Ala., 1959).

in cases of fires. Losses, it is felt, are somehow "paid by the insurance company." Insurance rates are not associated with fire rates. (It might be noted that in nearly all American states, fire-insurance rates are determined by the quality of *fire defense equipment* in each community, with no consideration given to actual *fire-loss* experience.)

The core cities of urban areas typically have modern, professional fire departments. The larger the city, the more specialized the equipment is likely to be. Suburbs and small cities, on the other hand, often depend upon amateur departments. Some small residential communities make it a practice to hire a few full-time members who man the station and equipment, with volunteer amateurs on call to follow along at each fire alarm. Other municipalities, especially suburbs, are following the practice of training men as both police and firemen.[43]

It is a peculiar phenomenon of American life, best left to the explanation of psychologists, perhaps, that citizens will be apathetic in responding to calls for volunteers for blood donations, civil defense, or even the manning of a charity booth at a church bazaar, but will establish waiting lists to join a volunteer fire department. In fact, volunteer companies were such powerful pressure groups in New York and Philadelphia that they were able to prevent the installation of professional systems in those cities until 1865 and 1870, respectively, even though the first paid department had been inaugurated in Boston as early as 1837. This urge to assist, or to offer "helpful" information, is useful to the city government, but is also a nuisance at times.

Fire Prevention. Fire departments have a responsibility for preventing fires as they do for fire fighting. Europeans have long placed heavy emphasis upon fire-prevention procedures, but the idea has received serious and general attention in the United States only since about the mid-1920s. In their prevention activities, fire departments depend heavily upon routine inspections performed by the men of neighborhood fire stations. They seek to correct common hazards (e.g., accumulated rubbish, dirty chimneys, defective heating equipment). Periodically, technical surveys by trained engineers are made in some cities to suggest major improvements in the use and construction of buildings.

Fire prevention also involves the granting of permits, licenses, and certificates of approval (e.g., for the design of fire escapes, the use of dry-cleaning materials, the licensing of motion-picture operators, and the installation of oil burners). It is the responsibility of the city council (and in some cases of the state legislature) to provide adequate fire-prevention codes. The department also investigates the causes of fires and seeks to give publicity to fire statistics so that the public may learn from the

[43] See C. S. James, "The Integration of Fire and Police Services," *Public Management,* vol. 36 (February, 1954), pp. 26–29.

experiences of others. Firemen cooperate with municipal, school, and private agencies in teaching school children and the adult public the principles of fire prevention.

Fire-fighting Equipment. Cities are heavy concentrations of what the professional fire fighter calls "burnable values." Fighting fires in cities crowded with people, with buildings close together and with some of them reaching many stories into the air, is a technical and complex profession. The basic equipment for all urban departments includes internal-combustion pumpers, ladder trucks, hose, and nozzles. High-pressure pumpers capable of delivering 1,000 gallons of water a minute are now available and within the budget possibilities of middle-sized cities. Mechanical aerial ladders are used to reach the higher stories of buildings. They are expensive for the city to buy, but they are safer than old-style ladders, can be put into use more quickly, and have a low operating cost. Cities of all sizes also need chemical equipment for fighting various types of fires against which water is ineffective or dangerous to use.

Larger departments must be equipped with gas masks, asbestos suits, Pulmotors, and other rescue-squad equipment. Often they use fire boats. Recent developments in equipment include the increasing use of water-fog and water-spray nozzles that were developed by the United States Navy and Coast Guard during World War II. (The fog or spray turns to steam. Expansion then pushes smoke and heat out of the building, thus greatly reducing the temperature, clearing smoke and gas from the building, and putting out the fire. The method is fast acting and results in reduced smoke and water damage.)

Fires were once commonly reported by following the instructions to "break glass, pull lever" at the nearest alarm box, but the increasingly commonplace telephone has now largely supplanted the boxes in use. About 400 cities of over 10,000 population no longer use alarm boxes. Cities as large as Little Rock and Des Moines have none.

Larger fire departments, with their decentralization of equipment, must have elaborate methods of relaying alarms to the station in the vicinity of the fire, of indicating the intensity of a fire, of sending additional equipment by a prearranged plan when the original equipment answering a call cannot cope with the problem it encounters, of keeping track of equipment that is out of the stations, and of transferring equipment to unguarded sections of the city if some area's regular equipment is out on call.

Departmental Organization. Fire-department organization in general parallels that of the police department. At least fifty cities still have a lay fire commissioner in charge, although in others the departments are headed by professional chiefs chosen from the departments or, in a few instances, from fire departments in other cities. Fire or safety boards still appoint the chief in quite a few cities, and in nearly 100 weak-mayor cities the council makes the appointment. Normally, however, the appointment is made by the chief executive. In all but small cities, district stations are established with a company under the command of a lieutenant or captain. In very large cities, several companies in a section of the city may be organized into a battalion or district. In suburbs and small cities the volunteer firemen usually learn a good deal about the government of the community (political gossip is one of the staples around the fire house) and often become important figures in local election campaigns. They may be active because the mayor has chosen them with an eye to developing a low-voltage political device, or because they have stakes in the decisions of the council (allowances for clothing, a new pumper), or simply because they are a well-knit group that enjoys politics as a game.

Professional firemen work a platoon (shift) system, since stations must be manned at all hours. It was once common for them to be on duty for an eighty-four-hour week. Much duty time is, of course, spent in eating, sleeping, and card playing, and many firemen take outside employment on their days off; thus firemen must spend a great deal of time away from their homes and families. The average duty hours have been decreasing, especially in large cities, and in 1960 were sixty-three hours, with continuing pressure for further reduction.

Training. Stemming from the traditions of volunteer days, fire department ments did not have trained personnel until recent decades. The result of lack of training was, of course, unnecessary property damage and unnecessary fire losses. Today large cities have facilities for training their own recruits in the use of the highly complicated equipment that is now common. About two-thirds of the states provide for state-wide training courses which are available to all cities and villages in the training of their personnel. Training programs involve not only physical conditioning, but also instruction in the use of equipment, chemicals, and explosives, in fire-fighting techniques, in ventilation, and in making fire-prevention inspections.

OTHER PUBLIC SAFETY FUNCTIONS

Weights and Measures. One of the oldest functions entrusted to local government, first in England and then in the United States, was the task of overseeing the use of devices for determining weights and measures. The job of checking for honesty and accuracy is handled in larger cities by specially trained persons and in smaller places by the police department.

Smoke Abatement. In years past, American industrial plants concentrated exclusively upon maximizing profits and increasing size. There was little interest in the side effects of factory life or in the community results of releasing smoke to irritate lungs and blacken buildings. Today factory management is much more concerned about its responsibility to the rest of society. City ordinances are coming to assert more and more

HOW DID YOU MANAGE TO QUIT SMOKING?

Figure 17-3. Note: St. Louis adopted an effective smoke-control ordinance (over powerful opposition) a generation ago. Fortunately for the core city, uncooperating industrial suburbs in Illinois were downwind. SOURCE: Used by permission of Daniel R. Fitzpatrick and the *St. Louis Post-Dispatch*.

that smoke, dirt, and noise from a factory are damaging to society and that their abatement is part of the cost of doing business.

Smoke-abatement ordinances with effective enforcement provisions are coming into being. The problem has been one, not of complexity of administration, but of a willingness to enforce such ordinances. "The most important element in handling the problem," T. H. Reed has said, "is an ordinance clearly defining prohibited practices and then a courageous and personable inspector to enforce it. Even in a large city, no considerable force is necessary for this purpose." [44] Cincinnati, for example, employs about twenty persons in its bureau.

Traffic Engineering. T. H. Reed has said: [45]

So far as the traffic problem is concerned with laying out new thoroughfares, widening old ones, locating traffic circles and medial strips, and placing buildings toward which traffic naturally converges, [traffic engineering] belongs to the local planning agency. Actual construction of new traffic facilities is a matter for the department of public works. The enforcement of traffic regulations and reporting of accidents are clearly part of the duty of the police department. There is much, however, which can be done by studying the movement of traffic to determine what regulations should be made for the use of existing streets and where traffic signals should be located. This is the field of traffic engineering in its narrower sense.

In the past, traffic engineering was often decentralized. There might be a traffic-safety bureau in the department of public works, another in the police department, and a traffic-study group in the planning agency. Today there is an increasing trend toward centralizing these functions in a separate agency whose main problem is to keep the principal business districts and the main traffic arteries from becoming choked with automobiles. As the number of automobiles increases, this function increases in importance.

Civil Defense. Despite the threatened use of thermonuclear weapons in the event of war, the American public, even in metropolitan areas that would appear to be prime H-bomb targets, has been almost completely apathetic toward the development of a system of defense. The public regards the problem either as futile or as a technical one not involving popular participation at this time. Even industry has resisted Federal-government policies of deconcentration.

The Federal government has developed a civil-defense program in cooperation with state and local agencies, but many cities have done little to further planning and preparation. While others have worked at it, they have had great difficulty in getting volunteers to fill positions.

[44] T. H. Reed, *Municipal Management* (McGraw-Hill Book Company, Inc., New York, 1941), p. 401.
[45] *Ibid.*, p. 405.

Statements made from time to time by authorities on nuclear physics have added to resigned apathy by indicating that there is no real defense for urban areas except by evacuation. But no warning system is adequate to allow time for evacuation. It would appear, then, that the best defense for American cities is the prevention of World War III. It is likely, however, that a municipal civil-defense program is of *psychological* value as a means of reminding the public of the danger and horrible destructiveness of war. Some city officials have effectively combined the program with a disaster plan, so that the city is prepared for such emergencies as floods and tornadoes.[46]

[46] For a criticism of civil defense, see Robert Moses, "The Civil Defense Fiasco," *Harper's,* vol. 215 (November, 1957), pp. 29–34. On city governments in emergencies, see Morton Kroll, "The Challenge of Disaster to Administration," *Public Administration Review,* vol. 19 (Summer, 1959), pp. 203–204; and R. H. Marden, "Disaster," *ibid.,* vol. 20 (Spring, 1960), pp. 100–104.

Chapter 18

PUBLIC UTILITIES AND TRANSPORTATION

Public utilities provide services that are essential to urban living, given the American system of values. Of them all, public transportation has probably offered the biggest problem to municipal administrators in all except the smallest cities in the period after World War II. In addition to public utilities, this chapter will also examine the general topic of urban transportation.

PUBLIC UTILITIES [1]

Public utilities are not necessarily publicly owned. Many of them are, but the majority are actually owned and operated by private corporations, and some by individual proprietors. A list of utilities within a municipality would include street railways and buses, and telephone, telegraph, electricity, water, and gas services. Other functions that are of the nature of utilities, although not always fully accepted as such, are auditoriums, port facilities, slaughterhouses, airports, and possibly toll bridges, toll roads, sewers, and public markets.

Public utilities, then, are businesses affected with a more than usual amount of public interest and are therefore expected by the public to be subjected to more than a normal amount of governmental control. They are usually granted a monopoly within their areas of operation. This is because experience has shown that competition in these areas is impractical and uneconomical. Competitive utilities have existed in the past—a few still do—but generally they have proved to be wasteful of resources and have offered inferior and costly services to the public. A public utility normally has a right to use public property (over which to string electric wires, or to operate buses) and to exercise the state's power of eminent domain. It usually charges for services rendered on a benefits-received basis, and it is subject to the control of some type of public

[1] Many manuals and pamphlets on applied administration of public utilities are published by the American Public Works Association, Chicago, the Public Administration Service, Chicago, and other professional organizations.

service commission whose legal responsibility it is to protect both the provider and the purchaser of services.

Regulation. In the nineteenth century, utilities were normally operated on the basis of a *franchise* which was granted to local utilities, most commonly, by the city government. A franchise is a license stipulating the conditions under which a utility may operate and the privileges it is to enjoy. The franchise usually stated the quality of service that was expected of the utility and the rates that could be charged. In practice, the utilities were often little inhibited by their franchises. Sometimes they resorted to bribery of public officials, sometimes they won judicial interpretations of ambiguous provisions of the franchise by the use of superior legal talent, and in almost no cases was there a public body that had the legal authority to hold the utility to the terms of its agreement.

One of the major areas of activity of reform forces at the turn of the present century was that of public utility regulation. The method of control that gradually evolved centers around a public service commission (bearing various titles in various states) whose duty it is to determine rates after investigations and hearings, and to supervise both the service and the management of the utilities. Most commissions prescribe uniform accounting methods, they often must approve expansion plans and the issuance of new securities, and they may sometimes even be authorized to order such expansions. Commissions are constantly at work overseeing the activities of the utilities, but there is considerable variation in the degree to which they are effective.

Franchises are still granted, but they are no longer so detailed as they were in the days before public service commissions. They are usually limited to a term of years (perhaps twenty-five) rather than made to exist in perpetuity, as was once common. The franchise usually provides for the privileges to be enjoyed by the utility, it may provide for a special tax structure for it, and it prescribes some conditions which must be met by the utility. It leaves most other controls to the public service commissions. In the worst days of nineteenth-century corruption, control over franchises was assumed by the state, where it has remained for the most part.

The major questions in connection with public utilities have historically been three. First, how are utility rates to be determined? Second, should the state or the city control utilities operating in the city? Third, should utilities be privately or publicly owned?

The Determination of Rates. The question of rate determination is one that can easily take up most of a semester in a college course in public utility regulation without a satisfactory answer being arrived at. The problem in practice has evolved around a question that is almost impossible to answer: What is the true value of a large and complex corporation? If rates are so low that the utility does not receive a fair rate of return on its investment, confiscation of private property results, and this is prohibited by the due-process clause of the Fifth Amendment. But what is the "investment" or "worth" of a utility? Is it more equitable to calculate the revenue that a rate should produce on the basis of a percentage of the present cost of replacing the capital equipment of the utility, or of the actual total investment made over the years? The formula used may make a great difference in the allowable rates. Should changes in the price index be considered? Should any value be placed on the franchise, "good will," or "going concern"?

In an attempt to answer these questions, public service commissions have made valuation studies; but these often take years and are inconclusive, and by the time they are completed their results are no longer applicable to existing conditions. Since due process of law is involved, utilities controversies are commonly adjudicated in the courts on appeal from the commissions. In seeking equity, the United States Supreme Court has for years struggled between the "cost of reproduction" and the "actual amount of prudent investment" theories.[2] While the most recent decision leans toward actual investment in capital without considering the problem of subsequent influences of inflation or deflation, the Court still has not settled on a definitive formula. Even with a formula, there are many questions and problems. Rate determination, despite able research staffs, is still in large part based upon folklore and subjective evaluations, and it is very costly.[3]

Should the State Control Local Utilities? Advocates of a maximum of local self-government sometimes hold that utilities should be controlled by municipal public service commissions, since they operate locally, local people are their customers, and they make use of city property. Some cities do indeed control local utilities in this fashion. The general pattern, however, is for the state to control. An exception is often made in the case of *city-owned* utilities, where quality of service and charges made are left to local authorities.

A state commission is normally in a better position to control utilities, since it has broader jurisdiction. A utility is seldom limited to the boundaries of one city. The "local" telephone company will usually cover one or more states; bus systems include some of the suburbs in their

---

[2] See *Smyth v. Ames,* 169 U.S. 466 (1898), the first landmark case; *Southwestern Bell Telephone Co. v. Missouri,* 262 U.S. 276 (1923); *F.P.C. v. Hope Natural Gas Co.,* 320 U.S. 591 (1944), the ruling case at present.

[3] See John Bauer, *The Public Utility Franchise; Its Functions and Terms under State Regulation* (Public Administration Service, Chicago, 1948); R. E. Caywood, *Electric Utility Rate Economics* (McGraw-Hill Book Company, Inc., New York, 1957); Ellsworth Nichols, *Ruling Principles of Utility Regulation* (Public Utilities Reports, Inc., Washington, 1959).

operations. Even the state does not always have enough breadth of jurisdiction, so the Federal Power Commission controls interstate shipment
of electricity, while the Interstate Commerce Commission controls interstate telephone rates.

The interests to be regulated work hard to influence the behavior of
the public service commission members and their staffs, while these
people in turn usually seek to remain independent of such control. Legislatures often fail or refuse outright to provide adequate staff for effective enforcement activities. Pressures for favoritism, re-enforced by
contributions to political party campaign coffers, remain high. Problems
of this kind in the field of public utilities are chronic; yet the services
are generally provided at a fairly high level of efficiency and at prices
that most of the public probably regards (except perhaps for bus transportation within cities) as not unreasonable.[4]

The state can afford a more adequate technical staff than can communities. Its agency can use the experience gained in a utility proceeding in one community in other proceedings throughout the state. The
regulation of utilities is an enormously complicated problem of economics, law, accounting, and engineering. In general, most municipalities are
helpless in seeking to compete with the skilled experts of the large utility
corporations. Even the largest cities and the states can rarely match
them.

Should Utilities Be Privately or Publicly Owned? In nineteenth-
century America, when the businessman was paid great homage and
when business subsequently attracted the lion's share of talent, utilities
were commonly privately owned. This was in contrast to the practice in
Europe, where, apart from any arguments concerning the merits of socialism, state and municipal ownership of utilities has always been the
rule.

Americans in the past did not trust government, and, with business
proving on all sides that it could "get things done," it was quite natural
for Americans to expect private business to operate utilities. Nevertheless, starting in the nineteenth century it became customary for some
functions to be publicly owned. Water supply, which is closely related
to public health and to fire protection, was the earliest to become commonly a public function.

Most utilities are still privately owned, however, and probably most
citizens regard this as preferable. This despite the fact that the reform
movement around the turn of the century had included in it persons who

---

[4] M. H. Bernstein, *Regulating Business by Independent Commission* (Princeton
University Press, Princeton, N.J., 1955), examines some of the above problems within
Federal agencies. Probably most of his findings apply, in general terms, to state
agencies as well.

strongly advocated the need for municipal ownership of utilities. They argued that private ownership had failed because the utilities acted irresponsibly, with little effective state control and with a policy of maximizing profits and minimizing service. They therefore argued for municipal ownership of various utilities, but especially of urban transportation.

Those who today advocate municipal ownership hold that such a system has many advantages. It creates a system of operation for *use* rather than for *profit*. It is pointed out that private companies often have watered stock, they fail to pass on to the consumers the economies of technological developments, and they frequently fail to pay off their indebtedness, continuing it in order to boost the rate base. Municipalities expand their services less expensively than do private companies because they can normally borrow money at lower interest rates than can private companies. The great cost of determining net investment, which must be done each time a private company asks for a rate increase, is eliminated. Control of the utility is held entirely within the city, for state public service commissions often do not extend their control over functions that are municipally owned. The utilities magnate, with bribe—or at least campaign contribution—in hand is eliminated from local politics.

There are, however, arguments, presented with equal vigor, against municipal ownership. It is held that private utilities have cleaned their own houses since the worst days of blatant corruption and rate gouging in the 1870s and 1880s. American business has proved its ability to produce needed goods and services. A change to relatively untried public ownership and especially public *management* involves an unnecessary risk. The absence of the profit motive produces lethargy, inefficiency, and a lack of interest in technical experimentation. Policy is based on political, rather than economic, considerations. Patronage in small or large degree creeps into the system. Workers who also act as voters—especially if organized into a trade union—are able to exert undue control. They force the wage bill to disproportionate levels. Management is transitory, depending upon elections that may turn on trivial or irrelevant issues, instead of being stable.

Emotion, rather than reason or empirical study, is often the basis of argumentation on both sides. In particular, there is an insufficient amount of data available to prove or disprove many of the arguments. Most of them involve the propaganda technique of "card stacking"—the use of half-truths, or the emphasizing of favorable statistics and considerations and the de-emphasizing of the unfavorable.

No categorical argument can be made for or against municipal ownership. It has worked well in some places, poorly in others. The local environment is an important consideration. So is the relative effectiveness of the local privately owned utilities. If these are very unsatisfactory,

municipal ownership may be less unsatisfactory. There is neither intrinsic good nor evil in public ownership, nor is it part of a philosophy
of socialism. In typical American fashion, the question of its desirability
must be decided on the merits of the individual situation.[5]

The Extent of Municipal Ownership Today. Certain functions are
commonly owned by municipalities today. Nearly three-fourths of the cities of over 5,000 own their own water-distribution systems. Nearly all of
them own their own sewerage systems, and one-half of them own sewage-
treatment plants. Municipal airports and auditoriums are quite common,
and large cities often own incinerators.

Electricity is in the large majority of cases in private hands, although
many cities own plants and lines for distributing power to street lights
and traffic signals. In some parts of the nation, especially in relatively
isolated cities, municipal systems exist—over 500 of them. Of America's
eighteen largest cities (those over one-half a million), only Cleveland
and Los Angeles have city-owned electrical generating and distributing
systems for general use. Municipal gas plants are very rare. Of these
largest cities, only Philadelphia and Houston produce and distribute
gas.

The street railway has all but disappeared in America, and only seven
municipal systems remained in 1960. Thirty-three cities of over 5,000
owned bus systems, however, in addition to the Boston transit, which is
controlled by a separate unit of government.

All of the largest cities own some utilities, except for Boston, which has
them operated on a regional basis by the Massachusetts Metropolitan
District Commission. One city in eight, however, owns no utilities of any
kind, and private ownership is the overwhelming rule even today for
most functions.

MUNICIPAL SERVICES AND UTILITIES

Books have been written about each of the services performed by the
modern city. They are available to the student who desires to make a
detailed study of the various municipal services. This and following
chapters treat municipal functions not from the point of view of the technician, but rather from that of the citizen or the layman who needs a
basic understanding but not a technical account of them.

Highways. All cities must cope with the problem of street paving,
cleaning, and lighting, and sidewalk installation. While basic engineering and financing practices have come to be applied to these functions,
more perplexing problems have arisen in recent years in connection with

[5] John Bauer and Peter Costello, *Public Organization of Electric Power* (Harper &
Brothers, New York, 1949).

the building of high-speed, limited-access expressways and with the finding of off-street parking.

It has become generally accepted, for example, that street width should be measured in terms of automobile lanes, 10 feet to a lane. The actual width of a particular street and its sidewalk is determined on the basis of traffic studies and surveys. The type of surfacing material is today determined largely upon the basis of technical studies known to qualified engineers. The abutting property owners were once permitted to choose the material, but this method is so obviously unsatisfactory that it has been abandoned nearly everywhere. Engineers know the relative merits of concrete, asphaltic concrete, asphalt, macadam, stone blocks, wood blocks, and bricks. They know, for example, that concrete is fine for suburban residential streets and that asphalt is better for most thoroughfares, but that the warehouse district needs something like stone blocks.[6] They, not the property owners, are in a position to choose the best material.

Sidewalks are usually installed shortly after an area is subdivided for development. The principal question of public policy in connection with their construction and maintenance is that of financing. In former days, the property owner constructed the sidewalk, which was then inspected by the municipality to ensure its meeting specifications. A crumbling sidewalk could be condemned by inspectors who would order the owner to replace it, if necessary. This practice is still quite common, although it would seem that a better quality of concrete and a more uniform and satisfactory job could be had if the city did the job itself, either from general taxes or by special assessment.[7]

Mighty Rome had no street lighting and neither did any city of Western civilization until the eighteenth century. Occasional delegations of housewives waiting upon the mayor in his office today sometimes suggest that things have not changed much even after twenty centuries. Although technical specifications as to the proper height, spacing, intensity, and maintenance of street lighting exist, most city streets do not meet them.[8]

Expressways. In large cities, the principal postwar problem and political issue has been in connection with the construction of modern highways within the city. What route should they follow? How often should

[6] The national government furnishes specifications for many technical functions of the municipality. The Public Roads Administration of the Department of Commerce does this for streets. See its publication, *Highway Practice in the U.S.A.* (1949).

[7] Street construction and maintenance, sidewalks, lighting, and cleaning are covered in the International City Managers' Association, *Municipal Public Works Administration* (5th ed., 1957).

[8] See *Public Lighting Practice* (American Public Works Association, Chicago, 1945). On professional standards as optimums, see above, chap. 13.

there be an entrance-and-exit interchange? Expressways are enormously expensive. The Hollywood Freeway in Los Angeles cost about 5 million dollars per mile. The John Lodge and Edsel Ford Expressways in Detroit cost almost 8.5 million dollars per mile. How should they be paid for? Would a toll road be feasible? Should they be paid for out of a rebate to the city from the state gasoline tax? Out of the general revenue fund? Out of a local tax on each automobile? Expressways damage property values along their routes but enhance the values of property at either end of them. One of their main purposes is to shore up sagging property values in the downtown area and to keep up the dollar volume of business in downtown stores. If these establishments benefit particularly from the highways, should they be asked to pay an extra tax to compensate for this advantage?

Congress anticipated a postwar need for road building after a backlog of several years had built up during the war. It also recognized that additional autos would soon be on the road and therefore provided in the Federal Aid Highway Act of 1944 that one-fourth of such Federal funds should be used for the extension of U.S. highways within cities. As a result, many cities are building roads with up to 90 per cent of the cost paid out of Federal grants-in-aid. Because this is the case, many questions of routing and technical specifications are settled, not by local considerations, but by the Public Roads Administration. This agency must approve the route and all technical details before the Federal funds are made available. In most cases the cost of building is so great that without these funds there could be no expressway.

Many states are granting aid money to cities for building these high-speed, limited-access highways, and they have helped in other ways, too. Michigan, for example, has allowed its cities to issue bonds in anticipation of their future receipts of state-collected, locally shared gasoline taxes.

The use of Federal and state grants and of revenue from gasoline taxes have been the most popular methods of financing highways. Asking the downtown property owner to contribute a larger share has been suggested by some labor-backed candidates for municipal office, but this has not proved popular with the owners or the public. In several cities the county has paid part of the cost.

As part of the Interstate System, all large cities have developed plans for expressways leading to the central business district and, for those who wish to bypass, belting the city along the periphery (see Figure 18-1). The negotiations among the various units of government involved —core city, suburbs, county, state, and the Federal Bureau of Public Roads—are complex, delicate, and time-consuming. The technicians in the state and Federal agencies are likely to dominate these discussions—

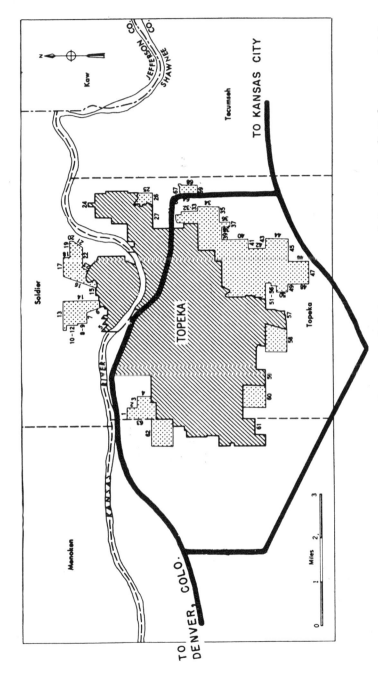

Figure 18-1a. Plans for the system of interstate highways include bypasses around the city and a limited-access route into the heart of it, if the community is of a certain size. SOURCE: Bureau of Public Roads, U.S. Department of Commerce, *General Location of National System of Interstate Highways* (1955), p. 25.

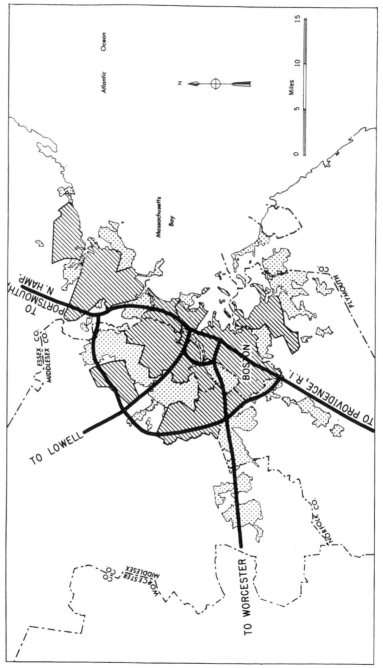

Figure 18-1b. SOURCE: *Ibid.*, p. 37.

though the often-dissenting views of community political figures may dominate the pages of the local newspaper—and these men are in many ways changing the face of the nation, for a modification in the arterial traffic pattern is likely to cause a great many changes in land use.[9] Meanwhile, back at the city hall, however, local interests urge the mayor or manager to intercede on their behalf. The engineers wish to maximize traffic flow in and around cities, and they want to prohibit later rule changes (e.g., in access privileges) that will modify the principal use of a road from a traffic to a business artery; real-estate operators will try to mold the shape of the new road to fit their speculations and investments; owners of unsalable land will try to convince the decision makers that their property lies directly along what is certainly the ideal route; the chamber of commerce manager will point out the significance of route choice to his campaign to attract new industry for the community; heavily mortgaged homeowners will claim that if the expressway goes within one-half a mile of their homes it will ruin the value of the property —though they may want an interchange located just beyond the sound of roaring truck exhausts; merchants along heavily traveled, free-access routes will complain that the siphoning off of the traffic onto a—to them —inaccessible expressway will threaten them with bankruptcy. With an occasional nod to overriding local demands—the kind that are powerful enough to potentially involve the intervention of a legislator or Congressman—the professional engineers go about their work of serving the most numerous interest of all, the motoring public.[10]

Traffic and Parking. Despite the expressways and a good deal of work in improving other streets, cities are not making progress against traffic congestion. The commonplace rectangular pattern of streets is inefficient for traffic flow; most streets are still expected to provide the impossible—to serve as rapid thoroughfares and as access routes to places of business; land is too scarce and valuable, wrecking operations too expensive to clear away many existing structures for parking or to widen existing streets; citizens refuse to use public transportation except as a matter of desperation.[11]

It has been estimated that one-third of the buildings in downtown Boston would have to be torn down to provide adequate parking space for the patrons of the remaining structures. The larger the city, the smaller the proportion of residents using their cars to get downtown. But

[9] See above, pp. 302–303; and E. M. Horwood and R. R. Boyce, *Studies of the Central Business District and Urban Freeway Development* (University of Washington Press, Seattle, Wash., 1959), chaps. 8–9.

[10] For more on highways, see Charles R. Adrian, *State and Local Governments* (McGraw-Hill Book Company, Inc., New York, 1960), pp. 472–480.

[11] See C. E. Stonier, "Metropolitan Traffic Crisis," *Traffic Quarterly*, vol. 11 (April, 1957), pp. 214–231, and other articles in the *Quarterly*.

despite this, the larger the city, the more difficult it is to find adequate parking.[12]

Beginning with its use in Oklahoma City in 1935, the parking meter has become an almost universal phenomenon along commercial streets in American cities. The meters are, in effect, yet another tax upon the motorist. They serve as a good source of revenue for cities. This income is used for street maintenance and traffic control in some cities and to construct off-street parking facilities in others. The meters themselves do not solve the parking problem, except perhaps to speed up the shopper and other parker and to discourage all-day parking along downtown streets.

Parking space is, economically speaking, a responsibility of the firm for whom the driver works or the store to which the driver-shopper is headed. Because the business districts were built before the automobile was developed, such provisions have not been made. Most cities now attempt to require all new commercial places to furnish adequate parking spaces off the street, though the practice is not universal.

A problem in many cities in procuring sufficient parking lots from private sources is found in the fact that the business is monopolized in the hands of one or a few large lot owners possessing considerable political power. There are several parking-lot corporations organized on a nationwide basis, each operating lots in numerous cities.

Cities are trying to keep up with the great increase in the population both of people and of autos. Buffalo offers a tax exemption on buildings used for off-street parking if they house at least 150 autos and are basically parking facilities. To hurry conversion of buildings, a time limit in order to qualify has been set. Milwaukee charges persons who park all night on the streets and uses the money to pay for off-street parking lots. Baltimore makes long-term loans from a 5-million-dollar fund for use in constructing parking garages by private operators. There is no tax exemption. The Municipal Parking Authority in Detroit acquires land by condemnation, issues revenue bonds, and constructs garages. The finished structures are then leased to private operators who run them at cost plus a fee. Other profits go to the authority. Low interest rates on bonds are secured by pledging garage revenues plus parking-meter profits.

Municipal Parking Lots. In 1960, three-fourths of the cities over 10,000 had publicly owned parking lots. Many cities are following the trend in this direction. Financing has been principally through general taxes or often through general-obligation bonds. Revenue bonds are also issued, and parking-meter receipts are often used as a partial method of finan-

---

[12] J. D. Carroll, Jr., "The Future of the Central Business District," *Public Management,* vol. 35 (July, 1953), pp. 150–153.

cing. A few cities have used special assessments against the benefiting property owners. This practice often encounters legal and political obstacles. Lots are usually administered by either the police or the public works departments. Over one-half of them in 1952 provided free parking, but by 1960, around 80 per cent of them involved a fee, reflecting a general trend toward greater use of service charges in cities.[13] It seems likely that the municipal parking lot, together with such elaborate devices as underground parking garages, will become increasingly common as municipal authorities fight to keep the streets clear and free for traffic.[14]

Airports: Public Subsidy for Transportation. American governments have traditionally subsidized methods of transportation, especially when they are new. We have subsidized facilities for canalboats, railways, automobiles and trucks, ocean transportation, and, after World World I, air travel. Beginning in the 1920s, cities were authorized to construct, and usually to operate, municipal airports. Today almost all of the nation's largest cities have city-owned airports. In some cases this is a county function and there are several *ad hoc* airport authorities to cover the metropolitan areas, while in other cities the airports are leased to private operators. But in most places the city owns and operates the facilities. (See Figure 18-2.)

So optimistic have people been about the future of air travel that municipal airports are common even in cities of under 10,000 population. The Federal Airport Act of 1946 undoubtedly encouraged many cities to construct airports that are not self-supporting, and for a long time into the future will not be self-supporting. The act made no allowance for aid in operation and maintenance, and these costs have proved to be a great burden for many municipalities.

In the first years after World War II, there were many rosy dreams in the thoughts of air-transport promoters, private flyers, returning armed forces pilots anxious to retain their newly learned skill, and the general public concerning the future of aviation. Some authorities believed that the number of airplanes would increase by 30 per cent a year in the ten years following the war—or by more than thirteen times the 1945 figure of 30,000 planes.[15] Airports were built and expanded. Helicopters were to

[13] See the current issue of the *Municipal Year Book* (International City Managers' Association, Chicago), for data.

[14] See G. Baker and B. Funaro, *Parking* (Reinhold Publishing Corporation, New York, 1958); and R. H. Burrage and E. G. Mogren, *Parking* (Eno Foundation, Saugatuck, Conn., 1957).

[15] See, for example, T. P. Wright, "The National Airport Program," in *City Problems of 1945–1946* (United States Conference of Mayors, Washington, 1946), pp. 83–94.

Figure 18-2. International Airport Building, New York International Airport at Idlewild. SOURCE: Courtesy of the Port of New York Authority.

carry people from far-outlying airports into the heart of the city. Airplanes that "anyone can fly" were soon to be on the market. Many cities expanded their facilities on the basis of such assumptions.

Air transportation is important, but it has not as yet supplanted the auto or train. There are many problems to be solved in airport facilities. Almost everyone in an urban area wants an airport, but no one wants it near his own home because of the noise, dirt, traffic, and threat of an accident. So airports are constructed many miles from the heart of the city, yet the time-saving helicopter has not come into widespread use because it is too expensive a device to serve as a shuttle bus. Many cities find themselves maintaining airports which are used to far less than capacity, some of them being hardly used at all. Almost no cities have broken even, much less shown a profit, on their airports, yet in some cases they are subsidizing airlines that are making comfortable profits on over-all business.

Airport Management. Municipal airports are administered in a variety of ways. They may be under the control of departments of public works, parks (because early airport management consisted largely of grass cutting), utilities, public service, or finance. Others are directly under city airport commissions enjoying semiautonomous status.

The airport manager, in cities with integrated forms of government, is appointed by the chief executive, or by the department head if the airport is a division of a larger department. The principal qualification for

an airport manager is not that he be a pilot (although that is not undesirable), but that he have administrative and business ability. He must
have high courage, too, for his airport is not unlikely to show a deficit
despite his best administrative efforts.[16]

Water and Sanitation. Probably no single governmental domestic policy is of more importance to the future pattern of development of the
United States than is that of water. It has been said, without exaggeration, that "you could write the story of man's growth in terms of his
epic concerns with water."[17] Man is utterly dependent upon it. It determined where he first settled as he moved into new lands. It dictates
the location of most heavy industry. It controls the size to which a city,
whether it be New York, Denver, or Los Angeles, may grow. It limits
possible land uses. Its quality affects the state of the public health, the
size of the municipal budget, and the taste of a highball. Its quantity
determines whether bluegrass lawns may be watered in August, a row-
boat must be kept in the garage as an escape vehicle from a flash flood,
or the economy of a resort area will flourish or wither. In all aspects of
water policy, government—national, state, and local—is involved.

Changing Needs. Although the population of the United States only
doubled between 1900 and 1955, per capita use of water quadrupled.
This was a result not only of changing agricultural and industrial uses
but also of the labor-saving devices that have been adopted in the contemporary home: the garbage grinder, the automatic washing machine,
the dishwasher, and the air-conditioning unit.

Here are some relevant facts:

1. The average American home used at least 145 gallons of water a
day for household needs in 1960. It used less than 95 gallons in 1890.

2. Homes with garbage grinders discharge 50 per cent more organic
matter into sewers than those without them. This adds greatly to the
sewage-treatment problem and potentially to water pollution and to the
existence of favorable conditions for the growth of fish in streams.

3. Industrial uses of water are enormous. Domestic uses of water account for only about 5 per cent of the total. The rest is divided about
equally between irrigation and industrial uses, the latter of which is
growing much faster than the former. It requires about 110 gallons of
water to manufacture a pound of rayon, 300 gallons for a gallon of beer,
65,000 gallons for a ton of steel, and 600,000 gallons for a ton of syn-
thetic rubber.[18]

[16] For airport developments immediately after World War II, see the *Municipal
Year Book, 1948*, pp. 309–323; and for airport administration, International City
Managers' Association, *op. cit.*

[17] Bernard Frank, "The Story of Water as the Story of Man," in Alfred Stefferud
(ed.), *Water* (U.S. Government Printing Office, 1955). This is probably the best
reference on the subject, though there is an extensive bibliography.

[18] *State Administration of Water Resources* (Council of State Governments, Chicago, 1957), p. 5, and Stefferud, *op. cit.*, pp. 636–643.

4. Both industrial and domestic effluents produce problems of water pollution that affect the welfare of downstream communities, of fish and game, and of recreation programs. Of approximately 16,000 American communities that have public water systems, only 9,000 have sewer systems, and of these no more than 6,000 are connected to sewage-treatment plants.

5. Increasing urban usage of lands adds to flood hazards and drainage problems, since land largely covered by roofs and concrete has much greater runoff than does other land.

6. The increasing concentration of the population in urban clusters involving a small percentage of the total land area has added greatly to the problem both of obtaining adequate water and of disposing of treated and untreated wastes.

Water Control and Supply Programs. The responsibility for getting the right amount of water of the right quality in the right place at the right time is shared by national, state, and local governments. The nature of the problems involved vary geographically and according to use. In the East, for example, the principal problems center around the distribution and quality of water; in the West, the major concern is with quantity. Some industries may be able to use raw water, whereas others need the highest quality; but much of the need is taken care of by industry itself, and governments need concern themselves only about regulation. Because water resources do not follow state or local boundaries, intergovernmental arrangements and potential problems and conflicts abound. Increasingly the states must arbitrate interlocal disputes and the Federal government those that are interstate.[19]

Water Supply. Many municipalities receive their water supply from wells. This is a relatively inexpensive method for small cities and villages, although the water is often very hard and, until one becomes accustomed to it, unpalatable. As core-city suburbs increase in size, their wells tend to become dry, for the table level of the ground water drops. It has been predicted, for example, that all of the thirty-odd suburbs of Chicago using wells in 1953 will eventually be forced to abandon them and obtain water from the core city.[20]

Few of the larger cities use wells. Memphis uses them. Brooklyn once

[19] See Albert Lepawsky, "Water Resources and American Federalism," *American Political Science Review*, vol. 44 (September, 1950), pp. 631–649; N. D. Hunter, "Problems of the Colorado River as Reflected in Arizona Politics," *Western Political Quarterly*, vol. 4 (December, 1951), pp. 634–643; L. L. Durisch and R. E. Lowry, "State Watershed Policy and Administration in Tennessee," *Public Administration Review*, vol. 15 (Winter, 1955), pp. 17–20; Duane Lockard, *New England State Politics* (Princeton University Press, Princeton, N.J., 1959), pp. 108–118.

[20] *Chicago Sanitary District* (Illinois Legislative Council, Springfield, Ill., 1953), p. 28.

did, but for many years citizens objected that the water was salty and brackish. This led to an abandonment of the privately owned wells in 1947 and the use throughout New York City of water from the Catskill reservoirs. In large cities, however, many wells have been sunk by business firms for air-conditioning purposes. In many cities the table level is sinking rapidly as a result, and strict regulation of these practices has become necessary. Some cities require all water withdrawn from the ground for air-conditioning purposes to be returned to the ground. New York has had such a rule since 1933. Business firms are not likely to do this voluntarily, since it adds to the expense of the system.

Most large cities depend for their water supply upon rivers or the damming of small streams, or they make use of lakes. The problem of securing a supply of relatively unpolluted water becomes increasingly difficult as urban populations grow and the amount of industrial and human waste dumped into streams increases. Cities along the Great Lakes have been able to get palatable, germ-free water with a minimum of treatment. Some cities, such as Philadelphia, which uses the Delaware River, must use a great amount of filtration and chemical treatment, for their sources are badly polluted.

Planning a water resources system

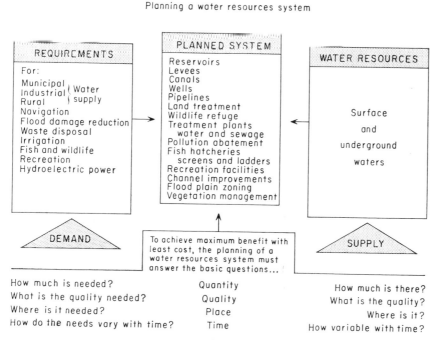

Figure 18-3. SOURCE: *Water for Your Ever-expanding Needs* (Delaware River Basin Research, Inc., Philadelphia, 1959), p. 12.

Cities along the ocean, such as New York and Los Angeles, have not been able to convert sea water inexpensively and have had to bring their supplies hundreds of miles from the mountains.[21] The 82d Congress authorized the Secretary of the Interior to cooperate with state and local governments in an effort to devise a process for making use of salt and brackish water for home and factory consumption.[22] Some growing inland cities have had to resort to desperate measures to ensure a water supply. Denver, for example, gouged a 23-mile tunnel through solid rock to reach the moisture-laden western slope of the Rocky Mountains.

A political issue in the area of water supply in the postwar period has centered in the fluoridation of water, a practice designed to reduce dental caries. For reasons that are not evident, fluoridation has been opposed by very conservative groups as being "un-American." [23] Others have questioned whether its beneficial results have been adequately demonstrated and the dangers of harmful side effects disproved. The American Dental Association and American Medical Association favor the adding of fluorides, and over 1,500 water systems do so.

Water-supply problems of cities are as old as are cities themselves. In America, searches for more and better water used to follow disastrous fires and terrible epidemics, such as the cholera wave of 1832 that convinced New Yorkers to try the then daring engineering feat of going 30 miles to the Croton River for safe water.[24]

Today, water supply is regarded as vital for the operation of a modern home and for the irrigation of suburban lawns and gardens. But it is also at times a matter of sheer survival, if we judge from the public reaction in New York, which had serious water-supply problems in 1949 and 1950 as a result of inadequate rainfall. At the time, there were: [25]

. . . daily front-page bulletins showing net gains and losses of precious water in city reservoirs; periodic prayers for rain offered at St. Patrick's Cathedral; fantastic solutions suggested by panicky citizens; bathless Fridays; official announcements that beards will be considered municipal "badges of honor"; official New York city rain-makers who drive around in the Catskill reservoir area, their trailers emitting the magical silver iodide smoke to squeeze water out of

[21] A worthwhile case study on water is Vincent Ostrom, *Water and Politics: A Study of Water Policies and Administration in the Development of Los Angeles* (Haynes Foundation, Los Angeles, 1953).

[22] R. D. Bugher, "Public Works Developments in 1952," *Municipal Year Book, 1953* (International City Managers' Association, 1953), p. 345. See Stefferud, *op. cit.*, pp. 109–118.

[23] See James M. Burns, "The Crazy Politics of Fluorine," *New Republic*, vol. 128 (July 13, 1953), pp. 14–15; B. Mausner and J. Mausner, "A Study of the Anti-scientific Attitude," *Scientific American*, vol. 192 (February, 1955), pp. 35–39.

[24] N. M. Blake, *Water for the Cities* (Syracuse University Press, Syracuse, N.Y., 1957).

[25] Lepawsky, *op. cit.*, p. 639. Used by permission.

reluctant clouds; complaints from sufficiently water-supplied suburbs that the city is thus causing unnecessary snow-storms.

Sanitation. Municipal and other local governments bear the primary responsibility for sewage treatment, including septic-tank installation practices, and for provision of means for carrying off rain water through storm drains and holding back floods through the construction (often with the aid of Federal funds) of levees and retaining walls. All of these activities cost a good deal of money. Sewerage and sewage-disposal plants are among the most expensive of municipal capital outlays, and great controversies center about the means of financing them and of holding costs to a minimum. Public forums in a city considering a new sewage-disposal plant give one the distinct impression that every taxpayer is also an expert in sanitary engineering. Storm drains, too, are matters of great concern to citizens—though usually only during wet springs. A complex cost-benefit problem is frequently involved. As a result, the citizen feels convinced in April that a new storm drain system in his neighborhood is necessary at any cost. By August, he has forgotten his earlier view and is now certain that larger water mains or better supply sources are needed so as to make it possible for him to preserve the color of his precious bluegrass during dry spells.

Boston, in 1823, was the first American city to install a system of sanitary sewers. Other cities followed as their populations increased. In those early days, the sewage was commonly dumped into a nearby stream or other body of water. This was in itself a scientific method of disposal. Contrary to a popular impression that the downriver town drank the raw sewage of the one above it, the chemical reaction of the oxygen in the water with the sewage would convert the organic matter into nitrates and other non-disease-bearing by-products. If a sufficient supply of water was available and cities were not too close together, this approach was reasonably safe.

Today, as a public health precaution, sewage must be treated before disposal. There are several methods of treatment, and they are all normally expensive. Because cities, and often their suburbs, may try to avoid this expense, several states have established water-pollution commissions. These commissions may, if they find that a municipality is endangering the public health or the fish and wildlife of the state, order a municipality to construct a sewage-treatment plant. The state has sometimes had to resort to its coercive power and force cities into safety precautions.

Sewage-treatment plants, like those for water treatment, are least expensive if used to full capacity and if one rather than a series of them exists in a metropolitan area.

Municipal sanitation also involves the disposal of ashes, rubbish, and garbage. These may be collected separately or in various combinations, depending upon the method of disposal. Ashes are becoming less of a municipal task. Industries normally dispose of their own, while each year fewer homes are heated by coal. Ashes, together with street dirt, make good fill for low places and are commonly disposed of in this fashion. Sometimes they are simply dumped.

Rubbish (nonorganic trash and discards) is also used for fill, or it may be dumped. Sometimes it is incinerated. Garbage (organic waste) may be disposed of by incineration, use of the reduction process, the sanitary fill, feeding to hogs, dumping, grinding at central locations, or grinding in the home. Incineration is expensive, but very effective. It is used particularly in larger cities and is becoming increasingly popular. The expensive reduction process, which is used to recover waste fats, has been tried in large cities but is passing from favor. The sanitary-fill method is used quite extensively, especially in small or medium-sized cities.

Feeding to hogs has been popular, since a part of the cost of collection and disposal can thereby be recouped. It is believed, however, that the feeding of raw garbage may be a method of transmitting vesicular exanthema among hogs and cholera and trichinosis to human beings. As a result, many states now require precooking of the garbage. This additional cost is causing municipalities to switch to other disposal methods, especially to incineration.

Garbage is sometimes dumped, either into a pit to be buried, or into a body of water. This is usually a temporary measure, although some small places use it as a regular disposal method.

Grinding of garbage has the effect of converting it into sewage. This is a method wherein solving the garbage problem adds to the sewage problem. Grinding at central locations is quite common and works satisfactorily if an adequate sewage-disposal plant exists. The home garbage grinder has become extremely popular in the postwar period, and new homes throughout the nation are frequently built to include them. In some places they are causing problems by overtaxing the sewerage system or the disposal plant. The increased amount of organic matter that is thereby dumped into bodies of water may constitute a threat to fish and wildlife by removing oxygen from the water to a dangerous extent.[26] But the grinders symbolize, to the housewife, another step in America's material progress.

Municipalities do not necessarily collect and dispose of ashes, rubbish, or garbage themselves. In some places the job is done by a collector holding a contract from the city. In others the city licenses several

[26] See the comments of William Vogt, *Road to Survival* (William Sloane Associates, New York, 1948), pp. 34–35.

"This model features worn-out equipment, which causes excitingly real hotboxes, delays, and other true-to-life malfunctions."

Figure 18-4. Around our largest cities, commuter trains are still important to the suburbanite—but are seldom profitable to railroad management, which tends to skimp on maintenance to cut down operating costs. SOURCE: Drawing by Stevenson; © 1960 The New Yorker Magazine, Inc.

collectors. A great many cities do the job themselves, however, through a department of public works. The sewerage system is almost always operated by the city itself, but an important question to be settled in connection with this activity is whether storm drains should be connected to the regular sewers or constructed separately. Engineers prefer the latter method.

Public Transportation. Public transportation systems within cities became white elephants after World War II. The development contains some elements of serious maladjustment, for while *most* people have automobiles and could get along entirely without public transportation if necessary, it still remains an absolutely vital utility to a small minority.

Virtually all transit systems in the United States were losing money in 1960. This was true of those privately owned as well as those publicly owned. No large-city system was earning the current rate on its investment. There were several reasons for the failure of these utilities to be able to pay their costs. First of all, of course, is the switch to auto transportation. There were 28 million autos in 1946 and about 61 million in 1960. Largely because of this, the number of passengers carried by transit systems fell from 23 billion to 15 billion between 1946 and 1953.[27]

[27] *Wall Street Journal,* July 20, 1953 (Chicago ed.).

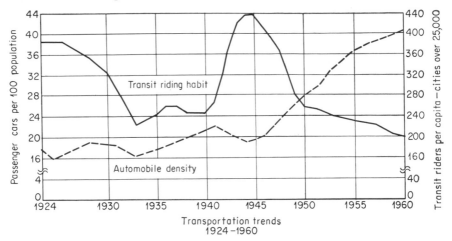

Transportation trends
1924–1960

Figure 18-5. SOURCE: To 1951, adapted from H. S. Simpson, "Mass Transit Can Be Saved," *Public Management,* vol. 35 (April, 1953), p. 79. Since 1951, based on figures in the *World Almanac* (New York World-Telegram and Sun, New York, 1960).

Further factors in reducing the load of transit systems include the suburban movement and television. Suburbanites, too far out to go to work or to shop downtown by public transportation, use commuter trains, or more likely, the auto. The lessening density of population of the core city spells trouble for transit lines. Television has a tendency to reduce entertainment travel, which does further damage. Entertainment travel is important to transit systems which are constantly confronted with the problem of the waste involved when equipment needed for peak-load hours lies idle in the evening.

As long ago as 1940, the number of persons entering the Chicago central business district daily by elevated train, streetcar, or bus amounted to only 47.8 per cent of the total number.[28] In 1916, 82.8 per cent of persons entering the St. Louis central business district each day came by streetcar. By 1946, only 46.9 per cent came by streetcar and bus. Almost an equal number came by private automobile. The decline in public transportation patronage since that time has been great—in most cities it was cut in half, at the least, between 1946 and 1960. (See Figure 18-5.)

The abnormal circumstances of World War II helped stave off the inevitable for a few years for many systems, but the shift from the six-day to the five-day work week since 1945 has reduced the number of riders considerably. In addition to the decreasing number of riders, postwar inflation brought increasing costs of operation and maintenance. This forced fare increases, which in turn encouraged switching to auto trans-

[28] G. W. Breese, *The Daytime Population of the Central Business District of Chicago* (University of Chicago Press, Chicago, 1949), pp. 106–109.

portation. The transit managers were then forced to reduce service or ask for another fare increase or both. Furthermore, the greater number of autos on the streets made it increasingly difficult to maintain schedules that were fast enough to satisfy the public. All of this added to the snowballing effect toward fewer passengers and greater deficits.[29] The problem was not helped by the rise of the bus as a replacement for the streetcar. The bus takes up less room on the street, interferes less with traffic, and costs less to buy and maintain, but it is uncomfortable, vexatiously slow —about one-half as fast as the private auto—and, if diesel fuel is used, a source of unpleasant odors.

Is There a Solution? In an attempt to solve the increasing financial difficulties of transit systems, various desperate measures have been recommended. There are some who urge that subways, monorails, or elevated-train systems be built, but it is unlikely that any but a few cities could, at this time, meet operating expenses out of fares from these, much less pay off any of the original capital investment.

Some laymen have urged that all would be well if cities would sell their systems to private companies, as if that were a panacea. Clearly, it is not, for Chicago had to take over its transportation system in 1947 after the private company had gone bankrupt and the system had been administered for years under the eye of a Federal judge. The Boston system lost money first under private and then under public management.

Other laymen, as well as some professional students of public administration, have said that the transit systems should be "taken out of politics," an old American antidote. Governor Thomas E. Dewey caused the New York transit system to be separated from the city government in 1953, and it was set up under an authority partly appointed by the Governor. The plan produced numerous cries of interference with local self-government, mostly from the Governor's political opponents.

Some have urged the inevitable proposal, Federal aid, others that people stop using their own autos and be persuaded to ride the public transit. This could be done by applying various pressures, such as a special tax on downtown parkers.[30] Few municipal or private managements, however, have made genuine appeals with meaningful promises behind them. As a result, urgings have fallen on deaf ears. For all except those who have no choice in the matter, public transportation is

[29] John Bauer, "Municipal Utilities Developments in 1952," *Municipal Year Book, 1953* (International City Managers' Association, 1953), pp. 352–357. The experience of the city where the population is most dependent upon public transportation is related in Mayor's Committee on Management Survey, *Modern Management for the City of New York* (1953), vol. 1, chap. 6.

[30] H. S. Simpson, "Mass Transit Can Be Saved," *Public Management*, vol. 35 (April, 1953), pp. 77–81; John Bauer, "The Crisis in Urban Transit," *ibid.*, vol. 34 (August, 1952), pp. 176–178.

too slow and the fare is too high. Besides, the problem is social as well as economic, and for that reason the solution is not easy. One authority on the subject has explained the shift as follows: [31]

. . . devolution of transit traffic and earning power has doubtless been due in part to gradual shifts in community life. But it has been due chiefly to everyone's desire to own an automobile and to have the satisfaction of driving to and from work in his own or jointly in his neighbor's car. This is not only a matter of assumed riding convenience and advantage, but perhaps principally one of inferred prestige.

Public tastes and dominant life styles, reflected in the decisions of city planners, also contribute to the decline of public transportation. Mass transit is used most in the older cities which have a relatively high density of population. It is here that disutility of the automobile is greatest. There might, thus, be something of a revival in the use of the bus if planners and redevelopers worked from the principle of concentration rather than deconcentration. They now have enough techniques in their professional bag of gimmicks to avoid the creation of slums and to provide for green spaces despite high-rise buildings. But such planning would defy the expectations of most Americans, and the fact that it would be compatible with the preservation of public transportation systems is not likely to be persuasive to many.[32]

The expressway, the off-street parking lot and garage, and the prestige factor seem to assure us that transit systems cannot hope to recapture much of their lost ridership. Should cities abandon public transportation as a thing of the past? This would work a great hardship upon enough people to be an unthinkable solution at this time. Furthermore, there are almost no cities that could handle either the street traffic or the parking problem if everyone were to ride by auto.

It seems likely that privately owned companies will have to be taken over by the cities in the future—perhaps as bankrupts. Municipally owned systems are faced with the need for subsidies in order to make up the difference between earnings and costs. Most such systems already enjoy some subsidies. Very often, for example, they need not pay property taxes. Sometimes the department of public works maintains the space between the tracks in the few remaining street railway systems, although private companies normally pay this cost themselves.

But is a subsidy equitable? If the loss is made up from the general-revenue fund, it means that the taxpayer is subsidizing the bus rider. If municipally owned transit systems are exempted from the property

[31] Bauer, "Municipal Utilities Developments in 1952," p. 355.
[32] See Joel Smith, *Some Social Aspects of Mass Transit* (Institute for Community Development, Michigan State University, East Lansing, Mich., 1959).

tax, the same result is obtained. Is this logical? Property-tax payers, for the most part, are not wealthy people.

Is a transit system a convenience to business? If it is, should some of the deficit be paid by a special tax on business? This plan is being tried in New York. The New York system receives a total subsidy equal to about 40 per cent of its expenses. This comes from business and real estate taxes. In any case, it seems unlikely that many transit systems will be able to break even in the future, given any type of ownership, management, or equipment.

THE ADMINISTRATION OF PUBLIC WORKS

Whenever a city is large enough to be organized on a departmental basis, it will have a department of public works operating under one title or another. The department usually includes many utility and other service functions—for example, divisions in charge of street maintenance, cleaning, and lighting, of bridges, of sewers and sewage disposal, of refuse collection and disposal, and of public property. Traffic engineering is frequently in the department of public works, as are municipally owned utilities, such as electricity, gas supply, public markets, and slaughterhouses, although any of these may be established as independent departments. Public transportation, airports, and water supply are in the great majority of cases, but not always, organized as separate departments.

The Department Head. The general view of authorities on municipal management holds that the public works department should be organized with a single department head responsible to the chief executive. The once-common autonomous board has generally been abandoned. This is not true, however, in the case of public transportation and water supply, where the board is still often found, even in strong-mayor and manager cities.

The director of public works (often called the city engineer, especially in smaller cities) is normally an engineer of one kind or another. In small cities, it is expected that the director will possess technical qualities. In large cities, administrative ability is imperative, while engineering ability is less important and may not be a requirement at all. In smaller cities, the director must supervise many technical functions himself. In large cities, say of over 100,000, the director often turns over technical matters to one or more assistant directors while he concerns himself with general administration. There may be two assistant directors, for example, one in charge of operations, the other in charge of departmental staff services.

In large cities, some of the functions performed by the public works department may be decentralized on an area basis. The object of such geographic decentralization is to save time and expense in moving men and materials about the city as they are needed. In most cities, however, the department is organized on a functional basis, each division operating under centralized control.

The Staff Services. In cities of less than about 10,000, the head of the public works department is likely to take care of the staff services himself —he does the planning, surveys, and inspections. In larger cities there are usually several divisions within the department which provide these services. The common ones deal with research and planning, design, and inspection. There may be a purchasing division, or the department may use the purchasing services existing for the city as a whole. Large departments may have a personnel officer, even though most personnel services are handled by the general agency established for that purpose. Cost accounting, a vital service that determines unit costs, may be performed by a staff division, or may be provided outside of the department by the central finance agency. Cost accounting is used by the department head to locate areas for possible economies, to compare costs with those of other cities, to compare costs from one year to the next, and for many other purposes.

The division of research and planning uses the city's master plan as a point of departure. It must establish priorities for the various projects proposed in the plan and then a timetable and capital budget for them. It takes careful planning to finance in the desired order such things as a new city hall, an additional water-pumping station, and a system of expressways. Planning provides further for the allocation of parts of the long-range plan in the annual budget and in the quarterly or monthly allotments within the department. Thus the division completes its job when work programs for construction and maintenance for each of the operating divisions have been readied for the next allotment period. Research and planning are part of a continuous, never-ending process. This division works closely with the division of design, which deals with the technical matters of the design of bridges, buildings, and other structures. It is through technical skills, over-all planning, and general knowledge of the local situation that the professionals become important as policy innovators. The public works department in cities of all sizes is a good case in point.

Because much of the work of construction and some of the maintenance is done by private contractors, the department of public works usually has a division of inspection. It is expected to make certain that contracts are fulfilled and that the quality of materials and workmanship meets the required standards. It was in the area of public works contracts that much corruption in city government once took place. There have been many forms of collusion among contractors and between city officials and contractors, not to mention the practices of skimping on materials and workmanship and the technical and financial incompetence of many contractors. Social pressures against these things are now great. The modern chief executive considers the public works department one of the best mediums through which to demonstrate his administrative ability to the public.[33]

[33] For an elaboration on the subjects of this section, see International City Managers' Association, *op. cit.* T. H. Reed, *Municipal Management* (McGraw-Hill Book Company, Inc., New York, 1941), explains the common methods of cheating used by private contractors. See chap. 23.

Chapter 19

URBAN HOUSING

Issues that urban citizens must now settle or must cope with in the future include these, among others: Should slum clearance be integrated with the development of public low-rent housing? Should slum clearance be effected by public or by private effort? If private effort is used, should the municipality grant a subsidy, or purchase land by condemnation for private companies, or otherwise grant assistance? Should low-rent housing be built only on the site of cleared slums, or should some or all of it be built upon vacant land? What policy should be followed in choosing vacant sites, if they are used? If cleared sites are used, where should the displaced families live while new projects are being constructed? Is it desirable or undesirable to clear slums and then build upon the site housing that the persons displaced cannot afford to rent? [1]

THE DIRECT APPROACH THROUGH GOVERNMENT

The Picture in 1960. American urban housing conditions have improved along with the rise in the American standard of living in the years since the end of World War II. [2] Owner occupancy was at an all-time high in 1960, and most homes had the basic services and amenities —electricity, radios, television sets, indoor plumbing, refrigerators, automatic washing machines—even among persons of quite modest income. Most of the figures revealed in the 1960 census exceeded by far comparable statistics in other nations.

Yet many Americans remain ill-housed by prevailing standards, and much blight and many dysfunctional buildings characterize our cities. In 1957, at least 15 million Americans lived in what society would regard as substandard dwellings. In 1950, New York City had, by official

[1] For a description of slum areas, see Daniel Seligman, "The Enduring Slums," in Editors of Fortune, *The Exploding Metropolis* (Doubleday Anchor Books, New York, 1958), chap. 4; or the citations in any textbook on urban sociology, some of those at the end of this chapter, or many in chap. 20.
[2] See the *1960 Census of Housing* for data.

444

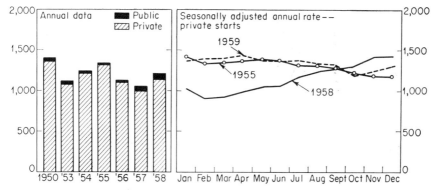

Figure 19-1. SOURCE: Annual housing starts. *Municipal Year Book, 1960* (International City Managers' Association, Chicago, 1960), p. 315.

measure, a housing shortage of 430,000 units. Ten years later the city was still short 430,000 units. Much of the inadequate housing had been destroyed in the meantime, with the land converted to other use. But the city still had a problem of housing low-income migrants, mostly Puerto Ricans, who crowded into the city, vastly increasing the density in blocks which they occupied.

Although over 1 million housing starts have been made in each year since the end of the war (see Figure 19-1), it is possible that deterioration is taking place at an ever greater rate.[3] Many labor and liberal leaders have argued that the rate of housing starts should be higher—perhaps double the figures of the late 1950s (see Figure 19-2). Is it economically feasible to seek to end the housing shortage, or must we expect that the lowest-income persons in urban areas must always live in what most citizens would regard as squalor? One study has concluded: [4]

There is no question that city dwellers could afford to put an end to slums and blight. An added $25 per capita to the tax burden (with Federal aid for only one-fourth of the cost) would not be intolerable. Nor, for that matter, would the extra taxes for the entire cost, approximately $33 annually per capita for a decade, according to the calculation for Chicago. If housing and slum clearance were high on the scale of personal and civic preference, such costs would be paid: the taxpayer would buy less gasoline, or smoke less, or even eat less. Compared to many "luxuries," the cost of a thoroughgoing housing program would be slight. There is little doubt, however, that consumers are likely to prefer the luxuries to the housing program for a long time to come.

[3] See, generally, E. C. Banfield and Morton Grodzins, *Government and Housing in Metropolitan Areas* (McGraw-Hill Book Company, Inc., New York, 1958).
[4] *Ibid.*, pp. 119–120.

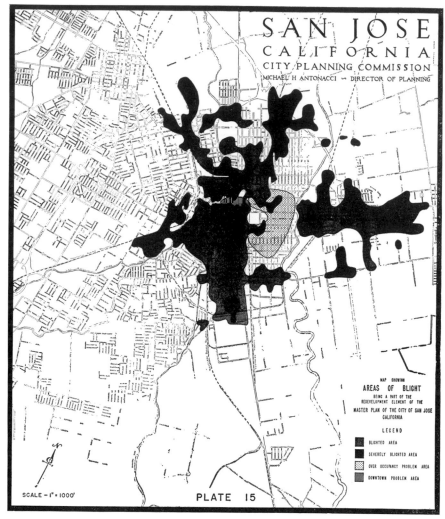

Figure 19-2. Blight may spread rapidly through cities, even those that are not old, and it may not be confined to the central core. SOURCE: *Planning San Jose* (City Planning Commission, San Jose, Calif., 1958), plate 15.

Enormous political difficulties face renewal and housing schemes on such a large scale. Support for these schemes might not come from the very groups that in the long run might benefit most from them. For example, dwellers in the Negro slums would see in such programs a great initial dislocation in residential patterns before any longer-run advantages would be apparent. (Negro groups currently lead the opposition to slum clearance projects.) Strong protests could be expected to come from many sides: from those making profits from present housing patterns; from suburban groups and the residents of the better city neighborhoods who would fear the infiltration of their communities by the dislocated populations; from political leaders of the areas to be rebuilt who would see their constituencies scattered, as well as from leaders of other areas who would fear the influx of new voters into already established constituencies; from taxpayers' organizations; and even, it is likely, from people who might see in such programs an unwarranted interference in the life patterns of the poor.[5]

Some Background. City governments have long had building codes providing for minimum standards for building and for human occupancy. The code (or series of codes, for they are not always unified or administered by a single agency) makes provisions for standards of lighting and ventilation, sanitation, and fire prevention and protection. Historically, these codes have often been subject to pressure demands of manufacturers, builders, real estate people, tenement owners, and building-trades unions. As a result they have often established minimum standards well below those that the contemporary society would accept as a rock-bottom minimum. Codes often become seriously outdated, so that their already meager standards in one era become grotesquely inadequate a few decades later as society's concept of a minimum standard of living changes. Trade unions have frequently used the code as a device to establish make-work rules or to prevent the use of cheaper and faster techniques of home building. Manufacturers have sometimes been able to get codes to require the use of their patented materials, thus creating a monopoly situation. Out-of-date codes have sometimes prevented the introduction of new devices, such as prefabricated homes or dry-wall construction, simply because they are not provided for in a code drawn up decades before these things appeared on the market.

Many cities bring their codes up to date, yet scores of others permit jerry-built housing, or do not allow modern building techniques, or permit the construction of low-rent housing (most likely by the *conversion* of old homes into tenements) that does not meet present standards for human living. On the other hand, in some cases building codes require materials of a quality far beyond what is reasonably necessary (for example, the use of metal conduits for basement wiring), thus raising the cost of housing. Some communities do not permit the construction of low-rent housing, thus depriving lower-income persons of adequate housing.[6]

The ecological pattern in American cities has been one of allowing

[5] On the slum dweller's opposition to ethnic dispersion, see Walter Firey, "Sentiment and Symbolism as Ecological Variables," in *Reader in Urban Sociology* (The Free Press, Glencoe, Ill., 1951), pp. 233–244.

[6] Banfield and Grodzins, *op. cit.*

the central parts of the city to decay and become low-rent housing while higher-priced housing moves outward along the periphery. Traditional American housing policy has been to let low-income people live in whatever is left over. In the days before the automobile some exceptions to this were made, since factories were located near the downtown area and workers were dependent upon public transportation or their own legs. In cities such as New York and Chicago, therefore, tenement buildings (multistoried apartments with minimal conveniences) were constructed specifically to provide housing for these people and to provide lucrative investments for absentee owners. In cities that have done most of their growing since World War I, however, few such buildings exist, and the poor live in converted and subdivided homes and apartments abandoned by the fleeing middle class.

A conservative writer has said, "In some respects, a 'slum' is like a used car lot. A 'slum area' offers a supply of second-hand housing of the kind which satisfies a need until such time as a person can afford and wants a better home." He argues further that "if people really want houses, let new ones be built or bought by those most able and anxious to build or buy." [7]

Public Housing. This approach to housing lasted until the Great Depression. At that time, the New Deal sought to encourage a revival of the home-building industry, which had ground to a complete stop, and at the same time to clear away some of the nation's worst slums. (Note that this was a characteristically New Deal effort in that it attempted to do two things simultaneously: to help business recover from the Depression and to effect social reforms.) In 1933, Federal offers of conditional loans for private housing projects were unsuccessful because, with only a few exceptions, private companies did not meet the established standards. Some states also attempted to encourage low-rent private housing, but almost all of these efforts were essentially unsuccessful. It was, and still is, more profitable, or at least a safer investment, to build homes for higher-income families.

Public housing had long been practiced abroad, but prior to 1933 it was generally regarded as unconstitutional in this country. The need for low-cost housing was especially great during the Depression, however, and the national government next turned its attention to public housing. Some fifty projects in thirty-six cities were Federally constructed and administered by the Public Works Administration (PWA). It was not, however, until the United States Housing Authority (now the Federal Public Housing Authority of the Housing and Home Finance Agency) was

---

[7] The laissez-faire argument against subsidized housing is presented in a pamphlet by Paul L. Poirot, *Public Housing* (Foundation for Economic Education, New York, 1954).

created under the Federal Housing Act of 1937 that public housing could become a new national policy.[8]

The act was bitterly opposed, however, as have been all subsequent acts and propositions calling for public housing. Opposition has come partly from realtors, bankers, and others who profit from the private housing industry. Others have said that public housing is wrong in theory, that housing, within the concepts of our prevailing economic system, belongs properly in the realm of private and not public endeavor. A third type of opposition has come from those persons who fear that public housing projects would in one way or another damage existing property values.

The Federal Housing Act of 1937. The act of 1937 provided for quasi-public corporations known as "housing authorities" to be established wherever state laws permitted. The authorities were made up of appointed officials serving without pay, in most cities. The authorities drew up the plans for Federal approval, received the loan, and constructed and operated the projects.[9] The authorities had to sign three contracts with the Federal agency. One provided for the loan and established conditions for qualifying. A second provided for conditions under which the United States would pay a subsidy to help bridge the gap between rent receipts and actual costs. A third provided for Federal accounting control and debt control. The city had to agree to eliminate unsafe and unsanitary dwelling units equal in number to the new units to be constructed. State and local governments had to contract to furnish municipal services either free or for a small payment in lieu of taxes by the national government. This generally meant that public housing would be subsidized, not only in the process of building, but afterward, too, and by both the national and local governments.

The status of the housing authority as a separate corporation had the effect of relieving the municipality of responsibility for its debts and could be used to avoid state constitutional debt limits. The local housing units, once constructed, remained to a large degree under Federal control, since questions of rent levels and eligibility to reside in the project were decided by its agency. Persons whose incomes came to exceed the established maximum were required to leave the projects.

Shortly before the start of World War II, by June, 1940, 210 local housing authorities had been established. During the war years, all pub-

---

[8] For historical background, see Jack Levin, *Your Congress and American Housing* (Legislative Reference Service, Library of Congress, 1952), a history of Congressional housing policy from 1892; Housing and Home Finance Agency, *Evolution of Housing Activities in the United States* (1950); Committee on Banking and Currency, *Federal Housing Programs: Chronology and Description* (1948).

[9] This section borrows from T. H. Reed, *Municipal Management* (McGraw-Hill Book Company, Inc., New York, 1941), pp. 506–512.

Figure 19-3. The passage of a post-World War II housing bill was delayed for several years. The dean of American cartoonists depicted the real estate lobby "playing footsie" with Congressmen while low-income families went without adequate shelter. SOURCE: By permission of Daniel R. Fitzpatrick and the *St. Louis Post-Dispatch*.

lic policy was directed toward a winning effort. Housing programs were aimed at giving millions of migrating people a place to live. A large number of units were constructed, mostly by private builders under a guaranteed-profit contract with the national government. These units were constructed in those cities with populations swollen by the construction of new war plants. Many of them were unsuitable for permanent postwar occupancy.

Postwar Policy. Since 1945, running warfare has been conducted between pressure groups representing or acting in the interest of low-income urbanites on the one hand, and the pressure groups of real estate interests on the other. The battle has been fought in Washington, in the state capitals, and in the city halls.

It was not even possible to get a new housing act through Congress until 1949, despite the powerful support given public housing by three leaders of the liberal Democrats, the southern Democrats, and the Republicans, in the Wagner-Ellender-Taft Bill (see Figure 19-3). The Federal Housing Act of 1949 reaffirmed the principle that providing for housing was basically a private business matter, and it did not change the fundamentals of the 1937 act. It made adjustments, however, in order to recognize inflation and the changing concepts of a minimum standard of human living.

The provisions of the act for an extensive Federal-municipal public housing program were immediately placed under attack by opponents. The opponents, again, were largely successful. In subsequent amendments, the number of unit starts authorized for each fiscal year was whittled away:

Year	No. of unit starts authorized
1949	135,000
1952	50,000
1953	35,000
1954	None
1955	35,000
1956	45,000
1957	35,000
1958	35,000

In 1958, over 1.7 million people lived in public housing controlled by some 900 public housing authorities in 1,225 communities.[10] About 30,000 additional units were added the next year. Opposition to public housing was strong, however. On the state level, attempts were made to require a local referendum before a public housing project could be begun. Five legislatures defeated such proposals in 1952, while Virginia passed one. On the local level, proposals are also placed before the voters from time to time to require referendums before launching into public housing.

The 1949 Detroit and 1953 Los Angeles municipal campaigns turned largely on the question of public housing policy. Los Angeles, Toledo, Indianapolis, Helena, and other municipalities attempted in 1952 to cancel their cooperation agreements on public housing with the Federal

[10] *Wall Street Journal,* May 2, 1958 (Midwest ed., Chicago).

government. They were generally blocked in the courts until Congress, by a 1953 law, prohibited new public housing units, even if under contract or construction, if the governing body of a municipality or a public referendum rejects the proposal. If some Federal money has already been spent in such cases, the municipality must make a "settlement" with the Public Housing Administration.

The Eisenhower Housing Policy. President Eisenhower, shortly after taking office, appointed an advisory committee on housing. It was made up principally of bankers, lenders, real estate men, and builders. Democrats charged that the group was prejudiced against low-rent and public housing.

Late in 1953, this committee made a report which contained no new recommendations on public housing, but committee members suggested that the whole approach be discontinued "when and if the new program induces private industry to provide enough good housing at a cost which low income workers could afford." [11] Some fifty recommendations were made by the committee. For low-cost housing, it suggested forty-year FHA mortgages with almost no down payment on homes costing less than $7,600. At the time of the report, the law allowed no more than thirty-year mortgages. Prospects that the plan would provide a substantial number of low-cost housing units and thus eliminate the need for public housing appeared to be small. Perhaps in recognition of this, President Eisenhower, in his 1954 housing message, urged that the public housing provisions of the 1949 act be continued.

In 1958, real estate interests once again showed their power in Congress. They blocked the enactment of a 2.4-billion dollar housing and slum-clearance bill.

Among the other factors militating against an expansion of public housing has been the change in clientele of municipal housing authorities in the years since the Great Depression. In the 1930s, when persons with many types of labor skills could not find jobs, social innovators thought of public housing as a facility that could care for every type of person. In the high-employment years after World War II, however, these housing authorities assumed the headaches of ministering to the needs of the marginal people of our society—those psychologically unable to work, alcoholics incapable of supporting their families, prostitutes, drug addicts, mothers with many illegitimate children. The number of these in public housing projects has probably been exaggerated by opponents, but they were common enough to take away the bloom of promise for many reformers.

Municipally administered public housing projects appear to be a permanent fixture as a local function of government. They will probably

[11] Associated Press dispatch, Dec. 16, 1953, citing the Housing Administrator.

"Oh dear! Low-cost housing."

Figure 19-4. Housing of a kind that would be efficient for rental to low-income people does not fit the American dream. As a result of this, together with unending attacks upon it, even those who would benefit often oppose it. SOURCE: Drawing by B. Tobey; © 1960 The New Yorker Magazine, Inc.

not expand beyond the small responsibility for total housing they now have, however, for the organized opposition to them is strong.[12] (See Figure 19-4.)

THE INDIRECT APPROACH THROUGH GOVERNMENT AID

Private Redevelopment with Public Assistance. A few efforts were made by state and local governments during the 1930s to encourage private endeavor to clear slums and build new homes. Tax exemptions were most commonly offered, but they were inadequate as inducements. The state of New York worked out a plan for redevelopment corpora-

[12] For a case study of conflict over public housing in Chicago, see Martin Meyerson and E. C. Banfield, *Politics, Planning and the Public Interest* (The Free Press, Glencoe, Ill., 1955). In March, 1961, President Kennedy recommended a housing program that included a great expansion of urban renewal aid; no-down-payment, forty-year mortgages for some housing; subsidies for private slum-clearance projects; and 100,000 public-housing units, one-half of them for the elderly. *The New York Times*, Mar. 12, 1961.

tions in 1941, but World War II interfered with putting it into effect. A few cities, notably Pittsburgh, completed outstanding renewal programs with local financing. Most communities were not able to do this.

The Federal Housing Act of 1949, among other things, offered aid to communities for slum clearance and urban redevelopment. Grants could be made to local units to acquire, clear, and prepare blighted areas for the construction of new dwellings. The cleared land could then either be used for public housing projects or be resold to private builders for redevelopment.

Some slums were cleared away as a result of the 1949 act, but only ten projects were completed in the ten years that followed its adoption. New slums developed at a faster rate than existing ones were cleared. The Housing Acts of 1954 and 1956, therefore, emphasized urban renewal. This orientation was re-enforced by the concern felt by local businessmen and realtors over the downward trend in land values in the older parts of cities.

Under the urban-renewal provisions, communities, private business, and the Federal government were to cooperate to prevent the spread of urban blight to new areas, to rehabilitate and conserve areas that could still be restored at reasonable cost, and to clear and redevelop areas that could not be saved. The community was required to prepare an urban renewal plan, to adopt adequate land-use controls, and to have a comprehensive physical plan for the whole community.

Federal aids are available to assist in the "main phases of project clearance, redevelopment or rehabilitation, rehousing of displaced families, and in community planning and other special operations." [13] Grants and loans cannot be used for the construction or rehabilitation of structures, but the FHA mortgage-insurance program was expanded to include such activities.

The 1954 and 1956 laws sought to overcome some of the earlier problems—of relocating displaced persons, of inducing private business to take part in renewal, of poor planning. But the amount of urban renewal that actually took place during the first few years after passage of the acts was relatively modest for several reasons: (1) Persons in areas to be renewed objected to relocation, fearing that adequate housing would not be available to them, or would be too costly; (2) slum owners feared loss of income and of valuable property if renewal plans went forward; (3) some conservatives, even though they owned deteriorating

[13] U.S. Housing and Home Finance Agency, *Urban Renewal: What It Is* (1956). See also G. Dugger and P. Ford, *Urban Renewal Administration* (Bureau of Public Administration, University of California, Berkeley, Calif., 1957), which analyzes state laws; C. F. Palmer, *Adventures of a Slum Fighter* (Tupper and Love, Atlanta, Ga., 1955); *Urban Development Guidebook* (Chamber of Commerce of the United States, Washington, 1955).

urban property, regarded government-assisted renewal as radicalism and thus undesirable. During 1959, only fifty-one slum clearance and urban-renewal projects were approved, and by the end of that year, the total of Federally assisted projects under way was only 699 in the entire nation.[14] A total of 417 communities were involved in these projects. According to past performances, some of these would take over ten years to complete. Some would not be completed at all.

There is mounting concern with the problem of blight in aging parts of urban areas, however. In 1957, cities indicated long-range plans to spend 3,000 million dollars for urban-renewal projects in the following ten years, and ten states adopted legislation providing new enabling authority for urban redevelopment. Housing needs of elderly persons—with attractive overtones for the politician seeking an additional support group—added another interest dimension at both the state and municipal levels. By the end of 1957, only eight states were without legislation which would permit communities to engage in effective urban-renewal plans.

More than 1 million housing starts have been made in the United States in each year beginning in 1949. The great bulk of these have been one- and two-family units. Despite the slum-clearance and urban-renewal provisions of the Federal housing acts and supportive state laws, blight continues to spread and the problem of housing low-income people has not been solved.[15]

Municipal Action against Blighting. It is likely that many deterio rated neighborhoods could be rehabilitated and others that are declining could be saved without rebuilding. This could be done by requiring landlords (largely absentees) to repair their properties and raise conditions to a minimum standard. An ordinance providing that the city would do the job if the owner failed to do so after adequate notice, with the cost being assessed against the property, would be greatly effective in retarding deterioration.

Political pressure by owners to prevent the adoption or enforcement of such ordinances has been great. The same is true of occupation density, and "safe-and-sanitary-condition" ordinances. They exist commonly enough, but are difficult to enforce. For one thing, the slum owner can frequently defy the inspector: "Go ahead, board up the place! See

---

[14] J. D. Lange, "Housing and Urban Renewal Developments in 1959," *Municipal Year Book, 1960* (International City Managers' Association, Chicago, 1960), pp. 313–315.

[15] On the general problem, see Coleman Woodbury, *The Future of Cities and Urban Redevelopment* (University of Chicago Press, Chicago, 1953); C. S. Stein, *Toward New Towns for America* (rev. ed.; Reinhold Publishing Corporation, New York, 1957); M. L. Colean, *Renewing Our Cities* (The Twentieth Century Fund, Inc., New York, 1953).

what happens!" What happens, of course, is that the slum dwellers are more concerned about being put out on the street, or forced into more expensive housing, or having to leave a comfortable, well-known neighborhood than they are about unsafe, unsanitary, and illegal conditions which exist. The owner knows this is the case. It is often his most powerful weapon. Owner and renter pressures are both applied against enforcement. Even so, in an increasing number of cities, the various ordinances dealing with the safety, sanitation, and physical appearance of buildings are being effectively enforced, at least to a greater degree than was once the case.

Closing Note. Despite a considerable amount of housing construction in the years following 1946, America seems not to be keeping pace with the increase in population. The problems posed by this will become considerably more complicated as the rate of new family formations increases in the 1960s—the marriage rate will increase, following along one generation after the sharp increase in the birth rate beginning in the war year 1942. Since the birth rate has remained high since that time, new family formations will not only increase at a rapid rate in the period 1962 to 1966, but will thereafter remain high. The result will be an increase in demand for housing.

Housing and urban-renewal programs demonstrate the interdependence of governments under a system of cooperative federalism. Municipalities acting alone cannot possibly provide an adequate housing policy for the nation. The resources and sanctions of state and national governments will also need to be invoked, and they will all have to be coordinated effectively if we are not to give in to unparalleled pressures for a decline in housing standards. As Banfield and Grodzins have noted: "Great urban problems are also great national problems; and the full pooling of resources . . . is necessary for their solution." [16]

[16] Banfield and Grodzins, *op. cit.*, p. 154. For further material on housing, see Coleman Woodbury, *The Future of Cities and Urban Redevelopment* (University of Chicago Press, Chicago, 1953); Julia Abrahamson, *A Neighborhood Finds Itself* (Harper & Brothers, New York, 1959), the story of urban renewal in the Hyde Park–Kenwood area of Chicago; Glenn H. Beyer, *Housing: A Factual Analysis* (The Macmillan Company, New York, 1958); Miles L. Colean, *Renewing Our Cities* (The Twentieth Century Fund, Inc., New York, 1953); R. M. Fisher, *Twenty Years of Public Housing* (Harper & Brothers, New York, 1959); Reuel Hamdahl, *Urban Renewal* (The Scarecrow Press, Inc., New York, 1959); Martin Millspaugh and Gurney Breckenfeld, *The Human Side of Urban Renewal* (Fight-Blight, Inc., Baltimore, Md., 1958); W. W. Nash, *Residential Rehabilitation; Private Profits and Public Purposes* (McGraw-Hill Book Company, Inc., New York, 1959); Stein, *op. cit.*; P. T. Van der Hoff and George S. Duggar (eds.), *Urban Renewal* (International Federation of Housing and Planning, The Hague, The Netherlands, 1959); *Toward Good Housing for the Aging* (National Association of Housing and Redevelopment Officials, Chicago, 1957).

Chapter 20

LAND-USE POLICIES

Planning "is the conscious and deliberate guidance of thinking so as to create logical means for achieving agreed-upon goals. Planning always and inevitably sets priorities and calls for value judgments. Planning is a basic and fundamental approach or way of dealing with the human problems which beset us. Planning is a point of view, an attitude, an assumption that says it is possible for us to anticipate, predict, guide, and control our own destiny." [1]

THE SETTING OF GOALS

The Meaning of Planning. While systematic planning in the United States might be said to date from William Penn's 1682 layout of the city of Philadelphia, most American cities had a chaotic growth until recent decades. In rural areas, planning was even less a community concern until the coming of the automobile and telephone which made possible the ribbon developments along arterial highways and fringe-area slums just beyond the reach of established land-use controls.

There has always been planning of some kind, of course. In the nineteenth century, informal committees composed of people interested in realty development or simply in what they considered to be civic improvement would sometimes present city plans to the council for consideration. Later, committees of the same sort were sometimes appointed by the mayor or council to study and make recommendations on city plans. Once they made a report, like most study groups, their task was finished.

In typical American fashion, land-use decisions were, until recently, made by private businessmen, the realtors, land developers, and bankers in particular. Characteristically, nineteenth-century Americans did not believe that a greater community interest stood above that of the profit motives of these men. Planners were thus concerned with their

[1] Harleigh B. Trecker, *The Group Process in Administration* (rev. ed.; Woman's Press, New York, 1950), p. 232.

profit-and-loss statements rather than with making Ackroyd City an attractive community with an imaginative physical design. It would be difficult to exaggerate the effect of their short-range concerns upon the face of urban America. Because bankers decide who gets loans and realtors decide, through their realty boards, who is to be allowed to buy where, their decisions determined, within the limits of cultural values, the face of American cities. They decided the areas in which Negroes would live and the quality of housing they would have. They determined when deteriorating areas were to be permitted to switch from single-family dwellings to multifamily apartments and rooming houses. They selected sites for parks (if any), business areas, and factories and established a basic policy of urban growth through exodus and conversion, so that home construction took place for the higher-income persons only (except in tenements), others taking the vacated property according to their status positions. It was a game of providing according to ability to pay with little concern for the decaying ugliness at the center.

But as American cities began to mature, this pattern changed. Persons in the community began to become concerned with the growing blight around them. Property owners began to fear for the income value of the older sections. The retreating upper middle class began to run into rural and fringe-area slums. Attitudes toward the uninhibited activities of private business began to change.

In 1907, a permanent planning commission as a municipal agency was established at Hartford, Connecticut. It set a pattern that has been followed ever since. Once begun, the movement spread rapidly, and in 1960 over 90 per cent of the cities of 10,000 population or larger had official planning commissions. At first, realtors sought to dominate the planning commissions and were often successful in doing so. Gradually, however, a broader representation has been developed, with various community interests, including homeowners, represented, though realtors remain dominant in many communities.

The Planning Commission. The central planning agency is almost always headed by a commission which coordinates the plans of the various municipal departments and carries on planning activities of a community-wide nature. The planning commission usually has five or seven members, but may have as many as fifty. It may be entirely ex officio, consisting of designated public officials, or it may be made up of citizens serving without pay, or some combination of these two.

The problems facing planning commissioners are many. They are usually subjected to great pressures from land developers or realtors who may regard them more as peculiar obstacles in their particular business than as guardians of broader community interests. Commissioners may be urged to seek locations for industry in order to strengthen the local tax base, but almost any sites they select will be highly controversial—each citizen wants the industrial zone as far from his home as is physically possible. The commissioners are typically laymen, lacking in any technical knowledge of planning or sometimes even a knowledge as to what planning seeks to do. Yet professional staff is expensive and usually is ill provided for in commission budgets, since this agency lacks a clear-cut constituency to fight for it before the governing board at budget time. It lacks status, too, for although membership on the commission may be sought by high-status citizens, the typical resident is likely to view it as a haven for idle dreamers. The commission often lacks public, political, or administrative support—the last of these because various administrative agencies, like the realtors and bankers, have their own vested interests to which the planning commission is a potential threat. Planners in the agencies dealing with education, streets, housing, recreation, traffic control, industrial development, and others may fear that the commission will not give sufficient attention to the items they consider of top priority.[2] Yet, lay concerns with the effects of possible land uses are becoming intensified, and with this trend planning commissions are rising in status as well as in power in public policy making.

Planning deals not only with streets, utilities, and the regulation of private property, but also with parks, recreation, housing, slum clearance, airports, traffic, parking, public health, and a host of other things. It "is essentially a process of understanding human needs and of influencing and shaping future public policy to serve those needs most effectively."[3] Using prevailing cultural values and professional criteria, it seeks to correct or minimize the effects of past mistakes and to avoid them in future development.

The Professionl Staff. Professional planners today enjoy high status, partly as a result of their own efforts to make the public conscious of their relatively new specialty, partly because their skills have become almost indispensable to the suburban leader anxious to mold a community to fit his image of the ideal and to the secretary-manager of the central business district association or chamber of commerce who wants to stop the leaks in his foundering vessel. Training for early planners was concentrated in engineering and landscape architecture (advocates of the City Beautiful movement were early supporters of planning). Knowledge from both these professions remains important to the planner today, but there is increasing emphasis upon much

[2] See Howard Miller, *Mr. Planning Commissioner* (Public Administration Service, Chicago, 1954); D. H. Webster, *Urban Planning and Municipal Public Policy* (Harper & Brothers, New York, 1958), chap. 1; F. Stuart Chapin, Jr., *Urban Land Use Planning* (Harper & Brothers, New York, 1957), chap. 1.

[3] Webster, *op. cit.*, p. 4.

broader training, particularly in public administration, economics, and sociology.

In the early days of planning, there was considerable doubt as to whom the commission and its staff should report. Sometimes they reported to the park board or some such secondary body. Usually they reported to the city council, and still do so in many cities, especially those of the weak-mayor type. But the council seldom took the planning commission seriously, often regarding it as a dumping ground for insistent cranks, a place where they could "play with pretty pictures."[4]

When urban planning came to be viewed as a vital municipal function after World War II, the tendency developed to center its activities under the mayor or manager and to make it a staff arm of the administration. This appears to be the dominant pattern today and the planner not only works through the commission, but directly with the chief executive, to whom he has, in many communities, become a major adviser and policy innovator.

Because of this trend, cities that have a resident planning staff have an advantage over cities that hire a planning consultant to visit the community occasionally, or hire the planner from a nearby larger city on an overtime basis, or receive technical assistance from a state agency. (About one-third of the cities over 10,000 population have a full-time planning director.) The resident planner, furthermore, has advantages in seeking to secure public support for the products of his staff. The non-resident consultant has much less opportunity to conduct a sales campaign on behalf of a new part of the over-all plan, or a new subdivision or zoning ordinance.[5]

The Plan. After a planning commission is established, surveys are made and basic data are gathered. The commission normally relies heavily upon professional help—from the city engineer if there is no planning staff. It is then the job of the commission to interpret the data and to develop plans. Space must be allocated for various types of home building, for commerce, for light and heavy industry, for recreation, and for traffic flow. A master capital-improvements plan may be developed to supplement the land-use recommendations. The plan as it finally emerges will be a compromise between the professional recommendations of the

---

[4] T. H. Reed, *Municipal Management* (McGraw-Hill Book Company, Inc., New York, 1941), p. 305.

[5] On the planner as a community organizer and educator, see Mel Scott, "Roots for Democracy," *Journal of the American Institute of Planners,* vol. 13 (Spring, 1947), pp. 11–16. The *Journal* is a major source of information on planning developments. The administration of the planning function is developed in Frederick N. Cleaveland, "Organization and Administration of Local Planning Agencies," in *Local Planning Administration* (3d ed.; International City Managers' Association, Chicago, 1959), pp. 40–75.

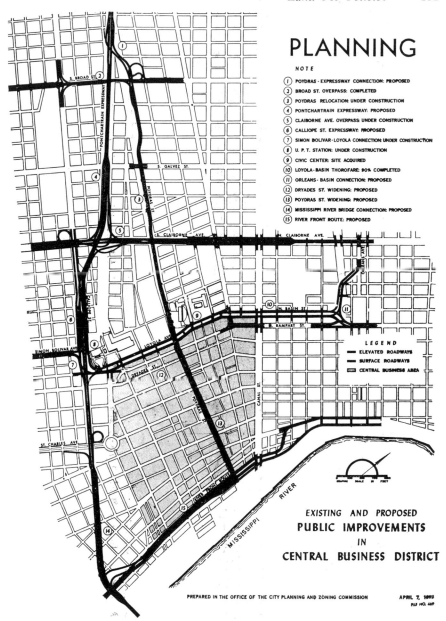

PLANNING

NOTE

1. POYDRAS - EXPRESSWAY CONNECTION: PROPOSED
2. BROAD ST. OVERPASS: COMPLETED
3. POYDRAS RELOCATION: UNDER CONSTRUCTION
4. PONTCHARTRAIN EXPRESSWAY: PROPOSED
5. CLAIBORNE AVE. OVERPASS: UNDER CONSTRUCTION
6. CALLIOPE ST. EXPRESSWAY: PROPOSED
7. SIMON BOLIVAR - LOYOLA CONNECTION: UNDER CONSTRUCTION
8. U. P. T. STATION: UNDER CONSTRUCTION
9. CIVIC CENTER: SITE ACQUIRED
10. LOYOLA - BASIN THOROFARE: 90% COMPLETED
11. ORLEANS - BASIN CONNECTION: PROPOSED
12. DRYADES ST. WIDENING: PROPOSED
13. POYDRAS ST. WIDENING: PROPOSED
14. MISSISSIPPI RIVER BRIDGE CONNECTION: PROPOSED
15. RIVER FRONT ROUTE: PROPOSED

LEGEND

ELEVATED ROADWAYS
SURFACE ROADWAYS
CENTRAL BUSINESS AREA

EXISTING AND PROPOSED
PUBLIC IMPROVEMENTS
IN
CENTRAL BUSINESS DISTRICT

PREPARED IN THE OFFICE OF THE CITY PLANNING AND ZONING COMMISSION   APRIL 7, 1953
FILE NO. 469

Figure 20-1. Existing and proposed improvements for the city of New Orleans.
SOURCE: *Annual Report of the Mayor* (City of New Orleans, La., 1953).

staff and the demands of various interests which make their views known to the commission and the local governing body (see Figure 20-1).

Planning is a continuous operation, however, since new data and new interpretations of the data must be constantly made by the commission in the light of unanticipated community developments. Master plans suffer from fairly rapid obsolescence. It is true that in 1791 Pierre L'Enfant was asked to draw up a master plan for the new city of Washington and that his imagination was so wonderful and his foresight so great that the plan has never needed serious alteration. Brigham Young, too, demonstrated real imagination in laying out Salt Lake City, but even his vision could not anticipate the crowded automobile traffic of today. The magnificent boulevards of his city came about because he wanted to allow room for a Conestoga wagon to make a U turn without backing up.

Most planners must start by accepting the existing situation, a heritage from the past that is not always fully welcome. They must make changes slowly and against inertia and the resistance of vested interests. The planners are rarely men of the vision of a L'Enfant. Even if they were, they would encounter difficulties in long-range planning. A plan in the early nineteenth century founded upon a system of water transportation would have to be seriously altered with the coming of the railroad. Later, the automobile would require even greater changes. And the best plans laid out in 1850 or 1900 could not have made proper arrangements for an airport at a logical and convenient location.

LAND-USE CONTROLS

The master plan drawn up by the commission is not usually enacted into law but serves as a basic guide for the legislative and administrative officials. The governing body may instead formally adopt a map that becomes the official statement of policy. The policies implied in the map or in statements of principle that sometimes accompany it are put into effect through three types of land-use controls: subdivision regulations, zoning, and building-construction codes.

Subdividing. Control over subdividing—the parceling of land into lots —is basic to the implementation of a plan. Subdividing is accomplished by requiring the land developer to present a "plat," that is, a map showing some or all of the following: lot sizes and shapes, utilities, topography, soil types, street sizes and patterns, and other relevant data. This plat must be in conformity with established policy and may be subject to review by the planning commission, as well as by health, highway, and other authorities before it is approved. No land can be built upon until a plat is approved, though platting may not be required in commercial, industrial, or rural nonfarm areas. With this control, planners can prevent the development of land without provision for necessary services.

Where subdivision regulations are few or nonexistent, ambitious land developers have subdivided far beyond the foreseeable needs of a community and have talked or pressured the governing body into furnishing utilities to an otherwise vacant subdivision. This, in effect, forces the taxpayers to subsidize speculation in real estate.[6]

Zoning.[7] The control of the height, area, and the use of buildings or lots may be achieved either by zoning or by subdivision deed restrictions. The former is public policy enforceable at law, while the latter are private contractual relationships enforceable in civil action before the courts. Subdivision deed restrictions are often used to protect property values where no or inadequate zoning exists. They are not a substitute for zoning, however, for in order to enforce their provisions, a resident must bring a court action against the violator. This is expensive, time-consuming, perhaps embarrassing, and often thought not worth the bother.

Zoning has now become the standard method of ensuring the efficient use of land and of promulgating many of the provisions of the master plan. The community is normally divided up into residential, commercial, and industrial zones, and perhaps into further subcategories. Zones should not be taken too literally, however, as being belts or areas of the community. A zone may be very small—it may be a narrow strip along a street or railroad track, or it may be a single lot. The location of a single lot or of a few lots of one classification in the midst of a more preferred type—"spot zoning"—may be very profitable to an owner able to sell a lot in an area zoned for single-family homes to a filling-station or grocery-store operator. But it means a loss in the total value of the community. Because this loss is socialized among many persons who individually have less incentive to exert pressure than does the single profiteer, such practices take place with considerable regularity in some communities, sometimes reducing to an absurdity the concept of zoning.

In addition to restrictions concerning *use* of land, the zoning ordinance will usually restrict the height of buildings in relation to the width of the street, the size of side yards, and the use to which the area is put. Residential and commercial zones normally have such restrictions. Further limitations are placed on *area* that is usable for building. In single-family-home areas, the building line may be 20 or 30 feet back of the sidewalk, for example. And apartment buildings are no longer allowed to take up the whole of the lot with little provision for

[6] See H. W. Lautner, *Subdivision Regulations* (Public Administration Service, Chicago, 1941); P. H. Cornick, *Premature Subdivision and Its Consequences* (Institute of Public Administration, Columbia University, New York, 1938).

[7] On the legal basis of zoning, see above, pp. 166–167.

sunlight and air. A building in a residential area is today generally required to come no nearer than a specified distance to the lot line—the distance being determined by the height of the buildings in the neighborhood.

Competent planning and zoning will not in itself guarantee a "city beautiful." This is clearly demonstrated by developments in New York skyscraper construction. Since the war a large number of moderate-sized skyscrapers—twenty to thirty stories in height—have been built. The financiers of these projects are anxious to make a maximum utilization of Manhattan's expensive land. The architects have therefore been forced to plan them, not with aesthetic considerations paramount, but rather so as to fit the minimum setback requirements of the zoning ordinance.[8] Lewis Mumford has given a fitting title to the resulting "style": wedding-cake modern.

The Zoning Ordinance. Zoning is intended, of course, to do more than merely protect property values. It is also used to ensure the availability of adequate light, air, and accessibility to all property. It protects the public health and minimizes the number of fire hazards. The zoning ordinance—which is sometimes the only formal and legal promulgation of the efforts of the planning commission—is logically based on the city's over-all plans and must, therefore, be adjusted to conform with the almost constant changes in the plans.

The zoning ordinance is sometimes primarily a mosaic of the pressures applied upon the councilmen. Professional planners prefer that it be drawn up by the planning staff and have the endorsement of the planning commission. If this procedure is followed, the ordinance is likely to enjoy some protection from the immediate, short-range demands of effective interests. Unless the zoning ordinance—which usually must be enacted by the council in order to have any legal validity—is coordinated with the work of the planning commission, the latter will lose its principal device for implementing its plans.

Building-construction Codes. A community with a complete set of land-use controls will have one or more building codes. These are usually known as building, plumbing, electrical, heating, and safe-and-sanitary-housing codes. They seek to enforce the subdivision and zoning regulations and the housing standards desired in the community by requiring permits to build or install equipment. This is coupled with inspections to determine whether or not compliance has taken place or, in the case of safe-and-sanitary-housing ordinances, is being maintained.

---

[8] The zoning rules regarding the height of buildings usually require a certain amount of *setback* as the number of stories increases. Thus, a building may use the full ground space for perhaps ten stories, after which there must be 1 foot of setback from the building line for, perhaps, 4 feet of height. This allows air and sunlight to reach the lower floors.

The building inspector, or zoning administrator, "can destroy the effectiveness of the [zoning ordinance or building code] by overlooking violations or permitting exceptions to the regulations. The integrity of such officer is, therefore, most essential."[9] Needless to say, he is subjected to great pressures and temptations. The physical appearance, not to say the reputation, of a community may depend upon his competence and incorruptibility. Because of inadequate codes and poor enforcement procedures, FHA regulations have, especially on the outer fringe, often given home buyers more protection than have those of the local government.

PLANNING IN THE URBAN REGION

Planning in the Suburbs. Urban areas have adopted procedures for planning and zoning—long after they were first needed, to be sure. Today, the principal growth in urban areas is on the periphery. And it is here, where planning and zoning are most needed today, that they are most often inadequate or entirely absent.

Suburbs, especially in their earliest years of development, suffer from several things that lead to blight. Premature subdividers are normally little enough controlled within the core city. In suburbs, and especially in unincorporated areas, they may encounter virtually no restrictions at all. They may be responsible for erratic and inefficient use of land. The outer fringe, which in a few years is to become an inner fringe, is characteristically the area where individuals try to build their own homes or purchase jerry-built shacks. With no building code or a very weak one, it may be possible for the person who cannot afford to build or buy a home in the city to construct one in the fringe area. He may be able to afford one that has too little floor space or is of too flimsy construction to meet the core-city building regulations.

In a few years, the outer fringe becomes truly suburban, with a great amount of subdividing and building. But the new homes are now interspersed with dilapidated shacks and nonconforming buildings according to the belatedly adopted zoning ordinances. In quite a number of metropolitan areas, there is a greater percentage of substandard and dilapidated homes in the suburbs than in the core city.[10]

There are some exceptional situations around the nation, and certainly the new homeowners of suburbia quickly grasp the importance of planning and effective land-use controls in relation to their investment. But the major problem remains—chaotic land usage until the area be-

[9] Webster, *op. cit.*, p. 424.
[10] Compare the approach in Australia: A. J. Brown and H. M. Sherrard, *Town and Country Planning* (Melbourne University Press, Melbourne, Australia, 1951).

comes quite heavily populated and then a belated attempt to prevent the building of any more individual shacks. But by this time the opportunity for maximum efficiency of land use is probably gone forever.

Efforts at Metropolitan Planning. Because our metropolitan areas are atomized politically while planning must, by its nature, extend continuously across the land, a hiatus exists between the need for planning and its political practicality. In order to fill this gap, there has been somewhat of a trend toward the development of metropolitan planning commissions or joint city-county commissions. Often these groups are private and unofficial, sometimes they are extralegal, sometimes they are provided for by state enabling acts, but almost always they are advisory only and have no coercive powers. Some of them have their own staffs, but quite a few share the staff of the core-city planning commission. Some have no staffs at all, but are merely operated through occasional meetings.

Planning for utilities, parks and recreation, highways, the location of industry, and many other urban matters might logically be approached on an area or regional rather than a city basis. But it has been generally impossible to find a politically expedient method of representing the many communities of the area in a planning organization with any real powers over land use. Although metropolitan-area studies often recommend that planning should be a function of any area-wide government that might be set up, this function is undoubtedly one over which local landowners themselves most want to keep close control.

Metropolitan planning: [11]

. . . assumes that it is possible to coordinate fully the making of important decisions regarding regional development with the result that each decision is made with due regard to every other decision and that all decisions together comprise a self-consistent system of decisions. In fact, however, even within any sizable city the power to make decisions of fundamental importance is too widely dispersed to permit a high level of coordination. . . . Many so-called plans are therefore really mere listings of anticipated actions by actors whose behavior is, and in the nature of the case must be, largely uncoordinated.

Though this is the case, at least one planner has noted that "if piecemeal planning is to be the rule, it is evident that the pieces are getting bigger and that a larger variety of factors are being taken into account than ever before." [12] Americans prefer to do their planning on an individual or small-area basis, but they are increasingly viewing the com-

[11] E. C. Banfield and Morton Grodzins, *Government and Housing in Metropolitan Areas* (McGraw-Hill Book Company, Inc., New York, 1958), pp. 67–68.

[12] Richard L. Meier, "Systems and Principles for Metropolitan Planning," *Centennial Review*, vol. 3 (Winter, 1959), pp. 79–94.

munity and the metropolitan area as a medium for some of society's systematic decision making.[13]

[13] There is considerable material dealing with planning and land-use controls. See the bibliography at the end of chap. 19, and that in Webster, *op. cit.*, and Chapin, *op. cit.* Lewis Mumford has written much on planning, especially of its aesthetic aspects. See his *City Development* (Harcourt, Brace & World, Inc., New York, 1945), and his occasional articles in *The New Yorker*.

Other basic references include *Local Planning Administration* (3d ed.; International City Managers' Association, Chicago, 1959); G. C. Bestor and H. R. Jones, *City Planning: A Basic Bibliography* (California Council of Civil Engineers and Land Surveyors, Sacramento, Calif., 1958); C. M. Haar, *Land-use Planning* (Little, Brown & Company, Boston, 1959); Harvey S. Perloff, *Education for Planning* (Johns Hopkins Press, Baltimore, 1957); Robert A. Walker, *The Planning Function in Urban Government* (2d ed.; University of Chicago Press, Chicago, 1950). The realtors' point of view is stated in R. L. Nelson and F. T. Aschmen, *Real Estate and City Planning* (Urban Land Institute, Washington, 1957). Land use is so important a factor in suburban politics that at least one mystery novel has been built around a zoning conflict: Richard and Frances Lockridge, *Burnt Offering* (J. B. Lippincott Company, Philadelphia, 1955).

Chapter 21

PUBLIC HEALTH AND WELFARE

Few functions of municipal government affect more urbanites in a greater variety of ways than do those involving health and welfare (which, for purposes of this chapter, includes recreation). Yet these are also largely technical and professional functions which rest on a foundation of stable cultural values. As a result, they provoke relatively little public controversy and tend to be dominated by a professional bureaucracy which administers them according to its own (culturally acceptable) standards.

Yet even though nearly complete consensus now exists, from time to time throughout history, health and welfare have become the subject of intense political controversy. Thus, discovery of the germ theory of disease, coupled with cholera and typhoid epidemics, resulted in sharp public debate and was followed by heavy public outlays and daring engineering projects designed to reach unpolluted water sources. Public welfare based on the harsh seventeenth-century poor law fitted so well into the American myth system that it was not seriously challenged until the Great Depression, when public attitudes quickly changed. Public welfare recipients and others who were potentially members of welfare clientele groups became politically conscious and active. Yet the long period of stable attitudes toward welfare could also block the development of concepts for a contemporary approach, thus delaying the maturation of a new public welfare system.

It is in the times of transition that a governmental function rises to the level of perception and concern of the average citizen. It is then that each of us may help to contribute to the construction of a new concept of the content of that function.

PUBLIC HEALTH

The Nation's Health Is a Municipal Trust. Great cities, with their high concentration of people in confined areas, are natural targets for communicable diseases. For this reason, local governments have long had responsibilities toward the protection of health. The idea that some diseases were in some manner contagious was discovered long ago. Resulting from this knowledge came the practice of having cities require the isolation of afflicted persons. The pesthouse was an early form of isolation. Quarantining of such persons in their houses also became a municipal responsibility. A flag or sign beside the doorway of the homes of those with contagious diseases was the responsibility of the public health officer.

During the Great Plague (bubonic plague) that struck London in 1665–1666, for example, the houses of the afflicted were marked with red crosses on the door, "searchers" were sent out to certify as to the cause of deaths, and municipal authorities sent a man out to kill the dogs of the city, for these creatures were mistakenly blamed for spreading the disease.[1] Cities, aided by a considerable amount of progress in medical knowledge, still perform these functions. In recent decades, their tasks have become ever greater and their successes in lowering the death rate ever more impressive.

Another development in municipal health activities, and a logical extension of the older practice of isolation, came with the discovery of the techniques of vaccination and inoculation against communicable diseases. A conflict has developed over the question of whether these practices are "treatments" that should be cared for by private physicians, or preventive medicine, and as such a public health function. In the United States, the former view has generally prevailed, except for the vaccination of school children in some cases and the emergency treatment of populations in the event of epidemics.[2]

A third factor in the development of public health departments was the popularity of the filth theory of disease in the middle years of the nineteenth century. This notion led to heavy emphasis upon sanitation, especially on the construction of sewers, the collection of garbage, and the abatement of nuisances. It was during this period that public health departments became common and were expanded in size beyond that of a local physician acting on a part-time basis. Although the collection and disposal of sewage and garbage is still a function of the health department in some cities, it has generally been transferred to the public works department. But the health department is still responsible for the health supervision of such activities, and it has been entrusted with an ever increasing number of other functions.

[1] See Johannes Nohl, *The Black Death* (Ballantine Books, New York, 1960), chap. 5, "Administrative Precautions."

[2] For an elaboration, see T. H. Reed, *Municipal Management* (McGraw-Hill Book Company, Inc., New York, 1941), chap. 18.

Public Health Administration. The American Public Health Association believes that specialization is so important in a proper health program that its Committee on Local Health Units has recommended the establishment of health units so organized as to contain not less than 50,000 people in each of them.[3] Smaller units not only cannot develop specialization, but are likely to be unable to finance a successful program. This means, of course, that the county or a special-purpose district would have to be used as the health unit, except for fair-sized cities. The professional organization also suggests that there should be one public health nurse for each 5,000 people and one sanitarian for each 25,000 people. Few communities in the nation meet these and other standards of the Association, however. Cities and villages are still the standard units established by state law, although county and city-county departments are increasingly taking over health functions in urban areas and standards are rising. For example, Michigan law provides that any city failing to maintain a full-time health officer comes automatically under the county health department, and that the city and county may, by mutual agreement, share the services of a single health officer to supervise both departments.[4] It is likely, however, that health units will be rapidly consolidated in the future only through the incentive of conditional Federal or state grants-in-aid.

There is a trend today toward municipal health departments under a single head responsible to the chief executive. Most municipalities, however, still make use of the traditional board of health. (General municipal health departments first became popular in the heyday of the independent board and commission.) Quite a few cities still have boards, but have stripped them of administrative powers, leaving them with but an advisory function. This is, in fact, the structure recommended by the American Public Health Association.

The board of health is often made up partly of physicians and partly of interested laymen. In some cities, at least one seat must be given to an engineer. The American Public Health Association and other medical groups favor a heavy representation of physicians on the board. This can perhaps be justified on the basis of the superior interest of these men, but undoubtedly they are also wanted there to "protect" the private medical profession against those who would expand the scope of public health functions.

The health officer in small cities is a local physician, often working on a part-time basis. In larger cities, a person with professional training in

[3] American Public Health Association, *Local Health Units for the Nation* (The Commonwealth Fund, New York, 1946).

[4] On the growth of local health units, see National Health Assembly, *America's Health* (Harper & Brothers, New York, 1949), p. 60.

public health and the degree of Doctor of Public Health, as well as that of M.D., is often employed. The specialized professional degree affords training in sanitation, public administration, and other fields in addition to medical training. In the largest cities, the health officer's time is fully occupied with administration, and technical functions are left to his subordinates.

Public Health Functions. A great many health activities are performed or aided by state health departments and by Federal agencies, especially by the U.S. Public Health Service of the Department of Health, Education and Welfare. But the principal direct health services are performed by local governments. Except in small communities, the health department is normally divided into several specialized divisions.

Communicable-disease Control. The traditional function of the health department deals with communicable-disease control. Despite limited funds, health departments have been so effective in reducing, with the help of private medicine, the incidence of these diseases that they have almost eliminated the need for this function. Almost—but never entirely. The communicable-disease division receives the required reports from physicians and enforces isolation in those cases where it is still required. It must sometimes prod lax physicians into the prompt reporting of diseases.

By keeping watch over water and milk supplies this division has almost eliminated typhoid fever. At the turn of the present century, there were more than thirty times as many deaths from this disease in the United States as there are today. Yellow fever and malaria, once common in swampy areas frequented by certain types of mosquitoes, have been virtually eliminated in this country by the draining of swamps and the treatment of other standing water. Typhus has been controlled through ratproofing programs and through health education, which has taught the dangers to be found in the body lice that transmit the disease. Smallpox is almost unknown today as a result of educating the public and the occasional use of compulsory vaccination laws. In recent years, trends in communicable-disease control have included (1) development of more effective medical treatment for communicable diseases; (2) realization that there are many more healthy disease carriers than sick ones—hence the abandonment of traditional quarantine practices after about 1945; and (3) the development of immunization techniques for an increased number of diseases.

Tuberculosis, less contagious than most communicable diseases, but requiring special equipment and methods, is handled by a separate division of the health department in larger cities. Clinics and special hospitals or hospital sections are needed for its treatment. The prevention of tuberculosis is possible largely through conditions beyond the control of the health department—through better housing and conditions of labor for many urban citizens.

Venereal diseases are also usually treated by a special division of the department. These diseases, like tuberculosis, must be controlled through treatment. Protection against them can be achieved only through health education. The venereal-disease-control section has the major task of persuading people to apply for its help voluntarily and of overcoming the sufferer's wish to keep secret his socially disapproved ailment. Health departments have sought to encourage people to come forward for treatment by making their services available to all, regardless of ability to pay, and by locating treatment clinics as inconspicuously as possible.

Federal grants for venereal-disease control have gone to local units. Some of the "wonder drugs" have been very effective in treatment. However, an unknown, but no doubt very large, number of cases requiring treatment are never brought to the attention of either private practitioners or public health clinics.[5]

Maternal and Child Care. The principal functions of this division are of an educational nature. It offers lectures, pamphlets, publicity releases, and other information services designed to reduce ignorance concerning childbearing among prospective mothers and fathers. The division also gives advice on child care and child rearing. Many cities operate prenatal and postnatal clinics and provide for home visits by public health nurses. The division works closely with hospitals offering free maternity service to the indigent, and it licenses and regulates midwifery in those states where its practice is still permitted.

Sanitation. Many municipal functions related to sanitation are administered outside of the health department. Swamps are drained, water is supplied, and sewage is disposed of by the public works department, or by independent departments, but health aspects are supervised by the health department.

The municipal department shares many inspection duties with state and Federal agencies. Milk must be inspected to guard against watering and against the presence of tuberculosis and typhoid as well as several other types of germs that may be found in raw milk. Local slaughterhouses, if not inspected by representatives of the U.S. Department of Agriculture, are often inspected by the local health department. Retail food establishments are inspected and food handlers examined for communicable diseases by the health department, or under its supervision.

In checking the premises of retail food establishments, sanitation-division personnel usually follow the practice of unexpected and irregular inspections. If illegal and unsanitary conditions are found, the usual prac-

[5] *Today's VD Control Program* (The Association of State and Territorial Health Officers, Chicago, 1957).

tice is to issue a warning. In the case of extreme or repeated violations, licenses may be suspended or revoked.

Municipal Hospitals. Municipal hospitals have become common throughout the nation as part of a public health program. There are over 250 city hospitals and over 60 city-county hospitals in the United States. Hospitals in cities under 100,000 are usually managed by semiautonomous boards, while in larger cities they tend to be controlled by the city health departments. In smaller cities, the budget is also usually autonomous, with the council having no power of review, but in larger cities, municipal hospitals as a rule are treated as simply another city agency.

Generally speaking, the smaller the city, the more likely its hospital is to be completely self-supporting, or nearly so. In very few cities of over 50,000 is the municipal hospital even 50 per cent self-supporting. The difference is made up from funds appropriated by the city, or sometimes the county or state. Municipal hospitals in larger cities exist to a large extent to care for police and indigent cases. The smaller the city, generally speaking, the more likely is the hospital to be a general-service institution. Larger cities are also likely to operate special hospitals for contagious diseases, tuberculosis, poliomyelitis, and mental disorders.[6]

The oldest municipal hospital in the United States, the Philadelphia General, dates from 1732. The largest municipal institution, New York's famed Bellevue, is only four years younger. The city of New York also operates thirteen other hospitals and sanatoria. There are, however, municipal hospitals in cities of all sizes, including about one hundred cities of under 5,000 population.

Public Health Education. This division seeks to increase longevity by teaching citizens the principles of personal hygiene and the need for proper medical care and consultation, and warning them about certain dangers to health. The division may conduct public lectures, issue news releases and public service announcements to press, radio, and television, and furnish lecturers to clubs, school assemblies, and other get-togethers. For example, the division may help the National Cancer Society warn the public of the "seven danger signals of cancer"; in the summer it may issue public service announcements to local radio stations reminding parents of the symptoms of poliomyelitis in children (or themselves); or it may issue news releases to the press warning of the dangers of food poisoning in an unrefrigerated cream puff.

The Staff Services. A staff function of general interest is the collection of vital statistics for the community: records of births, of deaths and their causes, and of communicable diseases. The public health laboratory furnishes analyses of blood, sputum, and other samples in helping

[6] Statistics are taken from the *Municipal Year Book, 1953* (International City Managers' Association, Chicago, 1953), pp. 310–326.

physicians diagnose diseases. It also may analyze food suspected of being tainted. As a staff service, public health nurses are furnished to aid the divisions in charge of communicable diseases, tuberculosis, venereal diseases, maternal and child care, public health education, and outpatient care.

Public Health and a Healthy Public. T. H. Reed, city manager, municipal consultant, and professor, writing in his usual style of realism tinged with satire, has said: [7]

There is no field of local public administration in which the professional staff comes into so many and so varied contacts with the public as does that of a department of health. Furthermore, it comes into contact not with any special section of the public but with representatives of every social and economic group. The marvelous development of the technical side of health work in the past generation has scarcely, if at all, reduced the importance of its human side. Health administration cannot, in spite of its scientific flavor, be reduced to a series of rigid formulas. It is still a matter of making rich landlords provide suitable sanitary conveniences for people who have to be taught not to use bathtubs for storing coal. It is as much as ever a question of inducing ignorant and wayward men and women to submit to restraints and treatments the nature of which they cannot understand. It furnishes the clearest possible illustration of the distinction between the pursuit of professional techniques and the application of such techniques to the service of real human beings. It is the human relationships involved which separate the science of epidemiology from the art of municipal management. [8]

Public Awareness and Attitudes. The public is not well informed concerning the services performed by public health agencies. There are many private organizations active in the health field (such as the American Social Hygiene Association, local tuberculosis organizations, The National Foundation), and these are often confused with public organizations. Furthermore, in one community, 84 per cent of the working-class, 51 per cent of the lower-middle-class, and 24 per cent of the upper-middle-class samples, could not name one specific activity that was

[7] Reed, *op. cit.*, p. 448.

[8] For further reading on public health functions, see Ira V. Hiscock, *Community Health Organization* (4th ed.; The Commonwealth Fund, New York, 1950); J. J. Hanlon, *Principles of Public Health Administration* (2d ed.; The C. V. Mosby Company, St. Louis, 1955); Peter Van Avery, *Public Health* (The H. W. Wilson Company, New York, 1959); *Urban Sprawl and Health* (National Health Council, New York, 1959); and two studies by political scientists, L. W. Wyatt, *Intergovernmental Relations in Public Health* (University of Minnesota Press, Minneapolis, Minn., 1951); and R. T. Daland, *Government and Health: The Alabama Experience* (Bureau of Public Administration, University of Alabama, University, Ala., 1955). For a case study in health administration involving a conflict between the elected leaders of a community and the professional staff of a municipal hospital, see Marianna Robinson and Corinne Silverman, *The Reorganization of Philadelphia General Hospital* (University of Alabama Press, University, Ala., 1959).

carried on by their local (county) public health agency.[9] This, despite the fact that "there is no field of local public administration in which the professional staff comes into so many and so varied contacts with the public as does that of a department of health." [10] This seeming paradox probably results from the high degree of professionalization in this field and the stable cultural attitudes that exist toward public health functions and administrators.

Important controversies before municipal governing bodies center around and are related to several items, especially the following: (1) the establishment of hospitals for the chronically ill (a group of increasing size in our society, a by-product of lengthening life expectancy); (2) the development of home-care programs by local health units at which patients not in need of hospitalization or other institutional care may be cared for and followed up in their own homes after hospital release; the public purchase of polio vaccine for children; and (3) the development of publicly financed medical-service centers in small towns with too little population to support hospitals or even physicians. All of these and some other items being urged as proper areas for public health activity are controversial, not only because they are potentially expensive, but also because they raise the long-standing question of the proper balance between public health and private medicine.

PARKS AND RECREATION

Recreational Administration.[11] In few areas of municipal activity have so many disputes arisen over the proper forms of organization as in the field of parks and recreation. Although the general public probably thinks of parks and recreation as two aspects of a single function, professionals in the field are not so sure. In the past, it was common for the city government to have separate departments for parks and for recreation, but the postwar trend has been away from this. In many cities, the school board also provides an organized summer recreation program.

[9] E. L. Koos, *The Health of Regionville* (Columbia University Press, New York, 1954), pp. 115–116. On public reactions to health programs, see B. J. Paul (ed.), *Health, Culture and Community* (Russell Sage Foundation, New York, 1955), and P. A. Miller, *Community Health Action* (Michigan State University Press, East Lansing, Mich., 1953); and C. Sower and others, *Community Involvement* (The Free Press, Glencoe, Ill., 1957), pt. 1.

[10] Reed, *op. cit.*, p. 448.

[11] See *Municipal Recreation Administration* (4th ed.; International City Managers' Association, Chicago, 1960); G. D. Butler, *Introduction to Community Recreation* (rev. ed.; McGraw-Hill Book Company, Inc., New York, 1959). For a case study of the mobilization of parks and recreation interests when New York's famed but controversial Parks Commissioner, Robert Moses, sought to convert a small portion of Central Park into a parking lot for the benefit of a private restaurant, see John B. Keeley, *Moses on the Green* (University of Alabama Press, University, Ala., 1959).

In the past, parks and recreation departments were commonly set up under autonomous administrative boards, and it was not uncommon for them to have independent sources of income so that they existed practically as separate *ad hoc* units of local government, similar in status to the school boards. Parks and recreation boards were (and still are) very often made up of well-known and prosperous members of the community —the type known to the irreverent as "do-gooders." Professional recreation workers have generally tended to favor the independent board because of the support which it gives to the recreation program, particularly when the budget is under consideration. They also argue that such a board offers a continuity of policy not to be found when the head of the department changes at the pleasure of the chief executive.

General administrators in the field of municipal management argue, however, that the parks and recreation function is not unique in its problems of management and that it should be administered as a regular department of the city under the control of the chief executive. They contend that this activity should be financed out of the general fund rather than a separate tax levy, that its budget should be treated like those of other city departments, and that the department should make use of the municipal staff services for purchasing, personnel, maintenance, and the like. In order to maintain organized community interest in parks and recreation, there is a tendency for a board to be retained as an *advisory* body and hence a watchdog, while at the same time leaving administrative control under the chief executive.

Concerning the question of combining parks and recreation, T. H. Reed has said: [12]

Many recreational facilities can be located most conveniently in parks. Recreationists used to deplore the preoccupation of park authorities with shrubs and flower beds. The idea, however, that parks are for the use of the public, not merely for the delectation of their eyes, has gained ground rapidly in recent years. A considerable portion of the area of all large parks within or adjacent to cities is nowadays devoted to active recreation. In other words, our traditional parks—laid out on the pattern of an English country gentleman's estate—have gone recreational in a large way. Today if there is any tendency which threatens the dominance of the recreational motive it is a weakness for turning park drives into motor speedways in an effort to relieve traffic congestion elsewhere.

Perhaps the number one problem of administration in the postwar era —at least in many cities—has been that of recruiting recreational leaders, and especially persons for top executive positions. In some cities salaries have increased at a greater rate than the cost of living, but leadership

[12] Reed, *op. cit.*, p. 461.

salaries have generally failed to keep pace with those offered in related professions. Qualified persons have thus been difficult to obtain, and turnover has been high.

The Recreation Program. Recreationists believe that every municipality should have a program designed to provide opportunity for all. It should provide a wide range of individual choices in different types of activities, not just sports, but games, music, arts and crafts, nature, drama, and social recreation. Passive forms of recreation are not neglected—watching, listening, and contemplation. The program usually continues throughout the year and serves people of all ages and of both sexes. As the normal work week decreases in length, the problem of providing for constructive and acceptable ways of using leisure time becomes ever greater. Recreationists believe that attention should be given to the needs of special groups, such as the family, the handicapped, and service personnel. The long-range goals of a recreation program include the development of creative expression as well as good citizenship through safe, healthful, and socially approved activities, and the teaching of activities that will persist after adulthood is reached.[13]

Parks. The inhabitants and public officials of cities have often been slow in providing for the benefits of spacious, beautiful, and useful parks. Parks are of great psychological value, especially to the apartment or slum dweller, to whom they may be the only available substitute for a front lawn or a back yard.

Cities such as New York and Philadelphia were allowed to grow up with almost complete disregard for the need for large open spaces, for grass, trees, and shrubs. (Slum dwellers will not use many playgrounds and green spaces that are beyond short walking distance. Magnificent open spaces such as Central Park are of limited value to low-income persons.) Even cities that expanded at a much later date, such as Detroit, failed to plan for parks. Today a belated attempt is being made in all large cities to provide small recreational playgrounds and indoor gymnasiums and swimming pools. In most cities it is now too late to provide areas for large parks that might have been set aside twenty-five, fifty, or more years ago. As a result, quite a few cities (or *ad hoc* park districts) have constructed parks and beaches outside of the urban areas. This practice began as long ago as 1893 in the Boston region. Outlying parks and "reservations" must sometimes be located 20, 30, or even more miles from the heart of the city. Where this is so, it at the least causes inconvenience and traffic hazards on week ends. To those in the lowest-income groups who have no automobiles, but who most need the facilities, these areas may be quite inaccessible.

[13] For an elaboration on the criteria for a successful recreation program, see International City Managers' Association, *Municipal Recreation Administration.*

Some municipalities have sought to require provisions for a reasonable amount of park and playground area at the time of, or in advance of, subdividing. The courts have not been particularly cooperative, however, and several types of such laws and ordinances have been declared unconstitutional. Of course, some cities have planned their parks carefully, fitting them into the long-range scheme of things and not waiting for a park to be located through the accident of a donated piece of land. Quite a few American cities have fine park systems. Minneapolis's is particularly beautiful, but Chicago, Boston, and other cities rate near the top, too.

Neighborhood parks offer a spot for relaxation, and their greenery breaks the monotony of a drab or uninteresting neighborhood. Large parks add to the beauty of a community and give opportunity for forms of recreation impossible in the small playground, such as golf, walking, bicycling, skiing and, very importantly, picnicking. With a lake, they may provide facilities for boating and swimming, and their trees and shrubs offer hours of pleasure to the nature lover and to that butt of television jokes, the bird watcher.

A large city often makes a zoo out of one of its parks. Zoos are sometimes operated by a board and department separate from the parks department. They are expensive to maintain but are immensely popular with children and adults alike. Zoos such as those in Chicago, Philadelphia, St. Louis, and Washington are among the finest in the world. All municipal institutions seem to have their opponents. Some people, for example, consider zoos to be either a waste of the taxpayers' money or a cruelty to the confined wild animals. But most people love animals and like to observe them, provided that they are given adequate and expert care and attention.

Places to Read and Learn. The first library that was tax-supported was established in Peterborough, New Hampshire, in 1833. Libraries are sometimes privately endowed and privately operated, but indirectly agencies of the city because they receive an annual appropriation either from the council or from a special property-tax levy. This type of library, especially common in New England and the South, is controlled by a self-perpetuating board of trustees. Other libraries are entirely public, controlled either by the school district or by the city government. They usually have autonomous control through a library board, but a few cities have a single librarian reporting directly to the chief executive.

Three problems, in particular, have vexed librarians in recent years. In the first place, the decentralizing tendency of cities means, in many places, that the main public library is often isolated in the center of the city from which the population is receding. This poses the threat that fewer people will use the libraries. The answer seems to be in a greater use of branch libraries in outlying residential areas. Such a movement has been under way for years but is now being accelerated. Connected with the problem is also the question of allowing suburbanites to use the core-city library, for which they do not pay taxes. Some cities allow free use of the library to anyone who is *employed* in the city regardless of where he may live. This is another form of subsidizing the suburbs. County libraries and *ad hoc* library districts are arising to supply the suburbs in many places.

A second problem lies in the threat posed by the coming of television. Have people stopped reading, thus making the library obsolete, or a luxury maintained only for scholars? Studies conducted to date indicate that people do, in fact, read less shortly after purchasing a television set, but that after the novelty wears off, they return to approximately their old habits.[14] There has been a decrease in library use in recent years, but television is probably only one of several causes.

A third area of controversy centers around the threatened censorship of reading materials in libraries. In times of tension, unrest, confusion, and doubt, people seek security through unity and conformity. Alien ideas become enemies to be fought along with the human enemies. In the period since the beginning of the cold war, and particularly during the period of McCarthyism (1950–1954), some citizens confused the study of communism with allegiance to it. In 1952, for example, the *Boston Post* conducted a campaign to have all materials concerned with communism removed from the public library. The effort was not successful in Boston, but in some smaller cities book burnings took place.

Potential attacks upon our libraries—the storehouses of the accumulated knowledge of mankind—are always with us. It does not take a threat as serious as that of communism to serve as the springboard of an assault. Headline seekers can create their own excuses. For example, in 1927, William Hale ("Big Bill") Thompson, Chicago's colorful demagogic mayor appointed a friend, Sport Herrmann, to the task of ridding the Chicago Public Library of books containing "pro-British propaganda and un-American statements." Herrmann explained his intended method: "I'm gonna burn every book in that there library that's pro-British! . . . The library's supported by public taxes and if this thing of undermining Americanism isn't stopped, the country'll go to pieces, that's all! . . . There must be thousands of propaganda books in the library system. I'll hunt them out and when I find them I'll burn them on the lake shore."[15]

---

[14] S. Janice Kee, "Public Libraries Developments in 1952," *Municipal Year Book, 1953* (International City Managers' Association, Chicago, 1953), p. 484.

[15] Quoted in Lloyd Wendt and Herman Kogan, *Big Bill of Chicago* (The Bobbs-Merrill Company, Inc., Indianapolis, 1953), pp. 288–289.

But our culture is made up of conflicting values. Some of them gave support to Herrmann, but the courts, which sometimes represent the long-range conscience and stable values of society, stood in his way. The threat of legal action stopped him.[16]

Museums and Art Galleries. There are far fewer museums and art galleries in the United States than there are libraries. Most large cities operate them, however. They are usually autonomously controlled in the same fashion as are libraries, and they enjoy the protection of the "patrons of the arts" in the political process. These patrons are often well-to-do and influential persons.

PUBLIC WELFARE

The ancient power of the state to protect the "welfare" of the people is not limited to public assistance programs. The problems of caring for the unemployed and those injured in industrial accidents, and of providing old-age and survivors' insurance, are largely beyond the scope of municipal administration. They are discussed in textbooks dealing with American and with state and local government.[17] But many other welfare functions are handled by municipalities, or jointly with the state. This includes the care of the poor, including children whose parents cannot or will not support them, and old people who can neither work nor support themselves from their savings. Delinquents, disabled persons, and the mentally handicapped are also taken care of by welfare agencies in some cities and states, as is the entire recreation program sometimes.

The Development of Welfare Programs. The responsibility for public assistance aid rests with the state, but it has been delegated to local units of government ever since the Elizabethan Poor Law of 1601, the principles of which were adopted in colonial America. The basic approach to the care of the poor taken in the days of the first Elizabeth in England remained unchanged in the American states until its archaism became obvious in the Great Depression. In the years since the Federal government set up its so-called categorical grants-in-aid program in the Social Security Act of 1935, however, there has been a shift of emphasis from the city or township as the administrative unit to the county or to the state itself.

---

[16] On libraries, see Oliver Garceau, *The Public Library in the Political Process* (Columbia University Press, New York, 1949); Robert D. Leigh, *The Public Library in the United States* (Columbia University Press, New York, 1950); and Ernestine Rose, *The Public Library in American Life* (Columbia University Press, New York, 1954).

[17] See Charles R. Adrian, *State and Local Governments* (McGraw-Hill Book Company, Inc., New York, 1960), chap. 20.

There were some activities by the states designed to modify the ancient poor law even before the Great Depression. In the 1880s, for example, some Eastern private child-welfare agencies would gather up whole trainloads of large-city waifs and bring them to the Midwest to be delivered to farmers who waited at railroad stations. The theory apparently was that any Midwest farmer who offered a child a home would provide a better place than could be found in a large city. The potential abuses of this method of child placement were so great that in the mid-1880s, Midwestern states enacted legislation bringing child placement under state control.

The needs of the elderly, as distinguished from those of the employable, became obvious as the special problems of urban living made impossible the old system of their being taken into the large farm homes of relatives. Even before the Great Depression, a number of states, including Montana, Kentucky, Wisconsin, and Nevada, had adopted some form of old-age assistance. But generally programs for the aged were adopted after the passage of the Social Security Act in 1935.

The Federal government furnishes grants-in-aid to the states to help in caring for certain categories of persons: old-age assistance, aid to the blind, aid to dependent children, and (since 1950) aid to the permanently and totally disabled. In 1956, Congress expanded these categorical aids by providing a program for hospital care for anyone eligible under the four programs. Some of the states administer these programs through field officers, but in most states they are administered by the counties or other local governments under state aid and supervision.

In some states, although the above categorical aids are administered by the county, general direct relief is left to the cities. The administration of these "welfare cases" is a major task taken alone. City public welfare agencies are often entrusted, in addition, with responsibility for the licensing of private child-caring agencies, the provision of foster care for children unable to live in their own homes, adoption services, work with children's courts, provision for medical and dental care for the needy, and the supervising of private charities.[18]

Persons Dependent upon Public Aid. The idea that some persons might not be capable of caring for their own basic economic needs was

[18] On welfare administration in general, see R. Clyde White, *Administration of Public Welfare* (2d ed.; American Book Company, New York, 1950); Wayne McMillen, *Community Organization for Social Welfare* (University of Chicago Press, Chicago, 1945); Ruth Raup, *Intergovernmental Relations in Public Welfare* (University of Minnesota Press, Minneapolis, 1952); and two fiscal studies, Lewis Meriam and others, *The Cost and Financing of Social Security* (Brookings Institution, Washington, D.C., 1950); and Ellen J. Perkins, *State and Local Financing of Public Assistance* (U.S. Department of Health, Education and Welfare, Bureau of Public Assistance, 1956).

long essentially alien to the American tradition of self-sufficiency. Those who went on relief were often characterized as lazy and shiftless. Although this idea has by no means been laid to rest in American folklore, the Great Depression made it clear that on some occasions, at least, the best efforts of a willing worker to find a job were unavailing. As a reaction to the earlier tendency to despise the destitute, some idealists came to describe the marginal members of the working force in glowing terms, ennobling them as martyrs, somewhat as the romantic Rousseau had considered the "noble savage."

In fact, welfare clients are a motley group made up of persons suffering from an extended period of bad luck; lazy persons; drunkards; psychologically unstable personalities; mentally retarded persons not requiring institutionalization; persons who married young, have several

Figure 21-1. Urban homes are smaller than were farm homes, and grown children today are often unable or unwilling to house their involuntarily retired parents. The result is yet another of the "problems of the aged"—housing. source: Federal Housing Administration, *Housing for the Elderly* (1957), p. 2.

children, but still have low seniority on their factory jobs and are thus often laid off; and many other types. The misfortunes that can bring a family onto public relief are many—exhaustion of unemployment-compensation benefits, successive years of crop failure on the farm, serious and prolonged illness on the part of the breadwinner, and dozens of others.

The attitude of social workers toward their clients is affected by both practical problems and social values that effect those problems. There are, in fact, two general philosophies toward people in need. One holds in essence that all men are rational beings who should be allowed to make decisions for themselves and that social service should provide emergency assistance only if it is wanted; the other is paternalistic in nature, with the caseworker often making decisions for the individual on behalf of society and with the welfare administrator deciding whether or not the client should receive a particular service.[19]

Welfare Administration. The department of welfare is ordinarily a separate agency of city government, although not all welfare functions are placed in such a department by any means. This is another function of government that has often been supervised by an administrative board, and weak-mayor cities, especially small cities, still treat it as an autonomous function. In large cities, it is normally organized under a single head, although quite a few cities retain an advisory welfare board. Professional social case workers and the influential persons of the community who frequently interest themselves in social work as an avocation tend to favor autonomy. Social workers point out that the welfare budget is very large and that the temptation for elective officials to use these funds in order to help win votes is great. This type of reasoning was implicit in the requirement of the Social Security Act, written by professional social workers, that merit systems of personnel administration be established in each state that wished to qualify for Federal aid. Conflicts of interest between politicians and professionals sometimes result.[20]

Late in the nineteenth century, persons interested in social welfare began to organize private charities on an increasing scale, and these institutions came to dominate the relief scene from that time until after World War I. It was through them that the casework system was developed, resulting in the administrative techniques still employed. These charities became so accepted that they were frequently subsidized by local governments, and they began to attract university-trained social

[19] See Alan Keith-Lucas, "The Political Theory Implicit in Social Casework Theory," *American Political Science Review*, vol. 47 (December, 1953), pp. 1076–1091; and, by the same author, *Decisions about People in Need* (University of North Carolina Press, Chapel Hill, N.C., 1957).

[20] For a case study, see P. N. Ylvisaker, *The Battle of Blue Earth County* (rev. ed.; University of Alabama Press, University, Ala., 1955).

workers.[21] During the Great Depression, basic responsibility was shifted to government. Today, private social-service agencies carry only a part of the total load, but they remain important in a great many areas, particularly in activities for the young and old.[22] Their professionally administered fund-raising campaigns are an annual feature of every community. The moneys collected are used to support the Boy Scouts, the YMCA, the Catholic Youth Organization; to provide care for polio and muscular dystrophy victims; to maintain nursing homes for the aged; to assist persons in need who cannot qualify for a public welfare program; to help in the rehabilitation of alcoholics; to care for unwed mothers; and for dozens of other purposes.

Under the contemporary casework system, a social worker is assigned to interview each person asking for assistance. He or she determines whether the individual is eligible for help on the basis of his residence, ability and willingness of the family to work, and reason for lack of self-support. Pending investigation of the facts gathered, temporary relief may be ordered. If investigation substantiates the facts gathered at the initial interview (called the "intake"), the budget to be granted is determined on the basis of established standard allowances. Since the purpose of the casework method is to provide individual attention, social workers follow up each relief case to ascertain whether there has been any change in eligibility status, to give advice, to try to bolster morale, and to help the family regain its self-support.

Despite many changes in the administration of governmental services in recent years, public relief, by its very nature, must be administered by some unit of local government. Any substantial unemployment in the future will find local relief agencies that have, for the most part, become professionalized, modernized, and prepared to fulfill their role.

FAIR EMPLOYMENT PRACTICE COMMISSIONS

". . . Because of Race, Color or Creed." In an attempt to bring social democracy abreast of political democracy, there was a movement after World War II to secure the adoption of municipal, state, and national fair employment practices commissions (FEPC laws). No nationwide FEPC has been adopted, but several states have established them. Where this is the case, the state enforces fair practices both among private employers in the cities and within the personnel structure of municipalities themselves.

[21] See Reed, *op. cit.*, chap. 20; A. Epstein, *Insecurity: A Challenge to America* (Random House, Inc., New York, 1938); and F. J. Bruno and L. Towley, *Trends in Social Work* (Columbia University Press, New York, 1957).

[22] See Alfred de Grazia (ed.), *Grass Roots Private Welfare* (New York University Press, New York, 1958), and D. L. Sills, *The Volunteers* (The Free Press, Glencoe, Ill., 1958).

Identifiable minority groups have, in recent years, been demanding equal rights. Their own potential political power as organized minorities has been re-enforced by a rising American conscience, a conscience that was pricked by both Nazi and Communist propaganda. Ethnic and racial groups, in addition, have become more verbally and politically skilled as time has passed and they tend to be concentrated in core cities where their political influence makes office seekers eager to support fair employment practices as well as intergroup-relations bodies.

A large number of cities of over 200,000 population, and many smaller places if they have substantial self-conscious minorities, have adopted charter amendments or ordinances providing for an FEPC. This is true of most of the largest cities of the nation outside the South.

The rules established by these commissions seek to prevent discrimination in employment because of race, religion, color, or national origin of the employee. They apply to cases of private employment in business and industry, to labor-union membership, and to discriminatory practices toward employees in governmental agencies.

Discrimination in employment is certainly not uncommon. Even city personnel agencies have permitted discrimination in the hiring of municipal employees, though their rules may formally forbid it. In some instances, personnel agencies have actually abetted such discrimination.

Most FEPC agencies have avoided coercion or punishment in attempts to eliminate discrimination. In fact, most municipal commissions have only advisory and noncoercive powers, although some of them have power to bring court actions against offenders which may result in both restraining orders and criminal punishments. Most FEPCs, however, depend upon education, conferences, persuasion, social pressure, and threat of unfavorable publicity to produce compliance.

There is some question as to whether the municipality has adequate jurisdiction to operate fair employment practices commissions. The problem is at least state-wide in nature.

Conservatives in general oppose FEPC legislation, not because they are bigoted, but because they feel that such legislation represents another area of governmental interference in private enterprise. They believe that it does more harm to freedom than it does good and are likely to argue that progress comes through education, not laws.

Some cities which lack FEPCs have established interracial or intergroup committees to help improve relations between persons of different ethnic, racial, or religious group membership. These are often known by the euphemism, "human relations" committees. They have no coercive powers, but they are sometimes objected to by improvement associations who fear that real equality would threaten property values.[23]

[23] For bibliography, see *Resource Handbook in Human Relations* (The Council on Human Relations, Cleveland, Ohio, 1959).

Chapter 22

GOVERNING URBAN AMERICA TOMORROW

There is likely to be a continued role—an important role—for city governments in the provision of services to people and in the making of policy decisions about those services. The task of municipalities in the future as in the past, will be to perform the functions that are demanded by influential groups—within the limits of revenues that can be raised through the political process. In determining types and levels of services and how to pay for them, municipalities will, as always, have to strike a balance among the effective interests seeking to influence the decisions that will be made. The method of political analysis suggested in this book has been based upon this approach, and it might be well at this point to review the analytical model given in Chapter 1.[1]

Great changes have taken place in American city government since the beginning of the present century. Honesty—as defined by the dominant American viewpoint—has replaced corruption and spoilsmanship. Highly professional municipal bureaucracies have been developed. Provision has been made, to a considerable degree at least, for effective policy innovation and leadership. But many issues of the past decades remain without effective resolution: issues concerning the scope of legal authority from the state, of access to the decision makers and representation in municipal policy making of all significant groups, of providing costly services at levels citizens expect, and of providing municipalities with the financial means with which to meet the increasing demands for services.

THE PAST

Reforms and Progress. The Jacksonian democracy of the 1820s and 1830s was a genuine reform movement. It helped to restore the common man's faith in government, it destroyed control of government by the aristocratic class, and it narrowed the gap between the people and those who operated the government. Even the much-criticized spoils system

[1] See chap. 1, pp. 2–3.

helped to do these things by putting the common man in control not merely of the elective positions, but of all the lesser positions of routine administration as well.[2] This movement accomplished much in bringing government into accord with the wants of the America of over a century ago. It produced universal manhood suffrage, which meant that all men could help choose their leaders. It devised a form of government to fit the personal politics of the informal, sparsely settled frontier. It applied this same type of democracy to our budding cities. But the movement also helped to make possible the city boss and machine. Its concepts proved to be inadequate when government became too complicated for "anyone" to hold official positions—positions which came to require professional and technical skills. Its weak-mayor system could not provide satisfactory services to impersonal, complex cities of a size unknown in Jackson's day.

A reaction to the demoralization of urban government that resulted when a theory of government developed in one epoch of history was applied to a different set of environmental circumstances came about in the shape of a reform movement headed largely by middle-class businessmen. The forty-year span from the 1880s until after World War I brought a great many changes in the apparatus for operating the present-day city. Contemporary forms of government—the strong-mayor and council-manager—evolved and have proved to be applicable to contemporary needs. The ballot was shortened somewhat so as to make it more comprehensible. The merit system for choosing employees was slowly but progressively applied to cities. New administrative techniques were developed. The idea that salaries of municipal employees should be equivalent to those in private endeavor was advanced. Graft and corruption in local government—and in private business, from whence the practices had come—were attacked until they have today declined to a fraction of what they once were. The boss and machine suffered a similar fate. Home rule and broad optional charter plans were devised so as to help fit government to the unique needs of particular cities and to reduce unwanted state control. The number and scope of municipal functions were—and have since continued to be—increased as demand for them arose.

But the reform movement, like Jacksonianism before it, had its limitations and defects. By the time of the onset of the Great Depression, it had become in part outmoded. Many of the reformers, in their distaste for the boss and machine, mistakenly named "politics," rather than "unethical politics," as the villain of the day. They condemned "political parties," rather than "political parties that are corrupt," as well. They

[2] See A. M. Schlesinger, Jr., *The Age of Jackson* (Little, Brown & Company, Boston, 1945), chap. 5.

were so concerned with the need for "efficiency and economy" in government that they overlooked the need for representativeness (except for the advocates of the ill-fated proportional representation). They were so vitally interested in what they were doing that many of them did not recognize that the great majority of urbanites were apathetic toward the problems of reform and would quickly forget reform campaigns. Many of them did not seem to realize that the common man might not respond to the same value appeals that inspired reformers, that he might want something in addition to "efficiency and economy" from government. The movement, which had developed in a day prior to the social-service state and the rise of organized labor as a powerful urban force, often found itself in opposition to interest groups that represented great numbers of working-class urbanites who had, by and large, been excluded from the movement.

Many of the reformers confused themselves through an exaggerated use of the business analogy. It is unrealistic to suppose that, by the simple method of selecting businessmen to apply business principles, satisfactory urban government can be achieved. Some reformers recognized this, but most apparently did not. Business institutions have profit making as their objective. Municipal governments have public service as their objective. The two can use the same procedural techniques to reach their goals; they cannot use the same techniques in policy formulation.

THE FUTURE

Unless there is a change in values of a scope and rapidity previously unequalled in American history, we can expect that the urbanizing trend in general and the suburban pattern of living in particular will continue into the indefinite future. Americans believe that the suburb offers the best available compromise between the advantages of the core city and those of the small town. In any case, the central portion of the metropolitan area could accept a larger population load only by great concentration in high-rise buildings, which do not fit into the American values of home ownership, single-family dwellings, and a private yard.

In What Direction Will the Present Course of Suburbanization Lead? One specialist is convinced that the suburban trend will become especially marked, in the coming years, in the outer fringe; that commercial and industrial suburbanization will continue; that the core cities will become increasingly the place of residence of migrants, of nonwhites, of lowest-income workers, of younger couples, and of the elderly.[3] As

[3] For a case study, see M. B. Dworkis (ed.), *The Impact of Puerto Rican Migration on Governmental Services in New York City* (New York University Press, New York, 1957).

the housing shortage becomes somewhat less acute, better-built houses will begin to appear—but by 1975, many of the postwar jerry-built project homes may be threatening to take on the appearance and social problems of slum areas.

Unless, as is possible, dramatic technological advances are made, adequate water and sewage-disposal problems will become increasingly serious and "both the metropolitan and the suburban bodies politic will remain split up into groups and classes unable to communicate effectively, mutually suspicious, incapable of defining their common interests or of cooperating to realize them."[4]

A New Kind of Segregation? Another specialist agrees that there are strong forces for continuing the present pattern of Balkanization in the suburbs. Noting that the present fragmented pattern of dozens of governments and special districts has long been criticized as irrational and inefficient, he points out that "despite our predictions, disaster has not struck: urban government has continued to function, not well perhaps, but at least well enough to forestall catastrophe. Traffic continues to circulate; streets and sewers are built; water is provided; schools keep their doors open; and law and order generally prevail."[5] But it is not simply because services have not collapsed that the present system continues. The existence of all shapes and sizes of communities within the metropolitan area allows for "the continued segregation of occupations, classes, and races [which] fits in well with modern doctrine on how to 'manage' social conflict. Let each man find his own, abstain from social contact with antagonistic elements, abjure political disagreement and debate by joining a constituency which shares his values, and his tensions, anxieties, and uncertainties are relieved."[6]

If this pattern does continue, if "local governments become truly a bundle of services, to be purchased by those who can afford them without regard to more general social consequences," pressures for conformity will increase even more, individualism will decline further, lack of understanding among differing subcultures will be perpetuated, a new kind of a class system may arise even though classlessness is the asserted goal.

While gross national product will have doubled between 1950 and 1975;[7] the public will feel the tremendous costs of increasing urbanization. Because this is the case, it is very possible that the past tendency

---

[4] Coleman Woodbury, "Suburbanization and Suburbia," *American Journal of Public Health*, vol. 45 (January, 1955), pp. 1–10.

[5] R. C. Wood, "Metropolitan Government, 1975: An Extrapolation of Trends," *American Political Science Review*, vol. 52 (March, 1958), pp. 108–122.

[6] *Ibid.*

[7] Joint Committee on the Economic Report, 83d Congress, *Potential Economic Growth of the United States during the Next Decade* (1954), p. 24.

to ignore appeals for efficiency and economy will be reconsidered. Furthermore, the fact that services have not so far broken down does not assure that they will not do so under ever increasing urbanization pressures. There may be a reconsideration of governmental organization in metropolitan areas based upon sheer economic cost.

The problems that result from urbanism and industrialism will become accentuated in the coming years. State and local governments will be called upon to help clear away old slums. Areas still in satisfactory condition in the 1960s will, in a decade or two, require rehabilitation. Industrial waste-disposal problems will become more widespread; water and air pollution will result from population increases and from industrial activity. These difficulties will have to be overcome.

The relocation and retraining of workers displaced as a result of changing agricultural economics and of automation will be a top-priority item. The organization and financing of ever more complicated metropolitan areas will require assistance from the states. Recreation facilities will have to be provided in an age of increased leisure time. Past failures to set aside enough land will cause serious shortages of space for parks and recreation and physical facilities will be expensive to procure.

Water and Power. States will be asked to help local communities to find water supplies in adequate amount. There may be considerable pressure for states to assist localities in financing water, sewage-disposal, and storm-drain improvements. The use of electricity in the United States doubled in the ten years following 1947. The rate of increased use will probably continue as population increases and industry makes greater use of this mobile power source. The states and communities may be called upon to help provide needed energy, especially in helping to develop atomic power sources.

Transportation. Highways between urban areas and within them will, with considerable Federal aid, be a major responsibility of state and local government. There will be 15 million more cars on the highways in 1975 than there were in 1960. Furthermore, the parking problem is far from being solved; with more automobiles on the streets each year, the solution will depend almost entirely upon local governments, perhaps with some state help.[8]

Representation and Democratic Government. Problems of representation will plague the public and cause untold conflicts. As yet, no satisfactory formula has been devised for representation of the various communities of a metropolitan area in any type of supergovernment that may be established in such areas in the future. Falling rural popula-

[8] See the Paley Report, President's Materials Policy Commission, *Resources for Freedom* (5 vols.; 1952).

tions and expanding urban populations will make constantly more serious the already widespread existence of gerrymandered state legislatures. In the 1960s and 1970s, we can expect rural and small-town areas to resist ever more vigorously efforts at reapportionment, but increasing needs for metropolitan services with the purse strings controlled at the state capital will cause build-ups of increasing counterpressures calling for a redistribution of representation in the state legislatures. The middle- and upper-income groups, having vacated to the suburbs for residential purposes, will find it ever more difficult to control core-city political decisions. The grandsons of municipal reformers will live in the suburbs and a new politics based on ethnic-group and lower-income group anxieties will come to replace reform values of efficiency and economy in the core cities.

Much has been said over the years concerning the apathy of the urbanite toward his local government. He has long been exhorted to become active in "the government closest to himself." He has been urged to take part in "citizen-action" groups. For the most part, he has preferred national politics—or baseball.

Perhaps a major cause of failure to interest the typical citizen in local political activities has been a lack of understanding of the urban political process. Floyd Hunter has stated the issue clearly: [9]

> The notion that city dwellers can or will act like persons inhabiting small New England towns and accustomed to town meetings has . . . been a pitfall for many efforts in community organization. Urban life is organized along the lines of organized interest groupings whether the particular interest be high wages, higher profits, lower tax rates or lower disease rates. Basic organizations have sprung up around a multiplicity of interests in urban communities and the possibility of the so-called "face-to-face relationship" of city dwellers is an illusion . . .

The suburban movement stimulated citizen interest and participation in local government as nothing in the last century has. This interest will probably be sustained in future decades, not through greater voter participation or greater awareness of the identity of officeholders, but through an increased feeling of common purpose, of effective representation, of easy access to the decision makers. None of these trends will likely apply to core cities, however, and there pervasive apathy will be set aside occasionally only by dramatic campaigns. Indirect representation through organized interests, with an absence of the consensus that characterizes many suburbs, will be normal.

[9] Floyd Hunter, *Community Power Structure* (University of North Carolina Press, Chapel Hill, N.C., 1953), p. 256. By permission of the University of North Carolina Press.

THE ROAD WE ARE TRAVELING

By judging from the direction society in America seems to be pointed, we can make some generalizations concerning the likely future. These must be noted, however, with the thought in mind that changing technology and social values, not to mention wars, among other things, may drastically change the path we see ahead of us. These changes can take place with great suddenness and can have enormous effects upon social institutions. Note, for example, that advances in medical knowledge that would greatly reduce the incidence of cancer and heart attacks could change the demands upon local governments in dozens of ways, for the average life span would suddenly increase. A drop of, say, 25 per cent in the birth rate could also throw off a great number of the statistical trends used here, as could a serious and persisting economic depression.

But, barring major changes in the pattern of life as it was when this was written, we can expect future trends in local government to include the following:

1. The political myth of the social-service state will probably remain dominant. It gives no indication of being fundamentally altered in the near future. If this assumption is correct, heavy service demands at all levels of government will continue and, as new problems arise, government will be one of the first, rather than one of the last, social institutions that people will turn to for help. The frontier traditions of individualism will continue to be influential, and political propaganda will be verbalized in part through its language, but it will serve only as a brake on the general trend.

2. Municipal functions will likely increase in number, and service levels will rise at least as rapidly as will the standard of living. As people come to depend increasingly upon government for services and for the compromising of various social conflicts (labor-management, interracial, etc.), trust in government will increase and so will the prestige of government officials and career employees.

3. Federal-state-local relationships will become more elaborate as the provision of many kinds of services is provided increasingly on an intergovernmental basis. This tendency away from a separation of functions by governmental level will not necessarily mean a decline in the policy-making importance of local government. As the bureaucracy continues to become professionalized at all levels, standards and values tend to become standardized, too. This, in turn, encourages a sense of cooperation rather than of exploitation on the part of officials and employees at one level working with their counterparts on a higher level. Further-

more, as mass communication, more years of education, and other factors diminish regional and subcultural differences in American society, the image of policy being imposed from the state capital or from Washington will tend to decline, thus re-enforcing the trend among public employees toward a common set of objectives.

4. The institutions which are a part of the process of public policy making will become increasingly important as governments become more important and they will be subjected to greater amounts of scrutiny and criticism. Struggles over legislative representation lie ahead. The struggle between the executive and legislative branches over policy domination will probably continue, but councils will very likely lose further ground as centers for innovation. Members of the professional bureaucracy of governments and of interest groups will be accorded a greater share in the development of policy, and the competence and responsibility of these persons will be of crucial importance.

5. Local parties (in nonpartisan cities) and especially interest groups will become generally of greater importance as they speak for citizens in a society that will become increasingly impersonal with social roles increasingly specialized. The individual will have much at stake in governmental decisions, and his best way to influence those decisions will normally be through membership and activity in interest groups.

6. The slow trend toward administrative organization integrated through the chief executive will continue. It is already far advanced at the municipal level. Counties and other local units, if they remain important units of government, will likely move in the same direction, and there is some evidence that the more urban counties and other units are already doing so.

7. The bureaucracy will become even more specialized in the coming years with an increasing sense of professional status. Resentment toward it will continue, if for no other reason than that many people resent to a degree those upon whom they must be dependent. But its prestige will continue to climb and its competence to expand. The percentage of the total labor force employed by governments will probably also continue to increase as the role of government expands.

8. Government in metropolitan areas will continue to be a problem. The need for cooperative or area-wide approaches to certain problems will become increasingly clear, but the suburbanite's preferences for access and homogeneity will militate against supergovernments. Administrative and structural arrangements will probably continue to be of an experimental, *ad hoc* character, with each area meeting issues as they come along, according to the existing balance of forces at the time a crisis appears.

9. The urban county will probably continue to show the effects of re-

vitalization that it has demonstrated in recent decades. It will continue to re-emerge as a unit for services that are wanted on a wider basis than that of the municipality. Nonschool special districts will continue to increase, but school districts will, for a while at least, continue to decline in number as educators continue to apply pressure for twelve-grade districts with substantial tax-carrying capacity.

10. Taxation will, as always, be viewed as a problem and will be the basis for much controversy. Cities and other local units will press for a tax base broader than that of the general property tax. They will, in some states, be given additional sources of tax revenue, but their expanded costs will be met, for the most part, by state grants-in-aid and shared taxes and by the use of self-liquidating revenue bonds. The gasoline tax will be increased over the years in order to pay for streets and highways made necessary by an expanding population and an increasing number of automobiles in proportion to population. Other taxes will increase, too, as a result of greater demands for governmental services. But it is doubtful if the typical citizen will show any increased tendency to associate taxes with services.

The citizen will continue his wishful thinking about electing a new council that will have spunk enough to lower taxes, just as happened at the turn of the century when New York was dominated by the Tammany machine under the control of Richard Croker. In 1901, various reform groups joined together in a strong effort to defeat the machine. They presented the voters with a slate, headed by Seth Low as the candidate for mayor. At a fusion-ticket conference, a "declaration of principles" was drawn up which included a promise for "a progressive, businesslike and nonpartisan administration of municipal affairs, with a special view to cutting down public expenses and reducing the present excessive burden of taxation." [10]

Seth Low was elected mayor. But his first budget, to the dismay and disillusionment of a great many reformers, was $600,000 *higher* than the estimates made by his Tammany predecessor. A wise editorial writer separated reality from wishful thinking: [11]

Some reformers expected a large reduction from Tammany expenditures, but the leaders of the reform movement have long since learned that good government means better public service rather than cheaper public service. The more alert the citizenship of a place and the greater their confidence in their city officials, the larger is the work which the municipality is required to perform for its members.

[10] Quoted in *The Outlook*, vol. 69 (Sept. 28, 1901), p. 199.
[11] *Ibid.*, vol. 71 (May 10, 1902), pp. 100–101.

These, then, are some of the probable trends in municipal govern-ment. They are not predictions, but they reflect the most likely develop-ments based upon what has happened in past decades.

Closing Statement. The American culture is a product created by all of the American people interacting upon one another. It is an independ-ent variable which must be accepted as a basis for understanding pres-ent and future American government. The projections that can be made seem to show that the future holds "more of the same," with increasing pressures, but of the same sort that have existed in the postwar years. Citizens in the coming years will be called upon to meet the problems of living together in vast numbers, problems that seemingly will be-come more complicated rather than simpler as time passes. By under-standing the political process as well as trends in municipal govern-ment services, these future challenges will become more understand-able, and workable programs perhaps somewhat easier to discover.

American cities and their governments have come a long way in the direction of the satisfaction of contemporary demands. Most of the tools and techniques that are needed have been found. The future of American cities looks bright. All great civilizations have centered in great cities.[12]

[12] For additional statistics and discussion of future trends in government, see Charles R. Adrian, *State and Local Governments* (McGraw-Hill Book Company, Inc., New York, 1960), chap. 23, and bibliography cited there.

SUGGESTED READINGS

PERIODICALS

In order for the student to keep abreast of current development in the fields of local government and administration, it is necessary for him to be acquainted with the periodical literature. The following are important periodicals, but they do not necessarily exhaust the field. In many states, the student can learn much about local municipalities through the periodical of his state municipal league. For a list of these publications, see the *Municipal Year Book* (International City Managers' Association, Chicago, annually).

American City. Monthly. Much detail on administrative developments and less attention to politics and reform action than is found in the *National Civic Review*. Many pictures and a great deal of advertising of the most recent municipal equipment.

American Journal of Public Health. Monthly. American Public Health Association.

American Municipal News. Monthly. Current municipal developments and practices.

City Managers' Newsletter. Biweekly. International City Managers' Association.

Journal of Housing. Monthly. National Association of Housing Officials. Housing and redevelopment news.

Municipal Finance. Quarterly. Municipal Finance Officers' Association. Also publishes a biweekly *News Letter*.

National Civic Review. Monthly. Formerly the *National Municipal Review.* Perhaps the best source of news of a general nature. Emphasizes political action, especially of the reform type.

National Tax Journal. Quarterly. National Tax Association. Features information on municipal taxation.

Newsletter. Monthly. American Society of Planning Officials.

New York Times. Daily. Reports important political and administrative developments throughout the country if of general interest.

Police Chief. Quarterly. International Association of Chiefs of Police.

Public Employee. Monthly. The American Federation of State, County, and Municipal Employees. The labor viewpoint, especially on personnel practices.

Public Management. Monthly. International City Managers' Association. A major source of news on administration.

Public Personnel Review. Quarterly. Public Personnel Association. Includes developments in municipal personnel administration.

Public Utilities Fortnightly. Management and technical problems of utilities operation.

Public Welfare. Quarterly. American Public Welfare Association.

Recreation. Monthly. National Recreation Association.

State Government. Monthly. Occasional articles on state-local relations.
The Tax Digest. Monthly. By California Taxpayers' Association, but with items of nationwide interest.
Taxes—the Tax Magazine. Monthly. Commerce Clearing House. Reports on local developments.
United States Municipal News. Monthly. U.S. Conference of Mayors.
Wall Street Journal. Daily, Chicago and New York. Frequent articles on municipal finance and other developments.

FOR SPECIFIC LOCALITIES

Local materials are scattered through periodicals, pamphlets, and books of all kinds. Many of them are given quite limited circulation. The student should consult his instructor, and the general reader his local librarian. Books dealing with state and local governments in specific states often contain valuable chapters on municipal government. Some of these are listed in Charles R. Adrian, *State and Local Governments* (McGraw-Hill Book Company, Inc., New York, 1960), pp. 517–521. On the vast bibliography concerning metropolitan-area governments, see footnote, p. 276, above.

BOSSES AND MACHINES

The old-time bosses, because they were glamorous, dramatic, and, to many people, immensely frustrating, produced perhaps more source material than any other aspect of city government. Since this material is now principally of historical value rather than a reflection of the contemporary scene, it is listed here rather than in the main part of the text. The following list is not complete; further material is cited in textbooks on political parties.

General materials that should be cited include Harold Zink, *City Bosses in the United States* (Duke University Press, Durham, N.C., 1930), a standard reference that draws conclusions from a study of twenty of them; F. R. Kent, *The Great Game of Politics* (Doubleday & Company, Inc., New York, 1923); and C. W. Van Devander, *The Big Bosses* (Howell, Soskin Company, New York, 1944). Journalistic surveys; J. T. Salter, *Boss Rule: Portraits in City Politics* (McGraw-Hill Book Company, Inc., New York, 1935), a study of political-leadership qualities in ward committeemen, based principally upon the Philadelphia machine of that time; S. Forthal, *Cogwheels of Democracy: A Study of the Precinct Captain* (The William-Frederick Press, New York, 1946). There are also famous early studies by Lincoln Steffens: *The Shame of the Cities* (McClure, Phillips and Company, New York, 1904), examines former machines in St. Louis, Minneapolis, Pittsburgh; and *Autobiography of Lincoln Steffens* (Harcourt, Brace & World, Inc., New York, 1931).

Boston. There is a bibliography in George Blackwood, "Boston Politics and Boston Politicians," in Murray B. Levin, *The Alienated Voter: Politics in Boston* (Holt, Rinehart and Winston, Inc., New York, 1960), chap. 1.

Chicago. See footnote, p. 152, above.

Jersey City. D. D. McKean, *The Boss: The Hague Machine in Action* (Houghton, Mifflin Company, Boston, 1940).

Kansas City. M. M. Milligan, *Missouri Waltz: The Inside Story of the Pendergast Machine by the Man Who Smashed It* (Charles Scribner's Sons, New

York, 1948), by the U.S. District Attorney; W. M. Reddig, *Tom's Town: Kansas City and the Pendergast Legend* (J. B. Lippincott Company, Philadelphia, 1947).

New York. A complete annotated bibliography will be found in Wallace S. Sayre and Herbert Kaufman, *Governing New York City* (Russell Sage Foundation, New York, 1960).

Philadelphia. James A. Bryce, *The American Commonwealth* (rev. ed.; The Macmillan Company, New York, 1911), vol. 2, pp. 354–371, deals with the "Gas Ring"; W. S. Vare, *My Forty Years in Politics* (Roland Swain Company, Philadelphia, 1933), is an autobiography of one of the bosses; the fall of the Philadelphia Republican machine is recorded in James Reichley, *The Art of Government: Reform and Organization Politics in Philadelphia* (The Fund for the Republic, New York, 1959); and Joseph D. Crumlish, *A City Finds Itself: The Philadelphia Home Rule Charter Movement* (Wayne State University Press, Detroit, Mich., 1959).

San Francisco. Walton Bean, *Boss Ruef's San Francisco* (University of California Press, Berkeley, Calif., 1952).

Access, concept of, 2–3, 64
Administration, municipal, as func-
    tion of local value systems,
    312
  future trends in, 493
  growth of, 305–307
  integration of, arguments for,
    310–311
    forces against, 308–310
  nature of, 312–314
  organization of, 314–316
  red tape as problem in, 321–322
  reform movement influence on
    307–308
  role of top management in, 322–
    324
  standards for, 319–320
Administrative code, 314–315
Aesthetics as basis for municipal pro-
    grams, 166–167
Airports, municipal, 429–431
Annexation, 276–278
Apathy toward municipal govern-
    ment, 6–7
  (See also Nonvoting)
Aristotle on metropolitan-area gov-
    ernment, 291–292
Assessor, 357–358, 380–381
Attorney, city, functions of, 253–254
Auditor, city, 382, 387

Ballot, long, 74–75
  nonpartisan, 99–102
  partisan, 98–100, 102–104

Banks and bankers, political influence
    of, 130
Billboard regulation, 166–167
Boards and commissions, 75, 316–
    319
Bonds, municipal, affected by na-
    tional-government policies,
    374
  characteristics of, 372
  debate over use of, 370–372
  Federal tax exemption of in-
    come, 374
  state limitations on, 355–356
  types of, 372–374
Boosterism, and city politics, 87–88
  and industrial recruitment, 376–
    377
Bosses and political machines, 79–
    81, 147–148
  challenged by reformers, 81–84
  in Chicago, 151–155
  decline of, 148–152
Bryce, James, 4
Budget, municipal, administration of,
    386–387
  enactment of, 386
  as executive function, 382–384
  parts of, 385
  performance-type, 383–384
  as policy statement, 384–385
  preparation of, 385–386
Building codes, 447–448, 464–465
Bureaucracy, municipal, as problem
    in democracy, 324–326
  professional, 87

Burgess, E. W., 33
Business groups, and council-man-
    ager plan, 228–229
    political action of, 128–134, 160–
        163

Central business district, threatened
    decline of, 59–60
Cermak, Anton J., 154
Charters (*see* City charters)
Chicago, 60–61
    political machine in, 151–155
    political power in, 129, 144–145
Cincinnati, Charter party in, 105–
    106
Cities, corrupt government in, 6
    development patterns, theories of,
        28–33
    growth of, 20–27
    life-style characteristics, 33–42
City, meaning of term, 19
City charters, nature of, 174–175
    types of, general act, 176–178
        home rule, 180–188
        optional, 178–180
        special act, 175–176
City employees, 138
    (*See also* Municipal employment)
City government, attitudes toward,
    3–8
    ideal images of, 87–89
    and New Deal, 85–87
City manager, duties of, 249, 256–
    257
    and elections, 250–251
    as professional, 251–252
    and public relations, 251
    qualifications of, 244–245
    relations with council, 249–250
    selection and tenure, 245–249
    (*See also* Council-manager plan)
City-national relations, advice and as-
    sistance to cities, 299–301
    approval of municipal activities,
        301
    grants-in-aid to cities, 301–303
    problems and issues, 303–304

City planning (*see* Planning)
City-state relations, 4–5
    oversight of cities, judicial, 189–
        191
        legislative, 188–189
        state administrative, 293–299
        state legislative control, 75–77
Civic associations (*see* Improvement
        associations)
Civil defense, 415–416
Civil service (*see* Municipal employ-
        ment)
Class system and political conflict,
        36–38
    urban, 34–35
Clerk, city, 252–253
Close corporations, 72
Commission plan, 83
    appraisal of, 216–218
    characteristics of, 215–216
    development of, 214, 217–218
Comptroller, city, 380
Consensus in village politics, 17–18
Contract liability, municipal, 191–
        192
Controller, city, 380
Cooley, Thomas M., 77–78
Cooperation, voluntary intergovern-
        mental, 289
Corporation, public, city as, 168–170
    creation and dissolution of, 173–
        174
    distinguished from quasi, 170–
        171
    powers of, 171–173
Corporation counsel, 253–254
Corrupt government in cities, 6
Council, city, as arbiter of conflict,
        257–258
    function of, 255–257
    members of, personal qualities,
        258
        practical problems, 271–273
        representatives of minority
            groups, 261–262
        salary, 262–263
        terms of office, 263–264

Council, city, members of, women as, 262
   organization and procedure, 268–270
   powers of, 270–271
   as ratifying agent for fiscal policies, 378
   relations with manager, 249–250
   structure of, election by wards or at-large, 265–267
      size, 264
      type of ballot, 267–268
      unicameral, 264–265
Council-manager plan, 83
   appraisal of, 223–230
   characteristics of, 220–223
   development of, 218–220
County as metropolitan government unit, 287–288
Courts, municipal, 408–410
Crime, causes of, 389–392
   and corruption of officials, 392–395
   as function of the culture, 395–396
   organized, 388–389
Crime rate, 396–397
Crump, Edward H., 151
Curley, James Michael, 151

Dearborn, Michigan, politics in, 155–160
Detroit, 41
   public awareness of political power in, 145–146
Dillon, John F., 171

Efficiency and economy movement, 79–85
Elections, nonpartisan, 99–102
   origin of, 82
   participation in, 96–98
   partisan, 98–100, 102–104
Ethnic and racial groups, 484–485
   and industrial recruitment, 377

Expenditures, municipal, 349–353
Extraterritorial jurisdiction, 288–289

Fair employment practice commissions, 484–485
Federal-city relations (*see* City-national relations)
Finance, municipal, administrators of, 378–382
   expenditures, 349–353
   nontax revenues, 361–367
      grants-in-aid, 301–303, 364–366
      special assessments, 368–370
      state-shared taxes, 365–366
      state limits on taxing and spending, 353–356
   (*See also* Bonds, Budget, Taxes)
Fire-fighting equipment, 412
Fire prevention, 411–412
Fire protection, organization for, 412–413
   problems of, 410–411
Forms of city government (*see* specific names of plans)
Friedland, Louis L., 344
Fromm, Erich, 33–34

Garbage disposal, 436
Good-government groups, 125–126
Governmental functions of city, defined, 170
   and tort liability, 192
Grants-in-aid to cities, 352, 481

Hague, Frank, 151
Health administration, public, 470
   functions of, 471–474
   as municipal function, 468
   public attitudes toward, 474–475
Hoan, Daniel W., 103, 232
Home rule, appraisal of, 187

Home rule, municipal, 180–181
  origin and spread of, 81, 183–185
  practical meaning of, 185–187
  procedure for adopting charter,
    181–183
Hospitals, municipal, 473
Housing, urban, building codes, 447–
    448
  continued shortage of, 444–447
  Federal programs, 86, 448–453
  (*See also* Public housing; Urban
    renewal)
Hoyt, Homer, 33
Hubbard, Orville L., 155–160

Improvement associations, 37–38,
    56–57
  as pressure groups, 127–128, 132
Industry, decentralization of, 48
  municipal recruitment of, 376–377
Inherent right of local self-govern-
    ment, theory of, 77–79
Initiative and referendum, 83–84,
    108–113
Interest groups (*see* Pressure groups)
Intergovernmental relations (*see*
    City-national relations; City-
    state relations; Cooperation;
    Extraterritorial jurisdiction)
Invasion, definition of term, 37
  as political issue, 165

Jacksonian democracy as theory of lo-
    cal government, 70–75, 486–488
Jail, municipal, 406
Jefferson, Thomas, on cities, 73
Jews in local politics, 55–56
Johnson, Tom L., 233
Jones, Victor, 274, 278, 282
Justice, concept of, 406–408
Justice of the peace, 408–409
  (*See also* Courts)

Kefauver committee, 388–389, 394
  (*See also* Crime)

Labor unions, leaders of, attitude to-
    ward council-manager plan,
    229–230
  in municipal employment, 341–
    345
  opposition to payroll tax, 360
  in political campaigns, 161–163
  as pressure groups, 134–136
  and urban-life styles, 41–42
La Guardia, Fiorello H., 104, 150,
    232
Land-use controls, building-construc-
    tion codes, 464–465
  subdivision regulations, 462–463
  zoning, 463–464
Lapham, Roger D., recall attempt of,
    114–116
Lausche, Frank J., 233
Law enforcement (*see* Police)
League of Women Voters, 83, 126
Lee, Eugene, 101
Legislative control over cities (*see*
    City-state relations)
Liability, municipal, for contracts,
    191–192
  for torts, 192–195
Libraries, municipal, 478–480
Long, Norton E., 291–292
Los Angeles County, city councils of,
    factions within, 257
  as metropolitan-area government,
    287
  voting behavior of cities in, 92–
    93
Low, Seth, 232, 494

Machines (*see* Bosses and political
    machines)
McKean, Dayton D., 151
Manager (*see* City manager)
Mayor, ceremonial functions of, 239–
    240
  as lobbyist, 240
  personal qualities of, 232–235
  powers of, 235–239
  salary and terms of office, 242–244

Mayor, selection method, 240–241
  (*See also* Strong-mayor-council
    plan; Weak-mayor-council
    plan)
Metropolitan-area government, atom-
    ization of, 274–276
  proposals, annexation, 276–278
    city-county consolidation, 283–
      284
    city-county separation, 284–285
    county as metropolitan unit,
      287–288
    extraterritorial jurisdiction, 288–
      289
    metropolitan federation, 285–
      287
    special districts, 278–283
      multipurpose, 283
    voluntary cooperation, 289
  unpopularity of, reasons for, 290–
    292
  (*See also* Suburbs)
Metropolitan areas, meaning of term,
    20
  as parts of urban regions, 23–24
  planning in, 11–12, 466–467
  studies of, 289–290
Minority groups (*see* Negroes; Racial
    and ethnic groups)
Model City Charter, 108
Municipal employees as pressure
    group, 138
Municipal employment, civil service
    commission, 333
  dismissal from, 338–339
  examination for, 336–337
  and organized labor, 341–345
  personnel director, 334–335
  police recruitment and training,
    404–405
  policies in, as function of the cul-
    ture, 335
  position classification in, 335–336
  public attitude toward, 332–333,
    339–341
  retirement systems, 347–348
  salaries, 346–347

Municipal home rule (*see* Home
    rule)
Murphy, Frank, 232–233

National-city relations (*see* City-na-
    tional relations)
National Municipal League, 82
Negroes, attitude toward urban re-
    newal, 446
  on city councils, 261–262
  pressure groups of, 136–137
  and property values, 57
  and suburban patterns, 55–57
  urbanization of, 24–27
New Deal and city government, 85–
    87
New York City, chief administrative
    officer in, 213
  political parties in, 104–106
Newspapers and local politics, 132–
    134
Nomination of candidates, methods
    of, 106–108
Nonvoting, consequences of, 95–96
  extent of, 91–93
  in Los Angeles County, 92–93
  reasons for, 93–95

Ordinance defined, 172*n.*
O'Rourke, Lawrence W., 92–93

Parking, municipal policies on, 427–
    429
Parks, administration of, 475–477
  function of, 477
Personnel administration (*see* Munic-
    ipal employment)
Philadelphia, 6, 151
Planning, urban, commission, func-
    tion of, 458–459
  defined, 457
  historical development of, 457–
    458
  influence on public transit sys-
    tems, 440

Planning, urban, metropolitan-wide, 466–467
　　procedures, 460–462
　　staff, 459–460
　　in suburbs, 465–466
　　(*See also* Land-use controls)
Police, corruption of, 394–395
　　detective division, 400–401
　　and gambling activities, 392–394
　　juvenile division, 403
　　mayor responsible for, 238
　　organization of, 397–399
　　patrol division, 399–400
　　recruitment and training of, 404–406
　　traffic division, 401–402
　　vice division, 395, 403
Political parties, local, 102–106
　　national, in local elections, 98–100
　　reform, 104–106
Political process, nature of, 2–3, 119–121
　　in suburbs, 163–165
　　(*See also* Power structures)
Population, urban, trends in, 21–27
Power structures, case studies, 143–146
　　and municipal government, 139–143
Preferential voting, systems of, 84, 117–118
Pressure groups, characteristics of, 121–124
　　function of, 2–3, 119–121
　　and government as arbiter, 88–89
Primary elections, 107–108
Property values, Negro influence on, 56–57
　　in suburban politics, 163
Proportional representation, 83, 117
Proprietary functions of city, defined, 170
　　and tort liability, 192
Public health (*see* Health)
Public hearing, function of, 116
Public housing, background of, 448–450

Public housing, recent policies for, 451–453
　　(*See also* Housing)
Public interest, as administrative guide, 320–321
　　concept of, 88–89
　　defined, 124–125
　　as viewed by councilmen, 258–259
Public relations, municipal, 326–331
Public utilities, definition of, 417–418
　　issues in, private versus public ownership, 420–422
　　state versus local control, 419–420
　　municipally owned, 422
　　as pressure groups, 130
　　rate determination, 418–419
　　regulation of, 418
Public welfare (*see* Welfare)
Public works department, 441–443
Purchasing agent, municipal, 381–382

Quasi corporation, 170–171

Racial and ethnic groups, political activities of, 484–485
　　and industrial recruitment, 377
　　(*See also* Negroes)
Realtors, political influence of, 131–132
Recall, 83–84, 113–116
Recreation administration, 475–477
Recreation program, 477
Red tape, 321–322
Referendum, 83–84, 108–113
Reform movement, 79–85
Religious groups in local politics, 137–138
Restrictive covenants, 37
Revenue, municipal (*see* Finance; Taxes)
Riesman, David, 34, 53

Roosevelt, Franklin D., 86–87
Rubbish disposal, 436

Salaries, municipal employee, 346–347
San Francisco, recall in, 114–116
Sanitation, 435–437
Schools as special districts, 252*n.*, 279–280
Sewage disposal, 431, 435–437
Slums, 444–447
    municipal action to prevent, 455–456
Smoke abatement, 414
Social-service state, 87
    future allegiance to, 492
Socialist parties in local elections, 102–103
Special assessments, 368–370
Special districts, 278–283
Special legislation, 75–77, 175–176
Standards, administrative, concept of, 319–320
State-city relations (*see* City-state relations)
Steffens, Lincoln, 84
Streets, 422–423
    expressways, 423–427
Strikes, municipal employee, 344–345
Strong-mayor-council plan, appraisal of, 209–210
    characteristics of, 206–209
    with chief administrative officer, 210–214
    (*See also* Mayor)
Subdivision regulations, 462–463
Suburban movement, and desire for political autonomy, 63–67
    effect of, on core city, 58–62
    in future, 488–489
    and metropolitan-wide problems, 69
    problems of suburbs created by, 62–69

Suburbs, ethnic and racial discrimination in, 55–58
    growth of, 43–46
    planning in, 11–12
    politics in, 18–19, 163–165
    subsidized by core city, 60–62
    types of, 47–57
Suffrage, municipal, extension of, 73–74
    present qualifications for, 90–91

Tammany Hall, 150
    (*See also* Bosses and political machines)
Tax appeal, board of, 381
Tax collector, 378–380
Tax exemption, municipal, of bond income, 374
    for industry, 375
Taxes, on admissions, 361
    on business, 360–361
    characteristics of, 349–350
    efforts to diversify, 359–361
    general property, 354, 356–359
    municipal, income, 360
    sales, 354, 360
    payroll, 360
    state-shared, 365–366
    (*See also* Finance)
Taxpayer groups as organized interests, 88, 128
Taxpayer suits, 189–191
Thompson, William H., 25, 152–153, 479–480
Toronto, metropolitan government for, 285–286
Tort, definition of, 191
    municipal liability for, 192–195
Town, meaning of term, 19–20
    in New England, structure of, 230–231
Township, meaning of term, 19–20
Traffic, 427–428
    police control of, 401–402
Traffic engineering, 415

Transportation, public, problems of, 437
    proposed policies for, 439–440
Treasurer, city, 378

Underwood, Kenneth W., 137–138
Urban region defined, 23–24
Urban renewal, 453–455
Urbanization, history of, 20–22
    (*See also* Cities)
Utilities (*see* Public utilities)

Veterans, political interests of, 138–139
Village, life style of, 15–16
    meaning of term, 19
Village politics, 16–18
Voting, preferential, 84, 117–118
    qualitative make-up of participants, 97–98
    (*See also* Elections; Nonvoting; Suffrage)

Water supply, 431–435
    fluoridation as political issue, 434
Weak-mayor-council plan, appraisal of, 204–206
    characteristics of, 200–204
    development of, 71–72
    (*See also* Mayor)
Weights and measures inspection, 413–414
Welfare, public, administration of, 483–484
    casework system, 484
    clients of, 481–483
    development of, 480–481
Whyte, William H., Jr., 40
Willbern, York, 311
Women in politics, 97, 164, 259, 262

Zoning, 463–464
    (*See also* Land-use controls)
Zoos, municipal, 478

32⁵⁰